América Central y el Caribe

0 100 200 300 400 Km.
0 100 200 300 400 Mi.

ESTADOS UNIDOS
Golfo de México
Miami
Estrecho de la Florida
Islas Bahamas
OCÉANO ATLÁNTICO
Trópico de Cáncer
La Habana
Matanzas
Pinar del Río
Cienfuegos
Morón
Camagüey
CUBA
Isla de Pinos
Canal de Yucatán
Guantánamo
Santiago de Cuba
REPÚBLICA DOMINICANA
Puerto Plata
Santiago de los Caballeros
Santo Domingo
HAITÍ
Puerto Príncipe
PUERTO RICO
San Juan
Bayamón
Río Piedras
Mayagüez
Ponce
Islas Vírgenes
Antigua
Guadalupe
Dominica
Martinica
Sta. Lucía
Barbados
San Vicente
Granada
Antillas Menores
Tobago
Puerto España
TRINIDAD
Antillas Mayores
JAMAICA
Kingston
Mar Caribe
MÉXICO
Tikal
PETÉN
Lago Petén Itzá
Lago Isabel
Belmopan
BELICE
Puerto Barrios
San Pedro Sula
GUATEMALA
Chichicastenango
Copán
HONDURAS
Tegucigalpa
Guatemala
Antigua
Quetzaltenango
EL SALVADOR
San Salvador
NICARAGUA
Managua
Lago de Nicaragua
Arenal
Poás
Irazú
Puerto Limón
Puntarenas
San José
Orosi
Quepos
COSTA RICA
Colón
Panamá
PANAMÁ
Canal de Panamá
OCÉANO PACÍFICO
COLOMBIA
Aruba
Curazao
Bonaire
Isla Margarita
AMÉRICA DEL SUR
VENEZUELA

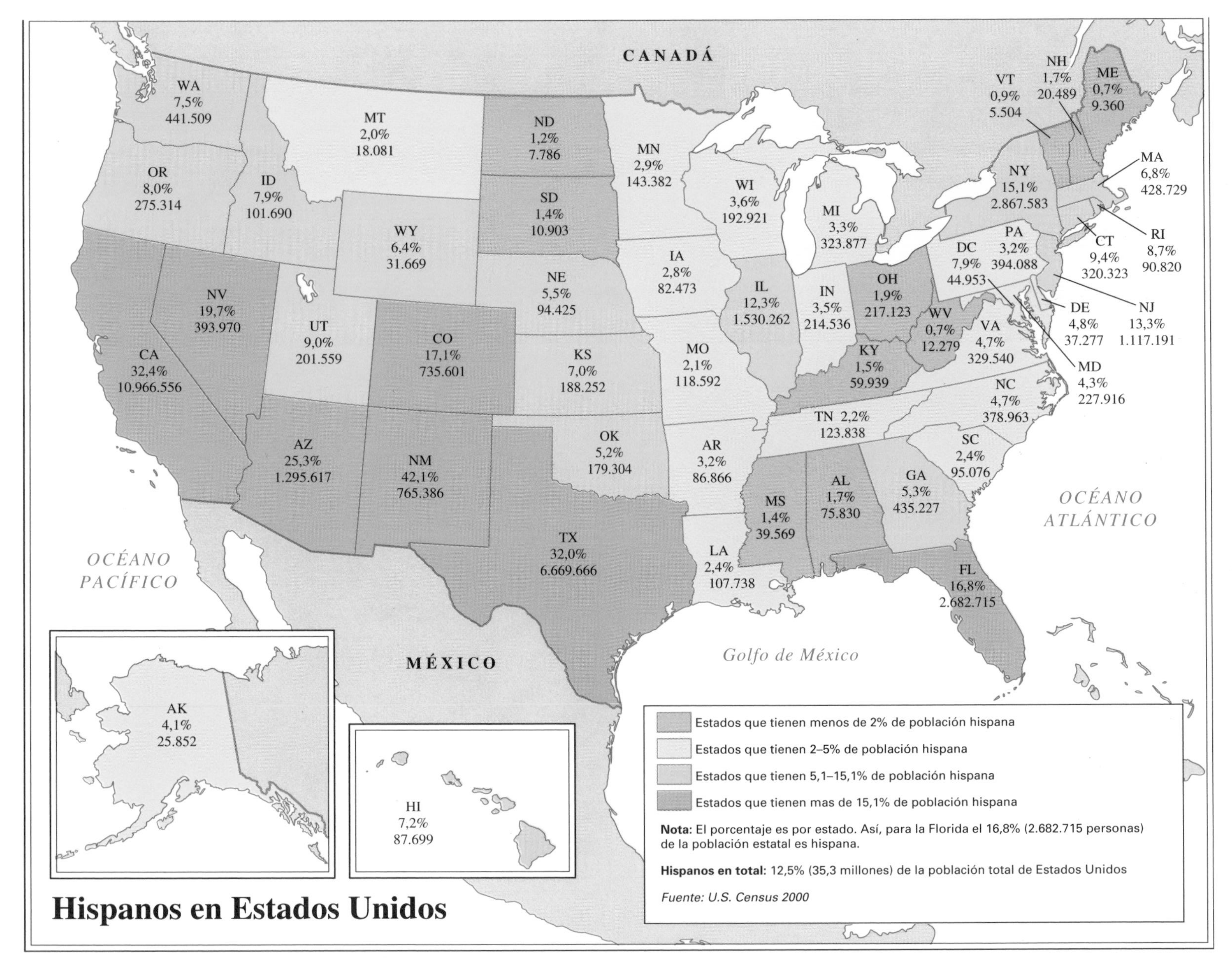

Hispanos en Estados Unidos
CANADÁ
MÉXICO
OCÉANO PACÍFICO
OCÉANO ATLÁNTICO
Golfo de México
WA 7,5% 441.509
OR 8,0% 275.314
CA 32,4% 10.966.556
ID 7,9% 101.690
NV 19,7% 393.970
MT 2,0% 18.081
WY 6,4% 31.669
UT 9,0% 201.559
AZ 25,3% 1.295.617
CO 17,1% 735.601
NM 42,1% 765.386
ND 1,2% 7.786
SD 1,4% 10.903
NE 5,5% 94.425
KS 7,0% 188.252
OK 5,2% 179.304
TX 32,0% 6.669.666
MN 2,9% 143.382
IA 2,8% 82.473
MO 2,1% 118.592
AR 3,2% 86.866
LA 2,4% 107.738
WI 3,6% 192.921
IL 12,3% 1.530.262
MI 3,3% 323.877
IN 3,5% 214.536
OH 1,9% 217.123
KY 1,5% 59.939
TN 2,2% 123.838
MS 1,4% 39.569
AL 1,7% 75.830
GA 5,3% 435.227
FL 16,8% 2.682.715
SC 2,4% 95.076
NC 4,7% 378.963
VA 4,7% 329.540
WV 0,7% 12.279
DC 7,9% 44.953
PA 3,2% 394.088
NY 15,1% 2.867.583
VT 0,9% 5.504
NH 1,7% 20.489
ME 0,7% 9.360
MA 6,8% 428.729
RI 8,7% 90.820
CT 9,4% 320.323
NJ 13,3% 1.117.191
DE 4,8% 37.277
MD 4,3% 227.916
AK 4,1% 25.852
HI 7,2% 87.699
Estados que tienen menos de 2% de población hispana
Estados que tienen 2–5% de población hispana
Estados que tienen 5,1–15,1% de población hispana
Estados que tienen mas de 15,1% de población hispana
Nota: El porcentaje es por estado. Así, para la Florida el 16,8% (2.682.715 personas) de la población estatal es hispana.
Hispanos en total: 12,5% (35,3 millones) de la población total de Estados Unidos
Fuente: U.S. Census 2000

Instructor's Annotated Edition

¡Hola, amigos!

Instructor's Annotated Edition

¡Hola, amigos!

SEVENTH EDITION

Ana C. Jarvis
Chandler-Gilbert Community College

Raquel Lebredo
California Baptist University, Emerita

Francisco Mena-Ayllón
University of Redlands, Emeritus

Houghton Mifflin Company
Boston New York

Publisher: Rolando Hernández

Senior Sponsoring Editor: Glenn A. Wilson

Executive Marketing Director: Eileen Bernadette Moran

Marketing Assistant: Lorreen Ruth Pelletier

Senior Development Editor: Judith Bach

Editorial Assistant: Erin Beasley

Project Editor: Amy Johnson

Art and Design Manager: Gary Crespo

Cover Design Manager: Anne S. Katzeff

Senior Photo Editor: Jennifer Meyer Dare

Composition Buyer: Chuck Dutton

Cover image © Will Terry/Images.com

Photo credits are listed on page 397, which is hereby considered an extension of the copyright page.

Printed in the U.S.A.

Library of Congress Control Number: 2006935838

Instructor's Annotated Edition
ISBN-10: 0-618-79405-0
ISBN-13: 978-0-618-79405-8
For orders, use student text ISBNs
ISBN-10: 0-618-79404-2
ISBN-13: 978-0-618-79404-1

23456789-VH-10 09 08 07

Introduction to the Instructor's Annotated Edition

Contents

¡Hola, amigos!, Seventh Edition, is a complete, fully integrated program for beginning students of Spanish at both two- and four-year colleges and universities. The purpose of this *Instructor's Annotated Edition* is to familiarize the instructor with the features of the *Student Edition* and with the other program components, as well as to offer suggestions for implementing the program effectively. To accomplish this, the *Annotated Edition* is divided into two parts. This first part describes the program and its objectives and offers teaching suggestions for implementing the various components. The remainder of the *Annotated Edition* consists of a complete *Student Edition,* with marginal annotations printed in color that offer suggested teaching strategies, supplementary cultural information, additional activities to enhance students' oral and written communicative skills, and in-text answers to all the exercises.

1. Instructor's Guide

The varying needs of foreign language programs in colleges and universities on two-semester and three-quarter schedules, with wide fluctuations in contact hours per week, demand flexibility in the instructional materials used. The broad range of ability levels often encountered in the foreign language classroom further heightens this need. In developing ***¡Hola, amigos!,*** Seventh Edition, our intention has been to provide a complete, adaptable beginning Spanish program that responds to the requirements of both the student and the instructor.

Student Components

All of the components of ***¡Hola, amigos!,*** Seventh Edition, are fully integrated with the *Student Edition* and are described in greater detail on the following pages. The extent to which each will be used in any given course will vary according to the course's objectives, the schedule requirements, and student ability and motivation. It is hoped that this range of teaching resources will give instructors the flexibility they require to meet these varying needs as well as the instructional goals of their curricula.

Student Text

The *Student Edition* contains all of the information and activities students need for in-class use. It is divided into seven units—consisting of two units each—that contain vocabulary presentations and activities, grammar presentations and activities, cultural information, reading selections, and writing practice. There are also valuable reference sections at the back of the book, including Spanish-English and English-Spanish glossaries, and verb charts showing the conjugations of different categories of verbs.

In-Text Audio CD

The *In-Text Audio CD* contains the recorded material for the listening-based activities in the *Student Edition,* such as lesson dialogues and pronunciation practice. This audio CD is packaged with the *Student Edition.* The in-text audio recordings are also available as .mp3 files at the *Online Study Center.* Instructors may play the recordings in the classroom during class time, or can assign listening activities to do outside of class.

Student Activities Manual (SAM)

The *Student Activities Manual* (*SAM*) includes out-of-class practice of the material presented in the *Student Edition.* It is divided into a *Workbook* **(Cuaderno de práctica),** which focuses on written vocabulary and grammar practice, reading, and writing, and a *Lab Manual* **(Manual de laboratorio),** which focuses on pronunciation and listening comprehension.

Online Multimedia eBook

WebCT
courses · campus · community

The *Online Multimedia eBook* provides students with the entire text online, integrated with links to a wide variety of resources—from audio pronunciations to video clips to Web expansion activities and interactive practice—for a completely interactive experience. By clicking on a link at the relevant point in the text, students can immediately practice and reinforce what they have learned. A real-time voice chat feature allows students to complete pair and group activities together, and audio pronunciations of every lesson's active vocabulary terms are included. The *Online Multimedia eBook* is available on Eduspace, Blackboard, and WebCT platforms.

eSAM

WebCT
courses · campus · community

The *eSAM* is the electronic version of the printed *SAM.* It enables students to work in a convenient, engaging online format and receive immediate feedback for most exercises. In addition, students can link to the textbook website for supplementary practice or to SMARTHINKING e-tutor for extra help. The audio associated with the *eSAM* is also included with an easy click. The *eSAM* is available on Quia, Eduspace, Blackboard, or WebCT platforms.

SAM Audio CDs

The *SAM Audio CDs* contain the pronunciation and listening practice that corresponds to the Lab Manual of the *SAM*. The material on the *SAM Audio CDs* is meant to be used by students outside of class at the language lab or communications center. The *SAM Audio CDs* may also be packaged for student purchase.

Online Study Center Online Study Center (college.hmco.com/PIC/holaamigos7e)

The *Online Study Center*, includes the following components:

- *Audio Flashcards:* Flashcards with integrated audio help students learn the chapter's new vocabulary.
- *Web Search Activites:* These activities are designed to give students further practice with lesson vocabulary and grammar while exploring existing Spanish-language web sites.
- *In-Text Audio:* Audio files from the *In-Text Audio CD*, provided in .mp3 format.
- *ACE Practice Tests:* Practice activities covering vocabulary, grammar, and video material. Additional language skills practice is also available.

Instructor Components

Instructor's Annotated Edition

The *Instructor's Annotated Edition (IAE)* provides marginal annotations with classroom tips, ideas for additional activities, and answers to *Student Edition* activities. The *Instructor's Guide* material at the beginning of the *Instructor's Annotated Edition* provides information about the program and ideas for teaching with ***¡Hola, amigos!***.

eSAM and Course Management

WebCT courses · campus · community

The electronic version of the *SAM* includes a comprehensive grade book and offers instructors the ability to make assignments, track performance, and view and manage the results of students' work. The audio associated with the *Lab Manual* portion of the *eSAM* is also included. Results from the Quia program can be exported into WebCT or Blackboard if desired. All of the resources included in the *HM ClassPrep CD* plus the *Testing Program* are included in Blackboard, WebCT, and Eduspace formats.

HM ClassPrep™ with HM Testing CD-ROM for Windows® and Macintosh®

This CD-ROM contains a variety of instructor resources, including:

- Complete *Testing Program* (PDFs for printing tests as is, as well as in Word so that instructors can modify the tests), *Testing Program Notes, Testing Audioscript,* and *Testing Program Answer Key*
- *Testing Audio* in .mp3 format
- *HM Testing*—a text-specific test generator program, which allows instructors to create customized multiple-choice and true/false tests.
- *SAM (Student Activities Manual) Answer Key*
- *Student Text Answer Key*
- *Online Teaching Center Link*—a direct link to additional instructor resources located on the *Online Teaching Center.*

All components are fully integrated, yet flexible enough to accommodate a range of scheduling factors, contact hours, and ability levels without sacrificing coverage of the key grammatical structures essential to communication in Spanish.

Online Teaching Center *Online Teaching Center* (college.hmco.com/PIC/holaamigos7e)

The *Online Teaching Center* includes

- *Integration Guide*
- *PowerPoint slides and Overhead Transparencies* featuring grammar charts and illustrations from the textbook.
- *Situation Cards and Guide to Situation Cards*
- *SAM Audioscript*
- *Video Transcript*
- *Translations of the Lesson Dialogues*

New to the Seventh Edition

The ***¡Hola, amigos!*** program continues to offer proven, flexible materials designed to develop students' ability to communicate effectively in Spanish. In preparing this new edition, we have kept in mind suggestions from reviewers and from users of previous editions. The following lists highlight the major changes in the *Student Edition* and in the individual components resulting from these suggestions.

New to the Student Edition

- ***¡Hola, amigos!,*** Seventh Edition, has a complete new design and art program.
- The distribution of the lessons has been streamlined to divide the book into seven units each split into two lessons, making it easier to cover the material in two semesters of seven lessons each.
- Unit openers have been expanded to include not only lesson objectives, but also comprehensive thematic cultural introductions presented through maps, flags, photos, and photo captions from the countries and regions represented in each unit.
- *Diálogos* are entirely new. A more robust selection of comprehension questions with a newly added true/false partner activity and an array of new illustrations help to contextualize these dialogues.
- Vocabulary sections have been updated to improve student recognition, comprehension, and retention of new terms. *Para hablar del tema: Vocabulario* now lists cognates separately without English translations, helping students to independently recognize cognates. *Amplíe su vocabulario* now showcases an innovative visual presentation of new terms making it easier for students to retain the new words. The new vocabulary feature, *De país a país,* highlights regional variations between "standard" Spanish and expressions used in different Spanish speaking countries. The vocabulary activities in *Para practicar el vocabulario* have also been expanded and diversified.
- Pronunciation activities are now a feature of *every* lesson. The newly added activities incorporate lines from the lesson dialogues and give the students opportunities to practice difficult words in context.
- *Entre nosotros,* found at the end of each lesson, features a new writing assignment after each *Encuesta* activity to give students additional writing practice and connect one skill to another. These activities add purpose to the interviews by asking students to critically relay their findings.
- The *El mundo hispánico* element provides unit-level cultural information with detailed visual presentations for many Hispanic countries. This section, found at the end of each unit, synthesizes each unit opener with the *Detalles culturales* and the *Diálogos* from each lesson.

New to the Components

- The marginal annotations in the *Instructor's Annotated Edition* now contain answers for all *Student Edition* activities.
- The *Student Activities Manual (SAM)* has been revised to reflect the changes in the textbook's organization and content. Some activities have been rewritten to provide more contextualized practice. Activity titles have been added in the *Puntos para recordar* sections of the *Lab Manual* section for easier navigation.
- The all new two-tier ***¡Hola, amigos!*** *Video* features a situational segment for each unit with recurring characters, and country specific-footage for selected countries, ethnic groups, and regions presented in each unit.
- The substantially upgraded ***¡Hola, amigos!*** web sites are now called *Online Teaching Center* and *Online Study Center.* The *Online Teaching Center* includes a technology integration guide, electronic versions of the *Audioscript,* the *Video Transcript,* the *Situation Cards,* the *Guide to the Situation Cards,* the *Translations of the Lesson Dialogues,* and *PowerPoint slides* that contain grammar charts and textbook illustrations. The *Online Study Center* provides online self-tests, audio flashcards, web search activities, and audio files in .mp3 format. Additional practice, including interactive multimedia practice, games, and video-based speaking, comprehension, and grammar activities, is also available.
- The new *HM ClassPrep™ with HM Testing* includes all the *Testing Program* materials and answer keys, as well as a test generator with testing items specifically written for this platform that enables instructors to assemble their own customized multiple-choice and true/false tests.

Objectives of the Program

¡Hola, amigos! is a balanced four-skills introduction to Spanish that endeavors to prepare students to use the language in a natural way for communication in a variety of situations. The basic structures of Spanish are presented as the tools without which communication ultimately breaks down, and they are practiced in a range of activities designed to prepare students to express themselves effectively in Spanish. Because our teaching experience has led us to conclude that no single method works as well in practice as a variety, we have chosen an eclectic approach that draws upon strategies associated with many different methodological trends. A prime consideration in making this decision was the need to use varied presentation strategies and provide an array of content formats to maintain students' interest in the language-learning process. The implementation of this program will vary with the goals of the course and the individual instructor's preferences. However, for courses meeting at least four hours weekly for approximately 26 weeks, the following are reasonable goals for each of the skill areas listed.

Speaking

- Pronunciation of all of the sounds of Spanish with sufficient accuracy to be understood by a native speaker of the language.
- Expression of ideas with the vocabulary covered in simple sentences, demonstrating control of the past, present, and future tenses and the most common subjunctive forms.
- Occasional use of subordinate clauses in spontaneous speech.

Listening

- Perception of all Spanish sounds and their distinction from one another.
- Comprehension of ideas expressed within the framework of the vocabulary and grammatical structures presented.

Reading

- Understanding of simple nonliterary Spanish prose on nontechnical, high-frequency topics. Understanding of the main ideas in short literary Spanish poetry and prose selections.
- Intelligent guessing at new vocabulary items based on context.
- Ability to demonstrate comprehension by answering questions on reading passages.

Writing

- Creating in class—and without a dictionary—a paragraph in Spanish on topics covered by the text with sufficient clarity to be understood without difficulty by a native speaker. (Major errors like verb or adjective agreement may appear.)
- Preparing at home a paragraph in Spanish without major errors on any topic covered by the text, with sufficient clarity to be understood upon first reading by a native speaker.

Culture

- Elementary knowledge of important aspects of culture in the Spanish-speaking world, such as climate and geography, family life, school and university life, rural and urban life, and how they differ from American culture.
- Elementary knowledge of cultural customs such as mealtimes, *el abrazo,* and shades of formality.
- The ability to discuss home culture's values and compare them with the target cultures' values, and the development of an enhanced appreciation of cultural differences and similarities.

Organization of the Textbook: Features and Teaching Strategies

¡Hola, amigos!, Seventh Edition, consists of seven units, each containing two thematically related lessons. Self-test review sections, called *Tome este examen,* follow each unit. Reference materials at the end of the text include an appendix on pronunciation, a summary of regular and irregular verb conjugations, a glossary of grammatical terms, an answer key to *Tome este examen,* the unit review sections, Spanish-English and English-Spanish vocabularies, and an index to the grammatical topics covered by the text.

To assist instructors in implementing the various features of the text, strategies for their use are provided as each is described in detail.

Lesson Features

Dialogues: To develop communicative competence, students must be exposed to language samples that function in realistic contexts of everyday situations. The dialogues serve this role as they introduce the vocabulary and structures that will be practiced throughout the remainder of the lesson.

Strategies: The dialogues may be introduced in class or given as a listening assignment outside of class. While they are not intended for memorization, it is important that students speak the lines aloud, preferably more than once (choral and individual repetition) and with a partner (role-playing the dialogues). Point out that the headphone icon indicates that the dialogues are recorded on the *In-text Audio CD* accompanying the text as well as the *SAM Audio CDs.* Also explain to students that the dialogues illustrate how the grammatical structures of the lesson are used for communication and that the grammatical explanations often draw upon the vocabulary from the dialogues in their example sentences. As students' familiarity with the dialogues and oral abilities increase, you may wish to encourage ad-libbing as students work with the dialogues in pairs.

Alternative methods of presenting the dialogues are (1) use of advance organizers (overhead transparencies or sketches on the board depicting the main action of the dialogue accompanied by questions, sentence completions, or other types of comprehension checks) that preview the content of the dialogue before students read it; (2) personalized questions related to the topic of the dialogue; (3) a brief brainstorming session in which students guess from the dialogue title or the accompanying illustrations where, when, and why the action takes place and who or what is involved; (4) use of realia or visuals to introduce key vocabulary; (5) a brief summary of the dialogue in Spanish by the instructor, followed by students' descriptions in simple sentences of the persons speaking, the location of the action, and other key information; and (6) assignment of the dialogue for individual listening and rehearsal before class.

Dialogue Translations: The dialogue translations, available at the *Online Study Center,* allow students working independently to check their comprehension. The translations are functional equivalents of the Spanish dialogues in idiomatic American English, not word-for-word translations.

Strategies: Alert students that the translations' purpose is to convey an immediate sense of the dialogues' meaning before the formal presentation of new structures. They should be encouraged to try to guess the meaning of the new words and structures from context before consulting the translations.

Para hablar del tema: Vocabulario: This two-page spread contains all the new vocabulary used in the dialogues. It is organized by grammatical functions to assist students in associating the various items with their role in communication. Cognates *(Cognados)* and regional variations *(De país a país)* are listed separately. All vocabulary must be memorized because all items will be used in the lesson's subsequent grammatical explanations, activated in practice exercises, and reentered in later lessons. The *Amplíe su vocabulario* section that follows expands on the thematic vocabulary introduced in the dialogues. The *Entre nosotros* section at the end of the lesson provides a general review of new vocabulary and structures through a variety of formats (see below).

Strategies: To check vocabulary acquisition, multiple-choice questions, open-ended completion statements, realia, and visual aids such as the ***¡Hola, amigos!*** *Transparency Masters* and the *Spanish Overhead Transparencies Kit* may be used. The following variation of "Bingo" is both a useful comprehension check and a welcome diversion. Have students fill in a 25-block grid with words chosen from the vocabulary list; then call out words from the list at random, telling students to mark these words with an "X" if they have them on their grids, until a student wins the game. This is also an excellent activity to check and improve comprehension of numbers. Additional activities for promoting vocabulary acquisition are (1) word association games in which students must respond to a stimulus word with a related vocabulary item; (2) team generation of crossword puzzles to be solved by classmates individually or in pairs, with simple definitions, cognates, synonyms, and antonyms as cues; and (3) an adaptation of the TV game *Jeopardy* in which rival teams select four or five categories and generate questions and answers for each; students on rival teams then individually pick a category, are shown the answer, and must supply the question to earn points for their team.

Pronunciación: Each lesson contains pronunciation and linking exercises designed to acquaint students with basic Spanish sounds, with those sounds that pose problems for English speakers, and with the ways that words in Spanish are combined in natural speech. Because these factors will strongly influence students' listening comprehension and oral abilities, it is important to spend sufficient time to ensure that all students are thoroughly familiarized with the material these sections contain.

Strategies: Point out that the headphone icon indicates that these sections are recorded on the *In-Text Audio CD* so that they can easily practice on their own outside of class. Students should also be referred to Appendix A of the textbook for additional information on Spanish pronunciation and spelling.

Puntos para recordar: This section presents the grammatical topics of the lesson succinctly and clearly enough to be readily understood by students. Charts and diagrams are used wherever possible to provide visual summaries of the structures presented. English explanations and Spanish examples define and illustrate both the formation of the new structure and its potential communicative value to the learners. When appropriate, new structures are compared and contrasted with previously learned Spanish structures or with English equivalents. Areas of potential interference between Spanish and English are also pointed out.

To the extent possible, no unknown language is used in these structural presentations or in the examples that illustrate their use. However, students should be advised that in certain cases—for example, telling time, describing the weather, and giving the days of the week and dates—the material covered dictates the introduction of new vocabulary items for which they are responsible.

Strategies: Students should be asked to read these sections on their own, so that as little class time as possible will be spent on explaining grammar. You may wish to set aside five minutes at the beginning of the class following this assignment to answer students' questions or offer any necessary clarification.

Práctica and Práctica y conversación: Following each grammar point, the *Práctica* and *Práctica y conversación* sections provide immediate practice and reinforcement with activities that range from highly controlled to more open-ended, creative use of language. Among the many types of exercises featured in these sections are substitution drills, transformations, fill-ins, matching, translations, open-ended sentence completions, personalized questions, and illustration-based activities. Many of these exercises are designed to be done either orally or in writing at the instructor's discretion.

Strategies: Suggestions for variations of these activities and follow-up communicative activities are provided in the instructor annotations for additional practice. Once students have demonstrated control over the structure in the earlier manipulative activities, it is advisable to proceed to communicative, though still controlled, tasks to maintain students' interest.

Whenever possible, selection of the activities to be used during class should be based on the opportunities they provide for allowing students to work in pairs or small groups. Depending on your mix of students, you may find that pair work functions best in the early stages of practice since it is generally perceived by students as less threatening. Small group activities are often more complex, demanding a higher degree of familiarity with vocabulary and structures, and should largely be deferred to later parts of the lesson.

Entre nosotros: This final section of each lesson consists of several activities that employ a variety of strategies to recombine and synthesize the various grammatical topics and lexical items introduced in the lesson. Students can use these open-ended activities to apply what they have learned to communicate in Spanish both orally and in writing.

- *¡Conversemos!* offers two interview activities, *Para conocernos mejor* and *Una encuesta,* that allow students to ask and answer questions related to the lesson theme and structures as well as relate the lesson material to their own experience. Follow-up activities may include students reporting on selected questions from their pair work, the class sharing results of the poll activity, or the reporting of responses for selected items.
- *¿Cómo lo decimos?* places students in a variety of high-frequency situations to be resolved through creative use of the language. As the course progresses, you may wish to copy the situations on cards, combining them with those from previous lessons for more sustained speaking practice and added review. These cards may also be used for individual oral testing.
- The photo-, realia-, or illustration-based activities in the *¿Qué pasa aquí?* and *¿Qué dice aquí?* sections develop speaking, writing, or reading skills in a creative, communicative manner.
- *Para escribir* affords the opportunity to use Spanish in some form of free written communication, such as an e-mail or a journal entry.
- The authentic, popular sayings (*Un dicho* or *Un proverbio*) at the end of the lesson enhance students' knowledge of Hispanic culture through cross-cultural comparison of language while simultaneously empasizing major preceding grammatical themes.

Strategies: It is important to stress the practical nature of all the motivating, creative activities in the *Entre nosotros* section. Instructors should emphasize their cultural authenticity and their similarity to situations that students would encounter in Spanish-speaking countries. Especially in the earlier lessons, brainstorming sessions that focus on the vocabulary needed to respond appropriately in each situation would help to prepare students. Assigning pairs or groups can also help those students who may experience difficulty.

End-of-Unit Features

Lectura: Following the second lesson of each unit, the *Lectura* sections feature reading selections based on authentic materials and, in Units 5, 6, and 7, literary selections. The pre-reading activity, *Estrategia de lectura,* is designed to help students predict and anticipate content based on the nature of the reading, visuals, and titles. You may want to encourage students to look for cognates when reading and to focus on general meaning rather than trying to understand every word. Ask questions based on information obtained from the title of the reading as well as from skimming through the passage. Also encourage students to read the questions in *Vamos a leer* prior to reading to help focus their reading or have them scan for answers to key questions before reading. Finally, an important part of the reading experience is the degree of personalization of material read. This is provided in the *Díganos* activity following each selection.

Strategies: Students should be encouraged to skim, scan, and get the gist of passages rather than to comprehend all of the details of the text as they read. Using advance organizers such as pictures and the other strategies covered in the *Estrategia de lectura* sections will help students become more independent readers.

El mundo hispánico: The end-of-unit cultural sections—in conjunction with the visuals, maps, and flags on the unit opener—have several goals. First, they expose students to geographic, ethnic, and sociocultural aspects of a particular area of the Spanish-speaking world. They also offer practical information on culturally conditioned behavioral norms and customs as they affect daily life in the Spanish-speaking world at large. These are thematically related to the situation portrayed by the dialogues. The cultural sections are all written in Spanish to provide opportunities for students to use reading strategies such as skimming, scanning, getting the gist, and identifying cognates. New thought-provoking questions have been added to engage students in comparing their own cultural norms and values with those from the Spanish-speaking countries they are studying.

Strategies: The *Comentarios* following the cultural sections may be used to invite comparisons between the target cultures and students' own cultures. Alternatively, these notes may be used as reading assignments and followed up with a brief comprehension check. The ***¡Hola, amigos!,*** Seventh Edition *Video,* the maps from the text, and any personal photographs or realia may be used to further illustrate this section. Spanish-language newspapers and magazines are also excellent sources of authentic cultural information.

Tome este examen: This comprehensive review section follows each unit. The exercises are grouped by lesson, and their titles clearly indicate whether their purpose is to check vocabulary control or mastery of a specific grammatical structure or cultural concept. A complete answer key to these review sections is provided in Appendix D so that students may immediately verify their responses. Upon completion of each review section, learners will know precisely which of the unit objectives they have attained and which they must review in greater detail. While these exercises are of necessity manipulative in nature, every effort has been made to ensure that the correct response entails natural use of Spanish.

Additional Features

Vocabularies: The Spanish-English vocabulary contains all active vocabulary items from the *Vocabulario* and *Puntos para recordar* sections, as well as all optional vocabulary items from the *El mundo hispánico* and *Lectura* sections not activated elsewhere in the text. The English-Spanish vocabulary contains the same items, with English entries and Spanish equivalents. Each vocabulary item is followed by the number of the lesson in which it is introduced.

2. Sample Lesson Plan

The following lesson plan assumes an elementary Spanish class meeting four times a week over a 14-week semester, for a total of 56 contact hours to cover the first seven lessons. This schedule allows for an average of six to seven hours per lesson, with ample time for review, quizzes, and major exams, as well as for the inclusion of video and other components in the program. Institutions organized on the quarter system can use this lesson plan as a guide. Classes meeting three times weekly, for a total of 42 contact hours, will devote five hours per lesson. Instructors may reduce or eliminate activities in order to cover material in a semester. Activities skipped in class may be assigned as written exercises. Pronunciation exercises from the textbook are recorded on the In-text Audio CD and may form part of a language laboratory assignment. This sample lesson represents a six-hour presentation of Lesson 8.

Lesson 8

Day I

1. Warm up with a review of the concepts presented in Lesson 7 to prepare for work on irregular and stem-changing verbs in the preterit, and direct and indirect object pronouns used together. Explain the communicative goals of Lesson 8.
2. Present the dialogues with choral repetition. Check comprehension using the true/false exercise and the comprehension questions. Review and discuss *Detalles culturales* cultural notes along with the dialogues.
3. Present the vocabulary in *Amplíe su vocabulario.* Have students do exercises A, B, C, and D in *Para practicar el vocabulario* (pages 176–177) orally. Alternatively you could assign exercises A and C as homework.

Homework: Have students review the dialogues and vocabulary and read *Puntos para recordar 1,* Preterit of some irregular verbs and *2,* Direct and indirect object pronouns used together. Students should write the answers to Exercises A and B (page 179) and Exercises A and B (pages 181–182).

Day 2

1. Divide the class into pairs and have students role-play the dialogues.
2. Present *Puntos para recordar 1,* Preterit of some irregular verbs, following the suggestions in the annotations.
3. Go over the answers to Exercises A and B (page 179) or have students check their answers against those written on an overhead transparency.
4. Do Exercises C and D on page 180 orally as a class or in pairs.
5. Present *Puntos para recordar 2,* Direct and indirect object pronouns used together, following the suggestions in the annotation on pages 180–181.
6. Review Exercises A and B (pages 181–182) as necessary; have students do Exercises C, D, and E (page 182) orally.

Homework: Have students write answers to Exercise C or D (page 182), read *Puntos para recordar 3,* Stem-changing verbs in the preterit and *4,* The imperfect tense, and complete Exercise A (page 184).

Day 3

1. Warm up by asking students questions involving irregular verbs in the preterit and object pronouns used together.
2. Present *Puntos para recordar 3,* Stem-changing verbs in the preterit, following the teaching suggestions in the annotation.
3. Have students give answers to Exercise A (page 184).
4. Have students do Exercise B (page 184) in pairs, and Exercise C (page 184) in groups. Have individual students write answers on the board.
5. Begin to present *Puntos para recordar 4,* The imperfect tense, following the teaching suggestions in the annotations.

Homework: Have students write the answers to Exercise A (page 187), and read *Puntos para recordar 5.*

Day 4

1. Warm up by asking students questions using the imperfect. Complete presentation, if necessary, and do a quick review of Exercise A on page 187.
2. Have students do Exercises B and C on pages 187–188 in pairs. Complete Exercise D on page 188 as a class.
3. Present *Puntos para recordar 5,* Formation of adverbs. Have students do Exercises A and B, (page 189) orally in class, and Exercise C (page 189) in pairs.
4. Have students do *Para conocernos mejor* (page 190), in pairs.
5. Have students do *Una encuesta* (page 190). Have students discuss what they have learned about their classmates. As a variation, have students write a summary for homework.
6. Divide students in groups, and have each group read about one country from *El mundo hispánico* (pages 194–195). Students should be prepared to talk about "their" country in class.

Homework: Have students prepare *¿Cómo lo decimos?* (page191) and read *De versos sencillos.* Students should be prepared to answer questions about the poems in class. Tell students to read the information about the country they have selected and be ready to answer questions in class the next day.

Day 5

1. In pairs, have students compare their answers to *¿Cómo lo decimos?* (page 191), then role-play them for the class.
2. Have students work in groups on *¿Qué pasa aquí?* (page 191). Each group presents their story to the class.
3. Read *De versos sencillos* and ask students the questions in the Vamos a leer section (page 192).
4. Ask students questions about the country they have selected, and ask them what impressed them most.

Homework: Assign *Para escribir* (page 191). Assign the Lesson 8, *Tome este examen* (pages 198–199). Instruct students to check their answers by comparing them to the answer key in Appendix D. Tell students to prepare for a quiz on Lesson 8 for the next class.

Day 6

1. Administer Lesson 8 quiz.
2. Introduce the dialogue and vocabulary in Lesson 9.

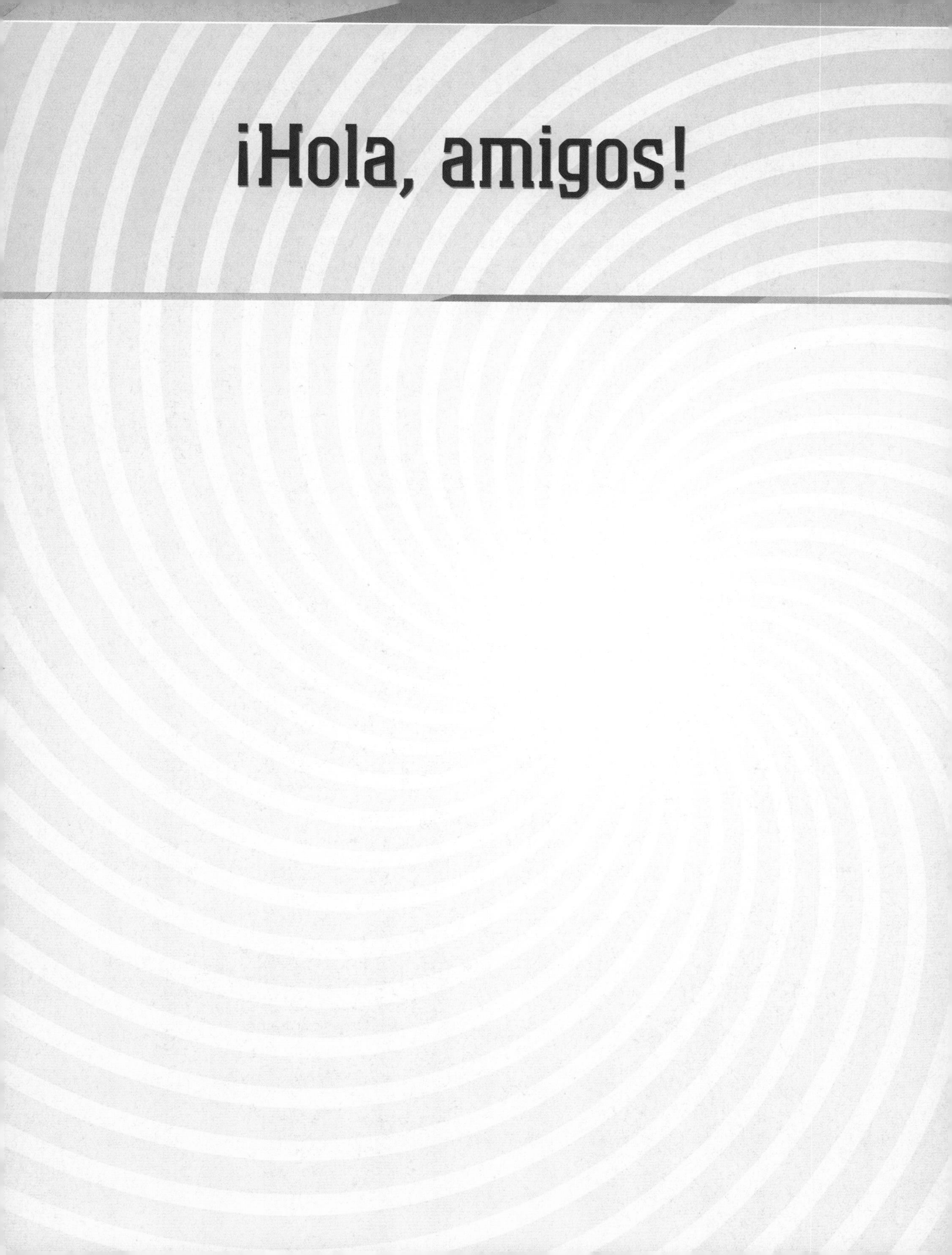

¡Hola, amigos!

¡Hola, amigos!

SEVENTH EDITION

Ana C. Jarvis
Chandler-Gilbert Community College

Raquel Lebredo
California Baptist University, Emerita

Francisco Mena-Ayllón
University of Redlands, Emeritus

Houghton Mifflin Company
Boston New York

Publisher: Rolando Hernández

Senior Sponsoring Editor: Glenn A. Wilson

Executive Marketing Director: Eileen Bernadette Moran

Marketing Assistant: Lorreen Ruth Pelletier

Senior Development Editor: Judith Bach

Editorial Assistant: Erin Beasley

Project Editor: Amy Johnson

Art and Design Manager: Gary Crespo

Cover Design Manager: Anne S. Katzeff

Senior Photo Editor: Jennifer Meyer Dare

Composition Buyer: Chuck Dutton

Cover image © Will Terry/Images.com

Photo credits are listed on page 397, which is hereby considered an extension of the copyright page.

Printed in the U.S.A.

Library of Congress Control Number: 2006935838

Instructor's Annotated Edition
ISBN-10: 0-618-79405-0
ISBN-13: 978-0-618-79405-8
For orders, use student text ISBNs
ISBN-10: 0-618-79404-2
ISBN-13: 978-0-618-79404-1

23456789-VH-10 09 08 07

Scope and Sequence

1 Los estudiantes universitarios (pp. 2–51)

	Lección 1 ¡Bienvenidos!	Lección 2 Nuestras clases
Para hablar del tema	*(pp. 6–7)* Títulos Expresiones de cortesía Saludos y despedidas Preguntas y respuestas Colores Vocabulario para la clase **De país a país**	*(pp. 24–25)* Asignaturas Expresiones Para pedir bebidas **De país a país**
Para practicar el vocabulario	*(pp. 8–9)* Online Study Center A. Los estudiantes B. Yo soy el anfitrión (la anfitriona) C. ¡Somos pintores! D. ¿Qué color te gusta? E. ¿Qué necesitamos? F. ¿Necesitas algo? **Pronunciación** Las vocales	*(pp. 26–27)* Online Study Center A. Palabras y más palabras B. Preguntas y respuestas C. ¿Qué deciden? D. ¿Qué clases necesito? **Pronunciación** Linking
Puntos para recordar	*(pp. 10–19)* Online Study Center 1. Gender and number of nouns, part I *(p. 10)* 2. Definite and indefinite articles *(p. 11)* 3. Subject pronouns *(p. 13)* 4. Present indicative of *ser* *(p. 15)* 5. Forms of adjectives and agreement of articles, nouns, and adjectives *(p. 16)* 6. The alphabet *(p. 18)* 7. Numbers 0 to 39 *(p. 18)*	*(pp. 28–41)* Online Study Center 1. Present indicative of *–ar* verbs *(p. 28)* 2. Interrogative and negative sentences *(p. 30)* 3. Possessive adjectives *(p. 32)* 4. Gender of nouns, part II *(p. 34)* 5. Numbers 40 to 200 *(p. 35)* 6. Telling time *(p. 36)* 7. Days of the week, and months and seasons of the year *(p. 39)*
Entre nosotros	*(pp. 20–21)* **¡Conversemos!** **Para escribir** Un mensaje electrónico **Un dicho**	*(pp. 42–43)* **¡Conversemos!** **Para escribir** Tu horario **Un dicho**

Lectura *(pp. 44–45)*	Universidad Nacional	**Video** Online Study Center
El mundo hispánico *(pp. 46–47)*	Los mexicoamericanos Los cubanoamericanos Los puertorriqueños	**Video** Calle 8 Online Study Center
Tome este examen *(pp. 48–51)*	Lección 1	Lección 2

2 En familia (pp. 52–97)

	Lección 3 Los trabajos de la casa	Lección 4 Una fiesta de cumpleaños
Para hablar del tema	*(pp. 56–57)* La casa Aparatos electrodomésticos Batería de cocina **De país a país**	*(pp. 76–77)* La familia Los amigos Una fiesta **De país a país**
Para practicar el vocabulario	*(pp. 58–59)* Online Study Center A. Preguntas y respuestas B. ¡Hay mil cosas que hacer! C. ¿Qué necesitas? D. Los trabajos de la casa **Pronunciación** Las consonantes *b, v*	*(pp. 78–79)* Online Study Center A. Preguntas y respuestas B. Planes para la fiesta C. El parentesco D. De mi álbum de fotos **Pronunciación** La consonante *c*
Puntos para recordar	*(pp. 60–71)* Online Study Center 1. Present indicative of *–er* and *–ir* verbs *(p. 60)* 2. Possession with *de (p. 62)* 3. Present indicative of *tener* and *venir (p. 64)* 4. Expressions with *tener (p. 65)* 5. Demonstrative adjectives and pronouns *(p. 67)* 6. Numbers from 300 to 1,000 *(p. 70)*	*(pp. 80–87)* Online Study Center 1. Verbs with irregular first-person forms *(p. 80)* 2. *Saber* vs. *conocer (p. 81)* 3. Personal *a (p. 82)* 4. Contractions: *al* and *del (p. 83)* 5. Present indicative of *ir, dar,* and *estar (p. 84)* 6. *Ir a* + infinitive *(p. 86)*
Entre nosotros	*(pp. 72–73)* **¡Conversemos!** **Para escribir** Para dividir el trabajo **Un dicho**	*(pp. 88–89)* **¡Conversemos!** **Para escribir** Un mensaje electrónico **Un dicho**
Lectura *(pp. 90–91)*	Sociales	**Video** Online Study Center
El mundo hispánico *(pp. 92–93)*	México Guatemala El Salvador	**Video** Online Study Center
Tome este examen *(pp. 94–97)*	Lección 3	Lección 4

3 ¿Qué comemos hoy? (pp. 98–147)

	Lección 5 El menú, por favor	Lección 6 En el mercado
Para hablar del tema	*(pp. 102–103)* La comida En el restaurante Para poner la mesa **De país a país**	*(pp. 122–123)* En el mercado Más comestibles **De país a país**
Para practicar el vocabulario	*(pp. 104–105)* Online Study Center A. En el restaurante B. Preguntas y respuestas C. Voy a pedir... D. Para poner la mesa **Pronunciación** Las consonantes *g, j, h*	*(pp. 124–125)* Online Study Center A. Preguntas y respuestas B. Dime... C. ¿Qué les servimos? D. En el supermercado **Pronunciación** Las consonantes *ll, ñ*
Puntos para recordar	*(pp. 106–117)* Online Study Center 1. Present progressive *(p. 106)* 2. Uses of *ser* and *estar (p. 108)* 3. Stem-changing verbs: *e* > *ie (p. 111)* 4. Comparative and superlative adjectives, adverbs, and nouns *(p. 113)* 5. Pronouns as objects of prepositions *(p. 116)*	*(pp. 126–137)* Online Study Center 1. Stem-changing verbs: *o* > *ue (p. 126)* 2. Stem-changing verbs: *e* > *i (p. 127)* 3. Direct object pronouns *(p. 129)* 4. Affirmative and negative expressions *(p. 133)* 5. *Hace... que (p. 135)*
Entre nosotros	*(pp. 118–119)* **¡Conversemos!** **Para escribir** En un restaurante **Un dicho**	*(pp. 138–139)* **¡Conversemos!** **Para escribir** Un invitado importante **Un proverbio**
Lectura *(pp. 140–141)*	Sección gastronómica	**Video** Online Study Center
El mundo hispánico *(pp. 142–143)*	Costa Rica Panamá Honduras Nicaragua	**Video** Online Study Center
Tome este examen *(pp. 144–147)*	Lección 5	Lección 6

4 Para divertirse (pp. 148–199)

	Lección 7 Un fin de semana	Lección 8 Las actividades al aire libre
Para hablar del tema	*(pp. 152–153)* El fin de semana Para invitar a alguien a salir **De país a país**	*(pp. 174–175)* Los deportes Más sobre las actividades al aire libre **De país a país**
Para practicar el vocabulario	*(pp. 154–155)* Online Study Center A. Preguntas y respuestas B. Todos se divierten C. ¿Adónde vamos...? D. ¿Quieres ir...? **Pronunciación** Las consonantes *l, r, rr*	*(pp. 176–177)* Online Study Center A. Preguntas y respuestas B. ¿Lógico o ilógico? C. Palabras y más palabras D. Planes de vacaciones **Pronunciación** Pronunciation in context
Puntos para recordar	*(pp. 156–169)* Online Study Center 1. Preterit of regular verbs *(p. 156)* 2. Preterit of *ser, ir,* and *dar (p. 158)* 3. Indirect object pronouns *(p. 159)* 4. The verb *gustar (p. 162)* 5. Reflexive constructions *(p. 165)* **RODEO:** Summary of the Pronouns *(p. 168)*	*(pp. 178–189)* Online Study Center 1. Preterit of some irregular verbs *(p. 178)* 2. Direct and indirect object pronouns used together *(p. 180)* 3. Stem-changing verbs in the preterit *(p. 183)* 4. The imperfect tense *(p. 185)* 5. Formation of adverbs *(p. 188)*
Entre nosotros	*(pp. 170–171)* **¡Conversemos!** **Para escribir** Un día típico **Un dicho**	*(pp. 190–191)* **¡Conversemos!** **Para escribir** De vacaciones **Un dicho**
Lectura *(pp. 192–193)*	*De versos sencillos* (José Martí)	**Video** Online Study Center
El mundo hispánico *(pp. 194–195)*	Cuba Colombia Puerto Rico Venezuela La República Dominicana	**Video** Online Study Center
Tome este examen *(pp. 196–199)*	Lección 7	Lección 8

5 ¿Qué hacemos hoy? (pp. 200–245)

	Lección 9 No tengo nada que ponerme	Lección 10 Diligencias
Para hablar del tema	*(pp. 204–205)* La ropa El tiempo **De país a país**	*(pp. 224–225)* En el banco En la oficina de correos Un poco de tecnología **De país a país**
Para practicar el vocabulario	*(pp. 206–207)* Online Study Center A. En la tienda y en la zapatería B. ¿Qué se ponen? C. Hablando del tiempo D. Haciendo compras **Pronunciación** Pronunciation in context	*(pp. 226–227)* Online Study Center A. Preguntas y respuestas B. Rubén y Eva hacen diligencias C. ¿Qué necesito o qué tengo que hacer? D. ¿Qué necesita hacer? **Pronunciación** Pronunciation in context
Puntos para recordar	*(pp. 208–219)* Online Study Center 1. Some uses of *por* and *para (p. 208)* 2. Weather expressions *(p. 211)* 3. The preterit contrasted with the imperfect *(p. 213)* 4. *Hace...* meaning *ago (p. 216)* 5. Possessive pronouns *(p. 218)*	*(pp. 228–235)* Online Study Center 1. Past participles *(p. 228)* 2. Present perfect tense *(p. 230)* 3. Past perfect (pluperfect) tense *(p. 232)* 4. Formal commands: *Ud.* and *Uds. (p. 233)*
Entre nosotros	*(pp. 220–221)* **¡Conversemos!** **Para escribir** ¿Cómo era Ud.? **Un dicho**	*(pp. 236–237)* **¡Conversemos!** **Para escribir** En el banco **Un dicho**

Lectura *(pp. 238–239)*	*Lecciones de inglés* (Adaptado) (Germán Arciniegas)	**Video** Online Study Center
El mundo hispánico *(pp. 240–241)*	Ecuador Perú Bolivia Paraguay	**Video** Online Study Center
Tome este examen *(pp. 242–245)*	Lección 9	Lección 10

6 De vacaciones (pp. 246–291)

	Lección 11 ¡Buen viaje!	Lección 12 ¿Dónde nos hospedamos?
Para hablar del tema	*(pp. 250–251)* En la agencia de viajes En el aeropuerto Más sobre los viajes **De país a país**	*(pp. 270–271)* En el hotel Más sobre los hoteles **De país a país**
Para practicar el vocabulario	*(pp. 252–253)* Online Study Center A. Preguntas y respuestas B. ¿Qué hago? ¿Adónde voy? C. Definiciones D. En la agencia de viajes **Pronunciación** Pronunciation in context	*(pp. 272–273)* Online Study Center A. Preguntas y respuestas B. En el hotel C. ¿Cuál es la solución? D. Minidiálogos **Pronunciación** Pronunciation in context
Puntos para recordar	*(pp. 254–265)* Online Study Center 1. Introduction to the subjunctive mood *(p. 254)* 2. Subjunctive with verbs of volition *(p. 257)* 3. Subjunctive with verbs of emotion *(p. 260)* 4. Some uses of the prepositions *a*, *de*, and *en (p. 262)*	*(pp. 274–281)* Online Study Center 1. Subjunctive to express indefiniteness and nonexistence *(p. 274)* 2. Familiar commands *(p. 276)* 3. Verbs and prepositions *(p. 278)* 4. Ordinal numbers *(p. 280)*
Entre nosotros	*(pp. 266–267)* **¡Conversemos!** **Para escribir** En una agencia de viajes **Un dicho**	*(pp. 282–283)* **¡Conversemos!** **Para escribir** En un hotel **Un dicho**

Lectura *(pp. 284–285)*	*El canario y el cuervo* (Tomás Iriarte)	**Video** Online Study Center
El mundo hispánico *(pp. 286–287)*	Chile Uruguay Argentina Brasil	**Video** Online Study Center
Tome este examen *(pp. 288–291)*	Lección 11	Lección 12

7 ¿Cómo te sientes? (pp. 292–339)

	Lección 13 En la sala de emergencia	Lección 14 Hablando con el médico
Para hablar del tema	*(pp. 296–297)* En el hospital El cuerpo Otras partes del cuerpo **De país a país**	*(pp. 314–315)* Medicinas Algunos especialistas El botiquín **De país a país**
Para practicar el vocabulario	*(pp. 298–299)* Online Study Center A. Preguntas y respuestas B. En la sala de emergencia C. ¿Qué sabes de anatomía? D. En el hospital **Pronunciación** Pronunciation in context	*(pp. 316–317)* Online Study Center A. Preguntas y respuestas B. ¿Qué debo tomar? C. ¿Qué especialista debo ver? D. En nuestro botiquín **Pronunciación** Pronunciation in context
Puntos para recordar	*(pp. 300–309)* Online Study Center 1. Subjunctive to express doubt, denial, and disbelief *(p. 300)* 2. Subjunctive with certain conjunctions *(p. 304)* 3. First-person plural commands *(p. 306)* **RODEO:** Summary of the Command Forms *(p. 307)* 4. *¿Qué?* and *¿cuál?* used with *ser* *(p. 309)*	*(pp. 318–329)* Online Study Center 1. Future tense *(p. 318)* 2. Conditional tense *(p. 320)* **RODEO:** Summary of the Tenses of the Indicative *(p. 322)* 3. The imperfect subjunctive *(p. 323)* 4. *If*-clauses *(p. 325)* **RODEO:** Summary of the Uses of the Subjunctive *(p. 328)*
Entre nosotros	*(pp. 310–311)* **¡Conversemos!** **Para escribir** Un accidente **Un dicho**	*(pp. 330–331)* **¡Conversemos!** **Para escribir** Con el doctor **Un dicho**
Lectura *(pp. 332–333)*	*Rimas* (Gustavo Adolfo Bécquer)	**Video** Online Study Center
El mundo hispánico *(pp. 334–335)*	España	**Video** Online Study Center
Tome este examen *(pp. 336–339)*	Lección 13	Lección 14

Brief Contents

An Overview of Your Textbook's Main Features

¡Hola, amigos!, Seventh Edition, consists of fourteen lessons thematically organized into seven units

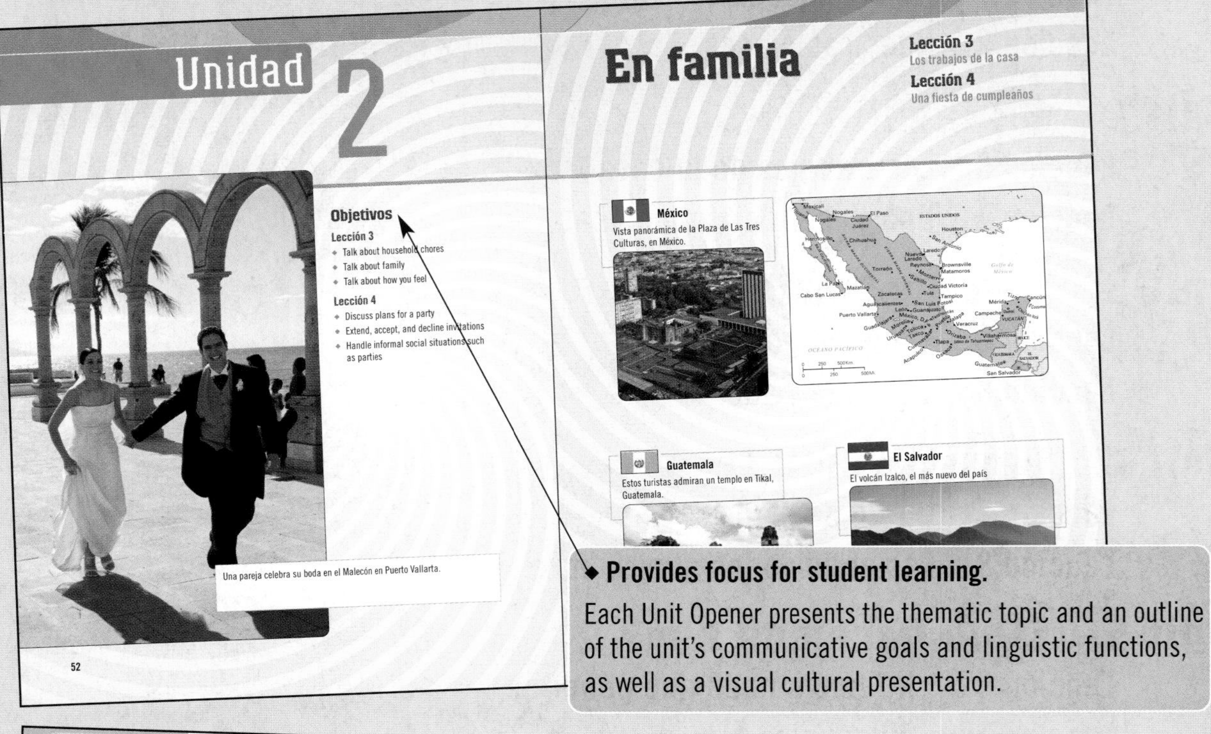

◆ **Provides focus for student learning.**

Each Unit Opener presents the thematic topic and an outline of the unit's communicative goals and linguistic functions, as well as a visual cultural presentation.

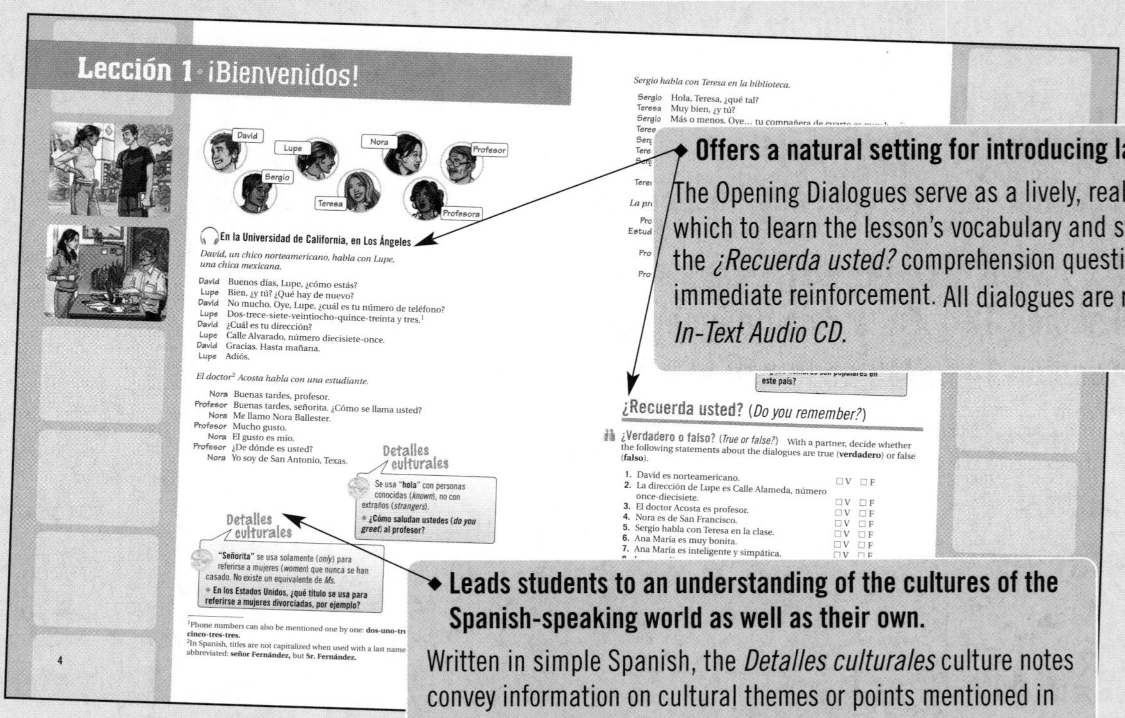

Lección 1 · ¡Bienvenidos!

David · Lupe · Nora · Profesor · Sergio · Teresa · Profesora

En la Universidad de California, en Los Ángeles

David, un chico norteamericano, habla con Lupe, una chica mexicana.

David: Buenos días, Lupe, ¿cómo estás?
Lupe: Bien, ¿y tú? ¿Qué hay de nuevo?
David: No mucho. Oye, Lupe, ¿cuál es tu número de teléfono?
Lupe: Dos-trece-siete-veintiocho-quince-treinta y tres.[1]
David: ¿Cuál es tu dirección?
Lupe: Calle Alvarado, número diecisiete-once.
David: Gracias. Hasta mañana.
Lupe: Adiós.

El doctor[2] Acosta habla con una estudiante.

Nora: Buenas tardes, profesor.
Profesor: Buenas tardes, señorita. ¿Cómo se llama usted?
Nora: Me llamo Nora Ballester.
Profesor: Mucho gusto.
Nora: El gusto es mío.
Profesor: ¿De dónde es usted?
Nora: Yo soy de San Antonio, Texas.

Detalles culturales

Se usa "**hola**" con personas conocidas (*known*), no con extraños (*strangers*).

◆ **¿Cómo saludan ustedes (*do you greet*) al profesor?**

Detalles culturales

"**Señorita**" se usa solamente (*only*) para referirse a mujeres (*women*) que nunca se han casado. No existe un equivalente de *Ms.*

◆ **En los Estados Unidos, ¿qué título se usa para referirse a mujeres divorciadas, por ejemplo?**

[1]Phone numbers can also be mentioned one by one: **dos-uno-tr...** **cinco-tres-tres.**
[2]In Spanish, titles are not capitalized when used with a last name ... abbreviated: **señor Fernández**, but **Sr. Fernández**.

4

Sergio habla con Teresa en la biblioteca.

Sergio: Hola, Teresa, ¿qué tal?
Teresa: Muy bien, ¿y tú?
Sergio: Más o menos. Oye... tu compañera de cuarto ...

¿Recuerda usted? (*Do you remember?*)

¿Verdadero o falso? (*True or false?*) With a partner, decide whether the following statements about the dialogues are true (**verdadero**) or false (**falso**).

1. David es norteamericano. ☐V ☐F
2. La dirección de Lupe es Calle Alameda, número once-diecisiete. ☐V ☐F
3. El doctor Acosta es profesor. ☐V ☐F
4. Nora es de San Francisco. ☐V ☐F
5. Sergio habla con Teresa en la clase. ☐V ☐F
6. Ana María es muy bonita. ☐V ☐F
7. Ana María es inteligente y simpática. ☐V ☐F

◆ **Offers a natural setting for introducing language.**

The Opening Dialogues serve as a lively, realistic context in which to learn the lesson's vocabulary and structures, and the *¿Recuerda usted?* comprehension questions provide immediate reinforcement. All dialogues are recorded on the *In-Text Audio CD.*

◆ **Leads students to an understanding of the cultures of the Spanish-speaking world as well as their own.**

Written in simple Spanish, the *Detalles culturales* culture notes convey information on cultural themes or points mentioned in the lesson's opening passage. To promote classroom discussion, cross-cultural reflection questions follow each note.

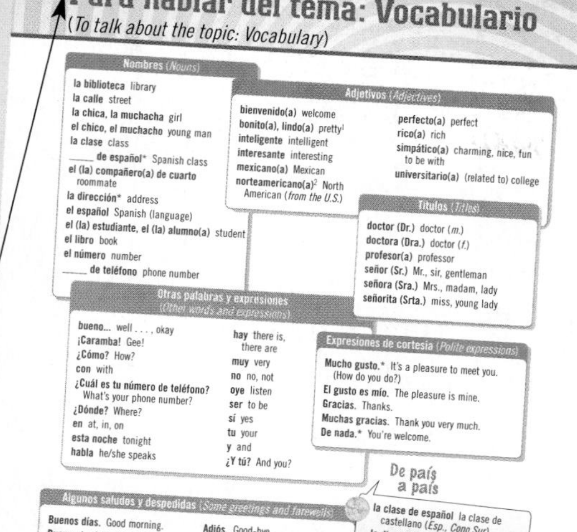

Para hablar del tema: Vocabulario

(*To talk about the topic: Vocabulary*)

Nombres (*Nouns*)

la biblioteca library
la calle street
la chica, la muchacha girl
el chico, el muchacho young man
la clase class
____ de español* Spanish class
el (la) compañero(a) de cuarto roommate
la dirección* address
el español Spanish (language)
el (la) estudiante, el (la) alumno(a) student
el libro book
el número number
____ de teléfono phone number

Adjetivos (*Adjectives*)

bienvenido(a) welcome
bonito(a), lindo(a) pretty[1]
inteligente intelligent
interesante interesting
mexicano(a) Mexican
norteamericano(a)[2] North American (*from the U.S.*)
perfecto(a) perfect
rico(a) rich
simpático(a) charming, nice, fun to be with
universitario(a) (related to) college

Títulos (*Titles*)

doctor (Dr.) doctor (*m.*)
doctora (Dra.) doctor (*f.*)
profesor(a) professor
señor (Sr.) Mr., sir, gentleman
señora (Sra.) Mrs., madam, lady
señorita (Srta.) miss, young lady

Otras palabras y expresiones (*Other words and expressions*)

bueno... well . . . , okay
¡Caramba! Gee!
¿Cómo? How?
con with
¿Cuál es tu número de teléfono? What's your phone number?
¿Dónde? Where?
en at, in, on
esta noche tonight
habla he/she speaks
hay there is, there are
muy very
no no, not
oye listen
ser to be
sí yes
tu your
y and
¿Y tú? And you?

Expresiones de cortesía (*Polite expressions*)

Mucho gusto.* It's a pleasure to meet you. (How do you do?)
El gusto es mío. The pleasure is mine.
Gracias. Thanks.
Muchas gracias. Thank you very much.
De nada.* You're welcome.

De país a país

la clase de español la clase de castellano (*Esp., Cono Sur*)
la dirección el domicilio (*Méx.*)

Algunos saludos y despedidas (*Some greetings and farewells*)

Buenos días. Good morning.
Buenas tardes. Good afternoon
Adiós. Good-bye.

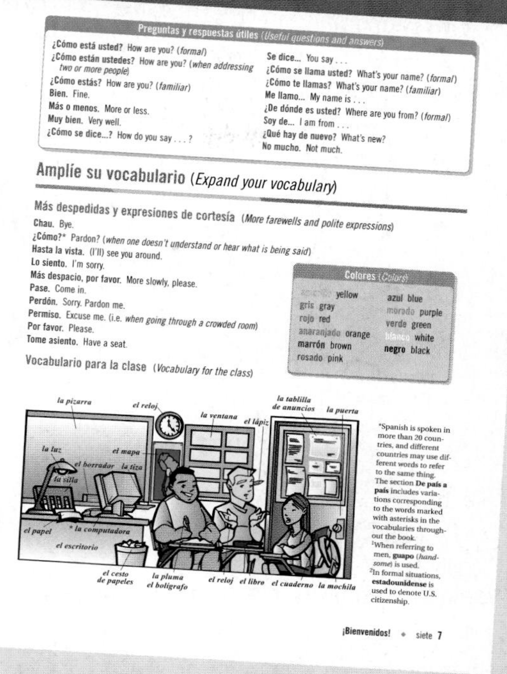

Preguntas y respuestas útiles (*Useful questions and answers*)

¿Cómo está usted? How are you? (*formal*)
¿Cómo están ustedes? How are you? (*when addressing two or more people*)
¿Cómo estás? How are you? (*familiar*)
Bien. Fine.
Más o menos. More or less.
Muy bien. Very well.
¿Cómo se dice...? How do you say . . . ?
Se dice... You say . . .
¿Cómo se llama usted? What's your name? (*formal*)
¿Cómo te llamas? What's your name? (*familiar*)
Me llamo... My name is . . .
¿De dónde es usted? Where are you from? (*formal*)
Soy de... I am from . . .
¿Qué hay de nuevo? What's new?
No mucho. Not much.

Amplíe su vocabulario (*Expand your vocabulary*)

Más despedidas y expresiones de cortesía (*More farewells and polite expressions*)

Chau. Bye.
¿Cómo?* Pardon? (*when one doesn't understand or hear what is being said*)
Hasta la vista. (I'll) see you around.
Lo siento. I'm sorry.
Más despacio, por favor. More slowly, please.
Pase. Come in.
Perdón. Sorry. Pardon me.
Permiso. Excuse me. (*i.e. when going through a crowded room*)
Por favor. Please.
Tome asiento. Have a seat.

Colores (*Colors*)

amarillo yellow
gris gray
rojo red
anaranjado orange
marrón brown
rosado pink
azul blue
morado purple
verde green
blanco white
negro black

Vocabulario para la clase (*Vocabulary for the class*)

*Spanish is spoken in more than 20 countries, and different countries may use different words to refer to the same thing. The section **De país a país** includes variations corresponding to the words marked with asterisks in the vocabularies throughout the book.
[1]When referring to men, **guapo** (*handsome*) is used.
[2]In formal situations, **estadounidense** is used to denote U.S. citizenship.

¡Bienvenidos! ◆ siete 7

◆ **Provides a solid foundation for building students' communication skills.**

The *Vocabulario* section lists all active vocabulary, new words, and expressions introduced in the opening dialogue, as well as other words and phrases related to the lesson theme in the *Amplíe su vocabulario* section.

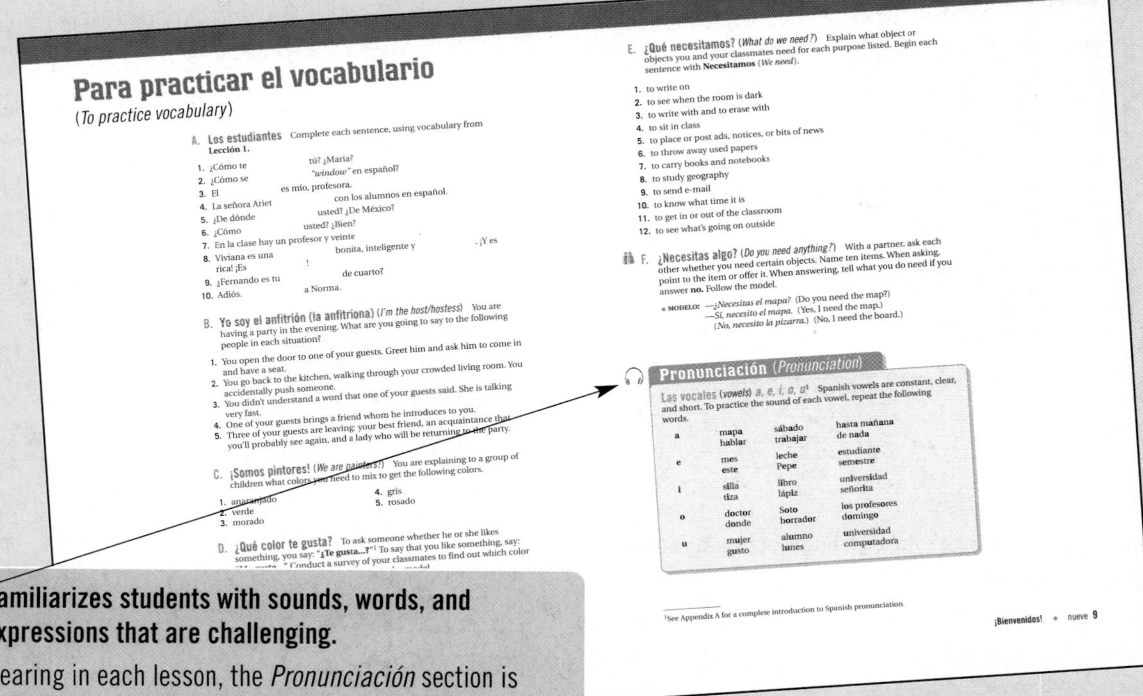

Para practicar el vocabulario

(*To practice vocabulary*)

A. **Los estudiantes** Complete each sentence, using vocabulary from **Lección 1.**

1. ¿Cómo te ____ tú? ¿María?
2. ¿Cómo se ____ "*window*" en español?
3. El ____ es mío, profesora.
4. La señora Ariet ____ con los alumnos en español.
5. ¿De dónde ____ usted? ¿De México?
6. ¿Cómo ____ usted? ¿Bien?
7. En la clase hay un profesor y veinte ____ . ¡Y es
8. Viviana es una ____ bonita, inteligente y ____ rica! ¡Es ____ !
9. ¿Fernando es tu ____ de cuarto?
10. Adiós. ____ a Norma.

B. **Yo soy el anfitrión (la anfitriona)** (*I'm the host/hostess*) You are having a party in the evening. What are you going to say to the following people in each situation?

1. You open the door to one of your guests. Greet him and ask him to come in and have a seat.
2. You go back to the kitchen, walking through your crowded living room. You accidentally push someone.
3. You didn't understand a word that one of your guests said. She is talking very fast.
4. One of your guests brings a friend whom he introduces to you.
5. Three of your guests are leaving: your best friend, an acquaintance that you'll probably see again, and a lady who will be returning to the party.

C. **¡Somos pintores!** (*We are painters!*) You are explaining to a group of children what colors you need to mix to get the following colors.

1. anaranjado
2. verde
3. morado
4. gris
5. rosado

D. **¿Qué color te gusta?** To ask someone whether he or she likes something, you say: "**¿Te gusta...?**"[1] To say that you like something, say: "Me gusta..." Conduct a survey of your classmates to find out which color ...

E. **¿Qué necesitamos?** (*What do we need?*) Explain what object or objects you and your classmates need for each purpose listed. Begin each sentence with **Necesitamos** (*We need*).

1. to write on
2. to see when the room is dark
3. to write with and to erase with
4. to sit in class
5. to place or post ads, notices, or bits of news
6. to throw away used papers
7. to carry books and notebooks
8. to study geography
9. to send e-mail
10. to know what time it is
11. to get in or out of the classroom
12. to see what's going on outside

F. **¿Necesitas algo?** (*Do you need anything?*) With a partner, ask each other whether you need certain objects. Name ten items. When asking, point to the item or offer it. When answering, tell what you do need if your answer **no.** Follow the model.

◆ MODELO: —*¿Necesitas el mapa?* (Do you need the map?)
—*Sí, necesito el mapa.* (Yes, I need the map.)
(*No, necesito la pizarra.*) (No, I need the board.)

Pronunciación (*Pronunciation*)

Las vocales (*vowels*) *a, e, i, o, u*[1] Spanish vowels are constant, clear, and short. To practice the sound of each vowel, repeat the following words.

a	mapa hablar	sábado trabajar	hasta mañana de nada
e	mes este	leche Pepe	estudiante semestre
i	silla tiza	libro lápiz	universidad señorita
o	doctor donde	Soto borrador	los profesores domingo
u	mujer gusto	alumno lunes	universidad computadora

[1]See Appendix A for a complete introduction to Spanish pronunciation.

¡Bienvenidos! ◆ nueve 9

◆ **Familiarizes students with sounds, words, and expressions that are challenging.**

Appearing in each lesson, the *Pronunciación* section is designed to acquaint students with the basic Spanish sounds. This section is recorded on the *In-Text Audio CD.*

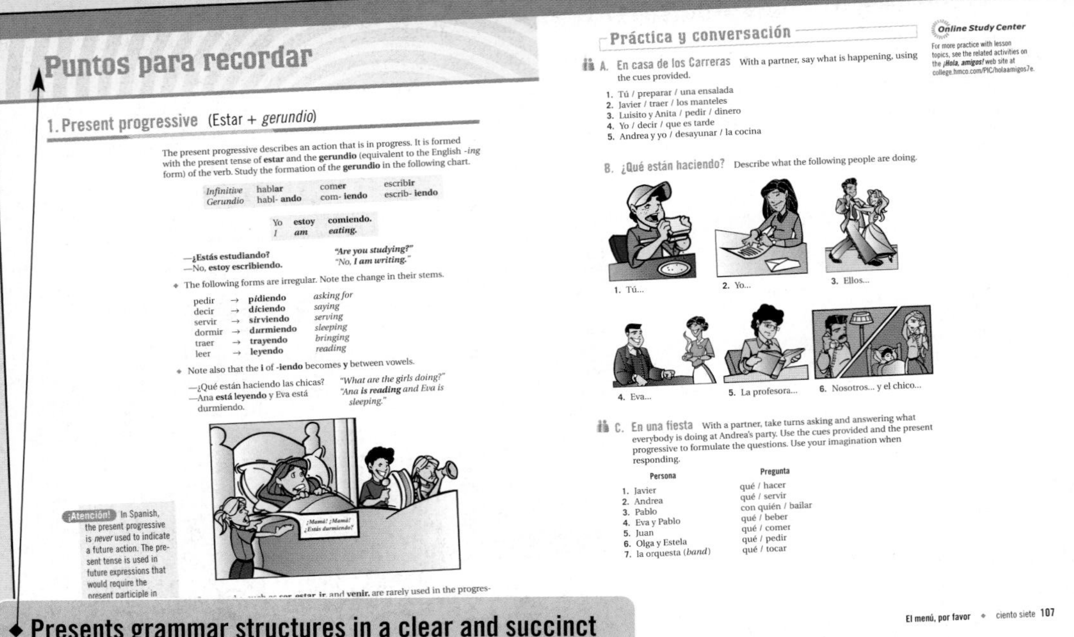

Puntos para recordar

1. Present progressive (Estar + *gerundio*)

The present progressive describes an action that is in progress. It is formed with the present tense of **estar** and the **gerundio** (equivalent to the English *-ing* form) of the verb. Study the formation of the **gerundio** in the following chart.

Infinitive	hablar	comer	escribir
Gerundio	habl- **ando**	com- **iendo**	escrib- **iendo**

Yo **estoy** **comiendo.**
I ***am*** ***eating.***

—¿**Estás estudiando?** *"Are you studying?"*
—No, **estoy escribiendo.** *"No, I am writing."*

- The following forms are irregular. Note the change in their stems.

pedir → **pidiendo** *asking for*
decir → **diciendo** *saying*
servir → **sirviendo** *serving*
dormir → **durmiendo** *sleeping*
traer → **trayendo** *bringing*
leer → **leyendo** *reading*

- Note also that the **i** of **-iendo** becomes **y** between vowels.

—¿Qué están haciendo las chicas? *"What are the girls doing?"*
—Ana **está leyendo** y Eva está durmiendo. *"Ana is reading and Eva is sleeping."*

¡Atención! In Spanish, the present progressive is *never* used to indicate a future action. The present tense is used in future expressions that would require the present participle in

Práctica y conversación

Online Study Center
For more practice with lesson topics, see the related activities on the *¡Hola, amigos!* web site at college.hmco.com/PIC/holaamigos7e.

A. En casa de los Carreras With a partner, say what is happening, using the cues provided.

1. Tú / preparar / una ensalada
2. Javier / traer / los manteles
3. Luisito y Anita / pedir / dinero
4. Yo / decir / que es tarde
5. Andrea y yo / desayunar / la cocina

B. ¿Qué están haciendo? Describe what the following people are doing.

1. Tú... 2. Yo... 3. Ellos... 4. Eva... 5. La profesora... 6. Nosotros... y el chico...

C. En una fiesta With a partner, take turns asking and answering what everybody is doing at Andrea's party. Use the cues provided and the present progressive to formulate the questions. Use your imagination when responding.

Persona	Pregunta
1. Javier	qué / hacer
2. Andrea	qué / servir
3. Pablo	con quién / bailar
4. Eva y Pablo	qué / beber
5. Juan	qué / comer
6. Olga y Estela	qué / pedir
7. la orquesta (*band*)	qué / tocar

El menú, por favor ◆ ciento siete 107

◆ **Presents grammar structures in a clear and succinct manner.**

The *Puntos para recordar* section presents an average of four or five grammar points in English. Each structure is immediately followed by a *Práctica* or *Práctica y conversación* section that ranges from controlled drills to open-ended activities, including illustration-based activities.

◆ **Presents opportunities to actively use the language in the classroom.**

¡Conversemos! consists of a series open-ended activities, including personalized pair activities, activities for vocabulary review, and pair and small group activities. The *Entre nosotros* section ends with *Para escribir,* a writing activity on a topic related to the thematic goals of the lesson.

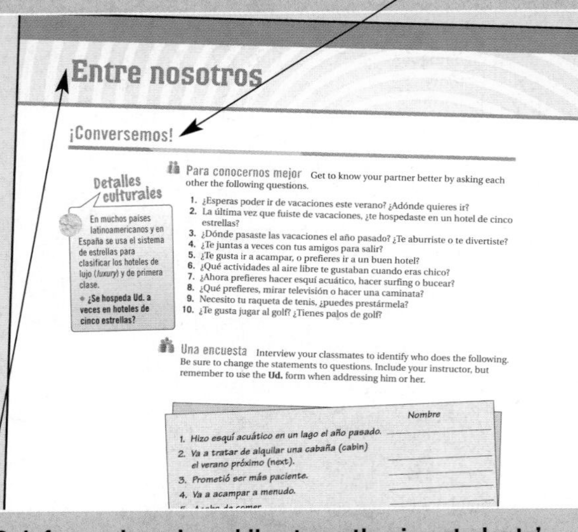

Entre nosotros

¡Conversemos!

Para conocernos mejor Get to know your partner better by asking each other the following questions.

1. ¿Esperas poder ir de vacaciones este verano? ¿Adónde quieres ir?
2. La última vez que fuiste de vacaciones, ¿te hospedaste en un hotel de cinco estrellas?
3. ¿Dónde pasaste las vacaciones el año pasado? ¿Te aburriste o te divertiste?
4. ¿Te juntas a veces con tus amigos para salir?
5. ¿Te gusta ir a acampar, o prefieres ir a un buen hotel?
6. ¿Qué actividades al aire libre te gustaban cuando eras chico?
7. ¿Ahora prefieres hacer esquí acuático, hacer surfing o bucear?
8. ¿Qué prefieres, mirar televisión o hacer una caminata?
9. Necesito tu raqueta de tenis, ¿puedes prestármela?
10. ¿Te gusta jugar al golf? ¿Tienes palos de golf?

Detalles culturales
En muchos países latinoamericanos y en España se usa el sistema de estrellas para clasificar los hoteles de lujo (*luxury*) y de primera clase.
◆ **¿Se hospeda Ud. a veces en hoteles de cinco estrellas?**

Una encuesta Interview your classmates to identify who does the following. Be sure to change the statements to questions. Include your instructor, but remember to use the **Ud.** form when addressing him or her.

	Nombre
1. Hizo esquí acuático en un lago el año pasado.	
2. Va a tratar de alquilar una cabaña (*cabin*) el verano próximo (*next*).	
3. Prometió ser más paciente.	
4. Va a acampar a menudo.	

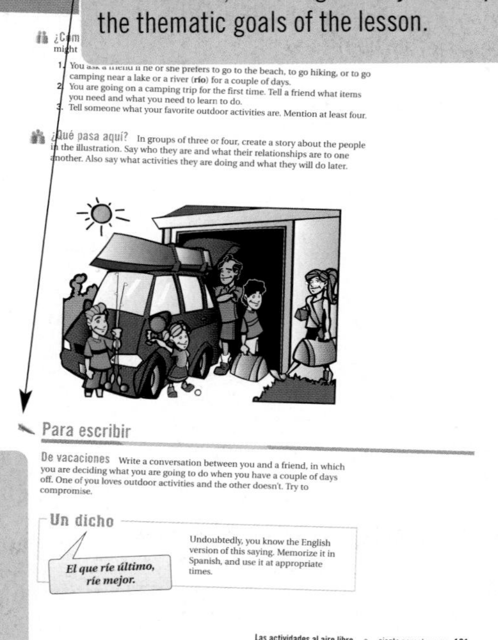

1. You ask a friend if he or she prefers to go to the beach, to go hiking, or to go camping near a lake or a river (**río**) for a couple of days.
2. You are going on a camping trip for the first time. Tell a friend what items you need and what you need to learn to do.
3. Tell someone what your favorite outdoor activities are. Mention at least four.

¿Qué pasa aquí? In groups of three or four, create a story about the people in the illustration. Say who they are and what their relationships are to one another. Also say what activities they are doing and what they will do later.

Para escribir

De vacaciones Write a conversation between you and a friend, in which you are deciding what you are going to do when you have a couple of days off. One of you loves outdoor activities and the other doesn't. Try to compromise.

Un dicho

El que ríe último, ríe mejor.

Undoubtedly, you know the English version of this saying. Memorize it in Spanish, and use it at appropriate times.

Las actividades al aire libre ◆ ciento noventa y uno 191

◆ **Reinforces learning while strengthening students' communication skills.**

The activities in *Entre nosotros* ask students to synthesize what they've learned in order to communicate in real-life situations.

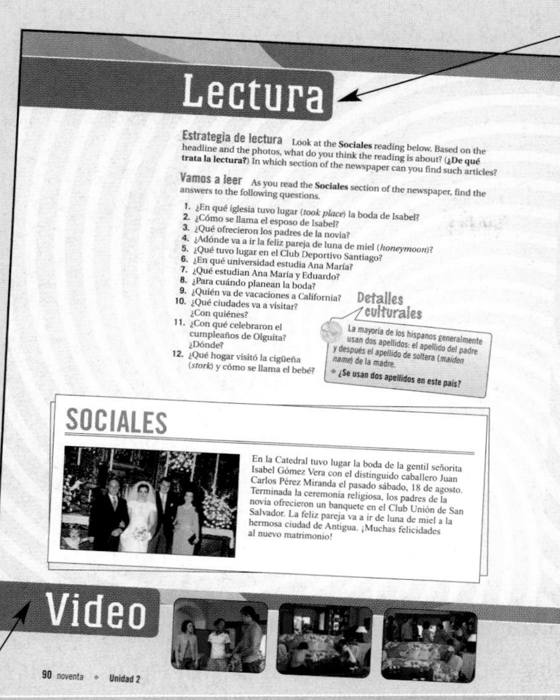

Lectura

Estrategia de lectura Look at the **Sociales** reading below. Based on the headline and the photos, what do you think the reading is about? (**¿De qué trata la lectura?**) In which section of the newspaper can you find such articles?

Vamos a leer As you read the **Sociales** section of the newspaper, find the answers to the following questions.

1. ¿En qué iglesia tuvo lugar (*took place*) la boda de Isabel?
2. ¿Cómo se llama el esposo de Isabel?
3. ¿Qué ofrecieron los padres de la novia?
4. ¿Adónde va a ir la feliz pareja de luna de miel (*honeymoon*)?
5. ¿Qué tuvo lugar en el Club Deportivo Santiago?
6. ¿En qué universidad estudia Ana María?
7. ¿Qué estudian Ana María y Eduardo?
8. ¿Para cuándo planean la boda?
9. ¿Quién va de vacaciones a California?
10. ¿Qué ciudades va a visitar? ¿Con quiénes?
11. ¿Con qué celebraron el cumpleaños de Olguita? ¿Dónde?
12. ¿Qué hogar visitó la cigüeña (*stork*) y cómo se llama el bebé?

Detalles culturales

La mayoría de los hispanos generalmente usan dos apellidos: el apellido del padre y después el apellido de soltera (*maiden name*) de la madre.

◆ **¿Se usan dos apellidos en este país?**

SOCIALES

En la Catedral tuvo lugar la boda de la gentil señorita Isabel Gómez Vera con el distinguido caballero Juan Carlos Pérez Miranda el pasado sábado, 18 de agosto. Terminada la ceremonia religiosa, los padres de la novia ofrecieron un banquete en el Club Unión de San Salvador. La feliz pareja va a ir de luna de miel a la hermosa ciudad de Antigua. ¡Muchas felicidades al nuevo matrimonio!

Video

90 noventa ◆ Unidad 2

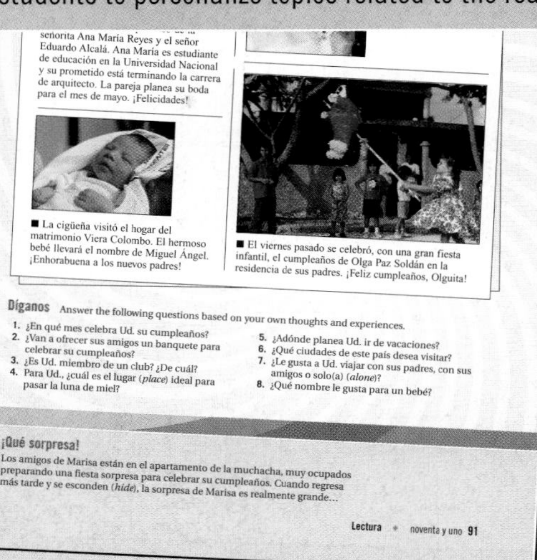

señorita Ana María Reyes y el señor Eduardo Alcalá. Ana María es estudiante de educación en la Universidad Nacional y su prometido está terminando la carrera de arquitecto. La pareja planea su boda para el mes de mayo. ¡Felicidades!

■ La cigüeña visitó el hogar del matrimonio Viera Colombo. El hermoso bebé llevará el nombre de Miguel Ángel. ¡Enhorabuena a los nuevos padres!

■ El viernes pasado se celebró, con una gran fiesta infantil, el cumpleaños de Olga Paz Soldán en la residencia de sus padres. ¡Feliz cumpleaños, Olguita!

Díganos Answer the following questions based on your own thoughts and experiences.

1. ¿En qué mes celebra Ud. su cumpleaños?
2. ¿Van a ofrecer sus amigos un banquete para celebrar su cumpleaños?
3. ¿Es Ud. miembro de un club? ¿De cuál?
4. Para Ud., ¿cuál es el lugar (*place*) ideal para pasar la luna de miel?
5. ¿Adónde planea Ud. ir de vacaciones?
6. ¿Qué ciudades de este país desea visitar?
7. ¿Le gusta a Ud. viajar con sus padres, con sus amigos o solo(a) (*alone*)?
8. ¿Qué nombre le gusta para un bebé?

¡Qué sorpresa!

Los amigos de Marisa están en el apartamento de la muchacha, muy ocupados preparando una fiesta sorpresa para celebrar su cumpleaños. Cuando regresa más tarde y se esconden (*hide*), la sorpresa de Marisa es realmente grande...

Lectura ◆ noventa y uno 91

◆ **Promotes the development of students' reading skills.**

Appearing at the end of each unit, the *Lectura* section develops reading comprehension while reinforcing the structures and vocabulary introduced in the preceding lessons. Pre-reading questions focus students' attention on detail and open-ended post-reading questions, and allow students to personalize topics related to the reading.

◆ **Fosters student understanding of spoken language.**

The situational video clips on the Video DVD and VHS, shot on location in Costa Rica, relate in theme and language level to each unit. Activities relating to each clip can be found at the *Online Study Center.*

El mundo hispánico

Costa Rica

- Costa Rica es uno de los países más pequeños del continente americano (51.000 km² —kilómetros cuadrados). Está situado en América Central y su capital es San José. Los productos principales del país son el café, las bananas, el cacao y la caña de azúcar (*sugar cane*).
- La mayoría de los "ticos" (como se les llama a los costarricenses) son católicos y de origen español. De todos los países centroamericanos, Costa Rica es el que tiene el menor número de analfabetos (*illiterates*). Tiene el mayor ingreso (*income*) per cápita y un gobierno democrático con muy pocos problemas políticos.
- En Costa Rica se le da una gran importancia a la educación, la cultura y las artes. Se dice (*It is said*) que en Costa Rica "hay más maestros (*teachers*) que soldados". Este país tiene excelentes programas para proteger la ecología, sobre todo (*especially*) la selva (*rainforest*).

▲ Miles de peregrinos visitan la Basílica de la Virgen de los Ángeles en Cartago, Costa Rica

Panamá

- Panamá está situado en el istmo (*isthmus*) que une (*joins*) Suramérica con América del Norte. El país, que está dividido por el Canal de Panamá, tiene una superficie de unos 78.000 km² y una población de más de dos millones y medio de habitantes. Su cultura es una mezcla (*mixture*) de las tradiciones españolas, africanas, indígenas y norteamericanas. El idioma oficial del país es el español, pero también se usa mucho el inglés.
- La principal fuente de ingresos (*source of income*) del país está asociada con las operaciones del Canal, que es administrado por Panamá desde el año 2000. La construcción del Canal por parte del gobierno de los Estados Unidos duró (*lasted*) diez años y fue terminada en 1914. El Canal mide 82,4 km y tiene tres esclusas (*locks*) a cada lado del istmo que cruza.
- Junto al Canal están las dos ciudades más grandes del país: Ciudad de Panamá, la capital, y Colón, la segunda ciudad más importante del país.

▲ El Fuerte de Santiago de la Gloria en Portobello, Panamá

142 ciento cuarenta y dos ◆ Unidad 3

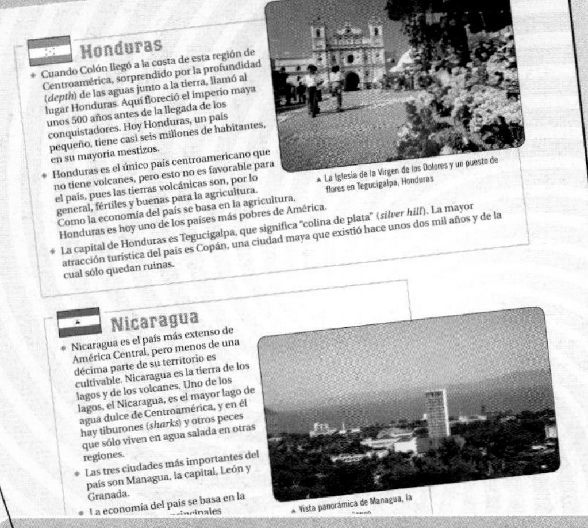

Honduras

- Cuando Colón llegó a la costa de esta región de Centroamérica, sorprendido por la profundidad (*depth*) de las aguas junto a la tierra, llamó al lugar Honduras. Aquí floreció el imperio maya unos 500 años antes de la llegada de los conquistadores. Hoy Honduras, un país pequeño, tiene casi seis millones de habitantes, en su mayoría mestizos.
- Honduras es el único país centroamericano que no tiene volcanes, pero esto no es favorable para el país, pues las tierras volcánicas son, por lo general, fértiles y buenas para la agricultura. Como la economía del país se basa en la agricultura, Honduras es hoy uno de los países más pobres de América.
- La capital de Honduras es Tegucigalpa, que significa "colina de plata" (*silver hill*). La mayor atracción turística del país es Copán, una ciudad maya que existió hace unos dos mil años y de la cual sólo quedan ruinas.

▲ La Iglesia de la Virgen de los Dolores y un puesto de flores en Tegucigalpa, Honduras

Nicaragua

- Nicaragua es el país más extenso de América Central, pero menos de una décima parte de su territorio es cultivable. Nicaragua es la tierra de los lagos y de los volcanes. Uno de los lagos, el Nicaragua, es el mayor lago de agua dulce de Centroamérica, y en él hay tiburones (*sharks*) y otros peces que sólo viven en agua salada en otras regiones.
- Las tres ciudades más importantes del país son Managua, la capital, León y Granada.
- La economía del país se basa en la

▲ Vista panorámica de Managua, la

◆ **Reinforces understanding of the cultures of the Spanish-speaking world.**

A longer cultural section, *El mundo hispánico,* provides unit-level cultural information with detailed visual presentations for many Hispanic countries. This section, found at the end of each unit, presents in more detail the Hispanic cultures introduced throughout the unit.

Tome este examen

Lección 11

Lección 11

A. Subjunctive with verbs of volition Write sentences in the present tense, using the elements given below. Use the present subjunctive or the infinitive, as appropriate, and add any necessary words.

1. Yo / querer / ella / ir / Viña del Mar
2. Nosotros / desear / viajar / avión
3. Ella / sugerirme / ir / Buenos Aires
4. El agente / querer / venderme / el pasaje
5. Ellos / aconsejarnos / comprar / seguro (*insurance*)
6. Yo / no querer / llevar / muchas maletas
7. Ellos / no querer / ella / llevarlos / en su coche
8. Nosotros / no querer / ir / contigo
9. ¿Tú / sugerirme / venir / luego?
10. Ella / necesitar / Uds. / darle / la maleta

B. Subjunctive with verbs of emotion Rewrite the following sentences, beginning each with the phrase in parentheses and using the subjunctive or the infinitive, as appropriate.

1. Ella se va pronto. (Espero...)
2. Los pasajes son muy caros. (Elsa teme...)
3. Yo estoy aquí. (Me alegro de...)
4. Ella se va de vacaciones. (Ella espera...)
5. Mamá se siente bien hoy. (Esperamos...)
6. Ellos no pueden ir a la fiesta. (Siento...)

C. Some uses of the prepositions *a, de,* and *en* Complete with **a, de,** or **en,** as necessary.

1. Anoche llamé ______ mi hermano por teléfono y hablamos nuestros planes para el fin de semana. Pensamos ir ______ Chile. Él quiere viajar ______ tren pero yo prefiero ir ______ coche. Mi hermana no quiere ir con nosotros; prefiere quedarse ______ casa porque no tiene con quién dejar ______ su perro.
2. Ayer Marta llegó ______ la agencia ______ las ocho y media ______ la mañana, pero no empezó ______ trabajar hasta las diez.
3. Mi hija es muy bonita; es morena, ______ ojos verdes y yo pienso que es la más inteligente ______ todos mis hijos.

D. Vocabulary Complete the following sentences, using vocabulary from **Lección 11.**

1. No quiero un ______ de pasillo; quiero uno de ______.
2. Voy a poner el bolso de ______ en el ______ de equipaje.
3. Voy a la ______ de viajes para comprar los pasajes.
4. Tiene que darle la tarjeta de ______ a la ______ de vuelo.
5. Tengo que pagar ______ de equipaje porque tengo cuatro maletas.
6. Quiero sentarme cerca de la ______ de emergencia.
7. Los paquetes ______ el pasaje, el hotel y algunas ______.
8. ¿A cuánto está el ______ de moneda?
9. No podemos viajar hoy. Tenemos que ______ la reservación.
10. Cuando viajo siempre llevo cheques de ______.
11. Este verano vamos a hacer un ______ por el Caribe.
12. Necesito una lista de los ______ de interés de la ______ de Chile.

E. Culture Complete the following sentences, based on the cultural notes you have read.

1. En Argentina se usa la forma ______ en lugar de **tú.**
2. La música típica de Argentina es el ______.
3. En los países hispanos no existe tanta ______ entre las generaciones como en este país.

Lección 11

◆ **Encourages self-assessment of learning objectives.**

Following each unit, the *Tome este examen* section contains exercises designed to review the vocabulary and structures of the two lessons in the previous unit. The Answer Key is available in Appendix D.

Preface

¡Hola, amigos!, Seventh Edition, continues to be the complete, flexible program that has made it a successful introduction to Spanish for beginning college and university students throughout six editions. It presents the basics of Spanish grammar using a balanced, eclectic approach that stresses all four skills—listening, speaking, reading, and writing. The program has always emphasized the active, practical use of Spanish for communication in high-frequency situations. The completely redesigned seventh edition features all new art and a streamlined, color-coded layout. A special effort has been made to enhance the cultural presentation and integration by focusing on culture on a unit level, and giving more substance to the smaller culture notes throughout each lesson. The program's goal is to help you achieve linguistic proficiency and cultural awareness, and to motivate you to continue your study of the Spanish language and the many cultures in which it is spoken.

The Student Text

¡Hola, amigos!, Seventh Edition has been reorganized into seven units, each containing two thematically-related lessons. Each of the seven units contains the following features:

Unit-Opener Spread

Each unit begins with a list of communicative objectives for the two lessons included in that unit. This list serves to focus your attention on important linguistic functions and vocabulary you will encounter and to help you gain a sense of accomplishment when you finish a unit. Captioned photos and maps give you a first impression of the countries presented in each unit.

Diálogos

New vocabulary and grammatical structures are first presented in the context of several brief conversations in idiomatic Spanish dealing with high-frequency situations that reflect the lesson's central themes. Each conversation is illustrated in the text and recorded on the *In-Text Audio CD* that accompanies your book. A headphone icon will remind you of recorded text. You can listen to the recordings and check your comprehension by doing the *¿Recuerda usted?* activities that follow the dialogues. The dialogues are also recorded on the *SAM Audio Program* where additional practice is available.

- *Detalles culturales* These short culture notes written in easy-to-read Spanish promote cultural awareness in the language-learning process. They can be found throughout the entire unit and will give you important and interesting cultural information that helps integrate the learning of language with the learning of culture.

Para hablar del tema: Vocabulario

All new words and expressions introduced in the conversations are listed by parts of speech or under the general headings *Cognados* and *Otras palabras y expresiones.* You should learn the entries in these lists for active use. The *Amplíe su vocabulario* section that follows expands on the thematic vocabulary introduced in the dialogues.

Para practicar el vocabulario

This practice section immediately follows the vocabulary presentation and encourages you to use the expressions you have just learned in a meaningful way.

- *Pronunciación* The section ends with a pronunciation feature to present and practice the sounds of the Spanish language with special attention to features that pose difficulty for most English speakers. A headphone icon indicates that the section is recorded on the *In-Text Audio CD.*

Puntos para recordar

Each new grammatical structure featured in the lesson-opening dialogue is explained clearly and concisely in English so that the explanations may be used independently as an out-of-class reference. All explanations include examples of practical use in natural Spanish and some explanations are illustrated by a cartoon.

- *Práctica* and *Práctica y conversación* After each grammar explanation, the activities in *Práctica* and *Práctica y conversación* offer immediate reinforcement through a variety of structured and communicative exercises. These activities are flexible in format so that you can do them in class or your instructor can assign them as written practice outside of class. Answers to these exercises are available at your instructor's discretion.
- *Rodeo* The Rodeo boxed sections in Lessons 7, 13, and 14 summarize and practice major grammatical topics such as pronouns, commands, and the indicative and subjunctive moods.

Entre nosotros

This final section provides for the recombination and synthesis of each lesson's new vocabulary and grammatical structures in a series of communicative activities. Because language is best learned through interpersonal communication, most of these exercises are designed to be done orally and require interactions with your classmates.

- *¡Conversemos!* features personalized activities such as pair interviews and class surveys that ask you to interact with your peers. Also included in this end-of-lesson cumulative section are activities that involve photos, realia, or illustrations, providing additional communicative practice based on authentic materials. This section has been expanded in the Seventh Edition to provide more interactive, communicative practice.
- *Para escribir* guides you to express yourself in writing in a variety of formats, such as e-mails, lists, and descriptions.
- *Un dicho* or *Un proverbio,* a thematically-related popular saying or proverb, provides cultural enrichment and concludes each lesson.

Lectura

A reading section at the end of each unit contains authentic, theme-related material from newspapers or magazines from the Spanish-speaking world, and in Units 4, 5, 6 and 7 you will find literary selections. One or two pre-reading activities emphasize the development of reading strategies and the selections are followed by comprehension and personalized questions for writing practice or discussion.

El mundo hispánico

This section, written in easy-to-read Spanish, provides an integrated cultural presentation of the countries and regions presented on the unit opener and throughout the lessons. It offers an overview of the locale in which the introductory dialogues were set, with attention to such details as climate, points of interest, customs, politics, economy, and inhabitants. It will also inform you about prevailing customs in the Spanish-speaking world that relate to the lesson themes. A map highlighting important geographic locations can be found on the unit opener spread. Color photos visually depict the country or custom(s) discussed.

Tome este examen

After each unit, these self-tests review and synthesize important vocabulary and grammatical structures you have learned in that unit. Because cultural awareness is as important as linguistic competence, the self-tests will also check your knowledge of cultural concepts. Organized by lesson, the self-tests quickly enable you to determine what material you have already mastered and which concepts you need to target for further review. An answer key for immediate verification is provided in Appendix D of the student textbook.

Reference Materials

The following sections provide you with useful reference tools throughout the course.

- **Maps.** Up-to-date maps of the Hispanic world appear on the inside front and back covers of the textbook for quick reference.
- **Appendices.** Appendix A summarizes the sounds and key pronunciation features of the Spanish language, with abundant examples. Conjugations of high-frequency regular, stem-changing, and irregular Spanish verbs constitute Appendix B. Appendix C is a glossary of all grammatical terms used in the text, with examples. Appendix D is the answer key to the *Tome este examen* self-tests.
- **Vocabularies.** Spanish-English and English-Spanish glossaries list all active, core vocabulary introduced in the dialogues and the *Amplíe su vocabulario* and grammar sections, as well as the passive vocabulary employed in the readings and the *El mundo hispánico* section. The number following each entry indicates the lesson in which it first appears.
- **Index.** An index provides ready access to all grammatical structures presented in the text.

Supplementary Materials for the Student

In-Text Audio CD

A free 90-minute In-Text *Audio CD* containing recordings of all the lesson opener-dialogues and pronunciation sections is packaged with each copy of the *Student Edition.* This *In-Text Audio CD* is designed to maximize your exposure to the sounds of natural spoken Spanish and to help improve pronunciation. It is designed so you can use it outside of class or in the Language Laboratory.

Student Activities Manual (SAM)

Each lesson of the *Student Edition* is correlated to the corresponding lesson in the *Student Activities Manual (SAM).* The *Workbook* section offers a variety of writing activities—sentence completion, matching, sentence transformation, and illustration-based exercises—that provide further practice and reinforcement of concepts presented in the textbook. Each lesson includes a crossword puzzle for vocabulary review and a reading comprehension passage. Writing strategies and topics appear in each lesson to further writing skills. In the Seventh Edition extra activities have been added to the workbook sections and new attention has been given to the cultural targets of each lesson. An answer key for all written exercises is available at your instructor's discretion. The *Laboratory Manual* section opens with an Introduction to Spanish Sounds designed to make learners aware of the differences between Spanish and English pronunciation. Each regular lesson of the *Laboratory Manual* includes pronunciation, structure, listening- and speaking practice, illustration-based listening comprehension, and dictation exercises to be used in conjunction with the audio program.

SAM Audio Program

Pronunciation exercises at the beginning of each lesson feature practice of isolated sounds; global pronunciation practice is also provided. The textbook dialogues then appear as listening and pronunciation exercises in each lesson. They are followed by comprehension questions on the dialogues, structured grammar exercises (one for each point in the lesson), a listening comprehension activity, and a dictation. Answers to all exercises, except the dictation, are provided on the SAM Audio CDs.

Video

The video features footage of locations presented in the *El mundo hispánico* section. The footage in each lesson consists of two parts, each part being approximately two to four minutes long. In the first part you will view a situational dialogue featuring recurring characters demonstrating everyday life. In the second part you will be able to see and hear country-specific footage for selected countries, ethnic groups, and regions presented in the units. Both parts are designed to develop your listening skills and cultural awareness as you view diverse images of the Hispanic world and Hispanic life and lifestyles. Pre-viewing, post-viewing, and expansion activities along with active vocabulary lists are correlated to each video segment and are located at the *Online Study Center*.

Online Multimedia eBook

The *Online Multimedia eBook* provides students with the entire text online, integrated with links to a wide variety of resources—from audio pronunciations to video clips to Web expansion activities and interactive practice—for a completely interactive experience. By clicking on a link at the relevant point in the text, you can immediately practice and reinforce what you have learned. A real-time voice chat feature allows you to complete pair and group activities with other students. The *Online Multimedia eBook* is available on Eduspace, Blackboard, and WebCT platforms.

eSAM

The electronic version of the *SAM* includes a comprehensive grade book and offers your instructor the ability to make assignments and track your performance. The audio associated with the Lab section of the *SAM* is also included.

Online Study Center *Online Study Center* (college.hmco.com/PIC/holaamigos7e)

The *Online Study Center* includes the following components:

- *Audio Flashcards:* Flashcards with integrated audio help students learn the chapter's new vocabulary.
- *Web Search Activites:* These activities are designed to give you further practice with lesson vocabulary and grammar while exploring existing Spanish-language websites.

- *In-Text Audio:* Audio files from the *In-Text Audio CD,* provided in .mp3 format.
- *ACE Practice Tests:* Practice activities covering vocabulary, grammar, and video material. Additional language skills practice is also available.

Acknowledgments

As always, we wish to express appreciation to the users of ***¡Hola, amigos!*** who have provided feedback on their experience with the program and to the following colleagues for the many valuable suggestions they offered in their reviews of this and previous editions of ***¡Hola, amigos!***

Amparo Font, Saddleback College
Pilar Hernández, Arizona Western College
Channing Horner, Northeast Missouri State University
Harriet Hutchinson, Bunker Hill Community College
Stephen Richman, Mercer County College
Dr. Tomás Ruiz-Fábrega, Albuquerque Technical Vocational Institute
Dr. Kristin Shoaf, Bridgewater State College
Vincent Spina, Clarion University of Pennsylvania
Susanna Williams, Macomb Community College
Lydia Bernstein, Bridgewater State College
Linda Burk, Manchester Community Technical College
Dimitrios Karayiannis, Southern Illinois University
David Korn, Anderson College
Barbar Kruger, Finger Lakes Community College
Ping Mei Law, McMaster University
Denis Mohan, University of Guelph
Stephen Richman, Mercer County Community College
Mercedes Rowinsky, Wilfred Laurier University
Virginia Vigil, Austin Community College at Rio Grande
Clementina Adams, Clemson University
Peter Alfieri, Salve Regina College
Jane Harrington Bethune, Salve Regina College
Joseph DiPaola, Macomb Community College
Rosita Marcella, Manhattan College
Joel B. Pouwels, University of Central Arkansas
Barbara Ross, Eastern Kentucky University

We also extend our sincere appreciation to the World Language Staff of Houghton Mifflin Company, College Division: Rolando Hernández, Publisher; Glenn A. Wilson, Senior Sponsoring Editor; Eileen Bernadette Moran, Executive Marketing Director; Judith Bach, Senior Development Editor; Amy Johnson, Project Editor; Erin Beasley, Editorial Assistant; and Lorreen Ruth Pelletier, Marketing Assistant.

Ana C. Jarvis
Raquel Lebredo
Francisco Mena-Ayllón

We would like to hear your comments on and reactions to *¡Hola, amigos!,* Seventh Edition. Reports on your experiences using this program would be of great interest and value to us. Please write us care of Houghton Mifflin Company, College Division, 222 Berkeley Street, Boston, MA 02116-3764, or e-mail us at college_mod_lang@hmco.com.

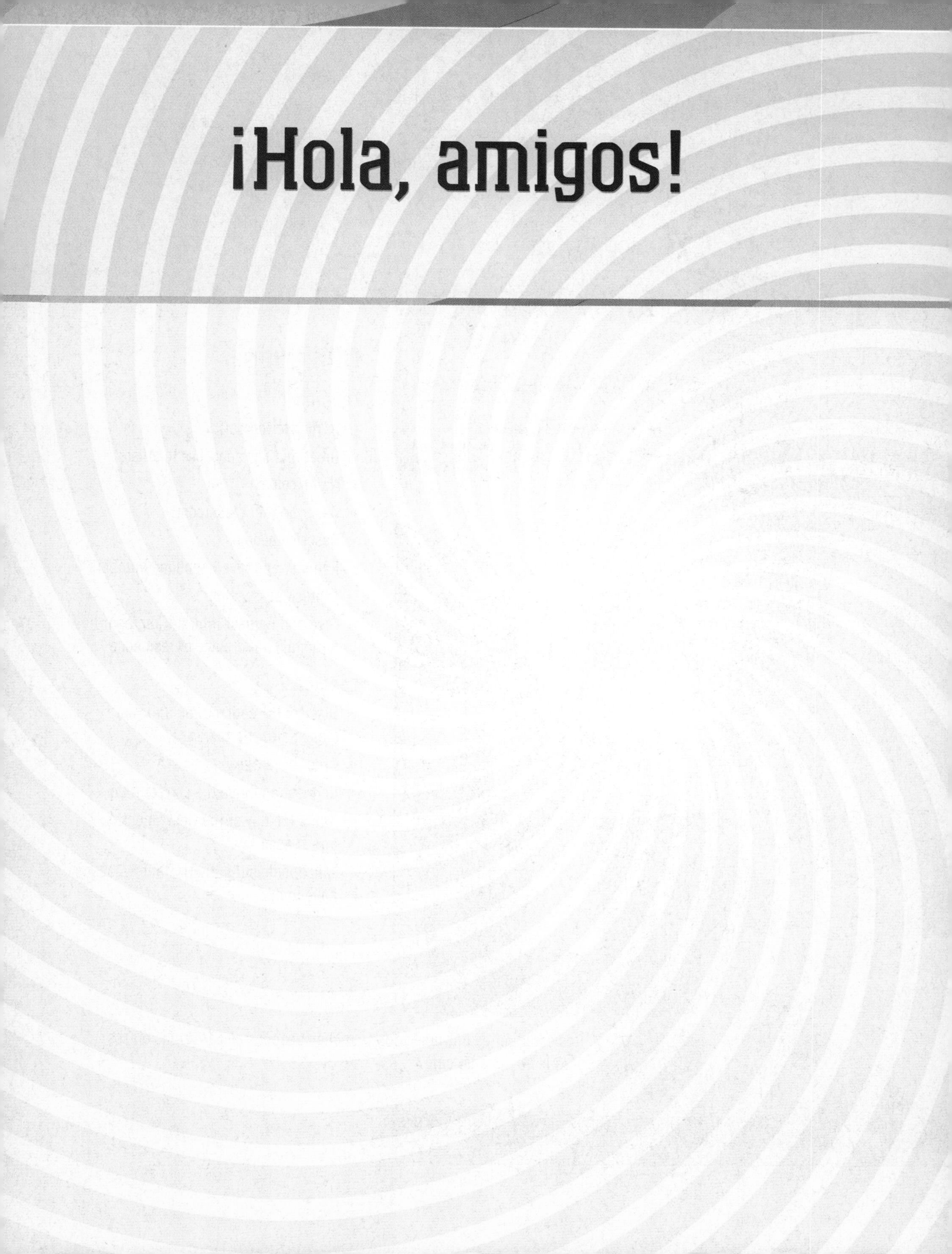

¡Hola, amigos!

Unidad

Objetivos

Lección 1

- Introduce yourself
- Greet and say good-bye to others
- Name colors
- Describe your classroom
- Describe people
- Request and give telephone numbers
- Express possession
- Give and request information regarding nationality and place of residence

Lección 2

- Discuss the courses you and your classmates are taking
- Order beverages
- Request and give the correct time
- Name the day of the week, months, and seasons
- Talk about your activities and what you have to do

Tres estudiantes universitarios se reúnen después de (*after*) las clases para ir (*to go*) a un café.

Los estudiantes universitarios

Lección 1
¡Bienvenidos!

Lección 2
Nuestras clases

Los mexicoamericanos

Una celebración del Cinco de Mayo con bailes folclóricos de México.

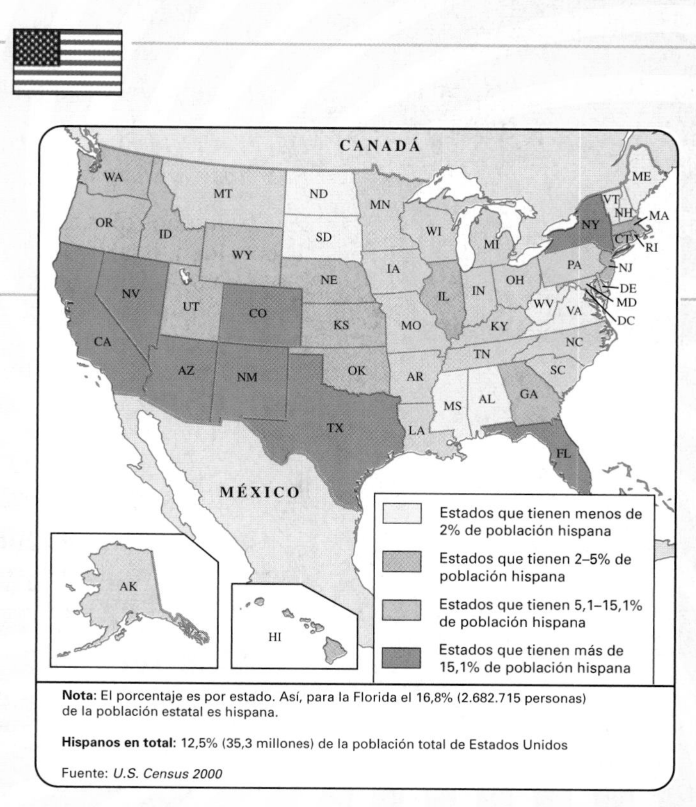

Los cubanoamericanos

Bebiendo jugo en una cafeteria cubana en Miami.

Los puertorriqueños

Celebrando el Día de Puerto Rico con un desfile en la ciudad de Chicago.

Lección 1 ◆ ¡Bienvenidos!

Suggestion: Use the **¡Hola, amigos!** transparency masters to create overheads of scenes from selected textbook dialogues and exercises. The overheads can be used for presentation and/or review with students.

En la Universidad de California, en Los Ángeles

David, un chico norteamericano, habla con Lupe, una chica mexicana.

Suggestion: Write the phone number with numerals on the board to convey meaning.

David Buenos días, Lupe, ¿cómo estás?
Lupe Bien, ¿y tú? ¿Qué hay de nuevo?
David No mucho. Oye, Lupe, ¿cuál es tu número de teléfono?
Lupe Dos-trece-siete-veintiocho-quince-treinta y tres.[1]
David ¿Cuál es tu dirección?
Lupe Calle Alvarado, número diecisiete-once.
David Gracias. Hasta mañana.
Lupe Adiós.

Suggestion: For presentation of dialogues, see Introduction, Instructor's Annotated Edition. English dialogue translations can be found in the Online Teaching Center. Students can listen to the dialogues on the student audio CD for additional practice.

El doctor[2] Acosta habla con una estudiante.

Nora Buenas tardes, profesor.
Profesor Buenas tardes, señorita. ¿Cómo se llama usted?
Nora Me llamo Nora Ballester.
Profesor Mucho gusto.
Nora El gusto es mío.
Profesor ¿De dónde es usted?
Nora Yo soy de San Antonio, Texas.

Expansion: Have students repeat or read the dialogues in pairs, replacing the characters' names with their own.

Detalles culturales

Se usa "**hola**" con personas conocidas (*known*), no con extraños (*strangers*).

◆ **¿Cómo saludan ustedes (*do you greet*) al profesor?**

Detalles culturales

"Señorita" se usa solamente (*only*) para referirse a mujeres (*women*) que nunca se han casado. No existe un equivalente de *Ms.*

◆ **En los Estados Unidos, ¿qué título se usa para referirse a mujeres divorciadas, por ejemplo?**

---

[1]Phone numbers can also be mentioned one by one: **dos-uno-tres-siete-dos-ocho-uno-cinco-tres-tres.**

[2]In Spanish, titles are not capitalized when used with a last name unless they are abbreviated: **señor Fernández,** but **Sr. Fernández.**

Sergio habla con Teresa en la biblioteca.

Sergio Hola, Teresa, ¿qué tal?
Teresa Muy bien, ¿y tú?
Sergio Más o menos. Oye… tu compañera de cuarto es muy bonita…
Teresa ¿Ana María? Sí, es una chica muy bonita y muy simpática.
Sergio ¡Muy interesante! ¿Es inteligente?
Teresa Sí… ¡y rica!
Sergio ¡Caramba! ¡Es perfecta! Bueno, nos vemos esta noche. Saludos a Ana María.
Teresa Hasta luego.

Expansion: Explain that **buenas noches** may be used both for greeting and for taking leave. The shortened form, **buenas**, and **muy buenas** may also be used. Also discuss the appropriate time of day for each greeting.

La profesora Rivas habla con los estudiantes en la clase de español.

Profesora Buenas noches. ¿Cómo están ustedes?
Estudiantes Bien, gracias.
David Profesora, ¿cómo se dice "*book*" en español?
Profesora Se dice **"libro".**
David Muchas gracias.
Profesora De nada.

Suggestions: You may wish to prepare name tags for students to wear until they know each other's names, so that they can greet each other after learning the appropriate vocabulary. For example:
Yo me llamo...
¿Y tú?

Have students turn to and greet the person next to them.

Detalles culturales

María es un nombre muy popular en España y en Latinoamérica. Se usa (*It's used*) frecuentemente con otros nombres: **Ana María, María Isabel,** etc. También (*Also*) se usa como segundo nombre para los hombres: **José María.**

◆ **¿Qué nombres son populares en este país?**

¿Recuerda usted? (*Do you remember?*)

¿Verdadero o falso? (*True or false?*) With a partner, decide whether the following statements about the dialogues are true (**verdadero**) or false (**falso**).

1. David es norteamericano. ☒ V ☐ F
2. La dirección de Lupe es Calle Alameda, número once-diecisiete. ☐ V ☒ F
3. El doctor Acosta es profesor. ☒ V ☐ F
4. Nora es de San Francisco. ☐ V ☒ F
5. Sergio habla con Teresa en la clase. ☐ V ☒ F
6. Ana María es muy bonita. ☒ V ☐ F
7. Ana María es inteligente y simpática. ☒ V ☐ F
8. Los estudiantes hablan con la profesora Rivas. ☒ V ☐ F

Alternative: Vary technique with this type of activity: have students work in pairs, do as a full-class activity, or have students do individually and then check answers with a partner.

Y ahora... conteste (*And now . . . answer*) Answer these questions, basing your answers on the dialogues.

1. ¿Cuál es el número de teléfono de Lupe? El número de teléfono de Lupe es dos-trece-siete-veintiocho-quince-treinta y tres.
2. ¿Cuál es la dirección de Lupe? La dirección de Lupe es Calle Alvarado, número diecisiete-once.
3. ¿De dónde es Nora Ballester? Nora Ballester es de San Antonio, Texas.
4. ¿Dónde hablan Sergio y Teresa? Sergio y Teresa hablan en la biblioteca.
5. ¿Ana María es rica? Sí, Ana María es rica.
6. ¿Cómo se dice "*book*" en español? Se dice "**libro**".

Para hablar del tema: Vocabulario
(*To talk about the topic: Vocabulary*)

Nombres (*Nouns*)

la biblioteca library
la calle street
la chica, la muchacha girl
el chico, el muchacho young man
la clase class
_____ **de español*** Spanish class
el (la) compañero(a) de cuarto roommate
la dirección* address
el español Spanish (language)
el (la) estudiante, el (la) alumno(a) student
el libro book
el número number
_____ **de teléfono** phone number

Adjetivos (*Adjectives*)

bienvenido(a) welcome
bonito(a), lindo(a) pretty[1]
inteligente intelligent
interesante interesting
mexicano(a) Mexican
norteamericano(a)[2] North American (*from the U.S.*)
perfecto(a) perfect
rico(a) rich
simpático(a) charming, nice, fun to be with
universitario(a) (related to) college

Títulos (*Titles*)

doctor (Dr.) doctor (*m.*)
doctora (Dra.) doctor (*f.*)
profesor(a) professor
señor (Sr.) Mr., sir, gentleman
señora (Sra.) Mrs., madam, lady
señorita (Srta.) miss, young lady

Otras palabras y expresiones (*Other words and expressions*)

bueno... well . . . , okay
¡Caramba! Gee!
¿Cómo? How?
con with
¿Cuál es tu número de teléfono? What's your phone number?
¿Dónde? Where?
en at, in, on
esta noche tonight
habla he/she speaks
hay there is, there are
muy very
no no, not
oye listen
ser to be
sí yes
tu your
y and
¿Y tú? And you?

Expresiones de cortesía (*Polite expressions*)

Mucho gusto.* It's a pleasure to meet you. (How do you do?)
El gusto es mío. The pleasure is mine.
Gracias. Thanks.
Muchas gracias. Thank you very much.
De nada.* You're welcome.

Algunos saludos y despedidas (*Some greetings and farewells*)

Buenos días. Good morning.
Buenas tardes. Good afternoon.
Buenas noches. Good evening; Good night.
Hola. Hello; Hi.
¿Qué hay de nuevo? What's new?
¿Qué tal? How is it going?
Adiós. Good-bye.
Hasta luego. (I'll) see you later.
Hasta mañana. (I'll) see you tomorrow.
Nos vemos. (I'll) see you.
Saludos a... Say hi to . . .

De país a país

la clase de español la clase de castellano (*Esp., Cono Sur*)
la dirección el domicilio (*Méx.*)
Mucho gusto Encantado(a) (*Arg., Cuba*) (The response is **igualmente**)
de nada por nada (*Méx.*)
¿Cómo? ¿Mande? (*Méx.*)
marrón café (*Méx.*); carmelita (*Cuba*)
la computadora el ordenador (*Esp.*)

Preguntas y respuestas útiles (*Useful questions and answers*)

¿Cómo está usted? How are you? (*formal*)
¿Cómo están ustedes? How are you? (*when addressing two or more people*)
¿Cómo estás? How are you? (*familiar*)
Bien. Fine.
Más o menos. More or less.
Muy bien. Very well.
¿Cómo se dice...? How do you say . . . ?
Se dice... You say . . .
¿Cómo se llama usted? What's your name? (*formal*)
¿Cómo te llamas? What's your name? (*familiar*)
Me llamo... My name is . . .
¿De dónde es usted? Where are you from? (*formal*)
Soy de... I am from . . .
¿Qué hay de nuevo? What's new?
No mucho. Not much.

Amplíe su vocabulario (*Expand your vocabulary*)

Más despedidas y expresiones de cortesía (*More farewells and polite expressions*)

Chau. Bye.
¿Cómo?* Pardon? (*when one doesn't understand or hear what is being said*)
Hasta la vista. (I'll) see you around.
Lo siento. I'm sorry.
Más despacio, por favor. More slowly, please.
Pase. Come in.
Perdón. Sorry. Pardon me.
Permiso. Excuse me. (i.e. *when going through a crowded room*)
Por favor. Please.
Tome asiento. Have a seat.

Colores (*Colors*)

amarillo yellow	**azul** blue
gris gray	**morado** purple
rojo red	**verde** green
anaranjado orange	**blanco** white
marrón brown	**negro** black
rosado pink	

Vocabulario para la clase (*Vocabulary for the class*)

*Spanish is spoken in more than 20 countries, and different countries may use different words to refer to the same thing. The section **De país a país** includes variations corresponding to the words marked with asterisks in the vocabularies throughout the book.

[1]When referring to men, **guapo** (*handsome*) is used.

[2]In formal situations, **estadounidense** is used to denote U.S. citizenship.

Para practicar el vocabulario

(*To practice vocabulary*)

A. Los estudiantes Complete each sentence, using vocabulary from **Lección 1.**

1. ¿Cómo te __llamas__ tú? ¿María?
2. ¿Cómo se __dice__ *"window"* en español?
3. El __gusto__ es mío, profesora.
4. La señora Ariet __habla__ con los alumnos en español.
5. ¿De dónde __es__ usted? ¿De México?
6. ¿Cómo __está__ usted? ¿Bien?
7. En la clase hay un profesor y veinte __estudiantes (alumnos)__.
8. Viviana es una __chica__ bonita, inteligente y __simpática__. ¡Y es rica! ¡Es __perfecta__!
9. ¿Fernando es tu __compañero__ de cuarto?
10. Adiós. __Saludos__ a Norma.

B. Yo soy el anfitrión (la anfitriona) (*I'm the host/hostess*) You are having a party in the evening. What are you going to say to the following people in each situation?

1. You open the door to one of your guests. Greet him and ask him to come in and have a seat. Buenas noches, ¿cómo está? Pase y tome asiento.
2. You go back to the kitchen, walking through your crowded living room. You accidentally push someone. Permiso. Perdón.
3. You didn't understand a word that one of your guests said. She is talking very fast. ¿Perdón? Más despacio, por favor.
4. One of your guests brings a friend whom he introduces to you. Mucho gusto.
5. Three of your guests are leaving: your best friend, an acquaintance that you'll probably see again, and a lady who will be returning to the party. Adiós (Chau). / Hasta la vista. / Hasta luego.

C. ¡Somos pintores! (*We are painters!*) You are explaining to a group of children what colors you need to mix to get the following colors.

1. anaranjado rojo y amarillo
2. verde azul y amarillo
3. morado azul y rojo
4. gris blanco y negro
5. rosado rojo y blanco

D. ¿Qué color te gusta? To ask someone whether he or she likes something, you say: "**¿Te gusta...?**"[1] To say that you like something, say: "**Me gusta...**" Conduct a survey of your classmates to find out which color is the most popular in class, following the model.

◆ **MODELO:** —¿Qué color te gusta?
—*Me gusta el color rojo.*

[1]When addressing someone as **usted,** use "**¿Le gusta...?**"

E. ¿Qué necesitamos? (*What do we need?*) Explain what object or objects you and your classmates need for each purpose listed. Begin each sentence with **Necesitamos** (*We need*).

1. to write on   cuadernos / papel / computadoras / una pizarra
2. to see when the room is dark   luz
3. to write with and to erase with   tizas / plumas (bolígrafos) / lápices / borradores
4. to sit in class   sillas
5. to place or post ads, notices, or bits of news   tablilla de anuncios
6. to throw away used papers   cesto de papeles
7. to carry books and notebooks   mochilas
8. to study geography   mapa
9. to send e-mail   computadoras
10. to know what time it is   relojes
11. to get in or out of the classroom   puerta
12. to see what's going on outside   ventana

F. ¿Necesitas algo? (*Do you need anything?*) With a partner, ask each other whether you need certain objects. Name ten items. When asking, point to the item or offer it. When answering, tell what you do need if you answer **no.** Follow the model.

◆ **MODELO:** —*¿Necesitas el mapa?* (Do you need the map?)
—*Sí, necesito el mapa.* (Yes, I need the map.)
(*No, necesito la pizarra.*) (No, I need the board.)

Pronunciación (*Pronunciation*)

Las vocales (*vowels*) ***a, e, i, o, u***[1] Spanish vowels are constant, clear, and short. To practice the sound of each vowel, repeat the following words.

a	m**a**p**a** h**a**bl**a**r	s**á**b**a**do tr**a**b**a**j**a**r	h**a**st**a** m**a**ñ**a**n**a** de n**a**d**a**
e	m**e**s **e**st**e**	l**e**ch**e** P**e**p**e**	**e**studiant**e** s**e**m**e**str**e**
i	s**i**lla t**i**za	l**i**bro láp**i**z	un**i**vers**i**dad señor**i**ta
o	d**o**ct**o**r d**o**nde	S**o**t**o** b**o**rrad**o**r	l**o**s pr**o**fes**o**res d**o**ming**o**
u	m**u**jer g**u**sto	al**u**mno l**u**nes	**u**niversidad comp**u**tadora

Suggestion: Stress the importance of using the lab program to develop good pronunciation skills. Refer students to Appendix A in this text and the student audio CD. You may want to add as additional practice: **Ana lava la sábana. / El nene bebe té. / Mimí dice que es difícil. / Yo no lo conozco. / Hugo usa uniforme azul.**

[1]See Appendix A for a complete introduction to Spanish pronunciation.

Puntos para recordar

1. Gender and number of nouns (*Género y número de los nombres*)

Suggestions: Point to various objects and people in the classroom and have students identify them using **el** or **la** to show gender.

Tell students to close their books. Pick nouns from the vocabulary lists in random order. Say each word and ask students to provide the definite article plus the noun.

I — tiza S1 — la tiza
I — día S2 — el día

Gender, part I

- In Spanish, all nouns—including those denoting nonliving things—are either masculine or feminine in gender.[1]

Masculine	Feminine
el profesor	la profesora
el cuaderno	la tiza
el lápiz	la ventana

- Most nouns that end in **-o** or denote males are masculine: **cuadern*o*, hombre** (*man*).
- Most nouns that end in **-a** or denote females are feminine: **ventan*a*, mujer** (*woman*).

¡Atención! Some common exceptions include the words **día** (*day*) and **mapa** (*map*), which end in **-a** but are masculine, and **mano** (*hand*), which ends in **-o** but is feminine.

Detalles culturales

En muchos países hispanos, los abogados (*lawyers*) y otros profesionales que tienen el equivalente de un *Ph.D.* tienen el título de **doctor** o **doctora.**

- **¿Qué títulos se usan con el apellido en este país?**

- Here are some helpful rules to remember about gender.
  - Some masculine nouns ending in **-o** have a corresponding feminine form ending in **-a: el secretari*o* / la secretari*a*.**
  - When a masculine noun ends in a consonant, you often add **-a** to obtain its corresponding feminine form: **el doctor / la doctora.**
  - Some nouns have the same form for both genders: **el estudiante / la estudiante.** In such cases, gender is indicated by the article **el** (masculine) or **la** (feminine).

[1]See Appendix C for a glossary of grammatical terms.

Práctica (*Practice*)

Online Study Center

For more practice with lesson topics, see the related activities on the ***¡Hola, amigos!*** web site at college.hmco.com/PIC/holaamigos7e.

¿Masculino o femenino? *Place **el** or **la** before each noun.*

1. el mapa
2. la tiza
3. el escritorio
4. la secretaria
5. la silla
6. la profesora
7. la pizarra
8. el libro
9. la mujer
10. la puerta
11. la ventana
12. el bolígrafo
13. el hombre
14. el día
15. el secretario
16. la mano
17. la computadora
18. el profesor

Plural forms of nouns

Spanish singular nouns are made plural by adding **-s** to words ending in a vowel and **-es** to words ending in a consonant. When a noun ends in **-z,** change the **z** to **c** and add **-es.**

Singular	*Plural*
silla	sillas
estudiante	estudiantes
profesor	profesores
borrador	borradores
lápiz	lápices

Suggestion: Write several examples of singular nouns ending in a vowel and singular nouns ending in a consonant. Make the nouns plural and ask students what rule is used in each case. Include nouns ending in **z: cruz, raíz, pez.**

¡Atención! When an accent mark falls on the *last* syllable of a word that ends in a consonant, it is omitted in the plural form:

lec**ción** → lec**ciones**[1]

Suggestion: Make sure students visualize what they are saying by using objects in the classroom to elicit singular and plural forms.

Práctica

Online Study Center

For more practice with lesson topics, see the related activities on the ***¡Hola, amigos!*** web site at college.hmco.com/PIC/holaamigos7e.

¿Cuál es el plural? *Give the plural of the following nouns.*

1. mapa mapas
2. profesor profesores
3. tiza tizas
4. lápiz lápices
5. ventana ventanas
6. mochila mochilas
7. lección lecciones
8. escritorio escritorios
9. borrador borradores
10. día días
11. luz luces
12. papel papeles

2. Definite and indefinite articles (*Artículos determinados e indeterminados*)

The definite article[2]

Spanish has four forms that are equivalent to the English definite article *the.*

Suggestion: To illustrate gender and number agreement, write the definite articles on the board in colored chalk to highlight them. Use different colors for masculine, feminine, singular, and plural; then write nouns next to them.

[1]For an explanation of written accent marks, refer to Appendix A.
[2]See Appendix C.

	Singular	Plural
Masculine	**el**	**los**
Feminine	**la**	**las**

el profesor	**la** profesora
el lápiz	**la** pluma
los profesores	**las** profesoras
los lápices	**las** plumas

Expansion: Divide the class into two or more teams. (Smaller teams offer more individual practice.) A member of one team must give a definite or indefinite article of either gender and number. If the opposing team responds with a noun that agrees with the article, it earns one point and gives the next article. If the opposing team cannot respond, the original team may give an appropriate noun to earn the point and then give the next article.

Suggestion: Have students close their books and practice changing the nouns from the vocabulary lists from singular to plural or vice versa, identifying the appropriate articles.

I — **profesor**
S1 — **el profesor, un profesor**
S2 — **los profesores, unos profesores**

Online Study Center

For more practice with lesson topics, see the related activities on the ***¡Hola, amigos!*** web site at college.hmco.com/PIC/holaamigos7e.

¡Atención! Always learn new nouns with their corresponding definite articles—this will help you remember their gender.

The indefinite article[1]

The Spanish equivalents of *a* (*an*) and *some* are as follows:

	Singular		Plural	
Masculine	**un**	a, an	**unos**	some
Feminine	**una**	a, an	**unas**	some

un libro	**unos** libros
un profesor	**unos** profesores
una silla	**unas** sillas
una ventana	**unas** ventanas

Práctica

A. ¿Qué es? For each of the following illustrations, identify the noun together with its corresponding definite and indefinite articles.

1. la (una) pizarra

2. el (un) estudiante

3. el (un) cuaderno

4. los (unos) libros

5. el (un) mapa

6. las (unas) chicas (muchachas)

[1]See Appendix C.

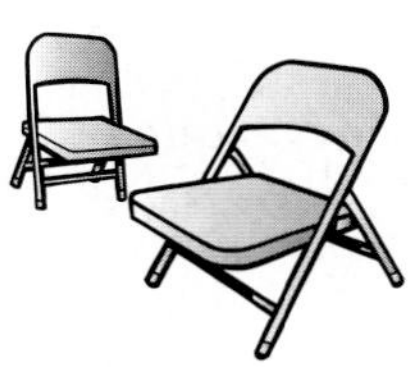

7. las (unas) sillas

8. el (un) escritorio

9. la (una) puerta

10. los (unos) relojes

B. ¿Qué necesitas? With a partner, go to p. 7 (*Vocabulario para la clase*) and, using indefinite articles, take turns indicating what you need. Name twelve items. *Answers will vary.*

◆ **MODELO:** *Necesito una silla.*

3. Subject pronouns (*Pronombres personales usados como sujetos*)[1]

Singular		Plural	
yo	I	**nosotros**	we (*m.*)
		nosotras	we (*f.*)
tú	you (*familiar*)	**vosotros**	you (*m., familiar*)
		vosotras	you (*f., familiar*)
usted	you (*formal*)	**ustedes**	you (*formal, familiar*[2])
él	he	**ellos**	they (*m.*)
ella	she	**ellas**	they (*f.*)

Suggestion: Write the subject pronouns on the board, then pronounce them while pointing to yourself and/or to one or more students, as appropriate. This method should help you later to elicit the pronouns through gestures. Note that the use of **vosotros** forms in this text is optional.

Alternative: Illustrate the uses of **tú** and **usted** with pictures of people of different ages, including well-known figures, asking students how they would address each person.

Cultural note: Tell students that in some Hispanic families children use **Ud.** with parents and/or grandparents.

- Use the **tú** form as the equivalent of *you* when addressing a close friend, a relative, or a child. Use the **usted** form in *all* other instances. In most Spanish-speaking countries, young people tend to call each other **tú,** even if they have just met.
- In Latin America, **ustedes** (abbreviated **Uds.**) is used as the plural form of both **tú** and **usted** (abbreviated **Ud.**). In Spain, however, the plural form of **tú** is **vosotros(as).**
- The masculine plural forms **nosotros, vosotros,** and **ellos** can refer to the masculine gender alone or to both genders together:

  Juan y Roberto → **ellos**   Juan y María → **ellos**

- Unlike English, Spanish does not generally express *it* or *they* as separate words when the subject of the sentence is a thing.

  Es una mesa.   *It is a table.*

[1]See Appendix C.
[2]In Latin America.

Online Study Center

For more practice with lesson topics, see the related activities on the *¡Hola, amigos!* web site at college.hmco.com/PIC/holaamigos7e.

Práctica

A. ¿Quiénes son? What subject pronouns do the following pictures suggest to you?

1. yo

2. tú

3. nosotros

4. nosotras

5. ellos

6. ustedes

7. él

8. ella

9. usted

Suggestion: Write a list of names on the board and ask students to give the pronoun that would be used to refer to those persons.

Teresa y José (ellos)
Enrique y yo (nosotros)
María y Linda (ellas)

B. ¿Tú, Ud. o Uds.? What pronoun would you use to address the following people?

1. the president of the university usted
2. two strangers ustedes
3. your best friend tú
4. your mother tú (usted)
5. a new classmate tú
6. your neighbor's children ustedes (**vosotros,** in Spain)

4. Present indicative of *ser* (*Presente de indicativo del verbo* ser)[1]

The verb **ser** (*to be*) is irregular. Its forms must therefore be memorized.

Expansion: Acquaint students with some important uses of the verb **ser**.

1. *Origin:* **¿De dónde *es* Ud.?**
2. *Nationality:* **María y Elena *son* mexicanas.**
3. *Profession:* **Él *es* profesor.**
4. *Description:* **Ana *es* alta y delgada.**

yo	**soy**	I am
tú	**eres**	you (*fam.*) are
Ud. / él / ella	**es**	you (*form.*) are / he is / she is
nosotros(as)	**somos**	we are
vosotros(as)	**sois**	you (*fam.*) are
Uds. / ellos / ellas	**son**	you are / they (*masc.*) are / they (*fem.*) are

—Ud. **es** el doctor Rivas, ¿no? *"**You are** Dr. Rivas, right?"*
—No, **soy** el profesor Soto. *"No, **I'm** professor Soto."*

—¿De dónde **son** Uds.? *"Where **are you** (all) from?"*
—**Somos** de Los Ángeles. ¿De dónde **eres** tú? *"**We are** from Los Angeles. Where **are you** from?"*
—Yo **soy** de Texas. *"**I am** from Texas."*
—¿Y Silvia? *"And Silvia?"*
—Ella **es** de Arizona. *"**She is** from Arizona."*

[1]See Appendix C.

Online Study Center

For more practice with lesson topics, see the related activities on the *¡Hola, amigos!* web site at college.hmco.com/PIC/holaamigos7e.

Práctica y conversación

A. ¿De dónde son? Miss Soto works in the Admissions Office and these out-of-state students are telling her where they are from. Using the verb **ser,** complete what they are saying.

1. David / Arizona
2. Yo / Colorado
3. Ana y Eva / Utah
4. Guadalupe / Nuevo México
5. Nosotros / Oregón
6. Raúl y Ángel / Idaho

Now indicate what Miss Soto would say to a girl, an older gentleman, and two young men to ask them where they are from.

Answers: 1. David es de Arizona. 2. Yo soy de Colorado. 3. Ana y Eva son de Utah. 4. Guadalupe es de Nuevo México. 5. Nosotros somos de Oregón. 6. Raúl y Ángel son de Idaho. Follow-up: ¿De dónde eres tú? / ¿De dónde es usted? / ¿De dónde son ustedes?

B. Compañeros de clase (*Classmates*) In groups of three or four, ask each other where you are from. Be prepared to have one person report to the class. *Answers will vary.*

5. Forms of adjectives and agreement of articles, nouns, and adjectives
(*La formación de adjetivos y la concordancia de artículos, nombres y adjetivos*)

Forms of adjectives[1]

- Most adjectives in Spanish have two basic forms: the masculine form ending in **-o** and the feminine form ending in **-a.** Their corresponding plural forms end in **-os** and **-as,** respectively.

profesor mexican**o**	profesores mexican**os**
profesora mexican**a**	profesoras mexican**as**
chico simpátic**o**	chicos simpátic**os**
chica simpátic**a**	chicas simpátic**as**

- When an adjective ends in **-e** or a consonant, the same form is normally used with both masculine and feminine nouns.

muchacho inteligent**e**	muchacha inteligent**e**
libro difíci**l** (*difficult*)	clase difíci**l**

- The only exceptions are as follows:
  - Adjectives of nationality that end in a consonant have feminine forms ending in **-a.**

señor españo**l** (*Spanish*)	señora españo**la**
señor inglé**s** (*English*)	señora ingle**sa**

- In forming the plural, adjectives follow the same rules as nouns.

mexican**o** → mexican**os**
feli**z** (*happy*) → feli**ces**
difíci**l** → difíci**les**

[1]See Appendix C.

Position of adjectives

- In Spanish, adjectives that describe qualities (*pretty, smart,* and so on) generally *follow* nouns, while adjectives of quantity precede them: Hay **dos** chicas **bonitas.**

Agreement of articles, nouns, and adjectives

- In Spanish, the article, the noun, and the adjective agree in gender and number.

El muchach**o** es simpátic**o.**	**Los** muchach**os** son simpátic**os.**
La muchach**a** es simpátic**a.**	**Las** muchach**as** son simpátic**as.**

Práctica y conversación

Online Study Center

For more practice with lesson topics, see the related activities on the ***¡Hola, amigos!*** web site at college.hmco.com/PIC/holaamigos7e.

Study these common adjectives that are used to describe people, places, or things.

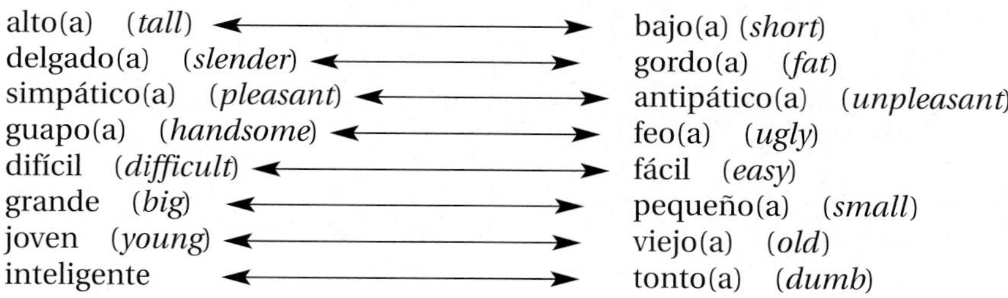

alto(a) (*tall*) ←→ bajo(a) (*short*)
delgado(a) (*slender*) ←→ gordo(a) (*fat*)
simpático(a) (*pleasant*) ←→ antipático(a) (*unpleasant*)
guapo(a) (*handsome*) ←→ feo(a) (*ugly*)
difícil (*difficult*) ←→ fácil (*easy*)
grande (*big*) ←→ pequeño(a) (*small*)
joven (*young*) ←→ viejo(a) (*old*)
inteligente ←→ tonto(a) (*dumb*)

A. ¿Cómo son...? With a partner, take turns asking and answering the following questions. In your answers, contradict what is stated.

- **MODELO:** —¿Eva es tonta?
  —*¡Al contrario* (On the contrary)*! Es muy inteligente.*

1. ¿Los chicos son bajos?
2. ¿Elena es joven?
3. ¿Eva y Gloria son antipáticas?
4. ¿Luis y Francisco son feos?
5. ¿Elsa es gorda?
6. ¿Las lecciones son fáciles?
7. ¿Las casas (*houses*) son grandes?
8. ¿Ellos son inteligentes?

Answers: **1.** ...son (muy) altos. **2.** ...es (muy) vieja. **3.** ...son (muy) simpáticas. **4.** ...son (muy) guapos. **5.** ...es (muy) delgada. **6.** ...son (muy) difíciles. **7.** ...son (muy) pequeñas. **8.** ...son (muy) tontos.

B. Para conversar (*To talk*) With a partner, take turns asking each other what these people are like. Ask: **¿Cómo es... ?** (*What is . . . like?*) *Answers will vary.*

1. Brad Pitt
2. Danny De Vito
3. Ricky Martin
4. Jennifer López
5. Roseanne
6. Leonardo Di Caprio
7. Cameron Díaz
8. Penélope Cruz

6. The alphabet (*El alfabeto*)[1]

¡Atención! All letters are feminine: la **a**, la **b**, and so on.

Suggestion: Remind students that **ch** and **ll** are not treated as separate letters in newer dictionaries.

Letter	Name	Letter	Name	Letter	Name
a	a	j	jota	r	ere
b	be	k	ca	rr	erre
c	ce	l	ele	s	ese
d	de	m	eme	t	te
e	e	n	ene	u	u
f	efe	ñ	eñe	v	ve
g	ge	o	o	w	doble ve
h	hache	p	pe	x	equis
i	i	q	cu	y	i griega
				z	zeta

Online Study Center

For more practice with lesson topics, see the related activities on the *¡Hola, amigos!* web site at college.hmco.com/PIC/holaamigos7e.

Práctica y conversación

A. Siglas *(Acronyms)* With a partner, take turns reading the following acronyms in Spanish.

1. FBI efe-be-i
2. CIA ce-i-a
3. IBM i-be-eme
4. D. C. de-ce
5. NAACP ene-a-a-ce-pe
6. NBA ene-be-a

B. Apellidos *(Last names)* In groups of three or four, ask each person in the group what his/her last name is and how to spell it. *Answers will vary.*

◆ **MODELO:** *¿Cuál es tu apellido?*
¿Cómo se deletrea?

7. Numbers 0 to 39 (*Números de 0 a 39*)

Learn the Spanish numbers from zero to thirty-nine.

0 cero	7 siete	14 catorce
1 uno	8 ocho	15 quince
2 dos	9 nueve	16 dieciséis[2]
3 tres	10 diez	17 diecisiete
4 cuatro	11 once	18 dieciocho
5 cinco	12 doce	19 diecinueve
6 seis	13 trece	20 veinte

[1]For a complete introduction to Spanish sounds, see Appendix A, p. 346, which appears on the in-text audio CDs.

[2]The numbers sixteen to nineteen and twenty-one to twenty-nine can also be spelled with a **y** (*and*): **diez y seis, diez y siete… veinte y uno, veinte y dos,** and so on. The pronunciation of each group of words, however, is identical to the corresponding word spelled with the **i.**

21 veintiuno	28 veintiocho	35 treinta y cinco
22 veintidós	29 veintinueve	36 treinta y seis
23 veintitrés	30 treinta	37 treinta y siete
24 veinticuatro	31 treinta y uno	38 treinta y ocho
25 veinticinco	32 treinta y dos	39 treinta y nueve
26 veintiséis	33 treinta y tres	
27 veintisiete	34 treinta y cuatro	

Suggestion: After students have asked for each other's phone numbers, ask for the information they have collected.

I — **¿Cuál es el número de Paul?**

S — **Es 432-5327.**

If students prefer not to disclose a private phone number, suggest they invent a phone number.

¡Atención! **Uno** changes to **un** before a masculine singular noun: **un libro** (*one book*). **Uno** changes to **una** before a feminine singular noun: **una silla** (*one chair*).

Online Study Center

For more practice with lesson topics, see the related activities on the ***¡Hola, amigos!*** web site at college.hmco.com/PIC/holaamigos7e.

Práctica y conversación

A. Números de teléfono Say the telephone number of each of the following people.

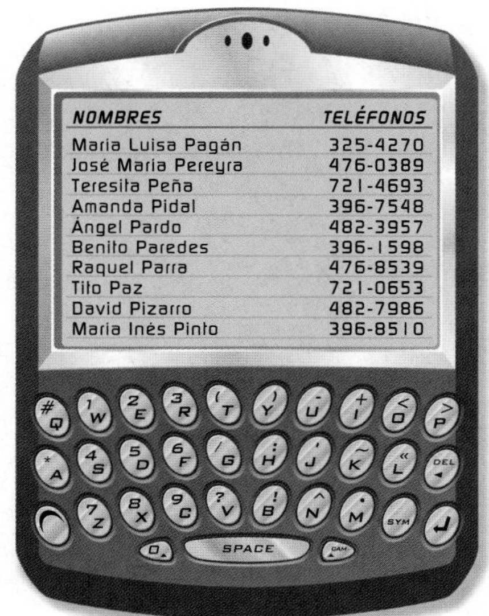
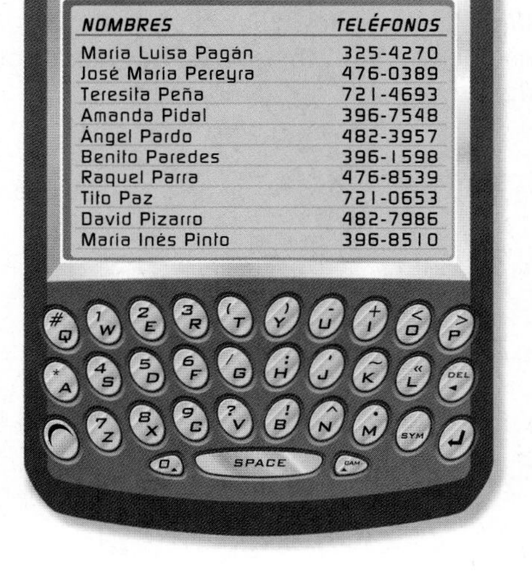

NOMBRES	TELÉFONOS
María Luisa Pagán	325-4270
José María Pereyra	476-0389
Teresita Peña	721-4693
Amanda Pidal	396-7548
Ángel Pardo	482-3957
Benito Paredes	396-1598
Raquel Parra	476-8539
Tito Paz	721-0653
David Pizarro	482-7986
María Inés Pinto	396-8510

Answers:
M. L. Pagán: tres-dos-cinco-cuatro-dos-siete-cero
J. M. Pereyra: cuatro-siete-seis-cero-tres-ocho-nueve
T. Peña: siete-dos-uno-cuatro-seis-nueve-tres
A. Pidal: tres-nueve-seis-siete-cinco-cuatro-ocho
A. Pardo: cuatro-ocho-dos-tres-nueve-cinco-siete
B. Paredes: tres-nueve-seis-uno-cinco-nueve-ocho
R. Parra: cuatro-siete-seis-ocho-cinco-tres-nueve
T. Paz: siete-dos-uno-cero-seis-cinco-tres
D. Pizarro: cuatro-ocho-dos-siete-nueve-ocho-seis
M. I. Pinto: tres-nueve-seis-ocho-cinco-uno-cero

B. ¿Cuál es tu número de teléfono? Ask three or four of your classmates for their names and phone numbers. Write down the response and show it to each one, asking, **¿Está bien?** (*Is it okay?*). He or she will say **"sí"** or **"no"** and will correct any mistakes. *Answers will vary.*

C. Sumas y restas *(Additions and subtractions)* Learn the following mathematical terms; then, with a partner, take turns adding and subtracting.

+ más   – menos   = son

◆ **MODELO:** 7 + 4 = 11   (Siete más cuatro son once.)
20 – 6 = 14   (Veinte menos seis son catorce.)

1. 20 + 15 =
2. 16 – 11 =
3. 17 – 13 =
4. 11 + 16 =
5. 19 + 11 =
6. 13 – 8 =
7. 30 – 12 =
8. 18 + 18 =
9. 23 – 14 =
10. 17 + 13 =

Answers: **1.** Veinte más quince son treinta y cinco. **2.** Dieciséis menos once son cinco. **3.** Diecisiete menos trece son cuatro. **4.** Once más dieciséis son veintisiete. **5.** Diecinueve más once son treinta. **6.** Trece menos ocho son cinco. **7.** Treinta menos doce son dieciocho. **8.** Dieciocho más dieciocho son treinta y seis. **9.** Veintitrés menos catorce son nueve. **10.** Diecisiete más trece son treinta.

Entre nosotros[1]

¡Conversemos!

 **Para conocernos mejor** (*To get to know each other better*) Get to know your partner better by asking each other the following questions. *Answers will vary.*

1. ¿Cómo te llamas?
2. ¿Cómo estás?
3. ¿Eres norteamericano(a)?
4. ¿De dónde eres?
5. ¿Cuál es tu número de teléfono?
6. ¿Cuál es tu dirección?
7. ¿Quién (*Who*) es tu profesor(a) favorito(a)?
8. ¿Cómo es tu mejor amigo(a) (*best friend*)?

Una encuesta (*A survey*) Interview your classmates to identify who fits the following descriptions. Include your instructor, but remember to use the **Ud.** form when addressing him or her. *Answers will vary.*

	Nombre
1. Es muy paciente.	______
2. Es inteligente.	______
3. Es muy liberal.	______
4. Es conservador(a).	______
5. Es popular.	______
6. Es eficiente.	______
7. Es perfeccionista.	______
8. Es atlético(a).	______
9. Es optimista.	______
10. Es pesimista.	

Suggestion: If needed, practice questions (**¿Eres muy paciente?**). Encourage students to get names for as many of the adjectives as possible. Tell them that once they receive an affirmative response and record a person's name, they must talk to another classmate. Discuss results of the survey by asking students, **¿Quién es muy paciente?**, etc.

Y ahora... Write a brief summary, indicating what you have learned about your classmates. *Answers will vary.*

---

[1] *Among us*

 **¿Cómo lo decimos?** (*How do we say it?*) What would you say in the following situations? What might the other person say? Act out the scenes with a partner.

1. You meet Mrs. García in the evening and you ask her how she is.
2. You ask Professor Vega how to say "I'm sorry" in Spanish.
3. You ask a young girl what her name is.
4. You ask a classmate what her roommate is like.
5. You ask a classmate where he or she is from.
6. You say good-bye to someone you expect to see at some point in the future.
7. You ask a friend how he or she is and what is new with him or her.
8. You offer Miss Vega a seat and then ask her what her address is.
9. You didn't understand what someone said. He or she is speaking too fast.
10. You are going through a crowded room. You stepped on someone's foot.
11. Someone is introduced to you.
12. You ask a classmate what his/her phone number is.

Suggestion: This may be assigned as homework or done orally by pairs of students.

Answers: **1.** Buenas noches, Sra. García. ¿Cómo está usted? **2.** ¿Cómo se dice "*I'm sorry*" en español? **3.** ¿Cómo te llamas? **4.** ¿Cómo es tu compañera de cuarto? **5.** ¿De dónde eres tú? **6.** Hasta la vista. **7.** ¿Cómo estás? ¿Qué hay de nuevo? **8.** Tome asiento. ¿Cuál es su dirección? **9.** ¿Perdón? Más despacio, por favor. **10.** Permiso. ¡Perdón! **11.** Mucho gusto. **12.** ¿Cúal es tu número de teléfono?

 **¿Qué pasa aquí?** (*What's going on here?*) With a partner, look at the photograph on page 1 and create a dialogue between two of the people in the photo. The two people should greet each other, introduce themselves and tell where they're from.

Para escribir (*To write*)

Un mensaje electrónico A new cyber friend wants to know what you are like. Write him/her an e-mail, describing yourself with as much detail as you can. At the end, ask your new friend for a description. *Answers will vary.*

Un dicho

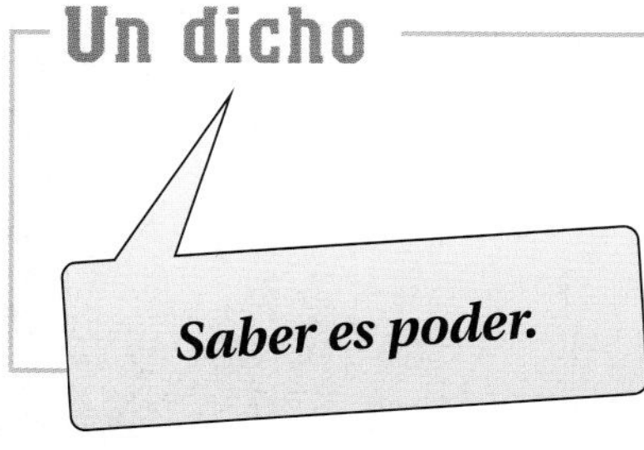

This is a popular saying in Spanish. Find out what it means. Does it have an equivalent in English? Learn it in Spanish. You might want to make it part of your philosophy . . .

Answers will vary.

Lección 2 ◆ Nuestras clases

Lisa, una chica norteamericana, habla con Alina, su nueva compañera de cuarto, que es cubanoamericana. Las dos estudian en la Universidad Internacional de la Florida, en Miami.

Lisa Alina, ¿cuántas clases tomas este semestre?

Alina Tomo cinco clases: inglés, matemáticas, física, psicología y biología. ¿Y tú?

Lisa Yo tomo historia, literatura y español.

Alina ¿Español? ¡Buena idea!, pero solamente tomas tres asignaturas.

Lisa Sí, porque yo trabajo los lunes, miércoles y viernes por la tarde porque necesito dinero.

Alina Yo también, pero trabajo en el verano, de julio a septiembre.

Lisa Tú tomas materias muy difíciles.

Alina Sí, pero todas mis clases son requisitos… además, la clase de psicología es fácil.

Lisa Pues, Alina, tu vida es muy aburrida. ¡Vamos a la playa!

Detalles culturales

En la mayoría de los países hispanos, el año escolar (*school year*) no se divide en semestres o trimestres; dura (*it lasts*) nueve meses. Los requisitos generales se toman en la escuela secundaria. En la universidad los estudiantes se concentran en su propio campo (*their own fields*).

◆ **En esta universidad, ¿el año escolar se divide en semestres o en trimestres?**

Detalles culturales

En los países de habla hispana, muchos estudiantes estudian con un(a) compañero(a) o en grupos. Generalmente viven con su familia o en pensiones. Hay muy pocas residencias universitarias (*dormitories*).

◆ **¿Cómo estudian los estudiantes en los Estados Unidos?**

Miguel habla con su amigo Pablo, un chico puertorriqueño. Los dos conversan en la cafetería de la universidad.

Miguel ¿Deseas tomar una taza de café?
Pablo No, un vaso de leche. Yo no tomo café. Oye, ¿qué hora es?
Miguel Es la una y media. ¿Por qué?
Pablo Porque a las dos de la tarde hay un programa de televisión muy interesante.
Miguel ¡Ah! Necesito mi horario de clases.
Pablo Aquí está. Nuestra clase de química es a las cuatro en el aula[1] ciento noventa y cinco.
Miguel ¿A qué hora terminan tus clases hoy?
Pablo A las ocho de la noche.
Miguel Estudiamos juntos mañana, ¿verdad?
Pablo Entonces, ¿mañana no vamos a la playa? Eres un aguafiestas. Bueno, me voy.

¿Recuerda usted?

¿Verdadero o falso? With a partner, decide whether the following statements about the dialogues are true (**verdadero**) or false (**falso**).

1. Lisa y Alina son estudiantes universitarias. ☒ V ☐ F
2. Alina toma cinco requisitos. ☒ V ☐ F
3. Lisa trabaja porque necesita dinero. ☒ V ☐ F
4. Alina solamente estudia en el verano. ☐ V ☒ F
5. La clase de psicología es muy difícil para Alina. ☐ V ☒ F
6. Pablo es de Cuba. ☐ V ☒ F
7. El programa de televisión es a las dos de la tarde. ☒ V ☐ F
8. La clase de química es a las cuatro. ☒ V ☐ F
9. Pablo termina sus clases a las seis de la tarde. ☐ V ☒ F
10. Pablo y Miguel estudian juntos. ☒ V ☐ F

Y ahora... conteste Answer these questions, basing your answers on the dialogue.

1. ¿Alina es norteamericana o cubanoamericana? Es cubanoamericana.
2. ¿Cuántas clases toma Lisa este semestre? Toma tres clases.
3. ¿Qué días trabaja Lisa? Trabaja los lunes, miércoles y viernes.
4. ¿La vida de Alina es muy aburrida? Sí, es muy aburrida.
5. ¿Dónde conversan Miguel y Pablo? Conversan en la cafetería de la universidad.
6. ¿Pablo desea tomar café o leche? Desea tomar leche.
7. ¿Miguel necesita el horario de clases o el libro? Necesita el horario de clases.
8. ¿Dónde es la clase de química? Es en el aula ciento noventa y cinco.

[1]The article **el** is used before a feminine noun that starts with a stressed **a** or **ha.**

Para hablar del tema: Vocabulario

Online Study Center

For more practice with lesson topics, see the related activities on the *¡Hola, amigos!* web site at college.hmco.com/PIC/holaamigos7e.

Suggestion: Remind students that the **Vocabulario** for each lesson appears on Audioflash cards in the Online Study Center (OSC).

Nombres

el (la) aguafiestas spoilsport
el (la) amigo(a) friend
la asignatura* course, subject
el aula (*f.*) classroom
el café coffee
el dinero* money
el horario de clases[1] class schedule
el inglés English (*language*)
el lunes Monday
la leche milk
el miércoles Wednesday
la noche night
la playa beach
el requisito requirement
la química chemistry
la tarde afternoon
la taza cup
el vaso (drinking) glass
el verano summer
la vida life
el viernes Friday

Cognados

la biología
la cafetería
cubanoamericano(a)
la física
la historia
la idea
internacional
julio
la literatura
las matemáticas
el programa
la psicología
puertorriqueño(a)
el semestre
septiembre
la televisión

Cognates are words that resemble one another and have similar meanings in Spanish and English. Note that English cognates are often spelled differently and pronunciation differs from their Spanish counterparts.

Suggestion: Have students pronounce all cognates and ask them to provide the English translation. Reverse the activity and have students come up with the Spanish word.

Otras palabras y expresiones

a at (*with time of day*); to
¿A qué hora...? (At) What time . . . ?
además besides
Aquí está Here it is
¿Cuántos(as)? How many?
de of
entonces then
este semestre this semester
hay there is, there are
hoy today
los (las) dos both
mañana tomorrow
Me voy I'm leaving
no vamos we are not going
pero but
por la tarde in the afternoon
¿Por qué? Why?
porque because
pues then
que who, that
¿Qué? What?
¿Qué hora es? What time is it?
solamente, sólo only
también also, too
¿verdad? right?, true?
y media half past
ya es tarde it's already late

Expansion: Consider the example of *a Spanish teacher:* Does he teach Spanish or was he born in Spain? Contrast **profesor de español** (teaches Spanish) with **profesor español** (teacher is from Spain). You may want to offer additional examples (**libro de español, clase de inglés,** and so on).

[1]Spanish uses prepositional phrases that correspond to the English adjectival use of nouns: **horario de clases** (*class schedule*).

Verbos

conversar* to talk, converse
desear to wish, want
estudiar to study
hablar to speak
necesitar to need
terminar to end, finish, get through
tomar to take (*a class*); to drink
trabajar to work

Adjetivos

aburrido(a) boring
bueno(a) good
juntos(as) together
nuestro(a) our
nuevo(a) new
todos(as) all

Amplíe su vocabulario

Para pedir bebidas (*Ordering drinks*)

Deseo una taza de
- café
- té — *tea*
- chocolate caliente — *hot chocolate*
- café con leche — *coffee and milk*

Deseo un vaso de
- agua con hielo — *ice water*
- leche
- cerveza — *beer*
- té helado, té frío — *iced tea*

Deseo jugo* de
- manzana — *apple*
- naranja* — *orange*
- tomate
- toronja — *grapefruit*
- uvas — *grapes*

Deseo una copa de vino (*wine*)
- blanco
- rosado — *rosé*
- tinto — *red*

Deseo una botella (*a bottle*) de agua mineral

De país a país

la asignatura la materia (*Arg., Esp.*)
el dinero la plata (*Cono Sur, Cuba*)
conversar platicar (*Méx.*)
el jugo el zumo (*Esp.*)
la naranja la china (*Puerto Rico*)

Más asignaturas (*More course subjects*)

la administración de empresas business administration
la antropología anthropology
el arte art
las ciencias políticas political science
la contabilidad accounting
la danza aeróbica aerobic dance
la geografía geography
la geología geology
la informática computer science
la música music
la sociología sociology

Para practicar el vocabulario

A. Palabras y más palabras ¿Qué palabra o frase corresponde a lo siguiente?

1. opuesto de día noche
2. asignatura donde estudiamos novelas y poemas literatura
3. Tiene seis meses. semestre
4. opuesto de invierno verano
5. clases que necesitamos tomar requisitos
6. Lo tomamos con leche. café
7. Debemos hacerlo antes de tomar un examen. estudiar
8. opuesto de malo bueno
9. sólo solamente
10. *Budweiser,* por ejemplo cerveza
11. idioma de Shakespeare inglés
12. opuesto de empezar terminar

B. Preguntas y respuestas Match the questions in column *A* with the answers in column *B*.

A	B
1. ¿Qué clases tomas este semestre? f	a. No, blanco.
2. ¿Es difícil la clase de biología? i	b. Sí, de julio a septiembre.
3. ¿Tú trabajas? j	c. A las ocho de la noche.
4. ¿Trabajas los lunes? h	d. Sí, de toronja.
5. ¿Deseas un vaso de leche? g	e. No, es aburrido.
6. ¿A qué hora terminas hoy? c	f. Química, inglés y física.
7. ¿Deseas vino tinto? a	g. No, una taza de café.
8. ¿Deseas jugo? d	h. No, los miércoles.
9. ¿Trabajas en el verano? b	i. No, es muy fácil.
10. ¿El programa es interesante? e	j. Sí, en la biblioteca.

C. ¿Qué deciden? With a partner, take turns offering each other something to drink. Choose what you will have to drink according to the circumstances described in each case. Then indicate your choice, using **Voy a tomar...**

1. You are allergic to citrus fruit. b
   a. un vaso de jugo de toronja
   b. un vaso de jugo de manzana
   c. un vaso de jugo de naranja

2. You are very hot and thirsty. b
   a. una taza de chocolate caliente
   b. un vaso de té helado
   c. una taza de café

3. You don't drink alcohol. a
   a. una botella de agua mineral
   b. una botella de cerveza
   c. una copa de vino tinto

4. You're having breakfast in Madrid. c
   a. una copa de vino rosado
   b. un vaso de agua con hielo
   c. una taza de café con leche

5. It's a cold winter night. b
   a. un vaso de jugo de uvas
   b. una taza de chocolate caliente
   c. un vaso de leche fría

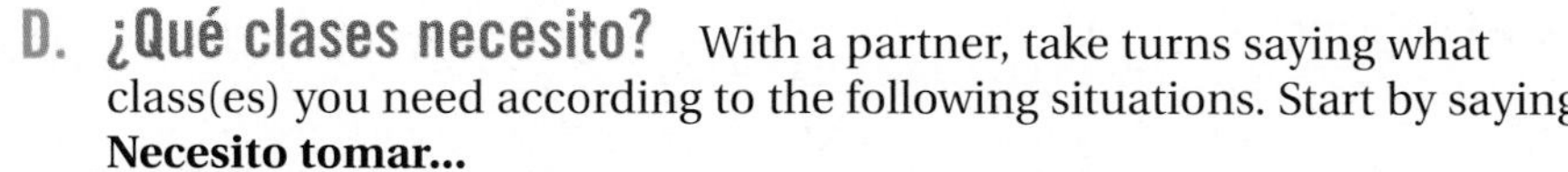

D. ¿Qué clases necesito? With a partner, take turns saying what class(es) you need according to the following situations. Start by saying **Necesito tomar...**

1. You need to get in shape. danza aeróbica
2. You would like to get a job in the business world. administración de empresas
3. You need two humanities classes. *Answers will vary.*
4. You need three social science classes. antropología, psicología y sociología
5. You know very little about other countries. *Answers will vary.*
6. You need to learn about computers. informática

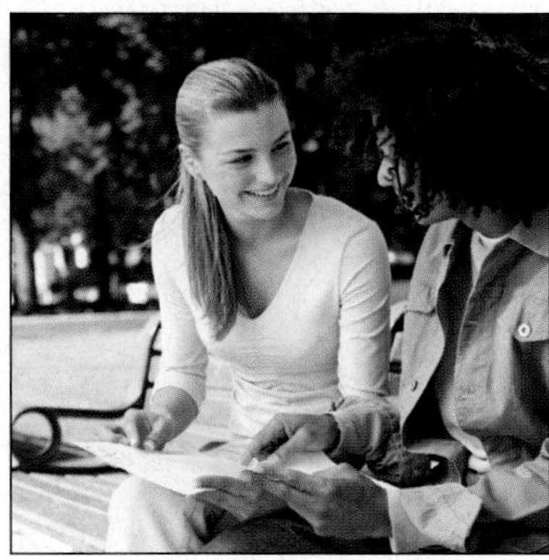

¿Qué clase cree Ud. que toman estos estudiantes?

Pronunciación

Linking[1] Practice linking by reading aloud the following sentences.

1. Habla en la universidad.
2. Juan habla con Norma Acosta.
3. Termino a la una.
4. ¿A qué hora es su clase de español?
5. Deseo un vaso de agua.

Suggestion: Now would be a good time to find out if students need additional Spanish vocabulary for other courses of interest to them. What do they need in order to graduate? **Necesito tomar...**

[1]See Appendix A for an explanation of linking.

Puntos para recordar

1. Present indicative of *-ar* verbs (*Presente de indicativo de los verbos terminados en* -ar)

Suggestions: To clarify what it means to "conjugate" a verb, have students conjugate the English verb *to be* orally.

Try to present verbs in complete sentences, rather than in isolation; also, gradually begin to drop subject pronouns before the verbs.

Alternative: You may want to use the following diagram when you present all verb conjugations.

habl- o	habl- amos
habl- as	habl- áis
habl- a	habl- an

Suggestion: Review subject pronouns by pointing to students or stick figures on the board or on index cards. Write the infinitive form of the verb on the board with additional choices to complete a simple sentence:

Ellos / Ud. / Yo / Ella (etc.)—hablar—español / inglés / francés

Then cue a pronoun and have students form complete sentences.

Suggestion: Write a short sentence builder on the board and ask students to combine the elements to form five original sentences.

- **Uds. / Yo / Pedro / Ellas / Tú**
- **tomar / trabajar / conversar / estudiar / necesitar**
- **el libro / español / café / con la profesora / en el laboratorio**

◆ Spanish verbs are classified according to their endings. There are three conjugations: **-ar, -er,** and **-ir.**[1]

—Rosa, tú **hablas** inglés, ¿no? *"Rosa, you **speak** English, don't you?"*
—Sí, **hablo** inglés y español. *"Yes, **I speak** English and Spanish."*

hablar (*to speak*)

	Stem Ending	
	Singular	
yo	habl- **o**	Yo **hablo** español.
tú	habl- **as**	Tú **hablas** español.
Ud.	habl- **a**	Ud. **habla** español.
él	habl- **a**	Juan **habla** español. Él **habla** español.
ella	habl- **a**	Ana **habla** español. Ella **habla** español.
	Plural	
nosotros(as)	habl- **amos**	Nosotros(as) **hablamos** español.
vosotros(as)	habl- **áis**	Vosotros(as) **habláis** español.
Uds.	habl- **an**	Uds. **hablan** español.
ellos	habl- **an**	Ellos **hablan** español.
ellas	habl- **an**	Ellas **hablan** español.

—¿Qué idioma **hablan** Uds. con el profesor? *"What language **do you speak** with the professor?"*
—**Hablamos** español. *"**We speak** Spanish."*

◆ Native speakers usually omit subject pronouns in conversation because the ending of each verb form indicates who is performing the action described by the verb. The context of the conversation also provides clues as to whom the verb refers. However, the forms **habla** and **hablan** are sometimes ambiguous even in context. Therefore, the subject pronouns **usted, él, ella, ustedes, ellos,** and **ellas** are used in speech with greater frequency than the other pronouns.

[1]The infinitive (unconjugated form) of a Spanish verb consists of a stem and an ending. The stem is what remains after the ending (**-ar, -er,** or **-ir**) is removed from the infinitive.

- Regular verbs ending in **-ar** are conjugated like **hablar.** Other verbs conjugated like **hablar** are **conversar, desear, estudiar, necesitar, terminar, tomar,** and **trabajar.**

—¿A qué hora **terminan** Uds. hoy?	*"What time **do you finish** today?"*
—**Terminamos** a las tres.	*"**We finish** at three o'clock."*
—¿Qué **necesitas**?	*"What **do you need**?"*
—**Necesito** el horario de clases.	*"**I need** the class schedule."*

¡Atención! In Spanish, as in English, when two verbs are used together, the second verb remains in the infinitive.

Expansion: Allowing students to act out or read the exchanges with a partner will give them additional pronunciation practice, reinforce conversational exchanges, and serve as a check of their responses.

Deseo **hablar** con Roberto. — *I want **to speak** with Roberto.*

- The Spanish present tense has three equivalents in English.

Yo hablo. — *I speak.* / *I am speaking.* / *I do speak.*

Práctica y conversación

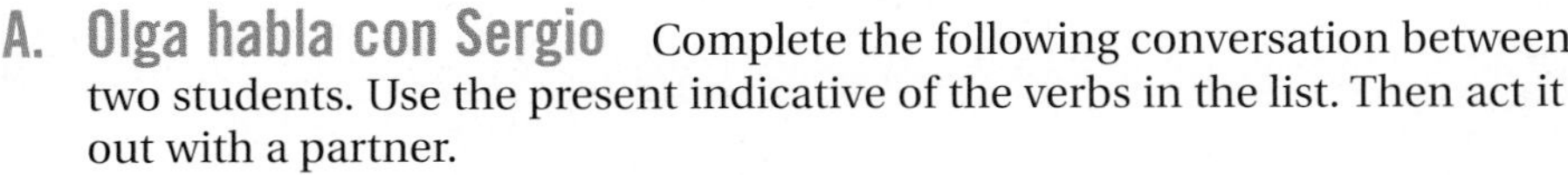

Online Study Center

For more practice with lesson topics, see the related activities on the *¡Hola, amigos!* web site at college.hmco.com/PIC/holaamigos7e.

A. Olga habla con Sergio

Complete the following conversation between two students. Use the present indicative of the verbs in the list. Then act it out with a partner.

desear   necesitar   tomar (2)   estudiar (2)   trabajar (2)   terminar (2)

Olga	¿Cuántas clases __tomas__ tú este semestre?
Sergio	__Tomo__ cuatro clases.
Olga	Tú y Álvaro __trabajan__ en la cafetería, ¿no?
Sergio	Sí, nosotros __trabajamos__ los lunes y miércoles. Oye, ¿tú __deseas__ tomar un vaso de agua?
Olga	Sí, gracias. ¿A qué hora __terminas__ tú hoy?
Sergio	Mis clases __terminan__ a las 4 de la tarde.
Olga	¿Tú y Álvaro __estudian__ juntos en la biblioteca?
Sergio	Sí, __estudiamos__ por la noche. Ah, (yo) __necesito__ tu número de teléfono.
Olga	Es el siete-treinta-veinticinco-doce.

B. Entreviste a su compañero(a) (*Interview your partner*)

Interview your partner, using the following questions. *Answers will vary.*

1. ¿Cuántas clases tomas este semestre?
2. ¿Qué asignaturas tomas? ¿Son fáciles o difíciles?
3. ¿Estudias en la biblioteca o en tu casa (*house*)?
4. ¿Trabajas en la universidad?
5. ¿Cuántas horas (*hours*) trabajas?
6. ¿Trabajas en el verano?
7. ¿Deseas un vaso de jugo o una botella de agua mineral?
8. ¿Tú tomas café o chocolate caliente? ¿Tú tomas vino?

Expansion: Encourage students to include at least two original questions in their conversations. Have students write paragraphs based on their partners' responses or describe their partners to the rest of the class.

2. Interrogative and negative sentences (*Oraciones interrogativas y negativas*)

Suggestion: Have the students ask you English questions that will elicit a *yes* or *no* response. Point out that intonation is the simplest way to form a question in English and in Spanish.

Interrogative sentences

- In Spanish, there are three ways of asking a question to elicit a *yes/no* response.

¿**Elena** habla español?
¿Habla **Elena** español? } Sí, Elena habla español.
¿Habla español **Elena**?

- The three questions above ask for the same information and have the same meaning. The subject may be placed at the beginning of the sentence, after the verb, or at the end of the sentence. Note that written questions in Spanish begin with an inverted question mark.

—¿**Trabajan Uds.** en la biblioteca? —No, trabajamos en la cafetería.	*"**Do you work** in the library?"* *"No, we work in the cafeteria."*
—¿**Habla** español **la profesora**? —Sí, y también habla inglés.	*"**Does the professor speak** Spanish?"* *"Yes, and she also speaks English."*
—¿**Carmen es** bonita? —Sí y muy simpática.	*"**Is Carmen** pretty?"* *"Yes, and very charming."*

Detalles culturales

Español y castellano son sinónimos. En muchos países de habla hispana para referirse al idioma no usan el término **español;** usan **castellano.** Este término también se usa para referirse al español como una asignatura en las escuelas (*schools*).

- **En su universidad, ¿cuál de los dos términos usan?**

¡Atención! Spanish does not use an auxiliary verb, such as *do* or *does,* in an interrogative sentence.

¿**Habla Ud.** inglés?	***Do you speak** English?*
¿**Necesita él** el horario de clases?	***Does he need** the class schedule?*

Suggestion: Write a short sentence builder on the board. Ask students to make as many negative sentences as possible in three to five minutes.

Yo / Ellas / Tú —trabajar / hablar / estudiar— hospital / inglés / cafetería

Negative sentences

- To make a sentence negative in Spanish, simply place the word **no** in front of the verb.

Yo tomo café.	*I drink coffee.*
Yo **no** tomo café.	*I **don't** drink coffee.*

- If the answer to a question is negative, the word **no** appears twice: once at the beginning of the sentence, as in English, and again before the verb.

—¿Trabajan Uds. en la cafetería?	*"Do you work in the cafeteria?"*
—**No,** nosotros **no** trabajamos en la cafetería.	*"**No,** we **don't** work in the cafeteria."*

¡Atención! Spanish does not use an auxiliary verb, such as the English *do* or *does,* in a negative sentence.

Ella no estudia inglés.	***She does not study*** *English.*
Yo no estudio hoy.	***I do not study*** *today.*

Práctica y conversación

A. ¿Qué preguntó? (*What did he ask?*) Complete the following dialogues by supplying the questions that would elicit the responses given. *Answers will vary.*

1. —¿ Estudian Uds. en la biblioteca ?
   —Sí, estudiamos en la biblioteca.
2. —¿ Tomas historia este semestre ?
   —No, este semestre tomo sociología.
3. —¿ Desean vino ?
   —No, deseamos agua mineral.
4. —¿ Trabajan ellos en el verano ?
   —Sí, ellos trabajan en el verano.
5. —¿ Tomas café ?
   —No, tomo jugo.
6. —¿ Deseas un vaso de leche ?
   —No, deseo una taza de chocolate.

Possible answers:

Online Study Center
For more practice with lesson topics, see the related activities on the ***¡Hola, amigos!*** web site at college.hmco.com/PIC/holaamigos7e.

Suggestion: You may want to pair students for this exercise.

Suggestion: Make a statement about yourself to a student and have him/her state whether that is true about him/her.
I: **Yo soy cubano.**
S: **Yo no soy cubano.**

Answers: 1. No, no necesito el libro; necesito el horario de clases. 2. No, no tomo café; tomo té frío. 3. No, no necesitan muchos libros; necesitan dos. 4. No, Rebeca no es puertorriqueña; es cubanoamericana. 5. No, Elsa no termina a las ocho; termina a las siete. 6. No, ellos no hablan español; hablan inglés. 7. No, la clase de geografía no es difícil; es fácil. 8. No, mi nueva compañera de cuarto no es baja; es alta.

B. ¿Quiere saber? This person wants to know many things. Use the cues provided to give him the information.

◆ **MODELO:** —¿Ud. es de Miami? (Nueva York)
—No, no soy de Miami; soy de Nueva York.

1. ¿Tú necesitas el libro? (el horario de clases)
2. ¿Tú tomas café? (té frío)
3. ¿Necesitamos muchos libros? (dos)
4. ¿Rebeca es puertorriqueña? (cubanoamericana)
5. ¿Elsa termina a las ocho? (a las siete)
6. ¿Ellos hablan español? (inglés)
7. ¿Es difícil la clase de geografía? (fácil)
8. ¿Tu nueva compañera de cuarto es baja? (alta)

C. Sobre el diálogo (*About the dialogue*) With a partner, reread the dialogue on p. 22. Then ask each other questions that you know will elicit negative answers about the people in the dialogue. *Answers will vary.*

◆ **MODELO:** —*¿Lisa es mexicana?*
—No, Lisa no es mexicana, es norteamericana.

3. Possessive adjectives (*Adjetivos posesivos*)

Forms of the Possessive Adjectives

Singular	*Plural*	
mi	**mis**	my
tu	**tus**	your (*fam.*)
su	**sus**	your (*form.*), his, her, its, their
nuestro(a)	**nuestros(as)**	our
vuestro(a)	**vuestros(as)**	your (*fam. pl.*)

Suggestion: Be sure students understand what is meant by "agreement."

◆ Possessive adjectives[1] always precede the nouns they introduce. They agree in number (singular or plural) with the nouns they modify.

Yo necesito **mi** < libro. / mochila.

Yo necesito **mis** < libro**s**. / mochila**s**.

[1]See Appendix C.

- **Nuestro** and **vuestro** are the only possessive adjectives that have the feminine endings **-a** and **-as.** The others take the same endings for both genders.

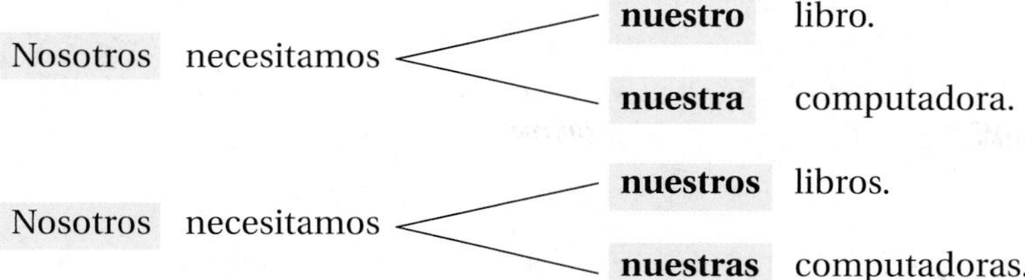

- Possessive adjectives agree with the thing possessed and *not* with the possessor. For instance, two male students would refer to their female professor as **nuestra profesora,** because **profesora** is feminine.
- Because **su** and **sus** have several possible meanings, the forms **de él, de ella, de ellos, de ellas, de Ud.,** or **de Uds.** can be substituted to avoid confusion. Use this pattern: *article* + *noun* + **de** + *pronoun*.

—¿Es **la amiga de él**? *"Is she **his** friend?"*
—Sí, es **su** amiga. *"Yes, she is **his** friend."*

Expansion: You might want to teach the saying **Mi casa es su casa,** which illustrates not only possessive adjectives but also the Hispanic tradition of hospitality.

Expansion: Tell students that there is a large network of Spanish-language radio stations in the U.S. If there are any such stations in your area, suggest that students tune in for additional practice outside of class. While on the topic of radio, you might ask, **¿Cuál es su estación de radio favorita?** Students can answer **Mi estación favorita es... (porque me gusta...).**

Práctica y conversación

Online Study Center

For more practice with lesson topics, see the related activities on the *¡Hola, amigos!* web site at college.hmco.com/PIC/holaamigos7e.

A. En la clase Complete the following exchanges using the appropriate possessive adjectives that correspond to each subject. Then act them out with a partner.

1. —¿Tú necesitas __tu__ bolígrafo rojo?
   —Sí, necesito __mi__ bolígrafo rojo y __mis__ lápices negros.
2. —¿De dónde es la profesora de Uds.?
   —__Nuestra__ profesora es de Los Ángeles.

3. —¿Qué necesita Roberto?
—Necesita ___sus___ cuadernos y ___su___ libro de español.
4. —Los alumnos de Uds., ¿son mexicanos?
—No, ___nuestros___ alumnos son argentinos.
5. —¿Qué necesita Ana? ¿ ___Su___ mochila?
—No, necesita ___su___ reloj.

B. Entreviste a su compañero(a) Interview your partner, using the following questions. *Answers will vary.*

1. ¿De dónde es tu mejor (*best*) amigo(a)?
2. ¿Tus padres (*parents*) son de Miami?
3. ¿Necesitas tus libros hoy?
4. ¿Son interesantes tus clases?
5. ¿Es simpático(a) tu compañero(a) de cuarto?
6. ¿Tú y tus amigos estudian juntos?
7. ¿Dónde estudian?
8. ¿Las clases de Uds. son fáciles o difíciles?

4. Gender of nouns, part II (*Género de los nombres, parte II*)

Suggestion: You may summarize the endings on the board thus:

Expansion: Ask students to guess the meaning of cognates they have never seen before (**corporación**, **medicina**, etc.).

Suggestion: Have students close their books and practice changing the nouns you give them from singular to plural, adding the appropriate definite and indefinite articles. Go quickly around the room.
I—**pared**
S1—**la pared**
S2—**las paredes**
S3—**una pared**
S4—**unas paredes**

Here are practical rules to help you determine the gender of those nouns that do not end in **-o** or **-a.** There are also a few important exceptions.

- Nouns ending in **-ción, -sión, -tad,** and **-dad** are feminine.

la lec**ción**	*lesson*	**la** liber**tad**	*liberty*
la televi**sión**	*television*	**la** universi**dad**	*university*

- Many words that end in **-ma** are masculine.

el progra**ma**	*program*	**el** cli**ma**	*climate*
el siste**ma**	*system*	**el** proble**ma**	*problem*
el te**ma**	*theme*	**el** poe**ma**	*poem*
el idio**ma**	*language*		

- The gender of nouns that have other endings and that do not refer to males or females must be learned. Remember that it is helpful to memorize a noun with its corresponding article.

el español	**el** borrador	**la** noche	**la** clase
el inglés	**el** reloj	**la** tarde	**la** leche
el café	**el** té	**la** luz	**la** calle

Práctica

Online Study Center

For more practice with lesson topics, see the related activities on the *¡Hola, amigos!* web site at college.hmco.com/PIC/holaamigos7e.

C. ¿Qué es...? For each illustration or set of words, give the Spanish noun together with its corresponding definite article.

1. la televisión

2. el café

3. francés, italiano, portugués
   los idiomas

4. Harvard, Yale, Stanford.
   las universidades

5. la lección

6. la luz

7. la noche

8. el borrador

9. Quito, Lima, Bogotá
   las ciudades

10. "The Raven"
    el poema

5. Numbers 40 to 200 (*Números de 40 a 200*)

40	cuarenta	90	noventa
41	cuarenta y uno	100	cien[1]
45	cuarenta y cinco	101	ciento uno
50	cincuenta	115	ciento quince
60	sesenta	175	ciento setenta y cinco
70	setenta	180	ciento ochenta
80	ochenta	200	doscientos

[1]When counting beyond 100, **ciento** is used: **ciento uno**

Answers: 1. cuarenta 2. cuarenta y nueve 3. ciento cinco 4. noventa y ocho 5. treinta y dos 6. ciento setenta 7. treinta 8. cuarenta y cinco 9. setenta y dos 10. sesenta y dos 11. ciento noventa 12. cien

Práctica y conversación

A. Sumas y restas

With a partner, take turns solving the problems.

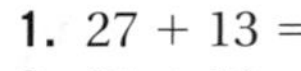

1. 27 + 13 =	**5.** 52 − 20 =	**9.** 16 + 56 =
2. 37 + 12 =	**6.** 200 − 30 =	**10.** 40 + 22 =
3. 90 + 15 =	**7.** 65 − 35 =	**11.** 200 − 10 =
4. 75 + 23 =	**8.** 80 − 35 =	**12.** 200 − 100 =

Online Study Center

For more practice with lesson topics, see the related activities on the *¡Hola, amigos!* web site at college.hmco.com/PIC/holaamigos7e.

B. Números de teléfono

Ask three or four classmates their phone numbers. To give a phone number, say the first number alone and the rest in pairs. This pattern is common in many Spanish-speaking countries.

Answers will vary.

◆ **MODELO:** *—¿Cuál es tu número de teléfono?*
—Es el 9–24–85–97.

6. Telling time (*La hora*)

Suggestion: A clock with movable hands may be used to provide practice in telling time. Add **el mediodía** (*noon*) and **la medianoche** (*midnight*) to vocabulary.

◆ The following word order is used for telling time in Spanish:

Es la				**y**		
or	+	*hour*	+	***or***	+	*minutes*
Son las				**menos**		

Es la una y veinte.

Son las cinco menos diez.

◆ **Es** is used with **una.**

Es la una y cuarto. — ***It is*** *a quarter after one.*

◆ **Son** is used with all the other hours.

Son las dos y cuarto. — ***It is*** *a quarter after two.*
Son las cinco y diez. — ***It is*** *ten after five.*

Programación de Telecaribe			
VIERNES			
6:00	Telecaribe	**9:00**	Noticiero Televisa
6:50	Noticiero Cartagena T.V.	**9:30**	Las Amazonas
7:00	Champagne	**10:00**	Amor gitano
7:30	Esta sí es la Costa	**11:00**	Noticiero Cartagena T.V.
8:00	Coralito	**11:10**	Cierre

- The feminine definite article is always used before the hour, since it refers to **la hora.**

  Es **la** una menos veinticinco. — *It is twenty-five to one.*
  Son **las** cuatro y media. — *It is four-thirty.*

- The hour is given first, then the minutes.

  Son las **cuatro** y **diez.** — *It is **ten** after **four.*** (literally, "four and ten")

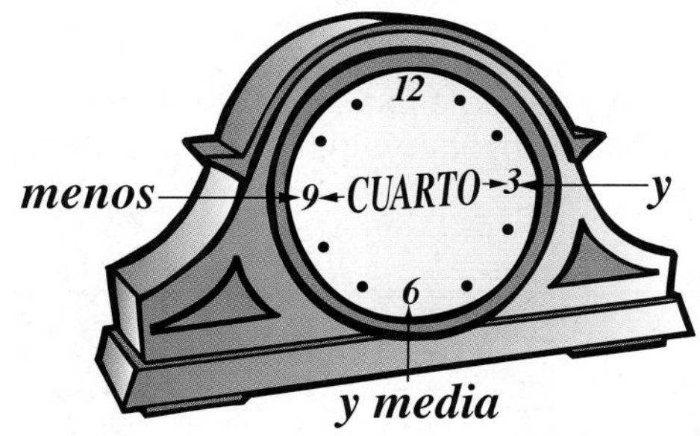

- The equivalent of *past* or *after* is **y.**

  Son las doce **y** cinco. — *It is five **after** twelve.*

- The equivalent of *to* or *till* is **menos.** It is used with fractions of time up to a half hour.

  Son las ocho **menos** veinte. — *It is twenty **to** eight.* (literally, "eight minus twenty")

¡Atención! To find out at what time an event will take place, use **¿A qué hora...?** as shown below. Observe that in the responses the equivalent of *at* + *time* is **a** + **la(s)** + *time.*

—¿**A qué hora** es la clase de arte? — *"**What time** is art class?"*
—**A la** una. — *"**At** one o'clock."*
—¿**A qué hora** termina Julio hoy? — *"**What time** does Julio finish today?"*
—**A las** cinco y media. — *"**At** five-thirty."*

Suggestion: Emphasize the difference between *it's* (**es, son**) and *at* (**a la, a las**).

- Note the difference between **de la** and **por la** in expressions of time.
  - When a specific time is mentioned, **de la (mañana, tarde, noche)** should be used. This is the equivalent to the English A.M. and P.M.

    Estudiamos a las **cuatro de la tarde.** — *We study at* **4 P.M.**

- When no specific time is mentioned, **por la (mañana, tarde, noche)** should be used.

Yo trabajo **por la mañana** y ella trabaja **por la noche.**	*I work **in the morning** and she works **at night.***

Detalles culturales

Para los horarios de aviones (*planes*), trenes, autobuses y algunas (*some*) invitaciones, se usa el sistema de veinticuatro horas. Por ejemplo, las cuatro de la tarde son las dieciséis horas.

- **¿Hay un sistema similar en este país?**

Online Study Center

For more practice with lesson topics, see the related activities on the ***¡Hola, amigos!*** web site at college.hmco.com/PIC/holaamigos7e.

Práctica y conversación

A. ¿Qué hora es? Give the time indicated on the following clocks, writing out the numerals in Spanish. Start with clock number one; then read the times aloud.

Suggestion: you may want to specify A.M. or P.M.

Answers: **1.** Son las doce. **2.** Es la una y cuarto. **3.** Son las cinco. **4.** Son las seis menos veinte. **5.** Son las seis menos cinco. **6.** Es la una y media. **7.** Es la una y veinte. **8.** Son las seis menos diez. **9.** Son las siete menos cuarto. **10.** Son las dos menos cuarto. **11.** Son las seis y cinco. **12.** Son las once menos cuarto.

B. Entreviste a su compañero(a) Interview your partner, asking the following questions. *Answers will vary.*

1. ¿A qué hora es tu primera (*first*) clase?
2. ¿A qué hora termina?
3. ¿A qué hora termina tu última clase?
4. ¿Estudias por la mañana, por la tarde o por la noche?
5. ¿Mañana estudiamos juntos(as)? ¿A qué hora deseas estudiar?
6. ¿A qué hora trabajas?
7. ¿A qué hora terminas de trabajar?
8. ¿A qué hora es tu programa de televisión favorito?

Expansion: Using a map of the world, ask students to tell you what time it is in different time zones.

I—Son las dos de la tarde en Dallas. ¿Qué hora es en Madrid? ¿Y en México? ¿Y en China?, etc.

C. Nuestros horarios With a partner, talk about your class schedule. Indicate whether your classes are in the morning, afternoon, or evening. *Answers will vary.*

Suggestion: You may want to bring a Spanish calendar to class. Emphasize that, except for **sábado** and **domingo**, the names of the days have the same form in the singular and in the plural.

7. Days of the week, and months and seasons of the year (*Los días de la semana, y los meses y las estaciones del año*)

MARZO 2007

lunes	martes	miércoles	jueves	viernes	sábado	domingo
			1	Estudiar con Ana 2	¡Fiesta! 3	4
Examen de arte 5	6	7	8	9	10	11
12	Clase de tenis 13	14	Conferencia 15	16	17	Programa religioso 18
19	20	21	22	23	24	25
26	27	Examen de inglés 28	29	Clase de yoga 30	31	

Days of the week (*Los días de la semana*)

- In Spanish-speaking countries, the week begins on Monday.
- Note that the days of the week are not capitalized in Spanish.
- The days of the week are masculine in Spanish. The masculine definite articles **el** and **los** are used with them to express *on:* **el lunes, los martes,** etc.
- To ask: "What day is today?" say: **"¿Qué día es hoy?"**

Suggestions: Give a day of the week. Have individual students say the day before and after.

Personalize the calendar by asking students to give days of familiar events.

¿Cuál es tu día favorito?

¿Qué día es tu clase de... (inglés, historia, psicología, etc.)?

Septiembre is also written **setiembre.**

Months of the year (*Los meses del año*)

enero	*January*	**mayo**	*May*	**septiembre**	*September*
febrero	*February*	**junio**	*June*	**octubre**	*October*
marzo	*March*	**julio**	*July*	**noviembre**	*November*
abril	*April*	**agosto**	*August*	**diciembre**	*December*

¡Atención! In Spanish, months are not capitalized.

Seasons of the year (*Las estaciones del año*)

la **primavera**

el **verano**

el **otoño**

el **invierno**

- Note that all the seasons are masculine except **la primavera.**
- To ask for the date, say:

Suggestion: Tell students that, from now on, the first one to get to class will write the day and the date on the board in Spanish.

¿Qué fecha es hoy?	***What's the date today?***

- When telling the date, always begin with the expression **Hoy es...**

Hoy es el 20 de mayo.	***Today is*** *May 20.*

- Note that the number is followed by the preposition **de** (*of*), and then the month.

el 15 de mayo	*May 15*
el 10 de septiembre	*September 10*
el 12 de octubre	*October 12*

Suggestion: Write on the board: **Mi cumpleaños es el... de...,** giving your birthday. Have students give their birthdays orally. You may want to point out that to Spanish speakers 7/9 means September 7, and not July 9.

- The ordinal number **primero** (*first*) is used when referring to the first day of the month.[1]

el primero de febrero	*February 1*
—¿Qué fecha es hoy, el **primero de octubre**?	*"What's the date today,* ***October 1****?"*
—No, hoy es el **2 de octubre.**	*"No, today is* ***October 2.****"*

[1]In Spanish today, many people say **el uno de: el uno de febrero.**

Práctica y conversación

A. Mi calendario
With a partner, look at the calendar on p. 39 and take turns asking each other on which day each event takes place. *Answers will vary.*

◆ **MODELO:** —*¿Cuándo estudio con Ana?*
—*El viernes 2.*

B. Fechas importantes
On what dates do the following annual events take place?

1. Independence Day el cuatro de julio
2. Halloween el treinta y uno de octubre
3. New Year's Day el primero de enero
4. Washington's birthday el veintidós de febrero (*may vary*)
5. Christmas el veinticinco de diciembre
6. the first day of spring el veintiuno de marzo
7. April Fool's Day el primero de abril
8. Veteran's Day el once de noviembre (*may vary*)

C. Las estaciones del año
In which season does each of these months fall in the Northern Hemisphere?

1. febrero el invierno
2. agosto el verano
3. mayo la primavera
4. enero el invierno
5. octubre el otoño
6. julio el verano
7. abril la primavera
8. noviembre el otoño

D. ¿Cuándo es?
On what dates do the following events occur? *Answers will vary.*

1. your mother's birthday
2. your father's birthday
3. your best friend's birthday
4. your birthday
5. the first day of classes this semester
6. the end of classes

E. Feliz cumpleaños
Ask four or five classmates when their birthday is. Ask: **¿Cuándo es tu cumpleaños?** Choose one of the birthdays and announce it to the rest of the class: *Answers will vary.*

El cumpleaños de _______ es el _______ de _______.

Online Study Center

For more practice with lesson topics, see the related activities on the ***¡Hola, amigos!*** web site at college.hmco.com/PIC/holaamigos7e.

Expansion: Additional questions you may want to use:

¿Qué día es hoy? ¿mañana?

Si hoy es lunes, ¿qué día es mañana?

Si hoy es lunes, ¿qué día es pasado mañana?

Expansion: Have students memorize this poem:

Treinta días trae noviembre
con abril, junio y septiembre.
De veintiocho, sólo hay uno
y los demás de treinta y uno.

Detalles culturales

Las estaciones ocurren en épocas opuestas en los dos hemisferios. Por ejemplo, cuando en Estados Unidos y Canadá (hemisferio norte) es verano; en Chile y Argentina (hemisferio sur) es invierno.

◆ **¿Cuál es su estación favorita?**

Detalles culturales

Los hispanos generalmente celebran, además del día de su cumpleaños, el día de su santo, que corresponde al santo de su nombre en el calendario católico. Patricio celebra su santo el 17 de marzo. (*St. Patrick's Day*)

◆ **¿Le gusta la idea de celebrar su santo? ¿Sabe Ud. cuándo es?**

Entre nosotros

¡Conversemos!

Para conocernos mejor Get to know your partner better by asking each other the following questions. *Answers will vary.*

1. ¿Qué asignaturas tomas tú este semestre?
2. ¿Cuál es tu clase favorita?
3. ¿Conversas con tus amigos en la cafetería? ¿Tomas café con ellos?
4. ¿Cuántas horas estudias? ¿Cuántas horas trabajas?
5. ¿Tú trabajas los sábados? ¿Y los domingos?
6. En el verano, ¿tomas clases o trabajas?
7. ¿Qué clases deseas tomar el próximo semestre?
8. ¿Qué estación te gusta?
9. ¿Deseas tomar café, leche o té?
10. ¿Deseas agua con hielo o jugo de naranja?

Una encuesta Interview your classmates to identify who does the following activities. Be sure to change the statements to questions. Include your instructor, but remember to use the **Ud.** form when addressing him or her.
Answers will vary.

	Nombre
1. Trabaja por la noche.	______
2. Trabaja cuatro horas al día (a day).	______
3. Toma clases en el verano.	______
4. Toma mucho café.	______
5. Toma cerveza o vino.	______
6. Estudia los domingos.	______
7. Estudia en la biblioteca.	______
8. Toma danza aeróbica.	______
9. Toma una clase de psicología.	______
10. Desea tomar una clase de música.	______

Suggestion: Encourage students to extend these roleplays by adding other information that is related to the topic.

Y ahora... Write a brief summary, indicating what you have learned about your classmates.

¿Cómo lo decimos? What would you say in the following situations? What might the other person say? Act out the scenes with a partner.

1. You want to ask a friend what subjects he or she is taking this semester.

2. You want to tell someone what subjects you are taking.
3. You want to ask someone where he or she works.
4. You want to order something to drink.
5. You want to know the time.
6. You want to ask a classmate if his/her classes are easy or difficult.

Answers: **1.** ¿Qué clases tomas este semestre? **2.** (Yo) tomo... **3.** ¿Dónde trabaja(s)? **4.** *Answers will vary.* **5.** ¿Qué hora es? **6.** ¿Tus clases son fáciles o difíciles?

¿Qué dice aquí?

With a classmate, study Virginia's schedule and take turns asking each other the following questions.

1. ¿Qué días tiene (*has*) Virginia la clase de historia? ¿A qué hora?
2. ¿Cuántas clases tiene Virginia por la noche?
3. ¿Qué clases tiene ella los (*on*) lunes, miércoles y viernes a las ocho?
4. ¿Qué idioma estudia Virginia? ¿Qué días?
5. ¿Cuándo estudia con el grupo?
6. ¿A qué hora almuerza (*has lunch*) Virginia? ¿Dónde?
7. ¿Dónde trabaja Virginia?
8. ¿Cuántas horas trabaja por semana (*per week*)?
9. ¿Qué clases incluyen laboratorio?
10. ¿Qué estudia Virginia los sábados?

Answers: **1.** Virginia tiene la clase de historia los lunes y miércoles a las siete (de la noche). **2.** Tiene una clase por la noche: historia. **3.** Tiene la clase de biología. **4.** Estudia japonés los lunes, martes, miércoles y jueves. **5.** Estudia con el grupo los lunes, miércoles y viernes a las diez (de la mañana). **6.** Almuerza a las doce en la cafetería. **7.** Trabaja en la biblioteca. **8.** Trabaja diez horas por semana. **9.** (Las clases de) Biología y japonés incluyen laboratorio. **10.** Los sábados estudia cibernética.

Horario de Virginia

	Lunes	Martes	Miércoles	Jueves	Viernes	Sábado
8:00	Biología		Biología		Biología	
9:00	Japonés	Japonés	Japonés	Japonés		
10:00	Estudiar con el grupo		Estudiar con el grupo		Estudiar con el grupo	Cibernética
11:00	↓	Educación física	↓	Educación física	↓	
12:00	Cafetería	Cafetería	Cafetería	Cafetería	Cafetería	
1:00		Biología (Laboratorio)		Japonés (Laboratorio)		
2:00	Trabajar en la biblioteca →					
3:00	↓	↓	↓	↓	↓	
4:00	↓	↓	↓	↓	↓	
5:00						
6:00						
7:00	Historia		Historia			
8:00	↓		↓			

Un dicho

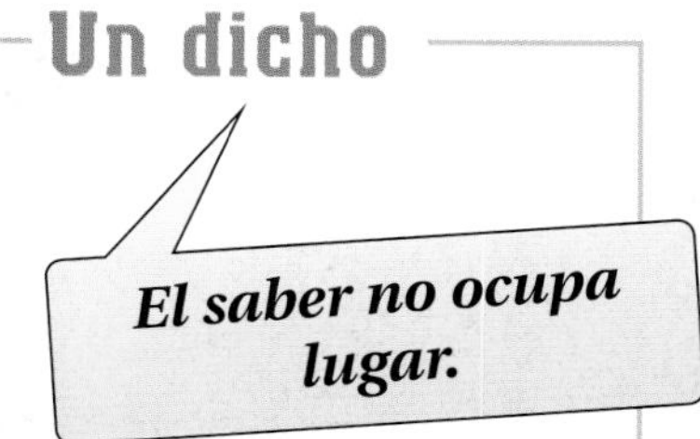

This is a popular saying in Spanish; find out what it means. It doesn't have an equivalent in English. Can you make up one?

Para escribir

Tu horario

With a partner, create a schedule for him or her. Use the following questions to ask about your partner's schedule. *Answers will vary.*

¿Qué clases tomas?
¿Qué días es la clase de...? ¿A qué hora?
¿Trabajas? ¿Qué días? ¿A qué hora?
¿Cuándo estudias? ¿A qué hora? ¿Dónde? ¿Con quién?

Lectura

Suggestion: Brainstorm items with students. Also, point out to students that using their background knowledge of a topic will give them a frame of reference and help them to understand more of what they read.

Answers: **1.** El estudiante debe revisar su horario de clases. **2.** Debe notificar cualquier error. **3.** Debe recibir la aprobación de la Administración para tomar más de 18 unidades. **4.** Sí, debe asistir a todas las clases. **5.** El carnet de estudiante debe tener su nombre, su número de identificación y su foto. **6.** Debe pagar la matrícula antes del primer día de clases. **7.** Debe llenar una solicitud en la Oficina de Administración si necesita un plan de pago especial. **8.** Debe hablar con un consejero si necesita cambiar una clase.

Estrategia de lectura The selection you are going to read talks about registration procedures at the **Universidad Nacional.** What types of information would you expect to find in such instructions? *Answers will vary.*

Vamos a leer As you read **Información sobre la matrícula,** find the answer to each of the following questions.

1. ¿Qué necesita revisar (*check*) el estudiante?
2. ¿Qué debe notificar?
3. ¿Qué debe hacer (*to do*) para tomar más de (*more than*) 18 unidades?
4. ¿Debe asistir (*attend*) a todas las clases?
5. ¿Qué información debe tener (*must have*) el carnet de estudiante?
6. ¿Cuándo debe pagar la matrícula (*pay tuition*)?
7. ¿Qué debe hacer si necesita un plan de pago (*payment*) especial?
8. ¿Con quién debe hablar si necesita cambiar (*to change*) una clase?

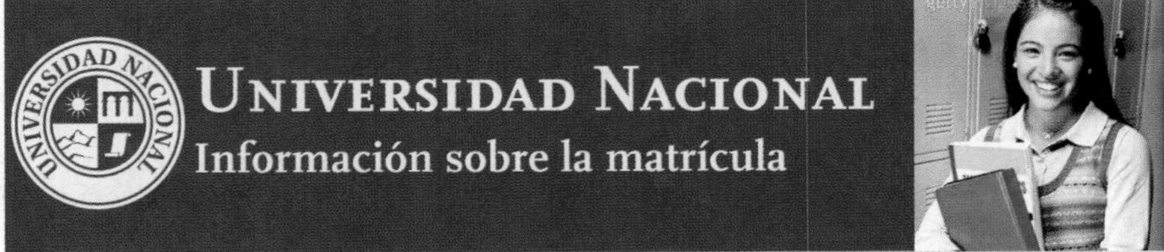

El estudiante debe:

- revisar su horario de clases
- notificar cualquier error
- recibir la aprobación de la Administración para tomar más de 18 unidades
- asistir a todas las clases
- sacar un carnet de estudiante con su nombre, su número de identificación y su foto
- pagar la matrícula antes del primer día de clases
- llenar una solicitud en la Oficina de Administración si necesita un plan de pago especial
- hablar con un consejero si necesita cambiar una clase

Video

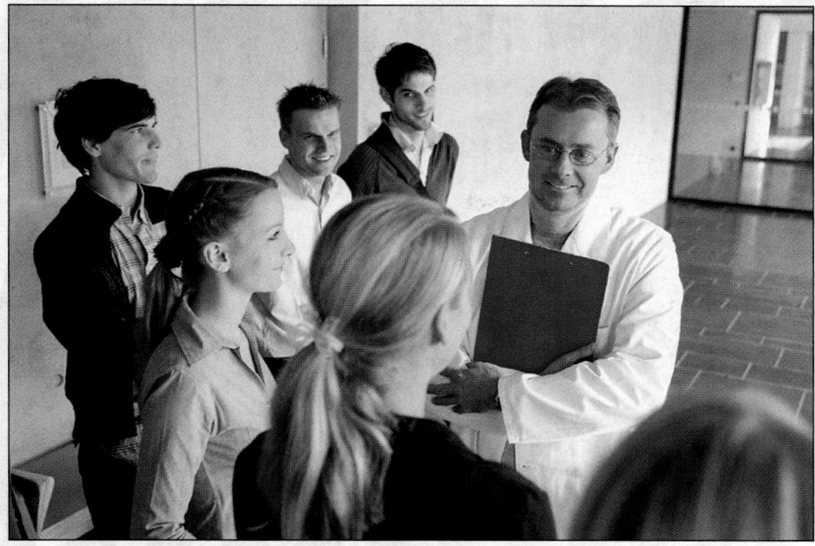

¿Cuántas clases toma cada (*each*) uno de estos estudiantes? ¿Trabajan o solamente estudian?

Díganos Answer the following questions, based on your own thoughts and experience. *Answers will vary.*

1. ¿Revisa Ud. su horario de clases cuidadosamente (*carefully*)?
2. ¿Toma usted más o menos de (*less than*) 18 unidades?
3. ¿Asiste usted a todas las clases?
4. ¿Qué información tiene su carnet de estudiante?
5. ¿Cuánto es la matrícula en su universidad?
6. ¿Necesita usted un plan de pago especial?
7. ¿Habla usted con un(a) consejero(a) (*adviser*) o con un(a) profesor(a) si necesita cambiar una clase?

Dos amigos

Pablo y Marisa, estudiantes de la Universidad de Costa Rica, estudian juntos y son buenos amigos. Cuando Marisa conoce a (*meets*) Fernando y Pablo conoce a Victoria, los dos amigos están un poco celosos (*jealous*).

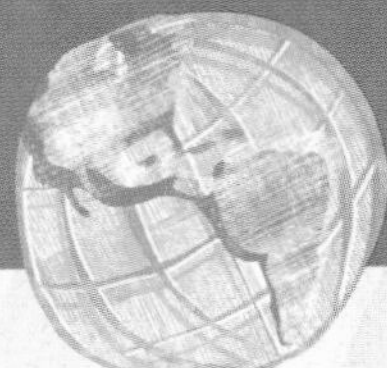

El mundo hispánico

Hispanos en los Estados Unidos 

Los mexicoamericanos

- En los Estados Unidos (*United States*) hay unos 40 millones de hispanos. El 66 por ciento (%) son de origen mexicano. La mayoría de ellos están (*are*) concentrados principalmente en California, Texas, Nuevo México y Arizona.
- El grado (*degree*) de asimilación a la cultura norteamericana de los mexicoamericanos es muy diverso. Unos se adaptan fácilmente (*easily*) y otros no. La mayoría conserva su lengua y su unidad familiar.
- Muchos mexicoamericanos se destacan (*stand out*) en la politica: Bill Richarson, gobernador de Nuevo México, Cruz Bustamante, vicegobernador de California y Ken Salazar, senador por Colorado; en educación: France Córdova, rectora de la Universidad de California, Riverside; en literatura: Rosaura Sánchez y Rolando Hinojosa; en música, cine y televisión: Carlos Santana, Eduardo James Olmos, George López y Eva Longoria. Muchos mexicoamericanos han ganado (*have earned*) honores en las fuerzas armadas.

▲ La famosa actriz hispana Eva Longoria en una fiesta en Pasadena, California.

Los cubanoamericanos

- Más de medio (*a half*) millón de cubanos viven en Miami, donde ejercen una gran influencia cultural y económica. Antes de la llegada (*arrival*) de los cubanos en 1959, Miami era (*was*) fundamentalmente un centro turístico. Hoy es un centro industrial y comercial de primer orden (*first-class*) y el puente (*bridge*) que une la economía de los Estados Unidos con la de América Latina y con la de España (*Spain*).
- Los cubanos son el 4 por ciento de los hispanos de este país, y como buena parte de ellos vinieron (*came*) por razones políticas, no económicas, son los inmigrantes hispanos más conservadores, con mayor nivel de escolaridad y mayor ingreso (*income*) per cápita. Entre los más conocidos se destacan en la política: Ileana Ros-Lehtinen y Rafael Díaz Balart, Representantes al Congreso de los Estados Unidos; en el cine: Andy García y Cameron Díaz; y en la música: Jon Secada, Gloria Estefan y Celia Cruz (1925–2003).
- En la Pequeña Habana, un barrio (*neighborhood*) cubano de Miami, el español es el idioma más hablado (*spoken*).

▲ La cantante cubana Celia Cruz, ganadora de un Premio Grammy en el año 2003.

Los puertorriqueños

- Los puertorriqueños son el segundo (*second*) grupo más grande (*largest*) de hispanos en los Estados Unidos. Como Puerto Rico es un Estado Libre Asociado a este país (*country*), los puertorriqueños son ciudadanos estadounidenses y no necesitan pasaporte ni visa para entrar en el país. En total, más de 2.700.000 puertorriqueños viven en los Estados Unidos, el 70 por ciento de ellos en Nueva York y Nueva Jersey. Más puertorriqueños viven en Nueva York que en San Juan, la capital de Puerto Rico.

▲ Marc Anthony y Jennifer López en una fiesta de Premios de la Vanity Fair Academy en Los Angeles.

- La mayoría de los puertorriqueños llegaron (*arrived*) a este país después de la Segunda Guerra Mundial (*World War II*) y, para muchos, fue (*it was*) muy difícil adaptarse a la vida (*life*) de la gran ciudad. En las últimas décadas, han llegado de Puerto Rico miles de profesionales, artistas y gente de negocios (*businesspeople*). Hoy hay puertorriqueños famosos en todos los campos (*fields*). Son buenos ejemplos de estos éxitos Nydia Velázquez y José Serrano, congresistas; Marc Anthony, Ricky Martin y Chayanne, cantantes (*singers*); Jennifer López, Benicio del Toro y muchos más, artistas de Hollywood; Félix (Tito) Trinidad, ex triple campeón de boxeo, etc.

Comentarios... With a partner, answer these questions about the different Hispanic groups found in this country.

1. ¿Cuál es el grupo más numeroso de hispanos en este país?
2. ¿La mayoría de los mexicoamericanos están (*are*) en el Suroeste (*Southwest*) o en el Sureste (*Southeast*) de los Estados Unidos?
3. ¿En qué campos se destacan muchos mexicoamericanos?
4. ¿Por qué razones vinieron (*came*) a este país la mayor parte de los cubanos?
5. ¿Cómo se llama el barrio cubano de la ciudad de Miami?
6. ¿En qué ciudad norteamericana viven más puertorriqueños que en San Juan, Puerto Rico?
7. ¿Puede Ud. (*can you*) mencionar algunos hispanos importantes?
8. En su estado, ¿cuál es el grupo de hispanos más numeroso?

Answers: **1.** El grupo más numeroso es el de los mexicoamericanos. **2.** La mayoría de los mexicoamericanos está en el Suroeste. **3.** Se destacan en la política, la educación, las artes y la literatura. **4.** La mayor parte de los cubanos vinieron por razones políticas. **5.** El barrio se llama la Pequeña Habana. **6.** Viven en la ciudad de Nueva York. **7.** *Answers will vary.* **8.** *Answers will vary.*

For more practice with lesson topics, see the related activities on the ***¡Hola, amigos!*** web site at college.hmco.com/PIC/holaamigos7e.

Tome este examen

Lección 1

Suggestion: Remind students about the Answer Key in Appendix D. Have them correct their mistakes and, if necessary, go back to the specific grammar point for review.

Lección 1

A. Gender of nouns; plural forms of nouns; definite and indefinite articles

Place the corresponding definite and indefinite article before each noun.

	Definite	Indefinite	Nouns
1.	los	unos	lápices
2.	los	unos	días
3.	el	un	hombre
4.	las	unas	mujeres
5.	la	una	mano
6.	la	una	silla
7.	los	unos	borradores
8.	los	unos	mapas

B. Subject pronouns

Say which pronoun would be used to talk about the following people.

1. Ana y yo (*f.*) nosotras
2. Jorge y Rafael ellos
3. la Dra. García ella
4. usted y el Sr. López ustedes
5. Amalia y Teresa ellas
6. el doctor Torres él

Now give the pronouns used to address the following people.

7. your professor usted
8. your best friend tú

C. Present indicative of *ser*

Complete the following sentences, using the present indicative of the verb ***ser.***

1. Yo __soy__ mexicana y John __es__ norteamericano.
2. ¿Uds. __son__ de Los Ángeles?
3. Teresa y yo __somos__ estudiantes.
4. Las plumas __son__ rojas.
5. ¿Tú __eres__ de San Diego?
6. ¿De dónde __es__ Ud.?

D. Forms of adjectives and agreement of articles, nouns, and adjectives Change each sentence according to each new element.

1. Las alumnas son norteamericanas. (*alumno*) El alumno es norteamericano.
2. Las tizas son verdes. (*lápices*) Los lápices son verdes.
3. El escritorio es blanco. (*mesas*) Las mesas son blancas.
4. Es una mujer española. (*hombre*) Es un hombre español.
5. El profesor es inglés. (*profesoras*) Las profesoras son inglesas.
6. La chica es rica. (*muchachos*) Los muchachos son ricos.
7. Es un hombre inteligente (*mujer*) Es una mujer inteligente.
8. La señora es muy simpática. (*señores*) Los señores son muy simpáticos.

E. The alphabet Spell the following last names in Spanish.

1. Díaz De-í-a-zeta
2. Jiménez Jota-i-eme-é-ene-e-zeta
3. Vargas Ve-a-ere-ge-a-ese
4. Parra Pe-a-erre-a
5. Feliú Efe-e-ele-i-ú
6. Acuña A-ce-u-eñe-a

F. Numbers 0–39 Write the following numbers in Spanish.

1. 8 ocho
2. 14 catorce
3. 26 veintiséis
4. 11 once
5. 35 treinta y cinco
6. 10 diez
7. 13 trece
8. 0 cero
9. 28 veintiocho
10. 17 diecisiete
11. 39 treinta y nueve
12. 15 quince

G. Vocabulary Complete the following sentences, using vocabulary from **Lección 1.**

1. ¿Cómo se __llama__ Ud.? ¿Teresa? ¿De __dónde__ es Ud.?
2. Mucho __gusto__, señor Vargas.
3. ¿Cómo se __dice__ *"desk"* en español?
4. Mi compañera de __cuarto__ es __muy__ bonita.
5. Hay una profesora y diez __alumnos (estudiantes)__ en la clase.
6. Rosa __habla__ con el profesor.
7. Buenos días. ¿Cómo __está__ usted? ¿Bien?
8. Adiós. __Saludos__ a Marisa.
9. ¿Cómo __es__ Sergio? ¿Guapo?
10. —Muchas gracias
    —De __nada__.

H. Culture Circle the correct answer, based on the cultural notes you have read.

1. El nombre María (no es/es) muy popular en los países hispanos. es
2. El título "señorita" se usa solamente para mujeres (casadas / que no se han casado). que no se han casado

Lección 2

Lección 2

A. Present indicative of *-ar* verbs

Complete each sentence with the correct form of the verb in parentheses.

1. ¿Tú ___tomas___ leche? (*drink*)
2. La señora Paz ___habla (conversa)___ con los alumnos. (*talks*)
3. Nosotros ___hablamos___ inglés con la doctora Torres. (*speak*)
4. Yo ___deseo___ tomar café. (*wish*)
5. ¿Ud. ___estudia___ matemáticas o biología? (*study*)
6. Ana y Paco ___trabajan___ en la biblioteca. (*work*)
7. Ernesto ___necesita___ la pluma roja. (*needs*)
8. Eva y yo ___terminamos___ en agosto. (*finish*)

B. Interrogative and negative sentences

Convert the following statements first into questions and then into negative statements.

1. Ellos hablan inglés con los estudiantes.
   a. ___¿Hablan ellos inglés con los estudiantes?___
   b. ___Ellos no hablan inglés con los estudiantes.___
2. Ella es de México.
   a. ___¿Es ella de México?___
   b. ___Ella no es de México.___
3. Ustedes terminan hoy.
   a. ___¿Terminan Uds. hoy?___
   b. ___Uds. no terminan hoy.___

C. Possessive adjectives

Complete these sentences, using the Spanish equivalent of the word in parentheses.

1. ¿Tú necesitas ___tu___ libro? (*your*)
2. Yo hablo con ___su___ profesor. (*her*)
3. Nosotros necesitamos hablar con ___nuestra___ profesora. (*our*)
4. Trabajo con ___mis___ compañeros de clase. (*my*)
5. ¿Ud. desea hablar con ___sus___ amigos? (*your*)
6. Carlos habla con ___nuestros___ profesores. (*our*)
7. Los estudiantes necesitan hablar con ___su___ profesor. (*their*)
8. Necesito ___su___ número de teléfono. (*his*)

D. Gender of nouns (Part II)

Write ***el, la, los,*** or ***las*** before each of the following nouns.

1. ___las___ lecciones
2. ___los___ relojes
3. ___el___ idioma
4. ___las___ unidades
5. ___los___ problemas
6. ___el___ café
7. ___la___ libertad
8. ___la___ televisión

E. Numbers 40–200

Write the following phrases in Spanish. (Write the numbers in words.)

1. 80 ballpoint pens
2. 46 backpacks
3. 72 clocks
4. 33 windows
5. 200 books
6. 115 notebooks

Answers: 1. ochenta bolígrafos 2. cuarenta y seis mochilas 3. setenta y dos relojes 4. treinta y tres ventanas 5. doscientos libros 6. ciento quince cuadernos

7. 68 students
8. 50 maps
9. 95 computers
10. 73 wastebaskets
11. 100 pens
12. 113 erasers

Answers: 7. sesenta y ocho estudiantes 8. cincuenta mapas 9. noventa y cinco computadoras 10. setenta y tres cestos de papeles 11. cien plumas 12. ciento trece borradores

F. Telling time

Write the Spanish equivalent of the words in parentheses.

1. Oye, ¿qué hora es? ¿ Es la una ? (*Is it one o'clock?*)
2. Luis toma química a las nueve y media de la mañana . (*at nine-thirty in the morning*)
3. Estudiamos español por la trade . (*in the afternoon*)
4. Son las ocho. (*It's*)
5. La clase es a las tres menos cuarto . (*at a quarter to three*)

G. Days of the week, and months and seasons of the year

Write the names of the missing days.

lunes, martes , miércoles , jueves, viernes , sábado , domingo

Give the following dates in Spanish.

1. March 1 el primero de marzo
2. June 10 el diez de junio
3. August 13 el trece de agosto
4. December 26 el veintiséis de diciembre
5. September 3 el tres de septiembre
6. October 28 el veintiocho de octubre
7. July 17 el diecisiete de julio
8. April 4 el cuatro de abril
9. January 2 el dos de enero
10. February 5 el cinco de febrero

What seasons do these months fall in the Northern Hemisphere?

1. febrero invierno
2. abril primavera
3. octubre otoño
4. julio verano

H. Vocabulary

Complete the following sentences, using vocabulary from **Lección 2.**

1. ¿Qué hora es? ¿Las dos?
2. Necesito el horario de clases. ¡Ah! ¡ Aquí está!
3. Yo tomo solamente dos clases.
4. Deseo una taza de café y un vaso de agua.
5. ¿Ellos toman café en la cafetería?
6. Este semestre tomo tres clases.
7. Marzo, abril y mayo son los meses de la primavera .
8. ¿Qué asignatura (materia) estudias? ¿Historia?
9. Él toma una copa de vino.
10. Deseo tomar jugo de manzana.
11. Eva es muy aburrida; es una aguafiestas .
12. Trabajo porque necesito dinero .

I. Culture

Circle the correct answer, based on the cultural notes you have read.

1. El (30 / 66) por ciento de los hispanos que viven en los Estados Unidos son de origen mexicano. 66
2. En las tiendas de la Pequeña Habana, el idioma más hablado es el (español / inglés). español
3. Los puertorriqueños son el (segundo / primer) grupo de hispanos más grande en los Estados Unidos. segundo

Unidad 2

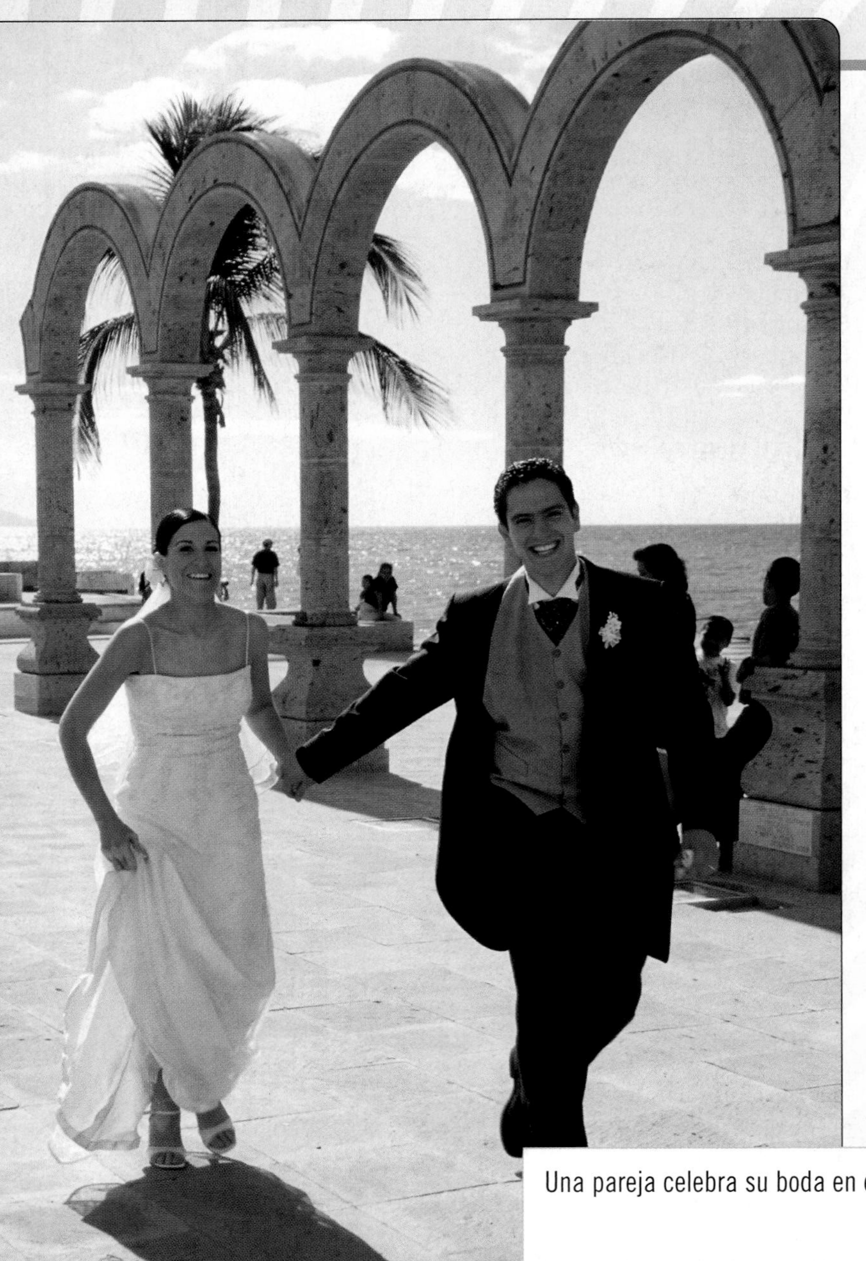

Una pareja celebra su boda en el Malecón en Puerto Vallarta.

Objetivos

Lección 3

- Talk about household chores
- Talk about family
- Talk about how you feel

Lección 4

- Discuss plans for a party
- Extend, accept, and decline invitations
- Handle informal social situations such as parties

En familia

Lección 3
Los trabajos de la casa

Lección 4
Una fiesta de cumpleaños

México

Vista panorámica de la Plaza de Las Tres Culturas, en México.

Guatemala

Estos turistas admiran un templo en Tikal, Guatemala.

El Salvador

El volcán Izalco, el más nuevo del país

Lección 3 ◆ Los trabajos de la casa

Hoy es un día muy ocupado para Susana, Alicia y Héctor, tres hermanos que viven con sus padres en la Ciudad de México.

Alicia Esta noche vienen papá y mamá de Guadalajara y esta casa es un desastre.

Susana Sí, especialmente el cuarto de Héctor. ¡Héctor! Tienes que limpiar tu recámara.

Alicia Y también tienes que sacar la basura y cortar el zacate.

Héctor Ustedes dos son muy mandonas. Yo siempre tengo que hacer todo el trabajo en esta casa.

Susana ¡Ja! Tu ocupación favorita es comer porque siempre tienes hambre.

Alicia Yo creo que lo mejor es dividir el trabajo: yo limpio la cocina y los baños, Susana sacude los muebles de la sala y Héctor barre el garaje.

Héctor ¡Yo hago todo eso! No tengo tiempo porque viene Carlos para estudiar conmigo.

Susana Tú siempre tienes excusas para no trabajar.

Detalles culturales

Actualmente (*At present*) muchos hombres hispanos, especialmente los más jóvenes, ayudan (*help*) a su esposa con los trabajos de la casa. Esto es debido a que, generalmente, los dos trabajan fuera de casa.

◆ **¿Los esposos norteamericanos ayudan con los trabajos de la casa?**

Detalles culturales

México tiene una comida típica excelente que hoy es popular en todo el mundo (*world*), pero en las grandes ciudades mexicanas los restaurantes sirven también comida internacional.

◆ **¿Qué comidas son típicas de su país?**

Esa tarde.

Alicia Todavía tenemos que lavar y planchar la ropa y lavar los platos.
Susana ¡Hay mil cosas que hacer!
Héctor ¿Por qué no descansamos un rato y bebemos una limonada? Yo tengo mucha sed.
Alicia Tienes razón. Hay limonada en el refrigerador.
Susana Bueno... descansamos un momento, pero después debemos pasar la aspiradora y preparar la comida.
Héctor Yo hago la ensalada y ustedes preparan las enchiladas.
Alicia ¿Y quién pone la mesa?
Susana Yo. Héctor, oye. Tocan a la puerta.
Héctor Debe ser Carlos. (*Héctor corre a abrir.*)

Esa noche, cuando llegan los padres, todos cenan y conversan en el comedor y después la mamá y las chicas miran su telenovela favorita.

Suggestion: Have students review the lesson dialogues and vocabulary prior to viewing the second segment of the **¡Hola, amigos!** video corresponding to **Lección 3**. Each lesson includes scenes and interviews related to the functional and thematic content of the lesson.

Detalles culturales

La música mexicana es conocida (*known*) en todos los países y sus telenovelas se ven (*are seen*) no solamente en el mundo hispano sino que también son populares en países como Rusia y Japón.

◆ **¿Qué telenovelas de su país son famosas?**

Suggestion: Have students correct false statements.

¿Recuerda usted?

¿Verdadero o falso?

With a partner, decide whether the following statements about the dialogue are true (**verdadero**) or false (**falso**).

1. Susana, Alicia y Héctor son hermanos. ☒ V ☐ F
2. Los padres de los chicos vienen de Acapulco. ☐ V ☒ F
3. Héctor tiene que limpiar su cuarto. ☒ V ☐ F
4. Héctor dice (*says*) que sus hermanas son muy mandonas. ☒ V ☐ F
5. Héctor come mucho. ☒ V ☐ F
6. Susana limpia la cocina y los baños. ☐ V ☒ F
7. Por la tarde, los chicos todavía tienen que lavar los platos. ☒ V ☐ F
8. Los chicos beben jugo de uvas. ☐ V ☒ F
9. Alicia prepara la ensalada. ☐ V ☒ F
10. Tocan a la puerta. Son los padres de los chicos. ☐ V ☒ F

Y ahora... conteste

Answer these questions, basing your answers on the dialogue.

1. ¿De dónde vienen los padres de los chicos?
2. Según (*According to*) Susana, ¿cuál es la ocupación favorita de Héctor?
3. ¿Quién sacude los muebles de la sala?
4. ¿Quién viene a estudiar con Héctor?
5. ¿Dónde hay limonada?
6. ¿Qué preparan las chicas?
7. ¿Dónde cenan todos?
8. ¿Qué miran la mamá y las chicas?

Answers: 1. Vienen de Guadalajara. 2. Según Susana, la ocupación favorita de Héctor es comer. 3. Susana sacude los muebles de la sala. 4. Carlos viene a estudiar con Héctor. 5. Hay limonada en el refrigerador. 6. Preparan las enchiladas. 7. Todos cenan en el comedor. 8. Miran su telenovela favorita.

Para hablar del tema: Vocabulario

Online Study Center

For more practice with lesson topics, see the related activities on the *¡Hola, amigos!* web site at college.hmco.com/PIC/holaamigos7e.

Cognados

el desastre
la ensalada
la excusa
la familia
favorito(a)
el garaje
la limonada
el momento
la ocupación
el refrigerador*

Nombres

el baño, el cuarto de baño bathroom
la basura garbage
la casa house
la ciudad city
la cocina kitchen
la comida meal, food
la cosa thing
el cuarto room
la hermana sister
el hermano brother
la mamá mom
los muebles furniture
los padres parents
el papá dad
el plato plate, dish
el dormitorio* bedroom
la ropa clothes
la sala living room
la telenovela soap opera
el tiempo time
el trabajo work
los trabajos de la casa housework
el césped* lawn

Adjetivos

este(a) this
mandón(ona) bossy
ocupado(a) busy

Verbos

abrir to open
barrer to sweep
beber to drink
cenar to dine
comer to eat
cortar to cut, to mow
deber to have to, must
descansar to rest
hacer (yo hago) to do, to make
lavar to wash
limpiar to clean
llegar to arrive
mirar to watch, to look at
planchar to iron
preparar to prepare
sacar to take out
sacudir* to dust
tener to have
venir to come
vivir to live

De país a país

el refrigerador la heladera (*Méx.*, Cono Sur)
la nevera (*Esp.*)
el dormitorio la recámara (*Méx.*)
el césped el zacate (*Méx.*)
sacudir limpiar el polvo (*Esp.*)

Otras palabras y expresiones

conmigo with me
cortar el césped to mow the lawn
cosas que hacer things to do
cuando when
después after
eso that
especialmente especially
mil a thousand
para for, in order to
pasar la aspiradora to vacuum
poner la mesa to set the table
¿Quién (es)? Who (is it)?
siempre always
tener hambre to be hungry
tener que + ***infinitivo*** to have to + *infinitive*
tener razón to be right
tener sed to be thirsty
tocar (llamar) a la puerta to knock at the door
todavía still
todo(a) all
un rato a while

Amplíe su vocabulario

Aparatos electrodomésticos y batería de cocina (*Home appliances and kitchen utensils*)

Para practicar el vocabulario

A. Preguntas y respuestas Match the questions in column *A* with the answers in column *B*.

A

1. ¿A qué hora cenan? ___i___
2. ¿Qué necesitas? ___l___
3. ¿Quién viene hoy? ___f___
4. ¿Ella es la hermana de Eva? ___a___
5. ¿Dónde viven? ___j___
6. ¿Qué deseas beber? ___c___
7. ¿Comes en tu cuarto? ___k___
8. ¿Con quién estudia Luis? ___b___
9. ¿Deseas una Coca-Cola? ___e___
10. ¿Quién hace los trabajos de la casa? ¿Tu hermano? ___d___
11. ¿No descansa? ___h___
12. ¿Qué miran por la noche? ___g___

B

a. No, la mamá.
b. Conmigo.
c. Limonada.
d. No, mi papá.
e. No, gracias; no tengo sed.
f. Mi hermano.
g. Una telenovela.
h. ¡No! ¡Siempre trabaja!
i. A las ocho de la noche.
j. En la ciudad de Lima.
k. No, en la cocina.
l. ¡Muchas cosas!

B. ¡Hay mil cosas que hacer! Complete these exchanges, using vocabulary from Lección 3. Then act them out with a partner.

1. —¿Qué ___tenemos___ (nosotros) que hacer hoy?
—Tenemos que ___sacudir___ los muebles, ___lavar___ los platos y ___limpiar___ el baño y la cocina.
2. —Tengo que ___pasar___ la aspiradora y ___preparar___ la comida.
—Yo tengo que ___barrer___ el garaje, ___cortar___ el césped y ___sacar___ la basura.
3. —Oye, Sara. Tienes que planchar la ___ropa___ y ___poner___ la mesa.
—Un ___momento___, mamá. Tengo mucha ___sed___ y deseo ___beber___ una limonada.

¿Quiénes son estas personas y qué tienen que hacer hoy?

C. ¿Qué necesitas? With a partner, look at the following list and take turns asking each other whether you need certain items.

◆ **MODELO:** —*¿Necesitas la lavadora?*
—*Sí, porque tengo que lavar la ropa.*

1. lavar la ropa
2. secar (*dry*) la ropa
3. planchar
4. lavar los platos
5. tostar el pan (*bread*)
6. preparar un batido (*shake*)
7. hacer sopa (*soup*)
8. preparar una ensalada
9. colar (*strain*) espaguetis
10. hacer café

Answers: **1.** ¿Necesitas la lavadora? / Sí, porque tengo que lavar la ropa. **2.** ¿Necesitas la secadora? / Sí, porque tengo que secar la ropa. **3.** ¿Necesitas la plancha? / Sí, porque tengo que planchar. **4.** ¿Necesitas el lavaplatos? / Sí, porque tengo que lavar los platos. **5.** ¿Necesitas la tostadora? / Sí, porque tengo que tostar el pan. **6.** ¿Necesitas la licuadora? / Sí, porque tengo que preparar un batido. **7.** ¿Necesitas la cacerola? / Sí, porque tengo que hacer sopa. **8.** ¿Necesitas el tazón? / Sí, porque tengo que preparar una ensalada. **9.** ¿Necesitas el colador? / Sí, porque tengo que colar espaguetis. **10.** ¿Necesitas la cafetera? / Sí, porque tengo que hacer café.

D. Los trabajos de la casa With a partner, play the roles of two family members trying to divide the housework by negotiating. *Answers will vary.*

◆ **MODELO:** —Si tú preparas la ensalada, yo lavo los platos.

¿Qué quehaceres de la casa tienen que hacer Estela y su mamá después de comer?

Pronunciación

Las consonantes (*consonants*) ***b, v*** In Spanish, **b** and **v** have the same bilabial sound. To practice this sound, pronounce the following words, paying particular attention to the sound of **b** and **v.**

b	**b**asura	**b**arrer	**b**e**b**er	**b**año	a**b**rir	**B**ena**v**ente
v	di**v**idir	**v**iene	**v**i**v**ir	la**v**ar	fa**v**orito	

Expansion: Additional practice: **Bárbara va a Varsovia con Vicente. Vas a buscar a Viviana a Burgos.**

Puntos para recordar

1. Present indicative of *-er* and *-ir* verbs (*Presente de indicativo de los verbos terminados en* -er *y en* -ir)

Suggestions: Before introducing the present indicative of regular **-er** and **-ir** verbs, review **-ar** verbs. You may wish to follow the presentation pattern suggested for **-ar** verbs in **Lección 2.**

Emphasize that the endings for **-er** and **-ir** verbs are the same except for the **nosotros(as)** and **vosotros(as)** forms.

comer (*to eat*)		**vivir** (*to live*)	
yo	com**o**	yo	viv**o**
tú	com**es**	tú	viv**es**
Ud. / él / ella	com**e**	Ud. / él / ella	viv**e**
nosotros(as)	com**emos**	nosotros(as)	viv**imos**
vosotros(as)	com**éis**	vosotros(as)	viv**ís**
Uds. / ellos / ellas	com**en**	Uds. / ellos / ellas	viv**en**

◆ Regular verbs ending in **-er** are conjugated like **comer.** Other regular **-er** verbs are **barrer, beber, correr** (*to run*), **creer, leer** (*to read*), and **deber.**

Suggestion: Write infinitive phrases on the board, cue pronouns, and have students form sentences:
beber té
vivir en...
correr por la mañana
escribir mucho

Suggestion: Stress the fact that English structure is the same. Give additional examples in Spanish using **deber** and other verbs:
Debemos estudiar esta tarde.
Necesito trabajar.
Deseo comer.

—Uds. **beben** café, ¿no? — *"**You drink** coffee, don't you?"*
—No, **bebemos** limonada. — *"No, **we drink** lemonade."*

—¿Nosotros **debemos** poner la mesa? — *"**Do we have to** set the table?"*
—No, Uds. **deben** preparar la comida. — *"No, **you must** prepare the food."*

◆ Regular verbs ending in **-ir** are conjugated like **vivir.** Other regular **-ir** verbs are **abrir, escribir** (*to write*), **recibir** (*to receive*), **sacudir,** and **dividir.**

—Tú **escribes** en inglés, ¿no? — *"**You write** in English, don't you?"*
—No, **escribo** en español. — *"No, **I write** in Spanish."*

—¿Uds. **viven** en D.F.[1]? — *"**Do you live** in D.F.?"*
—No, nosotros **vivimos** en Guadalajara. — *"No, **we live** in Guadalajara."*

—¿Qué **sacudes** tú? — *"What do **you dust**?"*
—Yo **sacudo** los muebles de la sala. — *"**I dust** the living room furniture."*

[1]Distrito Federal (Mexico City)

Práctica y conversación

Online Study Center

For more practice with lesson topics, see the related activities on the *¡Hola, amigos!* web site at college.hmco.com/PIC/holaamigos7e.

A. Minidiálogos Complete the following exchanges appropriately, using the present indicative of the verbs in the list. Then act them out with a partner.

1. vivir

   —¿Dónde __viven__ Uds.?

   —Nosotros __vivimos__ en Guanajuato.

   —¿Y Pablo?

   —Él __vive__ en Puebla.

2. comer

   —¿A qué hora __comes__ tú?

   —Yo __como__ a las dos.

3. leer

   —¿Qué libro __leen__ Uds.?

   —Nosotros __leemos__ *El Quijote.*[1]

4. beber

   —¿Ud. __bebe__ vino tinto?

   —No, yo __bebo__ vino blanco.

5. correr

   —¿Uds. __corren__ por la mañana?

   —Sí, nosotros __corremos__ por la mañana, pero Carlos __corre__ por la tarde.

6. sacudir

   —¿Tú __sacudes__ los muebles de la sala?

   —No, yo __sacudo__ los muebles del dormitorio.

---

[1] *El ingenioso hidalgo don Quijote de la Mancha,* Miguel de Cervantes's famous novel.

7. deber
   —¿Qué deben limpiar Uds.?
   —Yo debo limpiar el baño y Alicia debe limpiar la cocina.
8. barrer
   —¿Quién barre el garaje? ¿Tú?
   —No, Teresa y yo barremos la sala.
9. recibir
   —¿Uds. reciben cartas (*letters*)?
   —No, nosotros recibimos mensajes electrónicos.
10. escribir
   —¿Ud. escribe con lápiz?
   —No, yo escribo con pluma.

B. Entreviste a su compañero(a) Interview a partner, using the following questions. *Answers will vary.*

Expansion: Expand by listing things to eat and drink. Also teach: **Yo vivo en la calle** _______ . As an oral activity, ask individual students what they must do today and where they live. Then have the class review their answers: **Sandy, ¿dónde vives tú?** (*Answer.*) **Clase, ¿dónde vive Sandy?**, etc.

1. ¿Tú vives cerca de (*near*) la universidad? ¿Dónde vives?
2. ¿Bebes café por la mañana? Y por la tarde, ¿bebes té?
3. ¿Comes en la cafetería de la universidad? ¿A qué hora comes?
4. ¿Tú corres por la mañana?
5. ¿Tú escribes en inglés o en español? ¿Lees mucho?
6. ¿Tú abres la ventana de tu dormitorio por la noche?
7. ¿Qué días sacudes los muebles? ¿Qué días barres la cocina?
8. ¿Tú debes cortar el césped hoy? ¿Debes sacar la basura?

2. Possession with *de* (*El caso posesivo*)

Suggestion: Be sure students realize that in Spanish the apostrophe isn't used to show possession. Show the parallelism between the English construction *noun phrase + of + noun* and the Spanish construction *noun phrase* + **de** + *noun phrase*. First write a phrase expressing possession in English, such as *Ralph's wife.* Then express it thus:

English: *the wife of Ralph*
↓ ↓ ↓ ↓
Spanish: **la esposa de Raúl**

The **de** + *noun* construction is used to express possession or relationship. Unlike English, Spanish does not use the apostrophe.

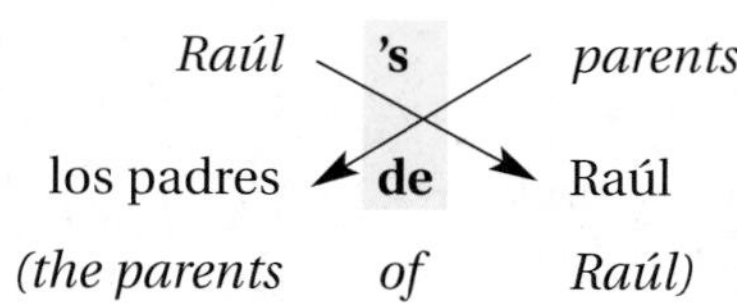

—¿Ellos son **los hermanos de** Rafael?	*"Are they Rafael's brothers?"*
—No, son **los** hijos **de** Oscar.	*"No, they are Oscar's children."*
—¿Dónde viven Uds.?	*"Where do you live?"*
—En **la** casa **de Pedro.**	*"At Pedro's house."*

¡Atención! Note the use of the definite article before the words **hijos** and **casa.**

Práctica y conversación

A. ¿Posesión o relación? Express the relationship of the people and/or objects in each illustration, using **de** + *noun* (i.e., the Spanish equivalent of *Marta's son*).

1. el hijo de Marta
2. el número de teléfono de la señorita Martínez

3. los libros de Elena
4. el escritorio de la profesora

B. ¿Quiénes son? According to the information given, you and a partner ask each other who everyone is. Answer expressing the relationship that exists among the people named.

◆ **MODELO:** La señora López tiene (*has*) dos estudiantes: Eva y Ana.

—¿Quiénes son Eva y Ana?
—Eva y Ana son las estudiantes de la señora López.

Online Study Center

For more practice with lesson topics, see the related activities on the *¡Hola, amigos!* web site at college.hmco.com/PIC/holaamigos7e.

Suggestion: Go around the class picking up objects belonging to students. Show the class each object and have students establish possession: **Es el lápiz *de* Tom.** For additional practice, have students follow up each identification with the appropriate possessive adjective: **Es su lápiz.**

Answers: 1. Roberto es el hermano de Elena. 2. Sergio, Daniel y Luis son los alumnos de la profesora Fernández. 3. Marisa es la hermana de Jorge. 4. Alicia es la secretaria de la señora Gutiérrez. 5. El señor Alba es el papá de Diana. 6. La doctora Vélez y la doctora Mena son las profesoras de Eva. 7. David es el compañero de clase de José Luis. 8. Silvia y Mónica son las compañeras de cuarto de Marta.

1. Elena tiene un hermano: Roberto.
2. La profesora Fernández tiene tres alumnos: Sergio, Daniel y Luis.
3. Jorge tiene una hermana: Marisa.
4. La señora Gutiérrez tiene una secretaria: Alicia.
5. Diana tiene un papá: el señor Alba.
6. Eva tiene dos profesoras: la doctora Vélez y la doctora Mena.
7. José Luis tiene un compañero de clase: David.
8. Marta tiene dos compañeras de cuarto: Silvia y Mónica.

3. Present indicative of *tener* and *venir* (*Presente de indicativo de* tener *y* venir)

Suggestions: Stress the similarity between the conjugations of **venir** and **tener.** Encourage students to study irregular verbs in groups, according to their shared irregular patterns.

Write on the board: **Yo *vengo* a pie** (*on foot*) **porque no *tengo* coche.** Have students repeat the sentence and change subjects.

tener (*to have*)		**venir** (*to come*)	
yo	**tengo**	yo	**vengo**
tú	**tienes**	tú	**vienes**
Ud. / él / ella	**tiene**	Ud. / él / ella	**viene**
nosotros(as)	**tenemos**	nosotros(as)	**venimos**
vosotros(as)	**tenéis**	vosotros(as)	**venís**
Uds. / ellos / ellas	**tienen**	Uds. / ellos / ellas	**vienen**

—¿**Tienes** la sartén? — *"**Do you have** the frying pan?"*
—Sí, **tengo** la sartén y la cacerola. — *"Yes, **I have** the frying pan and the sauce pan."*

—¿**Vienes** mañana por la mañana? — *"**Are you coming** tomorrow morning?"*
—No, **vengo** el jueves. — *"No, **I'm coming** on Thursday."*

—¿Cuántos platos **tienen** Uds.? — *"How many dishes **do you have?**"*
—**Tenemos** ocho platos. — *"**We have** eight dishes."*

—¿Uds. **vienen** a la universidad los martes y jueves? — *"**Do you come** to the university on Tuesdays and Thursdays?"*
—No, nosotros **venimos** los lunes, miércoles y viernes. — *"No, **we come** on Mondays, Wednesdays, and Fridays."*

—¿**Tienes que** limpiar la casa hoy? — *"**Do you have to** clean the house today?"*
—No, hoy no **tengo que** limpiar. — *"No, **I** don't **have to** clean today."*

¡Atención! **Tener que** means *to have to,* and it is followed by an infinitive: **Elsa *tiene que limpiar* la casa hoy.** (*Elsa **has to clean** the house today.*)

Práctica y conversación

For more practice with lesson topics, see the related activities on the *¡Hola, amigos!* web site at college.hmco.com/PIC/holaamigos7e.

A. Minidiálogos Supply the missing forms of **tener** and **venir** to complete the dialogues. Then act them out with a partner.

1. —¿Cuándo __vienen__ Uds.?
   —Pedro __viene__ el sábado y yo __vengo__ el domingo.
   —¿Con quién __vienes__ tú?
   —Yo __vengo__ con la Srta. Aranda.
2. —¿Tú __vienes__ a mi casa mañana?
   —No, yo __vengo__ el viernes.
3. —¿Uds. __tienen__ una licuadora?
   —Sí, y también una cafetera.
4. —¿Cuándo __vienes__ tú de Guadalajara?
   —__Vengo__ el jueves.
5. —¿Tú __tienes__ que lavar la ropa hoy?
   —No, yo no __tengo__ que lavar hoy.

B. ¿Quién puede ayudarme? (*Who can help me?*) You and your partner take turns playing the role of René, who keeps asking everyone for help. Use the elements given in your answers.

◆ **MODELO:** yo / la ensalada
—¿Tú puedes ayudarme?
—No, yo tengo que preparar la ensalada.

1. Elsa / los muebles
2. Ana y Eva / los platos
3. nosotros / la ropa
4. Marta / la aspiradora
5. Roberto / la basura
6. Sergio / el césped

Answers: 1. —¿Elsa puede ayudarme? —No, Elsa (ella) tiene que sacudir los muebles.
2. —¿Ana y Eva pueden ayudarme? —No, Ana y Eva (ellas) tienen que lavar los platos.
3. —¿Ustedes pueden ayudarme? —No, nosotros tenemos que lavar (planchar) la ropa.
4. —¿Marta puede ayudarme? —No, Marta (ella) tiene que pasar la aspiradora.
5. —¿Roberto puede ayudarme? —No, Roberto (él) tiene que sacar la basura.
6. —¿Sergio puede ayudarme? —No, Sergio (él) tiene que cortar el césped.

C. ¿Hay mucho trabajo? With a partner, ask each other five questions about what you have to do at different times and on different days. Follow the model. *Answers will vary.*

◆ **MODELO:** *—¿Qué tienes que hacer el sábado?*
—Tengo que barrer el garaje.

4. Expressions with *tener* (*Expresiones con* tener)

The following idiomatic expressions are formed with **tener.**

tener (mucho) frío	*to be (very) cold*
tener (mucha) sed	*to be (very) thirsty*
tener (mucha) hambre	*to be (very) hungry*
tener (mucho) calor	*to be (very) hot*
tener (mucho) sueño	*to be (very) sleepy*
tener prisa	*to be in a hurry*

Suggestion: Emphasize that idioms should not be translated literally, but learned as units of meaning. Point out that for these idioms **tener** + *noun* is used in Spanish while *to be* + *adjective* is used in English. It doesn't follow, however, that every English construction of this type has a Spanish counterpart with **tener.** Thus, *I am tired* is **Estoy cansado.**

Expansion: Use Transparency to introduce these idiomatic expressions. Ask students as a class and individually to describe each sketch by supplying the correct expression. You may also refer to the Instructor's Resource Manual (IRM) that accompanies the transparencies for additional activities and exercises related to **tener** expressions.

tener cuidado (*to be careful*); **tener suerte** (*to be lucky*); **tener éxito** (*to be successful*); **tener ganas de** (*to feel like*).

tener miedo	*to be afraid, scared*
tener razón	*to be right*
no tener razón	*to be wrong*
tener... años (de edad)	*to be . . . years old*

—¿Tienes hambre? — ***"Are you hungry?"***
—No, pero **tengo** mucha **sed.** — *"No, but **I am** very **thirsty.**"*

—¿Cuántos **años tiene** Eva? — *"How **old is** Eva?"*
—**Tiene** veinte **años.** — *"**She is** twenty **years old.**"*

Online Study Center

For more practice with lesson topics, see the related activities on the ***¡Hola, amigos!*** web site at college.hmco.com/PIC/holaamigos7e.

Práctica y conversación

A. ¿Qué tienen? Describe the following people according to the illustrations below, using an expression with **tener.**

Expansion: Introduce **tener... años de edad** by showing photos of famous people or by listing their names and professions on the board. Have students identify them and give their approximate ages. You may want to introduce **aproximadamente** at this time.

Shakira—Es una cantante colombiana. Tiene aproximadamente treinta años.

Brad Pitt—Es un actor norteamericano. Tiene unos cuarenta y tres años.

1. Elena ___________

2. Yo ___________

3. Nosotros___________

Answers: 1. Elena tiene sueño. 2. Yo tengo hambre. 3. Nosotros tenemos miedo. 4. Él tiene calor. 5. Ellos tienen prisa. 6. Tú tienes frío.

4. Él ___________

5. Ellos ___________

6. Tú ___________

B. ¿Cómo se sienten? How do these people feel? Answer, using expressions with **tener,** according to the information given.

Answers: 1. Tienen calor y sed. 2. Tiene hambre. 3. Tiene miedo. 4. Tienen prisa. 5. Tiene frío.

1. Carlos and Daniel are in the middle of the Sahara desert.
2. Luis hasn't had a bite to eat for fifteen hours.
3. Marta sees a snake near her feet.
4. Darío and Eva have to get to the airport in a few minutes.
5. Rosa is in South Dakota in February.

C. ¿Por qué...? With a partner, take turns indicating why you are or are not doing the following, using an expression with **tener.**

Answers: **1.** Porque tengo frío. (Porque no tengo calor.) **2.** Porque tengo prisa. **3.** Porque no tengo hambre. **4.** Porque no tengo sed. **5.** Porque tengo calor (frío).

1. ¿Por qué no abres las ventanas?
2. ¿Por qué corres?
3. ¿Por qué no comes ensalada?
4. ¿Por qué no tomas un vaso de limonada?
5. ¿Por qué cierras la puerta?

D. Entreviste a su compañero(a) Interview a partner, using the following questions. *Answers will vary.*

1. ¿Cuántos años tienes? ¿Cuántos años tiene tu mamá?
2. ¿Qué comes cuando tienes hambre?
3. ¿Qué bebes cuando tienes frío? ¿Y cuando tienes calor?
4. ¿Tienes sueño en este momento?
5. ¿Tú tienes miedo a veces (*sometimes*)?
6. En tu familia, ¿quién tiene razón siempre? ¿Y en la clase?

5. Demonstrative adjectives and pronouns (*Adjetivos y pronombres demostrativos*)

Demonstrative adjectives

Suggestion: Using classroom objects, ask choice questions to help make students aware of gender, number, and relative positions: **¿Quieres esta silla o aquélla? ¿Necesitas estos libros o ésos?** etc.

- Demonstrative adjectives point out persons and things. Like all other adjectives, they agree in gender and number with the nouns they modify. The forms of the demonstrative adjectives are as follows.

Masculine		Feminine		English Equivalent	
Sing.	*Pl.*	*Sing.*	*Pl.*	*Sing.*	*Pl.*
este	**estos**	**esta**	**estas**	this	these
ese	**esos**	**esa**	**esas**	that	those
aquel	**aquellos**	**aquella**	**aquellas**	that (*over there*)	those (*at a distance*)

—¿Qué necesitas? — *"What do you need?"*
—**Estos** vasos y **aquellas** tazas. — *"**These** glasses and **those** cups (over there)."*

Demonstrative pronouns

- The forms of the demonstrative pronouns are as follows.

Masculine		Feminine		Neuter		English equivalent	
Sing.	*Pl.*	*Sing.*	*Pl.*	*Sing.*	*Pl.*	*Sing.*	*Pl.*
éste	**éstos**	**ésta**	**éstas**	**esto**	**estos**	this (one)	these
ése	**ésos**	**ésa**	**ésas**	**eso**	**esos**	that (one)	those
aquél	**aquéllos**	**aquélla**	**aquéllas**	**aquello**	**aquellos**	that (over there)	those (at a distance)

- The masculine and feminine demonstrative pronouns are the same as the demonstrative adjectives, except that they have a written accent.
- Each demonstrative pronoun has a neuter form. The neuter forms have no gender and refer to unspecified situations, ideas, or things: *this, this matter; that, that business.*
- Note that the demonstrative pronouns replace a noun.

—¿Qué libro quiere Ud., **éste** o **ése**?	*"Which book do you want,* ***this one*** *or* ***that one****?"*
— Quiero **aquél.**	*"I want* ***that one over there.****"*
— ¿Qué es **eso**?	*"What is* ***that****?"*
— Es una plancha.	*"It's an iron."*

Online Study Center

For more practice with lesson topics, see the related activities on the ***¡Hola, amigos!*** web site at college.hmco.com/PIC/holaamigos7e.

Answers: 1. **a.** estas tostadoras **b.** este reloj **c.** esta chica (muchacha) **d.** estos vasos

Práctica y conversación

A. Este, ese y aquel Describe in Spanish the following illustrations, using the suggested demonstrative adjectives.

1. this, these:

a. ______________________

b. ______________________

c. ______________________

d. ______________________

2. that, those:

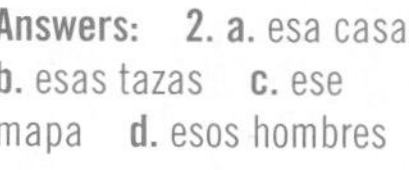
Answers: **2. a.** esa casa **b.** esas tazas **c.** ese mapa **d.** esos hombres

a. ______________________

b. ______________________

c. ______________________

d. ______________________

3. that (over there); those (over there):

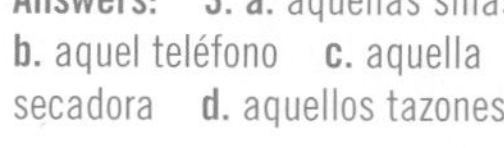
Answers: **3. a.** aquellas sillas **b.** aquel teléfono **c.** aquella secadora **d.** aquellos tazones

a. ______________________

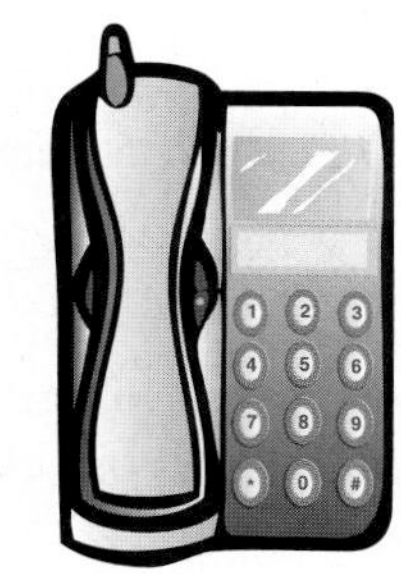

b. ______________________

c. ______________________

d. ______________________

Answers: a. Necesito esta mochila, este mapa y este cesto de papeles. b. Necesito esos libros, ese tazón y esas botellas.

B. Ud. está aquí Say what you need according to the objects in the illustration, using the corresponding demonstrative adjectives.

C. Minidiálogos Complete the following exchanges with the Spanish equivalent of the demonstrative pronouns in parentheses. Then act them out with a partner.

1. —¿Necesitas estos platos?
   —No, necesito ésos. (*those*)
2. —¿Cuál de las mesas necesitan Uds.?
   —Ésta. (*This one*)
3. —¿Cuáles son tus tazas? ¿Éstas o aquéllas? (*These / those over there*)
   —Ésas. (*Those*)
4. —¿Cuál es tu casa? ¿Ésta o ésa? (*This one / that one*)
   —Aquélla. (*That one over there*)

D. Nuestros compañeros You and your partner take turns asking each other who the people in your class are. According to the relative distance. Use the appropriate demonstrative adjectives. *Answers will vary.*

◆ **MODELO:** —*¿Quién es John?*
—***Ese** muchacho.*

6. Numbers from 300 to 1,000 (*Números de 300 a 1.000*)

Expansion: If time permits, play Bingo in Spanish to review the numbers learned so far.

You may wish to teach **un millón**, and point out that it requires the preposition **de** when used with nouns: **un millón de dólares.**

Suggestion: To review and practice numbers, write on the board: 5 (students say **cinco**): add 1 in front of the 5 (students say **quince**); add 3 in front of 15 (students say **trescientos quince**); and so on.

300	trescientos	600	seiscientos	900	novecientos
400	cuatrocientos	700	setecientos	1.000	mil
500	quinientos	800	ochocientos		

- In Spanish, one does not count in hundreds beyond one thousand; thus 1,100 is expressed as **mil cien.** Note that Spanish uses a comma where English uses a decimal point to indicate values below one: 1.095,99 (Spanish) = 1,095.99 (English).
- When a number from 200 to 900 is used before a feminine noun, it takes a feminine ending: **doscient*as* mes*as*.**[1]

[1]This is also true for higher numbers that incorporate the numbers 200–900: **mil doscientas treinta sillas, dos mil ochocientos libros.**

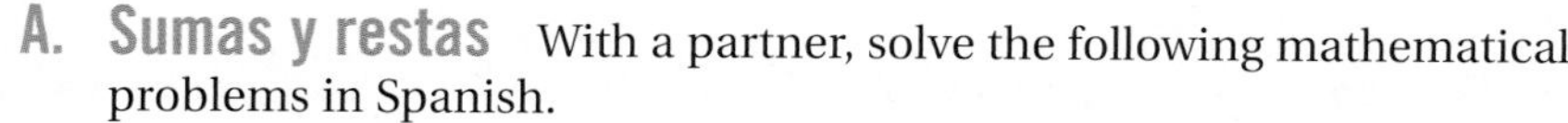

Práctica y comunicación

Online Study Center

For more practice with lesson topics, see the related activities on the *¡Hola, amigos!* web site at college.hmco.com/PIC/holaamigos7e.

A. Sumas y restas

With a partner, solve the following mathematical problems in Spanish.

1. 308 + 70 = trescientos setenta y ocho
2. 500 − 112 = trescientos ochenta y ocho
3. 653 + 347 = mil
4. 892 − 163 = setecientos veintinueve
5. 216 + 284 = quinientos
6. 1.000 − 450 = quinientos cincuenta
7. 700 + 280 = novecientos ochenta
8. 125 + 275 = cuatrocientos
9. 900 − 520 = trescientos ochenta
10. 230 + 725 = novecientos cincuenta y cinco

B. ¿Cuánto cuesta?

With a partner, take turns asking each other how much everything costs.

◆ MODELO: —¿Cuánto cuesta el refrigerador? (13.650)
—*Cuesta trece mil seiscientos cincuenta pesos.*[1]

1. ¿Cuánto cuesta la pluma?
2. ¿Cuánto cuesta el vino?
3. ¿Cuánto cuesta la silla?
4. ¿Cuánto cuesta la computadora?
5. ¿Cuánto cuesta el reloj?
6. ¿Cuánto cuesta la mesa?
7. ¿Cuánto cuesta el escritorio?
8. ¿Cuánto cuesta el libro?

Expansion: Extend this activity and review all the numbers by asking the price of various objects in the classroom: **¿Cuánto cuesta su libro de español (el diccionario,** etc)?

Using an overhead projector, show ads for houses, cars, and so on. Have students read and discuss the prices.

Answers: **1.** Cuesta doscientos nueve pesos. **2.** Cuesta cuatrocientos ocho pesos. **3.** Cuesta tres mil quinientos pesos. **4.** Cuesta dieciocho mil trescientos pesos. **5.** Cuesta setecientos setenta y cinco pesos. **6.** Cuesta cuatro mil ochocientos treinta pesos. **7.** Cuesta cinco mil novecientos noventa y siete pesos. **8.** Cuesta seiscientos veinte pesos.

[1]Mexican currency: 1 dollar = 10 pesos (more or less). Rate of exchange subject to change.

Entre nosotros

¡Conversemos!

Para conocernos mejor Get to know your partner better by asking each other the following questions. *Answers will vary.*

1. ¿En qué ciudad vives tú? ¿Y tus padres?
2. ¿Cuántos años tienes? ¿Y tu mejor (*best*) amigo(a)?
3. ¿Qué días limpias tu casa?
4. ¿Quién prepara la comida en tu casa?
5. ¿Te gusta cortar el césped? ¿Te gusta pasar la aspiradora?
6. ¿Tú trabajas todos los días?
7. ¿Quién lava y plancha tu ropa?
8. ¿Qué aparatos electrodomésticos tienes en tu cocina?
9. ¿Qué bebes cuando tienes sed? ¿Agua o limonada?
10. ¿Qué tienes que hacer mañana?
11. ¿Tu casa es un desastre a veces (*sometimes*)?
12. ¿Qué trabajo de la casa no te gusta hacer?

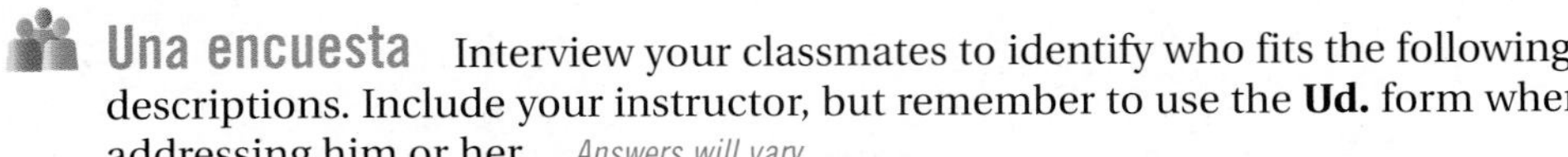

Una encuesta Interview your classmates to identify who fits the following descriptions. Include your instructor, but remember to use the **Ud.** form when addressing him or her. *Answers will vary.*

Suggestion: If needed, practice questions or model a few items. Encourage students to talk to as many students as possible.

	Nombre
1. Plancha su ropa los fines de semana.	
2. Corta el césped los domingos.	
3. Vive con sus padres.	
4. Limpia su casa los sábados.	
5. Llega a clase tarde (late).	
6. Tiene veinte años.	
7. Siempre tiene razón.	
8. Necesita descansar.	
9. Siempre tiene prisa.	
10. Es muy mandón (mandona).	

Y ahora... Write a brief summary, indicating what you have learned about your classmates. *Answers will vary.*

¿Cómo lo decimos?

What would you say in the following situations? What might the other person say? Act out the scenes with a partner.

1. You and a friend have invited guests for dinner and must decide what each of you has to do to prepare for them.
2. You tell your roommate that there is a knock at the door.
3. You ask a little boy how old he is.
4. You complain that there are a thousand things to do.

Suggestion: Assign as homework and select different pairs of students to roleplay each situation for the class.

Answers: 1. *Answers will vary.* 2. Tocan a la puerta. 3. ¿Cuántos años tienes? 4. Hay mil cosas que hacer.

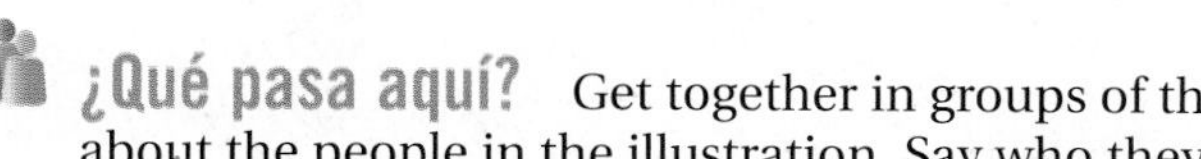

¿Qué pasa aquí?

Get together in groups of three or four and create a story about the people in the illustration. Say who they are, what their relationship is to one another, what they are doing, and what they might be getting ready for.
Answer will vary.

Para escribir

Para dividir el trabajo

You are in charge of organizing all the chores that must be done on a certain day. Indicate what you and everyone else has to do. Some of the chores must be done in pairs. To start out, brainstorm about all kinds of household chores and make a list. Then decide who is going to do what. *Answer will vary.*

Expansion: Assign as homework. For additional writing practice, have students write up dialogues and stories generated in the pair activities provided with each lesson.

Un dicho

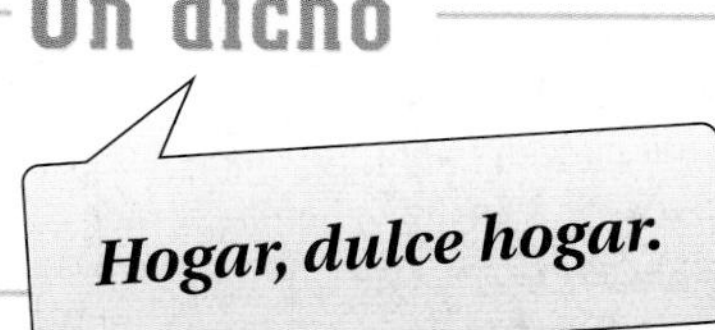

This is a saying about home life.
Can you guess the meaning?
Do you think it applies . . . ?

Lección 4 ◆ Una fiesta de cumpleaños

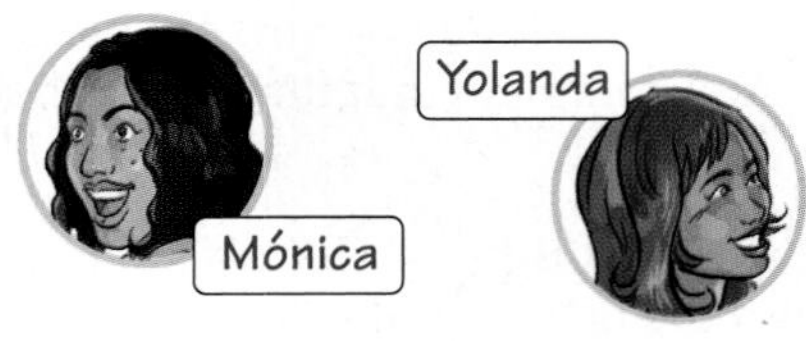

Silvia y Esteban deciden dar una fiesta para celebrar el cumpleaños de Mónica, una chica guatemalteca que ahora vive en San Salvador con la familia de Silvia.

Esteban Tenemos que mandar las invitaciones. ¿A quiénes vamos a invitar?

Silvia A todos nuestros amigos, a mis primos, al novio de Mónica y a Yolanda.

Esteban Yo no conozco a Yolanda. ¿Quién es?

Silvia Es la hermana del novio de Mónica.

Esteban ¿Ah, sí? ¿Es bonita? ¿Es rubia, morena o pelirroja? No es casada, ¿verdad?

Silvia Es morena, de ojos castaños, delgada, de estatura mediana… encantadora… y es soltera.

Esteban Bueno, si baila bien, ya estoy enamorado.

Silvia Oye, tenemos que planear la fiesta. Va a ser en el club, ¿no?

Esteban No, va a ser en la casa de mis abuelos. Ellos están en Costa Rica con mi madrina y yo tengo la llave de la casa.

Silvia ¡Perfecto! yo traigo los entremeses y la torta de cumpleaños.

Esteban Yo traigo las bebidas y los discos compactos. Yo sé que mis abuelos no tienen música para bailar.

Detalles culturales

Los jóvenes hispanos frecuentemente organizan fiestas en sus casas y casi siempre bailan.

◆ **En una fiesta, ¿los jóvenes de este país prefieren bailar o conversar?**

Detalles culturales

En los países hispanos, muchas personas pertenecen (*belong*) a un club. Allí pueden nadar, practicar deportes, asistir a fiestas o reunirse con sus amigos.

◆ **¿Qué clase de clubes hay en los Estados Unidos?**

En la fiesta

Cuando Mónica, su novio y Yolanda llegan a la casa, todos gritan: ¡Feliz cumpleaños!

Mónica (*Contenta*) ¡Qué sorpresa!
Silvia ¿Qué deseas tomar? ¿Champán, cerveza...? ¿O deseas comer algo?
Mónica Una copa de champán para brindar con todos mis amigos.
Silvia (*Levanta su copa*) ¡Un brindis! ¡Por Mónica! ¡Salud!
Todos ¡Salud!
Esteban (*A Yolanda*) Hola, soy Esteban Campos. Tú eres Yolanda, ¿verdad?
Yolanda Sí, mucho gusto.
Esteban ¿Bailamos? ¿Te gusta bailar salsa?
Yolanda Sí, me gusta, aunque no sé bailar muy bien.

Esteban y Yolanda bailan y conversan. Todos los invitados lo pasan muy bien.

Silvia (*A Mónica*) Veo que Yolanda y Esteban están muy animados.
Mónica Sí, hacen una buena pareja. Oye, Silvia, la fiesta es todo un éxito. ¡Muchas gracias!

Después de la fiesta, Esteban lleva a Silvia y a Mónica a su casa. Las chicas están cansadas, pero contentas.

Detalles culturales

La palabra **salsa** (*sauce* o *spice*) se usa para referirse a la música caribeña, basada en la música afrocubana.

◆ **¿Cuáles son los ritmos típicos de este país?**

¿Recuerda usted?

¿Verdadero o falso? With a partner, decide whether the following statements about the dialogue are true (**verdadero**) or false (**falso**).

1. Mónica es de Guatemala. ☒ V ☐ F
2. Mónica no tiene novio. ☐ V ☒ F
3. Esteban no sabe quién es Yolanda. ☒ V ☐ F
4. Yolanda es rubia, de ojos azules. ☐ V ☒ F
5. La fiesta es en el club. ☐ V ☒ F
6. Esteban hace la torta de cumpleaños. ☐ V ☒ F
7. Mónica desea brindar con champán. ☒ V ☐ F
8. Yolanda y Esteban bailan salsa. ☒ V ☐ F
9. Esteban y Yolanda están muy aburridos. ☐ V ☒ F
10. Todos lo pasan muy bien en la fiesta. ☒ V ☐ F

Y ahora... conteste Answer these questions, basing your answers on the dialogue.

1. ¿Qué deciden Silvia y Esteban?
2. ¿Quién es la hermana del novio de Mónica?
3. ¿Dónde están los abuelos de Esteban?
4. ¿Quién trae las bebidas?
5. ¿Yolanda sabe bailar bien?
6. ¿Con quién baila y conversa Yolanda?
7. ¿Quiénes hacen una buena pareja?
8. ¿Quién lleva a las chicas a su casa?

Answers: 1. Deciden dar una fiesta para celebrar el cumpleaños de Mónica. 2. La hermana del novio de Mónica es Yolanda. 3. Están en Costa Rica. 4. Esteban trae las bebidas. 5. No, no sabe bailar bien. 6. Yolanda baila y conversa con Esteban. 7. Yolanda y Esteban hacen una buena pareja. 8. Esteban lleva a las chicas a su casa.

Para hablar del tema: Vocabulario

Online Study Center

For more practice with lesson topics, see the related activities on the ***¡Hola, amigos!*** web site at college.hmco.com/PIC/holaamigos7e.

Cognados

el champán
el club
guatemalteco(a)
la invitación
la música
la sorpresa

Nombres

la bebida beverage
el brindis toast (i.e. *at a celebration*)
el cumpleaños birthday
el disco compacto CD
los entremeses appetizers, finger food
el éxito success
la fiesta party
el (la) invitado(a) guest
la madrina godmother
la novia girlfriend
el novio boyfriend
los ojos eyes
el padrino godfather
la pareja couple
el (la) primo(a) cousin
la torta* cake

De país a país

la torta la tarta (*Esp.*)
el pastel (*Méx.*)
moreno(a) trigueño(a) (*Cuba, Par.*)

Verbos

bailar to dance
brindar to toast
celebrar to celebrate
conocer to know, to be acquainted
dar to give
decidir to decide
estar to be
gritar to shout
invitar to invite
levantar to raise
llevar to take (*someone or something someplace*)
mandar, enviar to send
planear to plan
saber to know
traer to bring
ver to see

Adjetivos

animado(a) enthused
cansado(a) tired
casado(a) married
castaño brown (*eyes, hair*)
contento(a) happy, content
enamorado(a) in love
encantador(a) charming
feliz happy
moreno(a)* dark, brunet(te)
pelirrojo(a) red-haired
rubio(a) blond(e)
soltero(a) single

Otras palabras y expresiones

¿a quién(es)? whom
ahora now
aunque although
¿Bailamos? Shall we dance?
comer algo to have something to eat
de estatura mediana of medium height
de ojos castaños with brown eyes
pasarlo bien to have a good time
¡Salud! Cheers!
¡Qué sorpresa! What a surprise!
todo un éxito quite a success
ya already

Amplíe su vocabulario (*Expand your vocabulary*)

La familia

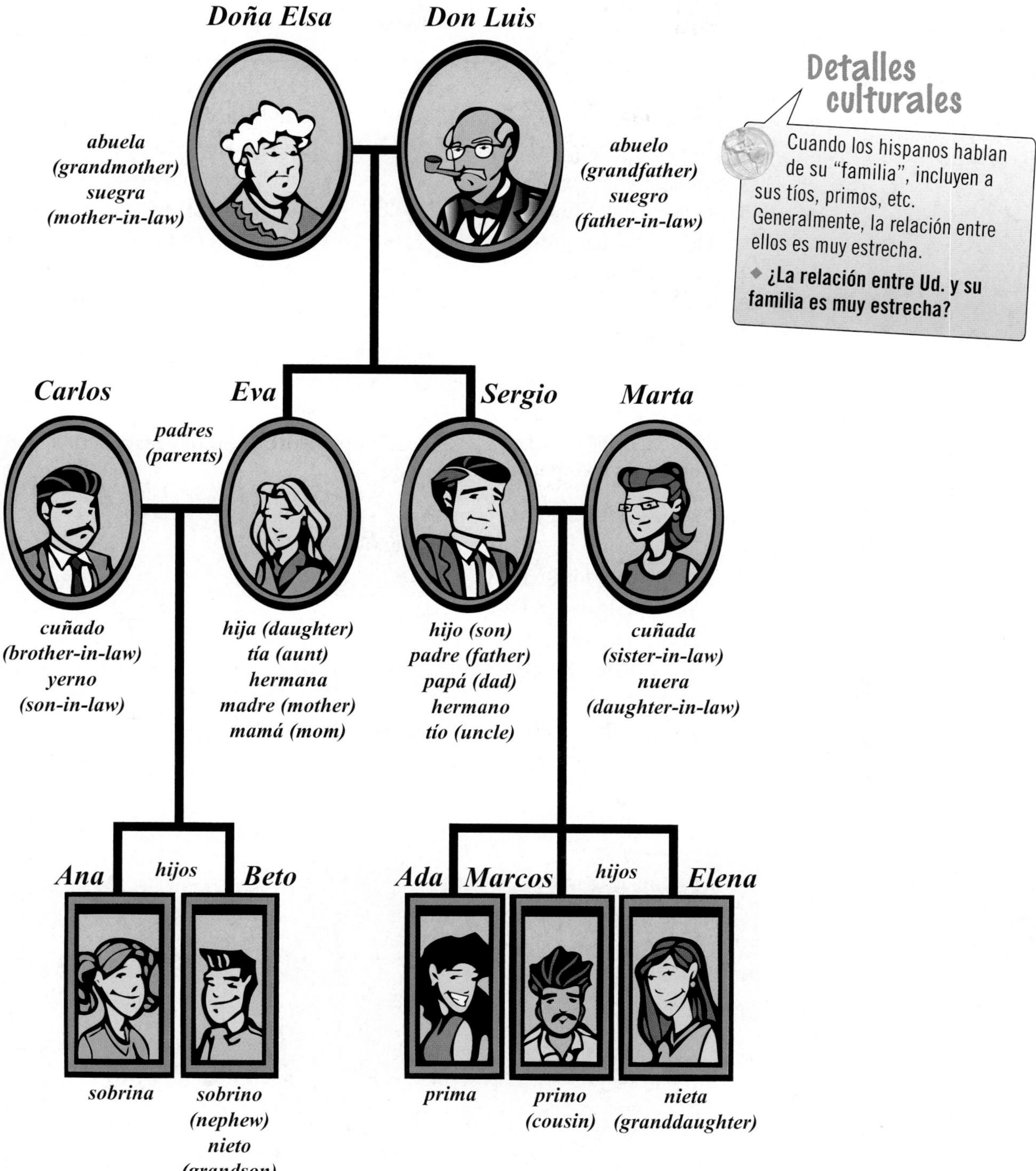

Detalles culturales

Cuando los hispanos hablan de su "familia", incluyen a sus tíos, primos, etc. Generalmente, la relación entre ellos es muy estrecha.

◆ **¿La relación entre Ud. y su familia es muy estrecha?**

Para practicar el vocabulario

A. Preguntas y respuestas With a partner, match the questions in column *A* with the answers in column *B*.

A		B
1. ¿Bailamos?	h	a. Champán.
2. ¿Es casada?	d	b. En la casa de mis abuelos.
3. ¿Es rubia o morena?	j	c. Las invitaciones.
4. ¿Qué bebida tienen?	a	d. No, es soltera.
5. ¿Qué celebran hoy?	i	e. No, es mi primo.
6. ¿Qué vas a mandar?	c	f. No, es guatemalteco.
7. ¿Luis es tu novio?	e	g. No, de estatura mediana.
8. ¿Dónde es la fiesta?	b	h. Ahora no; estoy cansada.
9. ¿Es alta?	g	i. Mi cumpleaños.
10. ¿Es de El Salvador?	f	j. Es pelirroja.

B. Planes para la fiesta Complete the following exchanges and then act them out with a partner.

1. —¿Qué vas a traer para comer?
   Entremeses y la __torta__ de cumpleaños.
2. —¿Los invitados lo __pasan__ bien?
   —Sí, la fiesta es todo un __éxito__.
3. —¿Vamos a brindar?
   —Sí. (__Levanta__ *su copa.*) ¡Un __brindis__!
   ¡Salud!
4. —¿Uds. __dan__ una fiesta el sábado?
   —Sí, y vamos a __invitar__ a todos nuestros amigos.

Una pareja de enamorados hace planes para una fiesta. ¿Qué creen Uds. que van a celebrar?

C. El parentesco (*Relationship with relatives*)

With a partner, take turns saying what the relationship of one person to another is in the family tree. Mention eight to ten relationships. *Answers will vary.*

◆ **MODELO:** —*Doña Elsa es la mamá de Eva.*

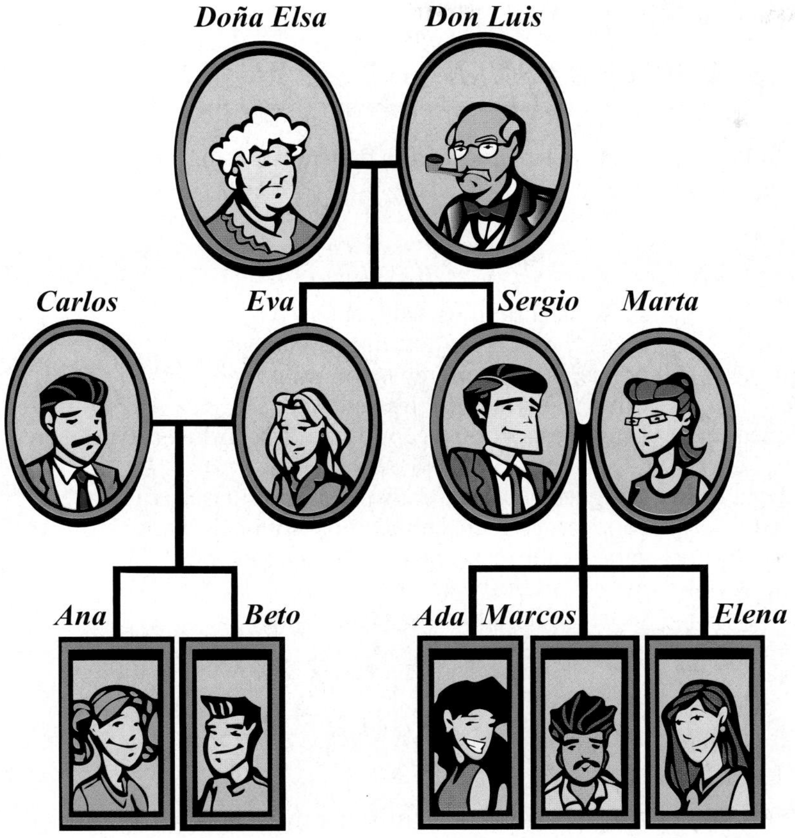

D. De mi álbum de fotos

Bring photos of family members and share information about them in small groups. Be prepared to present your family photos to the class. *Answers will vary.*

Pronunciación

La consonante *c*

In Spanish, **c** has two different sounds: [*s*] and [*k*]. The [*s*] sound occurs in **ce** and **ci**, the [*k*] sound in **ca, co, cu, cl,** and **cr.** Read the following words aloud.

[*s*]		[*k*]	
cerveza	**cie**n**ci**as	**Ca**rmen	**cu**ándo
gra**ci**as	ne**ce**sito	**ca**nsado	**cl**ub
invita**ci**ón	**ce**lebrar	**có**mo	**cr**eo

Puntos para recordar

1. Verbs with irregular first-person forms (*Verbos irregulares en la primera persona*)

- The following verbs are irregular in the first-person singular of the present tense.

Verb	yo form	Regular forms
salir (*to go out*)	**salgo**	sales, sale, salimos, salís, salen
hacer (*to do, make*)	**hago**	haces, hace, hacemos, hacéis, hacen
poner (*to put, place*)	**pongo**	pones, pone, ponemos, ponéis, ponen
traer (*to bring*)	**traigo**	traes, trae, traemos, traéis, traen
conducir (*to drive, to conduct*)	**conduzco**	conduces, conduce, conducimos, conducís, conducen
traducir (*to translate*)	**traduzco**	traduces, traduce, traducimos, traducís, traducen
conocer (*to know*)	**conozco**	conoces, conoce, conocemos, conocéis, conocen
caber (*to fit*)	**quepo**	cabes, cabe, cabemos, cabéis, caben
ver (*to see*)	**veo**	ves, ve, vemos, veis, ven
saber (*to know*)	**sé**	sabes, sabe, sabemos, sabéis, saben

Online Study Center

For more practice with lesson topics, see the related activities on the ***¡Hola, amigos!*** web site at college.hmco.com/PIC/holaamigos7e.

Práctica y conversación

A. Olga y yo... With a partner, take turns comparing what Olga does to what you do.

- **MODELO:** Olga traduce del inglés al español.
  Yo traduzco del español al inglés.

Olga:

1. ...sale de su casa a las ocho de la mañana.
2. ...pone su dinero en el Banco de América.
3. ...conoce Guatemala.
4. ...sabe bailar salsa.
5. ...trae a su amiga a la universidad.
6. ...conduce un Ford.
7. ...ve a sus abuelos los domingos.
8. ...hace ejercicio (*exercises*) por la mañana.

Answers: **1.** Yo salgo de mi casa a las... **2.** Yo pongo mi dinero en el banco... **3.** Yo (no) conozco Guatemala. **4.** Yo (no) sé bailar salsa... **5.** Yo (no) traigo a mi amiga. **6.** Yo conduzco un... **7.** Yo (no) veo a mis abuelos los domingos. **8.** Yo (no) hago ejercicio por la mañana.

B. ¿Y los otros...? Now get together with another pair and compare your answers to theirs. *Answers will vary.*

2. *Saber* vs. *conocer*

The verb *to know* has two Spanish equivalents, **saber** and **conocer,** which are used to express distinct types of knowledge.

Expansion: Write the following questions on the board and have students interview each other.

¿Cuántos idiomas sabes hablar?
¿Conoces a los padres de ____?
¿Qué sabes hacer muy bien?
¿Sabes tocar el piano?
¿Conoces un buen restaurante por aquí?
¿Conoces a alguien famoso?

- **Saber** means *to know something by heart, to know how to do something* (a learned skill), or *to know a fact* (information).

—¿**Sabes** el poema "The Raven" de memoria?	*"**Do you know** the poem 'The Raven' by heart?"*
—¡No!	*"No!"*
—¿Ana **sabe** bailar salsa?	*"**Does** Ana **know how** to dance salsa?"*
—No muy bien...	*"Not very well . . ."*
—¿Ud. **sabe** el número de teléfono de David?	*"**Do you know** David's phone number?"*
—Sí, es 8–26–49–30.	*"Yes, it's 8–26–49–30."*

- **Conocer** means *to be familiar or acquainted with a person, a thing, or a place.*

—¿**Conoces** a Hugo?	*"**Do you know** Hugo?"*
—Sí, es el primo de Alberto.	*"Yes, he's Alberto's cousin."*
—¿**Conocen** Uds. todas las novelas de Cervantes?	*"**Are you acquainted with** all of Cervantes's novels?"*
—No, no todas.	*"No, not all of them."*
—¿**Conoces** San Salvador?	*"**Do you know** (Have you been to) San Salvador?"*
— Sí, es una ciudad muy bonita.	*"Yes, it is a very pretty city."*

Extra Practice: Write the following phrases on the board: **Conozco a... Sé que...** Have students describe each other by completing the phrases.

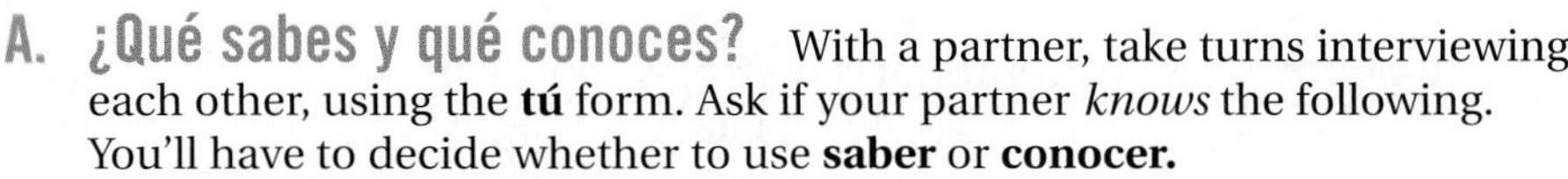

Práctica y conversación

Online Study Center

For more practice with lesson topics, see the related activities on the ***¡Hola, amigos!*** web site at college.hmco.com/PIC/holaamigos7e.

A. ¿Qué sabes y qué conoces? With a partner, take turns interviewing each other, using the **tú** form. Ask if your partner *knows* the following. You'll have to decide whether to use **saber** or **conocer.**

- **MODELO:** bailar rumba
  —¿Sabes bailar rumba?
  —Sí, yo sé bailar rumba. (No, no sé bailar rumba.)

1. el número de teléfono de la universidad
2. Guatemala
3. las novelas de Hemingway
4. hablar italiano
5. a los padres del profesor (de la profesora)
6. el poema "The Raven" de memoria
7. dónde vive el profesor (la profesora) de español
8. preparar entremeses

Questions: 1. ¿Sabes el número de teléfono de la universidad? 2. ¿Conoces Guatemala? 3. ¿Conoces las novelas de Hemingway? 4. ¿Sabes hablar italiano? 5. ¿Conoces a los padres del profesor (de la profesora)? 6. ¿Sabes el poema "The Raven" de memoria? 7. ¿Sabes dónde vive el profesor (la profesora) de español? 8. ¿Sabes preparar entremeses?

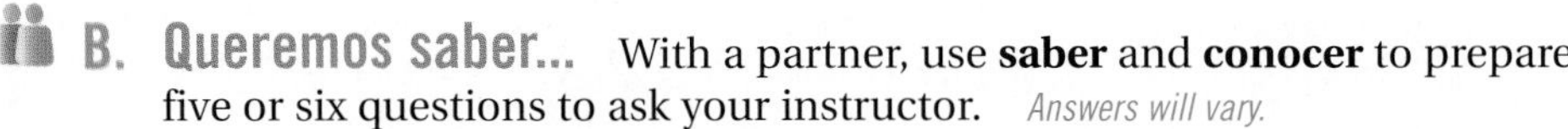

B. Queremos saber... With a partner, use **saber** and **conocer** to prepare five or six questions to ask your instructor. *Answers will vary.*

3. Personal *a* (*La a personal*)

Suggestion: For additional practice, discuss **llamar** (*to call*) at this point. Contrast: **Llamo a Rosa.** with **Llamo un taxi.**

- The preposition **a** is used in Spanish before a direct object (recipient of the action expressed by the verb) referring to a specific person or persons. When the preposition **a** is used in this way, it is called the *personal* **a** and has no English equivalent.

		(**Direct object**)
Yo conozco *I know*	**a**	Roberto. *Robert.*

—¿Tú conoces **a** Carmen y **a** Héctor? — *"Do you know Carmen and Héctor?"*
—Conozco **a** Carmen, pero no conozco **a** Héctor. — *"I know Carmen, but I don't know Héctor."*

¡Atención! When there is a series of direct object nouns, referring to people, the personal **a** is repeated: **¿Tú conoces *a* Carmen y *a* Héctor?**

- The personal **a** is *not* used when the direct object is a thing or place.

  Yo conozco Los Ángeles. *I know Los Angeles.*

- The personal **a** is seldom used following the verb **tener** even if the direct object is a person or persons.

  Tengo dos hermanas. *I have two sisters.*

- The personal **a** is also used when referring to pets.

  Yo llevo **a** mi perro a la veterinaria. *I take my dog to the vet.*

Online Study Center

For more practice with lesson topics, see the related activities on the ***¡Hola, amigos!*** web site at college.hmco.com/PIC/holaamigos7e.

Práctica y conversación

A. Minidiálogos Complete the following exchanges, using the personal **a** when appropriate. Leave the space blank if **a** is not needed.

1. —¿Tú conoces __a__ Silvia y __a__ Mónica?
   —Conozco __a__ Mónica, pero no conozco __a__ Silvia.
2. —¿__A__ quién llevas a la fiesta?
   —Llevo __a__ mi suegra y __a__ mi cuñada.
3. —¿Tienes __–__ hermanos?
   —Sí, tengo __–__ un hermano y __–__ dos hermanas.
4. —Qué tienes que hacer?
   —Tengo que llevar __a__ mi perro a caminar (*for a walk*).

B. Los sábados With a partner, take turns asking whom you call (**llamar**), visit (**visitar**), or see on Saturdays. *Answers will vary.*

◆ **MODELO:** —*¿A quién llamas todos los sábados?*
—*Yo llamo a mi abuela.*

4. Contractions: *al* and *del* (*Contracciones:* al *y* del)[1]

- The preposition **a** and the article **el** contract to form **al.**

Llevamos	**a**	+	**el**	profesor.
Llevamos		**al**		profesor.

- Similarly, the preposition **de** and the definite article **el** contract to form **del.**

Tiene los libros	**de**	+	**el**	profesor.
Tiene los libros		**del**		profesor.

¡Atención! **A** + **el** and **de** + **el** must *always* be contracted to **al** and **del.**

—¿Vienes **del** club? —No, vengo **de la** biblioteca.	*"Are you coming* ***from the*** *club?"* *"No, I'm coming* ***from the*** *library."*
—¿Vamos **al** cine? —Sí, vamos.	*"Shall we go* ***to the*** *movies?"* *"Yes, let's go."*

- None of the other combinations of preposition and definite article (**de la, de los, de las, a la, a los, a las**) is contracted.

El esposo **de la** profesora viene **a la** clase de español.

Extra Practice:
Write on the board:

Llamo a { el profesor / la señora / los estudiantes. / las profesoras.

Vengo de { la biblioteca. / el laboratorio. / las clases. / la cafetería.

Have students read the different combinations, using contractions when necessary. Make sure that students understand the distinction between the article **el** and the subject pronoun **él**.

[1]See Appendix C.

Online Study Center

For more practice with lesson topics, see the related activities on the *¡Hola, amigos!* web site at college.hmco.com/PIC/holaamigos7e.

Answers: **1.** Inés va al teatro. Lleva a la Sra. Vigo. **2.** El doctor Rojas va a la fiesta. Lleva al profesor Vega. **3.** Fernando va al club. Lleva a la Srta. Acosta. **4.** Paloma va al zoológico. Lleva a los niños. **5.** Ramiro va al parque. Lleva al perro. **6.** Sara va a la biblioteca. Lleva a los estudiantes.

Answers to Act. A follow up: **1.** Inés y la Sra. Vigo vienen del teatro. **2.** El doctor Rojas y el profesor Vega vienen de la fiesta. **3.** Fernando y la Srta. Acosta vienen del club. **4.** Paloma y los niños vienen del zoológico. **5.** Ramiro y el perro vienen del parque. **6.** Sara y los estudiantes vienen de la biblioteca.

Práctica y conversación

A. Ir y venir Using the list provided, you and your partner will take turns mentioning where everyone is going and whom everyone is taking.

◆ **MODELO:** Teresa / cine / Sr. López
*Teresa **va al** cine. Lleva **al** señor López.*

1. Inés / teatro / Sra. Vigo
2. El doctor Rojas / fiesta / profesor Vega
3. Fernando / club / Srta. Acosta
4. Paloma / zoológico / niños
5. Ramiro / parque / perro
6. Sara / biblioteca / estudiantes

Now you both use the same list to mention where everyone is coming from.

◆ **MODELO:** *Teresa y el Sr. López vienen **del** cine.*

B. Entreviste a su compañero(a) You and a partner take turns asking each other the following questions. *Answers will vary.*

1. ¿Tú conoces a los amigos del profesor (de la profesora)?
2. ¿Tú vienes a la universidad antes de (*before*) las ocho de la mañana?
3. ¿Tú llamas al profesor (a la profesora) a veces (*sometimes*)?
4. ¿Tú tienes el libro del profesor (de la profesora)?
5. ¿Tú vienes a la universidad los domingos?
6. ¿Tú ves al profesor (a la profesora) los sábados?

5. Present indicative of *ir, dar,* and *estar*
(*Presente de indicativo de* ir, dar *y* estar)

Expansion: Point out the similarities among these three verbs by writing the following sentence on the board: **Cuando yo estoy contento, voy a casa y doy una fiesta.** Have the students conjugate it in all persons.

Suggestion: Review the differences in usage between **ser** and **estar**, using the examples encountered thus far.

	ir (*to go*)	**dar** (*to give*)	**estar** (*to be*)
yo	**voy**	**doy**	**estoy**
tú	**vas**	**das**	**estás**
Ud. / él / ella	**va**	**da**	**está**
nosotros(as)	**vamos**	**damos**	**estamos**
vosotros(as)	**vais**	**dais**	**estáis**
Uds. / ellos / ellas	**van**	**dan**	**están**

—¿Dónde **está** Aurora? *"Where **is** Aurora?"*
—**Está** en el teatro. *"**She is** at the theater."*
—¿No **da** una fiesta hoy? *"**Isn't she giving** a party today?"*
—No, yo **doy** una fiesta. *"No, **I'm giving** a party."*

—¿Adónde **vas**? *"Where **are you going** (to)?"*
—**Voy** al cine. *"**I'm going** to the movies."*
—¿No **estás** cansada? *"**Aren't you** tired?"*
—No, no **estoy** cansada. *"**No, I am** not tired."*

¡Atención! The verb **estar** is used to indicate location and to describe condition at a given moment in time. **Estar** and **ser** are not interchangeable.

Location: Aurora está en el club.
Current condition: Estoy cansada.

Práctica y conversación

A. Fiestas y más fiestas Complete the following statements about Mónica's birthday party, using the appropriate forms of **dar, ir,** and **estar.**

1. Todos los amigos de Silvia ___van___ a la fiesta que ella y Esteban ___dan___ para Mónica. Esteban ___da___ dinero para la fiesta.
2. La abuela de Esteban no ___va___ a la fiesta; ella ___está___ en Costa Rica.
3. En la fiesta, Mónica ___está___ muy contenta y los invitados ___están___ muy animados.
4. Las bebidas y los entremeses ___están___ en la mesa (*table*).
5. Yo no ___voy___ a la fiesta porque no ___estoy___ invitado.
6. Yo no ___doy___ muchas fiestas en mi casa, pero mis amigos y yo ___damos___ fiestas en el club.

B. Entreviste a su compañero(a) You and your partner take turns interviewing each other, using the following questions. *Answers will vary.*

1. ¿Adónde vas los viernes?
2. ¿Vas al cine los sábados? ¿Con quién?
3. ¿Vas a la iglesia (*church*) los domingos?
4. ¿Tú y tus amigos van a muchas fiestas?
5. ¿Estás invitado(a) a una fiesta esta noche?
6. ¿Das muchas fiestas en tu casa?
7. ¿Estás cansado(a)?
8. ¿Dónde están tus padres ahora?

Now, you and your partner are interviewing Miss Muñoz. How would you ask her the same questions? Use the **Ud.** form.

Questions: 1. ¿Adónde va Ud. los viernes? 2. ¿Va al cine los sábados? ¿Con quién? 3. ¿Va a la iglesia los domingos? 4. ¿Ud. y sus amigos van a muchas fiestas? 5. ¿Está invitada a una fiesta esta noche? 6. ¿Da muchas fiestas en su casa? 7. ¿Está cansada? 8. ¿Dónde están sus padres ahora?

Online Study Center

For more practice with lesson topics, see the related activities on the ***¡Hola, amigos!*** web site at college.hmco.com/PIC/holaamigos7e.

Extra Practice: After introducing the verb **ir**, write the following list of places on the board.

cafetería
biblioteca
cine
club
clase de...
piscina
concierto
oficina de un(a) profesor(a)
residencia
fiesta
trabajo

Referring to the list, students work in groups of four and ask each other where they go after class, in the afternoon/evening, and at midnight.
S1—¿Adónde vas después de la clase (esta tarde/noche, a medianoche)?
S2—Voy a la cafetería.

Follow-up: Have students describe each other's activities to the rest of the class.

6. *Ir a* + infinitive (Ir a + *el infinitivo*)

Expansion: After explaining the use of **ir a** + *infinitive* and presenting the "formula" shown in the book, you may write on the board:

Yo **voy**
Tú **vas**
Usted **va**
Él **va**
Ella **va**
Nosotros **vamos**
Vosotros **vais**
Ustedes **van**
Ellos **van**
Ellas **van**
} a...

Have students personalize by making up sentences in response to your questions. For example, **¿Vas a estudiar español el semestre que viene? ¿Y tu mejor amigo(a)? ¿Qué va a estudiar? ¿Dónde van a trabajar?**

The **ir a** + *infinitive* construction is used in Spanish to express future time, in the same way English uses the expression *to be going to* + *infinitive.*

ir (*conjugated*)	+	**a**	+	*infinitive*
Voy		**a**		**estudiar.**
I am going				*to study.*

—¿Tú **vas a bailar** con Jorge? *"**Are you going to dance** with Jorge?"*
—No, **voy a bailar** con Carlos. *"No, **I'm going to dance** with Carlos."*

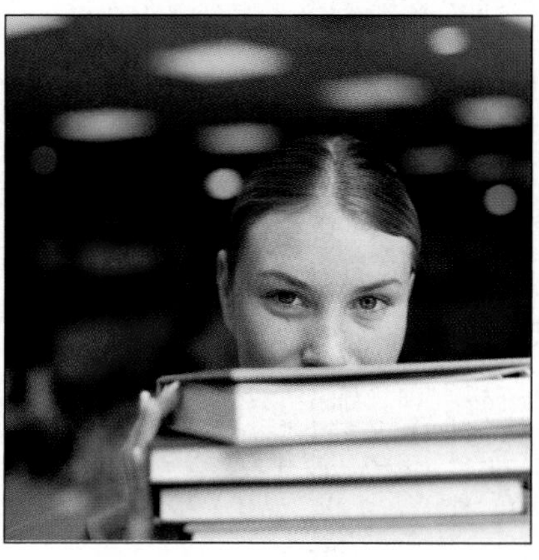

Elena va a estudiar ahora pero... ¿qué planea hacer después?

Práctica y conversación

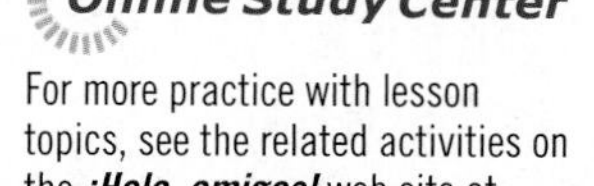

For more practice with lesson topics, see the related activities on the *¡Hola, amigos!* web site at college.hmco.com/PIC/holaamigos7e.

A. Entreviste a su compañero(a) You and your partner take turns interviewing each other, using the following questions. *Answers will vary.*

1. ¿Cuándo vas a estudiar? ¿Dónde?
2. ¿Cuántas horas vas a estudiar?
3. ¿Qué vas a hacer mañana?
4. ¿Dónde vas a comer mañana?
5. ¿Adónde van a ir tú y tus amigos el viernes?
6. ¿Vas a dar una fiesta el sábado?
7. ¿A quiénes vas a invitar a tu próxima (*next*) fiesta?
8. ¿Qué bebidas vas a servir (*serve*) en tu fiesta?

B. ¿Qué vamos a hacer? What will be the result of each of the following situations? Indicate what *is going to happen.*

◆ **MODELO:** Yo tengo hambre.
Voy a comer algo.

1. Ud. tiene un examen mañana.
2. Ud. y yo tenemos sed.
3. Mi tío tiene hambre.
4. Raquel y Luis van a ir a una fiesta.
5. Anita está cansada.
6. Marcelo quiere celebrar su cumpleaños.

Possible answers: **1.** Ud. va a estudiar. **2.** Vamos a beber algo. **3.** Va a comer algo. **4.** Van a bailar. **5.** Va a descansar. **6.** Va a dar una fiesta.

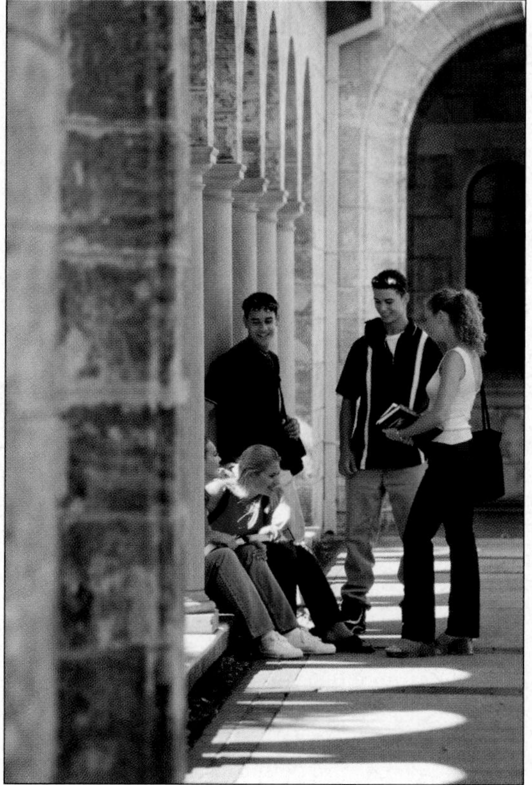

¿Qué va a hacer cada (*each*) uno de estos estudiantes el sábado por la noche?

Entre nosotros

¡Conversemos!

Para conocernos mejor Get to know your partner better by asking each other the following questions. *Answers will vary.*

1. ¿Cuándo planeas dar una fiesta?
2. ¿Tus discos compactos son de música para bailar o para escuchar (*to listen to*)?
3. ¿Sabes cantar (*to sing*) "Feliz cumpleaños" en español?
4. ¿Qué haces los sábados por la tarde? ¿Y por la noche?
5. ¿A qué hora sales de tu casa?
6. ¿Cuántas llaves (*keys*) de tu casa tienes?
7. ¿Tú conduces bien?
8. ¿Ves a tus abuelos frecuentemente?
9. ¿Estás enamorado(a)? ¿De quién?
10. ¿Tus ojos son azules, verdes o castaños?

Una encuesta Interview your classmates to identify who fits the following descriptions. Include your instructor, but remember to use the **Ud.** form when addressing him or her. *Answers will vary.*

	Nombre
1. Tiene un esposo muy guapo (una esposa muy bonita).	
2. Es la nieta favorita de su abuela.	
3. Visita a sus tíos frecuentemente.	
4. Da muchas fiestas en su casa.	
5. Va a muchas fiestas.	
6. Sabe bailar salsa.	
7. Conoce Canadá.	
8. Va a comer en la cafetería mañana.	
9. Está enamorado(a).	
10. Es soltero(a).	

Y ahora... Write a brief summary, indicating what you have learned about your classmates. *Answers will vary.*

¿Cómo lo decimos? What would you say in the following situations? What might the other person say? Act out the scenes with a partner.

1. You and a friend are planning a party. You ask him/her what beverages he/she is going to bring.
2. You ask a friend what he/she is going to do on Saturday and with whom.
3. You talk to a friend about some members of your family.

Answers: 1. ¿Qué bebidas vas a traer tú? 2. ¿Qué vas a hacer el sábado? ¿Con quién? 3. *Answers will vary.*

¿Qué pasa aquí? Get together in groups of three or four and create a conversation among the people in the picture. You might have them introduce one another and discuss their friends, their activities, the occasion, or the party itself. *Answers will vary.*

Para escribir

Un mensaje electrónico You are sending an e-mail to a friend, inviting him/her to a birthday party you are giving for someone.

Brainstorm about the place, the day, and the time, whom you are going to invite, what you are going to serve, and what you are going to do. Now make a list of all the details and then organize the e-mail. *Answers will vary.*

Un dicho

Come y bebe, porque la vida es breve.

This piece of advice reminds us of a similar one in English. Do you know what it is? Is it good advice? Memorize the Spanish saying!

Lectura

Reading strategy: Point out to students that looking at titles, subtitles, and visuals before they read will help orient them to the topic of a reading.

Estrategia de lectura Look at the **Sociales** reading below. Based on the headline and the photos, what do you think the reading is about? (**¿De qué trata la lectura?**) In which section of the newspaper can you find such articles?

Vamos a leer As you read the **Sociales** section of the newspaper, find the answers to the following questions.

Answers: **1.** En la Catedral. **2.** Se llama Juan Carlos Pérez Miranda. **3.** Ofrecieron un banquete. **4.** Va a ir a la hermosa ciudad de Antigua. **5.** La fiesta de compromiso de Ana María Reyes y Eduardo Alcalá. **6.** Estudia en la Universidad Nacional. **7.** Ana María estudia educación y Eduardo está terminando la carrera de arquitecto. **8.** Planean la boda para el mes de mayo. **9.** La Sra. Rosalía Mena de Castro va de vacaciones a California. **10.** Va a visitar Nueva York y Miami con sus padres. **11.** Celebraron su cumpleaños con una gran fiesta infantil en la residencia de sus padres. **12.** La cigüeña visitó el hogar del matrimonio Viera Colombo; el bebé se llama Miguel Ángel.

1. ¿En qué iglesia tuvo lugar (*took place*) la boda de Isabel?
2. ¿Cómo se llama el esposo de Isabel?
3. ¿Qué ofrecieron los padres de la novia?
4. ¿Adónde va a ir la feliz pareja de luna de miel (*honeymoon*)?
5. ¿Qué tuvo lugar en el Club Deportivo Santiago?
6. ¿En qué universidad estudia Ana María?
7. ¿Qué estudian Ana María y Eduardo?
8. ¿Para cuándo planean la boda?
9. ¿Quién va de vacaciones a California?
10. ¿Qué ciudades va a visitar? ¿Con quiénes?
11. ¿Con qué celebraron el cumpleaños de Olguita? ¿Dónde?
12. ¿Qué hogar visitó la cigüeña (*stork*) y cómo se llama el bebé?

Detalles culturales

La mayoría de los hispanos generalmente usan dos apellidos: el apellido del padre y después el apellido de soltera (*maiden name*) de la madre.

◆ **¿Se usan dos apellidos en este país?**

SOCIALES

En la Catedral tuvo lugar la boda de la gentil señorita Isabel Gómez Vera con el distinguido caballero Juan Carlos Pérez Miranda el pasado sábado, 18 de agosto. Terminada la ceremonia religiosa, los padres de la novia ofrecieron un banquete en el Club Unión de San Salvador. La feliz pareja va a ir de luna de miel a la hermosa ciudad de Antigua. ¡Muchas felicidades al nuevo matrimonio!

Video

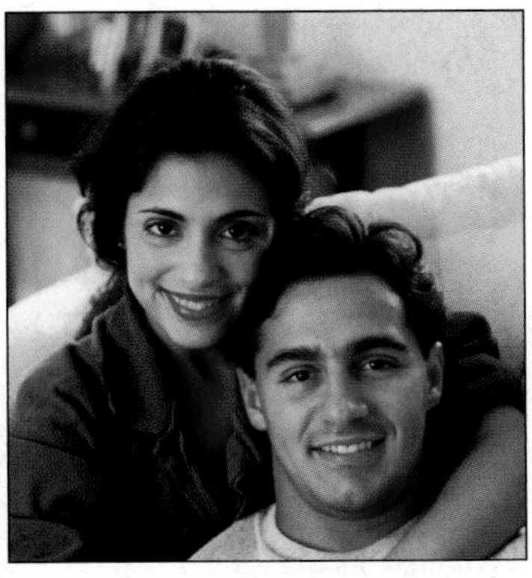

■ En el Club Deportivo Santiago tuvo lugar la fiesta de compromiso de la señorita Ana María Reyes y el señor Eduardo Alcalá. Ana María es estudiante de educación en la Universidad Nacional y su prometido está terminando la carrera de arquitecto. La pareja planea su boda para el mes de mayo. ¡Felicidades!

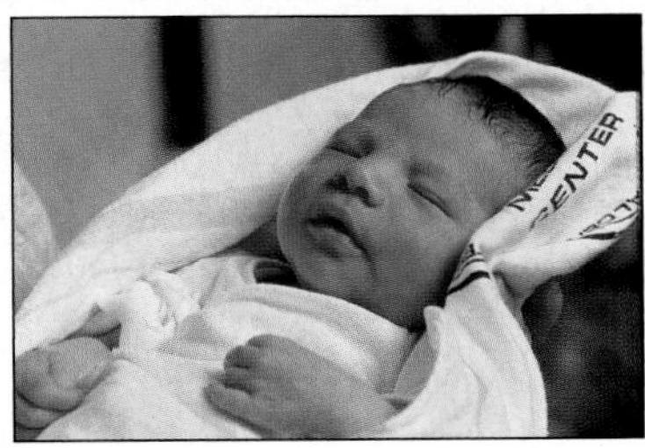

■ La cigüeña visitó el hogar del matrimonio Viera Colombo. El hermoso bebé llevará el nombre de Miguel Ángel. ¡Enhorabuena a los nuevos padres!

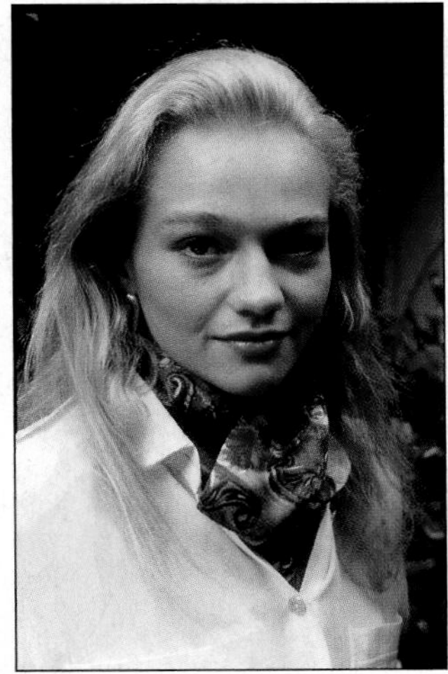

■ La semana próxima va de vacaciones a California la señora Rosalía Mena de Castro. Allí va a visitar a sus padres, que residen en San Diego. Acompañada de sus padres, visitará Nueva York y Miami. ¡Le deseamos buen viaje!

Expansion: The activity below can be done in pairs or in groups of 3. Follow up by polling the class to find out when birthdays are celebrated, where students want to travel, and so forth.

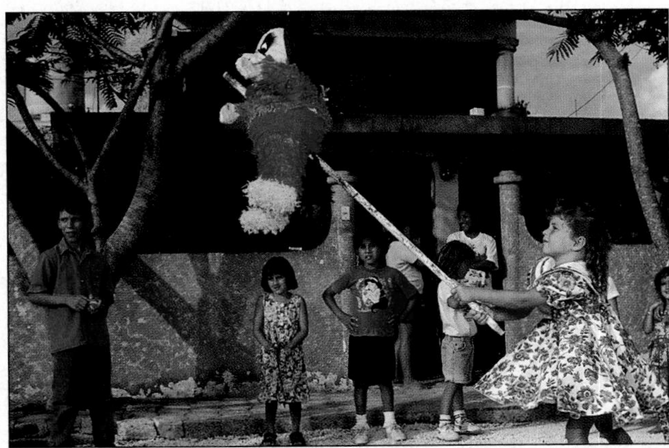

■ El viernes pasado se celebró, con una gran fiesta infantil, el cumpleaños de Olga Paz Soldán en la residencia de sus padres. ¡Feliz cumpleaños, Olguita!

Díganos Answer the following questions based on your own thoughts and experiences. *Answers will vary.*

1. ¿En qué mes celebra Ud. su cumpleaños?
2. ¿Van a ofrecer sus amigos un banquete para celebrar su cumpleaños?
3. ¿Es Ud. miembro de un club? ¿De cuál?
4. Para Ud., ¿cuál es el lugar (*place*) ideal para pasar la luna de miel?
5. ¿Adónde planea Ud. ir de vacaciones?
6. ¿Qué ciudades de este país desea visitar?
7. ¿Le gusta a Ud. viajar con sus padres, con sus amigos o solo(a) (*alone*)?
8. ¿Qué nombre le gusta para un bebé?

¡Qué sorpresa!

Los amigos de Marisa están en el apartamento de la muchacha, muy ocupados preparando una fiesta sorpresa para celebrar su cumpleaños. Cuando regresa más tarde y se esconden (*hide*), la sorpresa de Marisa es realmente grande…

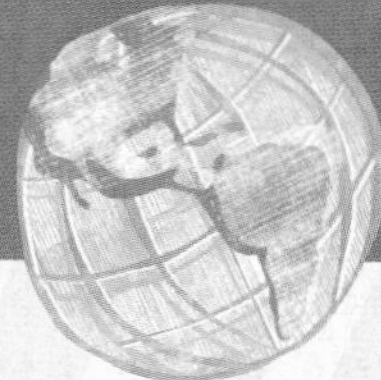

El mundo hispánico

México

- México, con más de cien millones de habitantes, ocupa por su población el primer lugar entre los países del mundo hispano, y tiene casi tres veces el área de Texas. Su capital, la Ciudad de México, D.F. (Distrito Federal), con unos 24 millones de habitantes, es el centro urbano más grande del mundo.
- La economía tradicional del país está basada en el petróleo y la agricultura, pero en las últimas décadas la industria, el turismo y el dinero que los emigrantes en los Estados Unidos envían a sus casas, son la principal fuente de ingreso (*source of income*).

▲ Vista del Ángel de la Independencia, en la ciudad de México.

- La importancia del turismo se debe a (*is due to*) la abundancia de bellezas naturales y de reliquias históricas y al servicio eficiente de sus centros turísticos. Playas famosas como Acapulco, Cancún y Puerto Vallarta; ruinas arquitectónicas como Teotihuacán, Chichén Itzá y Tulum, y la arquitectura de muchas ciudades atraen a turistas de todo el mundo. En México, D.F., coexisten restos arquitectónicos de la ciudad prehistórica Tenochtitlán, fundada en 1325 por los aztecas, edificios coloniales y modernas estructuras.
- Otras ciudades de gran interés turístico son Guadalajara, la segunda ciudad más grande del país, origen del mariachi y del tequila; Guanajuato, famosa por sus momias, y San Miguel de Allende, residencia de artistas de todo el mundo.
- En el mundo del arte, se destacan (*stand out*) pintores como Diego Rivera, José Clemente Orozco, David Alfaro Siqueiros y Frida Kahlo.

▲ Mural de Diego Rivera (1886–1957)

Guatemala

- Guatemala es uno de los países centroamericanos que fue (*was*) parte del imperio maya. Aunque el español es el idioma oficial, sólo lo habla el 60 por ciento de la población; el resto habla alguna lengua maya.
- Guatemala es un país de volcanes, montañas y bellos paisajes. Su clima es muy agradable y por eso se conoce como "el país de la eterna primavera". En Guatemala encontramos selvas tropicales (*jungles*), hermosas playas e innumerables centros arqueológicos. Uno de los más famosos es la ciudad maya de Tikal, que por su valor arqueológico fue declarada Patrimonio de la Humanidad por la UNESCO.
- La economía del país se basa en la agricultura. Los principales productos de exportación son café, bananas, algodón (*cotton*) y madera. En sus bosques hay numerosos pájaros (*birds*), entre ellos el quetzal, que le da nombre a la moneda del país, y que es el símbolo nacional de Guatemala.
- Una ciudad muy interesante de este país es Antigua, que fue la capital hasta 1776. Ciudad de Guatemala, la capital actual es, en su mayor parte, una ciudad moderna, aunque todavía hay algunas construcciones antiguas.

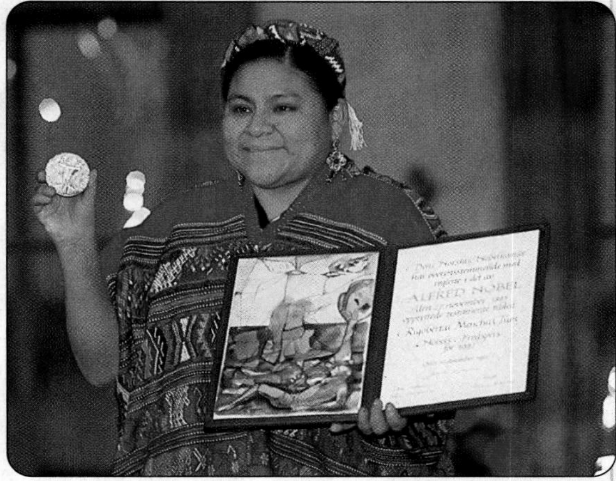

▲ Rigoberta Menchú (1959–), Premio Nobel de la Paz, 1992

El Salvador

- El Salvador es el país más pequeño de Centroamérica, pero es el más densamente poblado. Tiene más de seis millones de habitantes en un área aproximadamente del tamaño (*size*) del estado de Massachusetts.
- En El Salvador hay más de 200 volcanes y por eso lo llaman "la tierra (*land*) de los volcanes". El país tiene unos 300 kilómetros de costa, y sus playas están entre las más hermosas de América. El "surfing" es el deporte (*sport*) que más se practica en las playas.
- El clima del país es tropical, con dos estaciones: la estación de las lluvias (de mayo a octubre) y la estación de la seca (*dry season*) (de noviembre a abril).
- La capital de El Salvador es San Salvador, la ciudad más industrializada de América Central.

▲ La Catedral Metropolitana frente a la plaza Barrios, en San Salvador.

Comentarios... With a partner, discuss, in Spanish, what impressed you the most about these three countries, and compare them to your own. Which places do you want to visit and why?

Online Study Center

For more practice with lesson topics, see the related activities on the ***¡Hola, amigos!*** web site at college.hmco.com/PIC/holaamigos7e.

Tome este examen

Lección 3

Lección 3

A. Present indicative of *-er* and *-ir* verbs

Complete each sentence with the correct form of the Spanish equivalent of the verb in parentheses.

1. El profesor ___escribe___ en la pizarra. (*writes*)
2. Ana y yo ___vivimos___ en la casa de la Sra. Paz. (*live*)
3. Ellos ___deben___ limpiar el baño. (*must*)
4. ¿Tú ___corres___ por la noche? (*run*)
5. Yo ___bebo___ limonada. (*drink*)
6. Esteban ___come___ en la cocina. (*eats*)
7. María ___abre___ las ventanas. (*opens*)
8. ¿___Reciben___ Uds. libros de inglés? (*receive*)

B. Possession with *de*

Write the Spanish equivalent of the words in parentheses.

1. Estela es ___la amiga de Pedro___. (*Pedro's friend*)
2. Aquí está ___la ropa de Paco___. (*Paco's clothes*)
3. Ellos viven en ___la casa de la señora Peña___. (*Mrs. Peña's house*)
4. Ellos son ___los hermanos de Eva___. (*Eva's brothers*)

C. Present indicative of *tener* and *venir*

Complete the following sentences, using the present indicative of **tener** or **venir.**

1. ¿Tú ___vienes___ a la universidad los lunes?
2. Eva y yo ___venimos___ con Roberto porque no ___tenemos___ automóvil.
3. Ellos ___tienen___ mis libros de español, pero hoy no ___vienen___ a clase.
4. Yo no ___vengo___ a la universidad los viernes porque no ___tengo___ clases.
5. Sergio no ___tiene___ hijos.
6. Elvira ___tiene___ que planchar la ropa ahora.

D. Expressions with *tener*

Say how you and everybody else feel according to each situation, using expressions with **tener.**

1. It's July and you are in Phoenix, Arizona. (*Yo...*)
2. Marcelo hasn't had anything to eat for the last twelve hours. (*Marcelo...*)
3. Adela's throat is very dry. (*Adela...*)
4. I am in Alaska and it is winter. (*Tú...*)
5. We haven't slept for the last twenty-four hours. (*Nosotros...*)
6. The boys are being chased by a big dog. (*Los muchachos...*)
7. You have one minute to get to your next class, across campus. (*Yo...*)

Answers: **1.** ...tengo mucho calor. **2.** ...tiene mucha hambre. **3.** ...tiene mucha sed. **4.** ...tienes mucho frío. **5.** ...tenemos mucho sueño. **6.** ...tienen mucho miedo. **7.** ...tengo mucha prisa.

E. Demonstrative adjectives and pronouns Use the appropriate demonstrative adjective.

1. (*those*) a. esas cosas b. esos muebles
2. (*this*) a. esta cocina b. este dormitorio
3. (*that over there*) a. aquel café b. aquella limonada
4. (*that*) a. esa casa b. ese refrigerador
5. (*these*) a. estos platos b. estas casas

F. Numbers 300–1,000 Write the following numbers in Spanish.

1. 567 quinientos sesenta y siete
2. 790 setecientos noventa
3. 1.000 mil
4. 345 trescientos cuarenta y cinco
5. 615 seiscientos quince
6. 874 ochocientos setenta y cuatro
7. 965 novecientos sesenta y cinco
8. 825 ochocientos veinticinco
9. 481 cuatrocientos ochenta y uno
10. 13.816 trece mil ochocientos dieciséis

G. Vocabulary Complete the following sentences, using vocabulary from **Lección 3.**

1. No me gusta hacer los trabajos de la casa.
2. Tengo que descansar un rato.
3. ¿Quién es ese señor?
4. Yo corto el césped (zacate) los sábados.
5. Ellos tienen muchas cosas que hacer hoy.
6. Jorge, necesito los platos para poner la mesa.
7. Tenemos que sacudir los muebles.
8. Tocan a la puerta y Héctor corre a abrir.
9. Debes sacar la basura.
10. Mis amigos vienen dentro de un momento.
11. Yo bebo limonada cuando tengo sed.
12. Andrés tiene que pasar la aspiradora.

H. Culture Answer the questions based on the cultural information you have read.

1. Actualmente, ¿quiénes ayudan con los trabajos de la casa en los países hispanos?
2. ¿Dónde es popular la comida mexicana?
3. ¿En qué países son populares las telenovelas mexicanas?

Answers: 1. Los hombres ayudan con los trabajos de la casa.
2. La comida mexicana es popular en todo el mundo.
3. Son populares en Rusia y en Japón.

Lección 4

Lección 4

A. Irregular first person in the present indicative

Complete each sentence with the correct form of the verb in parentheses.

1. Yo ___salgo___ de mi casa a los ocho. (*leave*)
2. Yo ___conduzco___ el auto de mi papá. (*drive*)
3. Yo ___traduzco___ la lección al inglés. (*translate*)
4. Yo no ___hago___ ejercicio (*exercises*) hoy. (*do*)
5. Yo no ___quepo___ en este auto. (*fit*)
6. Yo ___traigo___ las bebidas. (*bring*)

B. *Saber* vs. *conocer*

Complete the following sentences, using the present indicative of **saber** or **conocer.**

1. ¿Tú ___conoces___ México? ¿___Sabes___ hablar español?
2. Yo no ___sé___ el número de teléfono de Ana.
3. Nosotros ___conocemos___ las novelas de Cervantes.
4. ¿Uds. ___conocen___ a Fernando Baños?
5. ¿Olga ___sabe___ bailar?

C. Personal *a*

Write a sentence with each group of words, adding any necessary words.

Answers: 1. Yo conozco a la tía de Julio. 2. Luis tiene tres tíos y dos tías. 3. Ana lleva a su prima a la fiesta. 4. Uds. conocen San Salvador.

1. Yo / conocer / la tía / Julio
2. Luis / tener / tres tíos / dos tías
3. Ana / llevar / su prima / fiesta
4. Uds. / conocer / San Salvador

D. Contractions *al* and *del*

Rewrite the following sentences, replacing the words in italics with the words in parentheses. Make all necessary changes.

Answers: 1. No conocemos al Sr. Vega. 2. Es la hermana del profesor. 3. Venimos del club. 4. Voy al laboratorio. 5. Vengo de la playa.

1. No conocemos a la *señora* Vega. (señor)
2. Es la hermana de la *profesora.* (profesor)
3. Venimos de la *fiesta.* (club)
4. Voy a la *clase.* (laboratorio)
5. Vengo del *aula.* (playa)

E. Present indicative of *estar, ir,* and *dar*

Complete the following sentences, using the present indicative of **dar, ir,** and **estar.**

1. Yo no ___doy___ mi número de teléfono.
2. Ella no ___está___ en el aula.
3. Nosotros ___vamos___ a la fiesta.
4. ¿Tú ___estás___ bien?
5. Ellos ___están___ en la cafetería.
6. ¿Ud. ___va___ a la universidad por la mañana?
7. ¿Uds. ___dan___ fiestas los sábados?
8. Yo ___voy___ al club.

F. *Ir a* + infinitive Write the question that originated each response, using the cues in italics.

1. Yo voy a estudiar *en el laboratorio.* (Use **tú.**)
2. Nosotros vamos a comer *sándwiches.*
3. Roberto va a ir *con Teresa.*
4. Yo voy a terminar *a las cuatro.* (Use **Ud.**)
5. Ellos van a trabajar *el sábado.*

Answers: **1.** ¿Dónde vas a estudiar? **2.** ¿Qué van a comer Uds.? **3.** ¿Con quién va a ir Roberto? **4.** ¿A qué hora va a terminar Ud.? **5.** ¿Cuándo van a trabajar ellos?

Lección 4

G. Vocabulary Complete the following sentences, using vocabulary from **Lección 4.**

1. Tenemos muchos __discos__ compactos.
2. Vamos a comer __algo__.
3. Mi madrina es morena de ojos __castaños__.
4. ¿Es rubia, morena o __pelirroja__?
5. Es de __estatura__ mediana.
6. Dan una fiesta de __cumpleaños__ para Ana hoy.
7. Elena no es casada; es __soltera__.
8. Paco y Rosa hacen una buena __pareja__.
9. Ellos traen los __entremeses__ para comer en la fiesta.
10. Están __tocando__ una salsa. ¿Quieres __bailar__?
11. Todos __levantan__ su copa y brindan: ¡__Salud__!
12. La fiesta es todo un __éxito__.

H. Culture Circle the correct answer based on the cultural information you have read.

1. La economía tradicional de México está basada en (el petróleo / la arquitectura).
2. Guanajuato es famosa por sus (momias / mariachis).
3. Guatemala es conocido como el país de la eterna (selva / primavera).
4. El Salvador tiene unos (200 / 300) kilómetros de costa.

Answers: **1.** el petróleo **2.** momias **3.** primavera **4.** 300

Unidad 3

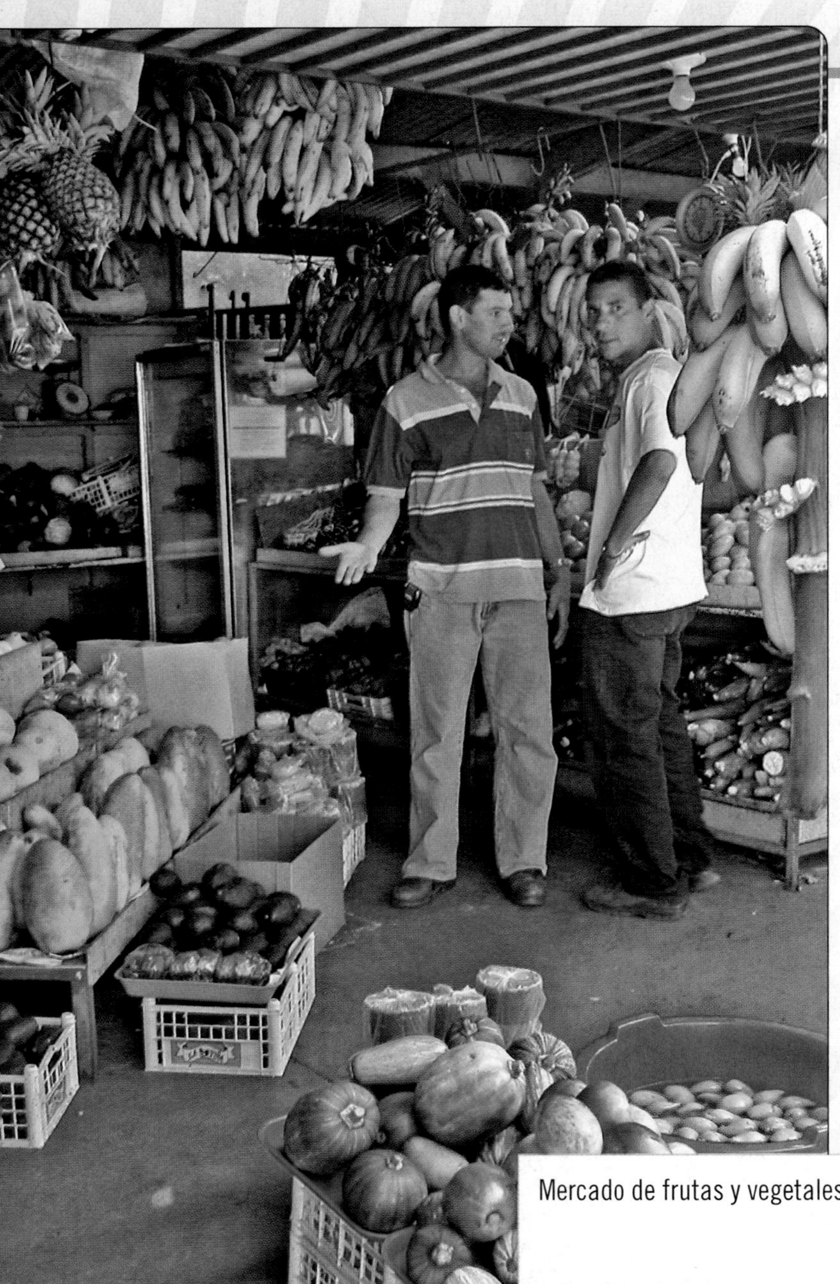

Mercado de frutas y vegetales en Costa Rica

Objetivos

Lección 5

- Order meals at cafés and restaurants
- Request and pay your bill
- Talk about what is going on
- Describe people and things
- Make comparisons

Lección 6

- Shop for groceries in supermarkets and specialty stores
- Avoid repetition
- Contradict what someone else is saying
- Talk about how long something has been going on

¿Qué comemos hoy?

Lección 5
El menú, por favor

Lección 6
En el mercado

Costa Rica

Turistas admirando la selva desde un puente en el Parque Selvatura, en Costa Rica

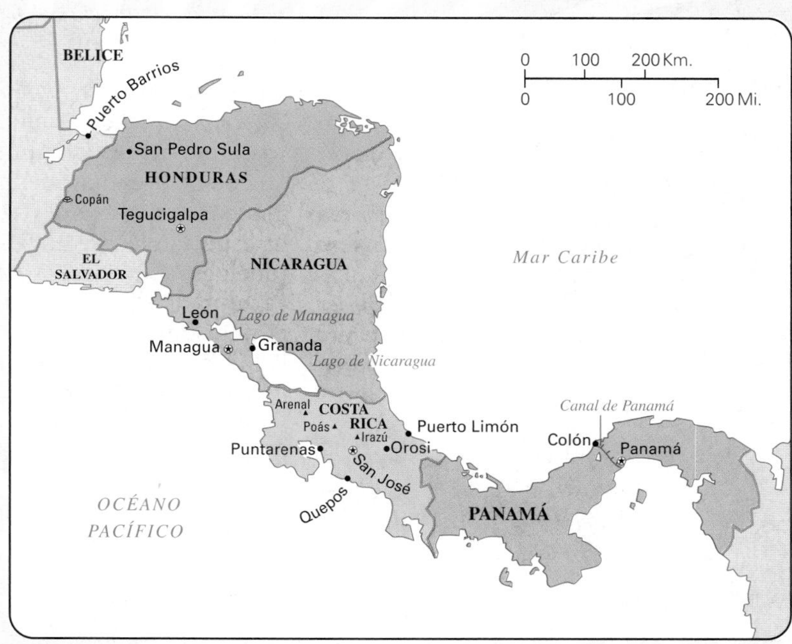

Panamá

Un barco de carga en el Canal de Panamá

Honduras

Ruinas mayas en Copán, Honduras

Nicaragua

Volcán Concepción, el más alto de Nicaragua, en la isla de Ometepe

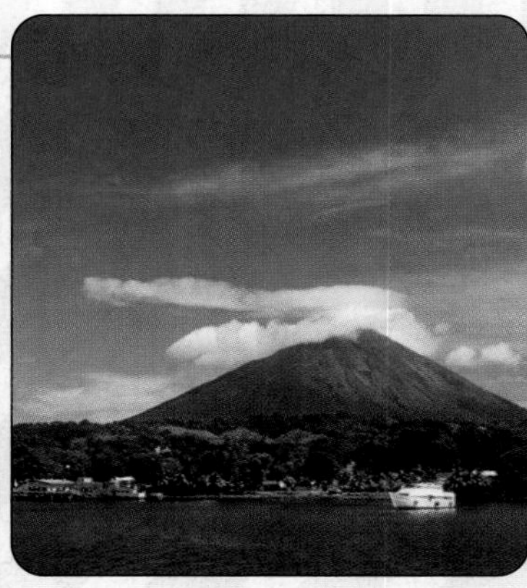

Lección 5 ◆ El menú, por favor

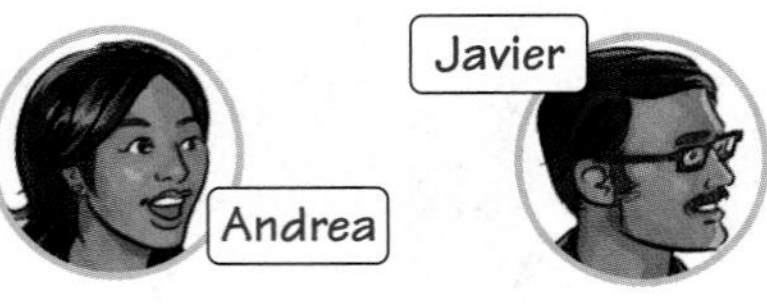

La familia Carreras, de Panamá, está de vacaciones en Costa Rica. Esta noche Andrea y Javier están en uno de los mejores restaurantes de San José, celebrando su aniversario de bodas. Ahora están conversando y esperando al camarero.

Andrea	(*Leyendo el menú*) ¡Ay, no sé qué pedir! Pollo a la parrilla, langosta, pescado asado...
Javier	Yo quiero bistec con puré de papas y verduras. ¡Oye!, ¿no quieres un coctel de camarones para empezar?
Andrea	¡Buena idea! Ah, aquí viene el camarero.
Camarero	La especialidad de hoy es cordero asado y bistec con langosta; ¿qué desean tomar?
Javier	Vermut.
Camarero	¿Y para comer?
Andrea	Para mí, sopa de cebolla, cordero asado y arroz.
Javier	Bistec con puré de papas y... una ensalada de tomates. Tráiganos también un coctel de camarones.
Camarero	¿Qué desean beber con la comida?
Javier	Dos copas de vino tinto.

Detalles culturales

Cada país latinoamericano tiene platos típicos, pero la mayoría de los restaurantes sirve también comida internacional.

◆ **¿Es fácil encontrar comida internacional en tu ciudad?**

Detalles culturales

En los países hispanos, los restaurantes tienen camareros profesionales que trabajan tiempo completo. Por lo general, son hombres y usan uniforme: pantalones negros y chaqueta blanca.

◆ **¿Qué diferencia ve Ud. entre los camareros hispanos y los de este país?**

Detalles culturales

◆ En los países de habla hispana, el café se sirve después del postre, nunca durante la comida. Generalmente es café tipo espresso, y se sirve en tazas muy pequeñas.

◆ La propina que se ofrece en los restaurantes generalmente es del 10%, pero hay variación según el país y el tipo de restaurante. Con frecuencia la propina está incluida en la cuenta. Si Ud. no está seguro de esto, debe preguntar (*ask*), **¿Está incluido el servicio?**

◆ El desayuno típico en Costa Rica es gallo pinto (arroz con frijoles negros), huevo, tortilla, jugo de mango y café.

1. ¿Se bebe mucho café en este país? ¿Qué tipo de café prefiere beber Ud.?
2. Generalmente, ¿cuánto se deja de propina en un restaurante en este país?
3. ¿Cuál es el desayuno típico en este país?

Más tarde.

Javier (*Lee la lista de postres*) Flan, torta, helado, arroz con leche, pastel...
Andrea Yo quiero helado de vainilla.
Javier Yo voy a pedir flan con crema y después tomamos un café.

Javier paga la cuenta y deja una buena propina.

Al día siguiente Andrea y Javier llevan a sus hijos a desayunar. Anita es una niña muy bonita y un poco tímida. Es mayor que Luisito, pero él es más alto que ella. El niño es simpático y travieso.

Javier (*Al mozo*) Jugo de naranja, huevos con jamón y pan tostado con mantequilla y mermelada.
Andrea Una ensalada de frutas y un café con leche. (*A Anita*) ¿Qué quieres tú?
Anita Yo quiero panqueques y un vaso de leche.
Luisito Yo quiero un perro caliente y una Coca-Cola.
Javier ¡No, no, no! Tienes que pedir algo mejor.
Luisito Bueno..., una hamburguesa y una taza de chocolate.
Andrea Está bien, pero en el almuerzo vas a comer pollo y verduras.
Luisito No me gusta el pollo. No es tan sabroso como la pizza.

Cuando terminan de desayunar son las diez de la mañana.

¿Recuerda usted?

¿Verdadero o falso?

With a partner, decide whether the following statements about the dialogue are true (**verdadero**) or false (**falso**).

1. La familia Carreras es de Costa Rica y está de vacaciones en Panamá. ☐ V ☒ F
2. Hoy Andrea y Javier celebran su aniversario de bodas. ☒ V ☐ F
3. Javier come pollo a la parrilla. ☐ V ☒ F
4. Andrea no quiere comer camarones. ☐ V ☒ F
5. Andrea va a pedir sopa. ☒ V ☐ F
6. Javier y Andrea comen postre. ☒ V ☐ F
7. Javier y Andrea no tienen hijos. ☐ V ☒ F
8. El niño es mayor que la niña. ☐ V ☒ F
9. Javier come más que Andrea. ☒ V ☐ F
10. La mamá de Luisito quiere comer una hamburguesa. ☐ V ☒ F
11. Luisito prefiere comer pizza. ☒ V ☐ F
12. La familia termina de desayunar a las doce. ☐ V ☒ F

Y ahora... conteste

Answer these questions, basing your answers on the dialogue.

1. ¿Dónde están Andrea y Javier ahora?
2. ¿Qué están haciendo?
3. ¿Qué beben Javier y Andrea?
4. ¿Qué quiere Andrea de postre? ¿Y Javier?
5. ¿Cómo es Anita? ¿Cómo es Luisito?
6. ¿Anita quiere panqueques o pan tostado?
7. ¿Qué bebe Luisito en el desayuno?
8. ¿Qué debe comer Luisito en el almuerzo?

Answers: **1.** Están en un restaurante. **2.** Están leyendo el menú. **3.** Beben vermut y vino tinto. **4.** Ella quiere helado y él quiere flan con crema. **5.** Anita es bonita y un poco tímida. Luisito es simpático y travieso. **6.** Quiere panqueques. **7.** Bebe una taza de chocolate. **8.** Debe comer pollo y verduras.

Para hablar del tema: Vocabulario

Online Study Center

For more practice with lesson topics, see the related activities on the *¡Hola, amigos!* web site at college.hmco.com/PIC/holaamigos7e.

Cognados

el aniversario
el coctel
la crema
la especialidad
la fruta
la hamburguesa
la lista
el menú
el panqueque*
el restaurante
la sopa*
la vainilla
el vermut

Nombres

el almuerzo lunch
el arroz rice
_____ **con leche** rice pudding
el bistec, el biftec steak
la boda wedding
el (la) camarero(a)* waiter, waitress
los camarones* shrimp
la cebolla onion
el cordero lamb
la cuenta check, bill
el flan caramel custard
el helado* ice cream
el huevo egg
el jamón ham
la langosta lobster
la mantequilla* butter
la mermelada jam
el (la) niño(a) child
el pan bread
_____ **tostado** toast
la papa* potato
el pastel pie
el perro caliente hot dog
el pescado fish
el pollo chicken
el postre dessert
la propina tip
el puré de papas mashed potatoes
la verdura, el vegetal vegetable

Verbos

dejar to leave (*behind*)
desayunar to have breakfast
empezar (e>ie), comenzar (e>ie) to begin, to start
esperar to wait
pagar to pay
pedir to order
preferir (e>ie) to prefer
querer (e>ie) to want, to wish

Adjetivos

asado(a) baked
mayor older, oldest
mejor better, best
sabroso(a), rico(a) tasty, rich
tímido(a) shy
travieso(a) mischievous

Otras palabras y expresiones

a la parrilla grilled
al día siguiente next day
algo something
aquí here
de postre for dessert
de vacaciones on vacation
más tarde later
tráiganos bring us

Amplíe su vocabulario

Para poner la mesa (*To set the table*)

De país a país

el panqueque el panqué (*Méx.*)
la sopa el caldo (*Méx.*)
el (la) camarero(a) el (la) mozo(a) (*Cono Sur*), el (la) salonero(a) (Costa Rica), el (la) mesonero(a) (*Ven.*), el (la) mesero(a) (*Méx.*)
los camarones las gambas (*Esp.*)
el helado la nieve (*Méx.*)
la mantequilla la manteca (*Arg.*)
la papa la patata (*Esp.*)

Para practicar el vocabulario

A. En el restaurante Choose the word or phrase that best completes each sentence.

1. Quiero una ensalada de (camareros, camarones, cuentas). camarones
2. La especialidad de hoy es biftec con (langosta, pastel, mantequilla). langosta
3. De postre quiero (cordero, pollo, helado). helado
4. No quiero salmón. No me gusta el (jamón, huevo, pescado). pescado
5. Quiero puré de (gambas, papas, arroz). papas
6. Quiero (almuerzo, pollo, mermelada) a la parrilla. pollo
7. Voy a pagar la (cuenta, cebolla, idea). cuenta
8. Javier deja una buena (boda, propina, verdura) para el mozo. propina

B. Preguntas y respuestas Match the questions in column *A* with the answers in column *B*.

A	B
1. ¿Qué quieres beber? g	**a.** No, perros calientes.
2. ¿Quieres langosta? j	**b.** Sí, a la parrilla.
3. ¿Quieren sopa? e	**c.** A las once y media.
4. ¿Comen hamburguesas? a	**d.** ¡Muy traviesos!
5. ¿Comes pan? i	**e.** Sí, de cebolla.
6. ¿A qué hora es el almuerzo? c	**f.** No, con helado.
7. ¿Quieres pollo? b	**g.** Vermut.
8. ¿Comen flan con crema? f	**h.** Quince dólares.
9. ¿Cómo son los niños? d	**i.** Sí, con mantequilla y mermelada.
10. ¿Cuánto dejas de propina? h	**j.** No, prefiero camarones.

C. Voy a pedir... With a partner, play the roles of two dining companions looking at the menu and talking about what they are going to order. Start by saying "Yo voy a pedir…". *Answers will vary.*

Marisa está leyendo el menú. ¿Qué cree Ud. que ella va a pedir para comer? ¿Y para tomar?

D. Para poner la mesa With a partner, decide what items you are going to need to set the table according to what is going to be served. Start out with a tablecloth and napkins.

You will serve soup, salad, steak and lobster, dessert, water, red wine, and coffee. *Answers will vary.*

Pronunciación

Las consonantes *g, j, h*

A. Practice the sound of Spanish **g** in the following words.

pa**g**ar	**g**racias
gambas	**g**uapo
lan**g**osta	trái**g**anos

B. Practice the sound of Spanish **j** (or **g** before **e** and **i**) in the following words.

ba**j**o	pare**j**a	**J**ulio
giro	anaran**j**ado	**J**avier
Gerardo	me**j**or	ve**g**etales

C. Repeat the following words. Remember that the Spanish **h** is silent.

a**h**ora	**h**asta	**h**elado
hoy	**h**ola	**h**amburguesas
hora	**h**istoria	**h**uevo

Suggestion: For additional practice:
Gustavo guardó la guitarra en el gabinete. / Gerardo y Ginés juegan con tarjetas. / Ahora Hugo habla con su hermano.

Puntos para recordar

1. Present progressive (Estar + *gerundio*)

Suggestion: Using colored chalk, write the endings for the gerund.

habl**ar**: habl **ando** (*speaking*)
com**er**: com **iendo** (*eating*)
escrib**ir**: escrib **iendo** (*writing*)

Suggestion: Emphasize that only **estar** is used in the present progressive. Write:

estar + *gerund*

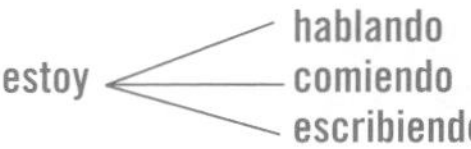

Act out an action and ask students **¿Qué estoy haciendo?**

Transparency: Use the transparency and ask students what activities are depicted.

Extra practice: Drill students on the following verb forms and encourage them to use the forms in sentences.

1. **Estoy leyendo... (Pedro, Ellas, Tú)**
   Student: Pedro está leyendo un libro.
2. **Estás pidiendo... (Yo, Uds., El profesor)**
3. **Él está durmiendo... (Los niños, Ana, Ellos)**

¡Atención! In Spanish, the present progressive is *never* used to indicate a future action. The present tense is used in future expressions that would require the present participle in English.

The present progressive describes an action that is in progress. It is formed with the present tense of **estar** and the **gerundio** (equivalent to the English *-ing* form) of the verb. Study the formation of the **gerundio** in the following chart.

Infinitive	habl**ar**	com**er**	escrib**ir**
Gerundio	habl- **ando**	com- **iendo**	escrib- **iendo**

Yo	**estoy**	**comiendo.**
I	***am***	***eating.***

—**¿Estás estudiando?** — ***"Are you studying?"***
—No, **estoy escribiendo.** — *"No, **I am writing.**"*

◆ The following forms are irregular. Note the change in their stems.

pedir	→	**p*i*diendo**	*asking for*
decir	→	**d*i*ciendo**	*saying*
servir	→	**s*i*rviendo**	*serving*
dormir	→	**d*u*rmiendo**	*sleeping*
traer	→	**tra*y*endo**	*bringing*
leer	→	**le*y*endo**	*reading*

◆ Note also that the **i** of **-iendo** becomes **y** between vowels.

—¿Qué están haciendo las chicas? — *"What are the girls doing?"*
—Ana **está leyendo** y Eva está durmiendo. — *"Ana **is reading** and Eva is sleeping."*

◆ Some verbs, such as **ser, estar, ir,** and **venir,** are rarely used in the progressive construction.

Suggestion: Remind students that *Are you coming?* and similar expressions would be expressed in Spanish using **ir a** + *infinitive,* not the present progressive.

Práctica y conversación

Online Study Center

For more practice with lesson topics, see the related activities on the *¡Hola, amigos!* web site at college.hmco.com/PIC/holaamigos7e.

A. En casa de los Carreras With a partner, say what is happening, using the cues provided.

1. Tú / preparar / una ensalada
2. Javier / traer / los manteles
3. Luisito y Anita / pedir / dinero
4. Yo / decir / que es tarde
5. Andrea y yo / desayunar / la cocina

Answers: **1.** Tú estás preparando una ensalada. **2.** Javier está trayendo los manteles. **3.** Luisito y Anita están pidiendo dinero. **4.** Yo estoy diciendo que es tarde. **5.** Andrea y yo estamos desayunando en la cocina.

B. ¿Qué están haciendo? Describe what the following people are doing.

1. Tú...

2. Yo...

3. Ellos...

4. Eva...

5. La profesora...

6. Nosotros... y el chico...

Answers: **1.** Tú estás comiendo (un sándwich). **2.** Yo estoy escribiendo. **3.** Ellos están bailando. **4.** Eva está sirviendo café. **5.** La profesora está leyendo un libro. **6.** Nosotros estamos hablando por teléfono y el chico está durmiendo.

C. En una fiesta With a partner, take turns asking and answering what everybody is doing at Andrea's party. Use the cues provided and the present progressive to formulate the questions. Use your imagination when responding.

	Persona	Pregunta
1.	Javier	qué / hacer
2.	Andrea	qué / servir
3.	Pablo	con quién / bailar
4.	Eva y Pablo	qué / beber
5.	Juan	qué / comer
6.	Olga y Estela	qué / pedir
7.	la orquesta (*band*)	qué / tocar

Preguntas: **1.** ¿Qué está haciendo Javier? **2.** ¿Qué está sirviendo Andrea? **3.** ¿Con quién está bailando Pablo? **4.** ¿Qué están bebiendo Eva y Pablo? **5.** ¿Qué está comiendo Juan? **6.** ¿Qué están pidiendo Olga y Estela? **7.** ¿Qué está tocando la orquesta? (*Answers to these questions will vary.*)

2. Uses of *ser* and *estar* (*Usos de* ser *y* estar)

Suggestion: List the uses of **ser** and **estar** on the board and have students give examples for each.

ser: basic characteristic; origin and nationality; professions; events; possession or relationship; material; times and dates

estar: location; condition; result of an action; sensory perceptions; in progressive forms

The English verb *to be* has two Spanish equivalents, **ser** and **estar,** which have distinct uses and are *not* interchangeable.

Uses of *ser*

Ser expresses a fundamental quality and identifies the essence of a person or thing: *who* or *what* the subject is.

- It describes the basic nature or inherent characteristics of a person or thing. It is also used with expressions of age that do not refer to a specific number of years.

Anita **es** tímida.	*Anita **is** shy.*
Estela **es** joven.	*Estela **is** young.*

- It is used with **de** to indicate origin and with adjectives denoting nationality.

Carmen **es** cubana; **es** de La Habana.	*Carmen **is** Cuban; she **is** from Havana.*

- It is used to identify professions and jobs.

Yo **soy** profesor de francés.	*I **am** a French professor.*

- With **de,** it is used to indicate possession or relationship.

El vaso **es** de Ana.	*The glass **is** Ana's.*
Ellas **son** las hermanas de Javier.	*They **are** Javier's sisters.*

- With **de,** it describes the material that things are made of.

El teléfono **es** de plástico.	*The telephone **is** (made of) plastic.*
La mesa **es** de metal.	*The table **is** (made of) metal.*

- It is used with expressions of time and with dates.

Son las cuatro y media.	*It **is** four-thirty.*
Hoy **es** jueves, primero de julio.	*Today **is** Thursday, July first.*

- It is used with events as the equivalent of "taking place."

La fiesta **es** en mi casa.	*The party **is (taking place)** at my house.*

Uses of *estar*

Suggestion: Contrast the following pairs of sentences. Notice how the use of **ser** or **estar** affects their meanings.

Somos de Boston. (origin)
Estamos en Boston. (location)

El chocolate es delicioso. (basic characteristic)
El chocolate (que estoy tomando ahora) está delicioso. (condition, sensory perception)

Estar is used to express more transitory qualities than **ser** and often implies the possibility of change.

- It indicates place or location.

Ana **está** en casa.	*Ana **is** at home.*

- It indicates a condition, often the result of an action, at a given moment in time.

Él **está** cansado.	*He's tired.*
La puerta **está** cerrada.	*The door **is** closed.*

- With personal reactions, it describes what is perceived through the senses—that is—how a subject tastes, feels, looks, or seems.

¡**Estás** muy bonita hoy!	***You look** very pretty today!*
La sopa **está** muy sabrosa.	*The soup **is** very tasty.*

- In present progressive constructions, it describes an action in progress.

Estoy desayunando.	***I am** having breakfast.*

Práctica y conversación

Online Study Center

For more practice with lesson topics, see the related activities on the ***¡Hola, amigos!*** web site at college.hmco.com/PIC/holaamigos7e.

A. Entreviste a su compañero(a) Interview a partner, using the following questions. *Answers will vary.*

1. ¿Eres norteamericano(a)?
2. ¿De dónde eres?
3. ¿Tu mejor amigo es alto, bajo o de estatura mediana?
4. ¿Tu mejor amiga es rubia, morena o pelirroja?
5. ¿Dónde están tus padres ahora?
6. ¿Estás cansado(a)?
7. ¿Qué día es hoy?
8. ¿Qué hora es?

Follow-up: As homework, have students write two or more personalized questions that illustrate each use of **ser** and **estar**. In class, have students work in pairs, asking and answering these questions.

B. Carlos Alberto y Marisa Complete the following story about Carlos Alberto and his girlfriend, Marisa, using the present indicative of **ser** or **estar,** as appropriate.

Suggestion: Students should be prepared to give reasons for choosing **ser** or **estar** in each case.

Carlos Alberto ___es___ joven, alto y delgado. ___Es___ estudiante de la Universidad Central. Él ___es___ de Panamá, pero ahora ___está___ en Costa Rica. ___Son___ las nueve de la noche y Carlos Alberto decide ir a la casa de Marisa. Marisa ___es___ su novia y ___es___ una chica muy inteligente y simpática. —¡Qué bonita ___estás___ hoy, Marisa! —exclama Carlos Alberto cuando ella abre la puerta. Los dos van a una fiesta. La fiesta ___es___ en casa de Andrea y Javier.

C. Ser o estar With a partner, take turns making statements about each illustration, using **ser** or **estar** as needed.

- **MODELO:** Pedro ________ y Luis ________.
  Pedro es alto y Luis es bajo.

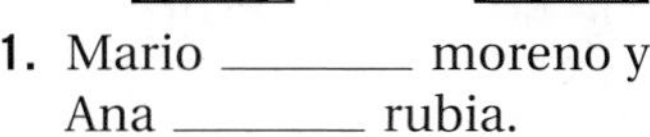

Some answers may vary.
1. es / es 2. está hablando con el cajero 3. está en la universidad (es profesor de matemáticas) 4. estoy cansada 5. es el seis de mayo (es lunes) 6. están en la clase 7. Es la una 8. somos norteamericanos

1. Mario _______ moreno y Ana _______ rubia.

2. Eva _______.

3. El doctor Torres _______.

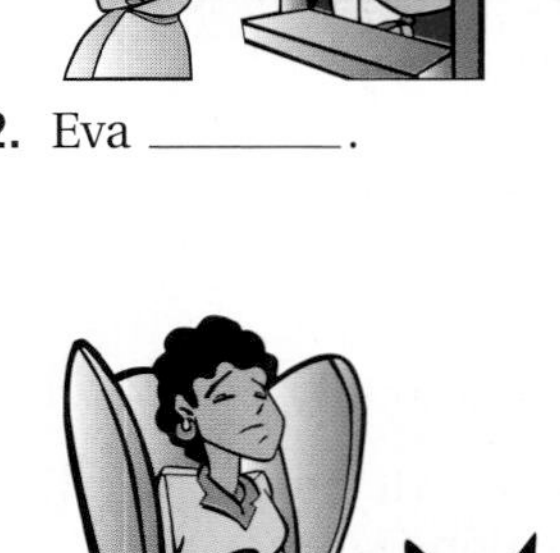

4. Yo _______.

5. Hoy _______.

6. Los estudiantes _______.

7. _______.

8. Nosotros _______.

Follow up: Have groups share their sentences with the class or another group.

 **D. En la clase** In groups of three or four, prepare twelve statements about objects and people in the classroom. Include as many uses of **ser** and **estar** as possible. *Answers will vary.*

3. Stem-changing verbs: *e > ie*
(*Verbos que cambian en la raíz:* e > ie)

As you have already seen, Spanish verbs have two parts: a stem and an ending (**-ar, -er,** or **-ir**). Some Spanish verbs undergo a change in the stem in the present indicative tense. When **e** is the last stem vowel and it is stressed, it changes to **ie** as shown below.

Suggestion: Drill students on the following verb forms and encourage them to use the forms in sentences.
1. **Yo cierro la puerta. (Uds., Ella, Tú, Nosotras)**
2. **Él piensa ir. (Yo, Tú, Ud. y ella, Mis amigos)**
3. **Nosotros empezamos hoy. (Tú, Uds., Yo, Ellas)**

preferir (*to prefer*)			
yo	pref**ie**ro	nosotros(as)	preferimos
tú	pref**ie**res	vosotros(as)	preferís
Ud. / él / ella	pref**ie**re	Uds. / ellos / ellas	pref**ie**ren

- Note that the stem vowel is not stressed in the verb forms used with **nosotros(as)** and **vosotros(as);** therefore, the **e** does not change to **ie.**
- Stem-changing verbs have the same endings as regular **-ar, -er,** and **-ir** verbs.
- Other verbs that also change from **e** to **ie** are **cerrar** (*to close*), **comenzar, empezar, entender**[1] (*to understand*), **pensar**[2] (*to think*), and **querer.**

—¿**Quieres** bistec?	*"**Do you want** steak?"*
—No, **prefiero** pollo.	*"No, **I prefer** chicken."*
—¿A qué hora **comienzan** Uds. a trabajar?	*"At what time **do you begin** to work?"*
—**Comenzamos** a las diez.	*"**We begin** at ten."*

Alternative: Write a short sentence builder on the board and ask students to combine the elements to form five original sentences.
Yo / Ellas / Tú / Nosotros / Uds. / La clase / La fiesta
pensar / empezar / cerrar / querer / preferir
a las nueve / la ventana / ir hoy / beber ponche / el próximo lunes

Práctica y conversación

Online Study Center
For more practice with lesson topics, see the related activities on the ***¡Hola, amigos!*** web site at college.hmco.com/PIC/holaamigos7e.

A. No están de acuerdo
Alicia and Sergio cannot agree on anything. Supply the correct form for each verb and act out the conversation with a partner.

Suggestion: Have students work in pairs, creating and asking their partners 5 questions using **pensar, preferir, querer, empezar, comenzar.**

Alicia ¿Tú _piensas_ (pensar) ir a la fiesta de Olga?
Sergio Yo no _quiero_ (querer) ir a fiestas; _prefiero_ (preferir) ir a un restaurante con los muchachos.
Alicia ¡Ellos también _quieren_ (querer) ir a la fiesta!
Sergio ¿A qué hora _empieza_ (empezar) la fiesta?
Alicia _Comienza_ (Comenzar) a las nueve, pero Beatriz y yo _queremos_ (querer) estar allí (*there*) a las ocho porque tenemos que llevar las bebidas.
Sergio Carlos y yo _pensamos_ (pensar) ir a la biblioteca.
Alicia ¡¿Uds. _piensan_ (pensar) ir a la biblioteca hoy?! Entonces yo voy a la fiesta con Roberto.
Sergio ¡Magnífico! Yo voy al restaurante con Marisa.

---

[1]For a complete list of stem-changing verbs, see Appendix B.
[2]When followed by an infinitive, **pensar** means *to plan:* **Pienso** estudiar hoy.

B. Dime... (*Tell me...*) With a partner, take turns asking and answering the following questions with complete sentences, using the illustrations as cues.

1. ¿Qué quieres tomar?

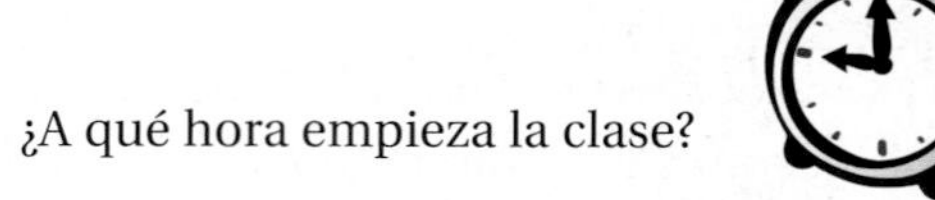

2. ¿A qué hora empieza la clase?

3. ¿Adónde quieren ir Uds.?

4. ¿Qué prefiere comer Adela?

5. ¿Cuándo comienzan las clases?

6. ¿A qué hora cierran la biblioteca?

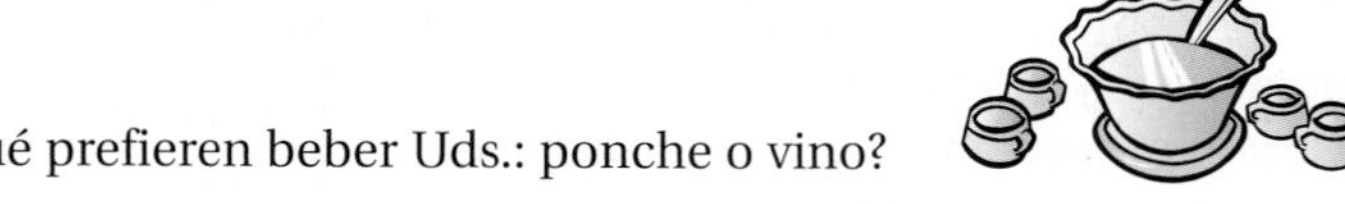

7. ¿Qué prefieren beber Uds.: ponche o vino?

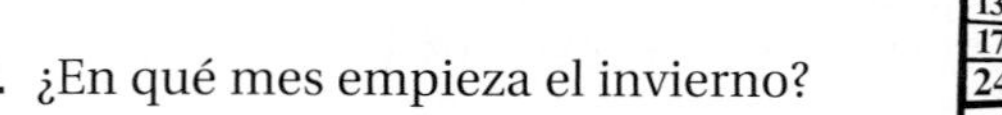

8. ¿En qué mes empieza el invierno?

Alternative: To vary the format, have students ask you their questions as a whole-group activity. Extend the activity by responding and then asking the same questions of individual students.

9. ¿Con quién piensas ir?

C. Quiero saber... Write five original questions to ask a partner, using **e:ie** stem-changing verbs. Your partner will, in turn, ask you five questions.
Answers will vary.

4. Comparative and superlative adjectives, adverbs, and nouns (*Comparativo y superlativo de adjetivos, adverbios y nombres*)

Comparisons of inequality

- In Spanish, the comparative of inequality of most adjectives, adverbs, and nouns is formed by placing **más** (*more*) or **menos** (*less*) before the adjective, the adverb, or the noun and **que** (*than*) after it.

Suggestion: Write the following sample sentence and list of adjectives on the board or on the overhead projector.
Yo soy más / menos... que...
alto(a) / moreno(a) / bajo(a) / rico(a) / simpático(a) / rubio(a) / inteligente / bonita / guapo bueno(a) / delgado(a) / joven / paciente

más (*more*) / **menos** (*less*)	+	*adjective* or *adverb* or *noun*	+	**que** (*than*)

—¿Tú eres **más alta que** Ana? *"Are you **taller than** Ana?"*
—Sí, ella es mucho **más baja que** yo. *"Yes, she is much **shorter than** I."*

¡Atención! **De** is used instead of **que** before a numerical expression of quantity or amount.

Luis tiene **más de** treinta años. *Luis is **over** thirty years old.*
Hay **menos de** veinte estudiantes aquí. *There are **fewer than** twenty students here.*

Comparisons of equality

- To form comparisons of equality with adjectives, adverbs, and nouns in Spanish, use the adjectives **tanto, -a, -os, as,** or the adverb **tan... como.**

When comparing adjectives or adverbs:	When comparing nouns:
tan (*as*) bonita / tarde **+ como**	**tanto** (*as much*) dinero / **tanta** plata (*money*) / **tantos** (*as many*) libros / **tantas** plumas **+ como**

Alternative: Using familiar adjectives, ask students to compare themselves to other classmates, friends, and family members.

I —¿Eres tan rico(a) como tu papá? (¿mamá?)
S1 —Sí, soy tan rico(a) como mi papá (mamá).
S2 —No, no soy tan rico(a) como mi papá (mamá).
I —¿Tienes tanto dinero como ellos?
S3 —Sí, tengo tanto dinero como ellos.

—¿Tu hermana habla bien el español? *"Does your sister speak Spanish well?"*
—Sí, habla español **tan bien como** nosotros. *"Yes, she speaks Spanish **as well as** we do."*

—Tú das muchas fiestas. *"You give many parties."*
—Sí, pero no doy **tantas fiestas como** Uds. *"Yes, but I don't give **as many parties as** you do."*

The superlative

- The superlative construction is similar to the comparative. It is formed by placing the definite article before the person or thing being compared.

Follow-up: Personalize by involving students in comparisons of each other (who is taller, shorter, and so forth).

definite article	+	(*noun*)	+	**más** or **menos**	+	*adjective*	+	**de**

—¿Quién es **el estudiante más inteligente** de la clase?
—Mario es **el**[1] **más inteligente** de todos.

*"Who is **the most intelligent student** in the class?"*
*"Mario is **the most intelligent** of all."*

¡Atención! Note that the Spanish **de** translates to the English *in* or *of* after a superlative.

Ellos son los más inteligentes **de** la clase. — *They are the most intelligent ones **in** the class.*

Suggestion: Show pictures of houses, cars, T.V. sets, clothes, etc., and have students establish comparisons (which is better, the best, more expensive, the most expensive, and so on).

Irregular comparative forms

- The following adjectives and adverbs have irregular comparative and superlative forms in Spanish.

Adjective	Adverb	Comparative	Superlative
bueno (*good*)	bien (*well*)	**mejor**	**el (la) mejor**
malo (*bad*)	mal (*badly*)	**peor**	**el (la) peor**
grande (*big*)		**mayor**	**el (la) mayor**
pequeño (*small*)		**menor**	**el (la) menor**

- When the adjectives **grande** and **pequeño** refer to size, the regular comparative forms are generally used.

Tu clase es **más grande que** la de Antonio. — *Your class is **bigger than** Antonio's.*

When these adjectives refer to age, the irregular comparative forms **mayor** and **menor** are used.

—¿Felipe es **mayor que** tú? — *"Is Felipe **older** than you?"*
—No, es **menor que** yo. — *"No, he's **younger** than I (am)."*

[1]The noun may be omitted in the superlative construction to avoid repetition when meaning is clear from context.

Práctica y conversación

Online Study Center

For more practice with lesson topics, see the related activities on the *¡Hola, amigos!* web site at college.hmco.com/PIC/holaamigos7e.

A. Más o menos... Complete the following sentences, giving the Spanish equivalent of the words in parentheses.

1. ¿Tu esposo tiene ___menos de___ cuarenta años? (*less than*)
2. Mi primo baila ___tan mal como___ yo. (*as badly as*)
3. Mi amigo(a) es ___menos inteligente que___ tú. (*less intelligent than*)
4. Andrea es ___mucho menor que___ su hermana. (*much younger than*)
5. Tú eres ___mucho más delgada que___ ella. (*much thinner than*)
6. Luis es ___tan simpático como___ Ariel. (*as nice as*)
7. Yo no tengo ___tantos libros como___ tú. (*as many books as*)
8. Nosotros damos ___tantas fiestas como___ Uds. (*as many parties as*)
9. Este restaurante es ___el mejor de___ todos. (*the best of*)
10. La langosta es ___más sabrosa que___ el pollo. (*tastier than*)

Follow-up: Write a number of adjectives of personality on the board (e.g., **paciente, trabajador, sincero,** etc.) and have students discuss who in class is "the most . . ." in each case. Use celebrities if students are uncomfortable discussing their classmates.

B. Comparaciones Establish comparisons between the following people and things, using the adjectives provided and adding any necessary words.

1. Hotel Hilton / Motel 6 / mejor
2. Einstein / yo / inteligente
3. Penélope Cruz / Meg Ryan / bonita
4. Maine / Texas / pequeño
5. Antonio Banderas / Danny De Vito / alto
6. Anita / Luisito / mayor
7. Brasil / Venezuela / grande
8. Jane Fonda / Jennifer López / menor

Answers: **1.** El Hotel Hilton es mejor que el Motel 6. **2.** Einstein es más inteligente que yo. (Yo soy menos inteligente que Einstein.) **3.** Penélope Cruz es más (menos) bonita que (tan bonita como) Meg Ryan. **4.** Maine es más pequeño que Texas. **5.** Antonio Banderas es más alto que Danny De Vito. **6.** Anita es mayor que Luisito. **7.** Brasil es más grande que Venezuela. **8.** Jennifer López es menor que Jane Fonda.

C. En la clase Read each statement; then answer the questions that follow.

1. Mario tiene A en español, José tiene B y Lolo tiene F.
   ¿Quién es el mejor estudiante?
   ¿Quién es el peor estudiante?
2. Juan tiene veinte años, Raúl tiene quince y David dieciocho.
   ¿Quién es el mayor de los tres?
   ¿Quién es el menor de los tres?

Answers: **1.** Mario es el mejor estudiante. Lolo es el peor estudiante. **2.** Juan es el mayor de los tres. Raúl es el menor de los tres.

3. Rosa es más inteligente que Beto. Lolo es menos inteligente que Beto. Rosa es la más inteligente de los tres. Lolo es el menos inteligente de los tres.

3. Lolo no es inteligente, Beto es inteligente y Rosa es muy inteligente.
¿Quién es más inteligente que Beto?
¿Quién es menos inteligente que Beto?
¿Quién es el (la) más inteligente de los tres?
¿Quién es el (la) menos inteligente de los tres?

D. En mi familia With a partner, ask each other questions to find out how you compare to members of your family with respect to height, age, intelligence, etc. *Answers will vary.*

5. Pronouns as objects of prepositions
(*Pronombres usados como complemento de preposición*)

The object of a preposition[1] is the noun or pronoun that immediately follows it.

La fiesta es *para María* (*ella*). **Ellos van *con nosotros.***

Alternative: Write on the board, using colored chalk for the **mí** and **ti** forms:

para, en, a, de, por, hacia, contra { mí, ti, **usted**, **él**, **ella**, **nosotros**, **vosotros**, **ustedes**, **ellos**, **ellas** }

con { ***conmigo***, ***contigo***, **usted**, **él**, **ella**, **nosotros**, **vosotros**, **ustedes**, **ellos**, **ellas** }

Singular		Plural	
mí	me	**nosotros(as)**	us
ti	you (*fam.*)	**vosotros(as)**	you (*fam.*)
Ud.	you (*form.*)	**Uds.**	you (*form. / fam.*)
él	him	**ellos**	them (*masc.*)
ella	her	**ellas**	them (*fem.*)

- Only the first- and second-persons singular, **mí** and **ti,** are different from regular subject pronouns.
- When used with the preposition **con, mí** and **ti** become **conmigo** and **contigo,** respectively. The other forms do not combine: **con él, con ella, con ustedes,** and so on.

—¿El café es para **mí**? *"Is the coffee for **me**?"*
—No, no es para **ti;** es para **él.** *"No, it's not for **you;** it's for **him.**"*

—¿Vas a la fiesta **conmigo**? *"Are you going **with me** to the party?"*
—No, no voy **contigo;** voy con **ellos.** *"No, I'm not going **with you;** I'm going with **them.**"*

Suggestion: To help students remember the exceptions, have one student go around the room and pick up various items (students' books, pens, pencils, and so on), asking the class: **¿Es (son) para mí?** Students are to answer: **No, no es (son) para ti.** Then have another student prepare to leave the room and ask classmates: **¿Vas conmigo?** They should answer: **No, no voy contigo.**

[1]See Appendix C.

Práctica y conversación

For more practice with lesson topics, see the related activities on the ***¡Hola, amigos!*** web site at college.hmco.com/PIC/holaamigos7e.

A. Entre amigos Complete the following sentences with the correct forms of the pronouns and prepositions in parentheses.

1. Elena no va ___contigo___, Anita. (*with you*)
2. Esas servilletas son para ___mí___ y el mantel es para ___ella___. (*me / her*)
3. Teresa está hablando de ___nosotros___. (*us*)
4. Elsa va a venir con ___ellos___. (*them, masc.*)
5. Olga no va a ir al restaurante ___con Uds.___; va a ir ___conmigo___. (*with you, pl. / with me*)
6. El vino no es para ___él___, Paco; es para ___ti___. (*him / you*)
7. El postre es para ___Ud.___, señorita. (*you*)
8. El café es para ___ellas___. (*them, fem.*)

Follow-up: Ask students personalized questions using the structures presented in this section. Remind them to respond using the appropriate preposition and pronoun.

I —¿Vienes conmigo o con Elena?
S1 —Voy contigo.
S2 —No, no voy contigo; voy con ella.

B. Entreviste a su compañero(a) Interview a partner, using the following questions. *Answers will vary.*

1. Cuando tú vas a un restaurante, ¿quién va contigo generalmente?
2. De postre, el camarero trae flan con crema; ¿es para ti?
3. Tú vas a preparar dos postres para tus padres: arroz con leche y pastel, ¿cuál es para él y cuál es para ella?
4. ¿Qué idioma hablan tú y tu familia entre (*among*) Uds.?
5. ¿Quiénes hablan bien de ti? (¿mal?)
6. ¿Quieres ir al restaurante conmigo hoy?

Entre nosotros

¡Conversemos!

Detalles culturales

En la mayoría de los países de habla hispana, el desayuno generalmente es café con leche y pan con mantequilla. El almuerzo (*lunch*), que es la comida principal del día, se sirve entre la una y las dos de la tarde; la cena generalmente no se sirve antes de las ocho o las nueve de la noche. La mayoría de los restaurantes no empiezan a servir la cena antes de las nueve de la noche.

◆ **Generalmente, ¿qué se desayuna en este país? ¿A qué hora se empieza a servir la cena en este país?**

Para conocernos mejor

Get to know your partner better by asking each other the following questions. *Answers will vary.*

1. ¿Cuál es el mejor restaurante de esta ciudad? ¿Cuál es la especialidad de la casa?
2. ¿A qué hora empiezan a servir el almuerzo en los restaurantes de tu ciudad?
3. Cuando pagas la cuenta en un restaurante, ¿dejas una buena propina?
4. ¿A qué hora es el almuerzo en tu casa? ¿A qué hora desayunas?
5. ¿Dónde piensas desayunar mañana? ¿Qué vas a desayunar?
6. ¿Prefieres tomar café con crema o café negro?
7. ¿Tú prefieres pollo a la parrilla, cordero asado, hamburguesas o perros calientes?
8. Generalmente, ¿qué comes de postre?
9. ¿Cuándo es el aniversario de bodas de tus padres? ¿Cómo lo celebran?
10. ¿Tu mamá es mayor o menor que tu papá?

Una encuesta

Interview your classmates to identify who fits the following descriptions. Be sure to change the statements to questions. Include your instructor, but remember to use the **Ud.** form when addressing him or her. *Answers will vary.*

	Nombre
1. Es de otro estado.	
2. Es tímido(a).	
3. Es el (la) más inteligente de la familia.	
4. Es tan alto(a) como su padre.	
5. Siempre está cansado(a).	
6. Piensa ir a comer más tarde.	
7. Está leyendo un buen libro.	
8. Comienza a trabajar a las ocho.	
9. Tiene más de un mes de vacaciones.	
10. Tiene un hermano(a) muy travieso(a).	

Y ahora...

Write a brief summary, indicating what you have learned about your classmates. *Answers will vary.*

¿Cómo lo decimos? What would you say in the following situations? What might the other person say? Act out the scenes with a partner.

1. You are at a café having breakfast. You are very hungry. Order a big breakfast.
2. You are having lunch with a friend. Suggest a few things he or she can have to eat and drink.
3. Call a restaurant and make reservations for dinner.
4. You have invited some friends to a party. Tell them it's at your house, and what time it starts.
5. Your friend has suggested having dinner at a restaurant you dislike. Tell him that it's the worst restaurant in town.

Suggestion: You may wish to assign this exercise as homework, and follow up by having students roleplay these situations in class.

Answers: **1.** *Answers will vary.* **2.** *Answers will vary.* **3.** *Answers will vary.* **4.** La fiesta es en mi casa. Empieza a la(s)... **5.** Ése es el peor restaurante del pueblo.

¿Qué pasa aquí? Get together in groups of three or four and create a conversation among some of the people in the picture. They discuss the menu, what they want to order, their preferences, etc. *Answers will vary.*

Para escribir

En un restaurante Following the style of the dialogues in this lesson, write a dialogue describing a dinner in a restaurant you may have had recently. Give as much details as you can. *Answers will vary.*

Un dicho

Donde hay hambre no hay pan duro.

If we tell you that **"pan duro"** refers to bread that's old and hard, what does the saying mean to you? Don't forget to learn all the sayings, and use them when applicable.

Lección 6 ◆ En el mercado

Marta y Ariel son una pareja de recién casados. Ellos son de Honduras, pero hace un mes que viven en Managua, la capital de Nicaragua, en un apartamento que está cerca de la universidad.

Marta No hay nada en el refrigerador, excepto un poco de carne. Tenemos que ir al supermercado.

Ariel ¿Podemos almorzar antes de ir? Yo estoy muerto de hambre.

Marta Bueno, puedes llevarme a comer algo antes...

Más tarde, en el supermercado.

Ariel Necesitamos azúcar, una docena de huevos, mantequilla, papel higiénico, detergente, lejía... ¿qué más? ¿Dónde está la lista?

Marta Yo la tengo. A ver... papas, zanahorias, brócoli, apio, pimientos...

Ariel ¡Caramba! ¡Tantos vegetales! ¿Quién los va a comer?

Marta ¡Tú y yo! Mi mamá dice que debemos comer cuatro vegetales y cuatro frutas al día.

Detalles culturales

En los países hispanos, la gente mayor (*elderly*), especialmente las mujeres que no tienen esposo, generalmente viven en casa de un pariente (*relative*).

◆ **En este país, ¿dónde viven, generalmente, los ancianos y las mujeres mayores que no son casadas?**

Detalles culturales

Muchas familias hispanas tienen criadas. Algunas viven en la casa donde trabajan y se les considera como parte de la familia.

◆ **¿Tiene Ud. criada? ¿Alguien lo (la) ayuda a Ud. con los trabajos de la casa?**

Don José y doña Ada, los padres de Ariel, están en un mercado al aire libre.

Don José	¿Cuánto cuestan las chuletas de cerdo?
Doña Ada	Son un poco caras, pero podemos comprarlas, si tú quieres. ¿Quieres chuletas de cerdo o chuletas de ternera?
Don José	Las dos, y también chuletas de cordero.
Doña Ada	¡No, no! Tienes que elegir una.
Don José	Está bien... elijo las chuletas de cerdo. Después tenemos que ir a la pescadería y a la panadería.
Doña Ada	Sí, pero antes voy a comprar pepinos, tomates y cebollas.
Don José	También necesitamos salsa de tomate porque quiero preparar mis famosos espaguetis con albóndigas.
Doña Ada	Buena idea. Tu hermana vuelve a las seis y puede cenar con nosotros.
Don José	¡Perfecto! La criada tiene el día libre hoy, de modo que yo soy el cocinero.
Doña Ada	¡Y tú cocinas mejor que ella!

¿Recuerda usted?

¿Verdadero o falso?

With a partner, decide whether the following statements about the dialogues are true (**verdadero**) or false (**falso**).

1. Marta dice que hay muchas cosas en el refrigerador. ☐ V ☒ F
2. Ariel no tiene hambre. ☐ V ☒ F
3. Marta tiene la lista de lo que necesitan comprar. ☒ V ☐ F
4. Marta quiere comprar muchos vegetales. ☒ V ☐ F
5. Don José es el suegro de Marta. ☒ V ☐ F
6. Don José quiere comprar tres tipos de chuletas. ☒ V ☐ F
7. Don José no piensa comprar pan. ☐ V ☒ F
8. Don José no sabe cocinar. ☐ V ☒ F

Y ahora... conteste

Answer these questions, basing your answers on the dialogue.

1. ¿De dónde son Marta y Ariel y dónde viven ahora?
2. ¿Qué quiere hacer Ariel antes de ir al supermercado?
3. ¿Qué van a comprar Ariel y Marta para lavar la ropa?
4. ¿Qué dice la mamá de Marta?
5. ¿Dónde están los padres de Ariel?
6. ¿Las chuletas de cerdo son baratas o son caras?
7. ¿Qué chuletas elige don José?
8. ¿Por qué va a cocinar don José hoy?

Answers: **1.** Son de Honduras y ahora viven en Managua, la capital de Nicaragua. **2.** Ariel quiere almorzar. **3.** Van a comprar detergente y lejía. **4.** Dice que deben comer cuatro vegetatales y cuatro frutas al día. **5.** Están en un mercado al aire libre. **6.** Son un poco caras. **7.** Elige las chuletas de cerdo. **8.** Porque la criada tiene el día libre.

Para hablar del tema: Vocabulario

Online Study Center

For more practice with lesson topics, see the related activities on the *¡Hola, amigos!* web site at college.hmco.com/PIC/holaamigos7e.

Cognados

el apartamento*
el brócoli
el detergente
la docena
los espaguetis
excepto
famoso(a)
la salsa

Nombres

el apio celery
la albóndiga meatball
el azúcar sugar
la carne meat
la chuleta chop
——— **de cerdo** pork chop
——— **de ternera** veal chop
el (la) cocinero(a) cook
el (la) criado(a) servant
la lejía bleach
el mercado market
——— **al aire libre** outdoor market
la panadería bakery
el papel higiénico toilet paper
el pepino cucumber
la pescadería fish market
el pimiento, el ají pepper
el supermercado supermarket
la zanahoria carrot

Suggestion: You may want to teach **confitería** and contrast it with **panadería.**

You may want to develop word families of related places of business and occupations:

confitería → **confitero;**
panadería → **panadero;**
lechería → **lechero;**
carnicería → **carnicero, etc.**

Verbos

almorzar (o>ue) to have lunch
cocinar to cook
comprar to buy
costar (o>ue) to cost
decir (e>i) to say, to tell
elegir (e>i), escoger to choose
poder (o>ue) to be able to, can
volver (o>ue) to return, to go (come back)

Adjetivos

caro(a) expensive
tantos(as) so many

Otras palabras y expresiones

a ver let's see
al día a day
antes (de) before
cerca (de) near, close
de modo (manera) que so
don a title of respect, used with a man's first name
doña a title of respect, used with a lady's first name
está bien all right, o.k.
estar muerto de hambre to be starving
libre off
nada nothing
qué más what else
los recién casados newlyweds
un poco (de) a little

Amplíe su vocabulario

Más comestibles

Additional vocabulary: habichuelas, judías verdes, guisantes, champiñones, frijoles.

De país a país

el apartamento el departamento (*Méx., Arg.*)
el piso (*Esp.*)
el aguacate la palta (*Arg.*)
el plátano la banana (*Cono Sur*)
la fresa la frutilla (*Cono Sur*)
el melocotón el durazno (*Méx., Cono Sur*)
la sandía el melón de agua (*Cuba, Puerto Rico*)
la patilla (*Col., Puerto Rico, R. Dom., Ven.*)

Para practicar el vocabulario

A. Preguntas y respuestas Match the questions in column *A* with the corresponding responses in column *B*.

Answers: 1. i 2. l 3. f 4. a 5. k 6. d 7. b 8. j 9. e 10. g 11. c 12. h

A	B
1. ¿Quieres comer algo?	**a.** Sí, necesito lejía y detergente.
2. ¿Son novios?	**b.** Al supermercado.
3. ¿Necesitas huevos?	**c.** En el baño.
4. ¿Vas a lavar la ropa?	**d.** La criada.
5. ¿Quieres chuletas de cerdo?	**e.** Cerca de la universidad.
6. ¿Quién va a cocinar?	**f.** Sí, una docena.
7. ¿Adónde vamos?	**g.** No, yo no como carne.
8. ¿Tienes que trabajar?	**h.** Que vuelve a las dos.
9. ¿Dónde está el apartamento?	**i.** Sí, estoy muerto de hambre.
10. ¿Quieres albóndigas?	**j.** No, tengo el día libre.
11. ¿Dónde está el papel higiénico?	**k.** No, de ternera.
12. ¿Qué dice Ariel?	**l.** No, son recién casados.

B. Dime... You and a partner take turns interviewing each other, using the following questions. *Answers will vary.*

Suggestion: Use a transparency to introduce some of the stores listed below. Ask students to write their grocery shopping list for the dinner they are going to give. Tell them to include the quantity (**una libra (pound)**, **½ libra**, **dos latas**, etc.) and the type of shop where each item can be purchased.

carnicería, frutería, verdulería, panadería, lechería, heladería, pastelería, dulcería

1. ¿Vives en una casa o en un apartamento?
2. ¿Vives cerca de la universidad? ¿Vives solo?
3. ¿Sabes cocinar? ¿Te gusta hacerlo?
4. En el desayuno, ¿tomas el café solo o con azúcar?
5. ¿Te gusta más comer carne o pescado?
6. ¿Comes mariscos? ¿Cuál prefieres?
7. ¿Qué frutas te gustan más?
8. ¿Prefieres comprar en un mercado al aire libre o en un supermercado? ¿Por qué?

C. ¿Qué les servimos? You and your partner have several guests. Discuss what you are going to serve them based on their likes and dislikes.

Possible answers: **1.** Le servimos helado de fresas o de vainilla. **2.** Le servimos chuleta de ternera. **3.** Les servimos espaguetis. **4.** Les servimos gambas, langosta o cangrejo. **5.** Le servimos piña, aguacate, etc. **6.** Le servimos pastel de cerezas. **7.** Le servimos frutas y vegetales. **8.** Le servimos pollo y vegetales. **9.** Le servimos una hamburguesa o un perro caliente.

1. A Marisa le gusta mucho el helado, pero no le gusta el chocolate.
2. A Raúl le gustan las chuletas, pero no come carne de cerdo.
3. A Sergio y a Daniel les gusta la comida italiana.
4. A Mirta y a Silvia les gustan los mariscos.
5. Raúl prefiere las frutas tropicales.
6. Mirta quiere comer pastel.
7. Alicia es vegetariana.
8. Raquel está a dieta (*on a diet*).
9. A Marisa le gusta mucho la comida típica americana.

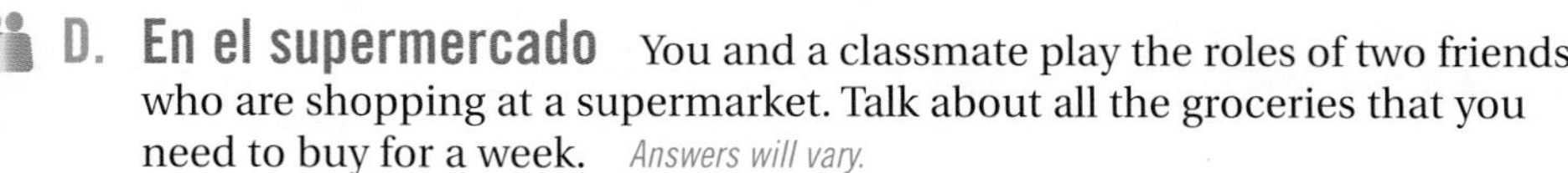

D. En el supermercado You and a classmate play the roles of two friends who are shopping at a supermarket. Talk about all the groceries that you need to buy for a week. *Answers will vary.*

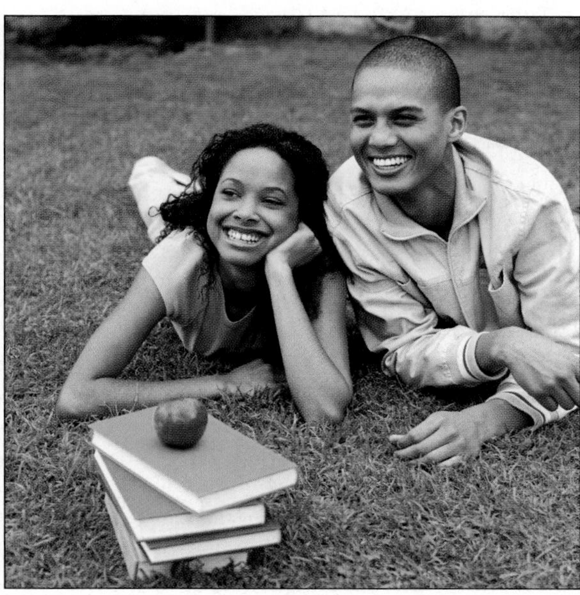

Eva va a comer una manzana mientras (*while*) descansa. ¿Qué frutas cree Ud. que va a comer Julio?

Pronunciación

Las consonantes *ll*, *ñ*

A. Practice the sound of Spanish **ll** in the following words.

llegar	cebo**ll**a	si**ll**a
llamar	A**ll**ende	a**ll**í
ca**ll**e	e**ll**os	mantequi**ll**a

B. Practice the sound of Spanish **ñ** in the following words.

se**ñ**or	se**ñ**ora	ni**ñ**o
a**ñ**o	oto**ñ**o	Pe**ñ**a
espa**ñ**ol	ma**ñ**ana	Espa**ñ**a

Extra practice: Ella llega a la ventanilla de sellos. / La Srta. Muñoz le da una muñeca a la niña.

Puntos para recordar

1. Stem-changing verbs: *o > ue* (*Verbos que cambian en la raíz:* o > ue)

- As you learned in **Lección 5,** some Spanish verbs undergo a stem change in the present indicative tense. When **o** is the last stem vowel and it is stressed, it changes to **ue,** as shown below.

poder (*to be able to*)			
yo	p**ue**do	nosotros(as)	podemos
tú	p**ue**des	vosotros(as)	podéis
Ud. / él / ella	p**ue**de	Uds. / ellos / ellas	p**ue**den

- Note that the stem vowel is not stressed in the verb forms used with **nosotros(as)** and **vosotros(as);** therefore, the **o** does not change to **ue.**

Some other verbs that undergo the **o > ue** changes:[1]

almorzar **costar** **dormir** (*to sleep*) **encontrar** **recordar** **volver**

—¿A qué hora **pueden** Uds. ir a la panadería?
—**Podemos** ir a las dos.

*"What time **can you** go to the bakery?"*
*"**We can** go at two o'clock."*

—¿A qué hora **vuelves** tú del mercado?
—**Vuelvo** a las tres.

*"At what time **do you return** from the market?"*
*"**I return** at three o'clock."*

Detalles culturales

Hoy los supermercados son muy populares en los países de habla hispana, pero todavía es costumbre (*custom*) comprar uno o dos productos en pequeñas tiendas especializadas: panaderías, pescaderías, fruterías, etc.

- **¿Hay tiendas especializadas en este país?**

[1]For a complete list of stem-changing verbs, see Appendix B.

Práctica y conversación

Online Study Center

For more practice with lesson topics, see the related activities on the ***¡Hola, amigos!*** web site at college.hmco.com/PIC/holaamigos7e.

A. Minidiálogos Complete the following exchanges appropriately, using the present indicative of the verbs given. Then act them out with a partner.

1. —¿A qué hora almuerzan (almorzar) Uds.?
   —Nosotros almorzamos (almorzar) a las dos y volvemos (volver) a casa a las cuatro. ¿A qué hora vuelves (volver) tú?
   —Yo vuelvo (volver) a las cinco.
2. —¿Ud. puede (poder) ir conmigo al supermercado?
   —Sí, yo puedo (poder) ir contigo esta tarde.
   —¿Ud. sabe cuánto cuesta (costar) el detergente?
   —No, no sé.
3. —Jorge no encuentra (encontrar) el número de teléfono de Nora. ¿Tú lo sabes?
   —No, no lo recuerdo (recordar), pero puedo (poder) buscarlo (*look it up*).
4. —¿Dónde duermen (dormir) los niños?
   —En mi cuarto; yo duermo (dormir) en el sofá de la sala.

B. Entreviste a su compañero(a) Interview a partner, using the following questions. *Answers will vary.*

1. ¿Puedes ir al mercado conmigo?
2. ¿Qué cuesta más, el pollo o el pescado?
3. ¿Sabes cuánto cuestan los camarones?
4. ¿Dónde puedo comprar frutas?
5. ¿A qué hora almuerzas tú? ¿Dónde?
6. ¿A qué hora vuelves a tu casa hoy?
7. ¿Recuerdas el número de teléfono de todos tus amigos?
8. Generalmente, ¿cuántas horas duermes? ¿Duermes bien?

2. Stem-changing verbs: *e > i* (*Verbos que cambian en la raíz:* e > i)

- Some **-ir** verbs undergo a stem change in the present indicative. For these verbs, when **e** is the last stem vowel and it is stressed, it changes to **i** as shown below.

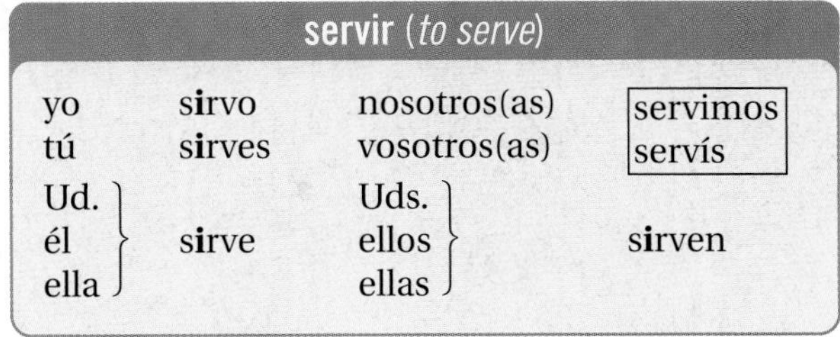

servir (*to serve*)			
yo	sirvo	nosotros(as)	servimos
tú	sirves	vosotros(as)	servís
Ud. / él / ella	sirve	Uds. / ellos / ellas	sirven

- Note that the stem vowel is not stressed in the verb forms used with **nosotros(as)** and **vosotros(as);** therefore, the **e** does not change to **i.**

Some other verbs that undergo the **e > i** change:

decir[1] (*to say, to tell*)
conseguir[2]
pedir[3]
seguir (*to follow, to continue*)

—¿A qué hora **sirven** Uds. el almuerzo?	*"What time **do you serve** lunch?"*
—**Servimos** el almuerzo a las doce.	*"**We serve** lunch at twelve o'clock."*
—¿Dónde **consigues** libros en español?	*"Where **do you get** books in Spanish?"*
—**Consigo** libros en la biblioteca.	*"**I get** books at the library."*

Práctica y conversación

Online Study Center

For more practice with lesson topics, see the related activities on the *¡Hola, amigos!* web site at college.hmco.com/PIC/holaamigos7e.

A. Minidiálogos Complete the following exchanges, using the present indicative of the appropriate verb from the list. Then act them out with a partner.

servir **pedir** **conseguir** **decir** **seguir**

1. —Yo nunca (*never*) ___consigo___ carne buena.
   —Mis padres ___consiguen___ carne muy buena en el Mercado Central.
2. —¿Marta y Ariel ___siguen___ viviendo en Managua?
   —Sí, ellos ___dicen___ que es una ciudad muy bonita.
3. —¿Qué ___sirven___ Uds. en sus fiestas?
   —Nosotros ___servimos___ hamburguesas y perros calientes.
4. —¿Qué ___pides___ tú cuando vas a ese restaurante?
   —Yo ___pido___ bistec con langosta.
   —Yo siempre ___digo___ que en ese restaurante (ellos) ___sirven___ los mejores mariscos.

B. Entreviste a su compañero(a) Interview a partner, using the following questions. *Answers will vary.*

1. Cuando vas a un restaurante mexicano, ¿qué pides para comer? ¿Qué eliges para beber?
2. ¿La comida mexicana es mejor que la italiana? ¿Qué dices tú?
3. ¿Dónde consigues mariscos frescos (*fresh*)?
4. ¿Qué sirves tú en tus fiestas para comer? ¿Y para beber?
5. Cuando tú y tus amigos dan una fiesta, ¿sirven cerveza o refrescos?
6. ¿Tú consigues discos en español? ¿Dónde?

---

[1]First person: **yo digo.**
[2]Verbs like **conseguir** drop the **u** before **a** or **o: yo consigo.**
[3]**Pedir** also means *to order* (at a restaurant).

3. Direct object pronouns (*Pronombres usados como complemento directo*)

- In addition to a subject, most sentences have an object[1] that directly receives the action of the verbs.

  Él compra **el café.** — *He buys **the coffee.***
  s. v. d.o.

  In the preceding sentence, the subject **él** performs the action, while **el café,** the direct object, directly receives the action of the verb. (The direct object of a sentence can be either a person or a thing.)

  The direct object can be easily identified as the answer to the questions *whom?* and *what?*

  Él compra **el café.** — (***What*** *is he buying?*)
  s. v. d.o.

  Alicia llama **a Luis.** — (***Whom*** *is she calling?*)
  s. v. d.o.

Extra practice: To practice direct object pronouns, pass out different objects to various students (a book, keys, a pen, pencils, etc.). Then ask, for example: **¿Quién tiene mi libro?** to elicit **Yo *lo* tengo.** Go to one who doesn't have it and ask: **¿Tú tienes mi libro? ¿Tú *lo* tienes?** to practice pronoun position in negative sentences.

- Direct object pronouns are used in place of direct objects. The forms of the direct object pronouns are as follows.

Singular		Plural	
me	me	**nos**	us
te	you (*fam.*)	**os**	you (*fam.*)
lo	him, you (*masc. form.*), it (*masc.*)	**los**	them (*masc.*), you (*masc. form. / fam.*)
la	her, you (*fem. form.*), it (*fem.*)	**las**	them (*fem.*), you (*fem. form. / fam.*)

Yo tengo **las sillas.** ¿Ustedes **las** necesitan?

*I have the **chairs.*** *Do you need **them**?*

- Position of direct object pronouns
  - In Spanish, object pronouns are normally placed before a conjugated verb.

    Yo compro **el café.** — *I buy **the coffee.***
    Yo **lo** compro. — *I buy **it.***

  - In a negative sentence, **no** must precede the object pronoun.

    Yo compro **el café.** — *I buy **the coffee.***
    Yo **lo** compro. — *I buy **it.***
    Yo **no lo** compro. — *I **don't** buy **it.***

Expansion: You may need to explain that the grammar examples use the direct object pronouns **la** because **silla** is feminine and **lo** because **café** is masculine.

[1]See Appendix C.

Suggestion: You may want to point out that **a Ud. (Uds.)** may be added for clarity or for courtesy: **Lo voy a visitar a Ud. / Voy a visitarlo a Ud.**

◆ When a conjugated verb and an infinitive appear together, the direct object pronoun is either placed before the conjugated verb or attached to the infinitive. This is also the case in a negative sentence.

La voy a llamar. Voy a llamar**la.**	}	*I'm going to call* ***her.***
No **la** voy a llamar. No voy a llamar**la.**	}	*I'm not going to call* ***her.***

◆ In the present progressive, the direct object pronoun can be placed either before the verb **estar** or after the present participle.[1]

Lo está leyendo. Está leyendo**lo.**	}	*He's reading* ***it.***

¡Atención! Note the use of the written accent on present participles that have pronouns attached: **está leyéndolo, estamos mirándola.**

Online Study Center

For more practice with lesson topics, see the related activities on the ***¡Hola, amigos!*** web site at college.hmco.com/PIC/holaamigos7e.

Práctica y conversación

A. Minidiálogos Complete the following exchanges supplying the missing direct object pronouns. Then act them out with a partner.

1. —¿Tú tienes la lejía?
   —No, yo no __la__ tengo. ¿Quién tiene el detergente?
   —Julián __lo__ tiene.
2. —¿A qué hora cierran el supermercado?
   —__Lo__ cierran a las diez. ¿Tú vas a comprar las frutas?
   —Sí, __las__ voy a comprar esta noche.
3. —Ariel, ¿Carlos __te__ va a llevar a ti o a mí?
   —__Me__ va a llevar a mí.
4. —¿Tú conoces a los hermanos de Marta?
   —No, yo no __los__ conozco.
5. —¿Ellos __los__ invitan a Uds. a sus fiestas?
   —Sí, siempre __nos__ invitan.

Detalles culturales

La mayoría de los pueblos hispanos tienen un mercado central, con pequeñas tiendas. Mucha gente compra en estos mercados donde los precios generalmente son más bajos y los clientes pueden regatear (*bargain*) con los vendedores (*merchants*).

◆ **¿Es costumbre regatear aquí o los precios son fijos?**

[1] *Present participle* is **gerundio** (**-ando** and **-iendo** forms) in Spanish.

B. Susana dice que sí

Susana has a car and her teacher and her friends often need rides. Susana always says yes. What does she say to the following people?

1. *Ana* —¿Puedes llevarme a casa?
2. *Raúl y Jorge* —¿Puedes llevarnos a la biblioteca?
3. *Profesora* —¿Puedes llevarme a mi apartamento?
4. *Teresa* —¿Puedes llevar a Rosa y a Carmen a casa?
5. *Sergio* —¿Puedes llevar a Pedro y a Luis al restaurante?
6. *Marta y Raquel* —¿Puedes llevarnos al Mercado Central?

Answers: **1.** Sí, puedo llevarte. (Sí, te puedo llevar.) **2.** Sí, puedo llevarlos (los puedo llevar). **3.** Sí, puedo llevarla (la puedo llevar). **4.** Sí, puedo llevarlas (las puedo llevar). **5.** Sí, puedo llevarlos (los puedo llevar). **6.** Sí, puedo llevarlas (las puedo llevar).

C. ¿Qué hacemos?

Use the appropriate direct object pronouns to say what we do with respect to the following people or things.

◆ **MODELO:** el café
Lo bebemos.

1. las cartas (*letters*)
2. las frutas
3. el pan
4. el coctel de camarones
5. los libros
6. la ensalada
7. el taxi
8. dos chicas (dos muchachos)

Possible answers: **1.** Las escribimos. **2.** Las compramos. **3.** Lo pedimos. **4.** Lo servimos. **5.** Los leemos. **6.** La preparamos. **7.** Lo tomamos. **8.** Las (Los) llamamos.

D. Planes

You and your friends Gustavo and Jaime are making plans to go out for the evening. Answer Gustavo's questions, using direct object pronouns and the cues provided.

1. ¿A qué hora me llamas? (a las cinco)
2. ¿Adónde nos llevas? (a un restaurante)
3. ¿Recuerdas el número de teléfono de Jaime? (no)
4. ¿Tienes tu licencia para conducir (*driver's license*)? (sí)
5. ¿Cuándo vas a llamar a Teresa y a Susana? (más tarde)
6. ¿El novio de Teresa los conoce a Uds.? (no)

Answers: **1.** Te llamo a las cinco. **2.** Los llevo a un restaurante. **3.** No, no lo recuerdo. **4.** Sí, la tengo. **5.** Voy a llamarlas (Las voy a llamar) más tarde. **6.** No, no nos conoce.

E. Necesitamos información With a partner, take turns answering the following questions, basing your answers on the illustrations. Use direct object pronouns in your responses.

1. ¿A qué hora llama Sara a Luis?
2. ¿Cuándo tiene que llamar Luis a Sara?
3. ¿Pepe puede llevar a los chicos a casa?
4. ¿Dónde tiene Pepe los libros?

Answers: **1.** Lo llama a las ocho y media. **2.** La tiene que llamar mañana. **3.** No, no los puede llevar. **4.** Los tiene en la mesa. **5.** Esteban lo sirve. **6.** Juan lo bebe. **7.** Eva las tiene. **8.** Paco la abre.

5. ¿Quién sirve el café?
6. ¿Quién bebe el refresco?

7. ¿Quién tiene las cartas?
8. ¿Quién abre la puerta?

4. Affirmative and negative expressions (*Expresiones afirmativas y negativas*)

Suggestion: You may want to add **a algún lado** (*somewhere, anywhere*) and **a ningún lado** (*nowhere*).

Affirmative		Negative	
algo	something, anything	**nada**	nothing
alguien	someone, anyone	**nadie**	nobody, no one
algún / **alguno(a)** / **algunos(as)**	any, some	**ningún** / **ninguno(a)**	none, not any; no one, nobody
siempre	always	**nunca** / **jamás**	never
alguna vez	ever		
algunas veces, a veces	sometimes		
también	also, too	**tampoco**	neither
o... o	either . . . or	**ni... ni**	neither . . . nor

—¿Uds. **siempre** van a Tegucigalpa? *"Do you **always** go to Tegucigalpa?"*
—No, **nunca** vamos. *"No, we **never** go."*
—Nosotros **tampoco.** *"**Neither** do we."*

—¿Conoces a **alguien** de Honduras? *"Do you know **anyone** from Honduras?"*
—No, no conozco a **nadie** de Honduras. *"No, I don't know **anyone** from Honduras."*

- **Alguno** and **ninguno** drop the final **-o** before a masculine singular noun, but **alguna** and **ninguna** keep the final **-a.**

Expansion: After explaining that the **-o** in **alguno** and **ninguno** is dropped, you may mention other words that follow the same rule: **uno, primero, tercero, bueno, malo.**

—¿Hay **algún** libro o **alguna** pluma en la mesa? *"Is there **any** book or pen on the table?"*
—No, no hay **ningún** libro ni **ninguna** pluma. *"No, there is **no** book or pen."*

- **Alguno(a)** can be used in the plural form, but **ninguno(a)** is used only in the singular.

—¿Necesita mandar **algunas** cartas? *"Do you need to send **some** letters?"*
—No, no necesito mandar **ninguna** carta. *"No, I don't need to send **any** letters."*

Suggestion: To emphasize the use of the double negative in Spanish, contrast these translations of the English sentence *He (She) doesn't want anything.*
No quiere algo. (incorrect)
No quiere nada. (correct)

- Spanish sentences frequently use a double negative. In this construction, the adverb **no** is placed before the verb. The second negative word either follows the verb or appears at the end of the sentence. **No** is never used, however, if the negative word precedes the verb.

—¿Habla Ud. francés siempre? —No, yo **no** hablo francés **nunca.**	*"Do you always speak French?"* *"No, I **never** speak French."*

or:

—No, yo **nunca** hablo francés.

—¿Compra Ud. **algo** aquí? —No, **no** compro **nada nunca.**	*"Do you buy **anything** here?"* *"No, I **never** buy **anything.**"*

or:

—No, yo **nunca** compro **nada.**

- In fact, Spanish often uses several negatives in one sentence.

Yo **nunca** pido **nada tampoco.** — *I **never** ask for **anything either.***

Expansion: Have students work in pairs and write a list of complaints frequently expressed by their peers. Remind them to use the negative expressions they just learned as frequently as possible in their statements.

Nunca podemos comer nada en la biblioteca.

Online Study Center

For more practice with lesson topics, see the related activities on the *¡Hola, amigos!* web site at college.hmco.com/PIC/holaamigos7e.

Práctica y conversación

A. No estoy de acuerdo (*I don't agree*) Contradict the following statements by saying that just the opposite is true.

- MODELO: Eva quiere comer algo.
  *Eva **no** quiere comer **nada.***

1. Jorge siempre va a ese mercado al aire libre.
2. Ellos tienen algunas verduras.
3. Ana siempre come langosta o cangrejo.
4. Pedro siempre va a ese restaurante y Eva también va.
5. Ella quiere hablar con alguien.

Answers: 1. Jorge nunca va a ese mercado al aire libre. 2. Ellos no tienen ninguna verdura. 3. Ana nunca come ni langosta ni cangrejo. 4. Pedro nunca va a ese restaurante y Eva tampoco va. 5. Ella no quiere hablar con nadie.

6. Luis tiene algunas amigas españolas.
7. Paco siempre compra algo.
8. Ella nunca habla con nadie.

6. Luis no tiene ninguna amiga española. 7. Paco nunca compra nada. 8. Ella siempre habla con alguien.

B. Entreviste a su compañero(a) Interview a partner, using the following questions. *Answers will vary.*

1. ¿Vas al mercado por la mañana a veces?
2. En el mercado, ¿siempre compras mariscos?
3. ¿Siempre llevas dinero contigo?
4. ¿Necesitas comprar algo en la panadería?
5. Yo nunca voy a la pescadería los domingos. ¿Y tú?
6. ¿Comes algunas frutas tropicales?
7. ¿Alguien va contigo al mercado?
8. ¿Tú comes pan tostado o panqueques por la mañana?

Extra practice: Have students follow up with a reporting phase so students also practice other forms: **nosotros(as), ellos(as),** and so on. Alternatively, for written practice, students can organize their answers into a brief paragraph.

C. Queremos saber... With a partner, prepare five affirmative and five negative questions to ask your instructor. *Answers will vary.*

D. Siempre... a veces... nunca... In groups of three, tell your classmates two things you always do, two things you sometimes do, and two things you never do. *Answers will vary.*

Follow up: Have students report the more interesting or amusing findings to the class.

5. *Hace... que*

- To express how long something has been going on, Spanish uses the following formula.

Suggestion: Have students prepare 3–4 questions to ask each other, using **¿Cuánto tiempo hace que...?**

> **Hace** + length of time + **que** + verb (*in the present tense*)
> **Hace** dos años **que** vivo aquí.
> *I have been living here for two years.*

—Oye, ¿dónde está Eva?	*"Listen, where is Eva?"*
—No sé. **Hace dos días que no viene** a clase.	*"I don't know. **She hasn't come** to class **for two days.**"*

- The following construction is used to ask how long something has been going on.

> **¿Cuánto tiempo hace que** + verb (*present tense*)?[1]

—**¿Cuánto tiempo hace que ella trabaja** aquí?	***"How long has she been working** here?"*
—**Hace una semana que trabaja** aquí.	***"She has been working** here **for a week.**"*

[1]Note that English uses the present perfect progressive or the present perfect tense to express the same concept.

Online Study Center

For more practice with lesson topics, see the related activities on the *¡Hola, amigos!* web site at college.hmco.com/PIC/holaamigos7e.

Práctica y conversación

A. ¿Cuánto tiempo hace? In complete sentences, tell how long each action depicted below has been going on. Use **hace... que** and the length of time specified.

1. veinte minutos

2. tres años

3. una hora

4. dos horas

5. seis meses

6. cinco días

Answers: 1. Hace veinte minutos que Marta y Alfredo bailan. 2. Hace tres años que Elisa vive en la calle Lima. 3. Hace una hora que ellos hablan (conversan). 4. Hace dos horas que José estudia. 5. Hace seis meses que Elena trabaja en el Banco Nacional. 6. Hace cinco días que Raquel está en el hospital.

 B. **Entreviste a su compañero(a)** Interview one of your classmates and then report to the class. *Answers will vary.*

Suggestion: Encourage students to say something about each person, such as where he/she lives.

1. ¿Cuánto tiempo hace que vives en esta ciudad?
2. ¿Cuánto tiempo hace que estudias en esta universidad?
3. ¿Cuánto tiempo hace que trabajas en esta ciudad?
4. ¿Cuánto tiempo hace que no comes?
5. ¿Cuánto tiempo hace que no ves a tus abuelos?
6. ¿Cuánto tiempo hace que no hablas con tus padres?
7. ¿Cuánto tiempo hace que no vas a la biblioteca?
8. ¿Cuánto tiempo hace que hablas español?

 C. **¿Dónde están?** In groups of three or four, mention three or four friends and relatives that you haven't seen for a while. *Answers will vary.*

◆ **MODELO:** *Hace dos años que no veo a mi prima Eva.*

Ésta es una reunión familiar, pero el abuelo no está aquí. ¿Cuánto tiempo hace que no lo ven?

Entre nosotros

¡Conversemos!

Para conocernos mejor Get to know your partner better by asking each other the following questions. *Answers will vary.*

1. ¿A qué hora almuerzas? ¿Con quién?
2. ¿Prefieres la comida italiana, la comida china o la comida mexicana?
3. ¿Qué prefieres: la ternera, la carne de cerdo o el pollo?
4. ¿Qué vegetales comes? ¿Cuáles no comes?
5. ¿Tú desayunas en tu casa o en la cafetería?
6. Generalmente, ¿qué días vas al mercado?
7. ¿Qué marca (*brand*) de detergente usas para lavar la ropa? ¿Usas lejía también?
8. Cuando das una fiesta, ¿sirves bebidas alcohólicas?
9. ¿Cuánto tiempo hace que vives en la misma (*same*) ciudad?
10. ¿Hay alguien en tu casa ahora?
11. ¿Tus amigos te llaman por teléfono todos los días?
12. ¿Tú puedes llamarme esta tarde?

Una encuesta Interview your classmates to identify who fits the following descriptions. Include your instructor, but remember to use the **Ud.** form when addressing him or her. *Answers will vary.*

	Nombre
1. Conoce a una pareja de recién casados.	
2. Vive cerca de la universidad.	
3. Tiene el día libre mañana.	
4. Está muerto(a) de hambre.	
5. Come cuatro vegetales y cuatro frutas al día.	
6. A veces va a la pescadería.	
7. Sabe preparar espaguetis con albóndigas.	
8. Es buen(a) cocinero(a).	
9. Cocina mejor que su madre.	
10. No bebe ni vino ni cerveza.	

Y ahora... Write a brief summary indicating what you have learned about your classmates. *Answers will vary.*

¿Cómo lo decimos? What would you say in the following situations? What might the other person say? Act out the scenes with a partner. *Answers will vary.*

Suggestion: Have students prepare this activity before class to do in pairs orally during class.

1. You are telling a friend that you need many things from the supermarket. Tell him or her what they are.
2. You are at an outdoor market in Managua and you need vegetables, fish, meat, and bread. You inquire about prices and so on.
3. You are telling someone what ingredients you need to make vegetable soup.
4. You tell someone what you serve to eat and to drink when you give a party.
5. You tell a friend what fruits you need to prepare a fruit salad (**ensalada de frutas**).

¿Qué pasa aquí? Working with classmates in groups of three or four, describe what is happening in the picture. Create a story, naming the characters and explaining who is who, and what these people plan to buy. Each group will compare its story with the rest of the class. *Answers will vary.*

Expansion: Students can individually write up their group's story for additional practice.

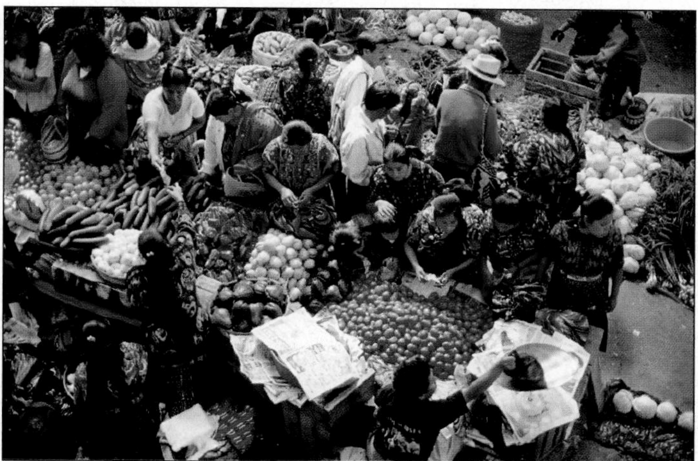

Para escribir

Un invitado importante Imagine that next Saturday you are hosting a very important guest. Who is the guest? What are you going to do to prepare for the occasion? What housework do you have to do? What do you need to buy and prepare for dinner? What else are you going to do in honor of your guest's arrival? *Answers will vary.*

Un proverbio

No sólo de pan vive el hombre.

You have probably heard this proverb before. Do you know where it comes from? What does it mean to you? Memorize it!

Lectura

Reading strategy: Point out to students that looking at titles, subtitles, and visuals before they read will help orient them to the topic of a reading.

Estrategia de lectura Look at the **Sección Gastronómica** of this paper. Based on the headline, what do you think the reading is about? What do you already know about the topic? Make a list in Spanish of key words that might appear in the reading. *Answers will vary.*

Vamos a leer As you read this section of the paper, find the answers to the questions that follow.

Sección gastronómica

por Juan Carlos Miró

Si Ud. quiere celebrar un cumpleaños o un aniversario en un ambiente elegante, visite el restaurante Miramar, donde va a encontrar sabrosísimos platos típicos e internacionales.

Si le gusta el pescado, yo recomiendo el salmón a la parrilla; si prefiere comer mariscos, pida la langosta Termidor. Además de pescados y mariscos, el restaurante ofrece una gran variedad de carnes, entre otras: bistec, pollo y chuletas preparadas por el conocido chef Antonio.

La lista de postres es muy variada y todos son excelentes, pero si tengo que elegir uno, pido la torta de fresas con crema chantilly.

En cuanto a los vinos, puede escoger entre los mejores de Chile, España y California.

¡Nos vemos en el restaurante Miramar!

Suggestion: Brainstorm items with students. Also, point out to students that using their back-ground knowledge of a topic will give them a frame of reference and help them to understand more of what they read.

1. ¿Cómo es el ambiente del restaurante Miramar?
2. ¿Qué tipos de platos va a encontrar en el restaurante?
3. Si Ud. quiere comer pescado o mariscos, ¿qué recomienda Miró?

Video

4. ¿Qué carnes ofrece el restaurante, entre otras?
5. ¿Quién es Antonio?
6. ¿Cuál es el postre favorito de Miró?
7. ¿Qué vinos tienen en el restaurante?

Answers: 1. Es un ambiente elegante. 2. Va a encontrar sabrosísimos platos típicos e internacionales. 3. Miró recomienda el salmón a la parrilla y la langosta Termidor. 4. El restaurante ofrece bistec, chuletas y pollo. 5. Antonio es el chef del restaurante. 6. El postre favorito de Miró es la torta de fresas con crema chantilly. 7. Tiene los mejores vinos de Chile, España y California.

Díganos Answer the following questions based on your own thoughts and experiences. *Answers will vary.*

1. ¿Cuál es su restaurante favorito? ¿Cuál es su especialidad?
2. Si Ud. va a un restaurante que tiene un menú similar del restaurante Miramar, ¿qué pide?
3. ¿Cuál es su postre favorito?
4. ¿De dónde cree Ud. que vienen los mejores vinos?
5. Si Ud. va a celebrar su cumpleaños, ¿prefiere ir a un restaurante o celebrarlo en su casa?

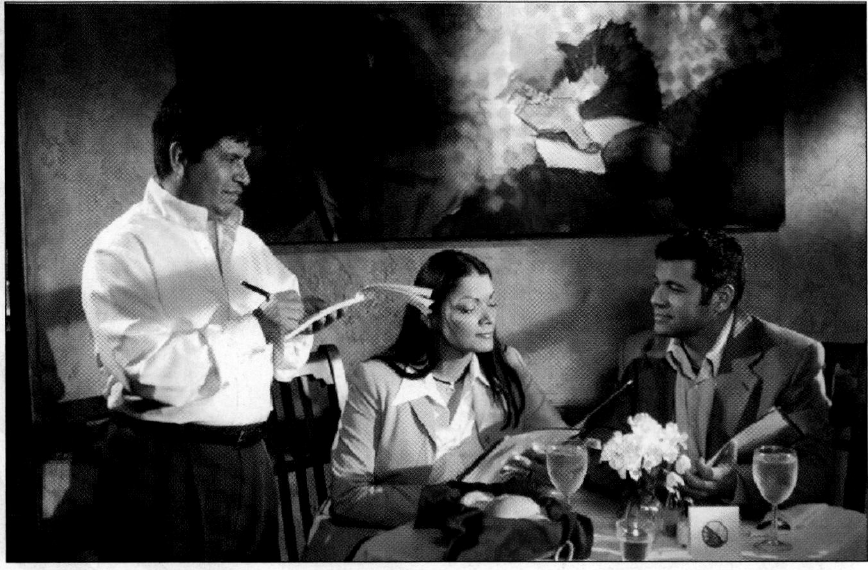

Esta pareja de recién casados está en un restaurante. ¿Qué comidas creen Uds. que hay en el menú?

Marisa en la cocina

Marisa está preparando una cena para el cumpleaños de Pablo. No tiene los ingredientes necesarios para el guiso (*stew*), y usa otros, con el resultado que podemos imaginar.

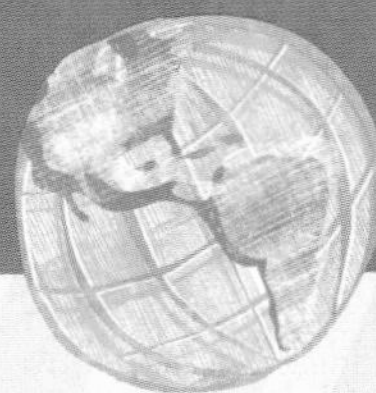

El mundo hispánico

Costa Rica

- Costa Rica es uno de los países más pequeños del continente americano (51.000 km^2—kilómetros cuadrados). Está situado en América Central y su capital es San José. Los productos principales del país son el café, las bananas, el cacao y la caña de azúcar (*sugar cane*).
- La mayoría de los "ticos" (como se les llama a los costarricenses) son católicos y de origen español. De todos los países centroamericanos, Costa Rica es el que tiene el menor número de analfabetos (*illiterates*). Tiene el mayor ingreso (*income*) per cápita y un gobierno democrático con muy pocos problemas políticos.
- En Costa Rica se le da una gran importancia a la educación, la cultura y las artes. Se dice (*It is said*) que en Costa Rica "hay más maestros (*teachers*) que soldados". Este país tiene excelentes programas para proteger la ecología, sobre todo (*especially*) la selva (*rainforest*).

▲ Miles de peregrinos visitan la Basílica de la Virgen de los Ángeles en Cartago, Costa Rica

▲ El Fuerte de Santiago de la Gloria en Portobello, Panamá

Panamá

- Panamá está situado en el istmo (*isthmus*) que une (*joins*) Suramérica con América del Norte. El país, que está dividido por el Canal de Panamá, tiene una superficie de unos 78.000 km^2 y una población de más de dos millones y medio de habitantes. Su cultura es una mezcla (*mixture*) de las tradiciones españolas, africanas, indígenas y norteamericanas. El idioma oficial del país es el español, pero también se usa mucho el inglés.
- La principal fuente de ingresos (*source of income*) del país está asociada con las operaciones del Canal, que es administrado por Panamá desde el año 2000. La construcción del Canal por parte del gobierno de los Estados Unidos duró (*lasted*) diez años y fue terminada en 1914. El Canal mide 82,4 km y tiene tres esclusas (*locks*) a cada lado del istmo que cruza.
- Junto al Canal están las dos ciudades más grandes del país: Ciudad de Panamá, la capital, y Colón, la segunda ciudad más importante del país.

Honduras

- Cuando Colón llegó a la costa de esta región de Centroamérica, sorprendido por la profundidad (*depth*) de las aguas junto a la tierra, llamó al lugar Honduras. Aquí floreció el imperio maya unos 500 años antes de la llegada de los conquistadores. Hoy Honduras, un país pequeño, tiene casi seis millones de habitantes, en su mayoría mestizos.
- Honduras es el único país centroamericano que no tiene volcanes, pero esto no es favorable para el país, pues las tierras volcánicas son, por lo general, fértiles y buenas para la agricultura. Como la economía del país se basa en la agricultura, Honduras es hoy uno de los países más pobres de América.
- La capital de Honduras es Tegucigalpa, que significa "colina de plata" (*silver hill*). La mayor atracción turística del país es Copán, una ciudad maya que existió hace unos dos mil años y de la cual sólo quedan ruinas.

▲ La Iglesia de la Virgen de los Dolores y un puesto de flores en Tegucigalpa, Honduras

Nicaragua

- Nicaragua es el país más extenso de América Central, pero menos de una décima parte de su territorio es cultivable. Nicaragua es la tierra de los lagos y de los volcanes. Uno de los lagos, el Nicaragua, es el mayor lago de agua dulce de Centroamérica, y en él hay tiburones (*sharks*) y otros peces que sólo viven en agua salada en otras regiones.
- Las tres ciudades más importantes del país son Managua, la capital, León y Granada.
- La economía del país se basa en la agricultura, y sus principales productos de exportación son café, algodón (*cotton*), carne de res (*beef*) y madera (*wood*). El país tiene una selva virgen mucho más extensa que la de Costa Rica, pero lamentablemente no está debidamente (*duly*) protegida contra la explotación excesiva.

▲ Vista panorámica de Managua, la capital nicaragüense

Comentarios... With a partner discuss, in Spanish, what impressed you the most about these four countries and compare them to your own. Which places do you want to visit and why?

For more practice with lesson topics, see the related activities on the *¡Hola, amigos!* web site at college.hmco.com/PIC/holaamigos7e.

Tome este examen

Lección 5

Lección 5

A. Present progressive Use the present progressive of the verbs **bailar, comer, dormir, leer,** and **servir** to complete the following sentences. Use each verb once.

1. Nosotros ___estamos sirviendo___ café.
2. Yo ___estoy leyendo___ un libro.
3. Fernando ___está bailando___ en la fiesta.
4. ¿Qué ___estás comiendo___ (tú)? ¿Pollo?
5. Carlos ___está durmiendo___ en su cuarto. (*room*)

B. Uses of *ser* and *estar* Complete each sentence, using the present indicative of **ser** or **estar.**

1. Paco ___es___ de Madrid, pero ahora ___está___ en Panamá.
2. Gabriela ___está___ estudiando italiano. ___Es___ una chica muy inteligente.
3. Las mesas ___son___ de metal.
4. ¡Tú ___estás___ muy bonita hoy!
5. La fiesta ___es___ en el club "Los Violines".
6. Alina ___es___ la novia de Marcos.
7. Nosotros ___estamos___ muy cansados.
8. ___Son___ las cinco de la tarde.
9. Los chicos ___son___ de Costa Rica.
10. Las frutas ___están___ muy sabrosas hoy.

C. Stem-changing verbs (*e* > *ie*) Complete each sentence with the Spanish equivalent of the verb in parentheses.

1. ¿Tú ___prefieres___ pollo o pescado? (*prefer*)
   Ana ___quiere___ bistec. (*wants*)
2. Las clases ___empiezan (comienzan)___ a las seis y terminan a las nueve. (*start*)
3. Nosotros ___pensamos___ estudiar esta noche. No tenemos ganas de ir a la fiesta de Eva. (*plan*)
4. Ellos ___prefieren___ comer aquí. (*prefer*)
5. Ana y yo ___queremos___ venir mañana. (*want*)
6. Yo no ___entiendo___ este menú; está en inglés. (*understand*)

D. Comparative and superlative of adjectives, adverbs, and nouns

Complete these sentences with the Spanish equivalent of the words in parentheses.

1. Mi novio es ___mucho mayor que___ yo. (*much older than*)
2. Mi primo no es ___tan alto como___ mi tío. (*as tall as*)
3. Elsa es ___la más inteligente de___ la familia. (*the most intelligent in*)
4. Yo no bailo ___tan bien como___ tú. (*as well as*)
5. Este hotel es ___el mejor de___ la ciudad. (*the best in*)
6. Clara es ___mucho más bonita que___ su hermana. (*much prettier than*)

E. Pronouns as object of prepositions

Complete each sentence with the Spanish equivalent of the words in parentheses.

1. ¿Tú vas ___conmigo___, Paquito? (*with me*)
   No, no voy ___contigo___, Anita. Voy ___con ellos (ellas)___. (*with you / with them*)
2. ¿Los camarones son ___para ti___, Tito? (*for you*)
   No, no son ___para mí___; son ___para ella___. (*for me / for her*)

F. Vocabulary

Complete the following sentences, using vocabulary from **Lección 5.**

1. Voy a ___pagar___ la cuenta y a dejar una buena ___propina___.
2. Julio quiere ___sopa___ de cebolla y yo ___coctel___ de camarones.
3. Ellos quieren pan ___tostado___ con ___mantequilla___ y ___mermelada___.
4. Yo prefiero el pollo ___asado___, no a la parrilla.
5. La ___especialidad___ de la casa es ___chuletas___ de cordero.
6. De postre quiero ___helado___ de vainilla.
7. Tráiganos ___puré___ de papas y ___ensalada___ de tomates.
8. Andresito no es tímido; es muy ___travieso___.
9. Para desayunar quiero huevos con ___jamón___.
10. ¿Qué deseas comer, una ___hamburguesa___ o un perro ___caliente___?

G. Culture

Circle the correct answer based on the cultural notes you have read.

1. En los países de habla hispana, el café se sirve (después de / durante) la comida.
2. En la mayoría de los países hispanos, el almuerzo es la comida (menos importante / principal) del día.

Answers: 1. después de 2. principal

Lección 5

Lección 6

Lección 6

A. Stem-changing verbs: *o > ue*

Complete each sentence, using one of the following verbs: **costar, encontrar, recordar, poder** (use twice), **volver, dormir.**

1. Yo no __recuerdo__ el número de teléfono de Raúl.
2. Jorge __vuelve__ a casa a las cinco.
3. ¿Cuánto __cuestan__ las chuletas?
4. ¿En qué __puedo__ (yo) servirle?
5. Nosotros no __encontramos__ el dinero. ¿Dónde está?
6. Nosotros no __podemos__ ir a la pescadería hoy.
7. Él __duerme__ en su cuarto.

B. Stem-changing verbs: *e > i*

Complete these sentences, using the present indicative of the following verbs: **conseguir, servir, pedir, decir.** (Use each verb twice.)

1. Ellos __piden__ trabajo en el hotel.
2. Nosotros __servimos__ ensalada y sándwiches en la fiesta.
3. ¿Dónde __consigues__ tú fresas?
4. Él __dice__ que está cansado.
5. Ella me __sirve__ una taza de café.
6. Yo __digo__ que van al mercado.
7. Mi esposo y yo siempre __pedimos__ vino cuando comemos en ese restaurante.
8. ¿Dónde __consigue__ Ud. las tarjetas de México?

C. Direct object pronouns

Answer the following questions in the negative, replacing the italicized words with direct object pronouns.

Answers: **1.** No, no voy a leerlos. (No, no los voy a leer.) **2.** No, no lo (la) conoce. **3.** No, no me llevan. **4.** No, ella no te llama mañana. **5.** No, no lo necesito. **6.** No, no la tengo. **7.** No, ellos no nos conocen. **8.** No, no las conseguimos.

1. ¿Vas a leer *estos libros*?
2. ¿Él *me* conoce? (*Use the* ***Ud.*** *form.*)
3. ¿*Te* llevan ellos al mercado?
4. ¿Ella *me* llama mañana? (*Use the* ***tú*** *form.*)
5. ¿Necesitas *el detergente*?
6. ¿Tienes *la lejía* aquí?
7. ¿Ellos *los* conocen a Uds.?
8. ¿Uds. consiguen *buenas frutas* en el supermercado?

D. Affirmative and negative expressions

Rewrite the following sentences, changing the negative expressions to the affirmative.

Answers: **1.** Tengo algo aquí. **2.** ¿Quiere algo más? **3.** Siempre vamos al supermercado. **4.** Quiero (o) la pluma roja o la pluma verde. **5.** Siempré llamo a alguien.

1. No tengo nada aquí.
2. ¿No quiere nada más?
3. Nunca vamos al supermercado.
4. No quiero ni la pluma roja ni la pluma verde.
5. Nunca llamo a nadie.

E. *Hace... que* Write the following sentences in Spanish.

1. I have been living in Honduras for five years.
2. How long have you been studying Spanish, Mr. Smith?
3. They have been writing for two hours.
4. She hasn't eaten for two days.

Answers: 1. Hace cinco años que (yo) vivo en Honduras. 2. ¿Cuánto tiempo hace que (Ud.) estudia español, Sr. Smith? 3. Hace dos horas que (ellos) escriben. 4. Hace dos días que (ella) no come.

F. Vocabulary Complete the following sentences, using vocabulary from **Lección 6.**

1. Yo le pongo __azúcar__ al café.
2. Ellos no quieren __chuletas__ de cerdo.
3. Va a comprar el pan en la __panadería__.
4. En mi casa __almorzamos__ a las doce.
5. ¿A qué hora __vuelven__ Uds. a su casa?
6. Ellos están __muertos__ de hambre.
7. Ana y Jorge son __recién__ casados.
8. Ellos viven __cerca__ de la universidad.
9. El __cangrejo__ y la __langosta__ son mariscos.
10. Necesito una __docena__ de huevos y __salsa__ de tomate para los espaguetis.

G. Culture Circle the correct answers, based on the cultural notes you have read.

1. La capital de Costa Rica es (San José / San Juan).
2. La principal fuente de ingresos de Panamá está asociada con (la agricultura / las operaciones del Canal).
3. Honduras (tiene / no tiene) volcanes.
4. La principal exportación de Nicaragua es (el café / el petróleo).

Answers: 1. San José 2. las operaciones del Canal 3. no tiene 4. el café

Unidad 4

Objetivos

Lección 7

- Discuss plans for a party
- Talk about what you like or dislike to do
- Extend, accept, and decline invitations
- Handle informal situations such as parties
- Talk about your daily routine

Lección 8

- Discuss activities you can do outdoors
- Discuss past actions and events
- Talk about the way things used to be

Venezuela

El Salto Ángel, en Venezuela, es la catarata más alta del mundo. Fue descubierto en 1935 y nombrado en honor de James Ángel, un piloto norteamericano que estrelló su avión cerca de allí en el año 1937.

Para divertirse

Lección 7
Un fin de semana

Lección 8
Las actividades al aire libre

Cuba
Vista del Capitolio Nacional de Cuba. Al frente, un anuncio de los tabacos Partagás.

República Dominicana
Una playa en Bayahibe La Romana, en la República Dominicana.

Puerto Rico
El Castillo del Morro, situado en la Bahía de San Juan, Puerto Rico.

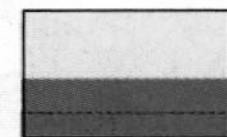

Colombia
Una réplica de la Balsa Muisca en el Museo del Oro en Colombia.

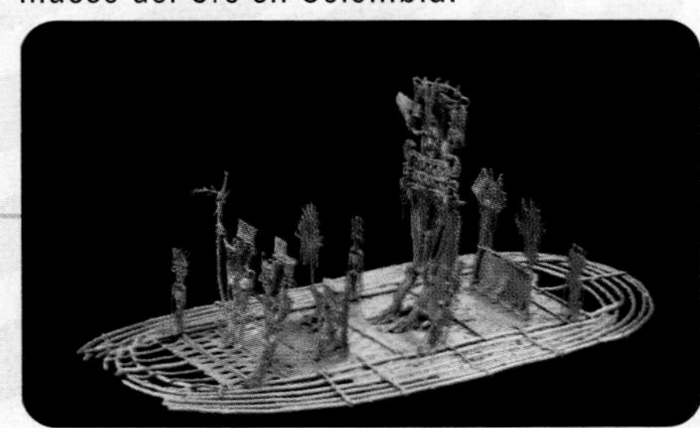

Lección 7 ◆ Un fin de semana

Carlos Aranda y su esposa Ester son cubanos, pero ahora viven en un apartamento grande y moderno en Santo Domingo. Tienen dos hijos: Olga, de dieciocho años, y Pablo, de quince años.

Carlos y Ester se levantan temprano hoy porque tienen muchos planes para el fin de semana. Los chicos duermen hasta las diez porque anoche fueron a una fiesta de cumpleaños en la casa de sus primos y volvieron muy tarde.

Ester ¿Vamos a ir al teatro con tus padres? Ellos nos invitaron la semana pasada.

Carlos Tú sabes que a mí no me gusta ir al teatro; me gusta más el cine. Papá quiere ver la película americana que ponen en el cine Rex…

Ester Bueno, voy a preguntarles si quieren cambiar sus planes.

Carlos ¡Ah! Recibimos una invitación a una boda. La recepción es mañana, en el club Náutico. ¿Quieres ir?

Ester Podemos ir un rato. ¿Ya se levantaron los chicos?

Carlos Sí, están desayunando. Olga se está quejando porque no puede ir a patinar con sus amigos esta tarde.

Ester Ella sabe que esta tarde tenemos que ir a visitar a tía Marcela, que nos invitó a merendar.

Carlos ¡Ay, pobre chica! En vez de divertirse con sus amigos se va a aburrir con tu tía Marcela…

Ester (*Se ríe*) ¡Está bien! Le voy a decir que no tiene que ir con nosotros.

Carlos (*Bromeando*) ¿Yo puedo ir a patinar con ella?

Detalles culturales

Las películas americanas son muy populares en el mundo hispánico. Generalmente tienen subtítulos en español o están dobladas (*dubbed*).

◆ **¿Le gusta ver películas extranjeras (*foreign*)?**

Olga y Pablo están hablando en la cocina.

Pablo Yo voy a ir a nadar con Beto y René esta tarde y después vamos a ir a ver un partido de béisbol.
Olga ¿Me estás diciendo que no tienes que ir a la casa de tía Marcela?
Pablo No, papá me dio permiso para salir con mis amigos.
Olga ¡Eso no es justo! ¡Mamá!
Ester (*Entra en la cocina.*) No tienes que ir con nosotros, Olga. La última vez que fuimos a la casa de tía Marcela, tú rompiste su florero favorito. A ella tampoco le gustan tus visitas... ¡Ella compró ese florero en San Juan!
Olga ¡No fui yo! ¡Fue Pablo! Bueno, no me importa. Esta noche, ¿puedo ir a bailar con María Inés y su hermano? Hay una discoteca nueva...
Ester ¡Ajá! ¿El hermano... ?
Olga A los dos nos gusta bailar... eso es todo...
Ester Bueno, pero tienes que volver antes de la medianoche.
Olga Les voy a decir que me tienen que traer a las doce menos cinco.

¿Recuerda usted?

¿Verdadero o falso?

With a partner, decide whether the following statements about the dialogue are true (**verdadero**) or false (**falso**).

1. Olga es mayor que Pablo. ☒ V ☐ F
2. Carlos y Ester no piensan hacer nada este fin de semana. ☐ V ☒ F
3. Carlos y su esposa están invitados a una boda. ☒ V ☐ F
4. Los chicos se levantaron muy temprano hoy. ☐ V ☒ F
5. Olga nunca se queja de nada. ☐ V ☒ F
6. A Pablo le gusta el béisbol. ☒ V ☐ F
7. A Marcela no le gustan las visitas de Ester. ☐ V ☒ F
8. Alguien rompió el florero. ☒ V ☐ F
9. María Inés no tiene hermanos. ☐ V ☒ F
10. Olga tiene que volver a su casa antes de las diez. ☐ V ☒ F

Y ahora... conteste

Answer these questions, basing your answers on the dialogue.

1. ¿Dónde viven Carlos Aranda y su familia?
2. ¿Adónde fueron los chicos anoche?
3. ¿Qué quiere ver el papá de Carlos? ¿En qué cine?
4. ¿Cuándo y dónde es la recepción?
5. ¿Carlos cree que su hija se va a divertir o que se va a aburrir con la tía de Ester?
6. ¿Con quiénes va a ir a nadar Pablo?
7. ¿Qué quiere hacer Olga esta noche?
8. ¿Adónde van a ir a bailar?

Answers: **1.** Viven en Santo Domingo. **2.** Fueron a una fiesta de cumpleaños. **3.** Quiere ver una película americana. En el cine Rex. **4.** Es mañana en el club Náutico. **5.** Cree que se va a aburrir. **6.** Va a ir a nadar con Beto y René. **7.** Quiere ir a bailar. **8.** Van a ir a una discoteca.

Para hablar del tema: Vocabulario

Online Study Center

For more practice with lesson topics, see the related activities on the *¡Hola, amigos!* web site at college.hmco.com/PIC/holaamigos7e.

Cognados

el béisbol
la discoteca
moderno(a)
el permiso
el plan
el teatro
la visita

Nombres

el cine movie theatre
el fin de semana weekend
el florero vase
la medianoche midnight
el partido, el juego game
la película movie, film
la semana week
la vez time

Verbos

aburrirse to be bored
bromear to kid, to joke
cambiar to change
divertirse (e>ie) to have a good time
entrar (en) to enter, to go in
gustar to like, to appeal
levantarse to get up
merendar (e>ie) to have an afternoon snack
nadar to swim
patinar to skate
preguntar to ask (*a question*)
quejarse to complain
reírse[1] to laugh
romper* to break
visitar to visit

Adjetivos

justo(a) fair
pasado(a) last
pobre poor
último(a) last (*in a series*)

Otras palabras y expresiones

anoche last night
en vez de instead of
hasta until
importarle (a uno) to matter
ir a patinar to go skating
poner una película* to show a movie
temprano early

[1]me río, te ríes, se ríe, nos reímos, os reís, se ríen

Amplíe su vocabulario

Para invitar a alguien a salir (*Asking someone out*)

¿Quieres ir...

a escalar una montaña? *mountain climbing*

a montar* en bicicleta? *bicycle riding*

a esquiar? *skiing (to ski)*

a montar a caballo? *horseback riding*

a un club nocturno? *to a nightclub*

a un concierto? *to a concert*

a la playa? *to the beach*

al museo? *to the museum*

al parque de diversiones*? *to the amusement park*

de picnic? *on a picnic*

al zoológico? *to the zoo*

De país a país

romper quebrar (*Méx.*)

poner una película dar una película (*Ecuador, Cono Sur*)

montar en bicicleta andar en bicicleta (*Arg.*)

el parque de diversiones el parque de atracciones (*Esp.*)

Para practicar el vocabulario

A. Preguntas y respuestas

Match the questions in column *A* with the answers in column *B*.

Answers: 1. g 2. j 3. a 4. c 5. b 6. i 7. e 8. d 9. h 10. f

A	B
1. ¿Se divierten en esas fiestas?	a. La semana pasada.
2. ¿Viste a Roberto en el club?	b. No, no tenemos hambre.
3. ¿Cuándo volvieron?	c. Sí, pero no me importa.
4. ¿Los niños rompieron el florero?	d. Sí, vamos a ir a patinar.
5. ¿Van a merendar?	e. No, porque yo trabajo los sábados.
6. ¿Tiene dinero?	f. ¡Sí! ¡No es justo!
7. ¿Vas los fines de semana?	g. No, se aburren.
8. ¿Tienen planes?	h. A la medianoche.
9. ¿A qué hora vienen?	i. No, es muy pobre.
10. ¿Tú haces todo el trabajo?	j. Sí, dos veces.

B. Todos se divierten

Complete the following statements about a great weekend.

1. Hoy __pasan (dan)__ una buena __película__ en el cine Victoria.
2. Los chicos van a ir a __montar__ a caballo.
3. Sergio va a ir a ver un __partido (juego)__ de béisbol.
4. Ana y sus amigos van a una __discoteca__ a bailar.
5. Esta tarde yo voy a ir a __patinar (nadar)__ con mi novio.
6. Estoy invitada a la __recepción__ de una boda.
7. Vamos a la piscina (*pool*) a __nadar__.
8. Vamos al __teatro__ a ver *Romeo y Julieta.*
9. Voy a __visitar__ a mi tía favorita.
10. Teresa y Armando van a un club __nocturno__.

C. ¿Adónde vamos...?

Your friend has accepted your invitation. Where are you going to go? Begin your answers with **Vamos a ir...**

Answers: 1. Vamos a ir a la playa. 2. Vamos a ir a escalar montañas. 3. Vamos a ir a un parque de diversiones. 4. Vamos a ir a una discoteca. 5. Vamos a ir al zoológico. 6. Vamos a ir al museo. 7. Vamos a ir de picnic. 8. Vamos a ir a un concierto. 9. Vamos a ir a esquiar. 10. Vamos a ir a montar a caballo o a montar en bicicleta.

1. You want to sunbathe and swim.
2. You feel like climbing a mountain.
3. You want to go to Disneyland.
4. You want to dance salsa.
5. You want to see animals.
6. You want to see Picasso's paintings.
7. You want to have lunch and commune with nature.
8. You want to hear some live music.
9. You want to go to Aspen, Colorado.
10. You want to go horseback riding or ride your bicycle.

D. ¿Quieres ir...? With a partner, play the roles of two friends who cannot agree on where to go or what to do on the weekend. *Answers will vary.*

◆ **MODELO:** —*¿Quieres ir al cine?*
—*No, prefiero ir al teatro.*

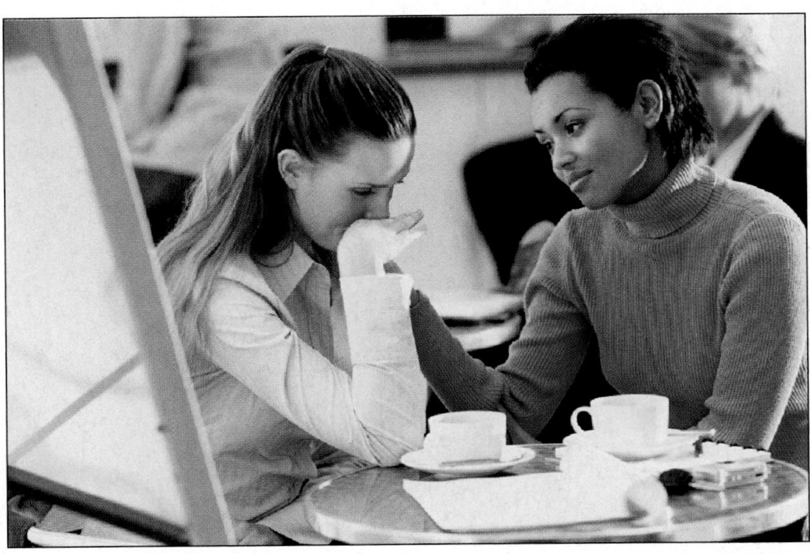

Es evidente que estas chicas no están muy contentas. ¿Qué pueden hacer para divertirse un poco?

Pronunciación

Las consonantes *l*, *r*, *rr*

A. Practice the Spanish **l** in the following words.

O**l**ga	abri**l**	ú**l**timo
mi**l**	Ánge**l**	béisbo**l**
Isabe**l**	ma**l**	vo**l**ver

B. Practice the Spanish **r** in the following words.

mode**r**no	teat**r**o	flo**r**e**r**o
prime**r**o	Pa**r**ís	cua**r**enta
pa**r**tido	favo**r**ito	de**r**echa

C. Practice the Spanish **rr** (spelled **r** both at the beginning of a word and after an **n**) in the following words.

recibir	bo**rr**ador	co**rr**er
En**r**ique	abu**rr**irse	**r**omper
recepción	piza**rr**a	**r**eírse

Extra practice:
1. Isabel y Aníbal faltan a clase los lunes.
2. Carolina quiere la cartera para el miércoles.
3. Los carros del ferrocarril parecen cigarros.

Puntos para recordar

1. Preterit of regular verbs (*El pretérito de los verbos regulares*)

Suggestion: Make sure students equate the preterit with the past tense by giving the English equivalent: **Tomé** = *I took, I drank.* Explain that the preterit ending **-ó** (3rd-person sing. **-ar** verbs) must be stressed clearly or the verb will sound like the present tense (1st-person sing. **-ar** verbs).

Extra practice: Write the following sentence builder on the board and ask students to form at least ten original sentences.

Ayer / La semana pasada / El año pasado / Anoche / Esta mañana / El viernes pasado

yo / tú / él / ella / nosotros / Ud. / el profesor / mi amigo(a)

escribirle una tarjeta postal a... / beber... / llegar a clase a la(s)... / leer... / empezar a estudiar a la(s)... / hablar con... / trabajar en... / estudiar en... / salir con... / vender...

Explanation: You may want to tell students that the spelling changes **c > qu** and **g > gu**, etc., occur in order to preserve the sound of the verb stem.

- Spanish has two simple past tenses: the preterit and the imperfect. (The imperfect will be presented in **Lección 8.**) The preterit of regular verbs is formed as follows. Note that the endings for **-er** and **-ir** verbs are identical.

-ar *verbs* ***tomar*** *(to take)*	-er *verbs* ***comer*** *(to eat)*	-ir *verbs* ***escribir*** *(to write)*
tom**é**	com**í**	escrib**í**
tom**aste**	com**iste**	escrib**iste**
tom**ó**	com**ió**	escrib**ió**
tom**amos**	com**imos**	escrib**imos**
tom**asteis**	com**isteis**	escrib**isteis**
tom**aron**	com**ieron**	escrib**ieron**

yo **tomé**	*I took; I did take*
Ud. **comió**	*you ate; you did eat*
ellos **decidieron**	*they decided; they did decide*

- Verbs ending in **-ar** and **-er** that are stem-changing in the present indicative are regular in the preterit.

encontrar	tú enc**ue**ntras	tú enc**o**ntraste
volver	yo v**ue**lvo	yo v**o**lví
cerrar	yo c**ie**rro	yo c**e**rré

- Verbs ending in **-gar, -car,** and **-zar** change **g** to **gu, c** to **qu,** and **z** to **c** before **é** in the first person of the preterit.

pagar → pag*ué* **buscar → bus*qué*** **empezar → empe*cé***

- Verbs whose stem ends in a strong vowel change the unaccented **i** of the preterit ending to **y** in the third-person singular and plural of the preterit.

leer → le*y*ó **le*y*eron**

- The preterit tense refers to actions or events that the speaker views as completed in the past.

—¿Qué **compraste** ayer? —**Compré** un florero.	*"What **did you buy** yesterday?"* *"**I bought** a vase."*
—¿Qué **comieron** Uds.? —**Comimos** ensalada.	*"What **did you eat**?"* *"**We ate** salad."*
—¿A qué hora **volvió** usted? —Yo **volví** a las seis.	*"What time **did you return**?"* *"I **returned** at six."*
—¿A qué hora **llegaste**? —**Llegué** a las seis.	*"What time **did you arrive?**"* *"**I arrived** at six."*

¡Atención! Note that Spanish has no equivalent for the English *did* used as an auxiliary verb in questions and negative sentences.

—¿**Encontraste** el dinero?	*"**Did you find** the money?"*
—No lo **busqué.**	*"**I didn't look for** it."*

Suggestion: Provide ample practice in interrogative and negative sentences to underscore this point.

Práctica y conversación

Online Study Center

For more practice with lesson topics, see the related activities on the ***¡Hola, amigos!*** web site at college.hmco.com/PIC/holaamigos7e.

A. Minidiálogos Complete the following dialogues, using the correct preterit forms of the verbs in parentheses. Then act them out with a partner.

1. —¿A qué hora volvieron (volver) Uds. ayer?
   —Yo volví (volver) a las siete y Mario volvió (volver) a las nueve. ¿A qué hora volviste (volver) tú?
2. —¿ Leyó (Leer) Ud. este libro, Sr. Vega?
   —Sí, lo leí (leer) ayer.
   —¿Ud. lo sacó (sacar) de la biblioteca o lo compró (comprar)?
   —Lo saqué (sacar) de la biblioteca.
3. —¿Cuándo empezaste (empezar) a trabajar tú?
   —Empecé (Empezar) la semana pasada.
   —¿En qué mes llegaste (llegar) aquí?
   —Llegué (Llegar) en noviembre del año pasado.
4. —¿Con quién hablaron (hablar) Uds.?
   —Yo hablé (hablar) con mi madrina y Ramiro hablό (hablar) con su abuela.

B. Ayer... Read what the following people typically do. Then complete each sentence telling how they varied from their normal routines yesterday. *Answers will vary.*

1. Yo siempre hablo con mis padres, pero ayer...
2. Yo siempre escribo en inglés, pero ayer...
3. Tú siempre estudias por la mañana, pero ayer...
4. Alberto siempre compra café, pero ayer...
5. Los chicos siempre toman café, pero ayer...
6. Nosotros siempre comemos en la cafetería, pero ayer...
7. Adela siempre sale con su novio, pero ayer...
8. Ustedes siempre vuelven a las seis, pero ayer...
9. Yo siempre llego a la universidad a las ocho, pero ayer...
10. Yo siempre empiezo a trabajar a las tres, pero ayer...

Answers: **1.** hablé... **2.** escribí... **3.** estudiaste... **4.** compró... **5.** tomaron... **6.** comimos... **7.** salió... **8.** volvieron... **9.** llegué... **10.** empecé...

C. Entreviste a su compañero(a) Interview a classmate about his / her activities yesterday, using the following questions. *Answers will vary.*

1. ¿A qué hora saliste de tu casa ayer?
2. ¿A qué hora llegaste a la universidad?
3. ¿Trabajaste mucho?
4. ¿Cuántas horas estudiaste?
5. ¿Dónde comiste? ¿Qué comiste?
6. ¿Qué tomaste?
7. ¿Compraste algo? ¿Qué?
8. ¿A qué hora volviste a tu casa?
9. ¿Qué programa de televisión viste?
10. ¿A qué hora cenaste?
11. ¿Leíste algo antes de acostarte?
12. ¿A qué hora te acostaste?

2. Preterit of *ser, ir,* and *dar* (*El pretérito de* ser, ir *y* dar)

Expansion: You might do sentence expansion exercises with students, using **ir** and **dar** with several subjects (e.g., **Yo fui... ¿adónde?, ¿con quién?, ¿cuándo? / Yo le di... ¿qué?, ¿a quién?, ¿cuándo?**).

- The preterits of **ser, ir,** and **dar** are irregular.

ser (*to be*)	ir (*to go*)	dar (*to give*)
fui	**fui**	**di**
fuiste	**fuiste**	**diste**
fue	**fue**	**dio**
fuimos	**fuimos**	**dimos**
fuisteis	**fuisteis**	**disteis**
fueron	**fueron**	**dieron**

—¿**Fuiste** al club ayer? — *"**Did you go** to the club yesterday?"*

—Sí, **fui** para comprar ropa. Papá me **dio** el dinero. — *"Yes, **I went** to buy clothes. Dad **gave** me the money."*

—¿Quién **fue** tu profesor de español? — *"Who **was** your Spanish professor?"*

—El Dr. Vega. — *"Dr. Vega."*

¡Atención! Note that **ser** and **ir** have identical preterit forms; however, there is no confusion as to meaning, because the context clarifies it.

Práctica y conversación

Online Study Center

For more practice with lesson topics, see the related activities on the *¡Hola, amigos!* web site at college.hmco.com/PIC/holaamigos7e.

A. Minidiálogos Complete the following dialogues, using the preterit of **ser, ir,** and **dar.** Then act them out with a partner, adding your own original lines of dialogue.

1. —¿Con quién __fuiste__ tú al cine?
   —__Fui__ con mi hijo.
   —¿__Fueron__ (Uds.) por la mañana o por la tarde?
   —__Fuimos__ por la tarde.
2. —¿Cuánto dinero __dieron__ Uds. para la fiesta?
   —Yo __di__ 10 dólares y Carlos __dio__ 5 dólares.
   —¿Luisa __fue__ a la fiesta con Roberto?
   —No, ella y Marisol __fueron__ con Juan Carlos al cine.
3. —¿Quién __fue__ el profesor de literatura de Uds. en la universidad?
   —El Dr. Rivas.
   —¿Uds. no __fueron__ estudiantes de la Dra. Torres?
   —No, no __fuimos__ estudiantes de ella.

B. Entreviste a su compañero(a) Interview a partner, using the following questions. *Answers will vary.*

1. ¿Quién fue tu profesor(a) favorito(a) el año pasado?
2. ¿Fuiste a la biblioteca ayer? ¿A qué hora?
3. ¿Adónde fuiste el fin de semana pasado?
4. ¿Tus amigos fueron también?
5. ¿Cuándo diste una fiesta?
6. ¿Dónde la diste?
7. ¿Fueron tú y tus amigos al cine el sábado pasado?
8. ¿Fuiste de vacaciones el verano pasado? ¿Adónde fuiste?

C. Queremos saber... With a partner, prepare five questions to ask your instructor about his/her activities. Use the preterit of **ser, ir,** and **dar.**
Answers will vary.

3. Indirect object pronouns (*Los pronombres usados como complemento indirecto*)

- In addition to a subject and direct object, a sentence can have an indirect object.[1]

Ella les da **el dinero a los muchachos.**

S.	V.	D.O.	I.O.

What does she give? **(el dinero)**

To whom does she give it? **(a los muchachos)**

In this sentence, **ella** is the subject who performs the action, **el dinero** is the direct object, and **a los muchachos** is the indirect object, the final recipient of the action expressed by the verb.

Suggestion: Review the concept of direct object. Be sure students know the difference between direct and indirect objects.

Él **la** llama Anita. (*direct*)
Él **le** escribe una carta. (*indirect*)
Yo **la** llevo. (*direct*)
Yo **le** llevo un libro. (*indirect*)

[1]See Appendix C.

You may want to write the indirect object pronouns and these two sentences on the board to show the contrasts in word order.

I give ***her*** *the stamps.*	Yo **le** doy las estampillas.

Suggestion: Point out that, unlike direct object pronouns, indirect object pronouns do not vary according to the gender of the object.

Extra practice: Have students practice the indirect object construction by giving objects to other members of the class while briefly stating the object given and the person who is to receive it. Remind students to use the preposition **a** and the recipient's name.

S1: **Yo le doy el libro a Juan.**
S2: **Yo les doy los cuadernos a Teresa y Pedro.**
S3: **Yo te doy la pluma a ti.**

- Indirect object nouns are for the most part preceded by the preposition **a.**
- An indirect object usually tells to whom or for whom something is done. Compare these sentences:

  Yo voy a mandar**lo** a México. (**lo:** *direct object*)
  I'm going to send ***him*** *to Mexico.*

  Yo voy a mandar**le** dinero. (**le:** *indirect object*)
  I'm going to send ***him*** *money.* (*I'm going to send money* ***to him.***)

- An indirect object pronoun can be used with or in place of the indirect object. In Spanish, the indirect object pronoun includes the meaning *to* or *for.* The forms of the indirect object pronouns are shown in the following table.

Singular		Plural	
me	(to/for) me	**nos**	(to/for) us
te	(to/for) you (*fam.*)	**os**	(to/for) you (*fam.*)
le	(to/for) you (*form.*) (to/for) him (to/for) her	**les**	(to/for) you (*form., fam.*) (to/for) them (*masc., fem.*)

- Indirect object pronouns have the same form as direct object pronouns, except in the third person.
- Indirect object pronouns are usually placed in front of the conjugated verb.

Le dimos una propina.	*We gave* ***him*** *a tip.*

- When used with an infinitive or in the present progressive, however, the indirect object pronoun may either be placed in front of the conjugated verb or attached to the infinitive or the present participle.

Le voy a escribir una carta. *or:* Voy a escribir**le** una carta.	*I'm going to write* ***you*** *a letter.*
Les estoy diciendo la hora. *or:* Estoy diciéndo**les**[1] la hora.	*I'm telling* ***them*** *the time.*

¡Atención! The indirect object pronouns **le** and **les** require clarification when the context does not specify the gender or the person to which they refer. Spanish provides clarification by using the preposition **a** + *pronoun or noun.*

Le doy la información.	*I give the information . . .*
but:	*(to whom? to him? to her? to you?)*
Le doy la información **a ella.**	*I give the information* ***to her.***

[1]When an indirect object pronoun is attached to a present participle, an accent mark is added to maintain the correct stress.

The prepositional phrase provides clarification or emphasis; it is not, however, a substitute for the indirect object pronoun. While the prepositional form can be omitted, the indirect object pronoun must always be used.

—¿Qué vas a compra**rle** a tu hija?	*"What are you going to buy (for) your daughter?"*
—**Le** voy a comprar un florero.	*"I'm going to buy **her** a vase."*

Práctica y conversación

Online Study Center

For more practice with lesson topics, see the related activities on the ***¡Hola, amigos!*** web site at college.hmco.com/PIC/holaamigos7e.

A. Frutas para todos

Mom went to the market and bought fruit for everyone. Indicate for whom she bought each fruit, using indirect object pronouns. Clarify when necessary.

◆ **MODELO:** Mamá compró duraznos *para él.*
*Mamá **le** compró duraznos **a él.***

1. Mamá compró manzanas *para mí.*
2. Mamá compró peras *para nosotros.*
3. Mamá compró uvas *para ella.*
4. Mamá compró una piña *para ti.*
5. Mamá compró melocotones *para Ud.*
6. Mamá compró una sandía *para ellos.*
7. Mamá compró cerezas *para Uds.*
8. Mamá compró fresas *para él.*
9. Mamá compró bananas *para Rodolfo.*
10. Mamá compró mangos *para Sofía.*

Answers: 1. Mamá me compró manzanas. 2. Mamá nos compró peras. 3. Mamá le compró uvas a ella. 4. Mamá te compró una piña. 5. Mamá le compró melocotones a Ud. 6. Mamá les compró una sandía a ellos. 7. Mamá les compró cerezas a Uds. 8. Mamá le compró fresas a él. 9. Mamá le compró bananas a Rodolfo. 10. Mamá le compró mangos a Sofía.

B. Entreviste a su compañero(a)

Interview a partner, using the following questions. *Answers will vary.*

1. ¿Cuándo vas a escribirles a tus amigos?
2. ¿Le escribiste a alguien ayer?
3. ¿Tú siempre le escribes a tu mejor amigo(a)?
4. ¿Tus padres te escribieron esta semana?
5. ¿Tus padres te dan dinero para comprar ropa?
6. ¿Tú vas a mandarle dinero a alguien? ¿A quién?
7. ¿Tus padres les hablan a Uds. en inglés o en español?
8. ¿Tú siempre les dices la verdad a tus padres?

Alternative: For written practice, students could also write up their response (or their partner's).

C. Son bilingües

What languages do the people below speak and what languages are spoken to them? With a partner, match each name to the most likely language.

alemán (*German*)	italiano
español	japonés
francés	portugués
inglés	ruso (*Russian*)

◆ **MODELO:** María del Pilar (a mí)
María del Pilar me habla en español.
Yo le hablo en español a ella.

1. Boris (a ti)
2. Giovanni (a ellos)
3. John (a mí)
4. El Sr. Toyota (a Uds.)
5. Monique y Pierre (a nosotros)
6. Hans (a Ud.)
7. Nelson (de Brasil) (a él)
8. Rosa y José (a ella)

Answers: 1. Boris te habla en ruso (a ti). Tú le hablas en ruso (a él). 2. Giovanni les habla en italiano (a ellos). Ellos le hablan en italiano (a Giovanni). 3. John me habla en inglés (a mí). Yo le hablo en inglés (a él). 4. El Sr. Toyota les habla en japonés (a Uds.). Uds. le hablan en japonés (al Sr. Toyota). 5. Monique y Pierre nos hablan en francés (a nosotros). Nosotros les hablamos en francés a Monique y a Pierre. 6. Hans le habla en alemán (a Ud.) Ud. le habla en alemán (a Hans). 7. Nelson le habla en portugués (a él). Él le habla en portugués (a Nelson). 8. Rosa y José le hablan en español (a ella). Ella les habla en español (a Rosa y a José).

 **D. Regalos** (*Presents*) In groups of three or four, tell each other about four or five gifts that you bought your friends and relatives for Christmas (*la Navidad*) or a birthday and describe what they bought you. *Answers will vary.*

◆ **MODELO:** *A mi mamá le compré una licuadora para su cumpleaños.*
El día de mi cumpleaños, mi mamá me compró un escritorio.

4. The verb *gustar* (*El verbo* gustar)

Expansion: Write a short sentence builder on the board and have students make up sentences that describe what they, their friends, and their families like and don't like. Remind them to include things that are not on the list.

A mí / A ti / A mi madre, padre / A mis amigos(as) / A (Tomás) / A los estudiantes / A nosotros

me / te / le(s) / nos

gusta(n)

estudiar / las cintas de... / bailar... / las vacaciones / hablar por teléfono con... / el café / los exámenes

Suggestion: Prepare students by talking about your own likes and dislikes. Have students work first in pairs and then in small groups, asking each other what they like to eat, drink, or do. Then have them report to you. All indirect object pronouns will thus be practiced. Follow up with a class survey of likes and dislikes (e.g., **¿A quién le gusta bailar?**).

◆ The verb **gustar** means to like something or somebody (literally, *to be pleasing*). A special construction is required in Spanish to translate the English *to like*. Note that the equivalent of the English direct object becomes the subject of the Spanish sentence. The English subject then becomes the indirect object of the Spanish sentence.

	*I like **your house.***
Me gusta **tu *casa.***	S. D.O.
I.O. S.	***Your house** is pleasing **to me.***
	S. I.O.

◆ **Gustar** is *always* used with an indirect object pronoun—in this example, **me.**

◆ The two most commonly used forms of **gustar** are the third-person singular **gusta** if the subject is singular or if the verb is followed by one or more infinitives, and the third-person plural **gustan** if the subject is plural.

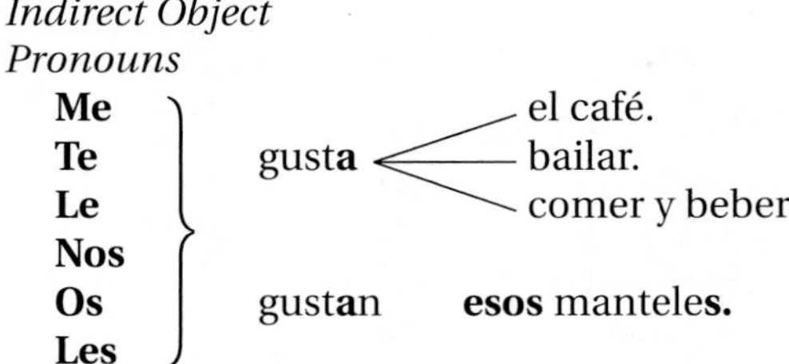

◆ Note that **gustar** agrees in number with the *subject* of the sentence, that is, the person or thing being liked.

Me gust**an las manzanas.**	***Apples are** pleasing to me.*

◆ The person who does the liking is the indirect object.

Me gustan las manzanas.	*Apples are pleasing **to me.***
—¿**Te** gusta este mantel rojo? —No, no **me** gustan los manteles rojos.	*"Do **you** like this red tablecloth?"* *"No, **I** don't like red tablecloths."*
—¿**Les** gusta el francés? —Sí, **nos** gusta mucho el francés, pero **nos** gusta más el español.	*"Do **you** like French?"* *"Yes, **we** like French very much, but **we** like Spanish better."*

¡Atención! Note that the words **más** and **mucho** immediately follow **gustar.**

- The preposition **a** + *a noun* or *pronoun* is used to clarify meaning or to emphasize the indirect object.

A Aurora (A ella) le gusta esa panadería, pero **a mí** no me gusta.	***Aurora** likes that bakery, but **I** don't like it.*
A Beto y **a Rosa** les gusta ese restaurante.	***Beto** and **Rosa** like that restaurant.*

¡Atención! If the thing liked is an action, the second verb is an infinitive: **Me gusta patinar.**

Detalles culturales

En la cultura hispánica, los sobrenombres son muy populares. Roberto: **Beto;** Enrique: **Quique;** Dolores: **Lola.**

- **¿Qué sobrenombres son populares en este país? ¿Ud. tiene sobrenombre?**

Práctica y conversación

A. ¿Qué les gusta? Tell who likes what.

- **MODELO:** Yo / ese cine
  Me gusta ese cine.

1. Nosotros / más / estos floreros
2. Tú / visitar / tus tíos
3. Yo / mucho / cocinar
4. Ellos / mucho / La Habana
5. Él / no / mucho / ese parque de diversiones
6. Uds. / más / esas ciudades
7. Ella / ese club nocturno
8. Yo / mucho / los restaurantes italianos
9. Uds. / no/ la música jazz
10. Mi mamá / mucho / esquiar

Online Study Center

For more practice with lesson topics, see the related activities on the ***¡Hola, amigos!*** web site at college.hmco.com/PIC/holaamigos7e.

Answers: **1.** (A nosotros) nos gustan más estos floreros. **2.** (A ti) te gusta visitar a tus tíos. **3.** (A mí) me gusta mucho cocinar. **4.** (A ellos) les gusta mucho La Habana. **5.** (A él) no le gusta mucho ese parque de diversiones. **6.** (A Uds.) les gustan más esas ciudades. **7.** (A ella) le gusta ese club nocturno. **8.** (A mí) me gustan mucho los restaurantes italianos. **9.** (A Uds.) no les gusta la música jazz. **10.** (A mi mamá) le gusta mucho esquiar.

B. Entreviste a su compañero(a) Interview a classmate, asking the following questions. *Answers will vary.*

1. ¿A ti te gusta más el invierno o el verano?
2. ¿Te gusta más venir a clase por la mañana o por la tarde?
3. ¿A ti te gusta más el rojo o el azul?
4. ¿Te gusta más vivir en una casa o en un apartamento?
5. ¿Te gustan más las ciudades grandes o las ciudades pequeñas?
6. ¿Te gustan más las peras o las manzanas?
7. ¿A tu mamá le gusta más bailar o cantar (*sing*)?
8. ¿A tus amigos les gusta más ir al cine o al teatro?

C. Los sábados With a partner, talk about what you, your parents, and your friends like and don't like to do on Saturdays. *Answers will vary.*

- **MODELO:** A mi papá...
  A mi papá le gusta leer. No le gusta trabajar.

1. A mí...
2. A mi mamá...
3. A mi papá...
4. A nosotros...
5. A mis amigos...
6. A mi mejor amigo(a)...

D. Preferencias... Look at these illustrations and say what these people like and what they don't like to do.

◆ **MODELO:**

A Juan le gusta leer.

1. ______________________

2. ______________________

3. ______________________

4. ______________________

5. ______________________

6. ______________________

7. ______________________

Answers: **1.** A Inés le gusta bailar. **2.** A Jorge y a Mario no les gusta el café. **3.** A mí me gustan las frutas. **4.** (A nosotras) nos gusta jugar al tenis. **5.** (A ti) te gustan las uvas, pero no te gustan las peras. **6.** A Ud. le gusta ir al teatro y al cine. **7.** A Carmen le gusta nadar y patinar.

E. Queremos saber With a partner, prepare three or four questions to ask your instructor about what he or she likes or doesn't like to do. *Answers will vary.*

5. Reflexive constructions (*Construcciones reflexivas*)

- The reflexive construction (e.g., *I introduce myself*) consists in Spanish of a reflexive pronoun and a verb.
- Reflexive pronouns[1] refer to the same person as the subject of the sentence does.

Subjects	Reflexive Pronouns	
yo	**me**	myself, to (for) myself
tú	**te**	yourself, to (for) yourself (*fam.*)
nosotros(as)	**nos**	ourselves, to (for) ourselves
vosotros(as)	**os**	yourselves, to (for) yourselves (*fam.*)
Ud.	**se**	yourself, to (for) yourself (*form.*)
Uds.	**se**	yourselves, to (for) yourselves (*form., fam.*)
él	**se**	himself, to (for) himself
ella	**se**	herself, to (for) herself
	se	itself, to (for) itself
ellos, ellas	**se**	themselves, to (for) themselves

¡Atención! Reflexive pronouns are positioned in the sentence in the same manner as object pronouns.

- Note that except for **se,** reflexive pronouns have the same forms as the direct and indirect object pronouns.
- The third-person singular and plural **se** is invariable, that is, it does not show gender or number.
- Any verb that can act upon the subject can be made reflexive in Spanish with the aid of a reflexive pronoun.

Julia **le** prueba el vestido **a su hija.**
(*Julia tries the dress on her daughter.*)

Julia **se prueba** el vestido.
(*Julia tries on the dress.*)

Suggestion: Conjugate a reflexive verb on the board, using colored chalk for the reflexive pronouns. Point out that in reflexive constructions the subject, the reflexive pronoun, and the verb must be in the same person and number.

Yo	**me**	**visto.**
(*1st pers. sing.*)	(*1st pers. sing.*)	(*1st pers. sing.*)

Alternative: Tell students that at the beginning of the semester they learned to use a reflexive construction: **¿Cómo se llama Ud.?** and **Yo me llamo...** Ask students: **¿Cómo se llama Ud.?** Have them ask each other: **¿Cómo te llamas tú?** Point to different students and ask the class: **¿Cómo se llama él (ella)? ¿Cómo se llaman Uds. (ellos)?**

Suggestions: Show pictures illustrating the difference between reflexive and nonreflexive constructions (e.g., someone washing his/her hair and someone washing dishes).

Dramatize the difference between a reflexive and a nonreflexive construction by lifting a chair and saying: **Yo levanto la silla.** Then sit on the chair and as you get up, say: **Yo me levanto.**

[1]See Appendix C.

vestirse (e > i) (*to dress oneself, to get dressed*)	
Yo **me visto.**	I dress myself.
Tú **te vistes.**	You dress yourself. (*fam.*)
Ud. **se viste.**	You dress yourself. (*form.*)
Él **se viste.**	He dresses himself.
Ella **se viste.**	She dresses herself.
Nosotros **nos vestimos.**	We dress ourselves.
Vosotros **os vestís.**	You dress yourselves. (*fam.*)
Uds. **se visten.**	You dress yourselves. (*form., fam.*)
Ellos **se visten.**	They (*masc.*) dress themselves.
Ellas **se visten.**	They (*fem.*) dress themselves.

Suggestion: Act out the verbs and have students tell what you're doing. Then have students act out some verbs while you ask their classmates: **¿Qué hace él? ¿Qué hacen ellas?**, etc. Play a game of charades.

- The following commonly used verbs are reflexive.

aburrirse *to get bored*	**lavarse** *to wash oneself*
acostarse (o>ue) *to go to bed*	**levantarse** *to get up*
afeitarse, rasurarse *to shave*	**ponerse** *to put on*
bañarse *to bathe*	**probarse (o>ue)** *to try on*
despertarse (e>ie) *to wake up*	**quitarse** *to take off*
divertirse (e>ie) *to have fun*	**sentarse (e>ie)** *to sit down*

—¿A qué hora **se levantan** Uds.?	*"What time do you **get up**?"*
—Yo **me levanto** a las seis y Jorge **se levanta** a las ocho.	*"I **get up** at six o'clock and Jorge **gets up** at eight."*
—Uds. **se levantaron** muy tarde hoy.	*"You **got up** very late today."*
—Sí, porque anoche **nos acostamos** a la medianoche.	*"Yes, because last night **we went to bed** at midnight."*

Online Study Center

For more practice with lesson topics, see the related activities on the ***¡Hola, amigos!*** web site at college.hmco.com/PIC/holaamigos7e.

Práctica y conversación

A. Entreviste a su compañero(a) Interview a partner, using the following questions. *Answers will vary.*

1. ¿A qué hora te despertaste esta mañana?
2. Generalmente, ¿te levantas temprano o tarde? ¿A qué hora te levantas?
3. ¿Te acuestas temprano? ¿Te acuestas antes de las once?
4. ¿Te bañas por la mañana o por la noche? ¿Con qué jabón (*soap*) te bañas?
5. ¿Puedes bañarte y vestirte en diez minutos?
6. ¿Con qué jabón te lavas las manos?
7. ¿Tu papá se afeita todos los días?
8. ¿Siempre te pruebas la ropa antes de comprarla?
9. En la clase de español, ¿prefieres sentarte cerca de la puerta o cerca de la pizarra?
10. ¿Te sientas cerca de la ventana? ¿Por qué?
11. ¿Te diviertes en la clase de español?
12. ¿En qué clase te aburres?

Verbs: 1. me desperté... 2. me levanto... 3. me acuesto... 4. me baño... 5. puedo bañarme y vestirme (me puedo bañar y vestir)... 6. me lavo... 7. se afeita... 8. me pruebo... 9. prefiero sentarme... 10. me siento... 11. me divierto... 12. me aburro...

B. ¿Qué pasó...? Use your imagination to complete the following sentences. *Answers will vary.*

1. Yo me levanté a las seis y Jorge…
2. Mi hermana se bañó por la noche y tú…
3. Yo me desperté temprano y Rosa…
4. Nosotras nos probamos los vestidos negros y ellas…
5. Tú te sentaste cerca de la puerta y ella…
6. Yo me vestí en diez minutos y tú…
7. Yo me afeité por la noche y él…
8. Nosotros nos acostamos a las once y Uds.…
9. Yo me aburrí en la fiesta y tú…
10. Yo me lavé las manos con jabón Dove y ellos…

Verbs: **1.** se levantó... **2.** te bañaste... **3.** se despertó... **4.** se probaron... **5.** se sentó... **6.** te vestiste... **7.** se afeitó... **8.** se acostaron... **9.** te aburriste... **10.** se lavaron...

C. La rutina diaria Look at the illustrations below. How would José describe his routine and that of his family?

Answers: **1.** Yo me levanto a las siete de la mañana. **2.** Mi papá se levanta a las cinco. **3.** Yo me baño por la mañana. **4.** Nosotros nos afeitamos los sábados. **5.** Mamá se viste a las siete y media de la mañana. **6.** Nosotros nos sentamos cerca de la puerta.

1. Yo...

2. Mi papá...

3. Yo...

4. Nosotros...

5. Mamá...

6. Nosotros...

7. Yo me acuesto a las diez de la noche. **8.** ¿Tú te acuestas a la medianoche?

7. Yo...

8. ¿Tú...?

Suggestion: Encourage students to add one or two original items. Follow up by asking questions such as, **¿Quién siempre / nunca se levanta antes de las siete?**

D. ¿Cada cuánto tiempo...? (*How often . . . ?*)

In groups of three or four, talk about how often you do the following things. Use **siempre, todos los días, nunca, a veces,** and **frecuentemente.** *Answers will vary.*

1. levantarse antes de las siete
2. despertarse muy tarde
3. bañarse por la noche
4. ponerse pijama para dormir
5. acostarse muy tarde
6. quejarse de sus profesores

Suggestion: You may want to assign the **Rodeo** grammar summary and **¡Vamos a practicar!** activity as homework.

Rodeo

Summary of the Pronouns (Resumen de los pronombres)

Subject	*Direct Object*	*Indirect Object*	*Reflexive*	*Object of Prepositions*
yo	**me**	**me**	**me**	**mí**
tú	**te**	**te**	**te**	**ti**
usted (*masc.*)	**lo**			**usted**
usted (*fem.*)	**la**	**le**	**se**	**usted**
él	**lo**			**él**
ella	**la**			**ella**
nosotros(as)	**nos**	**nos**	**nos**	**nosotros(as)**
vosotros(as)	**os**	**os**	**os**	**vosotros(as)**
ustedes (*masc.*)	**los**			**ustedes**
ustedes (*fem.*)	**las**	**les**	**se**	**ustedes**
ellos	**los**			**ellos**
ellas	**las**			**ellas**

Online Study Center

For more practice with lesson topics, see the related activities on the *¡Hola, amigos!* web site at college.hmco.com/PIC/holaamigos7e.

Práctica

Queridos padres Supply all the missing pronouns in the letter that Oscar wrote to his parents and read the letter aloud.

Queridos padres:

___Les___ escribo para decir-les___ que estoy bien y estoy trabajando mucho. Ayer hablé con Eva. ___Ella___ está estudiando en la universidad y dice que quiere conocer-los___ porque ___yo___ siempre ___le___ hablo de ___Uds.___. ___Me___ invitó a una fiesta que ella da esta noche.

Hoy ___me___ levanté muy temprano y fui de compras. Para ___ti___, papá, compré un reloj. A ___ti___, mamá, ___te___ compré un vestido. Para ___mí___, compré un par de zapatos para la fiesta de Eva.

¿Cómo está mi hermana? Hace mucho que no ___la___ llamo por teléfono ni ___le___ escribo. ¡Ah! A ___ella___ ___le___ compré un libro.

Bueno, ya son las seis y tengo que bañar-me___ y vestir-me___ para ir a la fiesta.

___Los___ quiero mucho.

Un abrazo,

Oscar

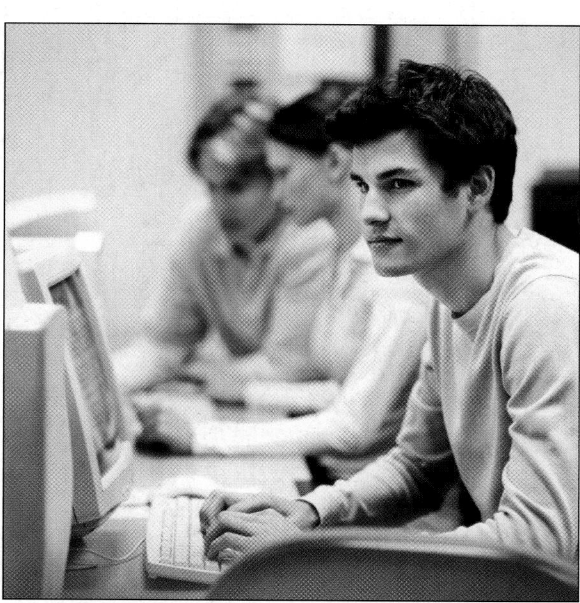

Sergio le envía un mensaje electrónico a su novia. ¿Qué le dice de sus planes para el sábado? ¿Va a salir con ella? ¿La va a llamar por teléfono?

Entre nosotros

¡Conversemos!

Para conocernos mejor Get to know your partner better by asking each other the following questions. *Answers will vary.*

1. ¿Te gusta levantarte temprano? ¿A qué hora te levantaste hoy?
2. ¿A qué hora te acostaste anoche?
3. ¿Qué te gusta hacer los fines de semana? ¿Qué no te gusta hacer?
4. ¿Qué actividades planeas para este fin de semana?
5. Si te invitan a un concierto de música clásica, ¿tú vas?
6. ¿Te gusta más patinar o esquiar?
7. ¿Adónde fuiste el sábado pasado? ¿Con quién fuiste?
8. ¿Le escribiste a alguien? ¿A quién?
9. ¿Cuándo fue la última vez que tus padres te dieron dinero para comprar ropa?
10. ¿Fuiste alumno(a) de esta universidad el año pasado?

Una encuesta Interview your classmates to identify who fits the following descriptions. Include your instructor, but remember to use the **Ud.** form when addressing him or her. *Answers will vary.*

	Nombre
1. Dio una fiesta el mes pasado.	
2. Fue al zoológico el año pasado.	
3. Va al cine todos los fines de semana.	
4. Fue a un parque de diversiones el verano pasado.	
5. Va a la playa frecuentemente.	
6. Fue de picnic con sus amigos.	
7. Sabe montar a caballo.	
8. Le gusta escalar montañas.	
9. Se queja de sus profesores a veces.	
10. Se despierta muy temprano.	

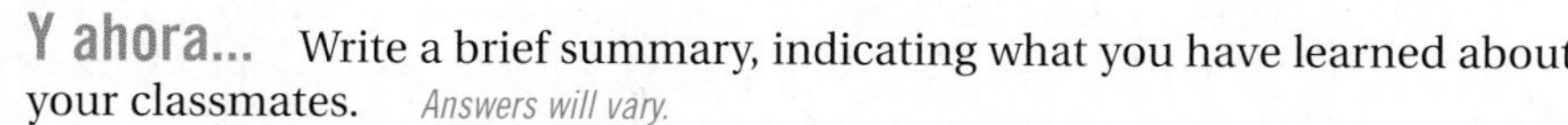

Y ahora... Write a brief summary, indicating what you have learned about your classmates. *Answers will vary.*

¿Cómo lo decimos? What would you say in the following situations? What might the other person say? Act out the scenes with a partner.

1. You ask a friend three questions about his/her daily routine.
2. While leaving a movie theatre, you see a friend. Ask him what movie he saw and whether he liked it.
3. You and a friend are making plans for the weekend and are discussing activities that you like.

Answers: 1. *Answers will vary.* 2. ¿Qué película viste? ¿Te gustó? 3. *Answers will vary.*

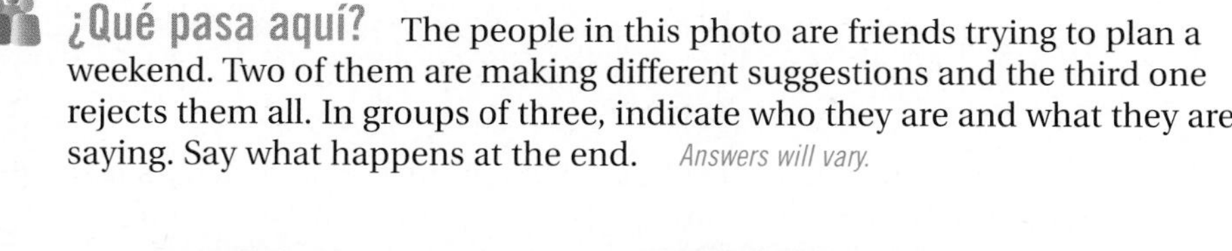

¿Qué pasa aquí? The people in this photo are friends trying to plan a weekend. Two of them are making different suggestions and the third one rejects them all. In groups of three, indicate who they are and what they are saying. Say what happens at the end. *Answers will vary.*

Para escribir

Un día típico Describe a typical day in your life: what time you get up, what you generally eat, where you go, what you do, and so on. *Answers will vary.*

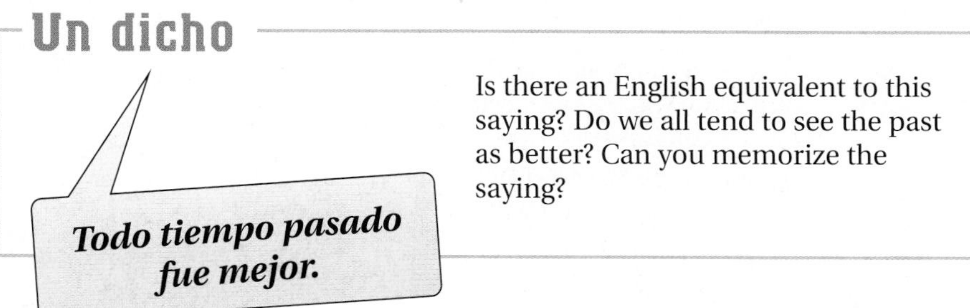

Un dicho

Todo tiempo pasado fue mejor.

Is there an English equivalent to this saying? Do we all tend to see the past as better? Can you memorize the saying?

Lección 8 · Las actividades al aire libre

Susana y Gloria son dos hermanas colombianas que están casadas con Jaime y David, de Venezuela. Los dos matrimonios viven en Caracas, y frecuentemente se juntan para ir a cenar, al cine o a la playa. Ahora están planeando un fin de semana.

Jaime Cuando yo era chico, mi familia y yo siempre íbamos a acampar al Parque Nacional de Canaima, de modo que soy un experto en armar tiendas de campaña, en hacer fogatas...

Susana En cambio Gloria y yo pasábamos nuestras vacaciones en ciudades grandes, y nos hospedábamos en hoteles muy buenos.

Gloria ¡Ay, sí! Ya te dije que nosotras no estábamos acostumbradas a todas estas actividades que te gustan a ti, mi amor.

Jaime ¡Les va a encantar dormir bajo las estrellas, en una bolsa de dormir!

David Oye, tu hermano prometió prestarte sus bolsas de dormir. ¿Te las trajo?

Jaime No, me las va a traer esta noche. También me va a prestar su caña de pescar.

David ¡Ah! No hay nada como comer pescado frito que uno acaba de pescar.

Detalles culturales

El Parque Nacional de Canaima es una de las áreas naturales más importantes de Venezuela y su mayor atracción turística. Aquí se encuentran las cataratas del Salto Ángel, las más altas del mundo. También existe en el parque una gran variedad de animales, muchos en peligro (*danger*) de extinción. Muchas de las plantas que hay en el parque son exclusivas de esta región.

◆ **¿Qué parques nacionales importantes hay en este país?**

Detalles culturales

En Latinoamerica son muy populares los vendedores ambulantes a los que se les pueden comprar diversos artículos. Los productos que ellos venden son más baratos y con ellos es más fácil regatear (*to haggle*).

◆ **¿Son populares los vendedores ambulantes en este país?**

Llegaron al parque el viernes por la tarde. Por la noche no durmieron muy bien y hoy están un poco cansados. Se levantaron muy temprano para hacer una caminata y ahora Jaime y David están tratando de pescar algo en el lago.

David Cuando veníamos para acá vi a unos hombres que vendían pescado. Si no pescamos nada...

Jaime Pronto vamos a tener pescado para el almuerzo. ¡Te lo prometo!

David Espero que sí, porque tengo mucha hambre. Jaime, ¿dónde pusiste el termo de café?

Jaime Se lo di a Gloria esta mañana, porque ella me lo pidió. Oye, después de almorzar podemos alquilar una canoa para ir a remar.

Dos horas más tarde.

David ¿Por qué no llamamos a Gloria y a Susana y les decimos que no pudimos pescar nada?

Jaime ¡Porque nos van a tomar el pelo! ¡Chist! ¡Ahí vienen!

Susana y Gloria traen dos cestas de picnic.

Susana Gloria y yo trajimos comida, por si acaso...

Gloria Pollo frito, ensalada de papas, pastel de manzana...

David ¡Excelente idea! ¡Vamos a comer!

¿Recuerda usted?

¿Verdadero o falso?

With a partner, decide whether the following statements about the dialogue are true (**verdadero**) or false (**falso**).

1. Los dos matrimonios viven en la capital de Venezuela. ☒ V ☐ F
2. Jaime sabe armar tiendas de campaña. ☒ V ☐ F
3. Gloria y su hermana siempre iban a acampar cuando eran ☐ V ☒ F
   niñas. ☒ V ☐ F
4. El hermano de David tiene bolsas de dormir. ☐ V ☒ F
5. A David y a Jaime no les gusta pescar. ☐ V ☒ F
6. El sábado todos se despertaron muy tarde. ☒ V ☐ F
7. Jaime es muy optimista. ☒ V ☐ F
8. Gloria tiene el termo de café. ☐ V ☒ F
9. A Jaime no le gusta remar. ☐ V ☒ F
10. Todos comieron pescado.

Y ahora... conteste

Answer these questions, basing your answers on the dialogue.

1. ¿Para qué se juntan, frecuentemente, los dos matrimonios?
2. ¿A dónde iban a acampar Jaime y su familia cuando él era chico?
3. ¿Dónde pasaban sus vacaciones Gloria y Susana?
4. Según (*According to*) Jaime, ¿qué les va a encantar a Gloria y a Susana?
5. ¿Cómo durmieron todos anoche?
6. ¿Qué le promete Jaime a David?
7. ¿Qué pueden hacer todos después de almorzar?
8. ¿Qué trajeron Susana y Gloria?

Answers: **1.** Se juntan para ir a cenar, al cine o a la playa. **2.** Iban al Parque Nacional de Canaima. **3.** Ellas pasaban sus vacaciones en ciudades grandes. **4.** Les va a encantar dormir bajo las estrellas, en una bolsa de dormir. **5.** No durmieron muy bien. **6.** Le promete que pronto van a tener pescado para el almuerzo. **7.** Pueden alquilar una canoa para ir a pescar. **8.** Trajeron pollo frito, ensalada de papas y pastel de manzanas.

Para hablar del tema: Vocabulario

Online Study Center

For more practice with lesson topics, see the related activities on the ***¡Hola, amigos!*** web site at college.hmco.com/PIC/holaamigos7e.

Cognados

la actividad
la canoa
experto(a)
excelente
el hotel
el termo

Nombres

la actividad al aire libre outdoor activity
la bolsa de dormir* sleeping bag
la caña de pescar fishing rod
la cesta basket
la estrella star
la fogata bonfire
el lago lake
el matrimonio married couple
la tienda de campaña tent

Verbos

acampar to camp
alquilar* to rent
armar to pitch (*a tent*), to put together
encantar[1] to love, to like very much
hospedarse to stay (i.e., *at a hotel*)
juntarse to get together
pasar to spend (time)
pescar to fish, to catch a fish
prestar to lend
prometer to promise
remar to row
tratar (de) to try to
vender to sell

Adjetivos

acostumbrado(a) accustomed or used to
chico(a), pequeño(a) little
frito(a) fried

Otras palabras y expresiones

acá here
acabar de + ***infinitive*** to have just (*done something*)
ahí there
bajo under
en cambio on the other hand
Espero que sí. I hope so.
frecuentemente, a menudo often
hacer una caminata to go hiking
ir a acampar to go camping
mi amor darling, my love
por si acaso just in case
pronto soon
tomarle el pelo a alguien to pull someone's leg
Vamos a comer. Let's eat.

De país a país

la bolsa de dormir el saco de dormir (*Col.*)
alquilar rentar (*Méx.*)
el velero el bote de vela (*Cuba, Arg.*)
el traje de baño la trusa (*Cuba*), el bañador (*Esp.*), la malla (*Cono Sur*)

[1]Conjugated like ***gustar***

Amplíe su vocabulario

Más sobre las actividades al aire libre

jugar al golf

cazar

jugar al tenis

Para practicar el vocabulario

A. Preguntas y respuestas

Match the questions in column *A* with the answers in column *B*.

Answers: 1. h 2. e 3. k 4. b 5. g 6. a 7. j 8. c 9. f 10. l 11. i 12. d

A	B
1. ¿Tienes hambre?	a. Sí, me encanta.
2. ¿Vas a ir a acampar?	b. Sí, soy un experto.
3. ¿Uds. se juntan para salir?	c. Sí, bajo las estrellas.
4. ¿Tú sabes armar tiendas de campaña?	d. En la cesta de picnic.
5. ¿Dónde se hospedaron?	e. Sí, necesito la tienda de campaña.
6. ¿Te gusta pescar?	f. En el termo.
7. ¿Compraste una caña de pescar?	g. En el hotel Hilton.
8. ¿Dormiste en una bolsa de dormir?	h. No, acabo de almorzar.
9. ¿Dónde pusiste el café?	i. No, no me gusta remar.
10. ¿Qué vendían esos hombres?	j. No, me la prestaron.
11. ¿Vas a ir en canoa?	k. Sí, frecuentemente.
12. ¿Dónde pusiste el pollo frito?	l. Pescado.

B. ¿Lógico o ilógico?

With a partner, indicate whether each of the following statements is logical (**L**) or illogical (**I**).

Answers: 1. I 2. L 3. I 4. I 5. L 6. I 7. L 8. I 9. I 10. I

1. Necesitamos el traje de baño para ir a cazar.
2. En la playa generalmente hay salvavidas.
3. Necesito la escopeta para hacer una fogata.
4. Voy a ir a bucear porque quiero tomar el sol.
5. Vamos a hacer esquí acuático en el lago.
6. Para remar usamos la tabla de mar.
7. Hicimos una caminata y ahora estamos muy cansados.
8. Traje los palos de golf para jugar al tenis.
9. Siempre dejamos el velero en el cuarto del hotel.
10. Anoche comimos arena.

C. Palabras y más palabras

¿Qué palabra o frase corresponde a lo siguiente?

1. La necesito para pescar. caña de pescar
2. Las vemos en el cielo (*sky*). estrellas
3. pequeño chico
4. a menudo frecuentemente
5. La necesito para jugar al tenis. raqueta
6. opuesto de comprar vender
7. muy, muy bueno excelente
8. Me gusta mucho. me encanta
9. quedarse (en un hotel) hospedarse
10. La necesito para cazar. escopeta

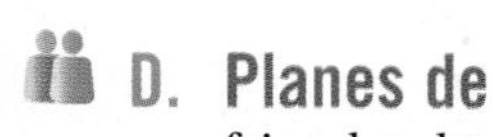

D. Planes de vacaciones You and a classmate play the roles of two friends who are planning a fun weekend. Talk about everything you can do. *Answers will vary.*

Estas chicas fueron a acampar el fin de semana pasado. ¿Qué hicieron?

Pronunciación

Pronunciation in context

In this lesson, there are some words or phrases that may be challenging to pronounce. Listen to your instructor and pronounce the following sentences.

1. **Pasábamos** nuestras **vacaciones** en ciudades grandes y **nos hospedábamos** en hoteles muy buenos.
2. Ya te dije que nosotras no estábamos **acostumbradas** a todas estas **actividades.**
3. **Se levantaron** muy temprano para **hacer** una caminata.
4. **Después** de almorzar podemos **alquilar** una canoa para ir a **remar.**
5. ¿Por qué no **llamamos** a Gloria y a Susana y les **decimos** que no pudimos pescar nada?

For continued pronunciation practice, the ***Pronunciation in context*** feature appears in lessons 8–14. Student may use the *In-text Audio CDs* to practice on their own. Assign pronunciation practice as homework.

Puntos para recordar

1. Preterit of some irregular verbs (*El pretérito de algunos verbos irregulares*)

Suggestion: To help students learn the irregular forms of these verbs, write the following chart on the board.

uv { tener, estar } u { poner, poder, saber }

i { hacer, venir, querer } j { decir, traer, conducir, traducir }

Work with each verb, asking questions and having students make statements about what they did.

◆ The following Spanish verbs are irregular in the preterit.

tener	tuve, tuviste, tuvo, tuvimos, tuvisteis, tuvieron
estar	estuve, estuviste, estuvo, estuvimos, estuvisteis, estuvieron
poder	pude, pudiste, pudo, pudimos, pudisteis, pudieron
poner	puse, pusiste, puso, pusimos, pusisteis, pusieron
saber	supe, supiste, supo, supimos, supisteis, supieron
hacer	hice, hiciste, hizo, hicimos, hicisteis, hicieron
venir	vine, viniste, vino, vinimos, vinisteis, vinieron
querer	quise, quisiste, quiso, quisimos, quisisteis, quisieron
decir	dije, dijiste, dijo, dijimos, dijisteis, dijeron
traer	traje, trajiste, trajo, trajimos, trajisteis, trajeron
conducir[1]	conduje, condujiste, condujo, condujimos, condujisteis, condujeron
traducir[1]	traduje, tradujiste, tradujo, tradujimos, tradujisteis, tradujeron

Extra practice: Write the following phrases on the board or on an overhead transparency. In pairs, have students take turns asking each other: **¿Cuándo fue la última vez que...?**
...tener un examen / estar en un mercado al aire libre / poder ir de compras / hacer un pastel / saber algo interesante / venir tarde a clase / querer ir al parque / conducir el coche de sus padres

¡Atención! The third-person singular of the verb **hacer** changes the **c** to **z** in order to maintain the original soft sound of the **c** in the infinitive. The **i** is omitted in the third-person plural ending of the verbs **decir, traer, conducir,** and **traducir.**

—¿Qué **trajeron** Uds. ayer? — *"What **did you bring** yesterday?"*
—**Trajimos** las cestas. — *"**We brought** the baskets."*

—Ayer no **viniste** a clase. ¿Qué **hiciste?** — *"**You did** not **come** to class yesterday. What **did you do**?"*
—**Tuve** que trabajar. ¿**Hubo** un examen? — *"**I had** to work. **Was there** an exam?"*
—No. — *"No."*

¡Atención! The preterit of **hay** (impersonal form of **haber**) is **hubo.**

[1]**conducir** = *to drive;* **traducir** = *to translate.*

Práctica y conversación

Online Study Center

For more practice with lesson topics, see the related activities on the *¡Hola, amigos!* web site at college.hmco.com/PIC/holaamigos7e.

A. Minidiálogos Complete the following exchanges, using the preterit of the verbs in parentheses. Then act them out with a partner.

1. —¿Dónde _estuviste_ (estar) tú la semana pasada?
   —(Yo) _estuve_ (estar) en el Parque Nacional de Canaima.
   —¿Y tus padres?
   —Ellos _estuvieron_ (estar) en Caracas.
2. —¿Qué _hizo_ (hacer) Roberto ayer?
   —Él _tuvo_ (tener) que trabajar.
3. —¿Tus padres te _trajeron_ (traer) las bolsas de dormir?
   —No, no _pudieron_ (poder) traerlas porque _vinieron_ (venir) en autobús.
4. —Cuando Uds. _vinieron_ (venir) al parque, ¿qué coche (car) _condujeron_ (conducir)?
   —_Condujimos_ (conducir) el coche de papá.
5. —¿Dónde _pusieron_ (poner) Uds. la cesta de picnic?
   —La _pusimos_ (poner) en la mesa.
   —¿Sergio comió con Uds.?
   —No, él no _quiso_ (querer) comer con nosotros.

B. La semana pasada Rewrite this paragraph, changing all the verbs to the preterite to indicate that everything happened last week.

Tengo que limpiar mi apartamento porque Ana y Eva vienen a visitarme. Después hago una torta para ellas. Las chicas traen bolsas de dormir porque no quieren dormir en mi cuarto. Las ponen en la sala y miran televisión hasta tarde. Mi prima Julia está con nosotras hasta las diez, pero no puede quedarse a dormir porque tiene que ir a trabajar.

Answer: Tuve que limpiar mi apartamento porque Ana y Eva vinieron a visitarme. Después hice una torta para ellas. Las chicas trajeron bolsas de dormir porque no quisieron dormir en mi cuarto. Las pusieron en la sala y miraron televisión hasta tarde. Mi prima Julia estuvo con nosotras hasta las diez, pero no pudo quedarse a dormir porque tuvo que ir a trabajar.

Expansion: Have students ask you their questions as a whole-group activity. After you respond, extend the activity by asking the same questions of individual students.

C. Entreviste a su compañero(a) Interview a partner, using the following questions. *Answers will vary.*

1. ¿A qué hora viniste a la universidad ayer?
2. ¿Condujiste tu coche o viniste en ómnibus (*bus*)?
3. ¿Tuviste algún examen? ¿En qué clase?
4. ¿Estuviste en la biblioteca por la tarde?
5. ¿Trajiste algún libro de la biblioteca a la clase?
6. ¿Dónde pusiste tus libros?
7. ¿Hiciste la tarea (*homework*) de la clase de español?
8. ¿Pudiste terminarla?
9. ¿Estuviste en tu casa por la noche?
10. ¿Tuviste una fiesta en tu casa? (¿Quiénes vinieron?)

Extra practice: Have students write compositions based on their partners' responses.

D. Queremos saber... In groups of three, prepare some questions for your instructor about what he or she did yesterday, last night, or last week. Use irregular preterit forms in your questions. *Answers will vary.*

2. Direct and indirect object pronouns used together
(*Los pronombres de complemento directo e indirecto usados juntos*)

Suggestion: To review the forms of the direct and indirect object pronouns, write on the board:

He gives it to me.
Él me lo da.

Emphasize the possible combinations:

me, te, nos, os, se + **lo, la** / **los, las**

Alternative: To illustrate the use of double object pronouns and their position in relation to the verb, hand a book to a student standing with you in front of the class. Pointing to yourself, the student, and the book, say: **Yo te lo doy.** Ask **¿Quién te lo da?** to elicit **Ud. me lo da.** Repeat with other students and other objects. Then proceed in a similar fashion, working with infinitives and gerunds: **¿A quién le vas a dar el libro? ¿Vas a dárselo a Roberto? Juan, ¿a quién le está dando el libro Antonio?**, etc.

- When an indirect object pronoun and a direct object pronoun are used together, the indirect object pronoun always comes first.

Ana **me** da la comida. Ana **me** la da.

- With an infinitive, the pronouns can be placed either before the conjugated verb or after the infinitive.

Ana **me la** va a dar.
Ana va a dár**mela**.[1]

*Ana is going to give **it to me**.*

- With a present participle, the pronouns can be placed either before the conjugated verb or after the present participle.

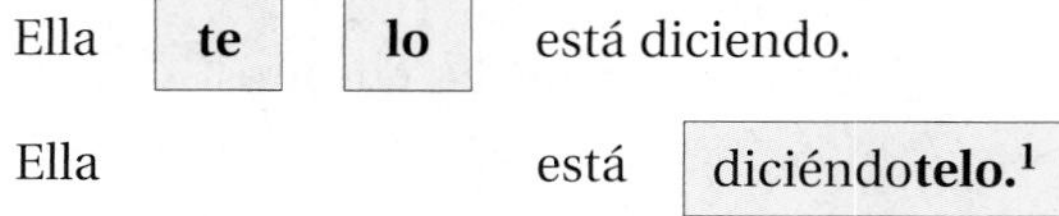

Ella **te lo** está diciendo.
Ella está diciéndo**telo**.[1]

*She is saying **it to you**.*

- If both pronouns begin with **l**, the indirect object pronoun (**le** or **les**) is changed to **se**.

Ana **le** da **la comida.** Ana **se la** da.

[1]Note that the use of the written accent follows the standard rules for the use of accents. See Appendix A.

For clarification, it is sometimes necessary to add **a él, a ella, a Ud., a Uds., a ellos,** or **a ellas.**

—¿A quién le dio la comida Ana? — *"To whom did Ana give the meal?"*
—**Se la** dio **a él.** — *"She gave **it to him.**"*

A proper name may also be given for clarification.

Se la dio **a Luis.** — *She gave **it to Luis.***

Online Study Center

For more practice with lesson topics, see the related activities on the ***¡Hola, amigos!*** web site at college.hmco.com/PIC/holaamigos7e.

Práctica y conversación

Expansion: Ask students to make a list of ten things they want. The other members of the class will tell them who will buy, lend, give, bring, or send them the items requested.

S1 —**Necesito un termo.**
S2 —**Yo te lo compro.**
S3 —**Necesito dinero.**
S4 —**Tus padres te lo prestan.**

A. Un tío generoso

We want to go camping, but we don't have anything that we need. Our generous uncle Ernesto provides everything. Rewrite the statements following the model.

◆ **MODELO:** No tenemos dinero. (dar)
Él nos lo da.

1. Yo necesito una caña de pescar. (prestar)
2. Tú no tienes traje de baño. (comprar)
3. Nosotros necesitamos tablas de mar. (traer)
4. Daniel no tiene esquíes acuáticos. (prestar)
5. Mis hermanas quieren una cesta de picnic. (conseguir)
6. Mis primos necesitan unas raquetas de tenis. (comprar)

Answers: 1. Él me la presta. 2. Él te lo compra. 3. Él nos las trae. 4. Él se los presta. 5. Él se la consigue. 6. Él se las compra.

Expansion: For more advanced students, have students respond to the initial question and then have them say how to obtain the item requested.

S1 —**Necesito 20 dólares. ¿Puedes dármelos?**
S2 —**No, no puedo dártelos. Pedro puede dártelos.**

Answers: 1. No te las traje porque no pude. 2. No se los mandé porque no tuve tiempo. 3. No me la compró porque no quiso. 4. No nos lo dio porque no vino a casa. 5. Me la escribió en inglés porque no sabe español. 6. No se lo llevé porque no lo hice.

B. Excusas, excusas

What excuses would you give in response to these questions? Follow the model and use the cues provided.

◆ **MODELO:** —¿Por qué no le diste el dinero a Ada? (no estuvo aquí)
—No se lo di porque no estuvo aquí.

1. ¿Por qué no me trajiste las raquetas? (no pude)
2. ¿Por qué no les mandaste los palos de golf? (no tuve tiempo)
3. ¿Por qué no te compró tu papá la escopeta? (no quiso)
4. ¿Por qué no les dio Lupe el dinero a Uds.? (no vino a casa)
5. ¿Por qué te escribió Johnny la carta en inglés? (no sabe español)
6. ¿Por qué no les llevaste el pastel a los niños? (no lo hice)

Possible answers: 1. —Susana quiere un traje de baño, ¿tú se lo puedes comprar? —No, lo siento, yo no puedo comprárselo. 2. —David quiere una caña de pescar, ¿tú se la puedes prestar? —No, lo siento, yo no puedo prestársela. 3. —Susana y Gloria quieren raquetas de tenis, ¿tú se las puedes traer? —No, lo siento, yo no puedo traérselas. 4. —Jaime quiere una tabla de mar, ¿tú se la puedes dar? —No, lo siento, yo no puedo dársela. 5. —Lucía quiere palos de golf, ¿tú se los puedes mandar? —No, lo siento, yo no puedo mandárselos. 6. —Jaime y David quieren comida, ¿tú se la puedes conseguir? —No, lo siento, yo no puedo conseguírsela.

C. Lo siento

With a partner, take turns asking and answering questions about what the following people want, saying you cannot help them. Use the verbs **mandar, dar, prestar, comprar, traer,** and **conseguir** and the cues provided.

◆ **MODELO:** —¿Qué quiere Elisa? (dinero)
—Elisa quiere dinero, ¿tú se lo puedes conseguir?
—No, lo siento, yo no puedo conseguírselo.

1. ¿Qué quiere Susana? (un traje de baño)
2. ¿Qué quiere David? (una caña de pescar)
3. ¿Qué quieren Susana y Gloria? (raquetas de tenis)
4. ¿Qué quiere Jaime? (una tabla de mar)
5. ¿Qué quiere Lucía? (palos de golf)
6. ¿Qué quieren Jaime y David? (comida)

D. Comprando comestibles

You went to the market to get groceries for your family. Talk about your errands.

◆ **MODELO:** ¿Quién te dio la lista? (mi mamá)
Mi mamá me la dio.

Answers: 1. Sí, (él) me la escribió. 2. Se lo pedí a mi papá. 3. Se las traje a mi mamá. 4. Se lo compré a mi hermana. 5. Me lo dio mi hermano. 6. Sí, se la traje. 7. No, no se las compré. 8. Se lo compré en la panadería.

1. ¿Tu papá te escribió la lista de los comestibles? (sí)
2. ¿A quién le pediste el dinero? (a mi papá)
3. ¿A quién le trajiste las naranjas? (a mi mamá)
4. ¿A quién le compraste el helado? (a mi hermana)
5. ¿Quién te dio el dinero para comprar la leche? (mi hermano)
6. ¿Le trajiste la carne a tu hermana? (sí)
7. Nosotros te pedimos uvas. ¿Nos las compraste? (no)
8. ¿Dónde le compraste el pan a tu mamá? (la panadería)

Suggestion: Have students suggest different friends or classmates who can help, including themselves.

E. Necesitamos ayuda (*help*)

With a partner, take turns indicating who does what for whom. Use the cues provided.

◆ **MODELO:** Raquel no sabe traducir las cartas. (Ana)
Ana se las traduce.

Answers: 1. Nosotros se la compramos. 2. Yo te la armo. 3. Papá nos la hace. 4. Mi abuelo me lo compra. 5. Mi hermana se las lleva. 6. Su padre se lo consigue.

1. Marta no tiene dinero para comprar una bolsa de dormir. (nosotros)
2. Tú no sabes armar la tienda de campaña. (yo)
3. Nosotras no sabemos hacer una fogata. (papá)
4. Yo no puedo comprar un velero. (mi abuelo)
5. Los chicos no pueden llevarle las raquetas a Teresa. (mi hermana)
6. Ud. no puede conseguir trabajo de salvavidas. (su padre)

3. Stem-changing verbs in the preterit
(*Los verbos con cambio radical en el pretérito*)

- As you will recall, **-ar** and **-er** verbs with stem changes in the present tense have no stem changes in the preterit. However, **-ir** verbs with stem changes in the present tense have stem changes in the third-person singular and plural forms of the preterit (**e** > **i** and **o** > **u**), as shown below.

Suggestion: Emphasize that **-ar** and **-er** stem-changing verbs are regular in the preterit. Practice the third-person forms of these verbs by telling a student something you did. This student repeats the information to the rest of the class.
Instructor: **Yo pedí café.**
Student: **El profesor (La profesora) pidió café.** Or,
Instructor: **David y yo pedimos café.**
Student: **El profesor (La profesora) y David pidieron café.**

servir (*e* > *i*)		dormir (*o* > *u*)	
serví	servimos	dormí	dormimos
serviste	servisteis	dormiste	dormisteis
s**i**rvió	s**i**rvieron	d**u**rmió	d**u**rmieron

- Other **-ir** verbs that follow the same pattern are **pedir** (*to order, to request*), **seguir** (*to continue, to follow*), **sentir(se)** (*to feel*), **conseguir, divertirse** (*to have fun*), and **morir** (*to die*).

—¿Qué te **sirvieron** en la cafetería?	*"What **did they serve** you at the cafeteria?"*
—Me **sirvieron** café y sándwiches.	*"**They served** me coffee and sandwiches."*
—¿Cómo **durmió** Ud. anoche?	*"How **did you sleep** last night?"*
—**Dormí** muy bien.	*"**I slept** very well."*
—¿Se **divirtieron** ayer?	*"Did **you have a good time** yesterday?"*
—Sí, nos **divertimos** mucho.	*"Yes, **we had a** very **good time.**"*

Práctica y conversación

Online Study Center

For more practice with lesson topics, see the related activities on the *¡Hola, amigos!* web site at college.hmco.com/PIC/holaamigos7e.

A. Minidiálogos Complete the following exchanges by supplying the preterit of the verbs given. Then act them out with a partner.

1. **dormir** —¿Cómo durmieron Uds. anoche?
   —Yo dormí muy bien, pero mamá no durmió bien.
2. **pedir** —¿Qué pidieron ellos?
   —Ana pidió pastel y los niños pidieron torta.
3. **seguir** —¿Hasta qué hora siguieron hablando Uds.?
   —Seguimos hablando hasta las doce.
4. **servir** —¿Qué sirvieron Uds. en la fiesta?
   —Servimos torta y Coca-Cola.
5. **divertirse** —¿Se divirtieron Uds. mucho?
   —Yo me divertí pero Julio no se divirtió mucho.
6. **conseguir** —¿Consiguieron ellos el dinero?
   —No, no lo consiguieron.
7. **morir** —Hubo un accidente, ¿no?
   —Sí, y murió mucha gente.

Answers: 1. Arturo durmió. 2. Ernesto le pidió dinero a Daniel. 3. Paco siguió a su mamá. 4. Mirta y Rafael se divirtieron mucho. 5. El mozo sirvió café. 6. Pilar consiguió trabajo.

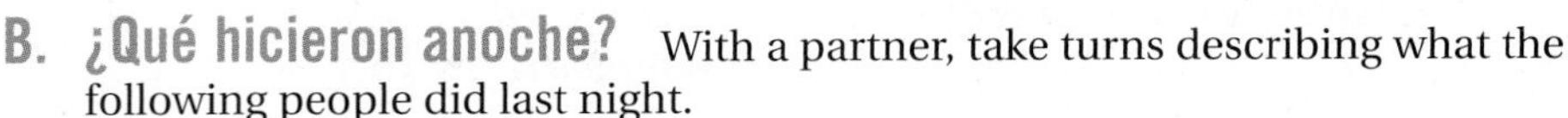

B. ¿Qué hicieron anoche? With a partner, take turns describing what the following people did last night.

1. Arturo ________. 2. Ernesto ________. 3. Paco ________.

4. Mirta y Rafael ________. 5. El mozo ________. 6. Pilar ________.

C. Fuimos a cenar In groups of three, tell your classmates about a recent meal at a restaurant. Tell where you went and with whom, what you ordered, and whether or not you had a good time. *Answers will vary.*

4. The imperfect tense (*El imperfecto de indicativo*)

Forms of the imperfect

Suggestion: Asking students questions like **¿Qué hora era cuando Ud.... llegó hoy? (...se acostó anoche?, se levantó esta mañana?,** and so on) will help them acquire a feeling for the use of the imperfect. Also, point out that English phrases like *used to live, was going,* and so on are often expressed in Spanish by the imperfect tense: **vivía, iba.**

- There are two simple past tenses in the Spanish indicative: the preterit, which you have been studying, and the imperfect. To form the imperfect, add the following endings to the verb stem.

-ar verbs	-er and -ir verbs	
hablar	***comer***	***vivir***
habl- **aba**	com- **ía**	viv- **ía**
habl- **abas**	com- **ías**	viv- **ías**
habl- **aba**	com- **ía**	viv- **ía**
habl- **ábamos**	com- **íamos**	viv- **íamos**
habl- **abais**	com- **íais**	viv- **íais**
habl- **aban**	com- **ían**	viv- **ían**

Extra practice: Ask students personalized questions about their childhoods that require simple affirmative or negative responses in the imperfect.

Examples: **1. ¿Qué querías ser? 2. ¿Hablabas mucho por teléfono? 3. ¿Sabías nadar? 4. ¿Estudiabas mucho? 5. ¿Dónde vivías? 6. ¿Tenías que limpiar tu casa? 7. ¿Comías mucho? 8. ¿Cuántas horas dormías?**

Note that the endings of the **-er** and **-ir** verbs are the same. Observe the accent on the first-person plural form of **-ar** verbs: **hablábamos.** Note also that there is a written accent on the first **í** of the endings of the **-er** and **-ir** verbs.

—Tú siempre te **levantabas** a las seis, ¿no?
—Sí, porque mis clases **empezaban** a las siete y media y yo **vivía** lejos de la universidad.

*"You always **used to get up** at six, didn't you?"*
*"Yes, because my classes **started** at seven-thirty and I **lived** far from the university."*

¡Atención! Stem-changing verbs are regular in the imperfect.

- Only three Spanish verbs are irregular in the imperfect tense: **ser, ir,** and **ver.**

ser	ir	ver
era	iba	veía
eras	ibas	veías
era	iba	veía
éramos	íbamos	veíamos
erais	ibais	veíais
eran	iban	veían

—Cuando yo **era** chica, siempre **iba** a acampar en el verano.
—Nosotros **íbamos** también.

*"When I **was** little, **I** always **went** camping in the summer."*
*"**We used to go** too."*

—¿Cuándo **veías** a tus amigos?
—Los **veía** sólo los sábados y los domingos.

*"When **did you see** your friends?"*
*"**I used to see** them only on Saturdays and Sundays."*

Uses of the imperfect

Suggestion: The contrast between the uses of the imperfect and the preterit is covered in **Lección 9**. You may want to use the examples here as a preview.

Point out that the imperfect is equivalent to the *was* (*were*) + *-ing* construction in English.

- The Spanish imperfect tense is equivalent to three English forms.

Yo **vivía** en Caracas.	*I* ***used to live*** *in Caracas.* *I* ***was living*** *in Caracas.* *I* ***lived*** *in Caracas.*

- The imperfect is used to describe actions or events that the speaker views as in the process of happening in the past, with no reference to when they began or ended.

Empezábamos a estudiar cuando él vino.	***We were beginning*** *to study when he came.*

- It is also used to refer to habitual or repeated actions in the past, again with no reference to when they began or ended.

—¿Uds. **hablaban** inglés cuando **vivían** en Bogotá?	*"**Did** you **speak** English when **you lived** in Bogotá?"*
—No, cuando **vivíamos** allí siempre **hablábamos** español.	*"No, when **we lived** there we always **spoke** Spanish."*

- It describes physical, mental, or emotional conditions in the past.

Mi casa **era** muy grande.	*My house **was** very big.*
No me **gustaba** estudiar.	***I didn't like*** *to study.*
Yo no me **sentía** bien.	*I **wasn't feeling** well.*

- It expresses time and age in the past.

—¿Qué hora **era**?	*"What time **was it**?"*
—**Eran** las seis.	*"**It was** six o'clock."*
Julia **tenía** veinte años.	*Julia **was** twenty years old.*

- The imperfect is used to describe or set the stage in the past.

Mi novia **era** bonita.	*My girlfriend **was** pretty.*
Era muy tarde.	***It was** very late.*

Práctica y conversación

Online Study Center

For more practice with lesson topics, see the related activities on the *¡Hola, amigos!* web site at college.hmco.com/PIC/holaamigos7e.

A. La vida cambia... Things have changed; tell how they used to be.

Answers will vary.

1. Ahora vivo en..., pero cuando era niño(a)...
2. Ahora hablamos español, pero cuando éramos niños(as)...
3. Ahora comemos pescado, pero cuando éramos niños(as)...
4. Ahora mis padres no se divierten mucho, pero cuando tenían veinte años...
5. Ahora Julia no ve a sus tíos, pero cuando era niña...
6. Ahora tú vas al teatro, pero cuando eras niño(a)...
7. Ahora mi hermana no da fiestas, pero cuando tenía dieciocho años...
8. Ahora me gustan los vegetales, pero cuando era niño(a)...
9. Ahora mi mamá nada muy bien, pero cuando era pequeña...
10. Ahora Ud. se levanta a las nueve, pero cuando era pequeño(a)...

Expansion: Assign as homework. As a variation, have students write five sentences about themselves following this pattern.

Verbs: **1.** (no) vivía... **2.** (no) hablábamos... **3.** (no) comíamos... **4.** se divertían... **5.** veía... **6.** (no) ibas... **7.** daba... **8.** (no) me gustaban... **9.** (no) nadaba... **10.** (no) se levantaba...

B. Entreviste a su compañero(a) Interview a partner, using the following questions.

Answers will vary.

1. ¿Dónde vivías cuando eras niño(a)?
2. ¿Con quién vivías?
3. ¿Tu casa era grande o pequeña?
4. ¿Cuántos dormitorios tenía?
5. ¿En qué idioma te hablaban tus padres?
6. ¿A qué escuela (*school*) ibas?
7. ¿Te gustaba estudiar?
8. ¿Qué te gustaba comer?
9. ¿Qué te gustaba hacer los sábados? ¿Y los domingos?
10. ¿Pasabas mucho tiempo con tus amigos los fines de semana?
11. ¿Sabías nadar? ¿Ibas a acampar?
12. ¿Jugabas al béisbol o al fútbol?

Follow-up: Have students use these questions as the basis of compositions about themselves.

Verbs: **1.** vivía... **2.** vivía... **3.** era... **4.** tenía... **5.** hablaban... **6.** iba... **7.** (no) me gustaba... **8.** me gustaba... **9.** me gustaba... **10.** (no) pasaba... **11.** (no) sabía... / (no) iba... **12.** (no) jugaba...

Detalles culturales

El béisbol es un deporte (*sport*) muy popular en Venezuela, Cuba, Puerto Rico y la República Dominicana. Muchos de los jugadores (*players*) de las Grandes Ligas de los Estados Unidos son de estos países. En España y en la mayoría de los otros países latinoamericanos el deporte más popular es el fútbol (*soccer*).

- **¿Cuáles son los deportes más populares en este país?**

Suggestion: Assign as homework and compare answers in class. You may want to develop several versions of the "story" or make up additional questions to continue it spontaneously in class (e.g., **¿Qué buscaban la chica rubia y el muchacho moreno? ¿Qué decían?**).

Verbs: 1. era(n)... 2. Estaba... 3. veníamos... 4. íbamos... 5. hablábamos... 6. era... 7. era... 8. (no) esperábamos...

C. En el parque Use your imagination to tell what was happening when you and your friends were seen in the park. *Answers will vary.*

Anoche te vi en el parque con unos amigos.

1. ¿Qué hora era?
2. ¿Con quiénes estabas?
3. ¿De dónde venían Uds.?
4. ¿Adónde iban?
5. ¿De qué hablaban?
6. ¿Quién era la chica pelirroja?
7. ¿Quién era el muchacho alto y moreno?
8. ¿Esperaban a alguien?

D. Queremos saber With a partner, prepare five questions to ask your instructor about what he or she used to do when he or she was a teenager (**adolescente**). *Answers will vary.*

5. Formation of adverbs (*La formación de los adverbios*)

Expansion: Point out that just as *easily* means *with ease*, **fácilmente** means **con facilidad.** Give similar phrases to elicit the corresponding adverbs: **con frecuencia, con lentitud, con rapidez, con claridad, por lo general, por completo, con franqueza,** etc.

- Most Spanish adverbs are formed by adding **-mente** (the equivalent of the English *-ly*) to the adjective.

general	*general*	general**mente**	*general**ly***
reciente	*recent*	reciente**mente**	*recent**ly***

—¿La fiesta de bienvenida es para Olga y sus amigas? *"The welcome party is for Olga and her friends?"*
—No, es **especialmente** para Olga. *"No, it's **especially** for Olga."*

- Adjectives ending in **-o** change the **-o** to **-a** before adding **-mente.**

lent**o**	*slow*	lent**amente**	*slow**ly***
rápid**o**	*rapid*	rápid**amente**	*rapid**ly***

- If two or more adverbs are used together, both change the **-o** to **-a,** but only the last one in the sentence ends in **-mente.**

Habla clar**a** y lent**amente.** *She speaks clear**ly** and slow**ly.***

- If the adjective has an accent mark, the adverb retains it.

fácil	*easy*	**fá**cilmente	*easily*

Práctica y conversación

Online Study Center

For more practice with lesson topics, see the related activities on the ***¡Hola, amigos!*** web site at college.hmco.com/PIC/holaamigos7e.

A. De adjetivos a adverbios You can recognize the following Spanish adjectives because they are cognates. Change them to adverbs.

1. real realmente
2. completo completamente
3. raro raramente
4. frecuente frecuentemente
5. posible posiblemente
6. general generalmente
7. franco francamente
8. normal normalmente

B. Lo entiendo perfectamente Use some of the adverbs you have learned to complete the following sentences appropriately.

1. Ellos hablan ________ y ________.
2. Viene a casa ________.
3. Yo ________ estudio por la mañana.
4. ________, no quiero bailar con Ud.
5. Ellos vuelven mañana, ________.
6. Los chicos escriben muy ________.
7. ________ estoy muy cansado.
8. Yo no escribo cartas; ________ escribo mensajes electrónicos (*e-mail*).

Possible Answers: **1.** lenta y claramente **2.** frecuentemente **3.** generalmente **4.** Francamente **5.** probablemente **6.** claramente **7.** Realmente **8.** normalmente

C. ¿Cuándo...? With a partner, talk about what you and your friends generally do, frequently do, and rarely do. *Answers will vary.*

Suggestion: To model, tell students something you generally do and rarely do. Follow up by having students report to the class.

Entre nosotros

¡Conversemos!

Detalles culturales

En muchos países latinoamericanos y en España se usa el sistema de estrellas para clasificar los hoteles de lujo (*luxury*) y de primera clase.

◆ **¿Se hospeda Ud. a veces en hoteles de cinco estrellas?**

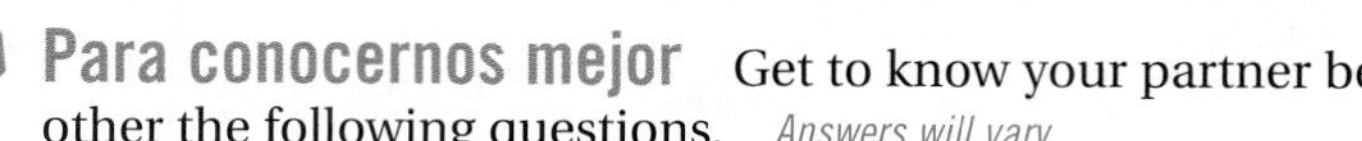

Para conocernos mejor Get to know your partner better by asking each other the following questions. *Answers will vary.*

1. ¿Esperas poder ir de vacaciones este verano? ¿Adónde quieres ir?
2. La última vez que fuiste de vacaciones, ¿te hospedaste en un hotel de cinco estrellas?
3. ¿Dónde pasaste las vacaciones el año pasado? ¿Te aburriste o te divertiste?
4. ¿Te juntas a veces con tus amigos para salir?
5. ¿Te gusta ir a acampar, o prefieres ir a un buen hotel?
6. ¿Qué actividades al aire libre te gustaban cuando eras chico?
7. ¿Ahora prefieres hacer esquí acuático, hacer surfing o bucear?
8. ¿Qué prefieres, mirar televisión o hacer una caminata?
9. Necesito tu raqueta de tenis, ¿puedes prestármela?
10. ¿Te gusta jugar al golf? ¿Tienes palos de golf?

Una encuesta Interview your classmates to identify who does the following. Be sure to change the statements to questions. Include your instructor, but remember to use the **Ud.** form when addressing him or her. *Answers will vary.*

	Nombre
1. Hizo esquí acuático en un lago el año pasado.	______
2. Va a tratar de alquilar una cabaña (cabin) el verano próximo (next).	______
3. Prometió ser más paciente.	______
4. Va a acampar a menudo.	______
5. Acaba de comer.	______
6. Pronto va a tener vacaciones.	______
7. Le gusta tomar el sol.	______
8. Compró un traje de baño recientemente.	______
9. Es experto(a) en armar tiendas de campaña.	______
10. Siempre les toma el pelo a sus amigos.	______

Y ahora... Write a brief summary, indicating what you have learned about your classmates. *Answers will vary.*

¿Cómo lo decimos? What would you say in the following situations? What might the other person say? Act out the scenes with a partner. *Answers will vary.*

1. You ask a friend if he or she prefers to go to the beach, to go hiking, or to go camping near a lake or a river (**río**) for a couple of days.
2. You are going on a camping trip for the first time. Tell a friend what items you need and what you need to learn to do.
3. Tell someone what your favorite outdoor activities are. Mention at least four.

Answers: 1. ¿Prefieres ir a la playa, hacer una caminata o ir a acampar cerca de un lago o de un río por un par de días? 2. *Answers will vary.* 3. *Answers will vary.*

¿Qué pasa aquí? In groups of three or four, create a story about the people in the illustration. Say who they are and what their relationships are to one another. Also say what activities they are doing and what they will do later. *Answers will vary.*

Para escribir

De vacaciones Write a conversation between you and a friend, in which you are deciding what you are going to do when you have a couple of days off. One of you loves outdoor activities and the other doesn't. Try to compromise. *Answers will vary.*

Un dicho

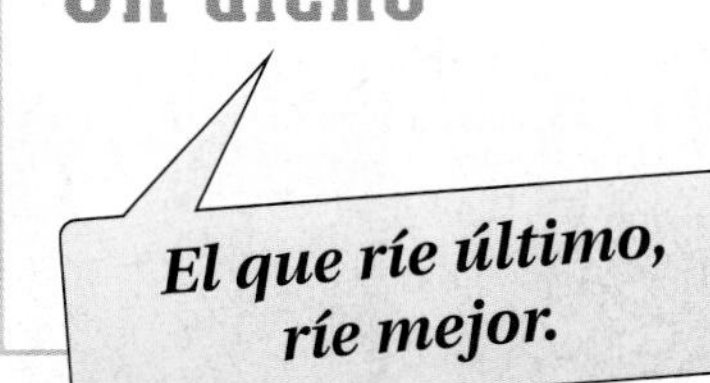

Undoubtedly, you know the English version of this saying. Memorize it in Spanish, and use it at appropriate times.

Lectura

Reading strategy: If needed, explain to students that, when they scan, they are looking for specific information and not reading every word. Help students recognize and interpret the images to comprehend the poem better.

Answers: 1. Nació en 1853. **2.** Murió en Cuba en 1895 en un campo de batalla. **3.** Los temas principales son la libertad, la justicia, la independencia de su patria y la defensa de los pobres y los oprimidos. **4.** Se describe como un hombre sincero. **5.** Quiere echar sus versos del alma. **6.** Dice que su verso es de un verde claro y de un carmín encendido. También dice que su verso es un ciervo herido que busca amparo en el monte. **7.** Quiere echar su suerte con los pobres de la tierra. **8.** Cultiva la rosa blanca. **9.** Cultiva la rosa para los dos. **10.** Simboliza el amor. **11.** No, no los odia.

Estrategia de lectura What images or ideas do you associate with the colors green, red, and white? Scan the two poems and make a list of the words associated with nature. *Answers will vary.*

Vamos a leer As you read the introduction to Martí and the poems, answer the following questions.

1. ¿En qué año nació (*was born*) el poeta?
2. ¿Dónde y en qué año murió?
3. ¿Cuáles son los temas principales de la poesía de Martí?
4. ¿Cómo se describe el poeta en el primer poema?
5. ¿Qué quiere hacer Martí antes de morirse?
6. ¿Qué imágenes usa Martí para describir sus versos?
7. ¿Con quiénes quiere echar su suerte el poeta?
8. ¿Qué flor (*flower*) cultiva el poeta?
9. ¿Cultiva el poeta la rosa solamente para sus amigos o también para sus enemigos?
10. ¿Qué simboliza la rosa blanca?
11. Según este poema, ¿el poeta odia a sus enemigos?

José Martí (Cuba: 1853–1895) dedicó su vida y su obra a la independencia de Cuba, donde murió en el campo de batalla° en 1895. Es famoso, no sólo como poeta y ensayista, sino también como orador.

Los poemas de Martí se caracterizan por la melodía, el ritmo y el uso de oraciones cortas, con las que expresa ideas muy profundas. Sus temas principales son la libertad, la justicia, la independencia de su patria y la defensa de los pobres y los oprimidos.°

Campo... *battlefield*

oppressed

Video

De Versos sencillos[1]

JOSÉ MARTÍ

I

Yo soy un hombre sincero
de donde crece° la palma;
y antes de morirme, quiero
echar° mis versos del alma.°

grows
to pour out / soul

V

Mi verso es de un verde claro,°
y de un carmín encendido°:
mi verso es un ciervo herido°
que busca en el monte amparo.°

light
***carmín...** bright red*
***ciervo...** wounded deer*
shelter

III

Con los pobres de la tierra,°
quiero yo mi suerte echar;°
el arroyo° de la sierra
me complace° más que el mar.

earth, land
***mi...** to share my destiny*
brook
pleases

XXXIX

Cultivo una rosa blanca,
en julio como en enero,
para el amigo sincero
que me da su mano franca.°

open

Y para el cruel que me arranca°
el corazón con que vivo,
cardo° ni ortiga° cultivo:
cultivo la rosa blanca.

tears out
thistle / nettle

[1]Este poema es la letra de la canción "La Guantanamera".

Díganos Answer the following questions based on your own thoughts and experiences. *Answers will vary.*

1. ¿Ha oído Ud. la canción "La Guantanamera"?
2. Al final del segundo poema, el poeta perdona (*forgives*) las ofensas de sus enemigos. ¿Haría Ud. (*Would you do*) lo mismo?

Expansion: You might want to play the song in class.

Recuerdos

Pablo y Marisa están en la casa de los padres de ella. Marisa y su mamá invitan a Pablo cenar y también a acampar con la familia ese fin de semana. El problema es que Pablo no sabe nada de acampar y ellas creen que él es un experto en actividades al aire libre.

El mundo hispánico

Cuba

- Cuba es la mayor de las islas del archipiélago de las Antillas. Su figura es similar a la de un cocodrilo y, como es larga (*long*) y estrecha (*narrow*), tiene extensas costas en las cuales hay playas de gran belleza (*beauty*). Muchos llaman a Cuba "la Perla de las Antillas".
- Hoy Cuba exporta azúcar, níquel, tabaco y frutas. El tabaco cubano tiene fama mundial. Sin embargo, las principales fuentes de ingreso (*sources of income*) del país son el turismo y el dinero que les envían a sus familiares más de un millón de cubanos que viven en el extranjero (*abroad*).

▲ La Catedral, construida entre 1748 y 1767, en La Habana Vieja.

- La Habana, la capital, es la ciudad más grande del Caribe. La Habana Vieja (*old*), su sección antigua, se caracteriza por sus iglesias, plazas, fortalezas, y edificios coloniales, como la Catedral y su plaza, y las fortalezas de El Morro y la Cabaña. En la Habana nació José Martí, escritor, poeta y el más famoso de los patriotas cubanos.
- La música cubana o afrocubana es muy popular en todo el mundo. De Cuba vienen el son, el danzón, la rumba, la conga, el cha cha cha, el mambo y, en buena parte, la salsa. El deporte más popular del país es el béisbol, al que los cubanos llaman "la pelota".

Colombia

- Colombia es la única nación nombrada en honor de Cristóbal Colón. Es el cuarto país suramericano en tamaño (*size*), y es el único con costas en el Pacífico y en el mar Caribe.
- Colombia produce y exporta café, bananas, flores y petróleo. El café colombiano tiene fama mundial por su alta calidad. Colombia es también famosa por sus esmeraldas, consideradas las mejores del mundo. El 90 por ciento de todas las esmeraldas provienen de este país.

▲ Vista panorámica de Bogotá de noche

- La música típica de Colombia es muy variada. Incluye la cumbia y el vallenato, que han alcanzado fama internacional. Shakira, Juanes y Carlos Vives son cantantes populares en los Estados Unidos.
- La capital de Colombia es Bogotá, una ciudad rodeada (*surrounded*) de montañas, por lo que el transporte entre ella y el resto del país es principalmente por vía aérea. En la ciudad hay muchos museos, pero el más famoso de ellos es el Museo del Oro, que tiene una de las mejores colecciones de la artesanía precolombina, incluidos unos 30.000 objetos de oro.
- El deporte más popular en todo el país es el fútbol, y Colombia es uno de los cuatro países latinoamericanos donde se celebran las corridas de toros (*bullfights*).

Online Study Center

For more practice with lesson topics, see the related activities on the ***¡Hola, amigos!*** web site at college.hmco.com/PIC/holaamigos7e.

Puerto Rico

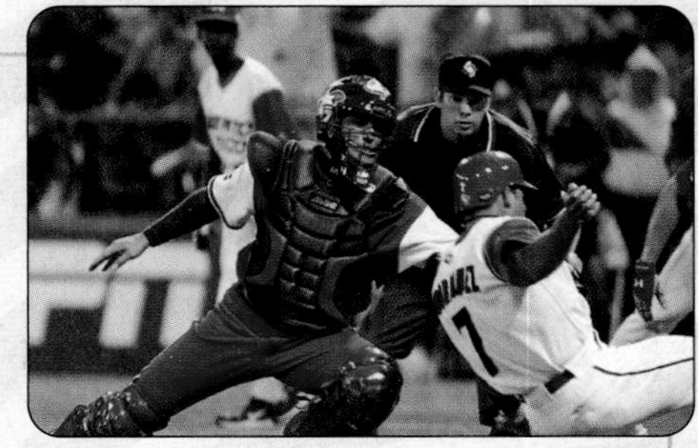

▲ Jugada (*play*) sensacional durante el Campeonato Mundial de Béisbol entre Cuba y Puerto Rico, 2006

- Puerto Rico, "la isla del encanto", es la menor de las islas de las Antillas Mayores. Los indios la llamaban **Boriquén** (modernizado luego como **Borinquen**), y aún hoy muchos la llaman así, y llaman **boricuas** a sus habitantes.
- Puerto Rico está muy densamente poblado; en un área de menos de 3.500 millas cuadradas de superficie, viven cerca de (*around*) 4 millones de habitantes. Desde 1952 el país es un Estado libre asociado de los Estados Unidos.
- San Juan, la capital, es la ciudad más grande y más poblada. Su parte antigua, el Viejo San Juan, es un centro de atracción turística por sus interesantes museos, sus edificios coloniales y las fortalezas de El Morro y San Cristóbal. Otros puntos de interés son sus playas y el Yunque, un bosque (*forest*) tropical.
- Igual que en Cuba, se ve la influencia de España, de África y de Estados Unidos en el arte y en la música. De los deportes, el más popular es el béisbol.

Venezuela

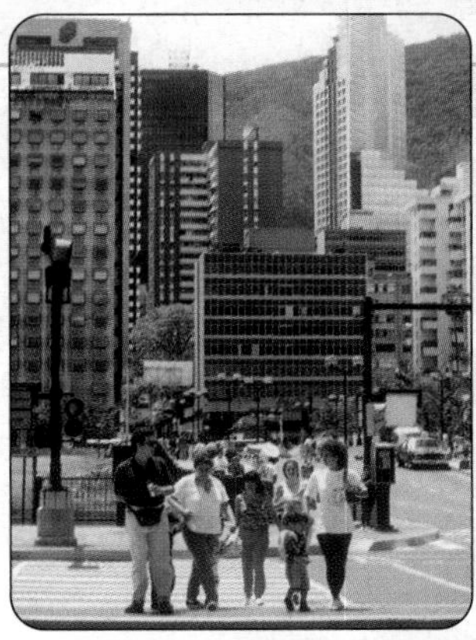

▲ Una familia cruza una calle en Caracas. Al fondo se ven los modernos edificios de la ciudad y una majestuosa montaña.

- Cuando los conquistadores españoles llegaron al lago Maracaibo, las construcciones de los indígenas a orillas del lago les recordaron las de Venecia, y por eso llamaron al país Venezuela, nombre que significa "pequeña Venecia".
- El país es uno de los diez mayores exportadores de petróleo del mundo. Más de la octava parte del petróleo importado por los Estados Unidos viene de Venezuela. La mayor parte de su gran reserva de petróleo se encuentra debajo del lago Maracaibo. Este lago es el mayor de Venezuela y de toda América del Sur.
- La principal atracción turística del país es el Salto Ángel, mucho más alto que las cataratas del Niágara.
- Caracas, la capital de Venezuela, es el centro gubernamental, financiero, cultural y artístico del país. En Caracas nació Simón Bolívar, llamado el Libertador de América.

▲ Juan Luis Guerra es un compositor y cantante (*singer*) de merengue

La República Dominicana

- La República Dominicana ocupa las dos terceras partes de la isla que Colón descubrió en su primer viaje y a la que llamó La Española. La parte occidental de la isla está ocupada por la República de Haití. Su economía se basa en la agricultura, pero el turismo comienza a ser una buena fuente de ingresos para el país. Sus principales atracciones son sus construcciones coloniales y sus hermosas playas.
- La música típica del país es el merengue, pero además son populares otros ritmos del Caribe como la rumba y la salsa. Como en Cuba y en Puerto Rico, el béisbol es el deporte más popular de la isla.
- Casi la mitad de la población del país vive en la capital, Santo Domingo, la primera ciudad europea fundada en el Nuevo Mundo. Aquí se encuentran algunas de las construcciones coloniales más antiguas de América.

Comentarios... With a partner, discuss in Spanish what impressed you most about these countries, and compare them to your own. Which places do you want to visit and why?

Tome este examen

Lección 7

Lección 7

Answers: 1. Ellos comieron tortilla y bebieron limonada. 2. Luis salió a las ocho y volvió a las cinco. 3. Tú cerraste la puerta y abriste las ventanas. 4. Yo empecé a las seis y terminé a las ocho. 5. Nosotros leímos un poema y ella leyó una novela. 6. Yo busqué el dinero y no lo encontré. 7. Yo llegué temprano y comencé a trabajar. 8. Yo compré carne aquí y pagué menos.

A. Preterit of regular verbs

Rewrite the following sentences, changing the verbs to the preterit.

1. Ellos comen tortilla y beben limonada.
2. Luis sale a las ocho y vuelve a las cinco.
3. Tú cierras la puerta y abres las ventanas.
4. Yo empiezo a las seis y termino a las ocho.
5. Nosotros leemos un poema y ella lee una novela.
6. Yo busco el dinero y no lo encuentro.
7. Yo llego temprano y comienzo a trabajar.
8. Yo compro carne aquí y pago menos.

Answers: 1. fue 2. Dieron 3. fue 4. fui 5. fueron 6. Di 7. fui 8. fuimos

B. Preterit of *ser, ir,* and *dar*

Change the verbs in the following sentences to the preterit.

1. Ella va a la discoteca.
2. Dan mucho dinero.
3. ¿Ud. es mi profesor?
4. Yo voy más tarde.
5. Ellos son mis alumnos.
6. Doy muchas fiestas.
7. Yo soy su novio.
8. Nosotros vamos al cine.

Answers: 1. No, no me traen el jugo. 2. No, no le doy el dinero a él. 3. No, no te voy a comprar los libros. (No, no voy a comprarte los libros). 4. No, no le voy a dar los cuadernos a Elsa. (No, no voy a darle los cuadernos a Elsa). 5. No, no me gusta el café. 6. No, no nos van a dar las invitaciones. (No, no van a darnos las invitaciones.)

C. Indirect object pronouns

Answer the following questions in the negative.

1. ¿Te traen el jugo?
2. ¿Le das el dinero a él?
3. ¿Me vas a comprar los libros?
4. ¿Le vas a dar los cuadernos a Elsa?
5. ¿Le gusta el café a Ud.?
6. ¿Ellos les van a dar las invitaciones a Uds.?

D. The verb *gustar*

Complete the following sentences with the Spanish equivalent of the words in parentheses.

1. Me gusta patinar, pero no me gusta nadar. (*I like / I don't like*)
2. ¿ Te gusta esta película, Anita? (*Do you like*)
3. A mi mamá le gusta más ese club. (*My mother likes better*)
4. Nos gusta levantarnos temprano. (*We like*)
5. A mi hermano le gusta bailar salsa. (*My brother likes*)

E. Reflexive constructions Complete these sentences, using the verbs from the following list appropriately. Use each verb once.

acostarse afeitarse bañarse levantarse probarse sentarse vestirse

1. Mis hijos se levantan muy temprano y se acuestan tarde.
2. Yo voy a afeitarme la barba (*beard*).
3. ¿Tú te pruebas el vestido (*dress*) antes de comprarlo?
4. Ella siempre se sienta en esa silla.
5. Nosotros nunca nos bañamos por la noche.
6. Él va a vestirse ahora. Necesita el traje (*suit*) azul.

F. Vocabulary Complete the following sentences, using vocabulary from **Lección 7.**

1. Este fin de semana voy a ir a la playa.
2. No me divertí; me aburrí.
3. Ellos se levantan a las siete de la mañana.
4. Mañana vamos a ir a un partido de fútbol.
5. En el cine Rex, ponen hoy una película muy buena.
6. El niño rompió el florero ayer.
7. En el zoológico hay muchos animales.
8. Ellos van a ir a escalar montañas este verano.
9. Carlos fue a montar a caballo.
10. Son las doce de la noche: es medianoche.
11. Voy a nadar en el lago (*lake*).
12. Esta noche vamos a estudiar, en vez de ir al teatro.

G. Culture Complete the following sentences, based on the cultural notes you have read.

1. El sobrenombre de Enrique es Quique.
2. Las películas americanas son muy populares en el mundo hispano.

Lección 8

Lección 8

Answers: 1. trajeron / traje 2. Tuve 3. hizo 4. dijiste / dijeron 5. vino / viniste 6. estuvimos / estuvieron 7. hicieron 8. supe 9. condujeron / conduje 10. quiso

A. Preterit of some irregular verbs

Change the verbs in the following sentences to the preterit tense.

1. Ellos traen la raqueta y yo traigo la caña de pescar.
2. Tengo que ir al hotel.
3. ¿Qué hace él con la escopeta?
4. Tú dices que sí y ellos dicen que no.
5. Laura viene al parque conmigo y tú vienes con Sergio.
6. Tú y yo estamos aquí y ellos están allá.
7. Ellas hacen el postre.
8. Yo sé toda la verdad.
9. Ellas conducen muy bien, pero yo conduzco muy mal.
10. Enrique no quiere ir a pescar.

Answers: 1. Sí, te (se) las compré. 2. Sí, se los trajimos. 3. Sí, me lo van a dar. (Sí, van a dármelo.) 4. Sí, nos los va a traer. (Sí, va a traérnoslos.) 5. Sí, se la va a comprar. (Sí, va a comprársela.) 6. Sí, me las traen.

B. Direct and indirect object pronouns used together

Answer the following questions in the affirmative, replacing the direct objects with direct object pronouns.

1. ¿Me compraste *las raquetas*?
2. ¿Nos trajeron Uds. *los palos de golf*?
3. ¿Ellos te van a dar *el traje de baño*? (*two ways*)
4. ¿Él les va a traer *los termos* a Uds.? (*two ways*)
5. ¿Ella me va a comprar *la canoa*? (*Use the **Ud.** form.*) (*two ways*)
6. ¿Ellos te traen *las cestas*?

C. Stem-changing verbs in the preterit

Complete the following sentences in the preterit tense, using the verbs listed.

conseguir	divertirse	dormir
morir	pedir	seguir

1. Ana y Eva __se divirtieron__ mucho en la fiesta. Cuando volvieron a casa, __siguieron__ hablando y no __durmieron__ mucho por la noche.
2. Elsa __pidió__ la comida y Juan se la trajo.
3. Hubo un accidente, pero no __murió__ nadie.
4. Roberto __consiguió__ el pescado en el mercado.

Answers: 1. ibas 2. era 3. hablaban 4. veíamos 5. pescaban 6. comía

D. The imperfect tense

Change the verbs in the following sentences to the imperfect.

1. ¿Tú vas al supermercado con tu papá?
2. Ella es muy bonita.
3. Ellos hablan español.
4. Nosotros no vemos a nuestros amigos.
5. Uds. nunca pescan en el lago.
6. Yo siempre como frutas por la mañana.

E. Formation of adverbs Write the following adverbs in Spanish.

1. easily
2. especially
3. slowly
4. rapidly
5. slowly and clearly
6. frankly

Answers: 1. fácilmente 2. especialmente 3. lentamente 4. rápidamente 5. lenta y claramente 6. francamente

Lección 8

F. Vocabulary Complete the following sentences, using vocabulary from **Lección 8.**

1. ¿Qué actividades al ___aire___ libre prefieres?
2. Voy a ir a ___cazar___; necesito la escopeta.
3. Él no sabe ___armar___ una tienda de campaña.
4. Voy a poner el pollo en la ___cesta___ de pícnic.
5. No quiero ir en la canoa porque no sé ___remar___.
6. Ellos siempre me toman el ___pelo___.
7. Un sinónimo de "a menudo" es ___frecuentemente___.
8. No me gusta hacer esquí ___acuático___.
9. Cuando voy a la playa, me gusta ___tomar___ el sol.
10. Necesito mi ___tabla___ de mar.
11. Ellos van a ___hacer___ una caminata.
12. Me gusta mucho nadar. Me ___encanta___.

G. Culture Complete the following sentences, based on the cultural notes you have read.

1. Cuba es la ___mayor___ de las Antillas.
2. La música típica de la República Dominicana es el ___merengue___.
3. Él ___Yunque___ es un bosque tropical de Puerto Rico.

Unidad

Objetivos

Lección 9

- Shop for clothing and shoes, conveying your needs with regard to sizes and fit
- Talk about the weather
- Discuss past actions and events
- Talk about possession

Lección 10

- Open an account and cash checks at the bank
- Mail letters and buy stamps at the post office
- Describe people and things
- Refer to actions, states, and events that have been completed in the past
- Tell others what to do

Una calle dedicada exclusivamente a los peatones *(pedestrians)* en la ciudad de Lima, Perú

¿Qué hacemos hoy?

Lección 9
No tengo nada que ponerme

Lección 10
Diligencias

Ecuador

Monumento Mitad del Mundo en la línea del ecuador, latitud 0°

Perú

Departmento de Química, Universidad de San Marcos, Lima

Bolivia

Lago Titicaca, el más alto del mundo, situado entre Bolivia y Perú

Paraguay

Represa hidroeléctrica de Itaipú, en el río Paraná

Lección 9 ◆ No tengo nada que ponerme

Sara y Pablo son muy buenos amigos. Los dos son de Ecuador pero ahora viven y estudian en Lima. Se conocieron en la facultad de medicina hace dos años. Ahora están en una tienda porque Pablo necesita comprar ropa y, según Sara, ella sabe exactamente lo que él necesita.

Sara ¿Por qué no te pruebas estos pantalones? No son muy caros y están de moda.
Pablo ¿Qué? Yo tenía unos pantalones como éstos cuando tenía quince años.
Sara (*Se ríe*) Bueno... todo vuelve... Tú usas talla mediana ¿no? Allí está el probador. Voy a buscarte una camisa.
Pablo Quiero una camisa blanca de mangas largas y una de mangas cortas.
Sara También necesitas un traje y una corbata para la boda de tu hermano... ¡y una chaqueta! Ya empezó el invierno y hace frío.
Pablo Oye, todo esto me va a costar un ojo de la cara.
Sara También tienes que comprar un regalo para tu mamá; me dijiste que era su cumpleaños.
Pablo No sé qué comprarle. ¿Un vestido? ¿Una blusa y una falda? Pero... no sé qué talla usa.
Sara No sé... quizá un par de aretes o una cadena de oro...
Pablo Sí, como la tuya. A ella le gusta mucho. A ver cuánto puedo gastar.

Detalles culturales

En la mayoría de los países hispanos la talla de la ropa se basa en el sistema métrico. Por ejemplo, la medida (*measure*) del cuello (*collar*) y el largo de las mangas (*sleeves*) de una camisa se dan en centímetros. Una talla 10 en los Estados Unidos es equivalente a la 30 en España. Estas equivalencias varían de país a país.

◆ **La talla de la ropa, ¿se basa en el sistema métrico en este país?**

Detalles culturales

El sistema métrico decimal se usa en todos los países de habla hispana. La unidad básica del sistema es el metro, que equivale a 3,28 pies.

◆ **¿Se estudia el sistema métrico en las escuelas de este país?**

Más tarde, en la zapatería.

Empleado ¿En qué puedo servirle, señor?
Pablo Necesito un par de zapatos. Creo que calzo el número cuarenta y cuatro.
Sara Las botas que compraste el mes pasado eran cuarenta y tres.
Pablo Sí, pero como me quedaban chicas y me apretaban un poco, se las mandé a mi hermano.
Sara Buena idea. ¡Los zapatos tienen que ser cómodos!
Pablo (*Se ríe.*) Entonces, ¿por qué usas esas sandalias de tacones altos?
Sara Las compré porque eran baratas, pero prefiero usar zapatos de tenis.
Pablo Yo prefiero andar descalzo. Cuando era chico, me quitaba los zapatos en cuanto llegaba de la escuela.
Sara Oye, ¿qué hora es?
Pablo No sé. Eran las cuatro cuando salimos de la tienda. ¿Quieres ir a comer algo?
Sara Bueno, voy a llamar a Teresa para decirle que no voy a cenar con ella.
Pablo Bueno, tú llamas a tu compañera de cuarto y yo llamo al mío.

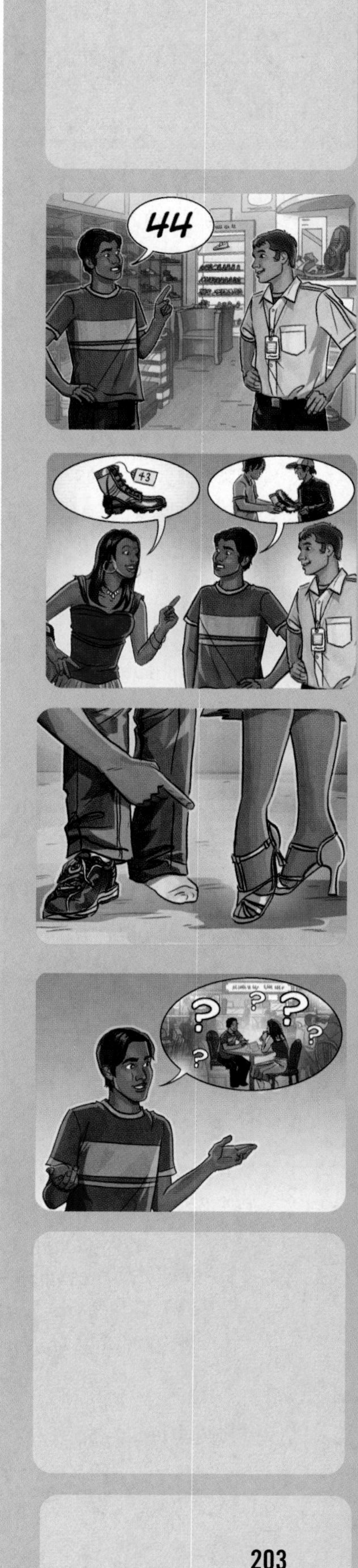

¿Recuerda usted?

Suggestion: Have students correct the false statements.

¿Verdadero o falso?

With a partner, decide whether the following statements about the dialogues are true (**verdadero**) or false (**falso**).

1. Hace tres años que Sara y Pablo se conocieron. ☐ V ☒ F
2. Pablo se va a probar unos pantalones de talla mediana. ☒ V ☐ F
3. Pablo quiere comprar una camisa. ☒ V ☐ F
4. Pablo necesita un traje para su boda. ☐ V ☒ F
5. Pronto va a empezar el verano. ☐ V ☒ F
6. Pablo compró botas el mes pasado. ☒ V ☐ F
7. A Pablo le quedaban grandes las botas. ☐ V ☒ F
8. Pablo usa tacones altos. ☐ V ☒ F
9. A Pablo no le gustaba usar zapatos cuando era chico. ☒ V ☐ F
10. Pablo y Sara salieron de la tienda a las cinco. ☐ V ☒ F

Y ahora... conteste

Answer the following questions, basing your answers on the dialogue.

1. ¿De dónde son Sara y Pablo y dónde viven ahora?
2. ¿Qué dice Sara de los pantalones?
3. ¿Pablo quiere una camisa de mangas cortas o de mangas largas?
4. ¿Qué más dice Sara que necesita Pablo?
5. ¿Qué número calza Pablo?
6. ¿Qué tipo de zapatos prefiere usar Sara?
7. ¿Qué hacía Pablo en cuanto llegaba de la escuela?
8. ¿A quiénes van a llamar Sara y Pablo?

Answers: 1. Son de Ecuador y ahora viven en Lima. 2. Sara dice que no son muy caros y están de moda. 3. Pablo quiere las dos. 4. Dice que necesita un traje, una corbata y una chaqueta. 5. Calza el número cuarenta y cuatro. 6. Sara prefiere usar zapatos de tenis. 7. Pablo se quitaba los zapatos. 8. Van a llamar a sus compañeros de cuarto.

Para hablar del tema: Vocabulario

Online Study Center

For more practice with lesson topics, see the related activities on the *¡Hola, amigos!* web site at college.hmco.com/PIC/holaamigos7e.

Cognados

la blusa
exactamente
la medicina
el par
las sandalias

Nombres

los aretes* earrings
la bota boot
la cadena chain
la camisa shirt
la chaqueta* jacket
la corbata tie
el (la) empleado(a) clerk
la escuela school
la facultad college
la falda skirt
la manga sleeve
el oro gold
los pantalones, el pantalón pants
el probador fitting room
el regalo gift
el tacón* heel
la talla size (*of clothing*)
la tienda store
el traje* suit
el vestido dress
la zapatería shoe store
el zapato shoe

Verbos

apretar (e>ie) to be tight
buscar to look for, to get
calzar to wear (*a certain shoe size*)
gastar to spend (i.e. *money*)
usar to wear, to use

Otras palabras y expresiones

andar descalzo(a) to go barefoot
como like
costar un ojo de la cara to cost an arm and a leg
en cuanto as soon as
¿en qué puedo servirle? how may I help you?
estar de moda to be in style
lo que what, that which
no tener nada que ponerse not to have anything to wear
quedarle chico(a) (grande) a uno to be too small (big) (on someone)
quizás, tal vez maybe, perhaps
según according to

De país a país

los aretes los pendientes (*Esp.*)
los aros (*Par., Arg.*)
las pantallas (*P.R.*)
la chaqueta la chamarra (*Méx.*)
el tacón el taco (*Arg.*)
el traje el vestido (*Colombia*)
el camisón la bata de dormir (*Cuba*)
el cinturón la correa (*P.R.*)

Adjetivos

alto(a) high
barato(a) inexpensive, cheap
cómodo(a) comfortable
corto(a) short
largo(a) long
mediano(a) medium

Amplíe su vocabulario

Más Ropa (*More clothes*)

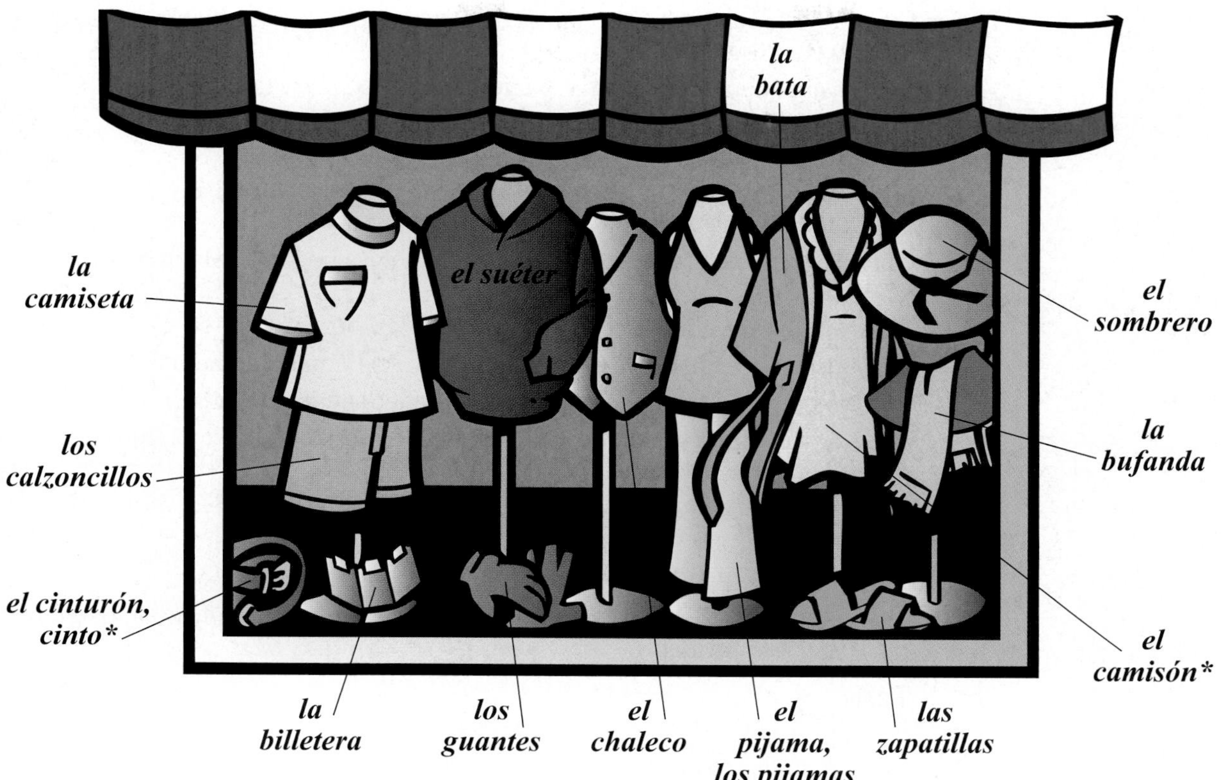

El tiempo (*The weather*)

El cielo está	nublado. despejado.	*The sky is*	*cloudy.* *clear.*

el grado *degree*

el clima	cálido templado frío seco húmedo	*hot* *warm* *cold* *dry* *humid*	*climate*

¿Qué temperatura hace? *What is the temperature?*

Hay... grados. *It's . . . degrees.*

Para practicar el vocabulario

A. En la tienda y en la zapatería Complete the following statements appropriately.

1. Pablo se va a probar la camisa de __mangas__ cortas y también los __pantalones__ en el __probador__.
2. La chaqueta no es __barata__; cuesta un __ojo__ de la cara.
3. Cuando él __usa__ el traje azul, se pone una camisa blanca y una __corbata__ roja.
4. Compré un __par__ de botas, pero me __quedan__ chicas; me __aprietan__ mucho.
5. Ella se puso una __falda__ blanca y una blusa negra. También se puso unas sandalias de __tacones__ altos.
6. No uso talla grande ni chica. Uso talla __mediana__.
7. Busco unos aretes y una __cadena__ de __oro__ para mi mamá.
8. No quiero usar zapatos en mi casa; prefiero andar __descalzo(a)__.
9. Voy a comprar el vestido. Está de __moda__ y no es muy caro. Cuesta solamente 50 dólares.
10. Tengo que comprar ropa. No __tengo__ nada que __ponerme__. ¿Vamos a la __tienda__?

B. ¿Qué se ponen? Describe what Pablo and Sara usually wear, based on the cues provided.

Pablo

Answers: 1. chaleco 2. calzoncillos 3. camiseta 4. cinturón (cinto, correa) 5. pijamas 6. guantes 7. zapatillas (zapatos, botas)

1. con el traje
2. debajo del pantalón
3. debajo de la camisa
4. para sujetarse (*hold*) los pantalones
5. para dormir
6. en las manos, cuando tiene frío
7. en los pies (*feet*)

Sara

Answers: 1. suéter 2. camisón 3. sombrero 4. bata ??? 5. zapatillas (sandalias, zapatos) 6. bufanda
Los dos ponen el dinero en la billetera.

1. cuando tiene frío
2. para dormir
3. en la cabeza (*head*)
4. con el camisón
5. en los pies
6. en el cuello (*neck*), cuando tiene frío

¿Y dónde ponen los dos el dinero?

C. Hablando del tiempo *Answers will vary.*

Possible answers: 1. a. Es frío. b. Es seco. c. Es húmedo d. Es cálido e. Es templado. 2. Está nublado. 3. Está despejado. 4. Hace...

1. ¿Cómo es el clima de
   - a. Alaska?
   - b. Arizona?
   - c. Oregón?
   - d. Miami?
   - e. San Diego?
2. Va a llover (*rain*). ¿Cómo está el cielo?
3. El cielo no está nublado. ¿Cómo está?
4. ¿Cuál es la temperatura de hoy?

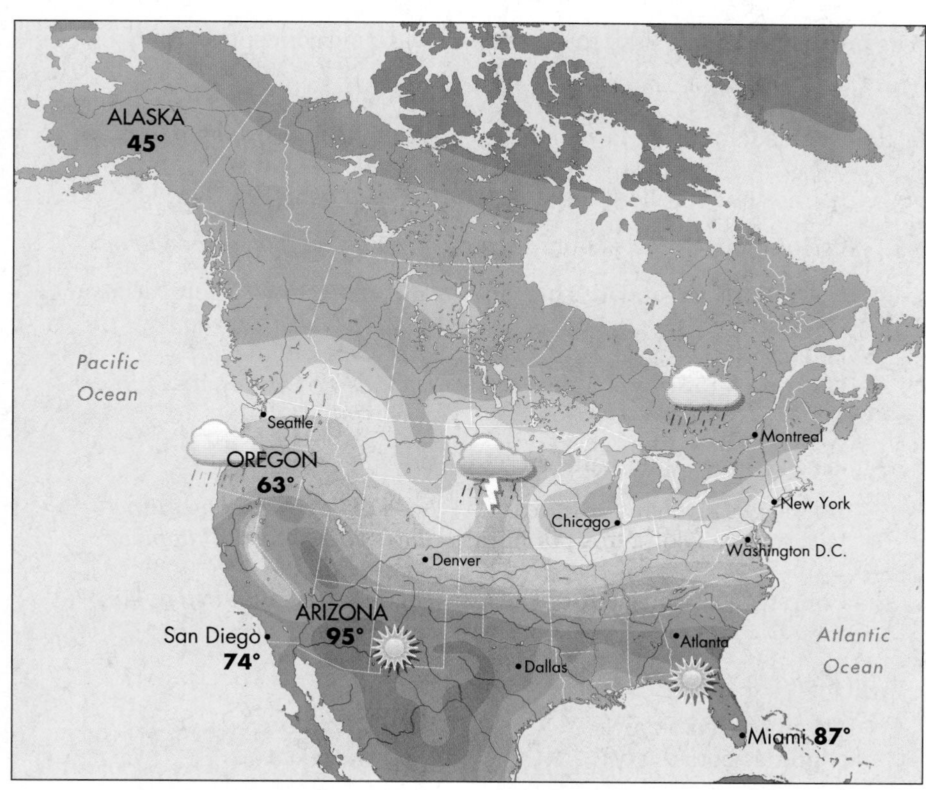

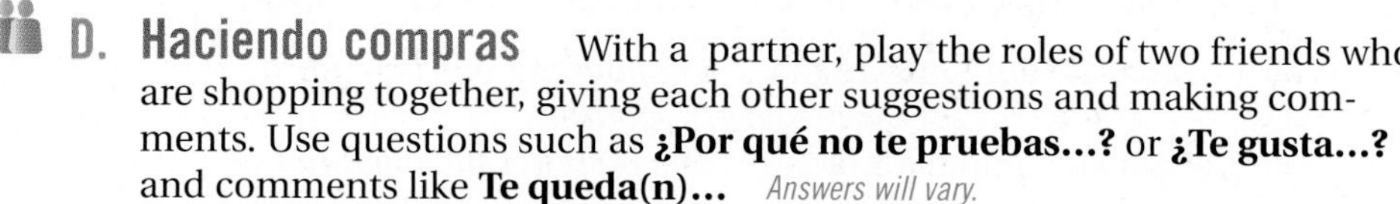

D. Haciendo compras

With a partner, play the roles of two friends who are shopping together, giving each other suggestions and making comments. Use questions such as **¿Por qué no te pruebas...?** or **¿Te gusta...?** and comments like **Te queda(n)...** *Answers will vary.*

Pronunciación

Pronunciation in context

In this lesson, there are some words or phrases that may be challenging to pronounce. Listen to your instructor and pronounce the following sentences.

1. **Se conocieron** en la **facultad** de **medicina** hace dos años.
2. **Ahora** están en una tienda porque Pablo necesita **comprar ropa.**
3. Necesito un par de **zapatos.** Creo que **calzo** el **número** cuarenta y cuatro.
4. Cuando era chico, **me quitaba** los zapatos en cuanto **llegaba** de la escuela.
5. Tú **llamas** a tu **compañera** de **cuarto** y yo llamo al mío.

Puntos para recordar

1. Some uses of *por* and *para* (*Algunos usos de* por *y* para)

Follow-up: After explaining the uses of **por** and giving several examples, you may write a summary of its uses on the board.

por
- motion
- cause
- means
- manner
- unit of measure
- *in exchange for*
- period of time

Ask students for examples of each use. Repeat this procedure for **para** using the following summary.

para
- destination in space
- goal in the future
- direction toward a recipient
- objective
- *in order to*

Again, request examples of each use.

The preposition **por** is used to express the following concepts.

- motion (*through, along, by, via*)

No puedo salir **por** la ventana.	*I can't go out* ***through*** *the window.*
Fuimos **por** la calle Quinta.	*We went* ***via*** *Fifth Street.*

- cause or motive of an action (*because of, on account of, on behalf of*)

No compré las sandalias **por** no tener dinero.	*I didn't buy the sandals* ***because*** *I didn't have any money.*
Lo hice **por** ti.	*I did it* ***on*** *your* ***behalf.***
Llegaron tarde **por** el tráfico.	*They arrived late* ***on account of*** *the traffic.*

- means, manner, unit of measure (*by, per*)

No me gusta viajar **por** tren.	*I don't like to travel* ***by*** *train.*
Va a setenta kilómetros **por** hora.	*She is doing seventy kilometers* ***per*** *hour.*
Cobran 100 dólares **por** noche.	*They charge a hundred dollars* ***per*** *night.*

- *in exchange for*

Pagamos cien dólares **por** las botas.	*We paid a hundred dollars* ***for*** *the boots.*

- period of time during which an action takes place (*during, in, for*)

Voy a quedarme aquí **por** un mes.	*I'm going to stay here* ***for*** *a month.*
Ella prepara la comida **por** la mañana.	*She prepares the meal* ***in*** *the morning.*

The preposition **para** is used to express the following concepts.

- destination

  ¿Cuándo sales **para** Quito? — *When are you leaving **for** Quito?*

- goal for a specific point in the future (*by* or *for* a certain time in the future)

  Necesito la camisa y el pantalón **para** mañana. — *I need the shirt and the pants **for** (**by**) tomorrow.*

- whom or what something is for

  La blusa es **para** ti. — *The blouse is **for** you.*

- objective or goal

  Mi novio estudia **para** profesor. — *My boyfriend is studying **to be** a professor.*

- *in order to*

  —Ayer fui a su casa. — *"Yesterday I went to his house."*
  —¿**Para** qué? — *"What **for**?"*
  —**Para** hablar con él. — *"**(In order) To** talk with him."*

Práctica y conversación

Online Study Center

For more practice with lesson topics, see the related activities on the *¡Hola, amigos!* web site at college.hmco.com/PIC/holaamigos7e.

A. Minidiálogos Supply **por** or **para** in each dialogue. Then act each one out with a partner.

1. —¿__Por__ qué calle fuiste?
   —Fui __por__ la calle Esperanza.
2. —¿__Para__ cuándo necesitas los pantalones?
   —Los necesito __para__ el sábado __por__ la noche.
3. —¿Para qué fuiste al mercado?
   —__Para__ comprar frutas. Lo hice __por__ ti, porque estabas muy cansada... Y no compré más carne __por__ no tener más dinero.
4. —¿Cuánto pagaron Uds. __por__ ese vestido?
   —Cien soles. Es __para__ nuestra hija.
   —¿Cuándo sale ella __para__ Cuzco?
   —El 3 de enero. Va a estar allí __por__ dos meses. Va __para__ visitar a su abuela.
   —¿Va __por__ tren?
   —Sí.
5. —¿Ofelia está en la universidad?
   —Sí, estudia __para__ profesora.

Detalles culturales

Sol: moneda peruana

◆ **¿Sabe Ud. cuáles son las monedas de otros países hispanos?**

B. Cosas que pasan Look at the illustrations and describe what is happening, using **por** or **para.**

1. Fuimos por tren a Lima.

2. Roberto salió por la ventana.

3. Marisa va a estar en Medellín por un mes.

4. La torta es para Ana.

5. Jorge pagó $35 por el vino.

6. Ana sale mañana por la mañana.

C. Diferentes circunstancias In groups of three, and using your imagination, add some details to the following circumstances. Use **por** or **para** and think of various possibilities. *Answers will vary.*

◆ **MODELO:** Marisa compró un vestido.
*Pagó 100 dólares **por** el vestido. El vestido es **para** su tía.*

1. Mi sobrino va a ir a Ecuador.
2. Mi prima está en la universidad.
3. Amalia trabaja de siete a once de la mañana.
4. Marité tiene una fiesta el sábado. Necesita comprar un vestido.
5. David compró una corbata.
6. Mi cuñado no pudo pagar la cuenta.

7. Este hotel es muy barato.
8. Julio conduce muy rápido (*fast*).
9. Ellos llegaron tarde a la fiesta.
10. Luis no pudo salir por la puerta.

2. Weather expressions (*Expresiones para describir el tiempo*)

- The following expressions are used when talking about the weather.

Suggestion: Refer students to **Amplíe su vocabulario** for additional related vocabulary.

Hace (mucho) frío.	*It is (very) cold.*
Hace (mucho) calor.	*It is (very) hot.*
Hace (mucho) viento.	*It is (very) windy.*
Hace sol.	*It is sunny.*
—¿Qué tiempo **hace** hoy?	*"What's the weather **like** today?"*
—**Hace buen (mal) tiempo.**	***"The weather is good (bad)."***

¡Atención! All of the expressions above use the verb **hacer** followed by a noun.

—¿Abro la ventana?	*"Shall I open the window?"*
—¡Sí! ¡**Hace** mucho **calor**!	*"Yes! **It's** very **hot!**"*

- The impersonal verbs **llover (o > ue)** (*to rain*) and **nevar (e > ie)** (*to snow*) are also used to describe the weather. They are used only in the third-person singular forms of all tenses, and in the infinitive, the present participle, and the past participle.

Expansion: You might want to teach the expression **llover a cántaros** *to rain cats and dogs.*

Aquí **llueve** mucho.	***It rains** a lot here.*
Creo que va a **nevar** hoy.	*I think it's going to **snow** today.*
Está **lloviendo;** no podemos salir.	*It's **raining;** we can't go out.*

Other weather-related words are **lluvia** (*rain*) and **niebla** (*fog*).

Hay **niebla.**	*It's **foggy.***
No me gusta **la lluvia.**	*I don't like **rain.***

Online Study Center

For more practice with lesson topics, see the related activities on the *¡Hola, amigos!* web site at college.hmco.com/PIC/holaamigos7e.

Expansion: Have the students prepare weather reports and read them in class. They can research the weather of some Spanish-speaking cities on the Internet and present the weather reports to the class.

Answers: **1.** Llueve (Está lloviendo). **2.** Hace buen tiempo (Hace sol). **3.** Hace calor y hace sol. **4.** Hace mucho viento. **5.** Hace mucho frío. **6.** Nieva (Está nevando).

Práctica y conversación

A. ¿Qué tiempo hace? Describe the weather in each illustration.

1. ____________________

2. ____________________

3. ____________________

4. ____________________

5. ____________________

6. ____________________

B. Minidiálogos With a partner, complete the exchanges in a logical manner.

1. —¿Necesitas un paraguas (*umbrella*)?
   —Sí, porque ___está lloviendo___.
2. —¿No necesitas un abrigo (*coat*)?
   —No, porque ___hace calor (no hace frío)___.
3. —¿Quieres un impermeable (*raincoat*)?
   —Sí, porque ___llueve (está lloviendo)___ mucho.
4. —¿No quieres llevar el suéter?
   —¡No! ¡Hace ___calor___!
5. —¿Vas a llevar el sombrero?
   —Sí, porque ___hace sol___.
6. —¿Necesitas un suéter y un abrigo?
   —Sí, porque ___hace mucho frío___.
7. —¿Un impermeable? ¿Por qué? ¿Está lloviendo?
   —No, pero ___nieva (está nevando)___.
8. —¡Qué ___lluvia___! Necesito un paraguas y un impermeable.
9. —No hay vuelos (*flights*) porque hay mucha ___niebla___.

C. De viaje (*On a trip*) A friend of yours from Lima is going to travel in the United States for a year. With a partner, discuss what kind of weather he's going to find in cities like Chicago, Boston, Phoenix, and San Francisco.

Answers will vary.

3. The preterit contrasted with the imperfect (*El pretérito contrastado con el imperfecto*)

- The difference between the preterit and imperfect tense can be visualized in the following way.

Suggestion: Before contrasting the preterit and the imperfect, review the forms of both. Use transparencies to present the contrast. To further illustrate the uses of these tenses, tell a well-known story like ***Caperucita Roja.*** Give key vocabulary (i.e., **Caperucita, bosque, leñador, lobo,** and so on). After the story, repeat certain passages and ask why the preterit or the imperfect is used.

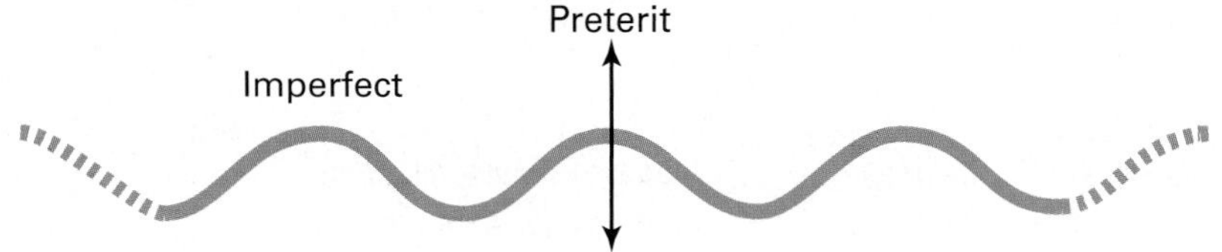

The wavy line representing the imperfect shows an action or event taking place over a period of time in the past. There is no reference as to when the action began or ended. The vertical line representing the preterit shows an action or event completed at a certain time in the past.

In many instances, the choice between the preterit and the imperfect depends on how the speaker views the action or event. The following table summarizes the most important uses of both tenses.

Preterit	Imperfect
• Reports past actions or events that the speaker views as completed Ella **vino** ayer.	• Describes past actions or events in the process of happening, with no reference to their beginning or end. **Íbamos** al cine cuando...
• Sums up a condition or state viewed as a whole (and no longer in effect). **Estuve** cansada todo el día.	• Indicates a repeated or habitual action (*used to . . . , would*) Todos los días **íbamos** con él.[1]
	• Describes a physical, mental, or emotional state or condition in the past. **Estaba** muy cansada.
	• Expresses time and age in the past. **Eran** las dos. **Tenía** veinte años.
	• Is used in indirect discourse. Dijo que **venía.**
	• Describes in the past or sets the stage. Mi novia **era** muy bonita. **Hacía** frío y **llovía.**

—¿**Viste** a Eva ayer? — *"**Did you see** Eva yesterday?"*
—Sí, **estaba** en el restaurante cuando la **vi.** — *"Yes, **she was** at the restaurant when **I saw** her."*

—¿Qué te **dijo** Raúl? — *"What **did** Raúl **say** to you?"*
—Dijo que **necesitaba** dinero. — *"He said **he needed** money."*

¡Atención! *Direct discourse:* Juan dijo: "Vengo mañana".
Indirect discourse: Juan dijo que **venía** mañana.

[1]Note that this use of the imperfect corresponds to the English *would* used to describe a repeated action in the past. *Every day **we used to** go with him. = Every day **we would** go with him.* Do not confuse this with the English conditional *would,* as in: *If I had the time **I would go** with him.*

Práctica y conversación

Online Study Center

For more practice with lesson topics, see the related activities on the *¡Hola, amigos!* web site at college.hmco.com/PIC/holaamigos7e.

A. Pequeñas historias

Complete the following stories, using the appropriate form of the preterit or the imperfect of the verbs provided. Then read the stories aloud.

1. ___Eran___ (Ser) las once y ___hacía___ (hacer) frío cuando Ada ___llegó___ (llegar) a su casa anoche. La chica ___estaba___ (estar) cansada y no ___se sentía___ (sentirse) bien. Su mamá ___se levantó___ (levantarse) y le ___hizo___ (hacer) una taza de té.
2. Cuando yo ___era___ (ser) niño yo ___vivía___ (vivir) en Chile. Todos los veranos ___iba___ (ir) a visitar a mis abuelos, que ___vivían___ (vivir) en el campo. El año pasado mi familia y yo ___nos mudamos___ (mudarse) a Cuzco y mis abuelos ___vinieron___ (venir) a vivir con nosotros.
3. Ayer Ana y Carlos ___fueron___ (ir) a la tienda La Peruana. Ana ___compró___ (comprar) una camisa. El empleado les ___dijo___ (decir) que ellos ___tenían___ (tener) mucha ropa buena y barata. Ana y Carlos ___volvieron___ (volver) a su casa a las siete, ___cenaron___ (cenar) y ___se acostaron___ (acostarse). Ana no ___durmió___ (dormir) muy bien.

B. Entreviste a su compañero(a)

Interview a partner, using the following questions. *Answers will vary.*

1. ¿Dónde vivías tú cuando eras niño(a)?
2. ¿Qué idioma hablabas tú cuando eras niño(a)?
3. ¿Tú siempre estudiabas mucho cuando eras niño(a)?
4. ¿Cómo era tu primer(a) novio(a)?
5. ¿En qué año comenzaste a estudiar en la universidad?
6. ¿De qué hablaste con tus amigos ayer?
7. ¿Tú estudiaste mucho anoche?
8. ¿Qué hora era cuando llegaste a la universidad hoy?
9. ¿Qué hacías cuando llegó el (la) profesor(a)?
10. ¿Qué te dijo el (la) profesor(a) que tenías que estudiar esta noche?

Expansion: You may wish to review weather expressions with the imperfect. **¿Qué tiempo hacía en la ciudad donde vivías? ¿Nevaba mucho? ¿Llovía mucho? ¿Hacía frío o hacía calor?**

C. ¿Qué hacíamos... qué hicimos...?

With a partner, talk about what you used to do when you were in high school and then discuss what you did last week. Use the following phrases to start. *Answers will vary.*

1. Cuando yo estaba en la escuela secundaria,
   a. todos los días yo...
   b. los fines de semana mi familia y yo...
   c. en mi clase de inglés mi profesor(a)...
   d. en la cafetería mis amigos y yo...
   e. mi mejor amigo(a) siempre...
   f. los viernes por la noche yo...
2. La semana pasada,
   a. el lunes por la mañana yo...
   b. en mi clase de español mi profesor(a)...
   c. el martes por la noche...
   d. el jueves por la tarde...
   e. el sábado mis amigos y yo...
   f. el domingo yo...

Suggestion: You may wish to teach the following.
la iglesia *church*
la sinagoga *synagogue*
la mezquita *mosque*

D. Ricitos de oro y los tres osos Working with your classmates in groups of three or four, write the Spanish version of the story "Goldilocks and the Three Bears." Some useful vocabulary is provided. *Answers will vary.*

Había una vez (*Once upon a time there was/were*)
Ricitos de oro (*Goldilocks*)
el oso (*bear*)
la avena (*porridge*)
mediana (*medium*)
el bosque (*forest*)
caliente (*hot*)
la cama (*bed*)
el tazón (*bowl*)

Suggestion: Assign as homework for students to read aloud in class.

E. Soy escritor (*I'm a writer*) Use your imagination to finish the following story. *Answers will vary.*

Eran las dos de la mañana y yo estaba durmiendo en mi apartamento. Tocaron a la puerta y yo fui a abrir. Cuando la abrí, vi...

4. *Hace...* meaning *ago* (Hace... *como equivalente de* ago)

Extra practice: Inform students that you will tell them when a series of events happened. Students must tell you how long ago each event took place, using **Hace... que...** (e.g., **Yo me casé en 1985. / Yo terminé mis estudios en 1990,** etc.)

In sentences in the preterit and in some cases the imperfect, **hace** + *period of time* is equivalent to the English *ago*. When **hace** is placed at the beginning of the sentence, the construction is as follows.

Hace + period of time	+ **que** + verb (*preterit*)
Hace + **dos años**	+ **que** + la conocí.
*I met her two years **ago**.*	

An alternative construction is:
La conocí hace dos años.

¡Atención! To find out how long ago something took place, ask:

¿Cuánto tiempo hace que... + *verb in the preterit*
¿ Cuánto tiempo hace que viniste a **Guayaquil?**

—**¿Cuánto tiempo hace que** tú llegaste?	*"**How long ago did** you arrive?"*
—**Hace tres años que** llegué.	*"I arrived **three years ago.**"*

Práctica y conversación

A. ¿Cuánto tiempo hace...? Say how long ago the following events took place.

◆ **MODELO:** Son las cuatro. Yo llegué a las tres.
Hace una hora que yo llegué.

Suggestion: Refer students to p. 137 for a review of **hace... que** + *present*.

1. Estamos en noviembre. Los García celebraron su aniversario de bodas en septiembre.
2. Son las seis. Yo almorcé a la una.
3. Hoy es viernes. Esteban salió para Bolivia el martes.
4. Son las diez. Pedimos el postre a las diez menos cuarto.
5. Estamos en el año 2008. Vinimos a California en el año 1994.
6. Son las diez. Ellos empezaron a estudiar a las siete.

Answers: 1. Hace dos meses que los García celebraron su aniversario de bodas. **2.** Hace cinco horas que yo almorcé. **3.** Hace tres días que Esteban salió para Bolivia. **4.** Hace quince minutos que pedimos el postre. **5.** Hace catorce años que vinimos a California. **6.** Hace tres horas que ellos empezaron a estudiar.

B. ¿Cuándo pasó eso? Discuss with a partner how long ago the following events happened in your life. *Answers will vary.*

1. ¿Cuánto tiempo hace que empezaste a estudiar español?
2. ¿Cuánto tiempo hace que Uds. tomaron el último examen?
3. ¿Cuánto tiempo hace que hablaste con tus padres?
4. ¿Cuánto tiempo hace que le escribiste a un(a) amigo(a)?
5. ¿Cuánto tiempo hace que tu mejor amigo(a) te llamó por teléfono?
6. ¿Cuánto tiempo hace que estuviste en un buen restaurante?
7. ¿Cuánto tiempo hace que compraste ropa?
8. ¿Cuánto tiempo hace que saliste con tus amigos?

Verbs: 1. Hace... que empecé a estudiar español. **2.** Hace... que tomamos el último examen. **3.** Hace... que hablé con mis padres. **4.** Hace... que le escribí a mi amigo(a). **5.** Hace... que me llamó por teléfono. **6.** Hace... que estuve en un buen restaurante. **7.** Hace... que compré ropa. **8.** Hace... que salí con mis amigos.

Online Study Center

For more practice with lesson topics, see the related activities on the ***¡Hola, amigos!*** web site at college.hmco.com/PIC/holaamigos7e.

Detalles culturales

En las ciudades hispanas hay excelentes tiendas donde se puede comprar ropa hecha (*ready-to-wear*), pero muchas personas prefieren utilizar los servicios de un sastre (*tailor*) o de una modista (*dressmaker*).

◆ **¿Le gusta a Ud. la idea de tener una modista (un sastre)?**

5. Possessive pronouns (*Pronombres posesivos*)

Suggestion: Take objects away from students and tell them they belong to you. They should react, and the rest of the class should help. For example:
Instructor: **Esta pluma es mía.**
Student: **No, no es suya. Es mía.**
Class: **Es la pluma de él (ella).**

Alternative: Stress the use of the definite article with the possessive pronoun by making statements about something of yours (or a student's). Then point to a different student, who will respond with a statement distinguishing his or her article from yours (or the classmate's).
Instructor: **Mi camisa es blanca.**
Student: **La mía es azul.**

- Possessive pronouns in Spanish agree in gender and number with the person or thing possessed. They are generally used with the definite article.

Singular		Plural		
Masc.	Fem.	Masc.	Fem.	
(el) mío	**(la) mía**	**(los) míos**	**(las) mías**	mine
(el) tuyo	**(la) tuya**	**(los) tuyos**	**(las) tuyas**	yours (*fam.*)
(el) suyo	**(la) suya**	**(los) suyos**	**(las) suyas**	yours (*form.*) / his / hers
(el) nuestro	**(la) nuestra**	**(los) nuestros**	**(las) nuestras**	ours
(el) vuestro	**(la) vuestra**	**(los) vuestros**	**(las) vuestras**	yours (*fam.*)
(el) suyo	**(la) suya**	**(los) suyos**	**(las) suyas**	yours (*form.*) / theirs

—Mis libros están aquí. ¿Dónde están los **tuyos**? — *"My books are here. Where are **yours**?"*
—Los **míos** están en la mesa. — *"**Mine** are on the table."*

¡Atención! Note that **los tuyos** substitutes for **los *libros* tuyos;** the noun has been deleted. Also note that after the verb **ser,** the article is usually omitted.

Suggestion: Mention that the phrase "a friend of mine" is expressed in Spanish as **un(a) amigo(a) mío(a).**

—¿Estas invitaciones son **tuyas**? — *"Are these invitations **yours**?"*
—Sí, son **mías.** — *"Yes, they're **mine.**"*

- Because the third-person forms of the possessive pronouns **(el suyo, la suya, los suyos, las suyas)** can be ambiguous, they can be replaced with the following for clarification.

el	de		**Ud.**
la	de		**él**
los	de		**ella**
las	de		**Uds.**
			ellos
			ellas

¿El diccionario? Es **suyo.** (*unclarified*) — *The dictionary? It's theirs.*

Es **el de ellas.** (*clarified*) — (*fem. pl. possessor*)

Práctica y conversación

Online Study Center

For more practice with lesson topics, see the related activities on the ***¡Hola, amigos!*** web site at college.hmco.com/PIC/holaamigos7e.

A. Todo es nuestro

Supply the correct possessive pronoun to agree with each subject. Clarify when necessary.

- **MODELO:** Yo tengo una camisa. Es ________.
  Es *mía.*

1. Nosotros tenemos un apartamento. Es ___nuestro___.
2. Ellos tienen una tienda. Es ___suya___. (Es ___la___ ___de___ ___ellos___.)
3. Él tiene dos trajes. Son ___suyos___. (Son ___los___ ___de___ ___él___.)
4. Yo tengo una billetera. Es ___mía___.
5. Tú tienes dos cinturones. Son ___tuyos___.
6. Uds. tienen muchos zapatos. Son ___suyos___. (Son ___los___ ___de___ ___ustedes___.)
7. Ella tiene dos camisones. Son ___suyos___. (Son ___los___ ___de___ ___ella___.)
8. Nosotros tenemos una casa. Es ___nuestra___.

B. ¿De quién es...?

Who owns the following items? Answer the questions affirmatively.

1. Aquí hay una blusa verde. ¿Es tuya?
2. Yo encontré 100 dólares. ¿Son tuyos?
3. ¿La cartera roja es de tu mamá?
4. El libro que tú tienes, ¿es mío?
5. Las plumas que están en mi escritorio, ¿son de ustedes?
6. Aquí hay un diccionario. ¿Es de ustedes?

Follow-up: Have students discuss items their friends or relatives have and explain how their own is / will be different.

Answers: **1.** Sí, es mía. **2.** Sí, son, míos. **3.** Sí, es suya (de ella). **4.** Sí, es tuyo. **5.** Sí, son nuestras. **6.** Sí, es nuestro.

C. Vamos a comparar

With a partner, make comparisons between the objects and people described. Use appropriate possessive pronouns when asking each other questions. *Answers will vary.*

- **MODELO:** —Mi hermano tiene... años. ¿Cuántos años tiene el tuyo?
  —*El mío tiene dieciocho.*

1. Mi casa está en la calle...
2. Mis abuelos son de...
3. Mi mejor amigo(a) se llama...
4. Mis profesores son...
5. Mis padres están en...
6. Mis tías viven en...

Entre nosotros

¡Conversemos!

Para conocernos mejor Get to know your partner better by asking each other the following questions. *Answers will vary.*

1. ¿Dónde conociste a tu mejor amigo(a)? ¿Cuántos años tenías cuando lo (la) conociste?
2. ¿Qué le compraste a tu mejor amigo(a) para su cumpleaños?
3. Cuando vas de compras, ¿prefieres ir solo(a) o con un(a) amigo(a)?
4. Yo compré mi ropa en la tienda _______. ¿Dónde compras tú la tuya?
5. ¿Cuándo fue la última vez que fuiste a la tienda? ¿Qué compraste?
6. Generalmente, ¿usas camisas (blusas) de mangas largas o de mangas cortas?
7. ¿Qué ropa te vas a poner mañana? ¿Te vas a poner sandalias o zapatos?
8. ¿Cuánto te costaron los zapatos? ¿Qué número calzas tú?
9. Si te gustan unos zapatos pero te quedan un poco chicos, ¿los compras?
10. ¿Qué te pones cuando hace mucho frío? ¿Te gustan más los climas fríos o los cálidos?

Una encuesta Interview your classmates to identify who fits the following descriptions. Include your instructor, but remember to use the **Ud.** form when addressing him or her. *Answers will vary.*

	Nombre
1. Prefiere los climas cálidos.	______
2. Usa impermeable cuando llueve.	______
3. Le gusta viajar por tren.	______
4. Llegó tarde a clase por el tráfico.	______
5. Siempre dice que no tiene nada que ponerse.	______
6. Estudia para profesor(a).	______
7. Celebró su cumpleaños el mes pasado.	______
8. Nació (was born) en el mes de julio.	______
9. Compró algo para un amigo (una amiga) recientemente.	______
10. Gastó mucho dinero en ropa este mes.	______

Y ahora... Write a brief summary, indicating what you have learned about your classmates. *Answers will vary.*

¿Cómo lo decimos? What would you say in the following situations? What might the other person say? Act out the scenes with a partner.

1. You are shopping for clothes in Lima. Tell the clerk what clothes you need, your size, and discuss colors and prices.
2. You go shopping for shoes, sandals, and boots. You try on several pairs, but have problems with them. You finally buy a pair of boots.
3. Your friends went to the store without you. Ask them what they bought and how much they spent.
4. You ask a new acquaintance from Ecuador where she lived when she was a child and what she liked to do. Give her the same information about you.

Answers: 1. *Answers will vary.* 2. *Answers will vary.* 3. ¿Qué compraron Uds. y cuánto gastaron? 4. ¿Dónde vivías cuando eras niña y qué te gustaba hacer? A mí me gustaba...

¿Qué dice aquí? Look at the following ad and help a friend of yours who is shopping at **La Limeña,** in Lima. Answer his or her questions, using the information provided in the ad.

1. ¿Cómo se llama la tienda?
2. ¿En qué mes son las rebajas (*sales*)?
3. Tengo una hija de nueve años. ¿Qué puedo comprarle en la tienda?
4. Mi esposo necesita zapatos. ¿Qué tipo de zapatos están en liquidación?
5. Además de (*Besides*) los zapatos, ¿qué puedo comprar para mi esposo?
6. Vamos a ir a la playa (*beach*). ¿Qué puedo comprar para mis hijos?
7. Soy profesora y necesito más ropa para el trabajo. ¿Qué puedo comprar?

Answers: 1. La tienda se llama La Limeña. 2. Las rebajas son en agosto. 3. Puedes comprarle camisetas, trajes de baño y playeros. 4. Los zapatos de cuero. 5. Puedes comprarle trajes y pantalones de sport y de vestir, y camisas. 6. Puedes comprarles playeros y bañadores. 7. Puedes comprar vestidos, blusas y faldas.

Un dicho

Do you only buy clothes that are of good quality? If you do, you will agree with this saying. What does it mean? Can you memorize it?

Para escribir

¿Cómo era Ud.? Write a short narration about your life when you were twelve. Where were you living? What were you like? What did you like to do? Make a list of all the facts and then organize them. *Answers will vary.*

Lección 10 • Diligencias

Roberto ha estado muy ocupado últimamente y no ha tenido tiempo de ir al banco. Hoy, por fin, tiene un par de horas para hacer diligencias. Primero va al Banco Nacional de Asunción.

Roberto — Buenas tardes. Dígame, ¿qué tengo que hacer para abrir una cuenta de ahorros?

Cajero — Siéntese, por favor. ¿Tiene usted alguna otra cuenta en este banco?

Roberto — Sí, tengo una cuenta corriente.

Cajero — ¿Quiere abrir una cuenta individual o una cuenta conjunta?

Roberto — Una cuenta individual.

Cajero — Bien, llene esta planilla, féchela y fírmela, por favor. ¿Cuánto va a depositar?

Roberto — Trescientos mil guaraníes.[1] También quiero cobrar este cheque por cuarenta mil guaraníes. ¿Cuál es el saldo de mi cuenta, por favor?

Cajero — Déjeme buscarlo en la computadora. A ver... quinientos mil guaraníes, señor.

Detalles culturales

Abrir una cuenta bancaria no es muy fácil en los países latinoamericanos, especialmente si es una cuenta corriente. La gente pobre que puede ahorrar, generalmente deposita su dinero en la caja postal de ahorros, un servicio que las oficinas de correo ofrecen en algunos países.

◆ **¿Existe ese tipo de servicio en este país?**

Detalles culturales

El uso de cheques no es tan común en América Latina como en los Estados Unidos y en Canadá, pero muchos bancos tienen sus propias (*own*) tarjetas de crédito.

◆ **¿Paga Ud. siempre con cheques o prefiere pagar en efectivo o con tarjetas de crédito?**

---

[1]Paraguayan currency

Media hora más tarde, Roberto está en la oficina de correos. Está haciendo cola, porque hay mucha gente.[1]

Roberto	Quiero mandar esta carta a La Paz, certificada.
Empleada	Sí, señor. Son diez mil guaraníes.
Roberto	¿Cuánto cuesta enviar un giro postal a Montevideo?
Empleada	Seis mil guaraníes. ¿Quiere mandar uno?
Roberto	No, voy a volver otro día.
Empleada	Bien, ¿necesita algo más, señor?
Roberto	Sí, deme estampillas para tres tarjetas postales.
Empleada	Aquí las tiene.
Roberto	Gracias. ¡Ah! ¿El correo está abierto mañana?
Empleada	No, señor. Está cerrado. Mañana es día feriado.

Roberto salió de la oficina de correos y trató de recordar dónde había estacionado su coche. Por fin lo encontró a una cuadra del correo. Como les había dicho a sus padres que iba a cenar con ellos, fue directamente a casa.

Detalles culturales

En muchos países de habla hispana, las estampillas sólo pueden comprarse en el correo o en tiendas especializadas que están autorizadas para venderlas.

◆ **¿Dónde puede Ud. comprar estampillas en este país?**

¿Recuerda usted?

¿Verdadero o falso? With a partner, decide whether the following statements about the dialogue are true (**verdadero**) or false (**falso**).

		V	F
1.	Roberto va a hacer algunas diligencias hoy.	☒ V	☐ F
2.	Roberto va a abrir una cuenta corriente.	☐ V	☒ F
3.	Roberto no tiene ninguna cuenta en el Banco Nacional.	☐ V	☒ F
4.	Roberto va a depositar más de 100.000 guaraníes.	☒ V	☐ F
5.	Roberto manda una carta certificada.	☒ V	☐ F
6.	Roberto manda un giro postal a Montevideo.	☐ V	☒ F
7.	Roberto puede ir al correo mañana.	☐ V	☒ F
8.	Roberto fue al correo en taxi.	☐ V	☒ F

Y ahora... conteste Answer these questions, basing your answers on the dialogue.

1. ¿En qué ciudad está el Banco Nacional?
2. ¿Por qué no ha tenido tiempo Roberto para ir al banco?
3. ¿Qué tipo de cuenta quiere abrir Roberto?
4. ¿Dónde va a buscar el empleado el saldo de la cuenta de Roberto?
5. En el correo, ¿por qué tiene que hacer cola Roberto?
6. ¿Cuántas tarjetas postales quiere enviar Roberto?
7. ¿Por qué está cerrado el correo mañana?
8. ¿Dónde encontró Roberto su coche?

Answers: **1.** Está en Asunción. **2.** Porque ha estado muy ocupado. **3.** Quiere abrir una cuenta de ahorros. **4.** Va a buscarlo en la computadora. **5.** Porque hay mucha gente. **6.** Quiere enviar tres tarjetas. **7.** Porque es día feriado. **8.** Lo encontró a una cuadra del correo.

---

[1] ***Gente*** (*People*) is considered singular in Spanish.

Para hablar del tema: Vocabulario

Online Study Center

For more practice with lesson topics, see the related activities on the *¡Hola, amigos!* web site at college.hmco.com/PIC/holaamigos7e.

Cognados

el banco
certificado(a)
el cheque
la computadora*
directamente
individual

Nombres

el (la) cajero(a) teller, cashier
la carta letter
el coche* car
la cuadra* block
la cuenta account
____ **corriente** checking account
____ **conjunta** joint account
____ **de ahorros** savings account
la estampilla* stamp
la gente people
el giro postal money order
la hora hour
la oficina office
____ **de correos, el correo** post office
la planilla form
el saldo balance
la tarjeta card
____ **postal** postcard

Verbos

cobrar to cash
depositar to deposit
estacionar* to park
fechar to date
firmar to sign
llenar to fill, to fill out

Adjetivos

abierto(a) open
cerrado(a) closed
medio(a) half
ocupado(a) busy
otro(a) another, other

Otras palabras y expresiones

¿Algo más? Anything else?
Aquí las tiene. Here you are.
día feriado holiday
hacer cola to stand in line
hacer diligencias to run errands
por fin finally
primero first
últimamente lately

De país a país

la computadora el ordenador (*Esp.*)
el coche el carro (*Méx.*)
la cuadra la manzana (*Esp.*)
la estampilla el timbre (*Méx.*)
estacionar parquear (*Antillas*)

Detalles culturales

El uso del "Internet" o la "Red", como se llama en español, es cada día más popular en el mundo hispánico, y muchas instituciones (empresas y organizaciones) tienen su propia página (*home page*).

◆ **En este país, ¿la mayoría de las instituciones tienen su propia página en la Red? ¿Cree Ud. que esto es importante? ¿Por qué?**

Amplíe su vocabulario

Más sobre el banco

ahorrar to save
la caja de seguridad safe-deposit box
el cajero automático automatic teller machine (ATM)
la casa central home office
en efectivo in cash
gratis free (of charge)
la libreta de ahorros passbook
el plan de ahorros savings plan
el talonario de cheques check book
solicitar un préstamo to apply (ask) for a loan
la sucursal branch office
la memoria memory
la microcomputadora laptop
el ordenador personal, la computadora personal personal computer
archivar la información to store information
navegar la Red to surf the net
tener acceso a la Red to have access to the Internet

Detalles culturales

Cada nación latinoamericana tiene un banco central encargado de (*in charge of*) emitir el dinero y de controlar la actividad de los bancos comerciales. En algunos países hay también sucursales de bancos extranjeros.

◆ **En su país, ¿qué institución está encargada de emitir el dinero?**

Additional vocabulary: entrar al sistema, guardar, la dirección electrónica, mandar por correo electrónico, el disco, el sitio web.

Un poco de tecnología (*A little about technology*)

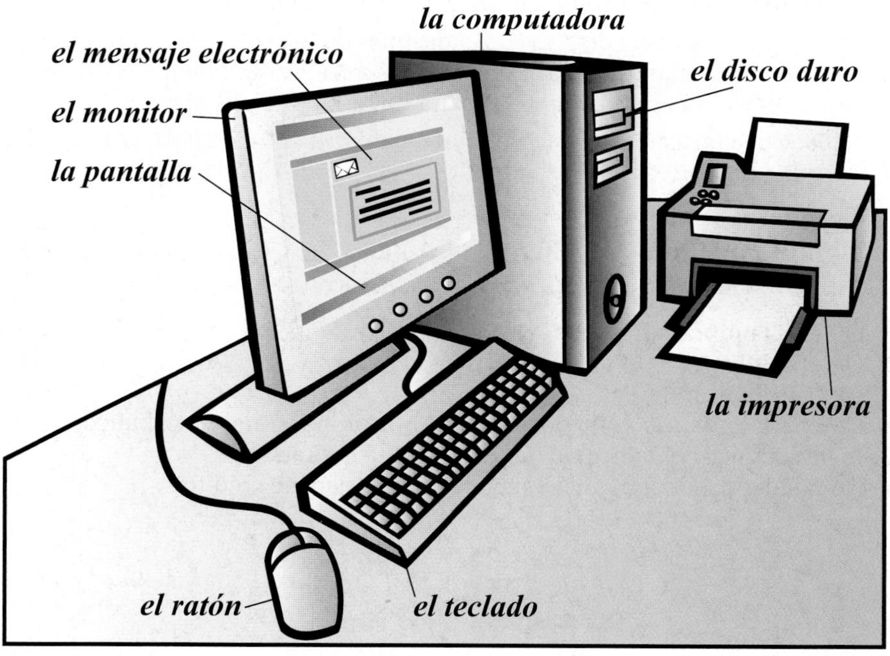

Para practicar el vocabulario

A. Preguntas y respuestas

Match the questions in column *A* with the answers in column *B*.

Answers: 1. f 2. d 3. g 4. j 5. h 6. b 7. i 8. a 9. c 10. e

A	B
1. ¿Cuál es el saldo de tu cuenta?	a. No, en una sucursal.
2. ¿Vas a depositar el cheque?	b. No, es un día feriado.
3. ¿Qué debo llenar?	c. No, abierto
4. ¿Qué vas a solicitar?	d. No, voy a cobrarlo.
5. ¿Necesitas algo más?	e. No, con un cheque.
6. ¿Trabajas hoy?	f. Quinientos dólares.
7. ¿Dónde pusiste el dinero?	g. Esta planilla.
8. ¿Trabajas en la casa central?	h. No, nada. Gracias.
9. ¿El banco está cerrado?	i. En la caja de seguridad.
10. ¿Pagas en efectivo?	j. Un préstamo.

Detalles culturales

En España y en la mayoría de los países latinoamericanos una persona debe tener por lo menos (*at least*) 18 años para obtener una licencia de conducir y los exámenes para obtenerla son muy difíciles.

◆ **¿A qué edad se puede obtener una licencia para conducir en este país?**

B. Rubén y Eva hacen diligencias

Complete the following description of Rubén and Eva's busy morning.

1. 8:15: Van al banco y abren una cuenta de __ahorros__ y una cuenta __corriente__. Las cuentas no son individuales; son __conjuntas__.
2. 8:50: Sacan dinero del __cajero__ automático.
3. 10:15: Van al Departamento de Vehículos. Eva llena una __planilla__ para sacar su licencia para conducir (*driver's license*); la fecha y la __firma__.
4. 11:30: Van a la oficina de __correos__ y después de hacer __cola__ por unos cinco minutos mandan una carta __certificada__ a La Paz. También envían un giro __postal__ y compran __estampillas__ para tres __tarjetas__ postales.
5. 12:00: Van a buscar el coche que Rubén había __estacionado (parqueado)__ a dos __cuadras__ del correo.

C. ¿Qué necesito o qué tengo que hacer?

Say what you need or what you have to do, according to each circumstance.

Answers: 1. Tengo que solicitar (pedir) un préstamo. 2. Tengo que preguntar cuál es el saldo de mi cuenta. 3. Necesito un plan de ahorros. 4. Necesito una caja de seguridad. 5. Tengo que ir a la casa central. 6. Tengo que pagar en efectivo.

1. Quieres comprar un automóvil, pero no tienes dinero.
2. Quieres saber cuánto dinero tienes en el banco.
3. Quieres ahorrar dinero.
4. Quieres guardar (*to keep*) documentos muy importantes en el banco.
5. En la sucursal del banco no tienen lo que necesitas.
6. No puedes pagar con un cheque ni con tu tarjeta de crédito.

D. ¿Qué necesita hacer? With a partner, take turns saying what parts of the computer you need to use or what you need to do, according to each circumstance. Use **Necesito** (+ *infinitive*)**...** or **Necesito usar...**

Answers will vary.

1. You need to write a report on the computer.
2. You need to print the report.
3. You need to read your e-mails.
4. You need to save a résumé.
5. You need to use a computer during a plane trip.
6. You need to look something up on the Internet.

Possible answers: 1. Necesito usar mi computadora personal. 2. Necesito usar la impresora. 3. Necesito mirar la pantalla. 4. Necesito archivar la información. 5. Necesito usar la microcomputadora. 6. Necesito tener acceso a la Red.

Miguel está comprando ropa por Internet. ¿Qué va a comprar?

Pronunciación

Pronunciation in context In this lesson, there are some words or phrases that may be challenging to pronounce. Listen to your instructor and pronounce the following sentences.

1. Hoy, por **fin,** tiene un par de **horas** para hacer **diligencias.**
2. ¿Qué tengo que **hacer** para abrir una cuenta de **ahorros**?
3. ¿Quiere abrir una cuenta **individual** o una cuenta **conjunta**?
4. Quiero mandar esta carta a **La Paz, certificada.**
5. Trató de **recordar** dónde había **estacionado** su coche.

Puntos para recordar

1. Past participles (*Los participios pasados*)

- In Spanish, regular past participles are formed by adding the following endings to the stem of the verb.

-ar *verbs*	-er *verbs*	-ir *verbs*
habl- **ado** (*spoken*)	com- **ido** (*eaten*)	recib- **ido** (*received*)

The following verbs have irregular past participles in Spanish.[1]

abrir	**abierto**	poner	**puesto**
decir	**dicho**	romper	**roto**
escribir	**escrito**	ver	**visto**
hacer	**hecho**	volver	**vuelto**
morir	**muerto**		

¡Atención! The past participle of **ir** is **ido.**

Suggestion: Open the classroom door, then have students tell you the result of your action. The students will say: **La puerta está abierta.** Say: **Cierren los libros.** The students then say: **Los libros están cerrados.**

- Past participles used as adjectives

  In Spanish, most past participles can be used as adjectives. As such, they agree in number and gender with the nouns they modify.

—¿**Las cartas** están **firmadas**?	*"Are **the letters signed?**"*
—Sí, ya están **firmadas** y **fechadas.**	*"Yes they are already **signed** and **dated.**"*
—¿**Las ventanas** están **abiertas**?	*"Are **the windows open**?"*
—No, están **cerradas.**	*"No, they're **shut.**"*

Extra practice: Divide the class into groups of three. Write the verb infinitives on pieces of paper and put them in containers for each group in the class. Have each student in the group choose an infinitive and give the past participle of that verb. The other students in the group should listen and make corrections.

Online Study Center

For more practice with lesson topics, see the related activities on the *¡Hola, amigos!* web site at college.hmco.com/PIC/holaamigos7e.

Práctica y conversación

A. Participios pasados

Give the past participles of the following verbs.

1. decir dicho
2. cerrar cerrado
3. hacer hecho
4. beber bebido
5. morir muerto
6. poner puesto
7. vivir vivido
8. ver visto
9. recetar recetado
10. volver vuelto
11. ir ido
12. tener tenido
13. romper roto
14. abrir abierto
15. parar parado
16. ser sido
17. escribir escrito
18. buscar buscado
19. leer leído
20. salir salido

[1]Verbs ending in **-er** and **-ir** whose stem ends in a strong vowel require an accent mark on the **i** of the **-ido** ending: **leer, leído; oír, oído; traer, traído; creer, creído.**

B. ¿Qué pasa? With a partner, take turns completing the description of each illustration, using the verb **estar** and the appropriate past participle.

1. El coche _está estacionado_ en la esquina (*corner*).

2. Los niños _están dormidos_.

3. El restaurante _está cerrado_.

4. La ventana _está rota_.

5. La puerta _está abierta_.

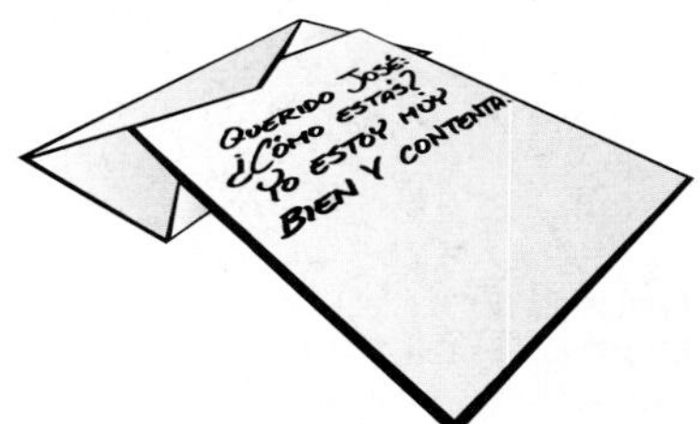

6. La carta _está escrita_ en español.

7. Los vestidos _están hechos_ en México.

8. El cuaderno _está abierto_.

9. La señora _está sentada_ cerca de la ventana.

C. Preguntas de un turista With a partner, take turns answering a tourist's questions. *Answers will vary.*

1. ¿Los bancos están abiertos a las ocho de la mañana?
2. Hoy es feriado, ¿están abiertas las tiendas?
3. ¿El correo ya está cerrado a las siete de la noche?
4. ¿Aquí todos los letreros (*signs*) están escritos en inglés?
5. ¿Dónde están hechos estos vinos?
6. ¿Los restaurantes están cerrados los domingos?

2. Present perfect tense (*Pretérito perfecto*)

Follow-up: After presenting the present perfect tense, move around the room, writing your name on the board, opening and closing a window, speaking to a student, etc. In each case, ask: **¿Qué he hecho?** Then have students do things and ask them or the rest of the class what they have done.

- The present perfect tense is formed by using the present tense of the auxiliary verb **haber** with the past participle of the verb that expresses the action or state.

Present Indicative of haber (*to have*)[1]	
he	**hemos**
has	**habéis**
ha	**han**

Expansion: Use the following activity to illustrate that when past participles are used as adjectives, they must agree in number and gender with the nouns they modify, but when they are used as part of a perfect tense, they are invariable. Go around the room doing things, telling students what you have done. Then have them tell you what the result of each action is using past participles as adjectives.

I: *Open the window and say:* **He abierto la ventana.**

S: **Sí, la ventana está abierta.**

Game: Present this as a test of students' powers of observation. Ask one student to leave the class. Select another to perform a prepared list of instructions. The rest of the class must observe carefully, then describe to their absent classmate what has taken place. This student will then duplicate the instructions exactly.

Formation of the Present Perfect Tense

	Present of haber	+ *Past Participle*	
yo	**he**	**hablado**	I have spoken
tú	**has**	**comido**	you (*fam.*) have eaten
Ud., él, ella	**ha**	**vuelto**	you (*form.*) have returned; he, she has returned
nosotros(as)	**hemos**	**dicho**	we have said
vosotros(as)	**habéis**	**roto**	you (*fam.*) have broken
Uds., ellos, ellas	**han**	**hecho**	you (*form., fam.*) have done, made; they have done, made

- The present perfect tense is equivalent to the use in English of the auxiliary verb *have + past participle,* as in *I have spoken.*

  —¿Nora **ha ido** al correo? *"**Has** Nora **gone** to the post office?"*
  —No, no **ha podido** ir. *"No, she **hasn't been** able to go."*

- Note that in Spanish, when the past participle is part of a perfect tense, its form does not vary for gender or number agreement.

  Él **ha estacionado** aquí. *"He has parked here."*
  Ella **ha estacionado** aquí. *"She has parked here."*

[1]Note that the English verb *to have* has two equivalents in Spanish: **haber** (used as an auxiliary verb) and **tener.**

- Unlike English, the past participle in Spanish is never separated from the auxiliary verb **haber.**

Ella **nunca ha hecho** nada.	*She **has never done** anything.*
Él **siempre ha escrito** las cartas en inglés.	*He **has always written** the letters in English.*

Online Study Center

For more practice with lesson topics, see the related activities on the *¡Hola, amigos!* web site at college.hmco.com/PIC/holaamigos7e.

Práctica y conversación

A. Hoy llega mamá Mrs. Aranda is coming home today after a business trip. With a partner, take turns saying what everybody has done to get ready for her homecoming. Use the cues provided.

MODELO: Viviana / preparar / comida
Viviana ha preparado la comida.

1. El Sr. Aranda / lavar / coche
2. Jorge / barrer / garaje
3. Yo / sacudir / muebles
4. Tú / hacer / una torta
5. Los niños / poner / mesa
6. Andrés / comprar / rosas
7. Raquel / pasar/ aspiradora
8. Rolando y yo / traer / bebidas

Answers: **1.** El Sr. Aranda ha lavado el coche. **2.** Jorge ha barrido el garaje. **3.** Yo he sacudido los muebles. **4.** Tú has hecho una torta. **5.** Los niños han puesto la mesa. **6.** Andrés ha comprado rosas. **7.** Raquel ha pasado la aspiradora. **8.** Rolando y yo hemos traído las bebidas.

B. Entreviste a su compañero(a) Interview a classmate, using the following questions. *Answers will vary.*

1. ¿Has ido al banco últimamente?
2. ¿Has pedido un préstamo recientemente?
3. ¿Has tenido que sacar dinero del cajero automático esta semana?
4. ¿Tus padres han abierto una cuenta conjunta contigo?
5. ¿Alguien te ha mandado tarjetas postales recientemente?
6. ¿Tú y tu familia han estado en Suramérica alguna vez (*ever*)?
7. ¿Dónde has estacionado tu coche hoy?
8. ¿Has llegado tarde a clase?

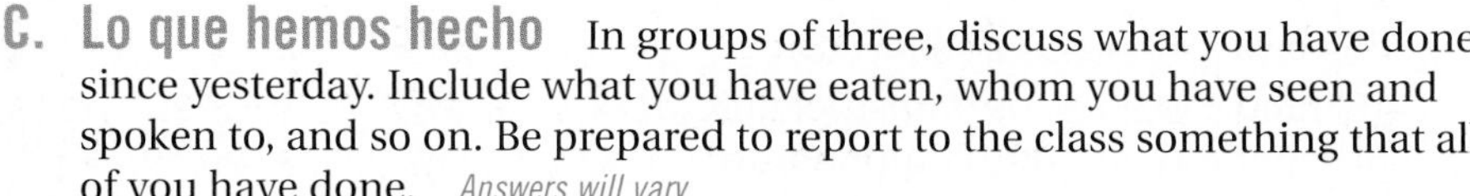

C. Lo que hemos hecho In groups of three, discuss what you have done since yesterday. Include what you have eaten, whom you have seen and spoken to, and so on. Be prepared to report to the class something that all of you have done. *Answers will vary.*

3. Past perfect (pluperfect) tense (*Pretérito pluscuamperfecto*)

Suggestion: Review the past participle before you present this tense.

- The past perfect tense is formed by using the imperfect tense of the auxiliary verb **haber** with the past participle of the verb that expresses the action or state.

Imperfect of haber	
había	**habíamos**
habías	**habíais**
había	**habían**

Formation of the Past Perfect Tense

	Imperfect of haber	+	*Past Participle*	
yo	**había**		**hablado**	I had spoken
tú	**habías**		**comido**	you (*fam.*) had eaten
Ud., él, ella	**había**		**vuelto**	you (*form.*), he, she had returned
nosotros(as)	**habíamos**		**dicho**	we had said
vosotros(as)	**habíais**		**roto**	you (*fam.*) had broken
Uds., ellos, ellas	**habían**		**hecho**	you (*form., fam.*) had done, made; they had done, made

Extra practice: Write the following incomplete statements on the board. Have students complete the sentences in pairs, using the past perfect.

Antes de 2004 yo no...
Antes de 1990 mis padres no...
Antes de 2000 mi(s) hermano (a, os, as) no...
Antes de cumplir dieciocho años mis amigos y yo...
Antes del semestre/trimestre pasado mi(s) amigo(s) no...

- The past perfect tense is equivalent to the use in English of the auxiliary verb *had* + *past participle,* as in *I had spoken.*

In Spanish, as in English, this tense refers to actions, states, or events that were already completed before the start of another past action, state, or event.

—¿Uds. **habían estado** en Chile antes del año pasado? — *"**Had** you **been** in Chile before last year?"*
—No, nunca **habíamos estado** allí. — *"No, **we had** never **been** there."*

—¿Ricardo está aquí? — *"Is Ricardo here?"*
—Sí, cuando yo vine, él ya **había llegado.** — *"Yes, when I came, he **had** already **arrived.**"*

Online Study Center

For more practice with lesson topics, see the related activities on the *¡Hola, amigos!* web site at college.hmco.com/PIC/holaamigos7e.

Práctica y conversación

A. Minidiálogos Complete the following exchanges with the past perfect of the verbs given.

1. —¿Qué __había hecho__ (hacer) el empleado?
   —Le __había traído__ (traer) las estampillas.
2. —¿Tú ya __habías visto__ (ver) a Roberto?
   —Sí, yo ya __había hablado__ (hablar) con él.
3. —¿El niño __había roto__ (romper) el florero?
   —Sí, y por eso tuve que comprar otro.

4. —Cuando papá vino a buscarnos, ¿Uds. ya habían ido (ir) al correo?
—No, no habíamos ido (ir) todavía.
5. —¿Qué había dicho (decir) tu mamá?
—Que necesitaba su talonario de cheques.
6. —¿Adónde habían ido (ir) Uds., a la casa central del banco?
—No habíamos ido (ir) a una sucursal.
7. —¿Dónde habías puesto (poner) tú los documentos?
—Los había puesto (poner) en la caja de seguridad.
8. —¿Qué le habían comprado (comprar) a Jorge Uds.?
—Le habíamos comprado (comprar) una computadora personal.

B. Están de vuelta Your parents just got back from a vacation. Say what everybody had done by the time they came back. *Answers will vary.*

1. yo
2. mi amiga
3. mis hermanos
4. mi tío y yo
5. tú
6. Uds.

C. Antes de los 16 Find out which of the following things your partner had done before turning 16. *Answers will vary.*

◆ **MODELO:** conducir
—*¿Habías conducido antes de cumplir dieciséis años?*
—*Sí (No),...*

1. abrir una cuenta corriente
2. trabajar
3. tener novio(a)
4. vivir en otro país (*country*)
5. estudiar un idioma
6. terminar la escuela secundaria

Verb forms: 1. Habías abierto / había abierto. 2. Habías trabajado / había trabajado. 3. Habías tenido / había tenido. 4. Habías vivido / había vivido. 5. Habías estudiado / había estudiado. 6. Habías terminado / había terminado.

4. Formal commands: *Ud.* and *Uds.* (*Mandatos formales:* Ud. *y* Uds.)

◆ The command forms for **Ud.** and **Uds.**[1] are formed by dropping the **-o** of the first-person singular of the present indicative and adding **-e** and **-en** for **-ar** verbs and **-a** and **-an** for **-er** and **-ir** verbs.

Infinitive	First-Person Sing. Present Indicative	Stem	Commands *Ud.*	Commands *Uds.*
habl**ar**	yo habl**o**	habl-	habl**e**	habl**en**
com**er**	yo com**o**	com-	com**a**	com**an**
abr**ir**	yo abr**o**	abr-	abr**a**	abr**an**
cerr**ar**	yo cierr**o**	cierr-	cierr**e**	cierr**en**
volv**er**	yo vuelv**o**	vuelv-	vuelv**a**	vuelv**an**
ped**ir**	yo pid**o**	pid-	pid**a**	pid**an**
dec**ir**	yo dig**o**	dig-	dig**a**	dig**an**

—¿Con quién debo hablar? *"With whom must I speak?"*
—**Hable** con el cajero. *"**Speak** with the teller."*

—¿Cuándo debemos volver? *"When must we come back?"*
—**Vuelvan** mañana. *"**Come back** tomorrow."*

Suggestion: Use TPR to introduce the command forms. Ask students to act out simple commands, for example:

Abra el libro.
Vaya a la pizarra.
Hable en inglés.
Siéntese.
Dele el libro a (*another student*).
Escriba su nombre en la pizarra.
Camine.
Ponga su libro en el pupitre de...
Salga de la clase.

Alternative: You may also write the infinitive phrases on the board and have students take turns giving each other commands.

[1]The command form for **tú** will be studied in **Lección 12.**

Suggestion: Spend sufficient time practicing the command forms of **-ar** verbs before going on to **-er** and **-ir** verbs. Begin by having students perform your commands. Then divide the class into pairs and have students take turns giving and responding to commands.

- The command forms of the following verbs are irregular.

	dar	estar	ser	ir
Ud.	**dé**	**esté**	**sea**	**vaya**
Uds.	**den**	**estén**	**sean**	**vayan**

—¿Vamos al correo ahora? — *"Shall we go to the post office now?"*

—No, no **vayan** ahora; **vayan** a las dos. — *"No, don't **go** now; **go** at two o'clock."*

Suggestions: Illustrate the fact that object pronouns are placed after an affirmative command and before a negative command by writing on the board:

Pída**selo**.
No **se lo** pida.

Highlight the accent on the affirmative form by using colored chalk.

- With all direct *affirmative* commands, object pronouns are placed after the verb and are attached to it, thus forming only one word. With all *negative* commands, the object pronouns are placed in front of the verb.

—¿Dónde pongo las cartas? — *"Where shall I put the letters?"*
—**Póngalas** aquí; **no las ponga** allí. — *"**Put them** here; **don't put them** there."*

¡Atención! Note the use of the written accent in **póngalas.**

Suggestion: It would be appropriate at this time to review the direct and indirect object pronouns used together presented in **Lección 8.**

Práctica y conversación

Online Study Center

For more practice with lesson topics, see the related activities on the *¡Hola, amigos!* web site at college.hmco.com/PIC/holaamigos7e.

A. Instrucciones A bank employee must give the customers certain instructions. Following the model, change each sentence to the appropriate command.

- **MODELO:** Tiene que llenar la planilla.
  Llene la planilla.

Answers: 1. Fechen y firmen la planilla. 2. Hagan cola.

1. Tienen que fechar y firmar la planilla.
2. Tienen que hacer cola.

3. Tienen que estar aquí a las tres.
4. Tiene que hablar con el cajero.
5. Tiene que sentarse y esperar unos minutos.
6. Tiene que venir más tarde y traer el número de su cuenta.
7. Tiene que darle su nombre al gerente (*manager*).
8. Tiene que dejarme su número de teléfono.
9. Tienen que decirle que los cheques son gratis.
10. Tiene que volver mañana.

3. Estén aquí a las tres. **4.** Hable con el cajero. **5.** Siéntese y espere unos minutos. **6.** Venga más tarde y traiga el número de su cuenta. **7.** Dele su nombre al gerente. **8.** Déjeme su número de teléfono. **9.** Díganle que los cheques son gratis. **10.** Vuelva mañana.

B. Mamá (Papá) y nosotros

Two teenagers are helping their Mom (Dad) and asking what to do. Take the role of the parent and answer their questions. Use the command forms and the cues provided.

1. ¿Adónde vamos ahora? (al mercado)
2. ¿Qué compramos? (frutas)
3. ¿A quién le pedimos el dinero? (a su abuelo)
4. ¿Qué más traemos? (detergente)
5. ¿Qué coche llevamos? (el mío)
6. ¿A qué hora empezamos a cocinar? (a las tres)
7. ¿Qué hacemos de postre? (arroz con leche)
8. ¿Invitamos a cenar a Roberto o a Miguel? (Miguel)

Answers: **1.** Vayan al mercado. **2.** Compren frutas. **3.** Pídanselo a su abuelo. **4.** Traigan detergente. **5.** Lleven el mío. **6.** Empiecen a las tres. **7.** Hagan arroz con leche. **8.** Inviten a Miguel.

C. ¿Que sí o que no?

Andrés says yes to everything, while Ana always says no. With your partner, play the roles of Ana and Andrés. Answer each question as he or she would, using a formal command and a direct object pronoun to replace each direct object.

1. ¿Mando las cartas hoy? (Andrés)
2. ¿Compramos los sellos? (Ana)
3. ¿Traigo el talonario de cheques? (Ana)
4. ¿Compramos las tarjetas postales? (Andrés)
5. ¿Llamo a Rafael? (Andrés)
6. ¿Llamamos a nuestros amigos? (Ana)
7. ¿Mando el giro postal? (Andrés)
8. ¿Hacemos las diligencias hoy? (Ana)

Answers: **1.** Sí, mándelas hoy. **2.** No, no los compren. **3.** No, no lo traiga. **4.** Sí, cómprenlas. **5.** Sí, llámelo. **6.** No, no los llamen. **7.** Sí, mándelo. **8.** No, no las hagan hoy.

Extra practice: Have students create 5–10 rules for improving their campus or workplace, using formal commands. This activity may be done orally individually, in pairs, in small groups, or written as homework.

D. A mi secretaria

Using commands, tell your secretary to do the following tasks.

1. *Escribirles* al Dr. López y al Dr. Smith. *Escribirle* al Dr. López en español y *escribirle* al Dr. Smith en inglés. *Decirles* que los documentos ya están listos. *Mandarles* las cartas hoy.
2. *Comprarle* (a él) papel y lápices.
3. *Darle* al Sr. Gómez su número de teléfono, pero no *darle* su dirección.
4. *No hablarles* a los empleados del nuevo horario.
5. *Llevarle* las planillas al Sr. Soto, pero *no llevarle* los cheques.
6. *No decirle* a la Sra. Castro que los cheques son gratis.

Answers: **1.** Escríbales al Dr. López y al Dr. Smith. Escríbale al Dr. López en español y escríbale al Dr. Smith en inglés. Dígales que los documentos ya están listos. Mándeles las cartas hoy. **2.** Cómpreme papel y lápices. **3.** Dele al Sr. Gómez mi número de teléfono, pero no le dé mi dirección. **4.** No les hable a los empleados del nuevo horario. **5.** Llévele las planillas al Sr. Soto, pero no le lleve los cheques. **6.** No le diga a la Sra. Castro que los cheques son gratis.

E. Una nota

You and your partner are going to be gone for a few days, and you have two very irresponsible roommates. Write them a note telling them four things to do and four things not to do in your absence. *Answers will vary.*

Entre nosotros

¡Conversemos!

Para conocernos mejor Get to know your partner better by asking each other the following questions. *Answers will vary.*

1. ¿En qué banco tienes tu cuenta de ahorros? ¿Y tu cuenta corriente?
2. ¿Usas el cajero automático a veces?
3. Cuando compras algo, ¿pagas en efectivo o con cheque?
4. ¿Vas a depositar dinero en tu cuenta de ahorros mañana?
5. ¿Tienes tu talonario de cheques contigo?
6. ¿Tú sabes cuál es el saldo de tu cuenta corriente?
7. ¿Tienes tus documentos importantes en una caja de seguridad?
8. Cuando vas al correo, ¿a veces tienes que hacer cola?
9. ¿Envías muchas tarjetas de Navidad (*Christmas*)?
10. ¿Usas microcomputadora o computadora personal?
11. ¿Navegas mucho la Red?
12. ¿Cuántos mensajes electrónicos recibes al día?

Una encuesta Interview your classmates to identify who fits the following descriptions. Include your instructor, but remember to use the **Ud.** form when addressing him or her. *Answers will vary.*

	Nombre
1. Hace sus diligencias los sábados.	
2. A veces manda giros postales.	
3. A veces envía cartas certificadas.	
4. Recuerda su número de Seguro Social (Social Security).	
5. Piensa abrir una cuenta en el banco.	
6. Tiene un buen plan de ahorros.	
7. Necesita ahorrar más.	
8. Tiene una cuenta conjunta.	
9. Siempre manda tarjetas postales cuando viaja (he/she travels).	
10. Deposita dinero en el banco todos los meses.	

Y ahora... Write a brief summary, indicating what you have learned about your classmates. *Answers will vary.*

¿Cómo lo decimos? What would you say in the following situations? What might the other person say? Act out the scenes with a partner. *Answers will vary.*

1. Ask for the necessary information to open a savings account.
2. You need to cash a check. Tell the teller how much you want to deposit in your checking account, and how much cash you want.
3. You are in Asunción, and you need to send some letters and postcards to the United States. Tell the employee what you need.
4. You are teaching a computer class for beginners. In Spanish, identify the parts of a computer for your students.
5. You are at a computer lab at closing time. Tell the attendant three things you need to do before you leave.

Suggestion: Have students prepare this activity before class to do in pairs orally during class.

Possible answers: **1.** Quiero abrir una cuenta de ahorros. ¿Qué interés pagan? ¿Puedo usar el cajero automático para sacar mi dinero en cualquier momento? **2.** Necesito cobrar un cheque. Quiero depositar... dólares en mi cuenta corriente y quiero... dólares en efectivo. **3.** Necesito enviar (mandar) algunas cartas y tarjetas postales a los Estados Unidos. Quiero enviar las cartas certificadas. ¿Cuánto cuesta? **4.** Algunas partes de la computadora son: el monitor, el teclado, el ratón y la pantalla. **5.** *Answers will vary.*

¿Qué dice aquí? Read the following ad, and answer the questions that follow.

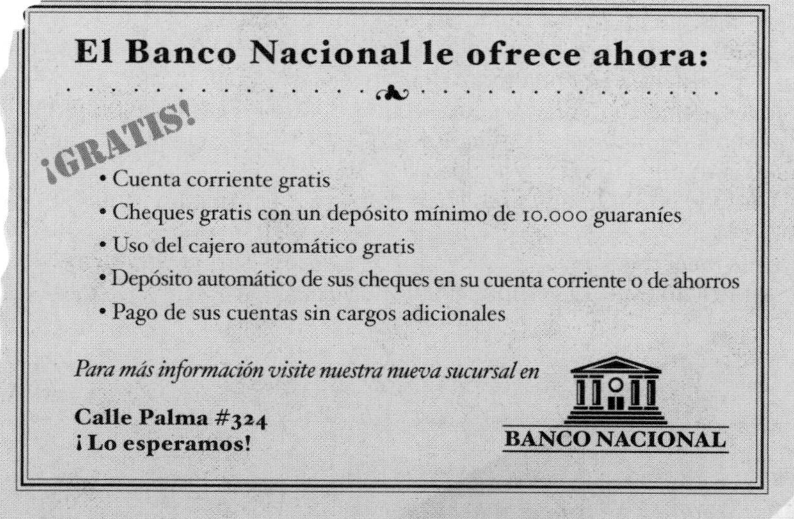

1. ¿Cuánto hay que pagar por tener una cuenta corriente?
2. ¿Cuánto se debe tener depositado para recibir los cheques gratis?
3. ¿Cuánto cobra el banco por el uso del cajero automático?
4. ¿En qué tipos de cuentas se pueden depositar los cheques automáticamente?
5. ¿Que otro servicio ofrece gratis el banco?
6. ¿Dónde se puede obtener más información sobre los servicios que da el banco?
7. ¿Cómo se llama el banco? ¿Cuál es la dirección de la nueva sucursal?

Un dicho

El tiempo es oro (gold).

As you can see, time is important in both cultures. Next time someone is wasting time you can quote this saying in Spanish.

Answers: **1.** Nada, la cuenta es gratis. **2.** Debe tener depositado un mínimo de 10.000 guaraníes. **3.** No cobra nada. Es gratis. **4.** Se pueden depositar en la cuenta corriente y en la cuenta de ahorros. **5.** El pago de las cuentas también es gratis. **6.** Se puede obtener más información en la nueva sucursal. **7.** Se llama Banco Nacional. Calle Palma 324.

Para escribir

En el banco Write about your banking practices. Mention . . . *Answers will vary.*

1. the name of your bank and types of accounts you have.
2. the interest (**interés**) your bank pays.
3. whether you need to pay for the checks or if they are free.
4. whether you pay for purchases by check or by a credit card.
5. whether you save money, and why.

Suggestion: Encourage students to memorize sayings and apply them when appropriate.

Lectura

Reading strategy: Have students work in small groups or brainstorm ideas with the class. Ask leading questions as needed.

Answers: 1. Un inglés deletrea su apellido. 2. Una palabra puede escribirse de mil maneras. 3. Sí, es más difícil. 4. Como tesis fundamental, se puede decir que toda palabra inglesa es un jeroglífico. 5. El título de su libro en español es *El caballero de El Dorado.* En inglés, es *The Knight of El Dorado.* 6. Porque en inglés, *"knight"* y *"night"* se pronuncian de la misma manera. 7. "Hoy da una conferencia sobre la América Latina el doctor Arthur Nagus." 8. La dificultad del inglés está en la emisión de los sonidos. 9. Dice que cada una de las vocales se pronuncia de cuatro o cinco modos distintos. 10. Causa una gran fatiga. 11. Deja una impresión de dolor o de gran torpeza. 12. Dice que él no es bobo; es que no sabe inglés.

Estrategia de lectura Make a list of some aspects of English that make it difficult to learn as a second language. Think about some of the problems that Spanish-speaking students might face. *Answers will vary.*

Vamos a leer As you read the story, find the answers to the following questions.

1. ¿Qué deletrea (*spell*) un inglés cuando se presenta?
2. Según el autor, ¿de cuántas maneras puede escribirse una palabra?
3. ¿Es más difícil el deletreo cuando se hace por teléfono?
4. ¿Qué se puede decir como tesis fundamental?
5. ¿Cuál es el título de su libro en español? ¿Y en inglés?
6. Cuando Arciniegas habla de su libro en inglés, nadie sabe si él escribió un nocturno o un libro de caballería. ¿Por qué?
7. ¿Cómo anunciaron un día una conferencia de Arciniegas en el periódico?
8. Para el autor, ¿dónde está la dificultad del inglés?
9. ¿Qué dice Arciniegas de las vocales?
10. ¿Qué causa el esfuerzo que un hispanohablante realiza para producir "eres" o "eses"?
11. ¿Qué deja en el rostro?
12. ¿Qué explicación les da siempre el autor a sus colegas?

Germán Arciniegas (1900–1999) es uno de los escritores colombianos más distinguidos. Sus brillantes ensayos° se centran en la cultura, la sociología, la historia, el arte y la literatura de su país y de toda Latinoamérica. Su estilo es ligero° y ágil. Su famosa biografía, El caballero de El Dorado *(1942), sobre la vida° de Gonzalo Jiménez de Quesada, conquistador de Colombia y fundador de Bogotá, es una de las mejor escritas° en este continente. Muchos de sus libros han sido traducidos al inglés.*

° ensayos: *essays*; ligero: *light*; vida: *life*; escritas: *written*

Video

Lecciones de inglés (Adaptado)

GERMÁN ARCINIEGAS

Un inglés que en algo se estima° se presenta de esta manera: "Soy Mr. John Nielsen, Ene-i-e-ele-ese-e-ene". Esto es porque en inglés se supone que una palabra se pronuncia de un modo —cosa que no es exacta— pero que en todo caso puede escribirse de mil maneras. Aun el deletreo° puede no ser suficientemente claro, principalmente si se hace por teléfono. En este caso lo más discreto y usual es decir: "Mr. Arciniegas, *A* como en Argentina, *R* como en Rusia, *C* como en Colombia, *I* como en Irlanda..." De esta manera, siendo el idioma de Shakespeare tan conciso, un apellido puede extenderse indefinidamente.

Las confusiones no quedan limitadas a los apellidos. Como tesis fundamental usted puede decir que toda palabra inglesa es un jeroglífico. Yo tengo un libro que, en la edición española, se llama *El caballero° de El Dorado*. Aquí, *The Knight of El Dorado.* Pero como en inglés "noche" y "caballero" se pronuncian de un mismo modo°, cuando estoy hablando de mi libro nadie sabe si escribí un nocturno° o una obra de caballería°. En la cubierta de este libro aparece la siguiente advertencia°: "Germán Arciniegas (se pronuncia *Hair-máhn Ar-seen-yay-gus*)". La advertencia es indispensable.

Pero si el lector° quiere saber más sobre los problemas de mi apellido en este país, puedo informarle que un día en el periódico anunciaron una conferencia mía así: "Hoy da una conferencia sobre la América Latina el doctor *Arthur Nagus*".

La dificultad del inglés está en la emisión de los sonidos. Cuando uno se da cuenta° de que cada letra de las vocales se pronuncia de cuatro o cinco modos distintos, desfallece°. El esfuerzo que uno realiza para producir "eres" o "eses" no sólo causa una gran fatiga a quienes estamos acostumbrados al español, sino que deja en el rostro° una impresión de dolor o de gran torpeza°. Yo siempre les doy esta explicación a mis colegas: "Yo no soy bobo; es que no sé inglés".

que... *who has some self esteem*
spelling
knight
way
nocturne / chivalry
warning
reader
se... *realizes*
one faints
face, stupidity

Díganos Answer the following questions, based on your own thoughts and experience. *Answers will vary.*

1. ¿Sabe usted deletrear en español?
2. ¿Qué cree usted que es lo más difícil en español? ¿Pronunciar las palabras? ¿Conjugar verbos? ¿Escribir?
3. ¿Qué problemas tiene usted para aprender español?
4. ¿Usted tiene que realizar un gran esfuerzo para hablar español?
5. ¿Cuánto tiempo hace que usted empezó a estudiar español? ¿Lo practica frecuentemente?
6. ¿Usted piensa continuar estudiando español?

Un día funesto

Marisa, Teresa y Pablo han tenido un día difícil en el que todo les fue mal (*went badly for them*). ¿Qué van a hacer? Los tres están demasiado cansados. ¿Encuentran una solución...?

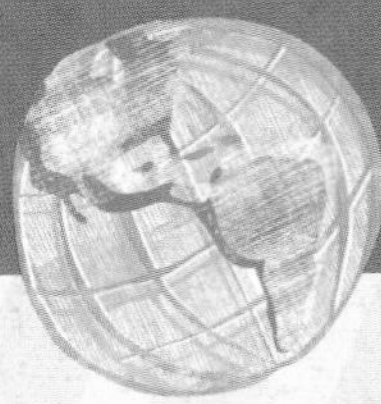

El mundo hispánico

Ecuador

- Ecuador debe su nombre a su posición geográfica. El país está situado justamente sobre la línea del ecuador. Su territorio, incluidas las islas Galápagos, es un poco menor que el de Nevada, y su población es de unos 13,5 millones de habitantes.
- Debido a la inestabilidad del sucre, su antigua moneda, en septiembre de 2000 el país adoptó el dólar de Estados Unidos como su moneda oficial.
- Quito, la capital de Ecuador, está situada en las laderas (*hillsides*) del volcán Pichincha, a más de 9.000 pies de altura sobre el nivel del mar. Por eso, aunque la ciudad está muy cerca de la línea del ecuador, su clima es templado (*mild*) y agradable. Quito es la capital más antigua de América del Sur, y todavía mantiene su aspecto colonial, con sus calles estrechas (*narrow*) y sus viejas iglesias.
- A 22 millas de Quito, cerca de la villa de San Antonio, está el monumento La Mitad del Mundo, que marca el sitio exacto por donde pasa la línea del ecuador.
- Las islas Galápagos, situadas frente a las costas de Ecuador, son una de las zonas ecológicas mejor conservadas del mundo. Charles Darwin hizo la mayor parte de sus estudios sobre la evolución de las especies en estas islas.

▲ Estas enormes tortugas les dieron nombre a las famosas Islas Galápagos.

Perú

- Perú es el tercer país más grande de Suramérica. Su territorio es un poco menor que el de Alaska, y su población es de unos 28 millones de habitantes. La moneda del país es el nuevo sol. La principal fuente de ingreso del país continúa siendo la industria pesquera.
- Entre los animales típicos de la fauna de Perú están las llamas, alpacas y vicuñas. De su lana dependen muchas de las artesanías del país. La llama, además, se usa como animal de carga y para el transporte.
- Las principales atracciones turísticas del país son Cuzco, la antigua capital de los incas, y las impresionantes ruinas de Machu Picchu, situadas en las montañas cerca de Cuzco a una altura de 2.350 metros. Machu Picchu fue una fortaleza incaica que después de la conquista quedó perdida hasta 1911, cuando fue descubierta por el arqueólogo norteamericano Hiram Bingham.
- La capital de Perú es Lima. En esta ciudad se encuentra la Universidad de San Marcos, que es la más antigua de Suramérica.

▲ Machu Picchu es el más conocido de los símbolos del Imperio Inca.

Online Study Center

For more practice with lesson topics, see the related activities on the ***¡Hola, amigos!*** web site at college.hmco.com/PIC/holaamigos7e.

Bolivia

▲ La plaza del estudiante en La Paz, Bolivia

- Bolivia, llamada así en honor del Libertador Simón Bolívar, es un país de superlativos. Tiene la capital (La Paz), el aeropuerto y el lago navegable más altos del mundo, y unas de las ruinas más antiguas. En realidad, La Paz es una de las dos capitales de Bolivia; la otra es Sucre. La Paz, situada a 12.000 pies de altura, es la capital administrativa, y Sucre, la capital política. El lago Titicaca está a 12.500 pies de altura y es, después del lago Maracaibo, el segundo más grande de América del Sur. El país es tan grande como los estados de California y Texas juntos, pero apenas puede explotar sus riquezas naturales porque no tiene salida al mar y su territorio es muy montañoso.
- Los indios quechua y aymará, que constituyen más de la mitad de su población, mantienen su cultura y sus lenguas tradicionales. El resto de la población lo constituyen las personas de ascendencia europea (un 15% de la población) y los mestizos producto de la integración de las razas indígenas y europeas. La mayor parte de los habitantes del país vive en el altiplano (*plateau*).
- Bolivia es uno de los más atractivos destinos turísticos por sus bellísimos paisajes andinos, que le han valido el nombre de "el Tibet de América", y por las ruinas doblemente milenarias de Tiahuanaco.

Paraguay

- Paraguay es casi tan grande como el estado de California, pero su población es de menos de 6 millones de habitantes. La mayoría de los paraguayos hablan dos idiomas: el español y el guaraní.
- Paraguay es un país principalmente agrícola y su economía depende de sus bosques y sus fértiles tierras (*lands*). Sin embargo, desde la construcción de la planta hidroeléctrica de Itaipú, el país ha comenzado a industrializarse. Itaipú, la mayor planta hidroeléctrica del mundo, obra del esfuerzo conjunto de Brasil y Paraguay, ha hecho de este país el mayor exportador de energía hidroeléctrica.
- Al igual que Bolivia, Paraguay no tiene salida al mar, pero tiene más de 1.800 millas de ríos navegables, que son sus principales vías de transporte. En la frontera de Paraguay, Argentina y Brasil están las famosas cataratas de Iguazú, nombre guaraní que significa "agua grande".
- Asunción, la capital de Paraguay, es también su principal puerto. Es una ciudad de más de dos millones de habitantes en la que se mezclan los edificios coloniales con modernas construcciones.

▲ El Panteón de los Héroes, en Asunción, Paraguay

 **Comentarios...** With a partner, discuss, in Spanish, what impressed you the most about these four countries, and compare them to your own. Which places do you want to visit and why?

Tome este examen

Lección 9

Lección 9

A. Some uses of *por* and *para* Complete each sentence, using **por** or **para.**

1. El vestido es __para__ ti, mamá.
2. ¿Cuánto pagaron __por__ los aretes?
3. Yo no trabajo __por__ la mañana.
4. Los chicos salieron __por__ la puerta principal.
5. Ellos fueron al club nocturno __para__ bailar.
6. Necesito la falda __para__ mañana __por__ la tarde.
7. El sábado salimos __para__ Lima. Vamos __por__ avión (*airplane*). Vamos a estar allí __por__ una semana.
8. En ese hotel cobran 100 dólares __por__ noche.

B. Weather expressions Complete each sentence with the appropriate word(s).

1. En verano __hace__ mucho __calor__ en Texas.
2. En invierno en Denver __hace__ mucho __frío__ y __nieva__ mucho.
3. En Oregón __llueve__ todo el año.
4. Hoy no hay vuelos (*flights*) porque __hay__ mucha __niebla__.
5. Necesito la sombrilla porque __hace__ mucho __sol__.

C. The preterit contrasted with the imperfect Complete each sentence, using the preterit or the imperfect tense of the verbs in parentheses.

1. Ayer nosotros __celebramos__ (celebrar) nuestro aniversario.
2. __Eran__ (Ser) las cuatro de la tarde cuando yo __salí__ (salir) del restaurante. __Llegué__ (Llegar) a mi casa a las cinco.
3. El mozo me __dijo__ (decir) que la especialidad de la casa __era__ (ser) cordero y yo lo __pedí__ (pedir).
4. Cuando Raúl __era__ (ser) pequeño __vivía__ (vivir) aquí.
5. Jorge __estaba__ (estar) en el café cuando yo lo __vi__ (ver).
6. Ella no __fue__ (ir) a la fiesta anoche porque __estaba__ (estar) muy cansada. __Prefirió__ (Preferir) quedarse en su casa.
7. Ayer yo __hice__ (hacer) las reservaciones.
8. Nosotros __estábamos__ (estar) almorzando cuando tú __llamaste__ (llamar).

D. *Hace...* meaning *ago* Indicate how long ago everything took place.

1. Llegué a las seis. Son las nueve.
2. Ellos vinieron en marzo. Estamos en julio.
3. Empecé a trabajar a las dos. Son las dos y media.
4. Terminaron el domingo. Hoy es viernes.
5. Llegaste en 1998. Estamos en el año 2008.

Answers: **1.** Hace tres horas que llegué. **2.** Hace cuatro meses que ellos vinieron. **3.** Hace media hora que empecé a trabajar. **4.** Hace cinco días que (ellos) terminaron. **5.** Hace diez años que tú llegaste.

Lección 9

E. Possessive pronouns Complete each sentence, giving the Spanish equivalent of the word in parentheses.

1. Mi vestido es mejor que __el tuyo__, María. (*yours*)
2. Las camisas azules son __mías__. (*mine*)
3. Yo voy a invitar a mis amigos. ¿Tú vas a invitar a __los tuyos__? (*yours*)
4. Estos zapatos son __nuestros__. (*ours*)
5. Mi abuelo es de México. __El suyo (El de ellos)__ es de Cuba. (*Theirs*)
6. Ese libro no es __mío__; es __suyo (de ella)__. (*mine / hers*)

F. Vocabulary Complete the following sentences, using vocabulary from **Lección 9.**

1. Estos zapatos no son caros, son muy __baratos__.
2. Voy a la __zapatería__ para comprar unas sandalias.
3. Estudia en la __facultad__ de medicina.
4. Necesito un __par__ de botas.
5. Necesito una camisa de __mangas__ largas.
6. ¿En que puedo __servirle__, Srta.?
7. Este traje no está de __moda__ ahora.
8. No me gusta andar __descalzo__. Siempre uso zapatos.
9. Voy a comprar ropa porque no tengo nada que __ponerme__.
10. Los aretes me costaron un __ojo__ de la __cara__.
11. ¿Qué número __calza__ Ud.?
12. El clima de este país no es seco, es __húmedo__.

G. Culture Complete the following sentences, based on the cultural notes you have read.

1. En los países hispanos se usa el sistema __métrico__ decimal.
2. La moneda de Perú es el __nuevo sol__.

Lección 10

A. Past participles

Complete each sentence, using the past participle of the verb in parentheses.

1. Las puertas están cerradas. (cerrar)
2. La oficina está abierta. (abrir)
3. El florero está roto. (romper)
4. Los niños están dormidos. (dormir)
5. Las cartas están escritas en italiano. (escribir)
6. La cena ya está hecha. (hacer)

B. Present perfect tense

Complete each sentence, using the present perfect of the verb in parentheses.

1. El cajero no ha llegado. (llegar)
2. Yo he roto los vasos. (romper)
3. Ellos no han traído las cartas. (traer)
4. Como los niños no han vuelto, nosotros no hemos podido salir. (volver / poder)
5. Ellos han muerto en el accidente. (morir)
6. Tú se lo has dicho antes. (decir)

C. Past perfect (Pluperfect) tense

Indicate what had taken place by the time Ana arrived home, using the past perfect tense.

Ana llegó a su casa a las diez.

Answers: **1.** habían vuelto **2.** había firmado **3.** habías hecho **4.** habíamos escrito **5.** había puesto **6.** habían ido

1. Los chicos volvieron a casa.
2. Yo firmé la planilla.
3. Tú hiciste los cheques.
4. Nosotros escribimos las cartas.
5. Carlos puso el dinero en su cuenta.
6. Uds. fueron al banco.

D. Formal commands

Complete each sentence, using the command form of the verb in parentheses. Use the **Ud.** or **Uds.** form, as needed.

1. Llame a su esposa, Sr. García. (Llamar)
2. Camine, Sr. Vega. (Caminar)
3. Salgan en seguida, señoritas. (Salir)
4. Esté aquí a las dos, señora. (Estar)
5. No venga ahora, Sr. Sosa. (venir)
6. Vayan a la izquierda, señores. (Ir)
7. No lo haga Ud. ahora. (hacerlo)
8. Señor, no dé su número de teléfono. (dar)
9. Chicos, sean buenos, por favor. (ser)
10. Póngala aquí. Srta. Pérez. (Ponerla)

E. Vocabulary Complete the following sentences, using vocabulary from **Lección 10.**

1. Ud. debe ___firmar___ y ___fechar___ esta planilla.
2. ¿Cuánto dinero va a ___depositar___ en su cuenta?
3. El banco no está ___abierto___ hoy, porque es un día ___feriado___.
4. Quiero saber cuál es el ___saldo___ de mi cuenta corriente.
5. Mi esposa y yo queremos abrir una cuenta de ahorros ___conjunta___.
6. Estacioné mi coche a dos ___cuadras___ de aquí.
7. Tengo que hacer ___cola___ porque hay mucha gente en el banco.
8. Necesito mi ___talonario___ de cheques.
9. No tengo mi dinero en el banco central, sino en una ___sucursal___.
10. Ellos van a sacar dinero del ___cajero___ automático.
11. Necesito dinero. Voy a solicitar un ___préstamo___ en el banco.
12. No quiero pagar con cheque, prefiero pagar en ___efectivo___.
13. Tengo mis documentos en una ___caja___ de seguridad.
14. Necesito comprar ___sellos (estampillas)___ para estas cartas.
15. Hoy tengo que hacer muchas ___diligencias___.

F. Culture Complete the following sentences, based on the cultural notes you have read.

1. Las islas ___Galápagos___ son una de las zonas ecológicas mejor conservadas.
2. Machu Picchu y ___Cuzco___ son las principales atracciones turísticas de Perú.
3. Bolivia tiene dos capitales: La Paz y ___Sucre___.
4. En Paraguay está ___Itaipú___, la mayor planta hidroeléctrica del mundo.

Unidad 6

Objetivos

Lección 11

- handle routine travel arrangements
- discuss tour features and prices
- request information regarding stopovers, plane changes, gate numbers, and seating
- express feelings and reactions

Lección 12

- register at a boarding house, discuss room prices, accommodations, and service
- tell others what to do
- describe needs and wants
- ordinal numbers

Situado entre lagos, ríos y glaciares, está el hotel Llao Llao en Bariloche, Argentina.

De vacaciones

Lección 11
¡Buen viaje!

Lección 12
¿Dónde nos hospedamos?

Argentina

El obelisco en la famosa Avenida 9 de Julio en Buenos Aires, Argentina

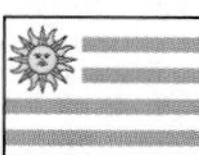

Uruguay

Vista del famoso balneario de Punta del Este

Chile

Vista del Lago Pehoé, Parque Nacional Torres del Paine, en la Patagonia

Lección 11 ◆ ¡Buen viaje!

Héctor Rivas y su esposa Sofía Vargas viven en Santiago, la capital de Chile. Ahora están planeando sus vacaciones de verano. No pueden ponerse de acuerdo porque ella quiere pasar un mes en Viña del Mar, y él quiere ir a Buenos Aires y a Mar del Plata.

Héctor Espero que hoy podamos decidir lo que vamos a hacer, porque tenemos que ir a la agencia de viajes para comprar los pasajes.

Sofía Yo te sugiero que averigües lo que cuestan dos pasajes de ida y vuelta a Buenos Aires, por avión. Podemos ahorrar dinero si vamos a Viña del Mar en coche...

Héctor ¡Pero hemos estado en Viña del Mar muchas veces! ¡Estoy empezando a cansarme de hacer siempre lo mismo!

Sofía ¡Y yo temo que el viaje a Buenos Aires nos cueste mucho dinero!

Héctor Yo busqué información en Internet. Hay paquetes que incluyen vuelo directo a Buenos Aires, hotel y algunas excursiones.

Sofía Siento no poder compartir tu entusiasmo, querido, pero viajar a otro país es complicado... Necesitamos pasaporte...

Héctor Eso no es problema. Un momento... ¿Es porque no quieres viajar en avión?

Sofía Bueno... en parte... un poco.

Héctor ¡Pero, mi amor! Sólo necesitas que tu médico te dé alguna pastilla para los nervios.

Sofía Está bien, pero te pido que me dejes pensarlo antes de tomar una decisión.

Detalles culturales

Viña del Mar es el más conocido de los balnearios (*resorts*) de Chile, y uno de los centros turísticos más populares de Suramérica. Allí hay numerosas playas, parques, hoteles y casinos. La ciudad es también un centro comercial e industrial importante.

◆ **¿Cuál es un famoso balneario de su país?**

Sofía decidió ir a Buenos Aires en avión. El día del viaje, hablan con el agente de la aerolínea en el aeropuerto.

Agente ¿Qué asientos desean? ¿De ventanilla o de pasillo?
Héctor Dos asientos juntos.
Sofía Cerca de la salida de emergencia.
Héctor El avión no hace escala, ¿verdad?
Agente No, señor. ¿Cuántas maletas tienen?
Sofía Cinco maletas y dos bolsos de mano.
Agente Tienen que pagar exceso de equipaje.
Héctor Pero, Sofía, ¿has puesto toda nuestra ropa en las maletas?
Sofía ¡Es que no sabía qué llevar!
Agente La puerta de salida es la número tres. ¡Buen viaje!

En la puerta número tres.

"Última llamada para los pasajeros del vuelo 340 a Buenos Aires. Suban al avión, por favor."

Héctor y Sofía le dan las tarjetas de embarque a la auxiliar de vuelo, suben al avión y ponen los bolsos de mano en el compartimento de equipajes.

Sofía Tenemos que abrocharnos el cinturón de seguridad. ¡Espero que el piloto tenga mucha experiencia!

¿Recuerda usted?

¿Verdadero o falso? With a partner, decide whether the following statements about the dialogue are true (**verdadero**) or false (**falso**).

1. Sofía quiere pasar las vacaciones en Chile. ☒ V ☐ F
2. Héctor piensa comprar los pasajes por Internet. ☐ V ☒ F
3. Sofía dice que es más barato viajar en coche. ☒ V ☐ F
4. Héctor y Sofía han pasado muchas vacaciones en Viña del Mar. ☒ V ☐ F
5. A Sofía le encanta viajar en avión. ☐ V ☒ F
6. Héctor y Sofía quieren dos asientos de ventanilla. ☐ V ☒ F
7. El vuelo a Buenos Aires es directo. ☒ V ☐ F
8. Héctor y Sofía viajan con poco equipaje. ☐ V ☒ F
9. Héctor y Sofía no llevan bolsos de mano. ☐ V ☒ F
10. Sofía espera que el piloto sepa lo que está haciendo. ☒ V ☐ F

Y ahora... conteste Answer these questions, basing your answers on the dialogue.

1. ¿Dónde quiere pasar sus vacaciones Héctor?
2. ¿De qué está empezando a cansarse Héctor?
3. ¿Qué incluyen los paquetes?
4. ¿Qué puede tomar Sofía para viajar en avión?
5. En el avión, ¿dónde quiere sentarse Sofía?
6. ¿Qué tienen que pagar Héctor y Sofía?
7. ¿Cuál es el número del vuelo?
8. ¿Qué le dan Héctor y Sofía a la auxiliar de vuelo?

Answers: **1.** Quiere pasarlas en Buenos Aires. **2.** De hacer siempre lo mismo. **3.** Incluyen el vuelo, el hotel y algunas excursiones. **4.** Puede tomar pastillas para los nervios. **5.** Quiere sentarse cerca de la salida de emergencia. **6.** Tienen que pagar exceso de equipaje. **7.** Es el vuelo 340. **8.** Le dan las tarjetas de embarque.

Para hablar del tema: Vocabulario

Online Study Center

For more practice with lesson topics, see the related activities on the ***¡Hola, amigos!*** web site at college.hmco.com/PIC/holaamigos7e.

Cognados

la aerolínea
el aeropuerto
la agencia
el (la) agente
la capital
complicado(a)
directo(a)
la emergencia
el entusiasmo
la experiencia
la información
los nervios
el pasaporte
el piloto

Nombres

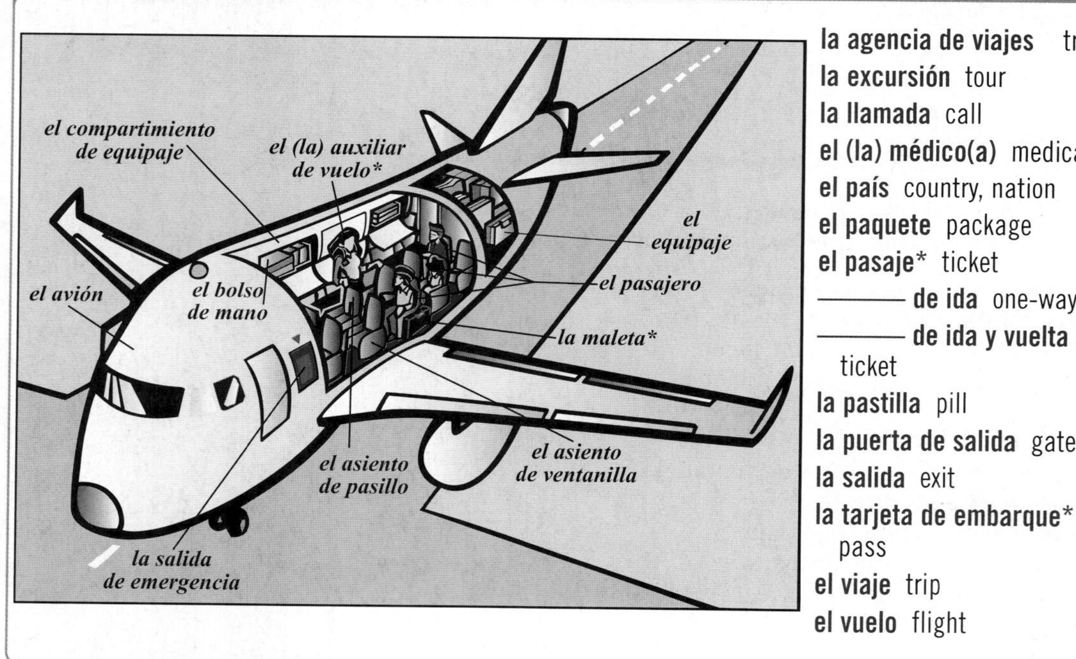

la agencia de viajes travel agency
la excursión tour
la llamada call
el (la) médico(a) medical doctor, MD
el país country, nation
el paquete package
el pasaje* ticket
——— **de ida** one-way ticket
——— **de ida y vuelta** round-trip ticket
la pastilla pill
la puerta de salida gate
la salida exit
la tarjeta de embarque* boarding pass
el viaje trip
el vuelo flight

Adjetivos

querido(a) dear

Verbos

ahorrar to save
averiguar to find out
cansarse to get tired
compartir to share
dejar to let
incluir to include
sentir (e>ie) to regret
subir, abordar to board
sugerir (e>ie) to suggest
temer to fear, to be afraid
viajar to travel

Otras palabras y expresiones

abrocharse el cinturón de seguridad to fasten the seat belt
¡Buen viaje! Have a good trip!
en parte in part
exceso de equipaje excess luggage
hacer escala to make a stop over
lo mismo the same thing
ponerse de acuerdo to come to an agreement, to agree upon
tomar una decisión to make a decision
¿verdad? right?

Amplíe su vocabulario

Más sobre los viajes

¿A cuánto está el cambio de moneda? What's the rate of exchange?
cancelar to cancel
el cheque de viajero traveler's check
(de) clase turista tourist class
confirmar to confirm
crucero cruise
la lista de espera waiting list
los lugares de interés places of interest
el maletín small suitcase, hand luggage
(de) primera clase first class

De país a país

la auxiliar de vuelo la azafata (*Esp.*)
la maleta la valija (*Cono Sur*)
el veliz (*Méx.*)
el pasaje el billete (*Esp.*)
la tarjeta de embarque la tarjeta de embarco (*Arg.*)

Para practicar el vocabulario

A. Preguntas y respuestas

With a partner, match the questions in column *A* with the answers in column *B*.

Answers: 1. j 2. d 3. k 4. b 5. h 6. i 7. a 8. e 9. f 10. l 11. g 12. c

A	B
1. ¿Dónde compraste los pasajes?	a. A la auxiliar de vuelo.
2. ¿Es un vuelo directo?	b. Estas pastillas.
3. ¿Quieres un asiento de pasillo?	c. No sé, voy a averiguar.
4. ¿Qué te dio el médico?	d. No, hace escala.
5. ¿Tienen que pagar exceso de equipaje?	e. En el compartimiento de equipaje.
6. ¿A qué país van a viajar?	f. Abrocharse el cinturón.
7. ¿A quién le doy la tarjeta de embarque?	g. No, no se pusieron de acuerdo.
8. ¿Dónde pongo el bolso de mano?	h. Sí, tienen cinco maletas.
9. ¿Qué deben hacer los pasajeros?	i. A Chile.
10. ¿Cuál es la puerta de salida?	j. En la agencia de viajes.
11. ¿Tomaron una decisión?	k. No, de ventanilla.
12. ¿A qué hora sale el avión?	l. La número cuatro.

B. ¿Qué hago? ¿Adónde voy?

Complete the following sentences.

1. Van a __cancelar__ el vuelo porque hay mucha niebla.
2. Los pasajes de __primera__ clase son más caros.
3. ¿Cuáles son los __lugares__ de interés en la ciudad donde Ud. vive?
4. Vamos a viajar. Tenemos que __confirmar__ la reservación del hotel.
5. ¿A cómo está el __cambio__ de __moneda__?
6. ¿Vas a llevar tu tarjeta de crédito o vas a llevar cheques de __viajero__?
7. No tenemos mucho dinero. Vamos a viajar en clase __turista__.
8. Solamente puede llevar un __maletín__ con Ud. en el avión.
9. Este verano vamos a hacer un __crucero__ por el Caribe.
10. No hay pasaje para hoy pero podemos ponerlo en la lista de __espera__.

C. Definiciones

Write the words or phrases that correspond to the following.

Answers: 1. aerolínea 2. aeropuerto 3. tomar una decisión 4. directo 5. país 6. equipaje 7. abordar 8. sugerir 9. ¡Buen viaje! 10. compartimiento de equipajes

1. Delta, Continental
2. Allí tomamos el avión.
3. decidir
4. que no hace escala
5. Argentina, por ejemplo
6. maletas y bolsos de mano
7. subir
8. dar una sugerencia
9. lo que le decimos a una persona que va a viajar
10. donde ponemos el bolso de mano durante el vuelo

D. En la agencia de viajes With a partner, play the roles of a travel agent and someone getting a round-trip-ticket to Buenos Aires. The "traveler" asks pertinent questions, talks about date of travel, and reserves a seat.

Answer will vary.

¿A qué ciudad suramericana van los pasajeros de este avión? ¿A qué hora llegan? ¿Qué quieren hacer allí?

Pronunciación

Pronunciation in context

In this lesson, there are some words or phrases that may be challenging to pronounce. Listen to your instructor and pronounce the following sentences.

1. Tenemos que ir a la **agencia de viajes** para comprar los **pasajes.**
2. Yo te **sugiero** que **averigües** lo que cuestan dos pasajes de ida y vuelta.
3. Hay **paquetes** que **incluyen** vuelo directo a Buenos Aires, hotel y algunas **excursiones.**
4. El día del viaje, hablan con el **agente** de la **aerolínea** en el **aeropuerto.**
5. **Héctor** y Sofía le dan las tarjetas a la **auxiliar** de vuelo.

Puntos para recordar

1. Introduction to the subjunctive mood
(*Introducción al modo subjuntivo*)

Alternative: Write a chart on the board to contrast the forms of the **-ar**, **-er**, and **-ir** verbs in the present indicative and present subjunctive. Indicate the change in the endings by writing them in different colored chalk.

Present indicative	Present subjunctive
habl- *o*	**habl-** *e*
habl- *as*	**habl-** *es*
habl- *a*	**habl-** *e*, etc.

Until now, you have been using verbs in the indicative mood. The indicative is used to express factual, definite events. By contrast, the subjunctive is used to reflect the speaker's feelings or attitudes toward events, or when the speaker views events as uncertain, unreal, or hypothetical. Because expressions of volition, doubt, surprise, fear, and the like all represent reactions to the speaker's perception of reality, they are followed in Spanish by the subjunctive.

Forms (*Formas*)

- Present subjunctive forms of regular verbs

To form the present subjunctive, add the following endings to the stem of the first-person singular of the present indicative, after dropping the **o.** Note that the endings for the **-er** and **-ir** verbs are identical.

Suggestion: Point out that the subjunctive forms for **Ud.** and **Uds.** are identical to the command forms they learned in **Lección 10.** Then draw the parallel between the use of the two forms to get others to adopt a course of action (e.g., compare **Hagan la tarea** with **Quiero / Sugiero / Espero que hagan la tarea**). Lead students to the conclusion that the subjunctive in this case is simply a veiled command. This will help students to deal with the subjunctive in the broad sense, as a perception of reality that may or may not be objectively true.

-ar *verbs*	-er *verbs*	-ir *verbs*
habl- **e**	com- **a**	viv- **a**
habl- **es**	com- **as**	viv- **as**
habl- **e**	com- **a**	viv- **a**
habl- **emos**	com- **amos**	viv- **amos**
habl- **éis**	com- **áis**	viv- **áis**
habl- **en**	com- **an**	viv- **an**

The following table shows how to form the first-person singular of the present subjunctive.

Verb	First-Person Sing. (Indicative)	Stem	First-Person Sing. (Subjunctive)
habl**ar**	hablo	habl-	habl**e**
aprend**er**	aprendo	aprend-	aprend**a**
escrib**ir**	escribo	escrib-	escrib**a**
conoc**er**	conozco	conozc-	conozc**a**
dec**ir**	digo	dig-	dig**a**
hac**er**	hago	hag-	hag**a**
tra**er**	traigo	traig-	traig**a**
ven**ir**	vengo	veng-	veng**a**

Práctica

Formas del subjuntivo I Give the present subjunctive forms of the following verbs.

1. *yo:* comer, venir, hablar, hacer, salir
2. *tú:* decir, ver, traer, trabajar, escribir
3. *él:* vivir, aprender, salir, estudiar, ver
4. *nosotros:* escribir, caminar, poner, desear, tener
5. *ellos:* salir, hacer, llevar, conocer, ver

Answers: 1. coma / venga / hable / haga / salga 2. digas / veas / traigas / trabajes / escribas 3. viva / aprenda / salga / estudie / vea 4. escribamos / caminemos / pongamos / deseemos / tengamos 5. salgan / hagan / lleven / conozcan / vean

Online Study Center

For more practice with lesson topics, see the related activities on the ***¡Hola, amigos!*** web site at college.hmco.com/PIC/holaamigos7e.

Suggestion: Assign as homework, but then do orally in class.

Present subjunctive forms of stem-changing and irregular verbs

- Verbs ending in **-ar** and **-er** undergo the same stem changes in the present subjunctive as in the present indicative.

recomendar (e > ie)		recordar (o > ue)	
recom**iende**	recomend**emos**	rec**uerde**	record**emos**
recom**iendes**	recomend**éis**	rec**uerdes**	record**éis**
recom**iende**	recom**ienden**	rec**uerde**	rec**uerden**

entender (e > ie) (*to understand*)		volver (o > ue)	
ent**ienda**	entend**amos**	v**uelva**	volv**amos**
ent**iendas**	entend**áis**	v**uelvas**	volv**áis**
ent**ienda**	ent**iendan**	v**uelva**	v**uelvan**

Extra practice: Have students practice switching from the indicative to the subjunctive by repeating quickly in groups of three the form you give them.

I: Yo entiendo	**S:** Que yo entienda
I: Ellos duermen	**S:** Que ellos duerman, etc.

- For verbs ending in **-ir,** the three singular forms and the third-person plural form undergo the same stem changes in the present subjunctive as in the present indicative. However, in addition, observe that unstressed **e** changes to **i** and unstressed **o** changes to **u** in the first- and second-person plural forms.

mentir (*to lie*)		dormir	
m**ienta**	m**intamos**	d**uerma**	d**urmamos**
m**ientas**	m**intáis**	d**uermas**	d**urmáis**
m**ienta**	m**ientan**	d**uerma**	d**uerman**

- The following verbs are irregular in the present subjunctive.

dar	estar	saber	ser	ir
dé	esté	sepa	sea	vaya
des	estés	sepas	seas	vayas
dé	esté	sepa	sea	vaya
demos	estemos	sepamos	seamos	vayamos
deis	estéis	sepáis	seáis	vayáis
den	estén	sepan	sean	vayan

Online Study Center

For more practice with lesson topics, see the related activities on the *¡Hola, amigos!* web site at college.hmco.com/PIC/holaamigos7e.

Suggestion: Assign as homework, but then do orally in class.

Answers: **1.** duerma / vaya / cierre / sienta / sea **2.** mientas / vuelvas / vayas / des/ recuerdes **3.** esté / sepa / pierda / duerma / sea **4.** pensemos / recordemos / demos / muramos / cerremos **5.** prefieran / den / vayan / sepan / duerman

¡Atención! The present subjunctive of **hay** (impersonal form of **haber**) is **haya.**

Práctica

Formas del subjuntivo II Give the present subjunctive forms of the following verbs.

1. *yo:* dormir, ir, cerrar, sentir, ser
2. *tú:* mentir, volver, ir, dar, recordar
3. *ella:* estar, saber, perder, dormir, ser
4. *nosotros:* pensar, recordar, dar, morir, cerrar
5. *ellos:* preferir, dar, ir, saber, dormir

Uses of the subjunctive (*Usos del subjuntivo*)

- The Spanish subjunctive is used in subordinate, or dependent, clauses. The subjunctive is also used in English, although not as often as in Spanish. For example:

Sugiero	que **llegue** mañana.	*I suggest*	*that **he arrive** tomorrow.*
Main clause	**Dependent clause**	**Main clause**	**Dependent clause**

The expression that requires the use of the subjunctive is in the main clause, *I suggest.* The subjunctive appears in the dependent clause, *that he arrive tomorrow.*

- There are four main conditions that call for the use of the subjunctive in Spanish.
  - *Volition:* demands, wishes, advice, persuasion, and other impositions of will

    Ella **quiere** que yo lo llame. — ***She wants** me to call him.*
    Te **aconsejo** que no **vayas** a ese viaje. — ***I advise** you not to **go** on that trip.*

  - *Emotion:* pity, joy, fear, surprise, hope, and so on

    Me **sorprende** que **llegues** tan temprano. — ***I am surprised** that **you are arriving** so early.*

  - *Unreality:* expectations, indefiniteness, uncertainty, nonexistence

    —¿**Hay alguien** aquí que **hable** español? — *"**Is there anyone** here who **speaks** Spanish?"*
    —No, **no hay nadie** que lo **sepa.** — *"No, **there is no one** who **knows** it."*

  - *Doubt and denial:* negated facts, disbelief

    No es verdad que Rosa **sea** azafata. — ***It isn't true** that Rosa **is** a flight attendant.*
    Dudo que **tengas** dinero. — ***I doubt** that **you have** money.*
    Roberto **niega** que ella **sea** su esposa. — *Roberto **denies** that **she is** his wife.*

2. Subjunctive with verbs of volition (*El subjuntivo con verbos que indican voluntad o deseo*)

All expressions of will require the use of the subjunctive in subordinate clauses. Note that the subject in the main clause must be different from the subject in the subordinate clause. Some verbs of volition that require the use of the subjunctive are:

aconsejar (*to advise*)	mandar (*to order*)	querer
decir	necesitar	recomendar
desear	pedir	sugerir

Mi	madre	**quiere**	**que**	yo	**trabaje.**
My	*mother*	*wants*		*me*	*to work.*

—¿Qué **quieres** que **haga**? — *"What **do you want me** to **do**?"*
—**Quiero** que **vayas** al aeropuerto. — *"**I want** you to **go** to the airport."*
—Necesito hablar con un médico. — *"**I need to talk** with a doctor."*
—Te **sugiero** que **hables** con el Dr. Paz. — *"**I suggest** that **you talk** with Dr. Paz."*

¡Atención! Note that the infinitive is used following verbs of volition if there is no change of subject: **Quiero comer.**

- Certain verbs of volition (**mandar, sugerir, aconsejar,** and **pedir**) are often preceded by an indirect object pronoun, which indicates the subject of the verb in the subjunctive.

Te sugiero que **vayas** al médico. — ***I suggest** that **you go** to the doctor.*
Le aconsejo que **venga** temprano. — ***I advise you** to **come** early.*

Extra practice: Write the following sentence builder on the board:

Ana {**quiere** / **desea** / **necesita** / **manda** / **aconseja** / **recomienda** / **sugiere**} que {yo / tú / Ud. / él / nosotros / Uds. / ellos}

Have students suggest ways to finish the sentences.

Suggestion: To illustrate the use of the infinitive versus the subjunctive following verbs of volition, have students tell you what they want to do, as opposed to what someone else (a friend, relative, co-worker, or professor) wants them to do.

Detalles culturales

En Argentina, como también en Costa Rica, Paraguay, Uruguay y Guatemala, la forma tú no se usa en la conversación. En lugar de (*In place of*) esta forma, se usa la forma **vos.** Por ejemplo, en estos países no dicen **"tú quieres"** sino **"vos querés".** Este fenómeno se llama **voseo.**

- **¿Se usa la forma tú en inglés?**

Online Study Center

For more practice with lesson topics, see the related activities on the *¡Hola, amigos!* web site at college.hmco.com/PIC/holaamigos7e.

Práctica y conversación

A. Minidiálogos Complete the following dialogues, using either the subjunctive or the infinitive, as appropriate. Then act them out with a partner.

1. —Marcos quiere que (nosotros) __vayamos__ (ir) a su casa esta noche. ¿Tú quieres __ir__ (ir)?
   —No, hoy me quiero __acostar__ (acostar) temprano porque no me siento bien.
   —Te sugiero que __tomes__ (tomar) dos aspirinas antes de acostarte.
   —No quiero __tomar__ (tomar) aspirina porque soy alérgica a la aspirina.
2. —Necesito que tú me __traigas__ (traer) las maletas hoy.
   —No puedo porque mamá quiere que la __lleve__ (llevar) a la agencia de viajes.
3. —Sofía me aconseja que __vaya__ (ir) al médico, pero yo no quiero __ir__ (ir) hoy.
   —Pues yo te sugiero que lo __veas__ (ver) lo más pronto posible (*as soon as possible*).
4. —Elena quiere que yo le __compre__ (comprar) un pasaje, pero yo no deseo __ir__ (ir) a la agencia de viajes ahora.
   —En ese caso te sugiero que le __digas__ (decir) que no puedes ir.
5. —Adela, quiero que hoy __vuelvas__ (volver) antes de las nueve y que te __acuestes__ (acostar) porque mañana tienes que levantarte a las cinco.
   —¿Por qué quieres que nos __levantemos__ (levantar) a las cinco?
   —Porque mamá quiere que nosotros __estemos__ (estar) en el aeropuerto a las seis.

B. Nadie está de acuerdo Complete each sentence creatively, using a verb in the infinitive or the subjunctive, as appropriate. *Answers will vary.*

◆ **MODELO:** Yo quiero volver en agosto, pero mi padre quiere que...
Yo quiero volver en agosto, pero mi padre quiere que vuelva en julio.

1. Luis quiere que yo hable sobre Chile, pero yo quiero...
2. El médico les aconseja que tomen las pastillas ahora, pero yo les aconsejo que...
3. Yo quiero ir a casa, pero mis amigos quieren...
4. Ellos le sugieren que pase todo el día aquí, pero ella quiere...
5. Mi esposo quiere que yo haga un crucero por el Mediterráneo, pero yo prefiero...
6. Ellos quieren ir al aeropuerto, pero nosotros queremos que...
7. Nora quiere viajar en avión, pero yo le sugiero que...
8. Los niños se quieren acostar a las once, pero su mamá quiere que...

C. Deseos y sugerencias (*Wishes and suggestions*) With a partner, take turns completing the following according to the illustrations below.

Answers: **1.** que Luis vaya al banco. **2.** que veas al Dr. Soto. **3.** que tomes pastillas. **4.** preste (dé) 20 dólares. **5.** que tome Tylenol. **6.** viaje en avión.

1. Ana quiere ________________.

2. Te sugiero ________________.

3. Te aconsejo ________________.

4. Olga quiere que Paco le ________________.

5. La doctora le recomienda ________________.

6. Pablo no quiere que su mamá ________________.

D. ¿Qué queremos? Say what you and these people want (or don't want) everybody to do. Compare notes with your partner. *Answers will vary.*

1. Yo quiero que mi mamá...
2. Mis padres no quieren que yo...
3. La novia de Julio quiere que él...
4. El profesor quiere que nosotros...
5. El médico quiere que mi padre...
6. Tu papá no quiere que tú...
7. Yo quiero que mis abuelos...
8. Nosotros no queremos que ellos...

Suggestion: Encourage students to make more than one suggestion for each situation. Follow up with a class sharing.

 **E. Soluciones** In groups of three, advise each of the following people what to do according to each circumstance. Use **sugerir, recomendar,** or **aconsejar.**

Answers will vary.

1. Julio no quiere viajar en avión.
2. A la Sra. Ruiz no le gusta viajar a otros países.
3. Mireya está muy nerviosa (*nervous*).
4. Ramiro quiere comprar un pasaje a Chile.
5. Aurora no quiere pagar exceso de equipaje.
6. A Nora no le gustan los asientos de ventanilla.
7. Enrique no quiere un vuelo que haga escala.
8. Rosario no puede viajar en primera clase.

3. Subjunctive with verbs of emotion (*El subjuntivo con verbos que expresan emoción*)

Suggestion: Write the following sentence builder on the board:

Have students suggest ways to finish the sentences.

Extra practice: Ask students to respond to your statements using a verb of emotion and the subjunctive. For example, *Instructor:* **No puedo ir con ustedes.** *Student:* **Siento que usted no pueda ir con nosotros.**

- In Spanish, the subjunctive mood is always used in the subordinate clause when the verb in the main clause expresses the emotions of the subject, such as fear, joy, pity, hope, regret, sorrow, surprise, and anger. Again, the subject in the subordinate clause must be different from the subject in the main clause for the subjunctive to be used.
- Some verbs of emotion that call for the subjunctive are **temer, esperar, alegrarse (de),** and **sentir.**

—Mañana salgo para Quito.	*"Tomorrow I leave for Quito."*
—**Espero** que **te diviertas** mucho.	*"**I hope you have a** very **good time.**"*
—**Temo** no **poder** ir de vacaciones con ustedes este verano.	*"**I'm afraid** that **I cannot** go on vacation with you this summer."*
—**Espero** que **puedas** ir con nosotros el verano que viene.	*"**I hope** that **you can** go with us next summer."*

¡Atención! If there is no change of subject, the infinitive is used.

Temo no **poder** ir. — ***I'm afraid*** *that* ***I can****not go.*

- The expression **ojalá** always takes the subjunctive.

Ojalá que **puedas** venir. — ***I hope you can*** *come.*

Práctica y conversación

For more practice with lesson topics, see the related activities on the ***¡Hola, amigos!*** web site at college.hmco.com/PIC/holaamigos7e.

A. Minidiálogos Complete the following exchanges, using the subjunctive or the infinitive, as appropriate. Then act them out with a partner.

1. —Temo que Estela no __vaya__ (ir) a la fiesta, porque tiene que trabajar.
   —Siento mucho que __tenga__ (tener) que trabajar; pero espero que __pueda__ (poder) ir la próxima vez.
2. —Me alegro de __estar__ (estar) aquí con Uds.
   —Y nosotros nos alegramos de que tú __estés__ (estar) aquí. Esperamos que te __diviertas__ (divertir) mucho.
3. —Necesito comprar un pasaje hoy. Espero que __haya__ (haber) una agencia de viajes cerca.
   —Hay una agencia cerca, pero temo que no __esté__ (estar) abierta a esta hora.
4. —Temo no __poder__ (poder) ir al aeropuerto a buscar a Rita. Espero que Ud. __pueda__ (poder) ir.
   —Rita va a sentir mucho que tú no __estés__ (estar) allí.
5. —Espero que Jorge no __deje__ (dejar) de ir hoy al banco.
   —Ojalá que le __den__ (dar) el préstamo que pidió.

Follow-up: After completion of the exercise, tell students to expand one of the dialogues into a conversation that includes one more problem and a solution that requires the use of the subjunctive. Have several students roleplay their dialogues the next day in class.

B. Emociones Complete each sentence in an original manner. Use the subjunctive or the infinitive, as appropriate. *Answers will vary.*

1. Ojalá que yo...
2. Siento mucho no poder...
3. Me alegro de que mi papá...
4. Temo no...
5. Mi amigo(a) espera...
6. El (La) profesor(a) siente que nosotros...
7. Mi madre se alegra de...
8. Tememos que las clases...

Suggestion: Assign as homework and compare answers in class.

Game: Divide the class into two teams. Team 1 gives the first word of a sentence (e.g., **Queremos**) and Team 2 adds a word. Play continues alternating between the two teams until one fails to find a word to add to the sentence. (You may want to limit the number of times **y**, **pero**, etc., may be used in a single sentence.)

Possible Answers: 1. Siento que esté enferma. 2. Me alegro de que tu papá esté mejor. 3. Siento que no puedas ir conmigo. 4. Temo que no llegues a tiempo. 5. Espero que consigas el dinero. 6. Me alegro de que vayas a México.

C. ¿Cómo reaccionas...? React appropriately to a friend's statements. *Answers will vary.*

1. Mi mamá está enferma (*sick*).
2. Mi papá está mejor.
3. No puedo ir contigo.
4. Son las cinco. Tengo que estar en casa a las cinco y media.
5. Quiero comprar un coche, pero es muy caro.
6. El mes próximo voy a México de vacaciones.

Suggestions: Start by sharing one or two hopes and fears that you have. Encourage students to react to what their classmates say. Follow up by having groups report to the class.

D. Amigos y parientes In groups of three, tell two or three things you hope your friends and relatives will do and one or two things you fear they can't or won't do. *Answers will vary.*

4. Some uses of the prepositions *a, de,* and *en*
(*Algunos usos de las preposiciones* a, de *y* en)

- The preposition **a** (*to, at, in*) expresses direction toward a point in space or a moment in time. It is used for the following purposes:
  - to indicate the time (hour) of day

A las cinco salimos para Lima.	***At** five we leave for Lima.*

  - after verbs of motion, when followed by an infinitive, a noun, or a pronoun

Siempre vengo **a** comprar aquí.	*I always come to buy here.*

  - after the verbs **empezar, comenzar, enseñar,** and **aprender,** when followed by an infinitive

Ellos empezaron **a** salir.	*They began to go out.*
Te enseñé **a** bailar el tango.	*I taught you to dance the tango.*

  - after the verb **llegar**

Cuando él llegó **a** su casa, le dieron los pasajes.	*When he arrived **at** his house, they gave him the tickets.*

Detalles culturales

El tango tuvo su origen en los suburbios de Buenos Aires a finales del siglo (*century*) XIX. Para muchos, Argentina es la tierra del tango, y éste se considera la música típica del país, pero hoy la música argentina es muy variada e incluye diferentes tipos de ritmos.

- **¿Cuál es la música típica de este país?**

- before a direct object noun that refers to a specific person. It may also be used to personify an animal or a thing

Yo no conozco **a** ese médico.	*I don't know that doctor.*
Bañé **a** mi perro.	*I bathed my dog.*

¡Atención! If the direct object is not a definite person, the personal **a** is not used.

Busco un buen médico.	*I'm looking for a good doctor.*

- The preposition **de** (*of, from, about, with, in*) indicates possession, material, and origin. It is also used in the following ways:
  - to refer to a specific period of the day or night when telling time

El sábado pasado trabajamos hasta las ocho **de** la noche.	*Last Saturday we worked until 8 P.M.*

  - after the superlative to express *in* or *of*

Orlando es el más simpático **de** la familia.	*Orlando is the nicest* ***in*** *the family.*

  - to describe personal physical characteristics

Es morena, **de** ojos negros.	*She is brunette,* ***with*** *dark eyes.*

  - as a synonym for **sobre** or **acerca de** (*about*)

Hablaban **de** todo menos **del** viaje.	*They were talking* ***about*** *everything except* ***about*** *the trip.*

- The preposition **en** (*at, in, on, inside, over*) in general situates someone or something within an area of time or space. It is used for the following purposes:
  - to refer to a definite place

Él siempre se queda **en** casa.	*He always stays* ***at*** *home.*

  - as a synonym for **sobre** (*on*)

Está sentada **en** la silla.	*She is sitting* ***on*** *the chair.*

  - to indicate means of transportation

Nunca he viajado **en** ómnibus.	*I have never traveled* ***by*** *bus.*

Online Study Center

For more practice with lesson topics, see the related activities on the *¡Hola, amigos!* web site at college.hmco.com/PIC/holaamigos7e.

Práctica y conversación

A. La carta de Isabel Complete the following letter, adding the missing prepositions **a, de,** or **en.**

Querida Alicia:

Como te prometí, te escribo en seguida. Ayer llegamos __a__ Quito. Es una __de__ las ciudades más antiguas __de__ Suramérica. Llegamos __a__ las tres __de__ la tarde y fuimos __a__ buscar hotel. __En__ el hotel conocimos __a__ unos chicos muy simpáticos que nos invitaron a salir con ellos. Yo salí con Carlos, que es alto, moreno, __de__ ojos verdes. Me ha dicho que me va __a__ enseñar __a__ bailar salsa. Espero aprender __a__ bailar otros bailes también. Mañana vamos __a__ ir __a__ visitar los museos. Vamos __a__ ir __en__ el coche __de__ Carlos.

Bueno, __en__ la próxima carta espero poder contarte más __de__ mi vida __en__ esta hermosa ciudad.

Isabel

B. Entre amigos Use the illustrations to complete the following information about a group of friends. Use appropriate prepositions.

Answers: 1. viajar en auto. 2. hablando de la clase de español. 3. de ojos azules. 4. en su casa.

1. Delia va a...

2. Sergio y Toña están...

3. Beatriz es rubia...

4. Teresa se quedó...

Answers: **5.** a bailar. **6.** a la una y cuarto. **7.** el más alto del. **8.** a Caracas mañana.

5. Rogelio quiere ir al club...

6. Tito salió de su casa...

7. Julio es... grupo.

8. Eva llega...

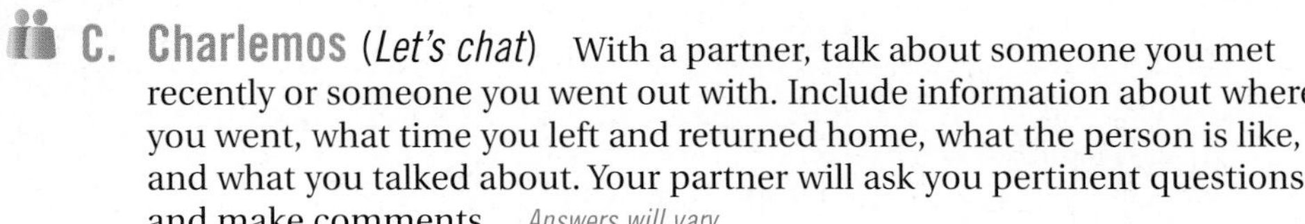

C. Charlemos (*Let's chat*) With a partner, talk about someone you met recently or someone you went out with. Include information about where you went, what time you left and returned home, what the person is like, and what you talked about. Your partner will ask you pertinent questions and make comments. *Answers will vary.*

Aurora llama a una amiga. ¿De qué están hablando?

Entre nosotros

¡Conversemos!

 **Para conocernos mejor** Get to know your partner better by asking each other the following questions. *Answers will vary.*

1. ¿Adónde piensas ir de vacaciones el verano que viene? ¿Con quién vas?
2. ¿Prefieres viajar solo(a) o con tu familia?
3. ¿Compras los pasajes en una agencia de viajes o por Internet?
4. Generalmente, ¿viajas en clase turista o en primera clase?
5. ¿Prefieres un asiento de ventanilla o de pasillo?
6. ¿Hiciste un crucero el verano pasado?
7. ¿Cuántas maletas llevaste la última vez que viajaste?
8. ¿Has tenido que pagar exceso de equipaje alguna vez?
9. ¿Dónde pones tu bolso de mano cuando viajas?
10. ¿Conoces a alguien que trabaje de auxiliar de vuelo?

 **Una encuesta** Interview your classmates to identify who fits the following descriptions. Include your instructor, but remember to use the **Ud.** form when addressing him or her. *Answers will vary.*

	Nombre
1. Hace muchos viajes.	
2. Le gusta viajar los fines de semana.	
3. Conoce muchos lugares de interés en este país.	
4. Prefiere volar por la noche.	
5. Tuvo que hacer escala la última vez que viajó.	
6. Necesita ahorrar más.	
7. Siempre lleva cheques de viajero cuando va de viaje.	
8. Lleva mucho equipaje cuando viaja.	
9. No fue de vacaciones el año pasado.	
10. Fue de excursión el mes pasado.	

Detalles culturales

En los países hispanos no existe tanta separación entre (*among*) las generaciones como en este país. Los niños, los padres y los abuelos frecuentemente van juntos a viajes o a fiestas y reuniones.

◆ **Generalmente, ¿Ud. viaja con otros miembros de su familia o prefiere ir con sus amigos?**

Y ahora... Write a brief summary, indicating what you have learned about your classmates. *Answers will vary.*

Suggestion: This exercise may be assigned as homework and presented orally in class. Encourage students to use commands in the last situation.

¿Cómo lo decimos? What would you say in the following situations? What might the other person say? Act out the scenes with a partner.

1. You want to find out how much a round-trip ticket to Santiago costs.
2. You ask the travel agent to give you information on several types of tours.
3. You need to know if there are flights to Buenos Aires on Sundays.
4. A friend of yours is traveling abroad for the first time. Give him suggestions and advice about what to do and what not to do.

Answers: 1. ¿Cuánto cuesta un pasaje de ida y vuelta a Santiago? 2. Necesito información de varios tipos de excursiones. 3. ¿Hay vuelos a Buenos Aires los domingos? 4. *Answers will vary.*

Expansion: You might wish to take the opportunity to discuss the marketing of U.S. products to Hispanics in the U.S. and overseas. Bring in newspaper and magazine ads in Spanish and English from other well-known companies such as Sears, Coca-Cola and Nike, and ask students to compare the two versions for cultural similarities and differences.

¿Qué dice aquí? Answer the questions about the new flight of Aerolíneas del Sur using the information provided in the ad. *Answers will vary.*

1. ¿Qué compañía ofrece más viajes a Latinoamérica?
2. ¿Qué puedo acumular si viajo por Aerolíneas del Sur?
3. ¿De qué ciudad sale el nuevo vuelo?
4. ¿Había antes vuelos a Buenos Aires desde Miami? ¿Cuándo comienza el nuevo vuelo?
5. Si tomo ese vuelo, ¿tengo que hacer escala?
6. ¿Qué puedo hacer para obtener más información y para hacer la reservación?
7. ¿Puedo llamar cualquier (*any*) día y a cualquier hora?
8. ¿Qué ventajas me ofrece Aerolíneas del Sur?

Answers: 1. Aerolíneas del Sur ofrece más viajes. 2. Puedes acumular millas. 3. Sale de Miami. 4. Sí, antes había vuelos a Buenos Aires. Comienza el 15 de enero. 5. No, no tienes que hacer escala. 6. Puedes hablar con tu agente de viajes, usar Internet o llamar a la aerolínea. 7. Sí, puedes llamar cualquier día a cualquier hora. 8. Te ofrece precios más bajos y mejor servicio.

Para escribir

En una agencia de viajes Write a dialogue between you and a travel agent. Choose your destination, ask about prices, flights, and any necessary documentation. Then make your reservations and choose your seat. *Answers will vary.*

Un dicho

Martes 13, no te cases ni te embarques.

This saying advices you not to get married or get on a ship . . . on what day? If you are superstitious, you now have two days to worry about! Remember the saying in Spanish.

Suggestion: Point out the use of the familiar command in this saying.

Lección 12 ◆ ¿Dónde nos hospedamos?

Estrella y Mariana, dos chicas peruanas, están de vacaciones en Montevideo.

Estrella	Tenemos que encontrar un hotel que no sea muy caro y que quede cerca de la playa.
Mariana	¡Estrella! ¡No hicimos reservaciones! ¡Y no hay ningún hotel que tenga habitaciones libres!
Estrella	No seas pesimista. A ver... queremos un hotel que tenga aire acondicionado, teléfono, televisor, servicio de habitación y, si es posible, vista al mar.
Mariana	¡Qué optimista! Hay muchos hoteles que tienen todo eso, pero están llenos. Hay un montón de turistas, y un montón de convenciones.
Estrella	¡Espera! Ahí hay un hotel...
Mariana	Pero, dime una cosa: ¿No ves que es un hotel de lujo? Probablemente cobran cinco mil pesos por noche. Nosotras necesitamos uno que cobre mucho menos...
Estrella	Pero tú tienes una tarjeta de crédito, ¿no? Bueno, ven. Vamos a buscar un taxi que nos lleve a Pocitos. Allí va a haber hoteles más baratos...
Mariana	O una pensión. ¡Acuérdate de que las pensiones son más baratas...!

Detalles culturales

En los países hispanos, los hoteles y restaurantes generalmente aceptan tarjetas de crédito como Visa o MasterCard.

◆ **¿Cuáles son las tarjetas de crédito que más se usan en este país?**

Detalles culturales

Las pensiones son muy populares en los países de habla hispana. Son más económicas que los hoteles y generalmente el precio incluye el cuarto y las comidas.

◆ **¿Dónde se hospeda Ud. cuando viaja?**

Estrella y Mariana están hablando con el Sr. Ruiz, el dueño de la pensión.

Estrella ¿Tiene un cuarto libre para dos personas?

Sr. Ruiz Sí, hay uno disponible en el segundo piso, con dos camas chicas. Cobramos 4.800 pesos por semana...

Mariana ¿Eso incluye las comidas?

Sr. Ruiz Sí, es pensión completa.

Estrella ¿Los cuartos tienen baño privado y televisor?

Sr. Ruiz No, señorita. Hay tres baños en el segundo piso. Tienen bañadera y ducha con agua caliente y fría... y hay un televisor en el comedor.

Mariana (*A Estrella*) ¿Por qué no nos quedamos aquí? La pensión parece limpia y está en un lugar céntrico.

Estrella ¿Hay alguna playa que esté cerca de aquí?

Sr. Ruiz Sí, hay una a dos cuadras. ¡Ah!, señorita, necesito el número de su cédula de identidad.

Mariana (*A Estrella*) ¡Uf! Estoy muy cansada. Ayúdame con las valijas, ¿quieres? Aquí no hay botones. Lo primero que voy a hacer es dormir un rato.

Estrella Bueno, pero después te voy a mostrar unos folletos sobre Río y San Pablo.

Mariana ¡Caramba! ¡Ya estás planeando nuestras próximas vacaciones!

¿Recuerda usted?

¿Verdadero o falso?

With a partner, decide whether the following statements about the dialogue are true (**verdadero**) or false (**falso**).

1. Estrella y Mariana son de Perú. ☒ V ☐ F
2. A Estrella le gusta estar cerca de la playa. ☒ V ☐ F
3. Mariana dice que los hoteles no tienen habitaciones libres. ☒ V ☐ F
4. Mariana quiere hospedarse en un hotel de lujo. ☐ V ☒ F
5. Las chicas llevaron su coche a Montevideo. ☐ V ☒ F
6. El señor Ruiz es el botones. ☐ V ☒ F
7. En la pensión hay un cuarto libre. ☒ V ☐ F
8. Las chicas tienen que pagar extra por la comida. ☐ V ☒ F
9. A Mariana le gusta la pensión. ☒ V ☐ F
10. El botones lleva las maletas al cuarto. ☐ V ☒ F

Y ahora... conteste

Answer these questions, basing your answers on the dialogue.

1. ¿En qué ciudad están de vacaciones las chicas?
2. ¿Qué están buscando las chicas?
3. ¿Estrella quiere un cuarto con vista al jardín?
4. ¿Por qué están llenos los hoteles?
5. ¿En qué piso está la habitación disponible?
6. ¿Qué tienen los baños?
7. ¿Qué es lo primero que va a hacer Mariana?
8. ¿Qué le va a mostrar Estrella a Mariana?

Answers: **1.** Están de vacaciones en Montevideo. **2.** Están buscando un hotel. **3.** No, Estrella quiere un cuarto con vista al mar. **4.** Porque hay un montón de turistas y de convenciones. **5.** La habitación está en el segundo piso. **6.** Los baños tienen bañadera y ducha con agua caliente y fría. **7.** Lo primero que va a hacer Mariana es dormir un rato. **8.** Le va a mostrar unos folletos sobre Río y San Pablo.

Para hablar del tema: Vocabulario

Online Study Center

For more practice with lesson topics, see the related activities on the ***¡Hola, amigos!*** web site at college.hmco.com/PIC/holaamigos7e.

Cognados

la convención
optimista
el (la) peruano(a)
pesimista
posible
privado(a)
probablemente
la reservación
el taxi
el (la) turista

Nombres

el aire acondicionado air conditioning
la bañadera* bathtub
el botones bellhop
la cama bed
——— **chica** twin bed
la cédula de identidad* I.D. card
la ducha* shower
el (la) dueño(a), propietario(a) owner
el folleto brochure
el lugar place
el lujo luxury
la pensión boarding house
la persona person
el piso floor
el servicio de habitación (cuarto) room service
la tarjeta de crédito credit card
el televisor TV set
la vista al mar ocean view

Verbos

acordarse (de) (o>ue) to remember
ayudar to help
parecer (yo parezco) to seem

Adjetivos

caliente hot
céntrico(a) central
libre, disponible vacant, available
limpio(a) clean
lleno(a) full
mostrar, enseñar to show
próximo(a) next
segundo(a) second

Otras palabras y expresiones

allí there
dime una cosa tell me something
la pensión completa room and board
por per
lo primero the first thing
¿Quieres? Will you?
si if
sobre about
un montón de a bunch of, many
un rato a while
va a haber there is going to be

Amplíe su vocabulario

Más sobre los hoteles

Quiero una habitación con vista
- **al jardín** garden
- **a la piscina*** swimming pool
- **al patio**
- **al mar** ocean, sea
- **a la playa** beach

Quiero una habitación
- interior
- exterior

desocupar to vacate
no funciona it doesn't work
ocupado(a) occupied
el precio price
el puesto* de revistas magazine stand
el sofá-cama sleeper sofa
la tienda de regalos souvenir shop
el vestíbulo lobby

De país a país

la bañadera la bañera (*Arg.*)
el baño (*Esp.*)
la cédula de identidad el carnet de identidad (*Esp.*)
la ducha la regadera (*Méx.*)
la piscina la alberca (*Méx.*)
el ascensor el elevador (*Méx., Cuba, Puerto Rico*)
el puesto de revistas el kiosko (*Arg., Esp.*)

Para practicar el vocabulario

A. Preguntas y respuestas

Match the questions in column *A* with the answers in column *B*.

Answers: 1. i 2. e 3. g 4. a 5. c 6. b 7. j 8. d 9. f 10. h 11. l 12. k

A	B
1. ¿Tenemos que ir a un restaurante?	a. No, con vista al mar.
2. ¿Hay cuartos libres?	b. Sí, pero yo no pienso ir.
3. ¿Elsa es argentina?	c. Sí, y calefacción.
4. ¿Tu habitación es interior?	d. Un folleto sobre Cuzco.
5. ¿Tiene aire acondicionado?	e. No, el hotel está lleno.
6. ¿Va a haber una fiesta?	f. Sí, y hablamos por un rato.
7. ¿El baño tiene bañadera?	g. Sí, es de Buenos Aires.
8. ¿Qué estás leyendo?	h. El inodoro no funciona.
9. ¿Viste a Susana?	i. Sí, porque el hotel no tiene servicio de habitación.
10. ¿Cuál es el problema?	j. No, ducha.
11. ¿Qué documento necesita?	k. La semana próxima.
12. ¿Cuándo llegan?	l. Una cédula de identidad.

B. En el hotel

With a partner, indicate whether the following statements are logical(L) or illogical(I). If it is illogical, say why.

Answers: 1. L 2. L 3. I (Si hace calor hay que poner el aire acondicionado.) 4. L 5. I (Si es un hotel de lujo, es caro.) 6. L 7. L 8. I (Si es pensión completa incluye las comidas.)

1. Mi cuarto está en el quinto (*fifth*) piso. Voy a tomar el ascensor.
2. Voy a llamar al empleado del hotel porque ni el inodoro ni el baño funcionan.
3. Hace mucho calor. Necesitamos poner la calefacción.
4. El baño tiene agua fría y caliente.
5. Es muy barato porque es un hotel de lujo.
6. No queremos comer en un restaurante. Preferimos el servicio de habitación.
7. No puedo llevar todas las maletas al cuarto. Necesito que me ayudes.
8. El precio no incluye las comidas; es pensión completa.

C. ¿Cuál es la solución?

What is the solution to these problems?

Answers will vary.

1. Quiero leer *Newsweek* pero no hay una copia en mi habitación.
2. No me gustan las habitaciones interiores.
3. Somos tres y sólo hay una cama doble en el cuarto.
4. Quiero comprar algo para llevarles a mis padres.
5. No sé cuánto cobran en el hotel.
6. No quiero recibir a mi amigo(a) en la habitación del hotel.
7. Tengo que subir a mi cuarto, que está en el décimo (*tenth*) piso.
8. Nos dieron una habitación con vista al patio, pero a nosotros nos gusta ver el mar.

D. Minidiálogos

Complete the following short exchanges in a logical manner, using vocabulary from **Lección 12.**

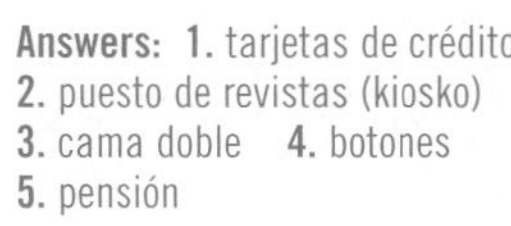
Answers: 1. tarjetas de crédito 2. puesto de revistas (kiosko) 3. cama doble 4. botones 5. pensión

1. —¿Tú usas *Visa*?
   —Bueno, yo uso varias ________.
2. —¿Dónde compraste la revista?
   —En el ________.
3. —¿Necesitan una cama chica?
   —No, una ________.
4. —¿Quién lleva las maletas al cuarto?
   —El ________.
5. —¿Están en un hotel?
   —No, en una ________.

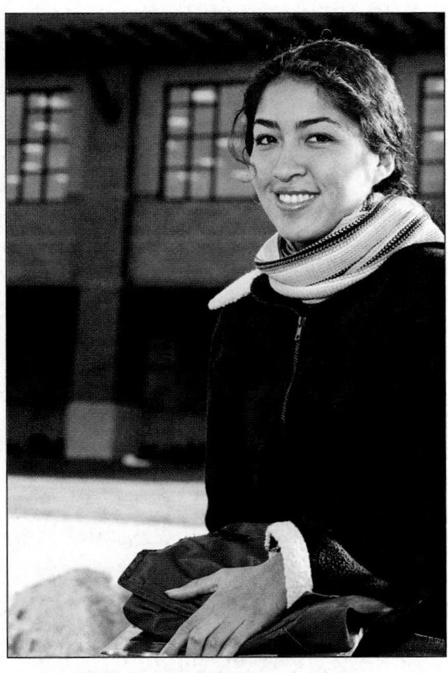

Silvia está de vacaciones en Lima. ¿En qué tipo de hotel está hospedada?

Pronunciación

Pronunciation in context

In this lesson, there are some words or phrases that may be challenging to pronounce. Listen to your instructor and pronounce the following sentences.

1. A ver... queremos un hotel que tenga **aire acondicionado.**
2. Vamos a buscar un taxi que nos lleve a **Pocitos. Allí va a haber** hoteles más baratos.
3. ¿Por qué no nos quedamos aquí? La **pensión** parece limpia y está en un lugar **céntrico.**
4. Necesito el número de su **cédula** de **identidad.**
5. Bueno, pero después te voy a mostrar unos **folletos** sobre **Río** y San Pablo.

Puntos para recordar

1. Subjunctive to express indefiniteness and nonexistence (*El subjuntivo para expresar lo indefinido y lo no existente*)

Suggestion: Write on the board:

MAIN CLAUSE
Él busca una casa
↓
nonspecific

SUBORDINATE CLAUSE
que **sea** grande.
↓
Verb: subjunctive

MAIN CLAUSE
Él tiene una casa
↓
specific

SUBORDINATE CLAUSE
que **es** grande.
↓
Verb: indicative

- The subjunctive is always used in the subordinate clause when the main clause refers to something or someone that is indefinite, unspecified, hypothetical, or nonexistent.

—¿**Hay alguna excursión** que **incluya** el hotel?	*"**Is there any tour** that **includes** the hotel?"*
—No, **no hay ninguna** que lo **incluya.**	*"No, **there is not any** that **includes** it."*
—**Necesito un secretario** que **hable** francés.	*"**I need a secretary** who **speaks** French."*
—**No conozco a nadie** que **hable** francés.	*"**I don't know anyone** who **speaks** French."*
—**Estamos buscando un restaurante** donde **sirvan** comida italiana.	*"**We're looking for a restaurant** where **they serve** Italian food."*
—**Hay varios restaurantes** donde **sirven** comida italiana.	*"**There are several restaurants** where **they serve** Italian food."*

¡Atención! If the subordinate clause refers to existent, definite, or specified persons or things, the indicative is used instead of the subjunctive.

Hay varios restaurantes donde **sirven** comida italiana.

MAIN CLAUSE
No hay nadie
↓
nonexistent

SUBORDINATE CLAUSE
que lo **sepa.**
↓
Verb: subjunctive

MAIN CLAUSE
Hay alguien
↓
existent

SUBORDINATE CLAUSE
que lo **sabe.**
↓
Verb: indicative

Ask students for other examples and have them explain why the subjunctive or the indicative is used in the subordinate clause.

Práctica y conversación

For more practice with lesson topics, see the related activities on the *¡Hola, amigos!* web site at college.hmco.com/PIC/holaamigos7e.

A. Minidiálogos Complete the following dialogues, using the indicative or the subjunctive, as appropriate. Then act out the dialogues with a partner.

1. —¿Hay algún hotel que _quede_ (quedar) cerca de la playa?
   —Sí, el hotel La Uruguaya _queda_ (quedar) a una cuadra de la playa.
2. —¿Sabes si hay algún cuarto libre que _tenga_ (tener) vista al mar?
   —No, pero hay uno que _tiene_ (tener) vista a la piscina.
3. —¿Hay alguien aquí que no _tenga_ (tener) pasaporte?
   —No, todos _tenemos_ (tener) pasaporte y visa.
4. —Necesito un botones que _pueda_ (poder) llevar las maletas.
   —No hay ninguno que no _esté_ (estar) ocupado.

B. Vienen los uruguayos A family from Uruguay has recently moved into your neighborhood. Answer their questions. *Answers will vary.*

Suggestion: Have students work in pairs to complete this exercise.

1. ¿Hay alguien que quiera vender su casa?
2. ¿Hay algún restaurante que sirva comida argentina?
3. ¿Hay alguien que sepa español y quiera trabajar de secretario(a)?
4. ¿Hay algún mercado que venda productos de Sudamérica?
5. Nuestro hijo es agente de viajes. ¿Sabe Ud. de alguna agencia que necesite empleados?
6. Queremos vender nuestro Ford. ¿Conoce Ud. a alguien que necesite un auto?

C. En la pensión Use your imagination to complete each statement.

Suggestion: Assign as homework and compare answers in class.

Possible verb forms: 1. que tenga 2. que tenga 3. que incluya 4. que esté 5. que sea

1. Nuestro cuarto tiene vista al jardín, pero preferimos uno... *Answers will vary.*
2. El baño tiene bañadera, pero yo quiero uno...
3. Esta pensión no incluye las comidas, pero yo necesito una...
4. Esta pensión es buena pero no está en un lugar céntrico; queremos una...
5. Este folleto es sobre Montevideo, pero nosotras necesitamos uno...

D. Dime una cosa You and a classmate want to find out about each other's relatives and friends. Ask each other questions about the following, always beginning with: *Answers will vary.*

¿Hay alguien en tu familia o entre tus amigos que...?

1. jugar al béisbol
2. viajar a México todos los veranos
3. bailar muy bien
4. tener una piscina en su casa
5. celebrar su aniversario de bodas este mes
6. ser muy optimista
7. conocer Brasil
8. hablar portugués
9. saber varios idiomas
10. trabajar para un hotel
11. ser empleado(a) de banco
12. ser peruano

Verb forms in questions: 1. ...juegue al béisbol? 2. ...viaje a México todos los veranos? 3. ...baile muy bien? 4. ...tenga una piscina en su casa? 5. ...celebre su aniversario de bodas este mes? 6. ...sea muy optimista? 7. ...conozca Brasil? 8. ...hable portugués? 9. ...sepa varios idiomas? 10. ...trabaje para un hotel? 11. ...sea empleado(a) de banco? 12. ...sea peruano?

E. Nuestro viaje a Brasil In groups of three or four, play the role of very wealthy and lazy travelers who want to make arrangements for a trip to Brazil. Say what you need people to do for you. *Answers will vary.*

◆ **MODELO:** *Necesitamos a alguien que vaya a la agencia de viajes.*

Follow-up: Have students specify at least seven or eight things. Follow up by having groups share some of their ideas.

2. Familiar commands (*Las formas imperativas de* tú *y de* vosotros)

Suggestion: Review the formal commands before teaching the familiar commands. Also, review the third-person present indicative, particularly of stem-changing verbs. Write several on the board and have students use them as commands.

- Regular affirmative commands in the **tú** form have exactly the same forms as the third-person singular (**él** form) of the present indicative.

Verb	Present Indicative Third-Person Sing.	Familiar Command (*tú*)
hablar	él habla	**habla**
comer	él come	**come**
abrir	él abre	**abre**
cerrar	él cierra	**cierra**
volver	él vuelve	**vuelve**
pedir	él pide	**pide**
traer	él trae	**trae**

—¿Qué quieres que haga ahora? *"What do you want me to do now?"*
—**Compra** los billetes para el viaje. *"**Buy** the tickets for the trip."*

—¿Vas a poner el equipaje aquí? *"Are you going to put the luggage here?"*
—Sí, **tráeme** las maletas y el bolso de mano. *"Yes, **bring me** the suitcases and the carry-on bag."*

¡Atención! As with the formal commands, direct, indirect, and reflexive pronouns are always placed *after* an affirmative command and are attached to it. A written accent must be placed on the stressed syllable.

Extra practice: To help students memorize the eight irregular commands, write on the board: **Eva, *ven* aquí. *Sé* buena y *hazme* un favor; *ve* a casa de Paco y *dile* que venga, pero *ten* cuidado porque tiene un perro muy grande. *Pon* tus libros aquí y *sal* por esta puerta.** For expansion, ask students to create their own sequence of commands.

- Eight Spanish verbs are irregular in the affirmative command for the **tú** form. They are listed below.

decir	**di**	salir	**sal**
hacer	**haz**	ser	**sé**
ir	**ve**[1]	tener	**ten**
poner	**pon**	venir	**ven**

—**Dime,** ¿a qué hora quieres que venga? *"**Tell me,** at what time do you want me to come?"*
—**Ven** a las ocho. *"**Come** at eight."*

—**Haz**me un favor: **pon** estos folletos en la mesa. *"**Do** me a favor: **put** these brochures on the table."*
—Sí, en seguida. *"Yes, right away."*

- The affirmative command form for **vosotros** is formed by changing the final **r** of the infinitive to **d.**

Infinitive	Familiar Command (*vosotros*)
habla**r**	habla**d**
come**r**	come**d**
escribi**r**	escribi**d**
ir	**id**
sali**r**	sali**d**

[1]Note that **ir** and **ver** have the same affirmative **tú** command, **ve.**

When the affirmative command of **vosotros** is used with the reflexive pronoun **os,** the final **d** is dropped.

bañar	bañad	**bañaos**
poner	poned	**poneos**
vestir	vestid	**vestíos**[1]

Bañaos antes de cenar.	***Bathe*** *before dinner.*
Poneos los zapatos.	***Put*** *your shoes* ***on.***
Vestíos aquí.	***Get dressed*** *here.*

Only one verb doesn't drop the final **d** when the **os** is added.

irse **¡Idos!** ***Go away!***

- The negative commands of **tú** and **vosotros** use the corresponding forms of the present subjunctive.

hablar	no **hables** tú	no **habléis** vosotros
vender	no **vendas** tú	no **vendáis** vosotros
decir	no **digas** tú	no **digáis** vosotros
salir	no **salgas** tú	no **salgáis** vosotros

—**No vayas** a la agencia de viajes hoy.	*"**Don't go** to the travel agency today."*
—Entonces voy mañana.	*"Then I'm going tomorrow."*
—**No** me **esperes** para comer.	*"**Don't wait for** me to eat."*
—¡**No** me **digas** que hoy también tienes que trabajar!	*"**Don't tell** me you have to work today also!"*

Suggestion: Review the **tú** form of the present subjunctive. On the board, write the affirmative commands and their corresponding negative forms:

habla	no **hables**
come	no **comas**
cierra	no **cierres**

Do the same with the irregular forms.

¡Atención! In a negative command, all object pronouns are placed before the verb.

No **me** esperes para comer.

Práctica y conversación

A. Órdenes Using command forms, tell your friend what to do.

- **MODELO:** Tienes que hablar con el dueño ahora.
  Habla con el dueño ahora.

1. Tienes que llamarme este fin de semana.
2. Tienes que hacer las camas.
3. Tienes que tener paciencia con él.
4. Tienes que decirle que no venga hoy.
5. Tienes que ir a la agencia de viajes y comprar los pasajes.
6. Tienes que salir en seguida.
7. Tienes que quedarte aquí.
8. Tienes que venir dentro de quince días.

Online Study Center

For more practice with lesson topics, see the related activities on the ***¡Hola, amigos!*** web site at college.hmco.com/PIC/holaamigos7e.

Answers: **1.** Llámame este fin de semana. **2.** Haz las camas. **3.** Ten paciencia con él. **4.** Dile que no venga hoy. **5.** Ve a la agencia de viajes y compra los pasajes. **6.** Sal en seguida. **7.** Quédate aquí. **8.** Ven dentro de quince días.

B. Now make all commands above negative.

Answers: **1.** No me llames... **2.** No hagas... **3.** No tengas... **4.** No le digas... **5.** No vayas... y no compres... **6.** No salgas... **7.** No te quedes... **8.** No vengas...

[1]Note that the **-ir** verbs take a written accent over the **i** when the reflexive pronoun **os** is added.

C. A mi hermanito You are going away for the day. Tell your younger brother what to do and what not to do.

Answers: 1. Levántate temprano y báñate. 2. Prepara el desayuno. 3. No tomes refrescos. 4. Haz la tarea. 5. No le abras la puerta a nadie. 6. Limpia tu cuarto. 7. No mires la televisión y no traigas a tus amigos a la casa. 8. Trae pan y ponlo en la mesa. 9. Ve al mercado y compra frutas. 10. Llama a papá y dile que venga temprano.

1. levantarse temprano y bañarse
2. preparar el desayuno
3. no tomar refrescos
4. hacer la tarea
5. no abrirle la puerta a nadie
6. limpiar su cuarto
7. no mirar la televisión y no traer a sus amigos a la casa
8. traer pan y ponerlo en la mesa
9. ir al mercado y comprar frutas
10. llamar a papá y decirle que venga temprano

Follow-up: Play a game of Simon says **(Simón dice...)**. Form groups and have students give the commands.

D. Haz esto... haz lo otro... (*Do this... do that...*) With a partner , take turns giving two commands, one affirmative and one negative, that the following people would likely give. *Answers will vary.*

1. una madre (un padre) a su hijo de quince años
2. un(a) estudiante a su compañero(a) de cuarto (de clase)
3. un muchacho a su novia (una muchacha a su novio)
4. un(a) doctor(a) a una niña
5. un(a) profesor(a) a un estudiante
6. un esposo a su esposa (una esposa a su esposo)

3. Verbs and prepositions (*Verbos y preposiciones*)

The prepositions **con, de,** and **en** can be used with verbs to form certain expressions. Some of the idioms are as follows:

casarse con	to marry, to get married (to)
comprometerse con	to get engaged to
acordarse de	to remember
alegrarse de	to be glad
darse cuenta de	to realize
enamorarse de	to fall in love with
olvidarse de	to forget
confiar en	to trust
convenir en	to agree on
entrar en	to go (come) into
fijarse en	to notice
insistir en	to insist on

—Celia **se comprometió con** David.	*"Celia **got engaged to** David."*
—Yo creía que iba a **casarse con** Alberto.	*"I thought **she** was going **to marry** Alberto."*
—No, ella **se enamoró de** David.	*"No, she **fell in love with** David."*
—**Insistieron en** venir esta noche.	*"**They insisted on** coming tonight."*
—Sí, no **se dieron cuenta de** que teníamos que trabajar.	*"Yes, **they didn't realize** that we had to work."*

¡Atención! Notice that the English translation of these expressions may not use an equivalent preposition.

Práctica y conversación

For more practice with lesson topics, see the related activities on the ***¡Hola, amigos!*** web site at college.hmco.com/PIC/holaamigos7e.

A. Lo que pasa... Look at the pictures below and complete each statement. *Answers will vary.*

Answers: **1.** Marisa decidió casarse con Daniel. **2.** Mirta y Raúl se comprometen. **3.** Graciela no se acuerda del número de teléfono de Pepe. **4.** Marisol se alegra de ver a Tito.

1. Marisa decidió ________________ ________________ Daniel.

2. Mirta ________________ ______. Piensan casarse en junio.

3. Graciela no ________________ ________________.

4. Marisol ________________ ________________ a Tito.

Answers: **5.** Rodolfo entra en la casa de Eva. **6.** Pedro insiste en ir con Alina.

5. Rodolfo ______________________
________________.

6. Pedro ______________________
________________.

Suggestion: For variation, have students work in pairs on this exercise or write the answers as homework.

B. Entreviste a su compañero(a) Interview your partner by asking the following questions.

1. ¿En quién confías?
2. ¿Prefieres casarte con un(a) médico(a) o con un(a) profesor(a)?
3. ¿De quién te enamoraste por primera vez?
4. ¿Algún amigo tuyo se ha comprometido últimamente? ¿Con quién?
5. ¿Te fijaste si la biblioteca estaba abierta?
6. ¿Te acordaste de traer tus libros a clase?
7. ¿Te alegras de estar en esta universidad?
8. ¿A qué hora entró el (la) profesor(a) en la clase?

4. Ordinal numbers (*Números ordinales*)

primero(a)[1]	first	**sexto(a)**	sixth
segundo(a)[1]	second	**séptimo(a)**	seventh
tercero(a)[1]	third	**octavo(a)**	eighth
cuarto(a)	fourth	**noveno(a)**	ninth
quinto(a)	fifth	**décimo(a)**	tenth

- Ordinal numbers agree in gender and number with the nouns they modify.

  el segundo **chico** — la segunda **chica**
  los primeros **días** — las primeras **semanas**

- Ordinal numbers are seldom used after **décimo.**

¡Atención! The ordinal numbers **primero** and **tercero** drop the final **-o** before masculine singular nouns.

el **primer**[2] día   el **tercer**[3] año

[1] abbreviated 1°, 2°, 3°, and so on
[2] abbreviated 1er
[3] abbreviated 3er

—Nosotros estamos en el **segundo** piso. ¿Y Uds.?	*"We are on the* ***second*** *floor. And you?"*
—Estamos en el **tercer** piso.	*"We are on the* ***third*** *floor."*

Práctica y conversación

For more practice with lesson topics, see the related activities on the ***¡Hola, amigos!*** web site at college.hmco.com/PIC/holaamigos7e.

A. Los meses del año With a partner, quiz each other on the order of the months of the year. Follow the model.

◆ **MODELO:** —*Septiembre.*
—*Septiembre es el noveno mes del año.*

Answers: **1.** Enero es el primer... **2.** Febrero es el segundo... **3.** Marzo es el tercer... **4.** Abril es el cuarto... **5.** Mayo es el quinto... **6.** Junio es el sexto... **7.** Julio es el séptimo... **8.** Agosto es el octavo... **9.** Octubre es el décimo...

B. ¿En qué piso estás? Imagine that the whole class is staying at a hotel in Punta del Este. Your classmates were assigned rooms on different floors. With a partner, take turns asking who is on what floor. *Answers will vary.*

Todos los hoteles están llenos. ¿Dónde va a poder hospedarse Carmen?

Entre nosotros

¡Conversemos!

Para conocernos mejor Get to know your partner better by asking each other the following questions. *Answers will vary.*

1. Cuando viajas, ¿te hospedas en un hotel o en una pensión?
2. Generalmente, ¿haces reservaciones en los hoteles antes de viajar?
3. ¿Prefieres un hotel que esté en un lugar céntrico o uno que quede lejos de todo?
4. Cuando vas a un hotel, ¿tú llevas tus maletas al cuarto o las lleva el botones?
5. Cuando vas a un hotel, ¿qué tipo de cuarto prefieres?
6. Si tu cuarto en el hotel está en el segundo piso, ¿usas el ascensor o la escalera (*stairs*)?
7. Cuando vas a un hotel, ¿a qué hora desocupas el cuarto?
8. ¿Tu casa tiene aire acondicionado y calefacción?
9. ¿Tenías televisor en tu cuarto cuando eras niño(a)?
10. En tu cuarto, ¿tienes una cama chica o una cama doble?

Una encuesta Interview your classmates to identify who fits the following descriptions. Include your instructor, but remember to use the **Ud.** form when addressing him or her. *Answers will vary.*

	Nombre
1. Tiene una piscina en su casa.	
2. Tiene un sofá-cama en su casa.	
3. Generalmente usa la ducha y no la bañadera.	
4. Compró algo en una tienda de regalos la semana pasada.	
5. Piensa viajar el próximo verano.	
6. Probablemente va a viajar con su familia.	
7. Nunca paga más de 100 dólares por noche en un hotel.	
8. Fue a una convención el año pasado.	
9. Es una persona pesimista.	
10. Tiene un montón de cosas que hacer.	

Y ahora... Write a brief summary indicating what you have learned about your classmates. *Answers will vary.*

¿Cómo lo decimos? What would you say in the following situations? What might the other person say? Act out the scenes with a partner. *Answers will vary.*

Suggestion: Assign as homework, then have students do in pairs orally during class.

1. You need a room for two people with a private bathroom and air conditioning. Find out the price, when you have to check out, whether the room overlooks the street, and whether the hotel has room service.
2. At a boarding house, find out what meals the price includes.
3. A friend will be staying at your house while you are away. Tell him or her what to do.

Answers: 1. Necesito una habitación para dos personas con baño privado y aire acondicionado. ¿Cuánto cuesta? ¿A qué hora tenemos que desocupar la habitación? ¿La habitación tiene vista a la calle? ¿El hotel tiene servicio de habitación? 2. ¿Qué comidas incluye el precio? 3. *Answers will vary.*

¿Qué dice aquí? Answer the questions about the Hotel Tabaré. Base your answers on the information provided in the ad. *Answers will vary.*

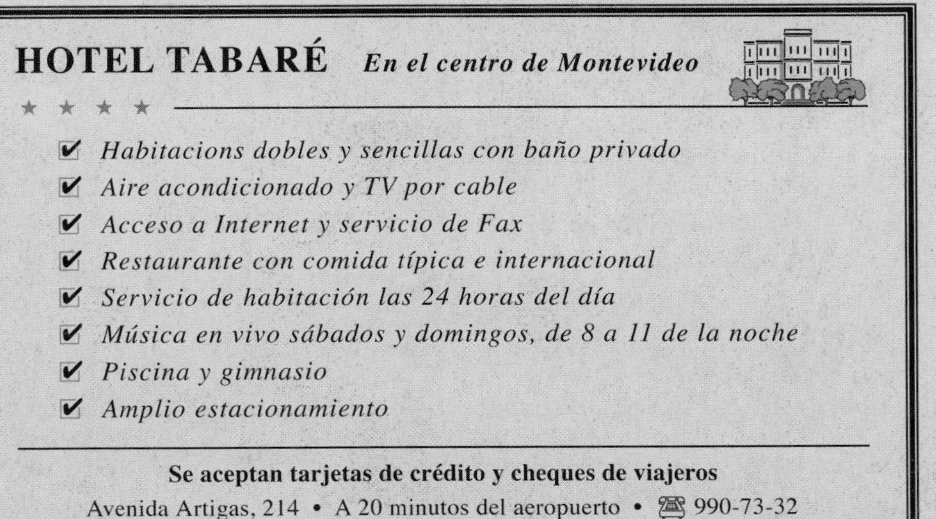

Answers: 1. Se llama Hotel Tabaré. Sí, está en el centro de Montevideo. Sí, es un hotel de lujo. 2. Son dobles o sencillas con baño privado. 3. No, tienen aire acondicionado. 4. Sí, el hotel tiene televisión por cable. 5. Sí, el hotel tiene servicio de Internet. 6. Sirven comida típica e internacional. Sí, tienen servicio de habitación. 7. Sí, pueden hacerlo; en el hotel hay gimnasio y piscina. 8. El hotel está a 20 minutos del aeropuerto y tiene amplio estacionamiento. 9. Pueden pagar con tarjetas de crédito y con cheques de viajero.

1. ¿Cómo se llama el hotel? ¿Está en un lugar céntrico? ¿Es un hotel de lujo?
2. ¿Cómo son las habitaciones?
3. ¿Vamos a tener calor en la habitación?
4. ¿Podemos ver la tele en nuestro cuarto?
5. Si necesitamos mandar mensajes electrónicos, ¿podemos hacerlo desde el hotel?
6. ¿Qué clase de comida sirven? ¿Tienen servicio de habitación?
7. Nos gusta hacer ejercicio y nadar todos los días, ¿podemos hacerlo en el hotel?
8. ¿El hotel está cerca del aeropuerto? ¿Podemos dejar el coche en el hotel?
9. ¿Con qué podemos pagar en el hotel?

Para escribir

En un hotel Write a conversation between you and a hotel clerk. Make reservations and ask about prices and accommodations. *Answers will vary.*

Un dicho

No hay mal que por bien no venga.

There is an English equivalent of this saying. Your challenge is to find out what it is.

Lectura

Reading strategy: Point out to students that predicting, based on the type of reading, the title, or illustrations, can help prepare them to better understand the content of the reading.

Suggestion: Have students read the list of comprehension questions before starting the reading.

Answers: 1. Sus fábulas se caracterizan por la originalidad de sus temas. 2. Los personajes son animales. 3. El canario cantaba muy bien. Lo elogió un ruiseñor extranjero. 4. Causó la envidia de todos. 5. Empezó a hablar mal del canario. 6. Lo comparó con un borrico. 7. Le dijo que quería oírle cantar. 8. Cuando el canario cantó, todos aplaudieron, incluyendo el águila. 9. Le pidió justicia para el canario. 10. Sólo se oyeron horribles chillidos. El que desacredita a otro, se desacredita a sí mismo.

Estrategia de lectura Before you read the fable of the canary (*el canario*) and the crow (*el cuervo*), think about what you know about the characteristics of these two types of birds and try to predict what might happen. *Answers will vary.*

Vamos a leer As you read the fable, try to find the answers to the following questions.

1. ¿Qué es lo que caracteriza las fábulas de Iriarte?
2. ¿Cuáles son las características de los personajes de las fábulas?
3. ¿Qué talento tenía el canario? ¿Quién lo elogió?
4. ¿Qué causó esta aprobación en otros pájaros?
5. ¿Qué hizo el cuervo para desacreditar al canario?
6. ¿Qué comparación hizo el cuervo?
7. ¿Qué hizo el águila cuando el canario dejó de cantar?
8. ¿Qué pasó cuando el canario cantó?
9. ¿Qué le pidió el águila al dios Júpiter?
10. ¿Qué pasó cuando el cuervo trató de cantar? ¿Cuál es la moraleja (*moral*) de la fábula?

La obra más importante de Iriarte fue ***Fábulas literarias.*** *Sus fábulas se caracterizan por la originalidad de sus temas. En la que se presenta aquí, los personajes son animales: un canario, un cuervo, un ruiseñor y un águila. El autor trata de demostrar que no se debe tratar de desacreditar a otros.*

El canario y el cuervo

UNA FÁBULA DE TOMÁS IRIARTE

Había una vez un canario que cantaba muy bien. ¡Todos aplaudían cuando lo escuchaban! Un ruiseñor° extranjero, generalmente acreditado, lo elogió° mucho, animándolo con su aprobación.

nightingale / praised

Video

La aprobación del ruiseñor causó la envidia de otros pájaros° que no cantaban tan bien como él. Al fin, un cuervo° que no podía lucirse° por su canto, empezó a hablar mal del canario. Como no podía decir nada malo de su canto, trató de desacreditarlo acusándolo de cosas que nada tenían que ver° con su manera de cantar. Los otros pájaros envidiosos aprobaron y repitieron las acusaciones del cuervo.

El cuervo, animado, empezó a decir que el canario era un borrico° y que lo que había en él no era verdadera música sino un rebuzno.° "¡Cosa rara!" —decían algunos. "El canario rebuzna; el canario es un borrico".

El canario, muy triste, dejó de° cantar, pero el águila,° reina° de las aves,° le dijo que quería oírlo cantar para ver si, en efecto, rebuznaba o no, porque si era verdad que rebuznaba, quería excluirlo del número de sus vasallos,° los pájaros. Cuando el canario cantó, lo hizo tan bien que todos aplaudieron, incluyendo el águila. Entonces el águila, indignada por la calumnia° del cuervo, le pidió a su señor, el dios Júpiter, justicia para el canario. El dios condescendió, diciéndole al cuervo: "Quiero escuchar tu canto". Cuando el cuervo trató de cantar, sólo se oyeron horribles chillidos.°

Moraleja: El que para desacreditar a otro recurre a medios injustos, se desacredita a sí mismo.°

birds
crow / shine
***tenían...** had to do*
donkey
braying
stopped / eagle / queen / birds
subjects
slander
screeches
***a...** himself*

Díganos Answer the following questions, based on your own thoughts and experiences. *Answers will vary.*

1. ¿Qué cosas hace Ud. bien?
2. ¿Recibe frecuentemente la aprobación de sus supervisores, sus profesores y sus amigos?
3. ¿Conoce a personas envidiosas que tratan de desacreditar a otros?
4. ¿Qué hace cuando ve que algunas personas son injustas?
5. ¿Qué trata de hacer para animar a sus parientes y amigos a desarrollar (*develop*) sus talentos?

¡Suban al avión!

Marisa tiene la oportunidad de viajar a California con su mamá, que tiene dos pasajes. El problema es que la señora tiene miedo de viajar en avión. Marisa le pide a Pablo que la ayude a convencer a su mamá de que ella puede viajar en avión.

El mundo hispánico

Chile

- Chile es un país largo y estrecho. En este país encontramos algunas de las montañas más altas de Suramérica, y por eso son muy populares los deportes de invierno. La cordillera de los Andes atraviesa (*goes through*) el país de norte a sur.
- Chile exporta pescados, mariscos y productos minerales y agrícolas. Exporta tanta fruta que se le considera la frutería del mundo. Sus vinos tienen fama internacional.
- Su capital, Santiago, es una ciudad cosmopolita que refleja la influencia de Europa y de Norteamérica. La ciudad tiene muchos lugares de recreo: hermosos parques, un estadio que tiene capacidad para ochenta mil personas y numerosos teatros y cines. Muy cerca de la ciudad hay excelentes lugares para esquiar.
- Dos escritores chilenos de fama internacional son Pablo Neruda y Gabriela Mistral, ganadores del Premio Nobel de Literatura. Otra escritora chilena de gran fama es Isabel Allende, autora de *La casa de los espíritus,* entre otras novelas.

▲ Pablo Neruda, famoso poeta chileno. Premio Nobel de Literatura 1971

Uruguay

- Uruguay, el país más pequeño de Suramérica, está situado entre Brasil y Argentina, en la costa oriental (*east*) de este continente. La mayoría de su territorio se dedica a la agricultura y a la ganadería (*livestock*), que son la base de la economía tradicional del país. Sin embargo, en las últimas décadas, el país se ha industrializado rápidamente gracias a la electricidad barata que producen sus plantas hidroeléctricas.
- Para los uruguayos, la carne es el plato esencial de su dieta, y el **mate,** su bebida favorita.
- Montevideo es una de las ciudades más cosmopolitas de Hispanoamérica, y es el centro administrativo, económico y cultural del país. Allí vive casi la mitad de su población, que es de unos tres millones de habitantes. Otra ciudad importante de Uruguay es Punta del Este, uno de los centros turísticos más famosos de América Latina. Punta del Este está situada a unas dos horas de Montevideo, y es muy popular por sus hermosas playas y por los festivales de cine que allí se celebran.

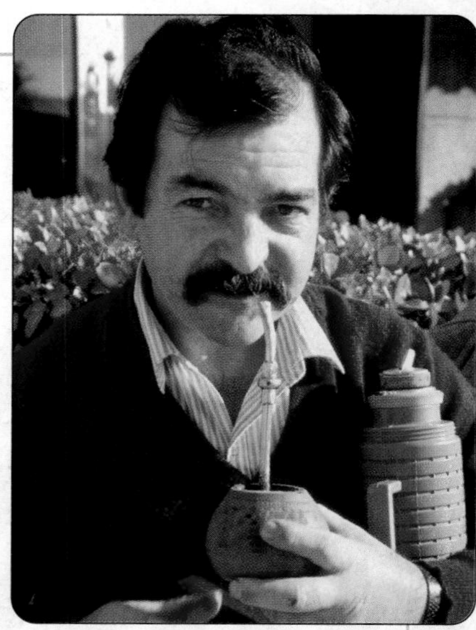

▲ Uruguayo bebiendo mate, una especie de té muy popular en todo el Cono Sur.

Argentina

- Argentina, por su extensión, es el país de habla hispana más grande, y ocupa el octavo lugar entre los países más extensos del mundo; sin embargo, es uno de los menos densamente poblados. La mayor parte de sus habitantes son de origen europeo, principalmente italianos.
- En este país se encuentra el pico más alto del mundo occidental: el Aconcagua. Una de sus mayores atracciones turísticas son las Cataratas de Iguazú, que comparte con Brasil y Paraguay.
- Su capital, Buenos Aires, es la ciudad más grande del hemisferio sur. A las personas de Buenos Aires se les llama **porteños,** que significa "gente del puerto." En esta ciudad hay más de cuarenta universidades y la ciudad tiene una vida cultural muy activa. Hay numerosos museos y teatros muy importantes; el Teatro Colón es uno de los más famosos del mundo. La ciudad tiene muchos parques muy hermosos y la Avenida 9 de Julio es la más ancha del mundo.

▲ Iguazú, una de las cataratas más espectaculares del mundo

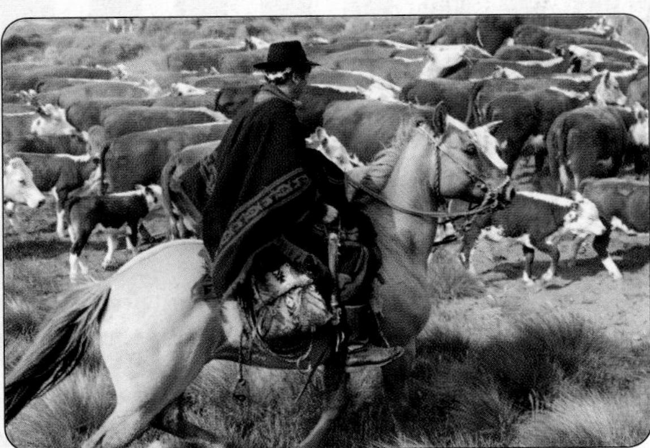

▲ Un gaucho con su ganado *(cattle herd).*

Brasil

- Brasil es el país más grande y más rico de América Latina. Limita con todos los países de Suramérica, excepto Chile y Ecuador. El idioma del país es el portugués, porque Brasil fue colonizado por Portugal.
- El país tiene muchos recursos naturales, incluidas extensas reservas de petróleo y de gas natural. Su principal producto agrícola es el café.
- Desde 1960 la capital de Brasil es Brasilia, la ciudad más moderna del mundo. Aislada del interior del país por la densa selva, la capital sigue prácticamente inaccesible excepto por avión y por eso Río de Janeiro, la antigua capital, y San Pablo siguen siendo las ciudades más importantes del país.
- Miles de personas de todas partes de Latinoamérica visitan Río de Janeiro, ciudad famosa por sus carnavales y por las populares playas de Copacabana e Ipanema.

For more practice with lesson topics, see the related activities on the *¡Hola, amigos!* web site at college.hmco.com/PIC/holaamigos7e.

 **Comentarios...** With a partner, discuss, in Spanish, what impressed you the most about these four countries and compare them to your own. Which places do you want to visit and why?

Tome este examen

Lección 11

Lección 11

A. Subjunctive with verbs of volition Write sentences in the present tense, using the elements given below. Use the present subjunctive or the infinitive, as appropriate, and add any necessary words.

Answers: **1.** Yo quiero que ella vaya a Viña del Mar. **2.** Nosotros deseamos viajar en avión. **3.** Ella me sugiere que yo vaya a Buenos Aires. **4.** El agente quiere venderme el pasaje. **5.** Ellos nos aconsejan que compremos seguro. **6.** Yo no quiero llevar muchas maletas. **7.** Ellos no quieren que ella los lleve en su coche. **8.** Nosotros no queremos ir contigo. **9.** ¿Tú me sugieres que venga luego? **10.** Ella necesita que Uds. le den la maleta.

1. Yo / querer / ella / ir / Viña del Mar
2. Nosotros / desear / viajar / avión
3. Ella / sugerirme / ir / Buenos Aires
4. El agente / querer / venderme / el pasaje
5. Ellos / aconsejarnos / comprar / seguro (*insurance*)
6. Yo / no querer / llevar / muchas maletas
7. Ellos / no querer / ella / llevarlos / en su coche
8. Nosotros / no querer / ir / contigo
9. ¿Tú / sugerirme / venir / luego?
10. Ella / necesitar / Uds. / darle / la maleta

B. Subjunctive with verbs of emotion Rewrite the following sentences, beginning each with the phrase in parentheses and using the subjunctive or the infinitive, as appropriate.

Answers: **1.** que ella se vaya pronto. **2.** que los pasajes sean muy caros. **3.** estar aquí. **4.** irse de vacaciones. **5.** que mamá se sienta bien hoy. **6.** que ellos no puedan ir a la fiesta.

1. Ella se va pronto. (Espero...)
2. Los pasajes son muy caros. (Elsa teme...)
3. Yo estoy aquí. (Me alegro de...)
4. Ella se va de vacaciones. (Ella espera...)
5. Mamá se siente bien hoy. (Esperamos...)
6. Ellos no pueden ir a la fiesta. (Siento...)

C. Some uses of the prepositions *a, de,* and *en* Complete with **a, de,** or **en,** as necessary.

1. Anoche llamé ___a___ mi hermano por teléfono y hablamos ___de___ nuestros planes para el fin de semana. Pensamos ir ___a___ Chile. Él quiere viajar ___en___ tren pero yo prefiero ir ___en___ coche. Mi hermana no quiere ir con nosotros; prefiere quedarse ___en___ casa porque no tiene con quién dejar ___a___ su perro.
2. Ayer Marta llegó ___a___ la agencia ___a___ las ocho y media ___de___ la mañana, pero no empezó ___a___ trabajar hasta las diez.
3. Mi hija es muy bonita; es morena, ___de___ ojos verdes y yo pienso que es la más inteligente ___de___ todos mis hijos.

D. Vocabulary

Complete the following sentences, using vocabulary from **Lección 11.**

1. No quiero un asiento de pasillo; quiero uno de ventanilla.
2. Voy a poner el bolso de mano en el compartimiento de equipaje.
3. Voy a la agencia de viajes para comprar los pasajes.
4. Tiene que darle la tarjeta de embarque (embarco) a la auxiliar de vuelo.
5. Tengo que pagar exceso de equipaje porque tengo cuatro maletas.
6. Quiero sentarme cerca de la salida de emergencia.
7. Los paquetes incluyen el pasaje, el hotel y algunas excursiones.
8. ¿A cuánto está el cambio de moneda?
9. No podemos viajar hoy. Tenemos que cancelar la reservación.
10. Cuando viajo siempre llevo cheques de viajero.
11. Este verano vamos a hacer un crucero por el Caribe.
12. Necesito una lista de los lugares de interés de la capital de Chile.

E. Culture

Complete the following sentences, based on the cultural notes you have read.

1. En Argentina se usa la forma vos en lugar de **tú.**
2. La música típica de Argentina es el tango.
3. En los países hispanos no existe tanta separación entre las generaciones como en este país.

Lección 11

Lección 12

Lección 12

A. Subjunctive to express indefiniteness and nonexistence

Rewrite each sentence, using the subjunctive or the indicative, as appropriate.

Answers: 1. hable español. 2. incluya el hotel. 3. no son caros. 4. salen a las seis. 5. pueda reservar los pasajes?

1. El agente habla español. (Necesitamos un agente que...)
2. Ese viaje incluye el hotel. (Aquí no hay ningún viaje que...)
3. No hay ningún pasaje que no sea caro. (Tenemos unos pasajes que...)
4. No hay ningún vuelo que salga a las seis. (Hay varios vuelos que...)
5. Hay una señora que puede reservar los pasajes. (¿Hay alguien que...?)

B. Familiar commands

Change the following negative commands to the affirmative.

Answers: 1. Compra el televisor. 2. Díselo. 3. Viaja mañana. 4. Sal con esa persona. 5. Pon la maleta debajo del asiento. 6. Invítalo. 7. Vete. 8. Ven entre semana. 9. Regresa tarde. 10. Haz la reservación. 11. Tráeme el folleto. 12. Pídele los comprobantes ahora.

1. No compres el televisor.
2. No se lo digas.
3. No viajes mañana.
4. No salgas con esa persona.
5. No pongas la maleta debajo del asiento.
6. No lo invites.
7. No te vayas.
8. No vengas entre semana.
9. No regreses tarde.
10. No hagas la reservación.
11. No me traigas el folleto.
12. No le pidas los comprobantes ahora.

C. Verbs and prepositions

Complete each sentence with the Spanish equivalent of the words in parentheses.

1. Olga _se enamoró de_ Daniel pero _se casó con_ Luis. (*fell in love with / she married*)
2. Mi papá _insiste en_ que yo compre los billetes hoy. (*insists on*)
3. Paco, _no te olvides de_ buscar los pasaportes. _Acuérdate de_ que viajas el lunes. (*don't forget / Remember*)
4. Yo _no me di cuenta de_ que mis padres _no confiaban en_ él. (*didn't realize / didn't trust*)

D. Ordinal numbers

Write the ordinal numbers that correspond to the following numbers.

2. segundo	8. octavo	3. tercero
7. séptimo	4. cuarto	6. sexto
5. quinto	9. noveno	10. décimo
1. primero		

E. Vocabulary Complete the following sentences, using vocabulary from **Lección 12.**

1. El baño vo tiene bañadera; tiene __ducha__.
2. El __ascensor (elevador)__ no funciona. Tiene que __subir__ por la escalera.
3. Tengo mucho frío y este cuarto no tiene __calefacción__.
4. Mi esposo(a) y yo queremos una __cama__ doble.
5. El __precio__ de la pensión incluye todas las comidas.
6. Hay mucha gente porque hay un __montón__ de convenciones.
7. ¿A qué hora debemos __desocupar__ el cuarto?
8. Mi cuarto no es con __vista__ a la calle; es interior.
9. La pensión no tiene __servicio__ de habitación.
10. Quiero una habitación exterior con __aire__ acondicionado.
11. Primero fui al __puesto__ de revistas y después a la tienda de __regalos__.
12. Un sinónimo de **dueño** es __propietario__.
13. Reservé un hotel con pensión __completa__.
14. No hay ninguna habitación __libre__. El hotel está lleno.
15. ¿En qué __piso__ está tu habitación?

F. Culture Circle the correct answer, based on the cultural notes you have read.

1. La ciudad de Santiago tiene (muy pocos / muchos) lugares de recreo.
2. La Avenida 9 de Julio en Buenos Aires es la (menos / más) ancha del mundo.
3. Uruguay está situado entre Brasil y (Argentina/Chile).
4. Desde 1960 la capital de Brasil es (Río de Janeiro/Brasilia).

Answers: 1. muchos 2. más 3. Argentina 4. Brasilia

Unidad 7

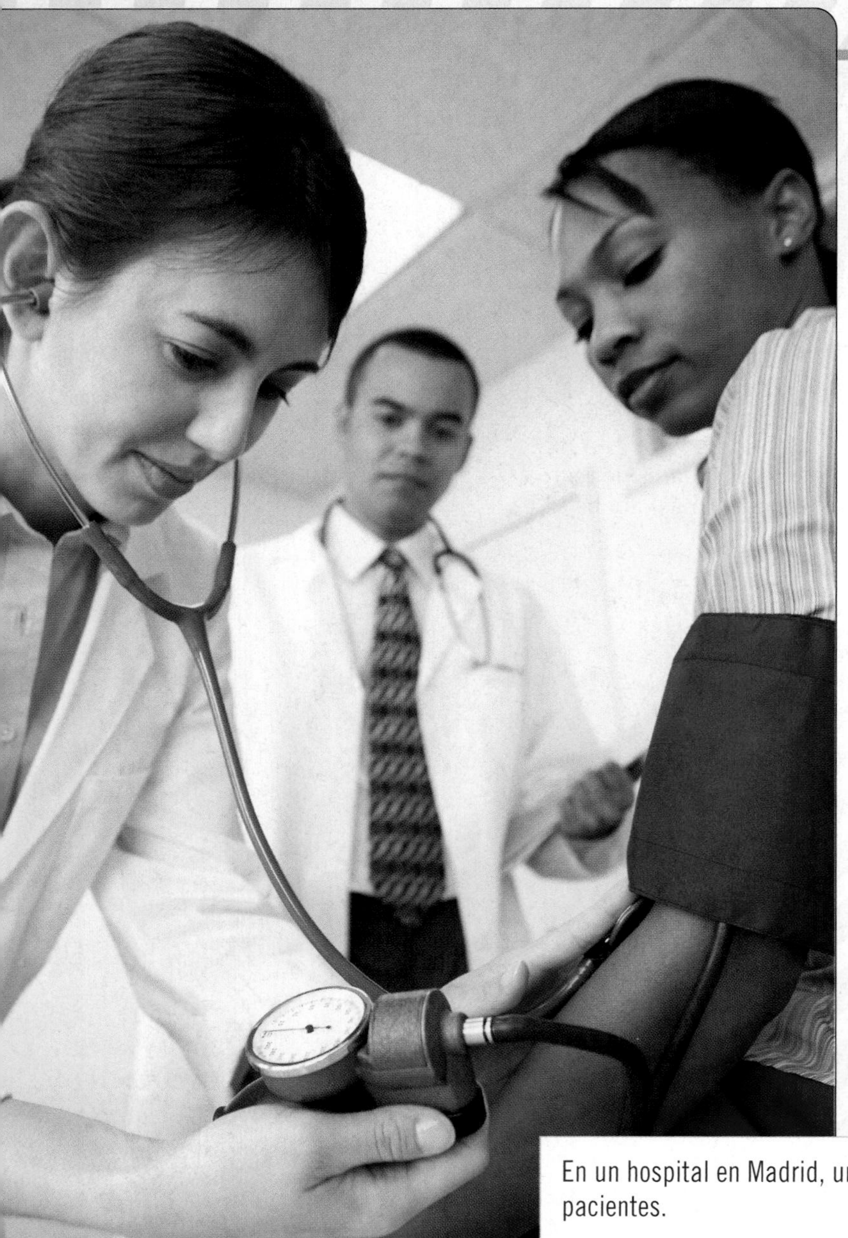

En un hospital en Madrid, una doctora le toma la presión a una de sus pacientes.

Objetivos

Lección 13

- Discuss health problems, medical emergencies, common medical procedures, and treatments
- Give and request information about physical symptoms and medications
- Express doubt, disbelief, and denial
- Tell others what to do

Lección 14

- Ask and respond to questions concerning personal medical history
- Make suggestions and give advice about health and other problems
- Talk about what will happen
- Talk about what would happen under different circumstances

¿Cómo te sientes?

Lección 13
En la sala de emergencia

Lección 14
Hablando con el médico

España

Un café al aire libre en la Plaza Mayor en Madrid, España

Jardines del Generalife, en el Palacio de la Alhambra, Granada

Playa de Fuengirola, en la Costa del Sol, Andalucía

Lección 13 ◆ En la sala de emergencia

En un hospital de Madrid

Hoy, como siempre, hay muchos pacientes en la sala de emergencia, y siguen llegando más. El Dr. Mena atiende a varios de ellos, y piensa que va a ser un día muy largo.

En este momento está hablando con un hombre que vino en una ambulancia y que los paramédicos acaban de traer en una camilla.

Dr. Mena	¿Qué le pasó?
Paciente I	Mi coche chocó con un árbol y me golpeé el hombro.
Dr. Mena	¿Perdió el conocimiento?
Paciente I	Sí, por unos segundos... pero me duele mucho...
Dr. Mena	Bueno, la enfermera lo va a llevar a la sala de rayos X. Vamos a hacerle unas radiografías para ver si hay fractura.

Ahora está hablando con una señora que trajo a su hijo. El niño se cayó en la escalera mecánica de una tienda y se lastimó.

Dr. Mena	Estoy casi seguro de que es una torcedura, pero vamos a hacerle unas radiografías por si acaso.
Madre	Se cortó la pierna. ¿Va a necesitar puntos?
Dr. Mena	Dudo que necesite puntos, pero cuando venga la enfermera va a limpiarle y desinfectarle la herida. Además, le vamos a poner una inyección antitetánica.

Detalles culturales

En la mayoría de los países de habla hispana, los hospitales son gratis y subvencionados por el gobierno. Hay clínicas privadas para la gente que no quiere ir a un hospital público.

◆ **¿Hay hospitales subvencionados por el gobierno en este país?**

Detalles culturales

En muchos países hispanos existen las llamadas casas de socorro, donde se ofrecen los primeros auxilios (*first aid*) y cuidados (*care*) médicos urgentes.

◆ **¿Hay en este país un equivalente a las casas de socorro?**

Ahora está hablando con un muchacho que tiene mucho dolor y náusea.

Paciente II Me duele mucho, doctor. Yo creo que tengo apendicitis...

Dr. Mena (*Lo revisa*) No creo que sea apendicitis, pero vamos a hacerle unos análisis.

El Dr. Mena continuó atendiendo a otros pacientes en la sala de emergencia: a una niña que se quemó la mano y lloraba mucho; a una señora que se rompió una pierna y tiene que usar muletas; a un señor que tuvo una reacción alérgica y tiene la cara hinchada... Cuando volvió a su casa, se dio cuenta de que no había almorzado.

Sra. Mena Cenemos temprano, porque hoy tenemos que ir a la escuela de los niños. ¡Ay! Estoy muy cansada. Descansemos un rato antes de que Paloma y Mario vuelvan de su clase de piano. ¿Qué tal fue tu día hoy?

Dr. Mena Bueno... fue un día como cualquier otro... ¡en la sala de emergencia!

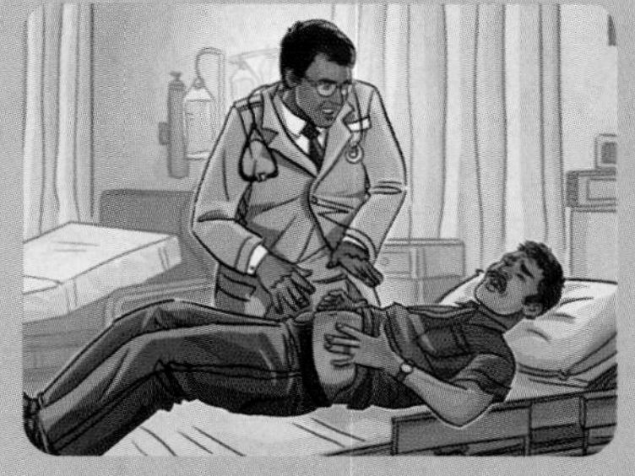

¿Recuerda usted?

¿Verdadero o falso?

With a partner, indicate whether these statements are true (**verdadero**) or false (**falso**).

1. Hoy no hay muchos pacientes en la sala de emergencia. ☐ V ☒ F
2. Un paciente se golpeó el hombro cuando su auto chocó con un árbol. ☒ V ☐ F
3. El Dr. Mena no sabe si el paciente tiene o no una fractura. ☒ V ☐ F
4. La mamá del niño se cayó de una bicicleta. ☐ V ☒ F
5. Le van a poner al niño una inyección antitetánica. ☒ V ☐ F
6. Uno de los pacientes cree que tiene apendicitis. ☒ V ☐ F
7. El Dr. Mena no tuvo que atender a nadie hoy. ☐ V ☒ F
8. El señor que tuvo una reacción alérgica tiene que usar muletas. ☐ V ☒ F
9. El Dr. Mena almorzó muy temprano hoy. ☐ V ☒ F
10. Hoy fue un día normal para el Dr. Mena. ☒ V ☐ F

Y ahora... conteste

Answer the following questions, basing your answers on the dialogues.

1. ¿Quiénes trajeron al primer paciente a la sala de emergencia?
2. ¿El hombre perdió el conocimiento?
3. ¿A quiénes les van a hacer radiografías?
4. ¿El Dr. Mena cree que el niño va a necesitar puntos?
5. ¿Qué problemas tiene el muchacho que viene a la sala de emergencia?
6. ¿Por qué lloraba mucho la niña?
7. ¿Qué va a tener que usar la señora que se rompió una pierna?
8. ¿De dónde vienen Paloma y Mario?

Answers: **1.** Los paramédicos lo trajeron. **2.** Sí, perdió el conocimiento por unos segundos. **3.** Les van a hacer radiografías al hombre y al niño. **4.** No, no cree que necesite puntos. **5.** Tiene mucho dolor y náusea. **6.** Lloraba mucho porque se quemó la mano. **7.** Va a tener que usar muletas. **8.** Vienen de su clase de piano.

Para hablar del tema: Vocabulario

Cognados

la ambulancia
la apendicitis
la fractura
el hospital
la náusea
el (la) paciente
el (la) paramédico(a)
el piano
la reacción

Nombres

el análisis test
el árbol tree
la cara face
el dolor pain
el (la) enfermero(a) male nurse, nurse
la escalera stairs
________ **mecánica*** escalator
la herida wound
el hombro shoulder
la inyección shot, injection
________ **antitetánica** tetanus shot
las muletas crutches
la pierna leg
el punto stitch
la radiografía X-ray
la sala ward (*at a hospital*)
________ **de emergencia** emergency room
________ **de rayos equis** X-ray room
la torcedura sprain

De país a país

la escalera mecánica la escalera automática (*Esp., Cuba*)
romperse quebrarse (*Méx.*)

Verbos

atender (e>ie) to see (*a patient*)
caerse (yo me caigo) to fall
chocar to collide
continuar to continue
cortar(se) to cut (oneself)
desinfectar to disinfect
doler (o>ue) to hurt, to ache
dudar to doubt
golpear(se) to hit (*oneself*)
lastimarse to hurt oneself
llorar to cry
pasar, suceder to happen
quemar(se) to burn (*oneself*)
revisar to check
romper(se)* to break

Adjetivos	
alérgico(a) allergic	**seguro(a)** sure
hinchado(a) swollen	**varios(as)** several

For more practice with lesson topics, see the related activities on the *¡Hola, amigos!* web site at college.hmco.com/PIC/holaamigos7e.

Otras palabras y expresiones	
casi almost	**hacer una radiografía** to take an X-ray
como siempre as usual	**perder el conocimiento, desmayarse** to faint
cualquier any	

Amplíe su vocabulario

Otras partes del cuerpo (*Other parts of the body*)

Para practicar el vocabulario

Answers: 1. f 2. j 3. l 4. a 5. c 6. h 7. k 8. d 9. g 10. i 11. b 12. e

A. Preguntas y respuestas Match the questions in column *A* with the answers in column *B*.

A	B
1. ¿Dónde tiene él la herida?	a. En la sala de rayos X.
2. ¿Qué te duele?	b. Me caí en la escalera.
3. ¿Qué te hizo la enfermera?	c. No, una torcedura.
4. ¿Dónde está Rita?	d. Sí, como siempre.
5. ¿Tiene una fractura?	e. A varios pacientes.
6. ¿Qué necesita el paciente?	f. En la cara.
7. ¿Qué le pasó a la niña?	g. No, tengo dudas.
8. ¿Tuviste mucho trabajo hoy?	h. Una radiografía.
9. ¿Estás seguro de eso?	i. No, sólo me lastimé.
10. ¿Te rompiste el brazo?	j. El hombro.
11. ¿Qué te pasó?	k. Se quemó la mano.
12. ¿A quiénes está atendiendo el médico?	l. Me desinfectó la herida.

B. En la sala de emergencia Complete the following statements about what goes on in the emergency room, using appropriate vocabulary.

1. Ayer el coche de Sergio __chocó__ con un árbol y él se __golpeó__ la cabeza. Los __paramédicos__ lo llevaron al hospital en una __ambulancia__.
2. Ayer Beto se __cayó__ de la bicicleta y se __rompió (quebró)__ un brazo. También se __cortó__ la pierna y va a necesitar puntos. Le van a __poner__ una inyección __antitetánica__.
3. Carlos tiene __náusea__ y mucho __dolor__ de estómago. Él cree que tiene __apendicitis__. El doctor le va a hacer unos __análisis__.
4. Marga se __rompió (quebró)__ la pierna y ahora tiene que usar __muletas__ para caminar (walk).
5. Ayer Amanda tuvo una __reacción__ alérgica y ahora tiene la cara y las manos __hinchadas__.

TELEFONOS DE EMERGENCIA

BOMBEROS INCENDIOS EMERGENCIA **19**

POLICIA **12**

SECRETARIA DE SALUD **15**
SERVICIO LAS 24 HORAS.
AMBULANCIAS

HOSPITALES

La Hortúa	246 4020
La Victoria	272 2028
Lorencita Villegas	231 8849
Militar	232 5333
Misericordia	246 7520
Samaritana	233 8880

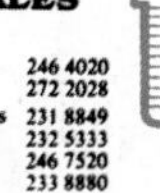

C. ¿Qué sabes de anatomía? Today you and your partner are the professors. Teach your students these parts of the body in Spanish.

Answers: 1. la nariz 2. la oreja 3. la boca 4. los dientes 5. la lengua 6. el ojo 7. el cuello 8. la cabeza 9. el pecho 10. el estómago 11. el dedo 12. la rodilla 13. la muñeca 14. el tobillo 15. los dedos del pie 16. el pie 17. el codo 18. el brazo 19. la espalda

D. En el hospital You and a classmate play the roles of two doctors talking about the patients they have seen during the day, and their problems.

Answers will vary.

Pronunciación

Pronunciation in context In this lesson, there are some words or phrases that may be challenging to pronounce. Listen to your instructor and pronounce the following sentences.

1. Hay muchos **pacientes** en la sala de **emergencia,** y **siguen** llegando más.
2. Vamos a hacerle una **radiografía** para ver si hay **fractura.**
3. **Además,** le vamos a poner una **inyección antitetánica.**
4. No creo que sea **apendicitis,** pero vamos a hacerle unos **análisis.**
5. Cuando volvió a su casa, se dio cuenta de que **no había almorzado.**

Puntos para recordar

1. Subjunctive to express doubt, denial, and disbelief
(*El subjuntivo para expresar duda, negación e incredulidad*)

Expansion: Write on the board:
MAIN CLAUSE
Dudo
↓
Expresses doubt
SUBORDINATE CLAUSE
que ellos **quieran** la casa.
↓
Verb: subjunctive
MAIN CLAUSE
Estoy seguro
↓
No doubt is expressed
SUBORDINATE CLAUSE
de que ellos **quieren** la casa.
↓
Verb: indicative

Ask students for other examples and have them explain why the subjunctive or the indicative is used in the subordinate clause.

Doubt

When the verb of the main clause expresses uncertainty or doubt, the verb in the subordinate clause is in the subjunctive.

—Te esperan a las cinco y son las cuatro y media. — *"They expect you at five and it is four-thirty."*
—**Dudo** que yo **pueda** estar ahí a esa hora. — *"**I doubt** that **I can** be there at that time."*

—Podemos tomar el desayuno a las once. — *"We can have breakfast at eleven."*
—**Dudo** que lo **sirvan** después de las diez. — *"**I doubt** that **they serve** it after ten."*
—Estoy segura de que lo sirven hasta las once. — *"I am sure that they serve it until eleven."*

¡Atención! Notice that when no doubt is expressed and the speaker is certain of the reality (**estoy seguro[a], no dudo, sé**), the indicative is used.

Estoy seguro de que lo **sirven** hasta las once. — ***I am sure** that **they serve** it until eleven.*

Online Study Center
For more practice with lesson topics, see the related activities on the ***¡Hola, amigos!*** web site at college.hmco.com/PIC/holaamigos7e.

Práctica y conversación

Answers: **1.** tenga una fractura. **2.** tiene que usar muletas. **3.** es apendicitis. **4.** está en la sala de rayos X. **5.** necesite radiografías.

A. ¿Cómo responde...? Respond to each of the following statements, beginning with the suggested phrases.

1. —Estoy seguro de que tiene una fractura.
   —Bueno, dudo que...
2. —Dudo que tenga que usar muletas.
   —Pues yo estoy seguro(a) de que...
3. —No estoy seguro de que sea apendicitis.
   —Pues yo no dudo que...
4. —Dudo que la enfermera esté en la sala de rayos X.
   —¿Sí? Yo estoy casi seguro(a) de que...
5. —Dudo que el paciente necesite radiografías.
   —Yo tampoco estoy seguro(a) de que...

B. En el hospital With a partner, read the following statements and take turns expressing doubt or certainty about them. Use **dudo, no dudo, estoy seguro(a),** and **no estoy seguro(a).** *Answers will vary.*

1. Todos los hospitales son gratis.
2. Las enfermeras trabajan solamente tres horas al día.
3. El médico puede desinfectar la herida.
4. Los paramédicos nunca vienen en la ambulancia.
5. Cualquier enfermera puede hacer una radiografía.
6. Si tienes un dolor en el pecho debes ir al hospital en seguida.
7. Los médicos ganan muy poco dinero.
8. Si te rompes una pierna necesitas usar muletas.

C. ¿Lo dudas...? With a partner, take turns telling each other three or four things about yourself. Give some false information to see if your partner doubts or doesn't doubt what you say. *Answers will vary.*

◆ MODELO: —*Tengo ocho clases este semestre.*
—*Dudo que tengas ocho clases.*
(*Estoy seguro[a] de que no tienes ocho clases.*)

Denial

When the main clause denies or negates what is expressed in the subordinate clause, the subjunctive is used.

—Ana **niega** que Carlos **sea** su novio.	*"Ana **denies** that Carlos **is** her boyfriend."*
—Sí, dice que son amigos...	*"Yes, she says that they are friends . . ."*
—Ellos trabajan mucho y siempre tienen dinero.	*"They work hard and always have money."*
—Es verdad que trabajan mucho, pero **no es cierto** que siempre **tengan** dinero.	*"It's true that they work hard, but **it's not true** that **they** always **have** money."*

¡Atención! Notice that when the main clause does not deny what is said in the subordinate clause, the indicative is used.

Es verdad que **trabajan** mucho. *It's true that they work hard.*

Expansion: Write on the board:
MAIN CLAUSE
No es verdad
↓
Denies
SUBORDINATE CLAUSE
que la fiesta **sea** hoy.
↓
Verb: subjunctive
MAIN CLAUSE
Es verdad
↓
Does not deny
SUBORDINATE CLAUSE
que la fiesta **es** hoy.
↓
Verb: indicative
Ask students for other examples and have them explain why the subjunctive or the indicative is used in the subordinate clause.

Online Study Center
For more practice with lesson topics, see the related activities on the ***¡Hola, amigos!*** web site at college.hmco.com/PIC/holaamigos7e.

Práctica y conversación

A. ¿Es verdad o no? With a partner, take turns saying whether each of the following statements is true or not.

◆ MODELO: Toda la gente tiene reacciones alérgicas a todo.
***No es verdad** que toda la gente **tenga** reacciones alérgicas a todo.*

1. Los médicos no trabajan en la sala de emergencia.
2. Generalmente hay muchos pacientes en la sala de emergencia.
3. Las enfermeras saben más que los médicos.

Extra practice: Have students make up five additional statements. Then in pairs or groups, students take turns asking each other to comment on the truth of their statements.

Answers: **1.** No es verdad que los médicos no trabajen en la sala de emergencia. **2.** Es verdad que generalmente hay muchos pacientes en la sala de emergencia. **3.** No es verdad que las enfermeras sepan más que los médicos. **4.** Es verdad que los paramédicos van en las ambulancias. **5.** No es verdad que los médicos no cobren mucho. **6.** Es verdad que hoy hace mucho frío. (No es verdad que hoy haga mucho frío.) **7.** Es verdad que está lloviendo. (No es verdad que esté lloviendo.) **8.** Es verdad que hoy hace buen tiempo. (No es verdad que hoy haga buen tiempo.)

4. Los paramédicos van en las ambulancias.
5. Los médicos no cobran mucho.
6. Hoy hace mucho frío.
7. Está lloviendo.
8. Hoy hace buen tiempo.

Disbelief

The verb **creer** is followed by the subjunctive in negative sentences, where it expresses disbelief.

—¿Teresa va al hospital hoy?	*"Is Teresa going to the hospital today?"*
—No, **no creo** que **vaya** hoy.	*"No, **I don't think she's going** today?"*

¡Atención! **Creer** is followed by the indicative in affirmative sentences, where it expresses belief.

Follow-up: Write on the board:

Disbelief
No creo que **sea** caro.
(subjunctive)

Belief
Creo que **es** caro.
(indicative)

Follow the same procedure as for subjunctive with verbs of denial.

—¿Qué va a pedir el médico?	*"What is the doctor going to ask for?"*
—**Creo** que **va** a pedir unos análisis.	*"**I think** he **is** going to order (ask for) some tests."*

Online Study Center

For more practice with lesson topics, see the related activities on the *¡Hola, amigos!* web site at college.hmco.com/PIC/holaamigos7e.

Práctica y conversación

Answers: **1.** Creo que (el hospital) es caro. **2.** No creo que (todos los cuartos) tengan aire acondicionado. **3.** No creo que tengan que llevarlo a la sala de emergencia. **4.** Creo que están allí. **5.** Creo que (él) necesita radiografías. **6.** No creo que necesite usar muletas.

A. El Sr. Contreras Mr. Contreras always contradicts everyone. How would he react to these statements?

◆ **MODELO:** Creo que ese médico es muy bueno.
__No creo__ que (ese médico) __sea__ muy bueno.

1. No creo que el hospital sea caro.
2. Creo que todos los cuartos tienen aire acondicionado.
3. Creo que tienen que llevarlo a la sala de emergencia.
4. No creo que estén allí.
5. No creo que él necesite radiografías.
6. Creo que necesita usar muletas.

B. En la universidad

Use your imagination to complete each statement, using the subjunctive or the indicative, as appropriate. Compare your statements to those of your partner. *Answers will vary.*

1. Yo creo que el profesor (la profesora)...
2. No es verdad que yo...
3. Es cierto que los estudiantes...
4. No creo que en la cafetería de la universidad...
5. No es verdad que la clase de español...
6. No es cierto que los norteamericanos...
7. Dudo que yo...
8. No estoy seguro(a) de que esta universidad...

Suggestion: Assign as homework and compare answers in class.

Mood: 1. indicative 2. subjunctive 3. indicative 4. subjunctive 5. subjunctive 6. subjunctive 7. subjunctive 8. subjunctive

C. Opiniones

Use the illustrations to complete the following sentences. *Answers will vary.*

1. Yo no creo que el papá de Beto...

2. Dudo que Paquito...

3. No es verdad que Carlos...

4. Rita cree que el hotel Granada...

5. No es cierto que el baño...

6. No es verdad que Esteban siempre...

Possible Answers: 1. le dé diez mil dólares. 2. sepa manejar. 3. tenga mucho dinero. 4. es muy caro. 5. tenga bañadera. 6. llegue tarde.

D. Viajando The following statements are made by someone who doesn't necessarily know what he or she is talking about. With a partner, take turns saying whether or not you think the comments are true. Use **creo, no creo, dudo, estoy seguro(a), es verdad,** or **no es verdad.** *Answers will vary.*

1. Hay vuelos directos de Nueva York a Madrid.
2. El pasaje a Madrid cuesta 200 dólares.
3. Los estudiantes siempre viajan en primera clase.
4. Puedo viajar por España en tren.
5. Todas las ciudades españolas son muy pequeñas.
6. Hay hoteles elegantes en Barcelona.
7. En los hoteles de Madrid, todas las habitaciones tienen vista al mar.
8. Podemos viajar de Los Ángeles a Madrid en tren.

2. Subjunctive with certain conjunctions (*El subjuntivo con ciertas conjunciones*)

Suggestion: Write on the board:

Lo haré cuando él **venga.**
Siempre lo hago cuando él **viene.**

Ask students to explain the use of **venga** as opposed to **viene.**

Follow-up: Ask students questions about their plans, such as **¿Qué vas a hacer cuando (en cuanto, tan pronto como) llegues a tu casa (tengas dinero, terminen las clases, te paguen)?**

Subjunctive after conjunctions of time

The subjunctive is used after conjunctions of time when the main clause refers to a future action or is a command. Some conjunctions of time are:

cuando when
hasta que until
tan pronto como,
en cuanto as soon as

Note in the following examples that the action in the subordinate clause has not yet taken place.

—¿Vamos a la pensión ahora? — *"Are we going to the boarding house now?"*
—No, vamos a esperar **hasta que venga** Eva. — *"No, we're going to wait **until** Eva **comes.**"*
—Bueno, llámeme **en cuanto llegue.** — *"Okay, call me **as soon as she arrives.**"*

—¿Cuándo vas a comprar las muletas? — *"When are you going to buy the crutches?"*
—**Cuando** mi papá me **dé** el dinero. — *"**When** my dad **gives** me the money."*

¡Atención! If the action has already taken place or if the speaker views the action of the subordinate clause as a habitual occurrence, the indicative is used after the conjunction of time.

Extra practice: Ask students personalized questions that require the use of the subjunctive, indicative, or infinitive.

1. **¿Qué vas a hacer en cuanto termine el curso?**
2. **¿Dónde quieres vivir cuando termines tus estudios?**
3. **¿Cuándo vas a comprar una casa?**

—¿Ya llamaste a Rodolfo? — *"Did you already call Rodolfo?"*
—Sí, lo llamé **en cuanto llegué.** — *"Yes, I called him **as soon as I arrived.**"*

—¿Cuándo llamas a Rodolfo? — *"When do you call Rodolfo?"*
—Siempre lo llamo **cuando llego** del trabajo. — *"I always call him **when I arrive** from work."*

Conjunctions that always take the subjunctive

Certain conjunctions by their very meaning imply uncertainty or condition; they are therefore always followed by the subjunctive. Examples include:

a menos que	unless	**con tal (de) que**	provided that
antes de que	before	**para que**	in order that, so that
en caso de que	in case	**sin que**	without

—Voy a llamar a la enfermera **para que** me **traiga** las radiografías	*"I'm going to call the nurse **so that she'll bring** me the x-rays."*
—Llámela **antes de que se vaya.**	*"Call her **before she leaves.**"*
—No puedo comprar la medicina **sin que** tú me **des** el dinero.	*"I can't buy the medicine **without you giving** me the money."*
—Puedo dártelo ahora.	*"I can give it to you now."*

Práctica y conversación

Online Study Center

For more practice with lesson topics, see the related activities on the ***¡Hola, amigos!*** web site at college.hmco.com/PIC/holaamigos7e.

A. Minidiálogos

Complete the following dialogues, using the indicative or the subjunctive of each verb. Then act them out with a partner.

1. **desocupar / llegar**

   —¿Podemos limpiar el cuarto ahora?

   —No, no podemos limpiarlo hasta que el paciente lo __desocupe__.

   —¿Cuándo lo va a desocupar?

   —En cuanto __llegue__ el taxi.

2. **llegar / atender**

   —¿Qué va a hacer en cuanto __llegue__ al hospital?

   —Voy a hablar con la recepcionista para que el médico me __atienda__ esta tarde.

3. **llamar**

   —¿Cuándo van a venir tus amigos?

   —Tan pronto como yo los __llame__.

4. **salir**

   —¿Los señores García te esperaron?

   —Sí, me esperaron hasta que yo __salí__ del hospital.

5. **hablar / ver**

   —Cuando Ud. __hable__ con el médico, dígale que el paciente no se siente bien.

   —Voy a decírselo en cuanto lo __vea__.

6. **irse / salir**

   —¿Tú puedes hablar con los paramédicos antes de que ellos __se vayan__?

   —Sí, a menos que (ellos) __salgan__ muy temprano.

B. Entreviste a su compañero(a) Interview your partner, using the following questions. *Answers will vary.*

1. ¿Siempre desayunas en cuanto te levantas?
2. ¿Siempre te lavas la cabeza cuando te bañas?
3. ¿Tú puedes salir de tu casa sin que nadie te vea?
4. ¿Qué le vas a decir a tu mejor amigo(a) cuando lo (la) veas?
5. ¿Tú llegas a veces a clase antes de que llegue el profesor (la profesora)?
6. ¿Qué vas a hacer para que el profesor (la profesora) te dé una "A" en esta clase?
7. ¿A veces te quedas en la biblioteca hasta que la cierran?
8. ¿Qué vas a hacer tan pronto como llegues a tu casa?

3. First-person plural commands (*El imperativo de la primera persona del plural*)

Suggestion: Review the first-person plural of the present subjunctive. Ask students for several examples, and write them on the board.

- In Spanish, the first-person plural of an affirmative command (*let's* + *verb*) can be expressed in two ways:
  - by using the first-person plural of the present subjunctive.

Preguntemos el precio de la habitación.	***Let's ask*** *the price of the room.*

  - by using the expression **vamos a** + *infinitive.*

Vamos a preguntar el precio de la habitación.	***Let's ask*** *the price of the room.*

Extra practice: You can use the verbs **subir, preguntar, llegar, viajar, tener, servir, pedir,** etc. Tell students that you will suggest places to go and things to do, and that they should disagree and suggest alternatives.

Instructor: **Vamos a Madrid.**
Student: **No, no vayamos a Madrid; Vamos a Barcelona.**

- The verb **ir** does not use the subjunctive form in the first-person plural affirmative command.

Vamos al teatro.	***Let's go*** *to the theatre.*

In a negative command, however, the subjunctive form is used.

No vayamos al teatro.	***Let's not go*** *to the theatre.*

- In all direct, affirmative commands, object pronouns are attached to the verb, and a written accent is then placed on the stressed syllable.

Comprémos**lo.**	*Let's buy* ***it.***
Llamémos**los.**	*Let's call* ***them.***

If the pronouns **nos** or **se** are attached to the verb, the final **-s** of the verb is dropped before adding the pronoun.

Sentémo**nos** aquí.	***Let's sit*** *here.*
Vistámo**nos** ahora.	***Let's get dressed*** *now.*
Démo**selo** a los niños.	***Let's give it*** *to the children.*
—Vamos a Madrid.	*"Let's go to Madrid."*
—No, no vayamos a Madrid; **quedémonos** en Barcelona.	*"No, let's not go to Madrid;* ***let's stay*** *in Barcelona."*
—¿Dónde queda el Museo del Prado?	*"Where's the Prado Museum located?"*
—No sé. **Preguntémoselo** a ese señor.	*"I don't know.* ***Let's ask*** *that gentleman."*

Práctica y conversación

For more practice with lesson topics, see the related activities on the *¡Hola, amigos!* web site at college.hmco.com/PIC/holaamigos7e.

A. ¿Qué hacemos...? With a partner, take turns saying what these people should do in the following situations. Use the first person plural command. Use pronouns wherever possible. *Answers will vary.*

1. Tenemos mucha hambre.
2. Estamos en un restaurante y necesitamos el menú.
3. No queremos salir hoy.
4. No sabemos qué hacer este fin de semana.
5. Un amigo nuestro tuvo un accidente.
6. No sabemos el precio de la medicina.
7. Estamos cansados.
8. Tenemos sueño.

Possibilites: **1.** Comamos algo. **2.** Pidámoselo al camarero. **3.** Salgamos mañana. **4.** Vamos al cine. **5.** Llevémoslo a la sala de emergencia. **6.** Preguntémoselo a alguien. **7.** Descansemos un rato. **8.** Durmamos. (Acostémonos)

B. ¡Vamos a España! You and a classmate are making plans to go on a trip to Spain. Take turns answering the following questions, using the first-person plural command. *Answers will vary.*

1. ¿A qué ciudad vamos?
2. ¿Cómo viajamos?
3. ¿Qué día y a qué hora salimos?
4. ¿Cuántas maletas llevamos?
5. ¿Nos hospedamos en un hotel o en una pensión?
6. ¿Pedimos una habitación con vista a la calle?
7. ¿Cuántos días nos quedamos en la ciudad?
8. ¿Comemos en un restaurante o en nuestra habitación?
9. ¿Dónde dejamos las joyas (*jewelry*)?
10. ¿Cuándo regresamos?

Verb forms: **1.** Vamos a... **2.** Viajemos en... **3.** Salgamos... **4.** Llevemos... **5.** Hospedémonos... **6.** Pidamos... **7.** Quedémonos... **8.** Comamos en... **9.** Dejémoslas en... **10.** Regresemos...

Rodeo

Summary of the Command Forms (*Resumen de las formas del imperativo*)

Usted	Ustedes	Tú		Nosotros
		Affirmative	*Negative*	
habl**e**	habl**en**	habl**a**	no habl**es**	habl**emos**
com**a**	com**an**	com**e**	no com**as**	com**amos**
abr**a**	abr**an**	abr**e**	no abr**as**	abr**amos**
cierr**e**	cierr**en**	cierr**a**	no cierr**es**	cerr**emos**
vay**a**	vay**an**	**ve**	no vay**as**	**vamos**[1]

[1]Remember that the affirmative command uses the indicative form **vamos,** but the negative command uses the subjunctive form **no vayamos.**

Notice that the command forms of these verbs are identical to the subjunctive forms, except for the affirmative forms for **tú,** which use the third-person singular of the present indicative. Also, the following verbs have irregular **tú** command forms.

decir	**di**	ir	**ve**	salir	**sal**	tener	**ten**
hacer	**haz**	poner	**pon**	ser	**sé**	venir	**ven**

Remember the position of direct, indirect, and reflexive pronouns with commands.

Affirmative	*Negative*
Cómpre**lo.**	No **lo** compre.
Dí**selo.**	No **se lo** digas.
Levanté**monos.**	No **nos** levantemos.

Práctica y conversación

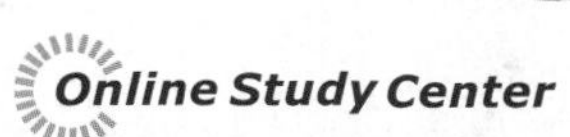

For more practice with lesson topics, see the related activities on the *¡Hola, amigos!* web site at college.hmco.com/PIC/holaamigos7e.

Planes y más planes You and a partner are busy making plans for a visit by some foreign students who will spend the weekend with you and your friends. One of your neighbors, Sra. Vega, and her young daughter, María, offer their help. Use the appropriate command form to say who is going to do each of the following chores and categorize them under the appropriate heading.

◆ **MODELOS:** Comprar frutas
Nosotros: *Compremos frutas.*
la señora Vega: *Compre frutas.*
María: *Compra frutas.*

1. limpiar el apartamento
2. ir al mercado
3. poner la mesa
4. preparar la comida
5. hacer las camas
6. invitar a otros estudiantes
7. ir al aeropuerto a esperar a los viajeros (*travelers*)
8. sacar entradas para el teatro
9. no levantarse tarde
10. llevarlos a visitar los lugares de interés
11. servir la comida
12. lavar los platos
13. darles una fiesta de bienvenida
14. pedirle los discos compactos a Roberto
15. llevarlos a las tiendas
16. no olvidarse de sacar dinero del banco

Nosotros	La Sra. Vega	María
1. limpiemos	limpie	limpia
2. vamos	vaya	ve
3. pongamos	ponga	pon
4. preparemos	prepare	prepara
5. hagamos	haga	haz
6. invitemos	invite	invita
7. vamos	vaya	ve
8. saquemos	saque	saca
9. no nos levantemos	no se levante	no te levantes
10. llevémoslos	llévelos	llévalos
11. sirvamos	sirva	sirve
12. lavemos	lave	lava
13. démosles	deles	dales
14. pidámoslos	pídalos	pídelos
15. llevémoslos	llévelos	llévalos
16. no nos olvidemos	no se olvide	no te olvides

4. *¿Qué?* and *¿cuál?* used with *ser*
(Qué *y* cuál *usados con el verbo ser*)

- *What?* translates as **¿qué?** when it is used as the subject of the verb and asks for a definition.

—¿**Qué** es una paella?	*"**What** is a paella?"*
—Es un plato español.	*"It's a Spanish dish."*

- *What?* translates as **¿cuál?** when it is used as the subject of a verb and asks for a choice. **Cuál** conveys the idea of selection from among several or many available objects, ideas, and so on.

—¿**Cuál** es su número de teléfono?	*"**What** is your phone number?"*
—712-4267.	*"712-4267."*

Práctica y conversación

Online Study Center

For more practice with lesson topics, see the related activities on the *¡Hola, amigos!* web site at college.hmco.com/PIC/holaamigos7e.

A. ¿Cuál es la pregunta? Write the questions you would ask to get the following information. Use **qué** or **cuál,** as needed.

1. —¿ Cuál es el nombre del hotel ?
   —El nombre del hotel es "El Alcázar".
   —¿ Cuál es la dirección del hotel ?
   —Calle del Prado, número 420.
   —¿ Cuál es el número de teléfono del hotel ?
   —6–35–42–37.
2. —Necesita mostrar su carnet de identidad.
   —¿ Qué es un carnet de identidad ?
   —Es una forma de identificación.
   —¿Cuánto cuesta una habitación en este hotel?
   —Cuesta doscientos euros.
   —¿ Qué es un euro ?
   —Es la moneda (*currency*) de España.

B. Entreviste a su compañero(a) Interview your partner, using the following questions. *Answers will vary.*

1. ¿Cuál es el hotel que tú prefieres?
2. ¿Cuál es la ciudad que más te gusta?
3. ¿Cuál es el programa de televisión que prefieres?
4. ¿Cuál es la comida que más te gusta?
5. ¿Cuál es el lugar que prefieres para ir de vacaciones?
6. ¿Cuál es tu color favorito?

Entre nosotros

¡Conversemos!

Para conocernos mejor Get to know your partner better by asking each other the following questions. *Answers will vary.*

1. ¿Has tenido un accidente alguna vez?
2. ¿Te han llevado al hospital en una ambulancia alguna vez?
3. ¿Cuándo fue la última vez que estuviste en una sala de emergencia?
4. ¿Cuándo fue la última vez que te pusieron una inyección antitetánica?
5. ¿Qué tomas cuando te duele la cabeza? ¿Y cuando te duele el estómago?
6. ¿Te han hecho una radiografía últimamente?
7. ¿Te has desmayado alguna vez (*ever*)?
8. ¿Tu médico te ha recetado alguna medicina últimamente?
9. ¿Te has roto una pierna o un brazo alguna vez?
10. ¿Te has quemado una mano alguna vez?

Una encuesta Interview your classmates to identify who fits the following descriptions. Include your instructor, but remember to use the **Ud.** form when addressing him or her. *Answers will vary.*

	Nombre
1. Se lastimó jugando al fútbol.	
2. Toma pastillas para el dolor a veces.	
3. Va a ir al médico el mes próximo.	
4. No se siente bien hoy.	
5. Se ha caído últimamente.	
6. Estuvo en la sala de rayos X el mes pasado.	
7. Va a tomar una medicina más tarde.	
8. Nunca se ha desmayado.	
9. Tiene problemas con el estómago a veces.	
10. Ha tenido que ir al hospital últimamente.	

Y ahora... Write a brief summary about what you have learned about your classmates. *Answers will vary.*

¿Cómo lo decimos? What would you say in the following situations? What might the other person say? Act out the scenes with a partner. *Answers will vary.*

Suggestion: This exercise may be assigned as homework and then role played in class.

1. You were in an accident and were brought to the hospital. Tell the doctor what happened and where it hurts. Ask him or her any relevant questions you may have regarding your injuries, any procedures the doctor may wish to perform, and your treatment.
2. You and your English-speaking friend are traveling in Spain. Your friend has fallen down the stairs in the hotel, so you take him/her to the doctor. Tell the doctor what happened, and ask any pertinent questions. (Does he/she need crutches? If so, how long must the crutches be used?, and so on).

¿Qué pasa aquí? In groups of three or four, create a story about the people in the illustrations. Say who they are, what happened to them, and what they need. *Answers will vary.*

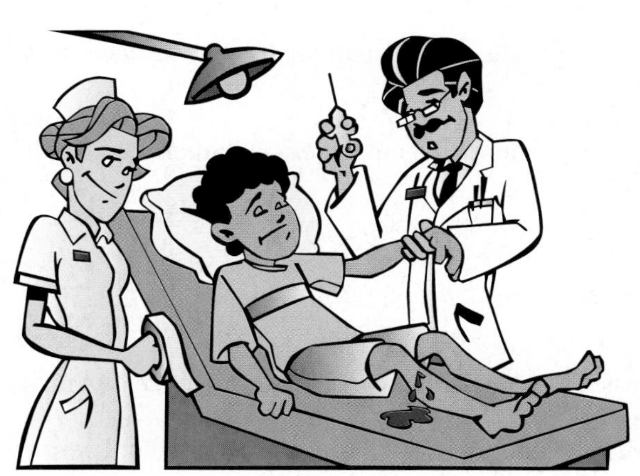

Para escribir

Un accidente Use your imagination to finish the following story, telling what happened to Julio. Tell how the accident happened, how he got to the hospital, what the doctor said and did, etc. *Answers will vary.*

Eran las ocho de la noche y Julio iba en su coche cuando tuvo un accidente...

Un dicho

Mente sana en cuerpo sano.

To have this shoud be everyone's goal! Keep repeating this wise saying in Spanish!

Lección 14 • Hablando con el médico

La Sra. Paz se despertó con dolor de garganta y una temperatura de 40 grados. Empezó a toser y le fue muy difícil levantarse. Pensó: "Tengo fiebre; tendré que ir al médico" y, afortunadamente, pudo hacer una cita para las diez de la mañana.

En el consultorio del Dr. Roca, la Sra. Paz habla con la recepcionista.

Recepcionista ¿Tiene su tarjeta de seguro médico? Tengo que hacer una fotocopia.
Sra. Paz Aquí la tiene.
Recepcionista Gracias. Tome asiento. La enfermera la llamará dentro de unos minutos.

Con la enfermera.

La enfermera la pesa y la lleva a uno de los cuartos. Allí le toma la temperatura y la presión.

Enfermera Tiene la presión un poco alta. ¿Cuánto tiempo hace que no se siente bien?
Sra. Paz Dos días. Mi esposo me aconsejó que viera al médico, pero yo fui a Barcelona a una conferencia.
Enfermera El médico probablemente le dirá que tiene que descansar. Bueno, en seguida vendrá el Dr. Roca a hablar con usted. ¿Es usted alérgica a alguna medicina?
Sra. Paz Que yo sepa, no.
Enfermera ¿Está embarazada?
Sra. Paz No.

Detalles culturales

En los países de habla hispana se mide la temperatura en grados *Celsius*, a los que también se les llama *Centígrados*. En la escala Celsius, 0° (temperatura de fusión del hielo) corresponde a 32° Fahrenheit. En el ejemplo, 40° Celsius corresponde a 104° Fahrenheit.

◆ **¿Sabe Ud. convertir grados Farenheit a centígrados?**

Detalles culturales

En muchos países hispanos, en cada barrio (*neighborhood*), hay una "farmacia de turno" que ofrece servicios durante la noche. A cada farmacia le corresponde estar abierta un día diferente de la semana. Un letrero en las farmacias cerradas indica dónde están las farmacias abiertas.

◆ **¿Hay en su ciudad farmacias que están abiertas 24 horas al día?**

Con el Dr. Roca.

Dr. Roca (*La examina*) A ver... Abra la boca y diga "ah". Ajá. Ahora, respire hondo... Otra vez...

Sra. Paz Me gustaría que me hiciera un buen chequeo, doctor.

Dr. Roca Sí, ésa sería una buena idea. Si tuviera tiempo, lo haría hoy, pero no será posible.

Sra. Paz Bueno, haré una cita para la semana que viene.

Dr. Roca Bien, usted tiene gripe pero, si no se cuida, puede convertirse en una pulmonía, y ésa es una enfermedad mucho más grave.

Sra. Paz ¿Me va a recetar algo?

Dr. Roca Sí, le voy a recetar un antibiótico y un jarabe para la tos. Lleve esta receta a la farmacia y empiece a tomar el antibiótico hoy mismo.

Sra. Paz Bueno, lo que tengo es contagioso, de modo que no podré ir a trabajar. Pero lo más difícil va a ser admitir que mi esposo tenía razón.

Dr. Roca ¿Tenía razón?

Sra. Paz Sí, él me dijo que viniera al médico y yo me fui a una conferencia... ¡Y me empeoré! ¡Ahora va a creer que él es infalible!

¿Recuerda usted?

¿Verdadero o falso?

With a partner, decide whether the following statements about the dialogues are true (**verdadero**) or false (**falso**).

1. La temperatura de la Sra. Paz es normal. ☐ V ☒ F
2. La Sra. Paz no tiene seguro médico. ☐ V ☒ F
3. La recepcionista pesa a la Sra. Paz. ☐ V ☒ F
4. La conferencia fue en Barcelona. ☒ V ☐ F
5. La Sra. Paz no está embarazada. ☒ V ☐ F
6. El Dr. Roca le va a hacer un buen chequeo a la Sra. Paz hoy mismo. ☐ V ☒ F
7. La Sra. Paz pedirá turno para la semana que viene. ☒ V ☐ F
8. El médico le dice a la Sra. Paz que debe cuidarse. ☒ V ☐ F
9. La Sra. Paz no quiere admitir que su esposo tenía razón. ☒ V ☐ F
10. La Sra. Paz fue a una conferencia y se mejoró. ☐ V ☒ F

Y ahora... conteste

Answer these questions, basing your answers on the dialogues.

1. ¿Qué le dolía a la Sra. Paz esta mañana?
2. ¿Cómo sabemos que la Sra. Paz tenía fiebre?
3. ¿Cuánto tiempo hace que la Sra. Paz no se siente bien?
4. ¿Qué le aconsejó el Sr. Paz a su esposa?
5. ¿Qué dice la Sra. Paz que ella necesita?
6. ¿En qué puede convertirse la gripe?
7. ¿Qué va a comprar la Sra. Paz en la farmacia?
8. Según la Sra Paz, ¿qué va a creer su esposo?

Answers: **1.** Le dolía la garganta. **2.** Porque tenía una temperatura de 40°. **3.** Hace dos días que no se siente bien. **4.** Le aconsejó que viera al médico. **5.** Dice que necesita un buen chequeo. **6.** Puede convertirse en pulmonía. **7.** Va a comprar un antibiótico y un jarabe para la tos. **8.** Él va a creer que es infalible.

Detalles culturales

En España y en algunos países latinoamericanos, las farmacias venden principalmente medicinas. En algunos países hispanos es posible comprar ciertas medicinas —como la penicilina— sin tener receta médica.

◆ **En este país, ¿se pueden comprar antibióticos sin tener receta médica?**

Para hablar del tema: Vocabulario

Online Study Center

For more practice with lesson topics, see the related activities on the *¡Hola, amigos!* web site at college.hmco.com/PIC/holaamigos7e.

Cognados

el antibiótico
contagioso(a)
la farmacia
la fotocopia
infalible
el minuto
(el) la recepcionista

Nombres

la cita, el turno appointment
el chequeo checkup
la conferencia lecture
el consultorio doctor's office
la garganta throat
el dolor de garganta sore throat
la enfermedad disease, sickness
la fiebre fever
la gripe* flu
el jarabe syrup
la presión pressure, (blood) pressure
la pulmonía pneumonia
la receta prescription
el seguro* insurance
_______ **médico** medical insurance
la tos cough

Verbos

admitir to admit
convertirse en (e>ie) to turn into
cuidar(se) to take care (of oneself)
empeorar(se)[1] to get worse
examinar to examine, to check
pesar to weigh
recetar to prescribe
respirar to breathe
toser to cough

Adjetivos

embarazada, en estado, encinta pregnant
grave, serio(a) serious

Otras palabras y expresiones

dentro de within
en seguida, enseguida right away
hoy mismo this very day
otra vez again
por suerte, afortunadamente luckily, fortunately
que viene next
que yo sepa that I know of
respirar hondo to take a deep breath

[1]**mejorar(se)** to get better

Amplíe su vocabulario

Más sobre la salud: Medicinas

Debe tomar
- un antiácido — *antacid*
- un calmante — *tranquilizer*
- un sedativo, un sedante — *sedative*
- vitaminas — *vitamins*

Algunos especialistas

el (la) cardiólogo(a)	*cardiologist*
el (la) cirujano(a)	*surgeon*
el (la) dermatólogo(a)	*dermatologist*
el (la) ginecólogo(a)	*gynecologist*
el (la) oculista	*oculist*
el (la) pediatra	*pediatrician*

De país a país

la gripe la gripa (*Méx.*)
el seguro la aseguranza (*Méx.*)

En el botiquín (*Medicine cabinet*)

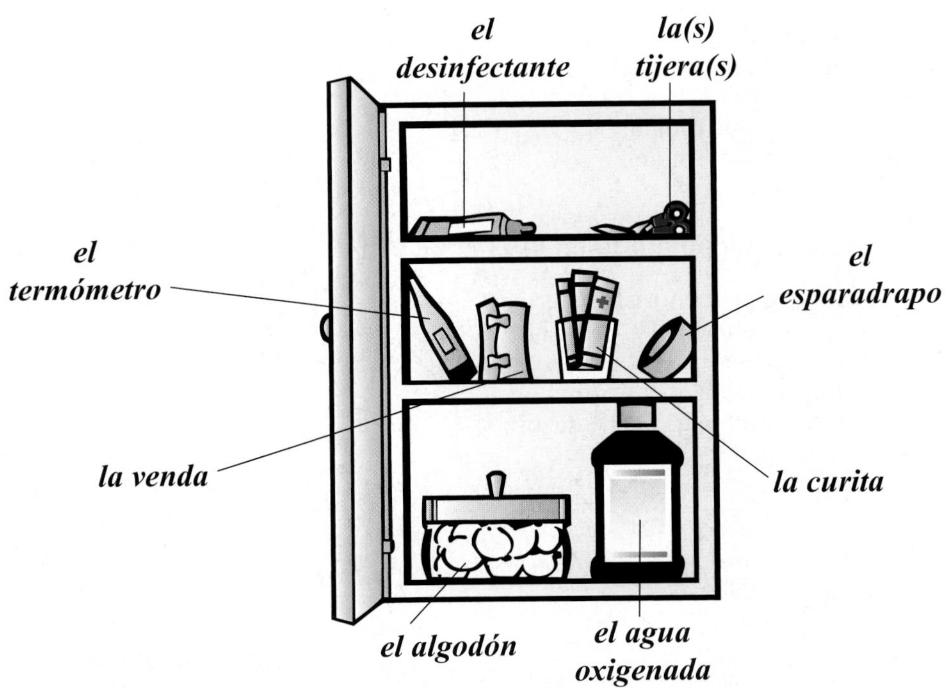

Para practicar el vocabulario

A. Preguntas y respuestas

With a partner, match the questions in column *A* with the answers in column *B*.

Answers: 1. i 2. f 3. k 4. b 5. h 6. a 7. l 8. d 9. g 10. c 11. e 12. j

A	B
1. ¿Qué te recetó el médico?	a. Aquí la tiene.
2. ¿Para cuándo tienes turno?	b. Sí, voy a la farmacia.
3. ¿Se mejoró?	c. No, normal.
4. ¿Necesitas la medicina ahora?	d. Que yo sepa, no.
5. ¿Tiene gripe?	e. Lo va a pesar.
6. ¿Dónde está la fotocopia?	f. Para hoy mismo.
7. ¿Debo volver mañana?	g. Sí, porque no tiene seguro.
8. ¿Es Ud. alérgica a alguna medicina?	h. Sí, pero puede convertirse en pulmonía.
9. ¿Rita tiene que pagar la cuenta?	i. Un jarabe para la tos.
10. ¿Tiene la presión alta?	j. Dentro de una semana.
11. ¿Qué va a hacer la enfermera?	k. No, se empeoró.
12. ¿Cuándo empieza a trabajar la recepcionista?	l. No, no es necesario.

B. ¿Qué debo tomar?

Answers: Debe tomar... 1. un antiácido 2. un sedante 3. vitaminas 4. un calmante 5. un antibiótico

1. Tengo acidez.
2. Estoy muy nervioso(a).
3. Estoy muy débil (*weak*).
4. Me duele una rodilla.
5. Tengo una infección.

C. ¿Qué especialista debo ver?

Answers: Debe ver a... 1. un pediatra 2. un ginecólogo 3. un oculista 4. un cirujano 5. un cardiólogo 6. un dermatólogo

1. si mi hijo pequeño está enfermo
2. si estoy embarazada
3. si no veo bien
4. si necesito una operación
5. si tengo problemas del corazón
6. si tengo acné

Detalles culturales

Especialmente en las grandes ciudades hispanas, la medicina está muy avanzada, pero en muchos pueblos (*towns*) remotos no hay hospitales ni médicos. En esos lugares, especialmente en Latinoamérica, hay curanderos (*healers*) que recomiendan hierbas (*herbs*) o tés, o que usan remedios tradicionales para sus curas.

◆ **En su país, ¿hay algunas personas que usan hierbas medicinales para curar ciertas enfermedades?**

 **D. En nuestro botiquín** With a partner, mention eight items you need for your medicine cabinet. *Answers will vary.*

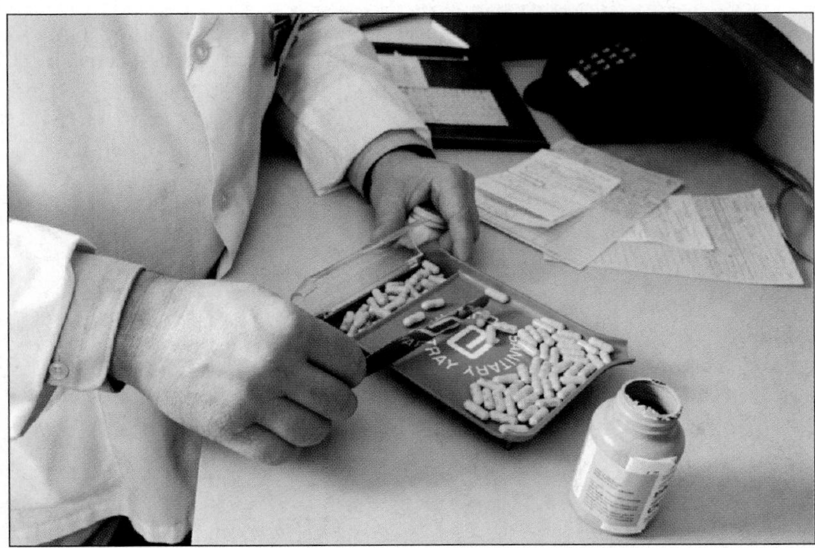

¿Para qué son las pastillas que está contando el farmacéutico?

Pronunciación

Pronunciation in context In this lesson, there are some words or phrases that may be challenging to pronounce. Listen to your instructor and pronounce the following sentences.

1. La Sra. Paz se despertó con dolor de **garganta** y una **temperatura** de 40 grados.
2. Mi esposo **me aconsejó** que fuera al médico, pero yo fui a **Barcelona** a una **conferencia.**
3. Me gustaría que me **hiciera** un buen **chequeo.**
4. Le voy a **recetar** un **antibiótico** y un **jarabe** para la tos.
5. Bueno, lo que tengo es **contagioso** y **no podré ir** a trabajar.

Puntos para recordar

1. Future tense (*Futuro*)

Extra practice: Ask students personalized questions about what they plan to do in the future.

1. **¿Adónde irás de vacaciones? ¿Cuándo? ¿Con quién?**
2. **¿Qué cursos tomarás el semestre / trimestre que viene? ¿Cuál será el más fácil / difícil?**
3. **¿Comprarás un coche nuevo el año que viene? ¿De qué marca?**
4. **¿Llevarás tu coche al taller de mecánica este fin de semana?**
5. **¿Trabajarás este verano? ¿Dónde?**

◆ Most Spanish verbs are regular in the future, and the infinitive serves as the stem of almost all verbs. The endings are the same for all three conjugations.

Formation of the Future Tense

Infinitive		*Stem*	*Endings*
trabajar	yo	trabajar-	**é**
aprender	tú	aprender-	**ás**
escribir	Ud., él, ella	escribir-	**á**
entender	nosotros(as)	entender-	**emos**
ir	vosotros(as)	ir-	**éis**
dar	Uds., ellos, ellas	dar-	**án**

¡Atención! Note that all the endings, except that of the **nosotros(as)** form, take accent marks.

—¿Adónde **irán** Uds. esta tarde? — *"Where **will** you **go** this afternoon?"*

—**Iremos** al consultorio del Dr. Báez. — *"**We will go** to Dr. Baez's office."*

◆ A small number of Spanish verbs are irregular in the future tense. These verbs have an irregular stem; however, the endings are the same as those for regular verbs.

Extra practice: Using the diagram that appears in the presentation of **-ar** verbs (p. 0), have students conjugate all irregular futures on the board. Work with each verb, asking questions and making statements in the future tense.

Expansion: Ask students personalized questions or have them interview each other in groups of three. Remind them to use the irregular future forms of the verbs in their responses.

S1 —**¿A qué hora vas a venir a la universidad mañana?**
S2 —**Vendré a las nueve de la mañana.**
S3 —**¿Harás la tarea antes de venir a clase?**
S2 —**Sí, la haré.**, etc.

Irregular Future Stems

Infinitive	*Stem*	*First-Person Sing.*
decir	dir-	**diré**
hacer	har-	**haré**
haber	habr-	**habré**
querer	querr-	**querré**
saber	sabr-	**sabré**
poder	podr-	**podré**
poner	pondr-	**pondré**
salir	saldr-	**saldré**
tener	tendr-	**tendré**
venir	vendr-	**vendré**

—¿A qué hora **saldrán** para el hospital?	*"At what time* ***will you leave*** *for the hospital?"*
—**Saldremos** tan pronto como lleguen mis padres.	*"****We will leave*** *as soon as my parents arrive."*
—¿**Podrás** venir mañana?	*"****Will you be able*** *to come tomorrow?"*
—Sí, **vendré** a menos que llueva.	*"Yes,* ***I will come*** *unless it rains."*

¡Atención! The future of **hay** (impersonal form of **haber**) is **habrá.**

¿**Habrá** una conferencia?	***Will there be*** *a lecture?*

- Uses of the future tense
  - The English equivalent of the Spanish future tense is *will* or *shall* plus a verb. As you have already learned, Spanish also uses the construction **ir a** plus an infinitive, or the present tense with a time expression, to refer to future actions, events, or states.

Esta noche **iremos** al cine.	*Tonight* ***we will go*** *to the movies.*
Esta noche **vamos a ir** al cine.	*Tonight* ***we're going to go*** *to the movies.*
Esta noche **vamos** al cine.	*Tonight* ***we're going*** *to the movies.*

  - Unlike English, the Spanish future is *not* used to express willingness. In Spanish, willingness is expressed by the verb **querer.**

—¿**Quieres** *llamar a Eva*?	*"****Will you*** *call Eva?"*
—Ahora no puedo.	*"I can't now."*

Online Study Center

For more practice with lesson topics, see the related activities on the *¡Hola, amigos!* web site at college.hmco.com/PIC/holaamigos7e.

Answers: 1. La Sra. Paz llamará al médico y preguntará si puede ir hoy. 2. La recepcionista le pedirá la tarjeta de seguro médico y le dirá que se siente. 3. La enfermera la pesará y le tomará la presión. 4. El médico le hará un chequeo y le dirá que se cuide. 5. La Sra. Paz irá a la farmacia y comprará la medicina. 6. Yo tendré que llevar a los niños a su casa porque la Sra. Paz no podrá llevarlos.

Follow-up: Involve students in a discussion of their futures by having them predict what will happen to each other. Start them off with your predictions (e.g., **Dentro de diez años, Miguel será profesor de química. Ángela estará casada,** etc.).

Expansion: After completion of this activity, have students work in pairs to write a paragraph describing what they will do to prepare for a trip from Maine to California; and what they will do during the trip.

Práctica y conversación

A. ¿Qué harán? Rewrite the following sentences, using the future tense. Follow the model.

◆ MODELO: Voy a comprar un jarabe y se lo voy a dar a Carlos.
Compraré un jarabe y se lo daré a Carlos.

1. La Sra. Paz va a llamar al médico y va a preguntar si puede ir hoy.
2. La recepcionista le va a pedir la tarjeta de seguro médico y le va a decir que se siente.
3. La enfermera la va a pesar y le va a tomar la presión.
4. El médico le va a hacer un chequeo y le va a decir que se cuide.
5. La Sra. Paz va a ir a la farmacia y va a comprar la medicina.
6. Yo voy a tener que llevar a los niños a su casa porque la Sra. Paz no va a poder llevarlos.

B. El verano pasado The following paragraph describes what happened last summer. Change all the verbs to the future to indicate what will happen in the upcoming summer.

En el verano, mi familia y yo **fuimos** a California. **Estuvimos** en San Diego por una semana. **Alquilamos** un apartamento cerca de la playa y unos amigos madrileños **vinieron** a quedarse con nosotros. Diego y Jaime **hicieron** surfing. Mi padre **pasó** un par de días pescando, y Gloria y yo **buceamos, tomamos** el sol y por la noche **salimos** con unos amigos. **Nos divertimos** mucho pero **tuvimos** que volver para empezar las clases. **Answers:** 1. iremos / Estaremos / Alquilaremos / vendrán / harán / pasará / bucearemos / tomaremos / saldremos / Nos divertiremos / tendremos

C. Planes para las vacaciones In groups of three, tell each other three or four things you plan to do during your summer vacations, using the future tense. Your classmates may ask for more details. *Answers will vary.*

2. Conditional tense (*Condicional*)

Extra practice: Write the following words on the board or on an overhead transparency, and have each student ask a classmate if he/she would do these things for him/her. Tell them to use the conditional to ask and respond.
1. limpiar / el apartamento
2. planchar / la ropa
3. preparar / la cena 4. lavar / la ropa 5. cortar / el césped
6. ir / de compras / mañana

◆ Like the future, the Spanish conditional uses the infinitive as the stem for most verbs and has only one set of endings for all three conjugations.

Formation of the Conditional Tense

Infinitive		*Stem*	*Endings*
trabajar	yo	trabajar-	**ía**
aprender	tú	aprender-	**ías**
escribir	Ud., él, ella	escribir-	**ía**
dar	nosotros(as)	dar-	**íamos**
hablar	vosotros(as)	hablar-	**íais**
preferir	Uds., ellos, ellas	preferir-	**ían**

—Me **gustaría** ir al parque. *"I **would like** to go to the park."*
—Nosotros **preferiríamos** ir a la piscina. *"We **would prefer** to go to the pool."*

—Voy a invitar a Julia. *"I'm going to invite Julia."*
—Yo no la **invitaría.** *"I **would** not **invite** her."*

- The verbs that are irregular in the future tense have the same irregular stems in the conditional. The endings are the same as those for regular verbs.

Irregular Conditional Stems

Infinitive	*Stem*	*First-Person Sing.*
decir	dir-	**diría**
hacer	har-	**haría**
haber	habr-	**habría**
querer	querr-	**querría**
saber	sabr-	**sabría**
poder	podr-	**podría**
poner	pondr-	**pondría**
salir	saldr-	**saldría**
tener	tendr-	**tendría**
venir	vendr-	**vendría**

—¿Qué **podría** hacer yo para ayudarte? *"What **could** I do to help you?"*
—**Podrías** traer las vendas. *"You could bring the bandages."*

¡Atención! The conditional of **hay** (impersonal form of **haber**) is **habría.**

Dijo que **habría** una reunión. *He said **there would be** a meeting.*

- Uses of the conditional
  - The Spanish conditional is equivalent to the English *would* plus a verb.

—¿Qué **harías** tú? *"What **would** you **do?**"*
—Yo **iría** al médico. *"I **would** go to the doctor."*

Extra practice: Have students work in pairs to practice giving excuses. One student should invite his or her partner to do something. The partner should then decline the invitation and offer an excuse using the conditional. Remind students to switch roles.

S1 —¿Quieres ir a una fiesta conmigo esta noche?
S2 —Iría contigo pero tengo que estudiar.

◆ In Spanish, the conditional is also used to soften a request or to express politeness.

—¿**Podrías** venir un momento?	*"**Could you** come for a minute?"*
—Sí, en seguida.	*"Yes, right away."*

Online Study Center

For more practice with lesson topics, see the related activities on the ***¡Hola, amigos!*** web site at college.hmco.com/PIC/holaamigos7e.

Práctica y conversación

A. En el consultorio de la Dra. Peña While waiting in Dr. Peña's office you overhear the following exchanges. Complete them, using the conditional of the verbs given.

1. —Carlitos tiene acné.
   —Yo lo llevaría (llevar) a un buen dermatólogo.
   —¿Tú crees que la Dra. Peña podría (poder) recomendarme uno?
   —Yo se lo preguntaría (preguntar).
2. —Mamá está muy nerviosa y no sé qué hacer.
   —Yo le daría (dar) un sedante.
   —Eso sería (ser) muy difícil porque a ella no le gusta tomar medicinas.
3. —¿Tú crees que Ana y yo podríamos (poder) ir al hospital a ver a Jorge?
   —Yo no iría (ir) hoy porque acaban de operarlo.
   —Pues sus padres dijeron que ellos lo visitarían (visitar) esta noche.
4. —Mi hijo tiene mucha acidez. ¿Qué le recomendarías (recomendar) tú?
   —Yo le sugeriría (sugerir) tomar un buen antiácido. Creo que mejoraría (mejorar) pronto.
5. —Pedro quiere que yo le compre un seguro médico; ¿qué harías (hacer) tú en mi caso? ¿Se lo comprarías (comprar)?
   —Bueno, yo no se lo compraría (comprar).

Suggestion: Encourage students to expand upon each answer by providing a reason.

B. Recomendaciones In groups of three or four, decide what you would recommend to a friend who has health problems, doesn't exercise, and has bad eating habits. Compare your recommendations with those of other groups, and select the best ones. *Answers will vary.*

Rodeo

Summary of the Tenses of the Indicative (*Resumen de los tiempos del indicativo*)

Simple Tenses

	-ar	**-er**	**-ir**
Presente	habl**o**	com**o**	viv**o**
Pretérito	habl**é**	com**í**	viv**í**
Imperfecto	habl**aba**	com**ía**	viv**ía**
Futuro	hablar**é**	comer**é**	vivir**é**
Condicional	hablar**ía**	comer**ía**	vivir**ía**

Compound Tenses			
Pretérito perfecto	**he** habl**ado**	**he** com**ido**	**he** viv**ido**
Pretérito plus-cuamperfecto	**había** habl**ado**	**había** com**ido**	**había** viv**ido**
Futuro perfecto[1]	**habré** habl**ado**	**habré** com**ido**	**habré** viv**ido**
Condicional perfecto[1]	**habría** habl**ado**	**habría** com**ido**	**habría** viv**ido**

[1]Optional material. See pages 340–345.

Práctica y conversación

Online Study Center

For more practice with lesson topics, see the related activities on the ***¡Hola, amigos!*** web site at college.hmco.com/PIC/holaamigos7e.

Entreviste a su compañero(a) Interview your partner, asking the following questions. *Answers will vary.*

1. ¿Cuánto tiempo hace que estudias español?
2. ¿En qué año empezaste a estudiar español?
3. ¿Quién fue tu profesor(a) de español el semestre pasado?
4. ¿Habías hablado con el (la) profesor(a) antes de comenzar esta clase?
5. ¿Sabías un poco de español antes de venir a la universidad?
6. ¿Continuarás estudiando español?
7. ¿Qué tendrás que hacer para hablar español perfectamente?
8. ¿Has visitado algún país de habla hispana?
9. ¿En qué país de habla hispana te gustaría vivir?
10. ¿Qué ciudades importantes de los Estados Unidos has visitado?
11. ¿Qué te gustaba hacer cuando estabas en la escuela secundaria?
12. ¿Qué películas has visto últimamente?
13. ¿Qué tuviste que hacer hoy antes de venir a la clase?
14. ¿Vives cerca o lejos de la universidad?

3. The imperfect subjunctive (*El imperfecto de subjuntivo*)

Forms

Suggestion: Review the preterit, especially the third-person plural, before you present this tense.

- To form the imperfect subjunctive of all Spanish verbs—regular and irregular—drop the **-ron** ending of the third-person plural of the preterit and add the following endings to the stem.

Imperfect Subjunctive Endings	
-ra	**-´ramos**
-ras	**-rais**
-ra	**-ran**

¡Atención! Notice that an accent mark is required in the **nosotros(as)** form:
...que nosotros habláramos
...que nosotros fuéramos

Suggestion: Point out that there is another form of the imperfect subjunctive: **-se, -ses, -se, -´semos, -seis, -sen.** Although the two forms may be used interchangeable in almost every case, the **-ra** ending is more commonly used.

Forms of the Imperfect Subjunctive

Verb	*Third-Person Preterit*	*Stem*	*First-Person Sing. Imperf. Subjunctive*
			(**-ra** *form*)
hablar	habla**ron**	habla-	**hablara**
aprender	aprendie**ron**	aprendie-	**aprendiera**
vivir	vivie**ron**	vivie-	**viviera**
dejar	deja**ron**	deja-	**dejara**
ir	fue**ron**	fue-	**fuera**
saber	supie**ron**	supie-	**supiera**
decir	dije**ron**	dije-	**dijera**
poner	pusie**ron**	pusie-	**pusiera**
pedir	pidie**ron**	pidie-	**pidiera**
estar	estuvie**ron**	estuvie-	**estuviera**

¡Atención! The imperfect subjunctive of **hay** (impersonal form of **haber**) is **hubiera.**

Online Study Center

For more practice with lesson topics, see the related activities on the ***¡Hola, amigos!*** web site at college.hmco.com/PIC/holaamigos7e.

Práctica

Conjugación Supply the imperfect subjunctive forms of the following verbs.

1. *que yo:* llenar, comer, vivir, decir, ir, admitir
2. *que tú:* dejar, atender, abrir, poner, estar, elegir
3. *que él:* volver, dormir, pedir, tener, alquilar, traer
4. *que nosotros:* ver, ser, entrar, saber, hacer, pedir
5. *que ellas:* leer, salir, llegar, sentarse, aprender, poder

Answers: 1. llenara / comiera / viviera / dijera / fuera / admitiera 2. dejaras / atendieras / abrieras / pusieras / estuvieras / eligieras 3. volviera / durmiera / pidiera/ tuvíera / alquilara / trajera 4. viéramos / fuéramos/entráramos / supiéramos / hiciéramos / pidiéramos 5. leyeran / salieran / llegaran / se sentaran / aprendieran / pudieran

Uses

- The imperfect subjunctive is always used in a subordinate clause when the verb of the main clause calls for the subjunctive and is in the past or the conditional.

Expansion: Write on the board:
MAIN CLAUSE
Yo **quería**
↓
Past tense
SUBORDINATE CLAUSE
que tú **vinieras.**
↓
Imperfect Subjunctive
MAIN CLAUSE
Siento
↓
Present tense
SUBORDINATE CLAUSE
que tú no **vinieras ayer.**
↓ ↓
Imperfect Subjunctive / Refers to past

—¿Por qué no compraste los billetes?	*"Why didn't you buy the tickets?"*
—**Temía** que no **pudiéramos** viajar hoy.	***"I was afraid we wouldn't be able** to travel today."*

- When the verb of the main clause is in the present, but the subordinate clause refers to the past, the imperfect subjunctive is often used.

—Oscar es un muchacho muy simpático.	*"Oscar is a very charming young man."*
—¡Sí! **Me alegro** de que **viniera** a vernos ayer.	*"Yes! **I'm glad** (that) **he came** to see us yesterday."*

Práctica y conversación

For more practice with lesson topics, see the related activities on the ***¡Hola, amigos!*** web site at college.hmco.com/PIC/holaamigos7e.

A. Instrucciones Indicate what Dr. Peña told some of her patients to do. Follow the model.

- **MODELO:** Sra. Paz, descanse.
  Le dijo a la Sra. Paz que descansara.

1. Sr. Mena, tome un jarabe para la tos.
2. Elena y Sara, pidan turno para mañana.
3. Srta. Rivas, vaya a ver a un oculista.
4. Sra. Ruiz, hable con la recepcionista.
5. Sr. López, esté aquí mañana a las ocho. Venga en ayunas (*fasting*).
6. Miguel y Pablo, pídanle la receta a la enfermera.
7. Señores, espérenme unos minutos.
8. Señora, abra la boca y diga "ah".
9. Juanito, respira hondo.
10. Señora, dele un calmante a su papá.

Answers: 1. Le dijo al Sr. Mena que tomara un jarabe para la tos. **2.** Les dijo a Elena y a Sara que pidieran turno para mañana. **3.** Le dijo a la Srta. Rivas que fuera a ver a un oculista. **4.** Le dijo a la Sra. Ruiz que hablara con la recepcionista. **5.** Le dijo al Sr. López que estuviera aquí mañana a las ocho y que viniera en ayunas. **6.** Les dijo a Miguel y a Pablo que le pidieran la receta a la enfermera. **7.** Les dijo a los señores que lo esperaran unos minutos. **8.** Le dijo a la señora que abriera la boca y que dijera "ah". **9.** Le dijo a Juanito que respirara hondo. **10.** Le dijo a la señora que le diera un calmante a su papá.

B. Mi primera cita In groups of three, talk about what your parents told you to do and what not to do when you went out on your first date.

Answers will vary.

4. *If*-clauses (*Cláusulas que comienzan con* si)

- When a clause introduced by **si** refers to a situation that is hypothetical or contrary to fact, **si** is always followed by the imperfect subjunctive.

Contrary-to-fact

—**Si** yo **tuviera** dinero, le daría 1.000 dólares a mi hijo.	*"**If** I **had** money, I would give my son a thousand dollars."*
—**Si** yo **fuera** tú, no le daría nada.	*"**If** I **were** you, I wouldn't give him anything."*

Hypothetical

Si yo **hablara** con el presidente...	***If** I **were to speak** to the president . . .*

Alternative: Give an English example of a hypothetical statement: If ***I were*** *you, I would go.* (Not *I was*, but *I were* = subjunctive.)

Extra practice: Write the following sentence builder on the board or on an overhead transparency. Have students tell, orally or in writing, what they or their friends would do if they followed certain careers. Remind them that they should use the imperfect subjunctive in the **si** clause and the conditional in the main clause.

Si yo fuera actriz, viajaría por todo el mundo.

Si

mi amigo(a) / tú / mi compañero(a) de cuarto / mi novio(a) / mi hermano(a)

ser

actor, actriz / médico(a) / psicólogo(a) / profesor(a) / arquitecto(a) / escritor(a) / científico(a)

hacer / tener / trabajar / participar / viajar / escribir / necesitar / ganar / estar

¡Atención! Note that the imperfect subjunctive is used in the *if*-clause, while the conditional is used in the main clause.

Si yo **tuviera** dinero, le **daría** 1.000 dólares a mi hijo.	*If I **had** money, **I would give** a thousand dollars to my son.*

- When the *if*-clause refers to something that is likely to happen or possible, the indicative is used.

—¿**Puedes** llevar a mi papá al cardiólogo?	*"**Can you** take my dad to the cardiologist?"*
—Lo llevaré si **tengo** tiempo.	*"I will take him if **I have** time."*

¡Atención! The present subjunctive is never used in an *if*-clause.

- The imperfect subjunctive is always used after the expression **como si** (*as if*) because it implies a condition that is contrary to fact.

—Marcos dice que necesito un antibiótico.	*"Marcos says that I need an antibiotic."*
—Sí, él habla **como si supiera** algo de medicina.	*"Yes, he talks **as if he knew** something about medicine."*

Práctica y conversación

Online Study Center

For more practice with lesson topics, see the related activities on the *¡Hola, amigos!* web site at college.hmco.com/PIC/holaamigos7e.

A. ¿Promesas o excusas? Complete each of the following statements with the correct form of the verb in parentheses. Use the imperfect subjunctive or the present indicative.

1. Si yo ___tengo___ (tener) tiempo te llevaré al médico.
2. Si nosotros ___pudiéramos___ (poder) compraríamos las medicinas.
3. Si Elba ___compra___ (comprar) las tijeras podemos ponerlas en el botiquín.
4. Si mis padres me ___dieran___ (dar) dinero yo podría pagar el seguro médico.
5. Si tú ___vienes___ (venir) temprano podremos llevar a los niños al pediatra.
6. Si Uds. ___trajeran___ (traer) a Nora el doctor podría examinarla.

Expansion: Have students interview each other using questions that require the use of the imperfect subjunctive and the conditional. Write the model and the infinitive phrases on the board or on an overhead transparency.

¿Qué harías si...
tuvieras mucho dinero
no poder tomar el examen final
necesitar comprar un coche nuevo
estar de vacaciones
tener hambre / sed
no tener clase hoy
tener tres días libres
ser invisible

B. Si... Referring to the pictures below for ideas, tell what the following people would do if circumstances were different. *Answers will vary.*

- **MODELO:** Yo no tengo dinero. Si...
  Si yo tuviera dinero, viajaría.

1. Ellos no tienen hambre. Si...

2. Nosotros no podemos estudiar hoy. Si...

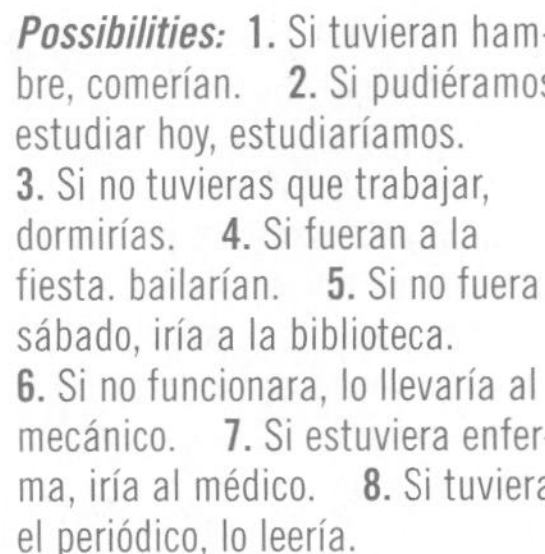

Possibilities: **1.** Si tuvieran hambre, comerían. **2.** Si pudiéramos estudiar hoy, estudiaríamos. **3.** Si no tuvieras que trabajar, dormirías. **4.** Si fueran a la fiesta. bailarían. **5.** Si no fuera sábado, iría a la biblioteca. **6.** Si no funcionara, lo llevaría al mecánico. **7.** Si estuviera enferma, iría al médico. **8.** Si tuviera el periódico, lo leería.

3. Tú tienes que trabajar. Si no...

4. Uds. no van a la fiesta. Si...

5. Hoy es sábado. Si...

6. El coche funciona. Si...

7. Laura no está enferma. Si...

8. La señora Soto no tiene el periódico. Si...

Suggestion: Start by giving one or two hypotheticals about your own life. If needed, write some phrases on the board: **si vivir en otra ciudad/otro país, si cambiar de universidad,** etc. Encourage students to mention three or four things each.

Suggestion: Have students provide new examples for all uses.

C. Si las cosas fueran diferentes In groups of three or four, discuss what you would do if circumstances in your lives were different. Include place of residence, schooling, work, and so on. *Answers will vary.*

Rodeo

Summary of the Uses of the Subjunctive (*Resumen de los usos del subjuntivo*)

Subjunctive vs. Infinitive

Use the subjunctive . . .	Use the infinitive . . .
1. After verbs of volition (when there is a change of subject). **Yo** quiero que **él salga.**	**1.** After verbs of volition (where there is no change of subject). **Yo** quiero **salir.**
2. After verbs of emotion (when there is a change of subject). **Me** alegro de que **tú estés** aquí.	**2.** After verbs of emotion (when there is no change of subject). **Me** alegro de **estar** aquí.
3. After impersonal expressions (when there is a subject). Es necesario que **él estudie.**	**3.** After impersonal expressions (when speaking in general). Es necesario **estudiar.**

Subjunctive vs. Indicative

Use the subjunctive . . .	Use the indicative . . .
1. To refer to something indefinite or nonexistent. Busco una casa que **sea** grande. No hay nadie que lo **sepa.**	**1.** To refer to something that exists or is specific. Tengo una casa que **es** grande. Hay alguien que lo **sabe.**
2. If the action is to occur at some indefinite time in the future as a condition of another action. Cenarán cuando él **llegue.**	**2.** If the action has been completed or is habitual. Cenaron cuando él **llegó.** Siempre cenan cuando él **llega.**
3. To express doubt, disbelief, and denial. Dudo que **pueda** venir. Niego que él **esté** aquí. No creo que él **venga.**	**3.** When there is no doubt, disbelief, or denial. No dudo que **puede** venir. No niego que él **está** aquí. Creo que él **viene.**
4. In an *if*-clause, to refer to something contrary to fact, impossible, or very improbable. Si **pudiera,** iría. Si el presidente me **invitara** a la Casa Blanca, yo aceptaría.	**4.** In an *if*-clause, when referring to something that is factual, probable, or very possible. Si **puedo,** iré. Si Juan me **invita** a su casa, aceptaré.

Práctica y conversación

For more practice with lesson topics, see the related activities on the *¡Hola, amigos!* web site at college.hmco.com/PIC/holaamigos7e.

A. La carta de Marisa Marisa wrote this letter to her parents from Sevilla. Complete it, using the subjunctive, indicative, or infinitive of the verbs that appear in parentheses.

Sevilla, 10 de junio

Queridos papá y mamá:

Recibí la tarjeta que me mandaron de Acapulco. Me alegro de que se __estén__ (estar) divirtiendo; cuando __vuelvan__ (volver) a México el año próximo, yo quiero __ir__ (ir) con Uds. También me gustaría que Uds. __pudieran__ (poder) visitar Sevilla, porque es una ciudad magnífica.

Ana y yo encontramos un piso que __está__ (estar) en el centro, cerca de la universidad. Si Uds. __deciden__ (decidir) venir a visitarme, tenemos un dormitorio extra. No creo que los padres de Ana __puedan__ (poder) venir, como nos habían dicho, porque no les dan vacaciones.

Mamá, es verdad que la comida de aquí __es__ (ser) muy buena, pero no hay nadie que __cocine__ (cocinar) tan bien como tú, así que en cuanto yo __llegue__ (llegar) a California, quiero que me __hagas__ (hacer) tu famoso pollo con mole[1].

Ayer fuimos con unos amigos a visitar la mezquita y después fuimos a un café en el barrio Santa Cruz. ¡Me estoy enamorando de Sevilla! Si __pudiera__ (poder), me quedaría a vivir aquí. ¡No se rían! Ya sé que no puedo vivir lejos de Uds.

Díganle a Héctor que quiero que me __escriba__ (escribir) y me __cuente__ (contar) cómo le va en la universidad.

Besos,

Marisa

B. ¿Qué recuerdan Uds.? With a partner, prepare five or six questions about Marisa's letter. Then join two classmates and ask them your questions and answer theirs. *Answers will vary.*

[1]**Mole,** a sauce made with many spices and unsweetened chocolate, is used in Mexican cuisine.

Entre nosotros

¡Conversemos!

Para conocernos mejor Get to know your partner better by asking each other the following questions. *Answers will vary.*

1. ¿Necesitas que el (la) médico(a) te examine?
2. ¿El consultorio de tu médico(a) está cerca de tu casa?
3. ¿Eres alérgico(a) a alguna medicina o comida? ¿A cuál?
4. ¿Qué tomas cuando tienes dolor de cabeza?
5. ¿Has tenido que tomar un sedante alguna vez?
6. ¿Qué haces cuando tienes gripe?
7. ¿Has tenido que ir al oculista últimamente?
8. La última vez que fuiste a tu médico, ¿qué te recetó?
9. ¿Cuándo tendrás que volver a ver al médico?
10. ¿Te gustaría ser médico(a) o enfermero(a)?

Una encuesta Interview your classmates to identify who fits the following descriptions. Include your instructor, but remember to use the **Ud.** form when addressing him or her. *Answers will vary.*

	Nombre
1. Trabajaría en un hospital.	
2. Necesita ir al oculista.	
3. Tiene turno para ver al médico el mes próximo.	
4. Toma Tylenol cuando tiene fiebre.	
5. Toma vitamina C todos los días.	
6. Es alérgico(a) a la penicilina.	
7. Ha tenido gripe recientemente.	
8. Toma antiácidos frecuentemente.	
9. Espera poder descansar este fin de semana.	
10. Da consejos como si fuera médico(a).	

Y ahora... Write a brief summary about what you have learned about your classmates. *Answers will vary.*

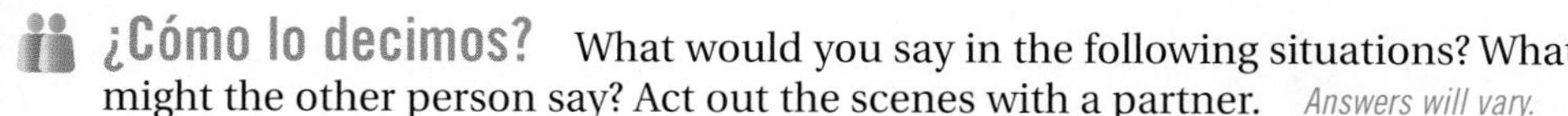

¿Cómo lo decimos? What would you say in the following situations? What might the other person say? Act out the scenes with a partner. *Answers will vary.*

1. You have the flu. Tell the doctor what your symptoms are.
2. You are giving advice to someone who has a cold and a bad cough.
3. Tell someone what your mother wants you to do when you are sick.

Suggestion: Have students work in pairs on dialogues for presentation in class on the subject of an appointment with the doctor. Dialogues may be real or fictitious, serious, or humorous.

¿Qué dice aquí? Read the ad, and answer the questions that follow.

1. Si una persona necesita perder peso (*weight*), ¿a que médico debe ir?
2. ¿Cuál es la especialidad de Luis Díaz?
3. Una amiga mía está embarazada. ¿Por qué debe ver a la Dra. Vega?
4. ¿Qué pruebas rutinarias debe hacerse una mujer?
5. ¿Qué servicios ofrece el Dr. Vargas?
6. ¿Por qué cree Ud. que el Dr. Díaz tiene más pacientes adolescentes?
7. Hace tiempo que no voy al médico. ¿Por qué debo ver a la Dra. López?
8. ¿Puedo ir al Centro Médico Regional el sábado? ¿Por qué ?
9. Yo no tengo seguro, ¿puedo ir a ver a alguno de los médicos del Centro?
10. ¿Cuál es la dirección y el número de teléfono del Centro Médico Regional?

Answers: **1.** Debe ver a la Dra. Rita López. **2.** Luis Díaz es dermatólogo. **3.** Porque la Dra. Vega es ginecóloga. **4.** Debe hacerse un Papanicolau y una mamografía. **5.** El Dr. Vargas ofrece un examen completo de la vista, anteojos y lentes de contacto, cirugía de cataratas y cirugía con laser. **6.** Creo que el Dr. Díaz tiene más pacientes adolescentes porque éstos generalmente tienen acné. **7.** Debe ver a la Dra. López porque ella es especialista en medicina general. **8.** No, no puede ir el sábado porque las consultas son de lunes a viernes. **9.** Sí, puede ir porque el Centro tiene planes de pago para pacientes que no tienen seguro. **10.** La dirección es Alonso Cano 192, Madrid. El teléfono es 3–27–93–84.

Un dicho

Es mejor prevenir que curar.

Another saying! What does it mean? Have you thought of an English equivalent? Use it every chance you get.

Para escribir

Con el doctor Write a dialogue between you and your doctor. Among the things you might discuss are: symptoms, general questions the doctor might ask, any questions you have, the advice and/or treatment the doctor offers. *Answers will vary.*

Suggestion: This exercise may be assigned as homework and presented orally in class.

Lectura

Suggestion: Stress to students that visualizing the words or images in a poem will help them better understand the feelings or message the poet is conveying.

Estrategia de lectura Reading a poem is different from reading a story or an essay. A poet often uses words in original ways to express his/her feelings. Think about the following words from *Rimas,* which you are going to read. Try to visualize them individually, and then together. What feelings do they convey? *Answers will vary.*

tierra	*earth*	mundo	*world*
cielo	*heaven*	beso	*kiss*
alma	*soul*	suspiros	*sighs*
sol	*sun*	lágrimas	*tears*
poesía	*poetry*	amor	*love*

Vamos a leer As you read this poem, try to answer the following questions.

1. ¿En quién cree hoy el poeta? ¿Por qué?
2. ¿De qué color son los ojos de la mujer que el poeta ama?
3. ¿Qué le pregunta la mujer al poeta?
4. ¿Qué le contesta el poeta?
5. ¿Qué daría el poeta por una mirada (*look*) de su amada?
6. ¿Qué daría por una sonrisa (*smile*)?
7. ¿Qué cree que sería lo más maravilloso para el poeta?
8. ¿Con qué compara el poeta los suspiros y las lágrimas?

Answers: **1.** Hoy cree en Dios porque ha visto a la mujer que ama. **2.** Los ojos de la mujer son azules. **3.** La mujer le pregunta, "¿Qué es poesía?" **4.** El poeta le contesta "Poesía... eres tú." **5.** El poeta daría un mundo por una mirada. **6.** Daría un cielo por una sonrisa. **7.** Lo más maravilloso sería un beso. **8.** Compara los suspiros con el aire y las lágrimas con el agua que va al mar.

Gustavo Adolfo Bécquer nació en Sevilla, España, en 1836 y murió en el año 1870. Se le considera un precursor de la poesía moderna, y se le conoce mayormente por sus Rimas *y sus* Leyendas. *Sus poemas son breves y suponen la máxima condensación lírica. Los temas principales de su poesía son el amor, la soledad y el misterio.*

Video

Rimas

Gustavo Adolfo Bécquer

XVII

Hoy la tierra y los cielos me sonríen;
hoy llega al fondo de mi alma el sol;
hoy la he visto..., la he visto y me ha mirado...
¡Hoy creo en Dios!

XXI

"¿Qué es poesía?," dices mientras clavas
en mi pupila tu pupila azul;
¿Qué es poesía? ¿Y tú me lo preguntas?
Poesía... eres tú.

XXIII

Por una mirada, un mundo;
por una sonrisa, un cielo;
por un beso... ¡yo no sé
qué te diera por un beso!

XXXVIII

¡Los suspiros son aire y van al aire!
¡Las lágrimas son agua y van al mar!
Dime, mujer, cuando el amor se olvida,
¿sabes tú a dónde va?

Díganos Answer the following questions based on your own thoughts or experiences. *Answers will vary.*

1. ¿Está Ud. enamorado(a)? ¿De quién?
2. ¿De qué color son los ojos de su amado(a)?
3. ¿A quién le ha dado Ud. un beso últimamente?
4. ¿Ha tenido Ud. un amor que ahora sólo es parte de su pasado?

¡Uno nunca sabe...!

Marisa y Pablo están estudiando juntos. Él se queja de un montón de problemas físicos y ella le dice que es un hipocondríaco.

Continúan hablando, y los dos admiten que se necesitan el uno al otro. ¿Continuarán siendo amigos...?

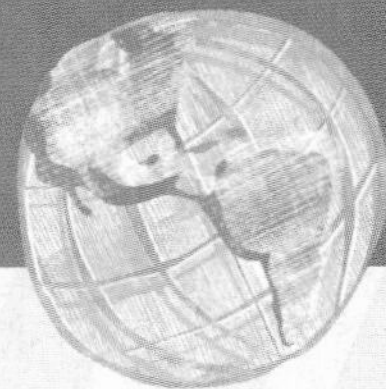

El mundo hispánico

España

Video/DVD

- España forma con Portugal la Península Ibérica, y es el tercer país europeo en cuanto a extensión. Por su situación entre el resto de Europa y África siempre ha poseído considerable valor (*value*) estratégico, y en su suelo se mezclaron (*mixed*) y fundieron (*melted*) diversos grupos étnicos provenientes (*coming*) de una gran variedad de civilizaciones; entre ellas, las más importantes fueron la romana, la judía y la árabe (*Arabic*).
- El relieve de España varía desde las cordilleras hasta los valles, llanuras (*plains*) y extensas mesetas. En los Pirineos, que sirven de frontera con Francia, se encuentran algunos de los picos más altos de Europa.
- Por su clima y sus magníficas playas, España es uno de los países de más turismo en el mundo.
- El sistema de gobierno español es una monarquía constitucional. El actual rey (*king*) es Juan Carlos de Borbón. España pertenece a la Unión Europea y su moneda es el euro.

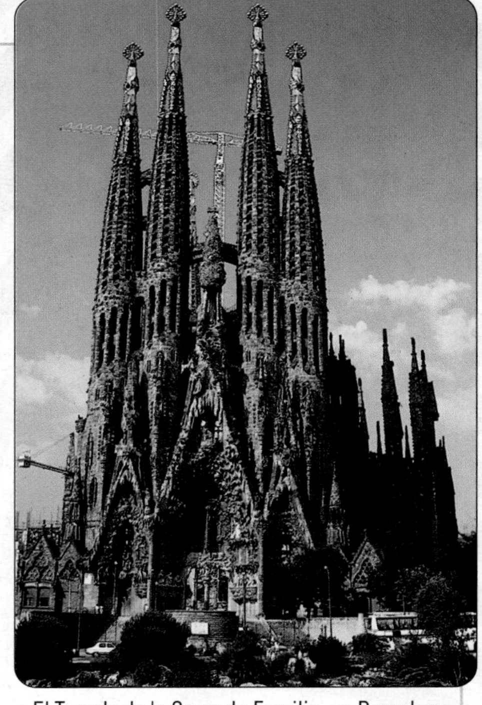

▲ El Templo de la Sagrada Familia, en Barcelona.

▲ Admirando unas pinturas en el famoso Museo del Prado en Madrid

- Madrid, la capital, es una ciudad moderna, y hoy en día es uno de los centros de negocios más importantes del mundo. Es una ciudad de gran movimiento y se dice que "Madrid nunca duerme". Sus grandes avenidas, centros culturales, plazas y museos son puntos de atracción turística. A pesar de ser una gran metrópoli, Madrid conserva grandes extensiones de áreas verdes, como el parque del Buen Retiro, La Rosaleda, el Parque del Oeste y el Prado. En Madrid está el Museo del Prado, uno de los mejores del mundo. Allí se conserva la colección más grande de las obras de pintores españoles como Murillo, Velázquez, El Greco y Goya, entre otros.
- En el norte de España están Barcelona, la segunda ciudad más grande del país y Pamplona, conocida por sus encierros y sus corridas de toros el día de San Fermín.
- En el sur de España se encuentran Granada, Sevilla y Córdoba, ciudades de gran belleza donde se ve la influencia árabe. La Alhambra de Granada, la Giralda de Sevilla y la Mezquita (*Mosque*) de Córdoba son verdaderas joyas arquitectónicas. Sevilla tiene además el maravilloso Parque de María Luisa, donde se encuentra la gran Plaza de España. En esta plaza, construida enteramente de azulejos (*ceramic tiles*) de tipo andaluz, están representadas escenas históricas de las cincuenta provincias de España.

◂ *Guernica,* uno de los cuadros más famosos de Picasso. Museo Reina Sofía, Madrid.

- Las playas de Andalucía, conocidas como la "Costa del Sol", están entre las más famosas atracciones turísticas del país, y son visitadas todo el año gracias a su clima cálido, aun en invierno.
- España es rica en tradiciones. Cada provincia tiene sus propios trajes regionales, música, artesanía y cocina típicas.
- Aunque no hay ninguna región española que no produzca su propio vino, Andalucía es la gran tierra del vino, por su gran calidad y variedad. Andalucía es famosa, además, por el cultivo del olivo y, en la música y en la danza, por el flamenco.
- España ha aportado (*exerted*) su influencia al mundo tanto en el campo de la ciencia como en el de la cultura, y ha obtenido premios Nobel en ambos campos. En la literatura, España se ha destacado desde la Edad Media. Entre sus numerosos escritores está Miguel de Cervantes, creador de *Don Quijote,* una de las obras literarias que más ha influido en todo el mundo. Tres grandes pintores del siglo XX, conocidos mundialmente, son españoles: Salvador Dalí, Joan Miró y Pablo Picasso.

▴ Corriendo delante de los toros en la Feria de San Fermín, en Pamplona

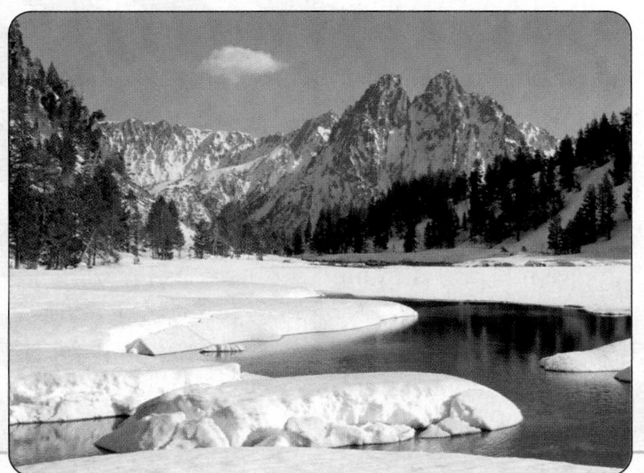

◂ Paisaje de invierno. Lago San Mauricio, Parque Nacional Aigüestortes, en los Pirineos.

Comentarios... With a partner, discuss in Spanish what impressed you the most about Spain. Compare this country to your own. Which places do you want to visit in this country and why?

For more practice with lesson topics, see the related activities on the *¡Hola, amigos!* web site at college.hmco.com/PIC/holaamigos7e.

Tome este examen

Lección 13

Lección 13

A. Subjunctive to express doubt

Complete the following sentences, using the subjunctive or the indicative of the verbs in parentheses.

1. Estoy seguro de que ellos ___son___ (ser) alérgicos a las fresas.
2. Dudo que ella ___esté___ (estar) en el hospital.
3. No estoy seguro de que él ___pueda___ (poder) llevarnos al hospital.
4. Estamos seguros de que ellos ___vienen___ (venir) hoy.
5. No dudo que ellos ___sirven___ (servir) el almuerzo a esa hora.

B. Subjunctive to express disbelief and denial

Rewrite each sentence, using the subjunctive or the indicative, as appropriate.

Answers: **1.** estén llamando la ambulancia. **2.** ellos vayan a quedarse en el hospital. **3.** prefiere venir con nosotros. **4.** cobran 50 dólares por las radiografías. **5.** el cuarto no tenga calefacción. **6.** ella esté en el hospital.

1. Están llamando la ambulancia. (No es cierto que...)
2. Ellos van a quedarse en el hospital. (No creo que...)
3. Ella prefiere venir con nosotros. (Es verdad que ella...)
4. Cobran 50 dólares por las radiografías. (Creo que...)
5. El cuarto no tiene calefacción. (No es verdad que...)
6. Ella está en el hospital. (Luis niega que...)

C. Subjunctive with certain conjunctions

Complete each sentence with the Spanish equivalent of the word(s) in parentheses.

1. Voy a llamar al médico en cuanto ellos ___terminen___. (*finish*)
2. No vamos a menos que ___podamos___ ir con él. (*we can*)
3. Voy a llamar a la enfermera para que nos ___traiga___ la radiografía. (*bring*)
4. Vamos a ir tan pronto como ellos ___empiecen___ a servir la comida. (*begin*)
5. Siempre voy a ese hospital cuando ___necesito un médico___. (*I need a doctor*)
6. En cuanto yo ___llegue___ a casa, voy a llamar a mis padres. (*arrive*)
7. Aunque ___no tengo hambre___, vamos al comedor. (*I'm not hungry*)
8. Mañana vamos a ir al cine aunque ___llueva___. (*it may rain*)

D. First-person plural commands

Answer the following questions, using the information provided in parentheses and first-person plural (**nosotros**) commands.

Answers: **1.** Quedémonos aquí. **2.** No se lo digamos a nadie. **3.** Levantémonos a las siete. **4.** Preguntemos el precio de los análisis. **5.** Démoselo a la enfermera. **6.** Vamos a la sala de rayos X.

1. ¿Dónde nos quedamos? (aquí)
2. ¿A quién se lo decimos? (a nadie)
3. ¿A qué hora nos levantamos? (a las siete)
4. ¿Qué preguntamos? (el precio de los análisis)
5. ¿A quién se lo damos? (a la enfermera)
6. ¿Adónde vamos? (a la sala de rayos X)

E. *¿Qué?* and *¿cuál?* with *ser* Complete the following, using **qué** or **cuál.**

1. ¿ Cuál es tu dirección?
2. ¿ Cuál es tu número de teléfono?
3. ¿ Qué es el béisbol?
4. ¿ Qué es una enchilada?
5. ¿ Cuál es su opinión?

F. Vocabulary Write the vocabulary words from **Lección 13** that correspond to the following words or descriptions.

1. Trabaja con el médico.
2. parte del brazo
3. perder el conocimiento
4. Tenemos diez en las manos.
5. Tenemos treinta y dos en la boca.
6. suceder
7. tener dudas
8. seguir
9. La usamos para subir y bajar.
10. Las uso para caminar.
11. Los necesitamos para ver.
12. Está dentro de la boca.
13. quebrarse
14. instrumento musical

Answers: **1.** enfermera **2.** codo **3.** desmayarse **4.** dedos **5.** dientes **6.** pasar **7.** dudar **8.** continuar **9.** escalera **10.** piernas **11.** ojos **12.** lengua **13.** romperse **14.** piano

Lección 13

G. Culture Complete the following sentences, based on the cultural notes you have read.

1. En la mayoría de los países hispanos, los hospitales son gratis .
2. En las casas de socorro se ofrecen cuidados médicos urgentes.

Lección 14

Lección 14

A. Future tense Change the verbs in these sentences to indicate what will take place.

Answers: 1. Irán/hablarán 2. pesarás/tomarás 3. traerá/pondrá 4. vendré/pediré 5. pondrá/dará

1. Van al consultorio y hablan con el médico.
2. Tú la pesas y le tomas la presión.
3. Rosa trae las radiografías y las pone en la oficina.
4. Yo vengo al hospital y pido turno.
5. La enfermera me pone una inyección y me da el jarabe.

B. Conditional tense Complete the following sentences, using the conditional form of the verbs in parentheses.

1. Nosotros no hablaríamos (hablar) con ellos.
2. Yo saldría (salir) temprano.
3. ¿Tú harías (hacer) eso?
4. Ella no sabría (saber) qué hacer.
5. ¿Adónde iría (ir) Ud. hoy?
6. Ellos le pedirían (pedir) turno.

C. Forms of the imperfect subjunctive Give the imperfect subjunctive of the following verbs according to the cues provided.

Answers: 1. pudiéramos 2. entendieras 3. pusieran 4. quisiera 5. trajera 6. tuvieran 7. supiéramos 8. dijera 9. fuera 10. fueras

1. nosotros / poder
2. tú / entender
3. ellos / poner
4. yo / querer
5. Ud. / traer
6. Uds. / tener
7. nosotras / saber
8. ella / decir
9. yo / ir
10. tú / ser

D. Uses of the imperfect subjunctive Complete the following sentences using the imperfect subjunctive of the verbs given.

1. Ella me pidió que trajera (traer) la receta.
2. Yo esperaba que mis padres vinieran (venir) hoy.
3. Ellos dudaban que yo estuviera (estar) enfermo.
4. No había nadie que supiera (saber) dónde estaba el médico.
5. Te dije que no era verdad que ella tuviera (tener) esa enfermedad.
6. Mi esposo quería que yo pidiera (pedir) turno para hoy.

E. *If*-clauses Complete each sentence with the equivalent of the words in parentheses.

1. Yo compraría el antibiótico... (*if I had the money*)
2. Vamos a ir a verte... (*if we have time*)
3. Nosotros iríamos a Barcelona... (*if we could*)
4. (*If you see her*)..., dígale que venga mañana.
5. Ella le habla a su esposo... (*as if she were his mother*)

Answers: **1.** si tuviera dinero. **2.** si tenemos tiempo. **3.** si pudiéramos. **4.** Si Ud. la ve **5.** como si (ella) fuera su madre.

Lección 14

F. Vocabulary Complete the following sentences, using vocabulary from **Lección 14.**

1. Tiene una temperatura de treinta y nueve __grados__.
2. El médico me recetó un jarabe para la __tos__.
3. Espero que Ud. se __mejore__ con estas medicinas.
4. El médico le va a __recetar__ un antibiótico.
5. Necesita un __calmante__ porque tiene mucho dolor.
6. Si tienes acné ve a un __dermatólogo__ y si tienes problemas con el corazón a un __cardiólogo__.
7. Necesito las __tijeras__ para cortar las vendas.
8. No se mejoró; se __empeoró__.
9. Mi __cita (turno)__ con el médico es para hoy.
10. No tuvo que pagar el hospital porque tiene __seguro__ médico.
11. Puse el esparadrapo en el __botiquín__.
12. Por __suerte__ no tiene pulmonía.

G. Culture Circle the correct answer, base on the cultural notes you have read.

1. (Barcelona / Madrid) es la capital de España.
2. Barcelona es la (segunda / tercera) ciudad más grande del país.
3. En el sur de España se encuentra (Sevilla / Valencia).
4. La música típica de Andalucía es el (tango / flamenco).

Answers: **1.** Madrid **2.** segunda **3.** Sevilla **4.** flamenco

Un poco más (*Material suplementario*)

1. Compound tenses of the indicative

Future perfect (*El futuro perfecto*)

◆ Forms

The future perfect tense in Spanish corresponds closely in formation and meaning to the same tense in English. The Spanish future perfect is formed with the future tense of the auxiliary verb **haber** + past participle of the main verb.

Formation of the Future Perfect Tense

	Future of haber	+ *Past Participle*	
yo	**habré**	**terminado**	I will have finished
tú	**habrás**	**vuelto**	you (*fam.*) will have returned
Ud., él, ella	**habrá**	**comido**	you (*form.*), he, she will have eaten
nosotros(as)	**habremos**	**escrito**	we will have written
vosotros(as)	**habréis**	**dicho**	you (*fam.*) will have said
Uds., ellos, ellas	**habrán**	**salido**	you (*form., fam.*), they will have left

◆ Use

Like its English equivalent, the Spanish future perfect tense is used to express an action that will have taken place by a certain time in the future.

—¿Tus padres estarán aquí para el dos de junio? *"Will your parents be here by June second?"*
—Sí, para esa fecha ya **habrán vuelto** de Madrid. *"Yes, by that date **they will have returned** from Madrid."*

Online Study Center

For more practice with lesson topics, see the related activities on the ***¡Hola, amigos!*** web site at college.hmco.com/PIC/holaamigos7e.

Práctica y conversación

A. Complete each sentence with the corresponding form of the future perfect tense.

1. Para junio nosotros _habremos vuelto_ (volver) del viaje, pero Carlos no _habrá llegado_ (llegar) de México todavía.
2. Para las nueve yo _habré servido_ (servir) la cena y ellos _habrán comido_ (comer).
3. ¿A qué hora _habrás terminado_ (terminar) tú el trabajo?
4. ¿Ya _habrán leído_ (leer) Uds. la novela para la próxima semana?
5. Para las doce la secretaria _habrá escrito_ (escribir) todas las cartas.

B. Interview a partner, using the following questions. *Answers will vary.*

1. ¿Habremos terminado esta lección para la semana que viene?
2. ¿Las clases habrán terminado para el 15 de junio?
3. ¿Te habrás graduado (*graduate*) para el año que viene?
4. ¿Tú habrás vuelto a tu casa para las 10 de la noche?
5. ¿Tú y tu familia habrán terminado de cenar para las siete de la noche?
6. ¿Te habrás acostado para las once de la noche?

C. Use your imagination to complete each statement, using the future perfect tense. *Answers will vary.*

1. Para el próximo año yo...
2. Para diciembre mis padres...
3. Para el sábado mi mejor amigo(a)...
4. Para la próxima semana el (la) profesor(a)...
5. Para el verano nosotros(as)...
6. Para esta noche tú...

Conditional perfect (*El condicional perfecto*)

- Forms

The conditional perfect tense is formed with the conditional of the verb **haber** + *past participle* of the main verb.

Formation of the Conditional Perfect Tense

	Conditional of haber +	*Past Participle*	
yo	**habría**	**hablado**	I would have spoken
tú	**habrías**	**comido**	you (*fam.*) would have eaten
Ud., él, ella	**habría**	**vuelto**	you (*form.*), he, she would have returned
nosotros(as)	**habríamos**	**dicho**	we would have said
vosotros(as)	**habríais**	**roto**	you (*fam.*) would have broken
Uds., ellos, ellas	**habrían**	**hecho**	you (*form., fam.*), they would have done, made

- Uses

The conditional perfect (expressed in English by *would have* + past participle of the main verb) is used:

- To indicate an action that *would have taken place* (*but didn't*), if a certain condition had been true.

De haber sabido[1] que venía, lo **habría llamado.** — *Had I known that he was coming, **I would have called** him.*

- To refer to a future action in relation to the past.

Él dijo que para mayo **habrían terminado** la clase. — *He said that by May **they would have finished** the class.*

[1]**De haber sabido** is an impersonal expression.

Online Study Center

For more practice with lesson topics, see the related activities on the *¡Hola, amigos!* web site at college.hmco.com/PIC/holaamigos7e.

Suggestion: Write the following infinitive phrases on the board. Then have students tell about the things they or their friends wanted to do or should have done over the weekend but for some reason did not.

Mi compañero habría limpiado el apartamento.
reunirse para planear una fiesta
ver a la familia
leer una novela interesante
lavar el coche
bañar al perro
pasar más tiempo en la biblioteca
ir al banco para sacar dinero
limpiar el apartamento
ir al supermercado para hacer las compras de la semana
tomar algo en la cafetería

Práctica y conversación

A. Complete each sentence, using the conditional perfect tense of the verbs given in parentheses.

1. De haber sabido que él no estaba aquí, yo no habría venido (venir).
2. De haber sabido que yo no tenía dinero, él me lo habría comprado (comprar).
3. Él dijo que para mayo nosotros habríamos vuelto (volver).
4. Carlos nos dijo que para septiembre tú habrías terminado (terminar).
5. De haber sabido que Uds. tenían los libros, ellos se los habrían pedido (pedir).
6. Él me dijo que para esta noche ellos habrían llamado (llamar).

B. Using the conditional perfect tense and the cues provided, tell what you and the other people would have done differently.

◆ **MODELO:** Tú fuiste de vacaciones a México. (yo)
Yo habría ido a España.

1. Ellos comieron hamburguesas. (yo) Yo habría comido...
2. Teresa salió con Ernesto. (tú) Tú habrías salido...
3. Yo preparé pollo para la cena. (ellos) Ellos habrían preparado...
4. Uds. estuvieron en México por una semana. (nosotras) Nosotras habríamos estado...
5. Nosotros invitamos a muchas personas. (Marta) Marta habría invitado...
6. Yo escribí las cartas en español. (Uds.) Uds. habrían escrito...

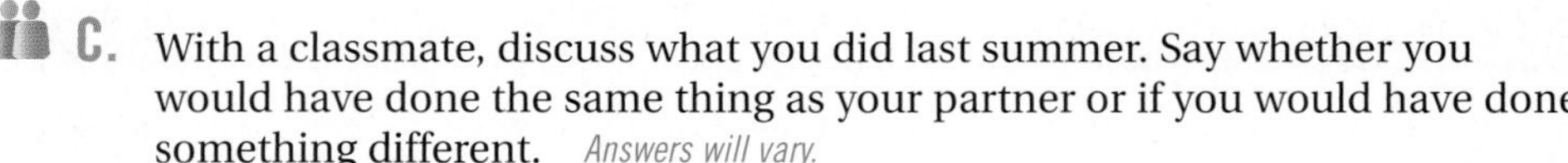

C. With a classmate, discuss what you did last summer. Say whether you would have done the same thing as your partner or if you would have done something different. *Answers will vary.*

2. Compound tenses of the subjunctive

Suggestion: Write the following sentence builder on the board or on an overhead transparency. Have students form, orally or in writing, as many sentences as possible in three minutes, using the present perfect subjunctive.

Me alegro de que / Es posible que / No creo que / Espero que / Siento que / Ojalá que

mis amigos(as) / el (la) profesor(a) / tú / mi(s) padre(s) / mi novio(a)

aprobar todos los cursos / terminar el examen de... / comprar un coche nuevo / poder obtener trabajo / solucionar los problemas / no estar enfermo(a) / tener tiempo para... / ir de vacaciones / ver... en la televisión

Present perfect subjunctive (*El pretérito perfecto de subjuntivo*)

◆ Forms

The present perfect subjunctive tense is formed with the present subjunctive of the auxiliary verb **haber** + *past participle* of the main verb.

Formation of the Present Perfect Subjunctive

	Present Subjunctive of haber	+	*Past Participle*
yo	**haya**		**hablado**
tú	**hayas**		**comido**
Ud., él, ella	**haya**		**vivido**
nosotros(as)	**hayamos**		**hecho**
vosotros(as)	**hayáis**		**ido**
Uds., ellos, ellas	**hayan**		**puesto**

Práctica

Conjugation For each subject below, conjugate the following verbs in the present perfect subjunctive.

1. *que yo:* escuchar, oír, divertirse, decir
2. *que tú:* llenar, despertarse, volver, pedir
3. *que ella:* celebrar, poner, estacionar, escribir
4. *que nosotros:* hacer, decidir, vestirse, ayudar
5. *que ellos:* conversar, abrir, morir, irse

Online Study Center

For more practice with lesson topics, see the related activities on the *¡Hola, amigos!* web site at college.hmco.com/PIC/holaamigos7e.

Answers: **1.** haya escuchado, haya oído, me haya divertido, haya dicho **2.** hayas llenado, te hayas despertado, hayas vuelto, hayas pedido **3.** haya celebrado, haya puesto, haya estacionado, haya escrito **4.** hayamos hecho, hayamos decidido, nos hayamos vestido, hayamos ayudado **5.** hayan conversado, hayan abierto, hayan muerto, se hayan ido

- Uses

The Spanish present perfect subjunctive tense is used in the same way as the present perfect tense in English, but only in sentences that call for the subjunctive in the subordinate clause.

—Espero que Eva **haya traído** las cintas.	*"I hope (that) Eva **has brought** the tapes."*
—Sí, y también ha traído la grabadora.	*"Yes, and she has also brought the tape recorder."*
—Álvaro prometió llevar a los niños al cine.	*"Álvaro promised to take the children to the movies."*
—Dudo que lo **haya hecho.**	*"I doubt that he **has done** it."*

Práctica y conversación

Online Study Center

For more practice with lesson topics, see the related activities on the *¡Hola, amigos!* web site at college.hmco.com/PIC/holaamigos7e.

A. Rewrite the following sentences, using the cues in parentheses. Make any necessary changes.

- **MODELO:** Ha llevado el coche al taller de mecánica.
  Espero que haya llevado el coche al taller de mecánica.

1. Ha estado aquí sólo un momento. (Dudo)
2. Han comprado una casa nueva. (Espero)
3. Ha podido celebrar su aniversario. (No creo)
4. Has perdido parte del interés. (Es posible)
5. No hemos comprado la alfombra. (Siento)
6. Me he divertido mucho en la fiesta. (No es verdad)
7. Han pasado unos días felices. (Me alegro de)
8. Le han dado la dirección del teatro. (Espero)
9. Le han mandado el dinero. (No creo)
10. Han ido al concierto. (No es cierto)

Answers: **1.** Dudo que haya estado... **2.** Espero que hayan comprado... **3.** No creo que haya podido... **4.** Es posible que hayas perdido... **5.** Siento que no hayamos comprado... **6.** No es verdad que me haya divertido... **7.** Me alegro de que hayan pasado... **8.** Espero que le hayan dado... **9.** No creo que le hayan mandado... **10.** No es cierto que hayan ido...

B. Complete the following dialogues by supplying the present perfect subjunctive of the verbs given. Then act them out with a partner.

1. —Espero que los chicos hayan vuelto (volver).
   —Dudo que ya hayan regresado (regresar) porque es muy temprano.
   —Temo que hayan tenido (tener) un accidente.
   —Tú te preocupas demasiado.
2. —¿Hay alguien que haya estado (estar) en Madrid alguna vez?
   —No, aquí no hay nadie que haya ido (ir) a España.

3. —Siento que Uds. no hayan podido (poder) terminar el trabajo.
   —No es verdad que no lo hayamos terminado (terminar).
4. —¿Ellos van a vivir en San Diego?
   —Sí, pero no creo que ya hayan alquilado (alquilar) un apartamento.
5. —Me alegro de que tú hayas conseguido (conseguir) el puesto.
   —Yo también.

C. Use your imagination to complete each statement, using the present perfect subjunctive tense. *Answers will vary.*

1. Me alegro mucho de que mis padres...
2. Siento mucho que los invitados...
3. Espero que la clase de español...
4. No creo que los estudiantes...
5. No es cierto que yo...
6. Me sorprende que el concierto...
7. Dudo que el (la) profesor(a)...
8. No es verdad que él...

Pluperfect subjunctive (*El pluscuamperfecto de subjuntivo*)

- Forms

The Spanish pluperfect subjunctive is formed with the imperfect subjunctive of the auxiliary verb **haber** + *past participle* of the main verb.

Formation of the Pluperfect Subjunctive Tense

	Imperfect Subjunctive of haber	+	*Past Participle*
yo	**hubiera**		**hablado**
tú	**hubieras**		**comido**
Ud., él, ella	**hubiera**		**vivido**
nosotros(as)	**hubiéramos**		**visto**
vosotros(as)	**hubierais**		**hecho**
Uds., ellos, ellas	**hubieran**		**vuelto**

- Use

The Spanish pluperfect subjunctive tense is used in the same way the past perfect is used in English, but in sentences in which the main clause calls for the subjunctive.

Yo dudaba que ellos **hubieran llegado.** — *I doubted that they **had arrived.***

Yo esperaba que tú **hubieras pagado** tus cuentas. — *I was hoping that you **had paid** your bills.*

Práctica

A. Rewrite the following sentences, using the cues in parentheses. Make any necessary changes.

◆ **MODELO:** Él se alegra de que ellos hayan hecho el trabajo. (Él se alegró)
Él se alegró de que ellos hubieran hecho el trabajo.

1. Nosotros sentimos que hayas estado solo en Lima. (Nosotros sentíamos)
2. Yo espero que Uds. hayan hecho el trabajo. (Yo esperaba)
3. Siente que yo no haya podido venir el sábado. (Sintió)
4. No creo que hayas comprado esas sábanas. (No creí)
5. Me sorprende que no hayas cambiado el pasaje. (Me sorprendió)
6. Me alegro de que hayamos conseguido la reservación. (Me alegré)
7. Es probable que ellos hayan tenido que transbordar. (Era probable)
8. No es verdad que él haya llegado tarde. (No era verdad)

B. Write the following sentences in Spanish.

1. We were hoping that they had done the work.
2. I was sorry you had been sick.
3. They were glad that he had bought the tickets for the trip.
4. I didn't think that they hadn't gotten a discount.
5. We were glad that you had brought your driver's license.

C. Use the pluperfect subjunctive to finish the following in an original manner. *Answers will vary.*

1. Mis padres se alegraron de que yo...
2. Yo esperaba que mis amigos...
3. Ellos sintieron que nosotros...
4. Aquí no había nadie que...
5. ¿Había alguien en esa familia que...?
6. Mi compañero de cuarto dudaba que yo...

Online Study Center

For more practice with lesson topics, see the related activities on the ***¡Hola, amigos!*** web site at college.hmco.com/PIC/holaamigos7e.

Answers: **1.** Nosotros sentíamos que hubieras estado solo en Lima. **2.** Yo esperaba que Uds. hubieran hecho el trabajo. **3.** Sintió que yo no hubiera podido venir el sábado. **4.** No creí que hubieras comprado esas sábanas. **5.** Me sorprendió que no hubieras cambiado el pasaje. **6.** Me alegré de que hubiéramos conseguido la reservación. **7.** Era probable que ellos hubieran tenido que transbordar. **8.** No era verdad que él hubiera llegado tarde.

Answers: **1.** Esperábamos que (ellos) hubieran hecho el trabajo. **2.** Sentí que hubieras estado enfermo. **3.** Se alegraron de que (él) hubiera comprado los pasajes para el viaje. **4.** No pensé que (ellos) hubieran recibido un descuento. **5.** Nos alegramos de que hubieras traído tu carnet de conducir.

Appendices

Appendix A

A: Spanish Sounds

Vowels

There are five distinct vowels in Spanish: **a, e, i, o, u.** Each vowel has only one basic, constant sound. The pronunciation of each vowel is constant, clear, and brief. The length of the sound is practically the same whether it is produced in a stressed or unstressed syllable.[1]

While producing the sounds of the English stressed vowels that most closely resemble the Spanish ones, the speaker changes the position of the tongue, lips, and lower jaw, so that the vowel actually starts as one sound and then *glides* into another. In Spanish, however, the tongue, lips, and jaw keep a constant position during the production of the sound.

English: ban*a*na **Spanish:** ban*a*na

The stress falls on the same vowel and syllable in both Spanish and English, but the English stressed *a* is longer than the Spanish stressed **a.**

English: ban*a*na **Spanish:** ban*a*na

Note also that the English stressed *a* has a sound different from the other *a*'s in the word, while the Spanish **a** sound remains constant.

a in Spanish sounds similar to the English *a* in the word *father.*

alta casa palma Ana cama Panamá alma apagar

e is pronounced like the English *e* in the word *eight.*

mes entre este deje ese encender teme prender

i has a sound similar to the English *ee* in the word *see.*

fin ir sí sin dividir Trini difícil

o is similar to the English *o* in the word *no,* but without the glide.

toco como poco roto corto corro solo loco

u is pronounced like the English *oo* sound in the word *shoot* or the *ue* sound in the word *Sue.*

su Lulú Úrsula cultura un luna sucursal Uruguay

[1]In a stressed syllable, the prominence of the vowel is indicated by its loudness.

Diphthongs and triphthongs

When unstressed **i** or **u** falls next to another vowel in a syllable, it unites with that vowel to form what is called a *diphthong.* Both vowels are pronounced as one syllable. Their sounds do not change; they are only pronounced more rapidly and with a glide. For example:

tr**ai**ga	Lid**ia**	tr**ei**nta	s**ie**te	**oi**go	ad**ió**s
Aurora	ag**ua**	b**ue**no	antig**uo**	c**iu**dad	L**ui**s

A triphthong is the union of three vowels, a stressed vowel between two unstressed ones (**i** or **u**) in the same syllable. For example: Parag**uay,** estud**iéi**s.

NOTE: Stressed **i** and **u** do not form diphthongs with other vowels, except in the combinations **iu** and **ui**. For example: **rí**-o, sa-**bí**-ais.

In syllabication, diphthongs and triphthongs are considered a single vowel; their components cannot be separated.

Consonants

p Spanish **p** is pronounced in a manner similar to the English *p* sound, but without the puff of air that follows after the English sound is produced.

pesca	pude	puedo	parte	papá
postre	piña	puente	Paco	

k The Spanish **k** sound, represented by the letters **k** and **c** before **a, o, u,** or a consonant, and **qu,** is similar to the English *k* sound, but without the puff of air.

casa	comer	cuna	clima	acción	que
quinto	queso	aunque	quiosco	kilómetro	kilo

t Spanish **t** is produced by touching the back of the upper front teeth with the tip of the tongue. It has no puff of air as in the English *t.*

todo	antes	corto	Guatemala	diente
resto	tonto	roto	tanque	

d The Spanish consonant **d** has two different sounds depending on its position. At the beginning of an utterance and after **n** or **l,** the tip of the tongue presses the back of the upper front teeth.

día	doma	dice	dolor	dar
anda	Aldo	caldo	el deseo	un domicilio

In all other positions the sound of **d** is similar to the *th* sound in the English word *they,* but softer.

medida	todo	nada	nadie	medio
puedo	moda	queda	nudo	

g The Spanish consonant **g** is similar to the English *g* sound in the word *guy* except before **e** or **i.**

goma	glotón	gallo	gloria	lago	alga
gorrión	garra	guerra	angustia	algo	Dagoberto

j The sound of Spanish **j** (or **g** before **e** and **i**) is similar to a strongly exaggerated English *h* sound.

gemir	juez	jarro	gitano	agente
juego	giro	bajo	gente	

b, v There is no difference in sound between Spanish **b** and **v.** Both letters are pronounced alike. At the beginning of an utterance or after **m** or **n, b** and **v** have a sound identical to the English *b* sound in the word *boy.*

vivir	beber	vamos	barco	enviar
hambre	batea	bueno	vestido	

When pronounced between vowels, the Spanish **b** and **v** sound is produced by bringing the lips together but not closing them, so that some air may pass through.

sábado autobús yo voy su barco

y, ll In most countries, Spanish **ll** and **y** have a sound similar to the English sound in the word *yes.*

el llavero	un yelmo	el yeso	su yunta	llama	yema
oye	trayecto	trayectoria	mayo	milla	bella

NOTE: When it stands alone or is at the end of a word, Spanish **y** is pronounced like the vowel **i.**

rey hoy y doy buey muy voy estoy soy

r The sound of Spanish **r** is similar to the English *dd* sound in the word *ladder.*

crema	aroma	cara	arena	aro
harina	toro	oro	eres	portero

rr Spanish **rr** and also **r** in an initial position and after **n, l,** or **s** are pronounced with a very strong trill. This trill is produced by bringing the tip of the tongue near the alveolar ridge and letting it vibrate freely while the air passes through the mouth.

rama	carro	Israel	cierra	roto
perro	alrededor	rizo	corre	Enrique

s Spanish **s** is represented in most of the Spanish world by the letters **s, z,** and **c** before **e** or **i.** The sound is very similar to the English sibilant *s* in the word *sink.*

sale	sitio	presidente	signo
salsa	seda	suma	vaso
sobrino	ciudad	cima	canción
zapato	zarza	cerveza	centro

h The letter **h** is silent in Spanish.

hoy	hora	hilo	ahora
humor	huevo	horror	almohada

ch Spanish **ch** is pronounced like the English *ch* in the word *chief.*

hecho	chico	coche	Chile
mucho	muchacho	salchicha	

f Spanish **f** is identical in sound to the English *f.*

difícil	feo	fuego	forma
fácil	fecha	foto	fueron

l Spanish **l** is similar to the English *l* in the word *let.*

dolor	lata	ángel	lago	sueldo
los	pelo	lana	general	fácil

m Spanish **m** is pronounced like the English *m* in the word *mother.*

mano	moda	mucho	muy
mismo	tampoco	multa	cómoda

n In most cases, Spanish **n** has a sound similar to the English *n.*

nada	nunca	ninguno	norte
entra	tiene	sienta	

The sound of Spanish **n** is often affected by the sounds that occur around it. When it appears before **b, v,** or **p,** it is pronounced like an **m.**

tan bueno	toman vino	sin poder
un pobre	comen peras	siguen bebiendo

ñ Spanish **ñ** is similar to the English *ny* sound in the word *canyon.*

señor	otoño	ñoño	uña
leña	dueño	niños	años

x Spanish **x** has two pronunciations depending on its position. Between vowels the sound is similar to English *ks.*

examen	exacto	boxeo	éxito
oxidar	oxígeno	existencia	

When it occurs before a consonant, Spanish **x** sounds like *s.*

expresión	explicar	extraer	excusa
expreso	exquisito	extremo	

NOTE: When **x** appears in **México** or in other words of Mexican origin, it is pronounced like the Spanish letter **j.**

Appendix A

Rhythm

Rhythm is the variation of sound intensity that we usually associate with music. Spanish and English each regulate these variations in speech differently, because they have different patterns of syllable length. In Spanish the length of the stressed and unstressed syllables remains almost the same, while in English stressed syllables are considerably longer than unstressed ones. Pronounce the following Spanish words, enunciating each syllable clearly.

es-tu-dian-te	bue-no	Úr-su-la
com-po-si-ción	di-fí-cil	ki-ló-me-tro
po-li-cí-a	Pa-ra-guay	

Because the length of the Spanish syllables remains constant, the greater the number of syllables in a given word or phrase, the longer the phrase will be.

Linking

In spoken Spanish, the different words in a phrase or a sentence are not pronounced as isolated elements but combined together. This is called *linking*.

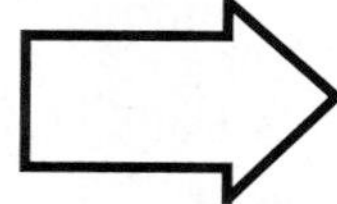

Pepe come pan.	Pe-pe-co-me-pan
Tomás toma leche.	To-más-to-ma-le-che
Luis tiene la llave.	Luis-tie-ne-la-lla-ve
La mano de Roberto.	La-ma-no-de-Ro-ber-to

1. The final consonant of a word is pronounced together with the initial vowel of the following word.

Carlos anda	Car-lo-san-da
un ángel	u-nán-gel
el otoño	e-lo-to-ño
unos estudios interesantes	u-no-ses-tu-dio-sin-te-re-san-tes

2. A diphthong is formed between the final vowel of a word and the initial vowel of the following word. A triphthong is formed when there is a combination of three vowels (see rules for the formation of diphthongs and triphthongs on page 347).

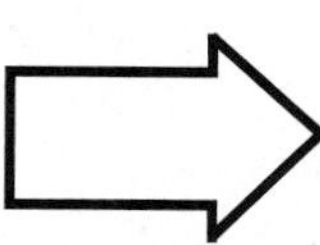

su hermana	suher-ma-na
tu escopeta	tues-co-pe-ta
Roberto y Luis	Ro-ber-toy-Luis
negocio importante	ne-go-cioim-por-tan-te
lluvia y nieve	llu-viay-nie-ve
ardua empresa	ar-duaem-pre-sa

3. When the final vowel of a word and the initial vowel of the following word are identical, they are pronounced slightly longer than one vowel.

Ana alcanza	A-n*a*l-can-za	tiene eso	tie-n*e*-so
lo olvido	l*o*l-vi-do	Ada atiende	Ad*a*-tien-de

The same rule applies when two identical vowels appear within a word.

crees	cr*e*s
Teherán	T*e*-rán
coordinación	c*o*r-di-na-ción

4. When the final consonant of a word and the initial consonant of the following word are the same, they are pronounced like one consonant with slightly longer than normal duration.

el lado	e-*l*a-do	tienes sed	tie-ne-*s*ed
Carlos salta	Car-lo-*s*al-ta		

Intonation

Intonation is the rise and fall of pitch in the delivery of a phrase or sentence. In general, Spanish pitch tends to change less than English, giving the impression that the language is less emphatic.

As a rule, the intonation for normal statements in Spanish starts in a low tone, raises to a higher one on the first stressed syllable, maintains that tone until the last stressed syllable, and then goes back to the initial low tone, with still another drop at the very end.

Tu amigo viene mañana.	José come pan.
Ada está en casa.	Carlos toma café.

Syllable formation in Spanish

Below are general rules for dividing words into syllables:

Vowels

1. A vowel or a vowel combination can constitute a syllable.

   a-lum-no a-bue-la Eu-ro-pa

2. Diphthongs and triphthongs are considered single vowels and cannot be divided.

   bai-le puen-te Dia-na es-tu-diáis an-ti-guo

3. Two strong vowels (**a, e, o**) do not form a diphthong and are separated into two syllables.

   em-ple-ar vol-te-ar lo-a

4. A written accent on a weak vowel (**i** or **u**) breaks the diphthong, separating the vowels into two syllables.

   trí-o dú-o Ma-rí-a

Consonants

1. A single consonant forms a syllable with the vowel that follows it.

   po-der ma-no mi-nu-to

   NOTE: **ch, ll,** and **rr** are considered single consonants: **a-ma-ri-llo, co-che, pe-rro.**

Appendix A

2. When two consonants appear between two vowels, they are separated into two syllables.

al-fa-be-to cam-pe-ón me-ter-se mo-les-tia

EXCEPTION: When a consonant cluster composed of **b, c, d, f, g, p,** or **t** with **l** or **r** appears between two vowels, the cluster joins the following vowel: **so-bre, o-tros, ca-ble, te-lé-gra-fo.**

3. When three consonants appear between two vowels, only the last one goes with the following vowel.

ins-pec-tor trans-por-te trans-for-mar

EXCEPTION: When there is a cluster of three consonants in the combinations described in rule 2, the first consonant joins the preceding vowel and the cluster joins the following vowel: **es-cri-bir, ex-tran-je-ro, im-plo-rar, es-tre-cho.**

Accentuation

In Spanish, all words are stressed according to specific rules. Words that do not follow the rules must have a written accent to indicate the change of stress. The basic rules for accentuation are as follows.

1. Words ending in a vowel, **n,** or **s** are stressed on the next-to-the-last syllable.

hi-jo	**ca**-lle	**me**-sa	fa-**mo**-sos
flo-**re**-cen	**pla**-ya	**ve**-ces	

2. Words ending in a consonant, except **n** or **s,** are stressed on the last syllable.

ma-**yor** a-**mor** tro-pi-**cal** na-**riz** re-**loj** co-rre-**dor**

3. All words that do not follow these rules must have a written accent.

ca-**fé**	sa-**lió**	rin-**cón**	fran-**cés**	sa-**lón**
án-gel	**lá**-piz	**dé**-bil	a-**zú**-car	**Víc**-tor
sim-**pá**-ti-co	**lí**-qui-do	**mú**-si-ca	e-**xá**-me-nes	de-**mó**-cra-ta

4. Pronouns and adverbs of interrogation and exclamation have a written accent to distinguish them from relative pronouns.

¿Qué comes?	*What are you eating?*
La pera que él no comió.	*The pear that he did not eat.*
¿Quién está ahí?	*Who is there?*
El hombre a quien tú llamaste.	*The man whom you called.*
¿Dónde está él?	*Where is he?*
En el lugar donde trabaja.	*At the place where he works.*

5. Words that have the same spelling but different meanings take a written accent to differentiate one from the other.

el	*the*	él	*he, him*	te	*you*	té	*tea*
mi	*my*	mí	*me*	si	*if*	sí	*yes*
tu	*your*	tú	*you*	mas	*but*	más	*more*

B: Verbs

Regular verbs

Model *-ar, -er, -ir* verbs

INFINITIVE

amar *(to love)*	**comer** *(to eat)*	**vivir** *(to live)*

PRESENT PARTICIPLE

amando *(loving)*	**comiendo** *(eating)*	**viviendo** *(living)*

PAST PARTICIPLE

amado *(loved)*	**comido** *(eaten)*	**vivido** *(lived)*

SIMPLE TENSES

Indicative Mood

Present

(I love)		*(I eat)*		*(I live)*	
am**o**	am**amos**	com**o**	com**emos**	viv**o**	viv**imos**
am**as**	am**áis**	com**es**	com**éis**	viv**es**	viv**ís**
am**a**	am**an**	com**e**	com**en**	viv**e**	viv**en**

Imperfect

(I used to love)		*(I used to eat)*		*(I used to live)*	
am**aba**	am**ábamos**	com**ía**	com**íamos**	viv**ía**	viv**íamos**
am**abas**	am**abais**	com**ías**	com**íais**	viv**ías**	viv**íais**
am**aba**	am**aban**	com**ía**	com**ían**	viv**ía**	viv**ían**

Preterit

(I loved)		*(I ate)*		*(I lived)*	
am**é**	am**amos**	com**í**	com**imos**	viv**í**	viv**imos**
am**aste**	am**asteis**	com**iste**	com**isteis**	viv**iste**	viv**isteis**
am**ó**	am**aron**	com**ió**	com**ieron**	viv**ió**	viv**ieron**

Future

(I will love)		*(I will eat)*		*(I will live)*	
amar**é**	amar**emos**	comer**é**	comer**emos**	vivir**é**	vivir**emos**
amar**ás**	amar**éis**	comer**ás**	comer**éis**	vivir**ás**	vivir**éis**
amar**á**	amar**án**	comer**á**	comer**án**	vivir**á**	vivir**án**

Conditional

(I would love)		*(I would eat)*		*(I would live)*	
amar**ía**	amar**íamos**	comer**ía**	comer**íamos**	vivir**ía**	vivir**íamos**
amar**ías**	amar**íais**	comer**ías**	comer**íais**	vivir**ías**	vivir**íais**
amar**ía**	amar**ían**	comer**ía**	comer**ían**	vivir**ía**	vivir**ían**

Subjunctive Mood

Present

([that] I [may] love)		*([that] I [may] eat)*		*([that] I [may] live)*	
am**e**	am**emos**	com**a**	com**amos**	viv**a**	viv**amos**
am**es**	am**éis**	com**as**	com**áis**	viv**as**	viv**áis**
am**e**	am**en**	com**a**	com**an**	viv**a**	viv**an**

Appendix B

	Imperfect	
([that] I [might] love)	*([that] I [might] eat)*	*([that] I [might] live)*
am**ara(-ase)**	com**iera(-iese)**	viv**iera(-iese)**
am**aras(-ases)**	com**ieras(-ieses)**	viv**ieras(-ieses)**
am**ara(-ase)**	com**iera(-iese)**	viv**iera(-iese)**
am**áramos(-ásemos)**	com**iéramos(-iésemos)**	viv**iéramos(-iésemos)**
am**arais(-aseis)**	com**ierais(-ieseis)**	viv**ierais(-ieseis)**
am**aran(-asen)**	com**ieran(-iesen)**	viv**ieran(-iesen)**

	Imperative Mood	
(love)	*(eat)*	*(live)*
am**a** (tú)	com**e** (tú)	viv**e** (tú)
am**e** (Ud.)	com**a** (Ud.)	viv**a** (Ud.)
am**emos** (nosotros)	com**amos** (nosotros)	viv**amos** (nosotros)
am**ad** (vosotros)	com**ed** (vosotros)	viv**id** (vosotros)
am**en** (Uds.)	com**an** (Uds.)	viv**an** (Uds.)

COMPOUND TENSES

PERFECT INFINITIVE

haber amado	**haber comido**	**haber vivido**

PERFECT PARTICIPLE

habiendo amado	**habiendo comido**	**habiendo vivido**

Indicative Mood

Present Perfect

(I have loved)		*(I have eaten)*		*(I have lived)*	
he amado	hemos amado	he comido	hemos comido	he vivido	hemos vivido
has amado	habéis amado	has comido	habéis comido	has vivido	habéis vivido
ha amado	han amado	ha comido	han comido	ha vivido	han vivido

	Past Perfect (Pluperfect)	
(I had loved)	*(I had eaten)*	*(I had lived)*
había amado	había comido	había vivido
habías amado	habías comido	habías vivido
había amado	había comido	había vivido
habíamos amado	habíamos comido	habíamos vivido
habíais amado	habíais comido	habíais vivido
habían amado	habían comido	habían vivido

	Future Perfect	
(I will have loved)	*(I will have eaten)*	*(I will have lived)*
habré amado	habré comido	habré vivido
habrás amado	habrás comido	habrás vivido
habrá amado	habrá comido	habrá vivido
habremos amado	habremos comido	habremos vivido
habréis amado	habréis comido	habréis vivido
habrán amado	habrán comido	habrán vivido

Conditional Perfect

(I would have loved)	*(I would have eaten)*	*(I would have lived)*
habría amado	habría comido	habría vivido
habrías amado	habrías comido	habrías vivido
habría amado	habría comido	habría vivido
habríamos amado	habríamos comido	habríamos vivido
habríais amado	habríais comido	habríais vivido
habrían amado	habrían comido	habrían vivido

Subjunctive Mood

Present Perfect

([that] I [may] have loved)	*([that] I [may] have eaten)*	*([that] I [may] have lived)*
haya amado	haya comido	haya vivido
hayas amado	hayas comido	hayas vivido
haya amado	haya comido	haya vivido
hayamos amado	hayamos comido	hayamos vivido
hayáis amado	hayáis comido	hayáis vivido
hayan amado	hayan comido	hayan vivido

Past Perfect (Pluperfect)

([that] I [might] have loved)	*([that] I [might] have eaten)*	*([that] I [might] have lived)*
hubiera(-iese) amado	hubiera(-iese) comido	hubiera(-iese) vivido
hubieras(-ieses) amado	hubieras(-ieses) comido	hubieras(-ieses) vivido
hubiera(-iese) amado	hubiera(-iese) comido	hubiera(-iese) vivido
hubiéramos(-iésemos) amado	hubiéramos(-iésemos) comido	hubiéramos(-iésemos) vivido
hubierais(-ieseis) amado	hubierais(-ieseis) comido	hubierais(-ieseis) vivido
hubieran(-iesen) amado	hubieran(-iesen) comido	hubieran(-iesen) vivido

Stem-changing verbs

The *-ar* and *-er* stem-changing verbs

Stem-changing verbs are those that have a spelling change in the root of the verb. Verbs that end in **-ar** and **-er** change the stressed vowel **e** to **ie,** and the stressed **o** to **ue.** These changes occur in all persons, except the first- and second-persons plural of the present indicative, present subjunctive, and imperative.

INFINITIVE	Indicative	Imperative	Subjunctive
cerrar	cierro	______	cierre
(*to close*)	cierras	cierra	cierres
	cierra	cierre	cierre
	cerramos	cerremos	cerremos
	cerráis	cerrad	cerréis
	cierran	cierren	cierren
perder	pierdo	______	pierda
(*to lose*)	pierdes	pierde	pierdas
	pierde	pierda	pierda
	perdemos	perdamos	perdamos
	perdéis	perded	perdáis
	pierden	pierdan	pierdan
contar	cuento	______	cuente
(*to count;*	cuentas	cuenta	cuentes
to tell)	cuenta	cuente	cuente
	contamos	contemos	contemos
	contáis	contad	contéis
	cuentan	cuenten	cuenten
volver	vuelvo	______	vuelva
(*to return*)	vuelves	vuelve	vuelvas
	vuelve	vuelva	vuelva
	volvemos	volvamos	volvamos
	volvéis	volved	volváis
	vuelven	vuelvan	vuelvan

Verbs that follow the same pattern are:

acordarse *to remember*
acostar(se) *to go to bed*
almorzar *to have lunch*
atravesar *to go through*
cocer *to cook*
colgar *to hang*
comenzar *to begin*
confesar *to confess*
costar *to cost*
demostrar *to demonstrate, show*
despertar(se) *to wake up*
empezar *to begin*
encender *to light; to turn on*
encontrar *to find*
entender *to understand*
llover *to rain*
mover *to move*
mostrar *to show*
negar *to deny*
nevar *to snow*
pensar *to think; to plan*
probar *to prove; to taste*
recordar *to remember*
rogar *to beg*
sentar(se) *to sit down*
soler *to be in the habit of*
soñar *to dream*
tender *to stretch; to unfold*
torcer *to twist*

The *-ir* stem-changing verbs

There are two types of stem-changing verbs that end in **-ir:** one type changes stressed **e** to **ie** in some tenses and to **i** in others, and stressed **o** to **ue** or **u;** the second type changes stressed **e** to **i** only in all the irregular tenses.

Type 1: -ir:e > ie or i / o > ue or u

These changes occur as follows.

Present Indicative: all persons except the first- and second-persons plural change **e** to **ie** and **o** to **ue.** *Preterit:* third person, singular and plural, changes **e** to **i** and **o** to **u.** *Present Subjunctive:* all persons change **e** to **ie** and **o** to **ue,** except the first- and second-persons plural, which change **e** to **i** and **o** to **u.** *Imperfect Subjunctive:* all persons change **e** to **i** and **o** to **u.** *Imperative:* all persons except the first- and second-persons plural change **e** to **ie** and **o** to **ue;** first-person plural changes **e** to **i** and **o** to **u.** *Present Participle:* changes **e** to **i** and **o** to **u.**

INFINITIVE	Indicative		Imperative	Subjunctive	
sentir *(to feel)*	PRESENT	PRETERIT		PRESENT	IMPERFECT
PRESENT PARTICIPLE s**i**ntiendo	s**ie**nto	sentí		s**ie**nta	s**i**ntiera(-iese)
	s**ie**ntes	sentiste	s**ie**nte	s**ie**ntas	s**i**ntieras
	s**ie**nte	s**i**ntió	s**ie**nta	s**ie**nta	s**i**ntiera
	sentimos	sentimos	s**i**ntamos	s**i**ntamos	s**i**ntiéramos
	sentís	sentisteis	sentid	s**i**ntáis	s**i**ntierais
	s**ie**nten	s**i**ntieron	s**ie**ntan	s**ie**ntan	s**i**ntieran
dormir *(to sleep)*	d**ue**rmo	dormí		d**ue**rma	d**u**rmiera(-iese)
	d**ue**rmes	dormiste	d**ue**rme	d**ue**rmas	d**u**rmieras
	d**ue**rme	d**u**rmió	d**ue**rma	d**ue**rma	d**u**rmiera
PRESENT PARTICIPLE d**u**rmiendo	dormimos	dormimos	d**u**rmamos	d**u**rmamos	d**u**rmiéramos
	dormís	dormisteis	dormid	d**u**rmáis	d**u**rmierais
	d**ue**rmen	d**u**rmieron	d**ue**rman	d**ue**rman	d**u**rmieran

Other verbs that follow the same pattern are:

advertir	*to warn*	divertir(se)	*to amuse (oneself)*	preferir	*to prefer*
arrepentirse	*to repent*	herir	*to wound, hurt*	referir	*to refer*
consentir	*to consent; to pamper*	mentir	*to lie*	sugerir	*to suggest*
convertir(se)	*to turn into*	morir	*to die*		

Appendix B

Type II: -ir: e > i

The verbs in the second category are irregular in the same tenses as those of the first type. The only difference is that they have just one change: **e > i** in all irregular persons.

INFINITIVE	Indicative		Imperative	Subjunctive	
pedir *(to ask for, request)*	PRESENT	PRETERIT		PRESENT	IMPERFECT
	pido	pedí		pida	pidiera(-iese)
PRESENT PARTICIPLE	pides	pediste	pide	pidas	pidieras
	pide	pidió	pida	pida	pidiera
pidiendo	pedimos	pedimos	pidamos	pidamos	pidiéramos
	pedís	pedisteis	pedid	pidáis	pidierais
	piden	pidieron	pidan	pidan	pidieran

Verbs that follow this pattern:

competir *to compete*
concebir *to conceive*
despedir(se) *to say good-bye*
elegir *to choose*
impedir *to prevent*
perseguir *to pursue*
reír(se) *to laugh*
reñir *to fight*
repetir *to repeat*
seguir *to follow*
servir *to serve*
vestir(se) *to dress*

Orthographic-changing verbs

Some verbs undergo a change in the spelling of the stem in some tenses in order to maintain the sound of the final consonant. The most common ones are those with the consonants **g** and **c.** Remember that **g** and **c** in front of **e** or **i** have a soft sound, and in front of **a, o,** or **u** have a hard sound. In order to keep the soft sound in front of **a, o,** or **u, g** and **c** change to **j** and **z,** respectively. In order to keep the hard sound of **g** or **c** in front of **e** and **i, u** is added to the **g (gu)** and the **c** changes to **qu.** The following are the most important verbs of this type that are regular in all tenses but change in spelling.

1. Verbs ending in **-gar** change **g** to **gu** before **e** in the first-person singular of the preterit and in all persons of the present subjunctive.

   pagar *to pay*
   Preterit: pa**gué**, pagaste, pagó, etc.
   Pres. Subj.: pa**gu**e, pa**gu**es, pa**gu**e, pa**gu**emos, pa**gu**éis, pa**gu**en

   Verbs that follow the same pattern: **colgar, jugar, llegar, navegar, negar, regar, rogar.**

2. Verbs ending in **-ger** or **-gir** change **g** to **j** before **o** and **a** in the first-person singular of the present indicative and in all the persons of the present subjunctive.

   proteger *to protect*
   Pres. Ind.: prote**j**o, proteges, protege, etc.
   Pres. Subj.: prote**j**a, prote**j**as, prote**j**a, prote**j**amos, prote**j**áis, prote**j**an

   Verbs that follow the same pattern: **coger, corregir, dirigir, elegir, escoger, exigir, recoger.**

3. Verbs ending in **-guar** change **gu** to **gü** before **e** in the first-person singular of the preterit and in all persons of the present subjunctive.

   averiguar *to find out*
   Preterit: averi**gü**é, averiguaste, averiguó, etc.
   Pres. Subj.: averi**gü**e, averi**gü**es, averi**gü**e, averi**gü**emos, averi**gü**éis, averi**gü**en

   The verb **apaciguar** follows the same pattern.

4. Verbs ending in **-guir** change **gu** to **g** before **o** and **a** in the first-person singular of the present indicative and in all persons of the present subjunctive.

   conseguir *to get*
   Pres. Ind.: consi**g**o, consigues, consigue, etc.
   Pres. Subj.: consi**g**a, consi**g**as, consi**g**a, consi**g**amos, consi**g**áis, consi**g**an

   Verbs that follow the same pattern: **distinguir, perseguir, proseguir, seguir.**

5. Verbs ending in **-car** change **c** to **qu** before **e** in the first-person singular of the preterit and in all persons of the present subjunctive.

   tocar *to touch; to play (a musical instrument)*
   Preterit: to**qu**é, tocaste, tocó, etc.
   Pres. Subj.: to**qu**e, to**qu**es, to**qu**e, to**qu**emos, to**qu**éis, to**qu**en

   Verbs that follow the same pattern: **atacar, buscar, comunicar, explicar, indicar, pescar, sacar.**

6. Verbs ending in **-cer** or **-cir** preceded by a consonant change **c** to **z** before **o** and **a** in the first-person singular of the present indicative and in all persons of the present subjunctive.

   torcer *to twist*
   Pres. Ind.: tuer**z**o, tuerces, tuerce, etc.
   Pres. Subj.: tuer**z**a, tuer**z**as, tuer**z**a, tor**z**amos, tor**z**áis, tuer**z**an

   Verbs that follow the same pattern: **convencer, esparcir, vencer.**

7. Verbs ending in **-cer** or **-cir** preceded by a vowel change **c** to **zc** before **o** and **a** in the first-person singular of the present indicative and in all persons of the present subjunctive.

   conocer *to know, be acquainted with*
   Pres. Ind.: cono**zc**o, conoces, conoce, etc.
   Pres. Subj.: cono**zc**a, cono**zc**as, cono**zc**a, cono**zc**amos, cono**zc**áis, cono**zc**an

   Verbs that follow the same pattern: **agradecer, aparecer, carecer, entristecer** (to sadden), **establecer, lucir, nacer, obedecer, ofrecer, padecer, parecer, pertenecer, reconocer, relucir.**

8. Verbs ending in **-zar** change **z** to **c** before **e** in the first-person singular of the preterit and in all persons of the present subjunctive.

   rezar *to pray*
   Preterit: re**c**é, rezaste, rezó, etc.
   Pres. Subj.: re**c**e, re**c**es, re**c**e, re**c**emos, re**c**éis, re**c**en

   Verbs that follow the same pattern: **abrazar, alcanzar, almorzar, comenzar, cruzar, empezar, forzar, gozar.**

9. Verbs ending in **-eer** change the unstressed **i** to **y** between vowels in the third-person singular and plural of the preterit, in all persons of the imperfect subjunctive, and in the present participle.

   creer *to believe*
   Preterit: creí, creíste, cre**y**ó, creímos, creísteis, cre**y**eron
   Imp. Subj.: cre**y**era(-ese), cre**y**eras, cre**y**era, cre**y**éramos, cre**y**erais, cre**y**eran
   Pres. Part.: cre**y**endo
   Past Part.: creído

   Verbs that follow the same pattern: **leer, poseer.**

Appendix B

Appendix B

10. Verbs ending in **-uir** change the unstressed **i** to **y** between vowels (except **-quir,** which has the silent **u**) in the following tenses and persons.

    huir *to escape; to flee*
    Pres. Part.: hu**y**endo
    Pres. Ind.: hu**y**o, hu**y**es, hu**y**e, huimos, huís, hu**y**en
    Preterit: huí, huiste, hu**y**ó, huimos, huisteis, hu**y**eron
    Imperative: hu**y**e, hu**y**a, hu**y**amos, huid, hu**y**an
    Pres. Subj.: hu**y**a, hu**y**as, hu**y**a, hu**y**amos, hu**y**áis, hu**y**an
    Imp. Subj.: hu**y**era(-ese), hu**y**eras, hu**y**era, hu**y**éramos, hu**y**erais, hu**y**eran

    Verbs that follow the same pattern: **atribuir, concluir, constituir, construir, contribuir, destituir, destruir, disminuir, distribuir, excluir, incluir, influir, instruir, restituir, sustituir.**

11. Verbs ending in **-eír** lose the **e** in all but the first- and second-persons plural of the present indicative, in the third-person singular and plural of the preterit, in all persons of the present and imperfect subjunctive, and in the present participle.

    reír *to laugh*
    Pres. Ind.: **rí**o, **rí**es, **rí**e, reímos, reís, **rí**en
    Preterit: reí, reíste, **ri**ó, reímos, reísteis, **ri**eron
    Pres. Subj.: **rí**a, **rí**as, **rí**a, **ri**amos, **ri**áis, **rí**an
    Imp. Subj.: **ri**era(-ese), **ri**eras, **ri**era, **ri**éramos, **ri**erais, **ri**eran
    Pres. Part.: **ri**endo

    Verbs that follow the same pattern: **sonreír, freír.**

12. Verbs ending in **-iar** add a written accent to the **i,** except in the first- and second-persons plural of the present indicative and subjunctive.

    fiar(se) *to trust*
    Pres. Ind.: (me) f**í**o, (te) f**í**as, (se) f**í**a, (nos) fiamos, (os) fiáis, (se) f**í**an
    Pres. Subj.: (me) f**í**e, (te) f**í**es, (se) f**í**e, (nos) fiemos, (os) fiéis, (se) f**í**en

    Verbs that follow the same pattern: **ampliar, criar, desviar, enfriar, enviar, guiar, telegrafiar, vaciar, variar.**

13. Verbs ending in **-uar** (except **-guar**) add a written accent to the **u,** except in the first- and second-persons plural of the present indicative and subjunctive.

    actuar *to act*
    Pres. Ind.: act**ú**o, act**ú**as, act**ú**a, actuamos, actuáis, act**ú**an
    Pres. Subj.: act**ú**e, act**ú**es, act**ú**e, actuemos, actuéis, act**ú**en

    Verbs that follow the same pattern: **acentuar, continuar, efectuar, exceptuar, graduar, habituar, insinuar, situar.**

14. Verbs ending in **-ñir** lose the **i** of the diphthongs **ie** and **ió** in the third-person singular and plural of the preterit and all persons of the imperfect subjunctive. They also change the **e** of the stem to **i** in the same persons and in the present indicative and present subjunctive.

    teñir *to dye*
    Pres. Ind.: t**i**ño, t**i**ñes, t**i**ñe, teñimos, teñís, t**i**ñen
    Preterit: teñí, teñiste, **tiñó,** teñimos, teñisteis, t**i**ñ**e**ron
    Pres. Subj.: t**i**ña, t**i**ñas, t**i**ña, t**i**ñamos, t**i**ñáis, t**i**ñan
    Imp. Subj.: t**i**ñ**e**ra(-ese), t**i**ñ**e**ras, t**i**ñ**e**ra, t**i**ñ**é**ramos, t**i**ñ**e**rais, t**i**ñ**e**ran

    Verbs that follow the same pattern: **ceñir, constreñir, desteñir, estreñir, reñir.**

Some common irregular verbs

Only tenses with irregular forms are given below.

adquirir *to acquire*
Pres. Ind.: adquiero, adquieres, adquiere, adquirimos, adquirís, adquieren
Pres. Subj.: adquiera, adquieras, adquiera, adquiramos, adquiráis, adquieran
Imperative: adquiere, adquiera, adquiramos, adquirid, adquieran

andar *to walk*
Preterit: anduve, anduviste, anduvo, anduvimos, anduvisteis, anduvieron
Imp. Subj.: anduviera (anduviese), anduvieras, anduviera, anduviéramos, anduvierais, anduvieran

avergonzarse *to be ashamed, embarrassed*
Pres. Ind.: me avergüenzo, te avergüenzas, se avergüenza, nos avergonzamos, os avergonzáis, se avergüenzan
Pres. Subj.: me avergüence, te avergüences, se avergüence, nos avergoncemos, os avergoncéis, se avergüencen
Imperative: avergüénzate, avergüéncese, avergoncémonos, avergonzaos, avergüéncense

caber *to fit; to have enough room*
Pres. Ind.: quepo, cabes, cabe, cabemos, cabéis, caben
Preterit: cupe, cupiste, cupo, cupimos, cupisteis, cupieron
Future: cabré, cabrás, cabrá, cabremos, cabréis, cabrán
Conditional: cabría, cabrías, cabría, cabríamos, cabríais, cabrían
Imperative: cabe, quepa, quepamos, cabed, quepan
Pres. Subj.: quepa, quepas, quepa, quepamos, quepáis, quepan
Imp. Subj.: cupiera (cupiese), cupieras, cupiera, cupiéramos, cupierais, cupieran

caer *to fall*
Pres. Ind.: caigo, caes, cae, caemos, caéis, caen
Preterit: caí, caíste, cayó, caímos, caísteis, cayeron
Imperative: cae, caiga, caigamos, caed, caigan
Pres. Subj.: caiga, caigas, caiga, caigamos, caigáis, caigan
Imp. Subj.: cayera (cayese), cayeras, cayera, cayéramos, cayerais, cayeran
Past Part.: caído

conducir *to guide; to drive* (All verbs ending in **-ducir** follow this pattern.)
Pres. Ind.: conduzco, conduces, conduce, conducimos, conducís, conducen
Preterit: conduje, condujiste, condujo, condujimos, condujisteis, condujeron
Imperative: conduce, conduzca, conduzcamos, conducid, conduzcan
Pres. Subj.: conduzca, conduzcas, conduzca, conduzcamos, conduzcáis, conduzcan
Imp. Subj.: condujera (condujese), condujeras, condujera, condujéramos, condujerais, condujeran

convenir *to agree* (see **venir**)

dar *to give*
Pres. Ind.: doy, das, da, damos, dais, dan
Preterit: di, diste, dio, dimos, disteis, dieron
Imperative: da, dé, demos, dad, den
Pres. Subj.: dé, des, dé, demos, deis, den
Imp. Subj.: diera (diese), dieras, diera, diéramos, dierais, dieran

decir *to say, tell*
Pres. Ind.: digo, dices, dice, decimos, decís, dicen
Preterit: dije, dijiste, dijo, dijimos, dijisteis, dijeron
Future: diré, dirás, dirá, diremos, diréis, dirán
Conditional: diría, dirías, diría, diríamos, diríais, dirían
Imperative: di, diga, digamos, decid, digan
Pres. Subj.: diga, digas, diga, digamos, digáis, digan
Imp. Subj.: dijera (dijese), dijeras, dijera, dijéramos, dijerais, dijeran
Pres. Part.: diciendo
Past Part.: dicho

detener *to stop; to hold; to arrest* (see **tener**)

entretener *to entertain, amuse* (see **tener**)

errar *to err; to miss*
Pres. Ind.: yerro, yerras, yerra, erramos, erráis, yerran
Imperative: yerra, yerre, erremos, errad, yerren
Pres. Subj.: yerre, yerres, yerre, erremos, erréis, yerren

estar *to be*
Pres. Ind.: estoy, estás, está, estamos, estáis, están
Preterit: estuve, estuviste, estuvo, estuvimos, estuvisteis, estuvieron
Imperative: está, esté, estemos, estad, estén
Pres. Subj.: esté, estés, esté, estemos, estéis, estén
Imp. Subj.: estuviera (estuviese), estuvieras, estuviera, estuviéramos, estuvierais, estuvieran

haber *to have*
Pres. Ind.: he, has, ha, hemos, habéis, han
Preterit: hube, hubiste, hubo, hubimos, hubisteis, hubieron
Future: habré, habrás, habrá, habremos, habréis, habrán
Conditional: habría, habrías, habría, habríamos, habríais, habrían
Pres. Subj.: haya, hayas, haya, hayamos, hayáis, hayan
Imp. Subj.: hubiera (hubiese), hubieras, hubiera, hubiéramos, hubierais, hubieran

hacer *to do, make*
Pres. Ind.: hago, haces, hace, hacemos, hacéis, hacen
Preterit: hice, hiciste, hizo, hicimos, hicisteis, hicieron
Future: haré, harás, hará, haremos, haréis, harán
Conditional: haría, harías, haría, haríamos, haríais, harían
Imperative: haz, haga, hagamos, haced, hagan
Pres. Subj.: haga, hagas, haga, hagamos, hagáis, hagan
Imp. Subj.: hiciera (hiciese), hicieras, hiciera, hiciéramos, hicierais, hicieran
Past Part.: hecho

imponer *to impose; to deposit* (see **poner**)

ir *to go*
Pres. Ind.: voy, vas, va, vamos, vais, van
Imp. Ind.: iba, ibas, iba, íbamos, ibais, iban
Preterit: fui, fuiste, fue, fuimos, fuisteis, fueron
Imperative: ve, vaya, vayamos, id, vayan
Pres. Subj.: vaya, vayas, vaya, vayamos, vayáis, vayan
Imp. Subj.: fuera (fuese), fueras, fuera, fuéramos, fuerais, fueran

jugar *to play*
Pres. Ind.: juego, juegas, juega, jugamos, jugáis, juegan
Imperative: juega, juegue, juguemos, jugad, jueguen
Pres. Subj.: juegue, juegues, juegue, juguemos, juguéis, jueguen

obtener *to obtain* (see **tener**)

oír *to hear*
Pres. Ind.: oigo, oyes, oye, oímos, oís, oyen
Preterit: oí, oíste, oyó, oímos, oísteis, oyeron
Imperative: oye, oiga, oigamos, oíd, oigan
Pres. Subj.: oiga, oigas, oiga, oigamos, oigáis, oigan
Imp. Subj.: oyera (oyese), oyeras, oyera, oyéramos, oyerais, oyeran
Pres. Part.: oyendo
Past Part.: oído

oler *to smell*
Pres. Ind.: huelo, hueles, huele, olemos, oléis, huelen
Imperative: huele, huela, olamos, oled, huelan
Pres. Subj.: huela, huelas, huela, olamos, oláis, huelan

poder *to be able to*
Preterit: pude, pudiste, pudo, pudimos, pudisteis, pudieron
Future: podré, podrás, podrá, podremos, podréis, podrán
Conditional: podría, podrías, podría, podríamos, podríais, podrían
Imperative: puede, pueda, podamos, poded, puedan
Imp. Subj.: pudiera (pudiese), pudieras, pudiera, pudiéramos, pudierais, pudieran
Pres. Part.: pudiendo

poner *to place, put*
Pres. Ind.: pongo, pones, pone, ponemos, ponéis, ponen
Preterit: puse, pusiste, puso, pusimos, pusisteis, pusieron
Future: pondré, pondrás, pondrá, pondremos, pondréis, pondrán
Conditional: pondría, pondrías, pondría, pondríamos, pondríais, pondrían
Imperative: pon, ponga, pongamos, poned, pongan
Pres. Subj.: ponga, pongas, ponga, pongamos, pongáis, pongan
Imp. Subj.: pusiera (pusiese), pusieras, pusiera, pusiéramos, pusierais, pusieran
Past Part.: puesto

querer *to want, wish; to like, love*
Preterit: quise, quisiste, quiso, quisimos, quisisteis, quisieron
Future: querré, querrás, querrá, querremos, querréis, querrán
Conditional: querría, querrías, querría, querríamos, querríais, querrían
Imp. Subj.: quisiera (quisiese), quisieras, quisiera, quisiéramos, quisierais, quisieran

resolver *to decide on, to solve*
Past Part.: resuelto

saber *to know*
Pres. Ind.: sé, sabes, sabe, sabemos, sabéis, saben
Preterit: supe, supiste, supo, supimos, supisteis, supieron
Future: sabré, sabrás, sabrá, sabremos, sabréis, sabrán
Conditional: sabría, sabrías, sabría, sabríamos, sabríais, sabrían
Imperative: sabe, sepa, sepamos, sabed, sepan
Pres. Subj.: sepa, sepas, sepa, sepamos, sepáis, sepan
Imp. Subj.: supiera (supiese), supieras, supiera, supiéramos, supierais, supieran

salir *to leave; to go out*
Pres. Ind.: salgo, sales, sale, salimos, salís, salen
Future: saldré, saldrás, saldrá, saldremos, saldréis, saldrán
Conditional: saldría, saldrías, saldría, saldríamos, saldríais, saldrían
Imperative: sal, salga, salgamos, salid, salgan
Pres. Subj.: salga, salgas, salga, salgamos, salgáis, salgan

ser *to be*
Pres. Ind.: soy, eres, es, somos, sois, son
Imp. Ind.: era, eras, era, éramos, erais, eran
Preterit: fui, fuiste, fue, fuimos, fuisteis, fueron
Imperative: sé, sea, seamos, sed, sean
Pres. Subj.: sea, seas, sea, seamos, seáis, sean
Imp. Subj.: fuera (fuese), fueras, fuera, fuéramos, fuerais, fueran

suponer *to assume* (see **poner**)

tener *to have*
Pres. Ind.: tengo, tienes, tiene, tenemos, tenéis, tienen
Preterit: tuve, tuviste, tuvo, tuvimos, tuvisteis, tuvieron
Future: tendré, tendrás, tendrá, tendremos, tendréis, tendrán
Conditional: tendría, tendrías, tendría, tendríamos, tendríais, tendrían
Imperative: ten, tenga, tengamos, tened, tengan
Pres. Subj.: tenga, tengas, tenga, tengamos, tengáis, tengan
Imp. Subj.: tuviera (tuviese), tuvieras, tuviera, tuviéramos, tuvierais, tuvieran

traducir *to translate* (see **conducir**)

traer *to bring*
Pres. Ind.: traigo, traes, trae, traemos, traéis, traen
Preterit: traje, trajiste, trajo, trajimos, trajisteis, trajeron

Imperative:	trae, traiga, traigamos, traed, traigan
Pres. Subj.:	traiga, traigas, traiga, traigamos, traigáis, traigan
Imp. Subj.:	trajera (trajese), trajeras, trajera, trajéramos, trajerais, trajeran
Pres. Part.:	trayendo
Past Part.:	traído

valer *to be worth*

Pres. Ind.:	valgo, vales, vale, valemos, valéis, valen
Future:	valdré, valdrás, valdrá, valdremos, valdréis, valdrán
Conditional:	valdría, valdrías, valdría, valdríamos, valdríais, valdrían
Imperative:	vale, valga, valgamos, valed, valgan
Pres. Subj.:	valga, valgas, valga, valgamos, valgáis, valgan

venir *to come*

Pres. Ind.:	vengo, vienes, viene, venimos, venís, vienen
Preterit:	vine, viniste, vino, vinimos, vinisteis, vinieron
Future:	vendré, vendrás, vendrá, vendremos, vendréis, vendrán
Conditional:	vendría, vendrías, vendría, vendríamos, vendríais, vendrían
Imperative:	ven, venga, vengamos, venid, vengan
Pres. Subj.:	venga, vengas, venga, vengamos, vengáis, vengan
Imp. Subj.:	viniera (viniese), vinieras, viniera, viniéramos, vinierais, vinieran
Pres. Part.:	viniendo

ver *to see*

Pres. Ind.:	veo, ves, ve, vemos, veis, ven
Imp. Ind.:	veía, veías, veía, veíamos, veíais, veían
Preterit:	vi, viste, vio, vimos, visteis, vieron
Imperative:	ve, vea, veamos, ved, vean
Pres. Subj.:	vea, veas, vea, veamos, veáis, vean
Imp. Subj.:	viera (viese), vieras, viera, viéramos, vierais, vieran
Past Part.:	visto

volver *to return*

Past Part.:	vuelto

C: Glossary of Grammatical Terms

adjective: A word that is used to describe a noun: *tall* girl, *difficult* lesson.

adverb: A word that modifies a verb, an adjective, or another adverb. It answers the questions "How?" "When?" "Where?": She walked *slowly.* She'll be here *tomorrow.* She is *here.*

agreement: A term applied to changes in form that nouns cause in the words that surround them. In Spanish, verb forms agree with their subjects in person and number (**yo** habl**o**, **él** habl**a**, etc.). Spanish adjectives agree in gender and number with the noun they describe. Thus, a feminine plural noun requires a feminine plural ending in the adjective that describes it (cas**as** amarill**as**), and a masculine singular noun requires a masculine singular ending in the adjective (libr**o** negr**o**).

auxiliary verb: A verb that helps in the conjugation of another verb: I *have* finished. He *was* called. She *will* go. He *would* eat.

command form: The form of the verb used to give an order or direction: *Go! Come back! Turn* to the right!

conjugation: The process by which the forms of the verb are presented in their different moods and tenses: I *am*, you *are*, he *is*, she *was*, we *were*, etc.

contraction: The combination of two or more words into one: *isn't, don't, can't.*

definite article: A word used before a noun indicating a definite person or thing: *the* woman, *the* money.

demonstrative: A word that refers to a definite person or object: *this, that, these, those.*

diphthong: A combination of two vowels forming one syllable. In Spanish, a diphthong is composed of one *strong* vowel (**a, e, o**) and one *weak* vowel (**u, i**) or two weak vowels: **ei, au, ui.**

exclamation: A word used to express emotion: *How* strong! *What* beauty!

gender: A distinction of nouns, pronouns, and adjectives, based on whether they are masculine or feminine.

indefinite article: A word used before a noun that refers to an indefinite person or object: *a* child, *an* apple.

infinitive: The form of the verb generally preceded in English by the word *to* and showing no subject or number: *to do, to bring.*

interrogative: A word used in asking a question: *Who? What? Where?*

main clause: A group of words that includes a subject and a verb and that by itself has complete meaning: *They saw me. I go now.*

noun: A word that names a person, place, or thing: *Ann, London, pencil,* etc.

number: Number refers to singular and plural: *chair, chairs.*

object: Generally a noun or a pronoun that is the receiver of the verb's action. A direct object answers the question "What?" or "Whom?": We know *her.* Take *it.* An indirect object answers the question "To whom?" or "To what?": Give *John* the money. Nouns and pronouns can also be objects of prepositions: The letter is *from Rick.* I'm thinking *about you.*

past participle: Past forms of a verb: *gone, worked, written,* etc.

person: The form of the pronoun and of the verb that shows the person referred to: *I* (first-person singular), *you* (second-person singular), *she* (third-person singular), etc.

possessive: A word that denotes ownership or possession: This is *our* house. The book isn't *mine.*

preposition: A word that introduces a noun or pronoun and indicates its function in the sentence: They were *with* us. She is *from* Nevada.

pronoun: A word that is used to replace a noun: *she, them, us,* etc. A **subject pronoun** refers to the person or thing spoken of: *They* work. An **object pronoun** receives the action of the verb: They arrested *us* (direct object pronoun). She spoke to *him* (indirect object pronoun). A pronoun can also be the object of a preposition: The children stayed with *us.*

reflexive pronoun: A pronoun that refers back to the subject: *myself, yourself, himself, herself, itself, ourselves,* etc.

subject: The person, place, or thing spoken of: *Robert* works. *Our car* is new.

subordinate clause: A clause that has no complete meaning by itself but depends on a main clause: They knew *that I was here.*

tense: The group of forms in a verb that show the time in which the action of the verb takes place: *I go* (present indicative), *I'm going* (present progressive), *I went* (past), *I was going* (past progressive), *I will go* (future), *I would go* (conditional), *I have gone* (present perfect), *I had gone* (past perfect), *that I may go* (present subjunctive), etc.

verb: A word that expresses an action or a state: We *sleep.* The baby *is* sick.

D: Answer Key to Tome Este Examen

Lección 1

A. 1. los / unos 2. los / unos 3. el / un 4. las / unas 5. la / una 6. la / una 7. los / unos 8. los / unos
B. 1. nosotras 2. ellos 3. ella 4. ustedes 5. ellas 6. él 7. usted 8. tú
C. 1. soy / es 2. son 3. somos 4. son 5. eres 6. es
D. 1. El alumno es norteamericano. 2. Los lápices son verdes. 3. Las mesas son blancas. 4. Es un hombre español. 5. Las profesoras son inglesas. 6. Los muchachos son ricos. 7. Es una mujer inteligente. 8. Los señores son muy simpáticos.
E. 1. De-i-a-zeta 2. Jota-i-eme-é-ene-e-zeta 3. Ve-a-ere-ge-a-ese 4. Pe-a-erre-a 5. Efe-e-ele-i-ú 6. A-ce-u-eñe-a
F. 1. ocho 2. catorce 3. veintiséis 4. once 5. treinta y cinco 6. diez 7. trece 8. cero 9. veintiocho 10. diecisiete 11. treinta y nueve 12. quince
G. 1. llama / dónde 2. gusto 3. dice 4. cuarto / muy 5. alumnos (estudiantes) 6. habla 7. está 8. Saludos 9. es 10. nada
H. 1. es 2. que no se han casado

Lección 2

A. 1. tomas 2. habla (conversa) 3. hablamos 4. deseo 5. estudia 6. trabajan 7. necesita 8. terminamos
B. 1. ¿Hablan ellos inglés con los estudiantes? / Ellos no hablan inglés con los estudiantes. 2. ¿Es ella de México? / Ella no es de México. 3. ¿Terminan Uds. hoy? / Uds. no terminan hoy.
C. 1. tu 2. su 3. nuestra 4. mis 5. sus 6. nuestros 7. su 8. su
D. 1. las 2. los 3. el 4. las 5. los 6. el 7. la 8. la
E. 1. ochenta bolígrafos 2. cuarenta y seis mochilas 3. setenta y dos relojes 4. treinta y tres ventanas 5. doscientos libros 6. ciento quince cuadernos 7. sesenta y ocho estudiantes 8. cincuenta mapas 9. noventa y cinco computadoras 10. setenta y tres cestos de papeles 11. cien plumas 12. ciento trece borradores
F. 1. Es la una 2. a las nueve y media de la mañana 3. por la tarde 4. Son 5. a las tres menos cuarto
G. martes / miércoles / viernes / sábado
1. el primero de marzo 2. el diez de junio 3. el trece de agosto 4. el veintiséis de diciembre 5. el tres de septiembre 6. el veintiocho de octubre 7. el diecisiete de julio 8. el cuatro de abril 9. el dos de enero 10. el cinco de febrero
1. invierno 2. primavera 3. otoño 4. verano
H. 1. hora 2. horario / Aquí 3. solamente 4. taza / vaso 5. toman 6. semestre 7. primavera 8. asignatura (materia) 9. copa 10. jugo 11. aguafiestas 12. dinero
I. 1. 66 2. español 3. segundo

Lección 3

A. 1. escribe 2. vivimos 3. deben 4. corres 5. bebo 6. come 7. abre 8. Reciben
B. 1. la amiga de Pedro 2. la ropa de Paco 3. la casa de la señora Peña 4. los hermanos de Eva
C. 1. vienes 2. venimos / tenemos 3. tienen / vienen 4. vengo / tengo 5. tiene 6. tiene
D. 1. ...tengo mucho calor. 2. ...tiene mucha hambre. 3. ...tiene mucha sed. 4. ...tienes mucho frío. 5. ...tenemos mucho sueño. 6. ...tienen mucho miedo. 7. ...tengo mucha prisa.
E. 1. esas / esos 2. esta / este 3. aquel / aquella 4. esa / ese 5. estos / estas
F. 1. quinientos sesenta y siete 2. setecientos noventa 3. mil 4. trescientos cuarenta y cinco 5. seiscientos quince 6. ochocientos setenta y cuatro 7. novecientos sesenta y cinco 8. ochocientos veinticinco 9. cuatrocientos ochenta y uno 10. trece mil ochocientos dieciséis
G. 1. trabajos 2. rato 3. Quién 4. césped (zacate) 5. cosas 6. poner 7. sacudir 8. puerta / abrir 9. sacar 10. vienen / momento 11. bebo / sed 12. pasar
H. 1. Los hombres ayudan con los trabajos de la casa. 2. La comida mexicana es popular en todo el mundo. 3. Son populares en Rusia y en Japón.

Lección 4

A. 1. salgo 2. conduzco 3. traduzco 4. hago 5. quepo 6. traigo
B. 1. conoces / Sabes 2. sé 3. conocemos 4. conocen 5. sabe
C. 1. Yo conozco a la tía de Julio. 2. Luis tiene tres tíos y dos tías. 3. Ana lleva a su prima a la fiesta. 4. Uds. conocen San Salvador.
D. 1. No conocemos al Sr. Vega. 2. Es la hermana del profesor. 3. Venimos del club. 4. Voy al laboratorio. 5. Vengo de la playa.
E. 1. doy 2. está 3. vamos 4. estás 5. están 6. va 7. dan 8. voy
F. 1. ¿Dónde vas a estudiar? 2. ¿Qué van a comer Uds.? 3. ¿Con quién va a ir Roberto? 4. ¿A qué hora va a terminar Ud.? 5. ¿Cuándo van a trabajar ellos?
G. 1. discos 2. algo 3. castaños 4. pelirroja 5. estatura 6. cumpleaños 7. soltera 8. pareja 9. entremeses 10. tocando / bailar 11. levantan / Salud 12. éxito
H. 1. el petróleo 2. momias 3. primavera 4. 300

Lección 5

A. 1. estamos sirviendo 2. estoy leyendo 3. está bailando 4. estás comiendo 5. está durmiendo
B. 1. es / está 2. está / Es 3. son 4. estás 5. es 6. es 7. estamos 8. Son 9. son 10. están
C. 1. prefieres / quiere 2. empiezan (comienzan) 3. pensamos 4. prefieren 5. queremos 6. entiendo
D. 1. mucho mayor que 2. tan alto como 3. la más inteligente de 4. tan bien como 5. el mejor de 6. mucho más bonita que
E. 1. conmigo / contigo / con ellos (ellas) 2. para ti / para mí / para ella
F. 1. pagar / propina 2. sopa / coctel 3. tostado / mantequilla / mermelada 4. asado 5. especialidad / chuletas 6. helado 7. puré / ensalada 8. travieso 9. jamón 10. hamburguesa / caliente
G. 1. después de 2. principal

Lección 6

A. 1. recuerdo 2. vuelve 3. cuestan 4. puedo 5. encontramos 6. podemos 7. duerme
B. 1. piden 2. servimos 3. consigues 4. dice 5. sirve 6. digo 7. pedimos 8. consigue
C. 1. No, no voy a leerlos. (No, no los voy a leer.) 2. No, no lo (la) conoce. 3. No, no me llevan. 4. No, ella no te llama mañana. 5. No. no lo necesito. 6. No, no la tengo. 7. No, ellos no nos conocen. 8. No. no las conseguimos.
D. 1. Tengo algo aquí. 2. ¿Quiere algo más? 3. Siempre vamos al supermercado. 4. Quiero (o) la pluma roja o la pluma verde. 5. Siempre llamo a alguien.
E. 1. Hace cinco años que (yo) vivo en Honduras. 2. ¿Cuánto tiempo hace que (Ud.) estudia español, Sr. Smith? 3. Hace dos horas que (ellos) escriben. 4. Hace dos días que (ella) no come.
F. 1. azúcar 2. chuletas 3. panadería 4. almorzamos 5. vuelven 6. muertos 7. recién 8. cerca 9. cangrejo / langosta 10. docena / salsa
G. 1. San José 2. las operaciones del Canal 3. no tiene 4. el café

Lección 7

A. 1. Ellos comieron tortilla y bebieron limonada. 2. Luis salió a las ocho y volvió a las cinco. 3. Tú cerraste la puerta y abriste las ventanas 4. Yo empecé a las seis y terminé a las ocho. 5. Nosotros leímos un poema y ella leyó una novela. 6. Yo busqué el dinero y no lo encontré. 7. Yo llegué temprano y comencé a trabajar. 8. Yo compré carne aquí y pagué menos.
B. 1. fue 2. Dieron 3. fue 4. fui 5. fueron 6. Di 7. fui 8. fuimos
C. 1. No, no me traen el jugo. 2. No, no le doy el dinero a él. 3. No, no te voy a comprar los libros. (No, no voy a comprarte los libros). 4. No, no le voy a dar los cuadernos a Elsa. (No, no voy a darle los cuadernos a Elsa). 5. No, no me gusta el café. 6. No, no nos van a dar las invitaciones. (No. no van a darnos las invitaciones.)
D. 1. Me gusta / no me gusta 2. Te gusta 3. A mi mamá le gusta más 4. Nos gusta 5. A mi hermano le gusta
E. 1. se levantan / se acuestan 2. afeitarme 3. te pruebas 4. se sienta 5. nos bañamos 6. vestirse
F. 1. fin 2. divertí 3. se levantan 4. partido 5. cine 6. rompió 7. zoológico 8. escalar 9. montar 10. medianoche 11. nadar 12. vez
G. 1. Quique 2. populares

Lección 8

A. 1. trajeron / traje 2. Tuve 3. hizo 4. dijiste / dijeron 5. vino / viniste 6. estuvimos / estuvieron 7. hicieron 8. supe 9. condujeron / conduje 10. quiso
B. 1. Sí, te (se) las compré. 2. Sí, se los trajimos. 3. Sí, me lo van a dar. (Sí, van a dármelo.) 4. Sí, nos los va a traer. (Sí, va a traérnoslos.) 5. Sí, se la va a comprar. (Sí, va a comprársela.) 6. Sí, me las traen.
C. 1. se divirtieron / siguieron / durmieron 2. pidió 3. murió 4. consiguió
D. 1. ibas 2. era 3. hablaban 4. veíamos 5. pescaban 6. comía
E. 1. fácilmente 2. especialmente 3. lentamente 4. rápidamente 5. lenta y claramente 6. francamente
F. 1. aire 2. cazar 3. armar 4. cesta 5. remar 6. pelo 7. frecuentemente 8. acuático 9. tomar 10. tabla 11. hacer 12. encanta
G. 1. mayor 2. merengue 3. Yunque

Lección 9

A. 1. para 2. por 3. por 4. por 5. para 6. para / por 7. para / por / por 8. por
B. 1. hace / calor 2. hace / frío / nieva 3. llueve 4. hay / niebla 5. hace / sol
C. 1. celebramos 2. Eran / salí / Llegué 3. dijo / era / pedí 4. era / vivía 5. estaba / vi 6. fue / estaba / Prefirió 7. hice 8. estábamos / llamaste
D. 1. Hace tres horas que llegué. 2. Hace cuatro meses que ellos vinieron. 3. Hace media hora que empecé a trabajar. 4. Hace cinco días que (ellos) terminaron. 5. Hace diez años que tú llegaste.
E. 1. el tuyo 2. mías 3. los tuyos 4. nuestros 5. El suyo (El de ellos) 6. mío / suyo (de ella)
F. 1. baratos 2. zapatería 3. facultad 4. par 5. mangas 6. servirle 7. moda 8. descalzo 9. ponerme 10. ojo / cara 11. calza 12. húmedo
G. 1. métrico 2. nuevo sol

Lección 10

A. 1. cerradas 2. abierta 3. roto 4. dormidos 5. escritas 6. hecha
B. 1. ha llegado 2. he roto 3. han traído 4. han vuelto / hemos podido 5. han muerto 6. has dicho
C. 1. habían vuelto 2. había firmado 3. habías hecho 4. habíamos escrito 5. había puesto 6. habían ido
D. 1. Llame 2. Camine 3. Salgan 4. Esté 5. venga 6. Vayan 7. lo haga 8. dé 9. sean 10. Póngala
E. 1. firmar / fechar 2. depositar 3. abierto / feriado 4. saldo 5. conjunta 6. cuadras 7. cola 8. talonario 9. sucursal 10. cajero 11. préstamo 12. efectivo 13. caja 14. sellos (estampillas) 15. diligencias
F. 1. Galápagos 2. Cuzco 3. Sucre 4. Itaipú

Lección 11

A. 1. Yo quiero que ella vaya a Viña del Mar. 2. Nosotros deseamos viajar en avión. 3. Ella me sugiere que yo vaya a Buenos Aires. 4. El agente quiere venderme el pasaje. 5. Ellos nos aconsejan que compremos seguro. 6. Yo no quiero llevar muchas maletas. 7. Ellos no quieren que ella los lleve en su coche. 8. Nosotros no queremos ir contigo. 9. ¿Tú me sugieres que venga luego? 10. Ella necesita que Uds. le den la maleta.
B. 1. que ella se vaya pronto. 2. que los pasajes sean muy caros. 3. estar aquí. 4. irse de vacaciones. 5. que mamá se sienta bien hoy. 6. que ellos no puedan ir a la fiesta.
C. 1. a / de / a / en / en / en / a 2. a / a / de / a 3. de / de
D. 1. asiento / ventanilla 2. mano / compartimiento 3. agencia 4. embarque (embarco) / auxiliar 5. exceso 6. salida 7. incluyen / excursiones 8. cambio 9. cancelar 10. viajero 11. crucero 12. lugares / capital
E. 1. vos 2. tango 3. separación

Lección 12

A. 1. hable español. 2. incluya el hotel. 3. no son caros. 4. salen a las seis. 5. pueda reservar los pasajes?
B. 1. Compra el televisor. 2. Díselo. 3. Viaja mañana. 4. Sal con esa persona. 5. Pon la maleta debajo del asiento. 6. Invítalo. 7. Vete. 8. Ven entre semana. 9. Regresa tarde. 10. Haz la reservación. 11. Tráeme el folleto. 12. Pídele los comprobantes ahora.

C. 1. se enamoró de / se casó con 2. insiste en 3. no te olvides de / Acuérdate de 4. no me di cuenta de / no confiaban en
D. 1. segundo / séptimo / quinto / primero / octavo / cuarto / noveno / tercero / sexto / décimo
E. 1. ducha 2. ascensor (elevador) / subir 3. calefacción 4. cama 5. precio 6. montón 7. desocupar 8. vista 9. servicio 10. aire 11. puesto / regalos 12. propietario 13. completa 14. libre 15. piso
F. 1. muchos 2. más 3. Argentina 4. Brasilia

Lección 13

A. 1. son 2. esté 3. pueda 4. vienen 5. sirven
B. 1. estén llamando la ambulancia. 2. ellos vayan a quedarse en el hospital. 3. prefiere venir con nosotros. 4. cobran 50 dólares por las radiografías. 5. el cuarto no tenga calefacción. 6. ella esté en el hospital.
C. 1. terminen 2. podamos 3. traiga 4. empiecen 5. necesito un médico 6. llegue 7. no tengo hambre 8. llueva
D. 1. Quedémonos aquí. 2. No se lo digamos a nadie. 3. Levantémonos a las siete. 4. Preguntemos el precio de los análisis. 5. Démoselo a la enfermera. 6. Vamos a la sala de rayos X.
E. 1. Cuál 2. Cuál 3. Qué 4. Qué 5. Cuál
F. 1. enfermera 2. codo 3. desmayarse 4. dedos 5. dientes 6. pasar 7. dudar 8. continuar 9. escalera 10. piernas 11. ojos 12. lengua 13. romperse 14. piano
G. 1. gratis 2. socorro

Lección 14

A. 1. Irán / hablarán 2. pesarás / tomarás 3. traerá / pondrá 4. vendré / pediré 5. pondrá / dará
B. 1. hablaríamos 2. saldría 3. harías 4. sabría 5. iría 6. pedirían
C. 1. pudiéramos 2. entendieras 3. pusieran 4. quisiera 5. trajera 6. tuvieran 7. supiéramos 8. dijera 9. fuera 10. fueras
D. 1. trajera 2. vinieran 3. estuviera 4. supiera 5. tuviera 6. pidiera
E. 1. si tuviera dinero. 2. si tenemos tiempo. 3. si pudiéramos. 4. Si Ud. la ve. 5. como si (ella) fuera su madre.
F. 1. grados 2. tos 3. mejore 4. recetar 5. calmante 6. dermatólogo / cardiólogo 7. tijeras 8. empeoró 9. cita (turno) 10. seguro 11. botiquín 12. suerte
G. 1. Madrid 2. segunda 3. Sevilla 4. flamenco

Vocabularies

The number following each vocabulary item indicates the lesson in which it first appears.

The following abbreviations are used:

abbr.	abbreviation	*indir. obj.*	indirect object	*pron.*	pronoun
adj.	adjective	*inf.*	infinitive	*refl. pron.*	reflexive pronoun
adv.	adverb	*m.*	masculine	*rel. pron.*	relative pronoun
conj.	conjunction	*Mex.*	Mexico	*sing.*	singular
dir. obj.	direct object	*neut. pron.*	neuter pronoun	*subj.*	subjunctive
f.	feminine	*obj.*	object	*v.*	verb
fam.	familiar	*pl.*	plural		
form.	formal	*prep.*	preposition		

Spanish-English

A

a at (with time of day), to, 2; **— la parrilla** grilled, 5; **— menos que** unless, 13; **— menudo** often, 8; **— poco más de** a little more than; **¿ — qué hora?** at what time?, 2; **¿— quién(es)?** whom, 4; **— veces** sometimes, 6; **— ver** let's see, 6

abierto(a) open, 10

abogado(a) *(m., f.)* lawyer

abordar to board, 11

abrigo *(m.)* coat, 9

abril April, 2

abrir to open, 3

abrochar: abrocharse el cinturón de seguridad to fasten the seat belt, 11

abuela *(f.)* grandmother, 4

abuelo *(m.)* grandfather, 4

abuelos *(m. pl.)* grandparents

aburrido(a) boring, 2

aburrirse to be bored, 7

acá here, 8

acabado(a) finished

acabar de + *inf.* to have just (done something), 8

acampar to camp, 8

accidente *(m.)* accident

aceite *(m.)* oil

acompañado(a) with someone else, accompanied

aconsejar to advise, 11

acordarse (de) (o > ue) to remember, 12

acostarse (o > ue) to go to bed, 7

acostumbrado(a) accustomed or used to, 8

actividad *(f.)* activity, 8; **— al aire libre** outdoor activity, 8

actualmente at present

además *(adv.)* besides, 2; **— de** *(prep.)* in addition to

adiós good-bye, 1

administración de empresas *(f.)* business administration, 2

admitir to admit, 14

¿adónde? where (to)?, 4

advertencia *(f.)* warning

aerolínea *(f.)* airline, 11

aeropuerto *(m.)* airport, 11

afeitarse to shave, 7

afortunadamente luckily, 14

agencia *(f.)* agency, 11; **— de viajes** *(f.)* travel agency, 11

agente *(m., f.)* agent, 11

agosto August, 2

agua (el) *(f.)* water, 2; **— con hielo** *(f.)* ice water, 2; **— mineral** mineral water, 2; **— oxigenada** hydrogen peroxide, 14

aguacate *(m.)* avocado, 6

aguafiestas *(m., f.)* spoilsport, 2

águila (el) *(f.)* eagle

ahí there, 8

ahora now, 4; **— mismo** right now

ahorrar to save *(money)*, 10

aire *(m.)* air; **— acondicionado** *(m.)* air conditioning, 12

ají *(m.)* green pepper, 6

al (a + el) to the, 4; **— día** a day, per day, 6; **— día siguiente** (on) the following day, 5

albóndiga *(f.)* meatball, 6

alegrarse (de) to be glad (about), 12

alemán *(m.)* German *(language)*

alérgico(a) allergic, 13

alfabeto *(m.)* alphabet

algo something, anything, 5; **¿— más?** anything else?, 10; **— para comer (tomar)** something to eat (drink)

algodón *(m.)* cotton, 14

alguien someone, anyone, 6

algún, alguno(s), alguna(s) any, some, 6; **en alguna parte** anywhere, somewhere; **alguna vez** ever, 6; **algunas veces** sometimes, 6

allá there

allí there, 12

alma (el) *(f.)* soul

almorzar (o > ue) to have lunch, 6

almuerzo *(m.)* lunch, 5

alquilar to rent, 8

alto(a) high, tall, 1

alumno(a) *(m., f.)* student, 1

amarillo(a) yellow, 1

ambulancia *(f.)* ambulance, 13

amigo(a) *(m., f.)* friend, 2

amistad *(f.)* friendship

amor love; **mi amor** darling, my love, 8

amparo *(m.)* shelter
ampliar to expand
analfabeto(a) *(m., f.)* illiterate
análisis *(m.)* test, 13
anaranjado(a) orange, 1
ancho(a) wide
anfitrión *(m.)* host
anfitriona *(f.)* hostess
animado(a) enthused, 4
aniversario *(m.)* anniversary, 5; **— de bodas** *(m.)* wedding anniversary
anoche last night, 7
anotar to write down
anteayer the day before yesterday
antes before; **— de** *(prep.)* before, 6; **— de que** *(conj.)* before, 13
antiácido *(m.)* antacid, 14
antibiótico *(m.)* antibiotic, 14
antiguo(a) old
antipático(a) unpleasant, 1
antropología *(f.)* anthropology, 2
añadir to add
año *(m.)* year, 2; **— escolar** *(m.)* school year
aparatos electrodomésticos *(m. pl.)* home appliances
apartamento *(m.)* apartment, 6
apellido *(m.)* last name; **— de soltera** maiden name
apio *(m.)* celery, 6
aprender (a) to learn (to), 11
apretar (e > ie) to be tight, 9
apurarse to hurry
aquel(los), aquella(s) *(adj.)* that, those *(distant)*, 3
aquél, aquéllos, aquélla(s) *(pron.)* that (one), those *(distant)*, 3
aquello *(neut. pron.)* that, 3
aquí here, 5; **— está** here it is, 2; **— las tiene** here you are, 10
árbol *(m.)* tree, 13
archivar la información to store information, 10
arena *(f.)* sand, 8
aretes *(m. pl.)* earrings, 9
argentino(a) Argentinian
armar to pitch (a tent), to put together, 8
arrancar to tear out
arroyo *(m.)* brook
arroz *(m.)* rice, 5; **— con leche** rice pudding, 5
arte *(m.)* art, 2
asado(a) baked, 5
ascensor *(m.)* elevator, 12
asegurado(a) insured
aseguranza *(f.)(Mex.)* insurance, 14
así que so, 7
asiento *(m.)* seat, 11; **— de pasillo** *(m.)* aisle seat, 11; **— de ventanilla** *(m.)* window seat, 11
asignatura *(f.)* course, subject, 2
asistir to attend
aspiradora *(f.)* vacuum cleaner
aspirina *(f.)* aspirin
atender (e > ie) to see *(a patient)*, 13
aula (el) *(f.)* classroom, 2
aunque although, 4; even if, 13
auto *(m.)* automobile, 10
autobús *(m.)* bus
automóvil *(m.)* automobile, 10
auxiliar de vuelo *(m., f.)* flight attendant, 11
ave (el) *(f.)* bird
avena *(f.)* porridge
averiguar to find out, 11
avión *(m.)* plane, 11
ayer yesterday, 7
ayuda *(f.)* assistance
ayudar to help, 12
azafata *(f.)* flight attendant, 11
azúcar *(m.)* sugar, 6
azul blue, 1

B

bailar to dance, 4; **¿Bailamos?** Shall we dance?, 4
bajar to go down
bajo *(prep.)* under, 8
bajo(a) short *(height)*, 5
balneario *(m.)* beach resort
banco *(m.)* bank, 10
bañadera *(f.)* bathtub, 12
bañarse to bathe, 7
baño *(m.)* bathroom, 3
barato(a) inexpensive, 9
barrer to sweep, 3
barrio *(m.)* neighborhood
basura *(f.)* garbage, 3
bata *(f.)* robe, 9
batería de cocina *(f. sing.)* kitchen utensils
batido *(m.)* milkshake
beber to drink, 3
bebida *(f.)* drink, 4
béisbol *(m.)* baseball, 7
biblioteca *(f.)* library, 1
bien fine, well, 1; **muy —** very well, 1; **no muy —** not very well, 1
bienvenido(a) welcome, 1
biftec *(m.)* steak, 5
billete *(m.)* ticket, 11
billetera *(f.)* wallet, 9
biología *(f.)* biology, 2
bisabuela *(f.)* great-grandmother
bisabuelo *(m.)* great-grandfather
bisnieta *(f.)* great-granddaughter
bisnieto *(m.)* great-grandson
bistec *(m.)* steak, 5
blanco(a) white, 1
blanquillo *(m.) (Mex.)* egg, 5
blusa *(f.)* blouse, 9
boca *(f.)* mouth, 13
boda *(f.)* wedding, 5
bolígrafo *(m.)* pen, 1
bolsa *(f.)* handbag, purse; **— de dormir** *(f.)* sleeping bag, 8
bolso *(m.)* handbag, purse; **— de mano** *(m.)* carry-on bag, 11
bonito(a) pretty, 1
borrador *(m.)* eraser, 1
borrico *(m.)* donkey
bosque *(m.)* forest
bota *(f.)* boot, 9
botella *(f.)* bottle, 2
botones *(m. sing.)* bellhop, 12
brazo *(m.)* arm, 13
brindar to toast, 4
brindis *(m.)* toast *(at a celebration)*, 4
brócoli *(m.)* broccoli, 6
bromear to joke, to kid, 7
bucear to scuba dive, 8
bueno... well . . . , okay, 1
bueno(a) good, 2; **buenas noches** good evening, good night, 1; **buenas tardes** good afternoon, 1; **buenos días** good morning, 1
bufanda *(f.)* scarf, 9
buscar to look for, to get, 9; to pick up

C

caballería *(f.)* chivalry
caballero *(m.)* gentleman; knight
caber to fit, 4
cabeza *(f.)* head, 13
cacerola *(f.)* saucepan, 3
cadena *(f.)* chain, 9

caerse to fall down, 13
café *(m.) (adj.)* brown, 1; coffee, 2; **— con leche** coffee with milk; **café** *(m.)* (restaurant), 5; **— al aire libre** outdoor café
cafetera *(f.)* coffeepot, 3
cafetería *(f.)* cafeteria, 2
caja de seguridad *(f.)* safe-deposit box, 10
cajero(a) *(m., f.)* teller, 10; **— automático** *(m.)* automatic teller machine, 10
calcetín *(m.)* sock
caldo *(m.)* soup *(Mex.)*, 5; broth
calefacción *(f.)* heating, 12
calidad *(f.)* quality
cálido(a) hot, 9
caliente hot, 12
calle *(f.)* street, 1
calmante *(m.)* tranquilizer, painkiller, 14
calumnia *(f.)* slander
calzar to wear a certain shoe size, 9
calzoncillos *(m. pl.)* undershorts, 9
cama *(f.)* bed, 12; **— chica (pequeña)** *(f.)* twin bed, 12; **— doble** *(f.)* double bed, 12; **— matrimonial** *(f.)* double bed
camarera *(f.)* waitress, 5
camarero *(m.)* waiter, 5
camarones *(m. pl.)* shrimp, 5
cambiar to change, 7; **— de avión** to change planes
cambio *(m.)* change; **en cambio** on the other hand, 8
cambio de moneda *(m.)* rate of exchange, 11; **¿a cómo está el —?** what's the rate of exchange?, 11
camilla *(f.)* gurney, stretcher
caminar to walk
camisa *(f.)* shirt, 9
camiseta *(f.)* T-shirt, 9
camisón *(m.)* nightgown, 9
campo *(m.)* country *(as opposed to city)*; field; **— de batalla** battlefield
cancelar to cancel, 11
cangrejo *(m.)* crab, 6
canoa *(f.)* canoe, 8
cansado(a) tired, 4
cansarse to get tired, 11
cantidad *(f.)* amount
caña de azúcar *(f.)* sugar cane
caña de pescar *(f.)* fishing rod, 8
capital *(f.)* capital, 11
cara *(f.)* face, 13
¡caramba! gee!, 1
cardiólogo(a) *(m., f.)* cardiologist, 14
cardo *(m.)* thistle
cargado(a) loaded
carmín *(m.)* red (Cuba)
carne *(f.)* meat, 6
carnicería *(f.)* meat market
caro(a) expensive, 6
carro *(m.)* automobile, 10
carta *(f.)* letter, 10
cartera *(f.)* handbag, purse
casa *(f.)* house, 3; **— central** main office, 10; **en —** at home
casado(a) married, 4; **recién casados** *(m. pl.)* newlyweds, 6
casarse (con) to marry, to get married (to), 12
casete *(m.)* (cassette) tape
casi almost, 13
caso *(m.)* case; **en ese —** in that case
castaño brown *(hair or eyes)*, 4
catarro *(m.)* cold
catorce fourteen, 2
cazar to hunt, 8
cebolla *(f.)* onion, 5
cédula de identidad *(f.)* I.D. card, 12
celebrar to celebrate, 4
cena *(f.)* dinner
cenar to have dinner (supper), 3
céntrico(a) central, 12
cerca (de) near, 6; **— de aquí** near here
cerdo *(m.)* pork, 6
cereal *(m.)* cereal
cereza *(f.)* cherry, 6
cero zero, 1
cerrado(a) closed, 10
cerrar (e > ie) to close, 5
certificado(a) certified, 10
cerveza *(f.)* beer, 2
césped *(m.)* lawn, 3
cesta *(f.)* basket, 8
cesto de papeles *(m.)* wastebasket, 1
chaleco *(m.)* vest, 9
champán *(m.)* champagne, 4
chaqueta *(f.)* jacket, 9
chau bye, 1
cheque *(m.)* check, 10; **— de viajero** *(m.)* traveler's check, 11
chequeo *(m.)* checkup, 14
chica *(f.)* young girl, 1
chico *(m.)* young man, 1
chico(a) little, small, 8
chillido *(m.)* screech
chocar (con) to collide, 13
chocolate *(m.)* chocolate; **— caliente** *(m.)* hot chocolate, 2
chorizo *(m.)* sausage
chuleta *(f.)* chop *(of meat)*, 6; **— de cerdo** pork chop, 6; **— de ternera** veal chop, 6
ciclón *(m.)* cyclone
cielo *(m.)* sky, 9; **el — está despejado** the sky is clear, 9; **el — está nublado** the sky is cloudy, 9
cien (ciento) one hundred, 2
ciencias políticas *(f. pl.)* political science, 2
cierto(a) true
ciervo *(m.)* deer
cigüeña *(f.)* stork
cinco five, 1
cincuenta fifty, 2
cine *(m.)* movies, movie theater, 7
cinta *(f.)* tape
cinto *(m.)* belt, 9
cinturón *(m.)* belt, 9
cirujano(a) *(m., f.)* surgeon, 14
cita *(f.)* appointment, 14
ciudad *(f.)* city, 3
claro(a) light
clase *(f.)* class, 1; **— de español (castellano)** Spanish class, 1; **— turista** tourist class, 11; **primera —** first class, 11
clima *(m.)* climate, 9
club *(m.)* club, 4; **— nocturno** *(m.)* nightclub, 7
cobrar to charge, 10; **— un cheque** to cash a check, 10
cocina *(f.)* kitchen, 3; stove
cocinar to cook, 6
cocinero(a) *(m., f.)* cook, 6
coche *(m.)* automobile, 10
codo *(m.)* elbow, 13
colador *(m.)* strainer, 3
colar (o > ue) to strain
color *(m.)* color, 1
combinación *(f.)* slip
comedor *(m.)* dining room
comenzar (e > ie) to start, to begin, 5
comer to eat, 3; **— algo** to have something to eat, 4
comestibles *(m. pl.)* groceries *(food items)*
comida *(f.)* food, meal, 3
comido(a) eaten, 10

como like, 9; as; **— si** as if, 14; **— siempre** as usual, 13

¿cómo? pardon, 1; how? 1; **¿— es... ?** what is . . . like?; **¿— está usted?** how are you? *(form.)*, 1; **¿— estás?** how are you? *(fam.)*, 1; **— no** of course, sure; **¿— se dice... ?** how do you say . . . ?, 1; **¿— se llama usted?** what is your *(form.)* name?, 1; **¿— te llamas?** what is your *(fam.)* name?, 1

cómodo(a) comfortable, 9

compañero(a) de clase *(m., f.)* classmate, 1; **— de cuarto** *(m., f.)* roommate, 1

comparativo *(m.)* comparative

compartimiento de equipajes *(m.)* luggage compartment, 11

compartir to share, 11

complacer to please

comprar to buy, 6

comprobante *(m.)* claim check

comprometerse (con) to get engaged (to), 12

computadora (personal) *(f.)* (personal) computer, 1

con with, 1; **¿— quién?** with whom?; **— razón** no wonder; **— tal (de) que** provided that, 13; **— vista a** overlooking (with a view of), 12

concierto *(m.)* concert, 7

condimentar to season (food)

conducir to drive, to conduct, 4

conferencia *(f.)* lecture, 14

confiar en to trust, 12

confirmar to confirm, 11

conmigo with me, 3

conocer to know, to be acquainted with, 4

conocido(a) known

conseguir (e > i) to obtain, to get, 6

consultorio *(m.)* doctor's office, 14

contabilidad *(f.)* accounting, 2

contento(a) happy, content, 4

contigo with you *(fam.)*, 5

continuar to continue, 13

convenir (en) to agree (on), 12

conversar to talk, to converse, 2

convertirse (e > ie) en to turn into, 14

copa *(f.)* wineglass, 2

corazón *(m.)* heart, 13

corbata *(f.)* tie, 9

cordero *(m.)* lamb, 5

correo *(m.)* post office, 10

correr to run, 3

corsario *(m.)* privateer

cortar to cut, 3; **— el césped** to mow the lawn, 3; **—se** to cut (oneself), 13; **—se el pelo** to get one's hair cut

corto(a) short, 9

cosa *(f.)* thing, 3; **cosas que hacer** things to do, 3

costar (o > ue) to cost, 6; **—un ojo de la cara** to cost an arm and a leg, 9

costumbre *(f.)* custom

crecer to grow

creer to think, to believe; **— que sí (no)** to think so (not), 13

crema *(f.)* cream, 5

criado(a) *(m., f.)* servant, 6

crucero *(m.)* cruise, 11

cuaderno *(m.)* notebook, 1

cuadra *(f.)* block, 10

¿cuál? (*pl.* **¿cuáles?**) which?, what?, 1; **¿— es tu número de teléfono?** what's your phone number?, 1

cualquier(a) any, 13; **en — momento** at any time

cuando when, 13

¿cuándo? when?, 2

¿cuánto(a)? how much?, 3; **¿por cuánto tiempo?** how long?

¿cuántos(as)? how many?, 2

cuarenta forty, 2

cuarto *(m.)* room, 3; **— de baño** *(m.)* bathroom, 3; **— de huéspedes** *(m.)* guest room; **menos —** quarter to, 2; **y —** quarter past or after, 2

cuatro four, 1

cuatrocientos(as) four hundred, 3

cubano(a) *(m., f.)* Cuban; **cubanoamericano(a)** Cuban American, 1

cuchara *(f.)* spoon, 5

cucharita *(f.))* teaspoon, 5

cuchillo *(m.)* knife, 5

cuello *(m.)* neck, 13; collar

cuenta *(f.)* account, 10; bill, check *(at a restaurant)*, 5; **— de ahorros** savings account, 10; **— conjunta** joint account, 10; **— corriente** checking account, 10

cuerpo *(m.)* body, 13

cuervo *(m.)* crow

cuidar(se) to take care (of oneself), 14

cumpleaños *(m. sing.)* birthday, 4

cuñada *(f.)* sister-in-law, 4

cuñado *(m.)* brother-in-law, 4

curita *(f.)* adhesive bandage, 14

D

danza aeróbica *(f.)* aerobic dance, 2

dar to give, 4

darse cuenta (de) to realize, 12

darse prisa to hurry up

de of, about, in, 2; from, with, 11; **— cortesía** polite; **¿— dónde eres?** where are you from?, 1; **— estatura mediana** of medium height, 4; **—modo (manera) que** so, 6; **— nada** you're welcome, 1

debajo de under

deber to have to, must, 3

débil weak

decidir to decide, 4

décimo(a) tenth, 12

decir (e > i) to say, 5; to tell, 6; **dime una cosa** tell me something, 12

dedo *(m.)* finger, 13; **— del pie** toe, 13

dejar to leave (behind), 5; to let, 11; **— de** to stop

del (de + el) of the, 4

deletrear to spell

deletreo *(m.)* spelling

delgado(a) slender, thin, 1

demasiado(a) too much

demostrativo(a) demonstrative

dentro de within, 14; **— quince días** in two weeks

departamento *(m.)* apartment, 6; **— de caballeros** *(m.)* men's department

dependiente(a) *(m., f.)* clerk

deporte *(m.)* sport

depositar to deposit, 10

derecho(a) right; **a la derecha** to the right

dermatólogo(a) *(m., f.)* dermatologist, 14

desarrollar to develop

desastre *(m.)* disaster, 3

desayunar to have breakfast, 5

desayuno *(m.)* breakfast

descalzo(a) barefoot; **andar —** to go barefoot, 9

descansar to rest, 3

descubierto(a) discovered

descuento *(m.)* discount

desde from

desear to wish, to want, 2

desfallecer to faint

desgraciadamente unfortunately

desinfectante *(adj.)* disinfectant, 14

desinfectar to disinfect, 13

desmayarse to lose consciousness, to faint, 13

desocupar to vacate, 12; **— el cuarto** to check out of a hotel room, 12

despedida *(f.)* farewell

despejado(a) clear *(sky)*, 9

despertarse (e > ie) to wake, 7

después then, 3; later, 5; **— de** after

detergente *(m.)* detergent, 6

día *(m.)* day, 1; **al — siguiente** next day, 5; **— feriado** holiday, 10

diario *(m.)* newspaper, diary

dicho(a) said, 10

diciembre December, 2

diecinueve nineteen, 2

dieciocho eighteen, 2

dieciséis sixteen, 2

diecisiete seventeen, 2

diente *(m.)* tooth, 13

diez ten, 1

difícil difficult, 1

diligencia *(f.)* errand

dinero *(m.)* money, 2

dirección *(f.)* address, 1

disco: — compacto *(m.)* compact disc (CD), 4; **— duro** hard drive, 10

discoteca *(f.)* club, disco, 7

diseñar programas to design, write programs

disponible vacant, available, 12

divertirse (e > ie) to have fun, 7

doce twelve, 2

docena *(f.)* dozen, 6

doctor (Dr.) *(m.)* doctor, 1; M.D., 13

doctora (Dra.) *(f.)* doctor, 1; M.D., 13

documento *(m.)* document

doler (o > ue) to hurt, to ache, 13

dolor *(m.)* pain, 13; **— de cabeza** *(m.)* headache; **— de garganta** sore throat, 14

domicilio *(m.)* address, 1

domingo *(m.)* Sunday, 2

don title of respect, used with a man's first name, 6

¿dónde? where?, 1

doña title of respect, used with a woman's first name, 6

dormir (o > ue) to sleep, 6; **—se** to fall asleep

dormitorio *(m.)* bedroom, 3

dos two, 1; **somos —** there are two of us

doscientos(as) two hundred, 2

ducha *(f.)* shower, 12

dudar to doubt, 13

dueño(a) *(m., f.)* owner, proprietor, 12

durante during

durar to last

durazno *(m.)* peach, 6

E

echar to share; to pour out

efectivo *(m.)* cash, 10

ejercicio *(m.)* exercise

el *(m. sing.)* the, 1

él he, 1; (*obj. of prep.*) him, 5

elegante elegant

elegir (e > i) to choose, 6

elevador *(m.)* elevator, 12

ella she, 1; *(obj. of prep.)* her, 5

ellas *(f.)* they, 1; *(obj. of prep.)* them, 5

ellos *(m.)* they, 1; *(obj. of prep.) them, 5*

elogiar to praise

embarazada pregnant, 14

emergencia *(f.)* emergency, 11

empeorar(se) to get worse, 14

empezar (e > ie) to start, to begin, 5

empleado(a) *(m., f.)* clerk, 9

en in, on, at, 1; inside, over; **— cambio** on the other hand, 8; **— casa** at home; **— caso de que** in case, 13; **— cuanto** as soon as, 9; **— efectivo** in cash, 10; **— español** in Spanish; **— inglés** in English; **—parte** in part, 11; **— seguida** right away, 14; **— vez de** instead of, 7

enamorado(a) in love, 4

enamorarse (de) to fall in love (with), 12

encantador(a) charming, 4

encantar to love, to like very much, 8

encargarse to take charge

encendido(a) bright

encontrar (o > ue) to find, 6

encuesta *(f.)* survey

enero January, 2

enfermedad *(f.)* disease, sickness, 14

enfermero(a) *(m., f)* nurse, 13

enfermo(a) sick

ensalada *(f.)* salad, 3; **— mixta** *(f.)* mixed salad

ensayo *(m.)* essay

enseguida right away, 14

enseñar to teach, 11; to show, 12

entender (e > ie) to understand, 5

enterrado(a) buried

entonces then, 2; in that case, 5

entrar (en) to enter, to go (in), 7

entre between; **— comidas** between meals; **— semana** during the week

entremeses *(m. pl.)* appetizers, finger food, 4

enviar to send, 4

enyesar to put a cast on

equipaje *(m.)* luggage, 11

escalar montañas to climb mountains, 7

escalera *(f.)* stairs, 13; **— mecánica** escalator, 13

esclusa *(f.)* lock *(in a canal)*

escoba *(f.)* broom

escoger to choose, 6

escopeta *(f.)* shotgun, 8

escribir to write, 3

escrito(a) written, 10

escritorio *(m.)* desk, 1

escuela *(f.)* school, 9

ese, esos, esa(s) *(adj.)* that those (*nearby*), 3

ése, ésos, ésa(s) *(pron.)* that (one), those, 3

eso *(neut. pron.)* that, 3

espaguetis *(m. pl.)* spaghetti, 6

espalda *(f.)* back, 13

español *(m.)* Spanish *(language)*, 1

español(a) *(m., f.)* Spanish *(person)*

esparadrapo *(m.)* adhesive tape, 14

especialidad *(f.)* specialty, 5

especialmente especially, 3

esperar to wait, 5; to hope, 11; **espero que sí** I hope so, 8

esposa *(f.)* wife, 4

esposo *(m.)* husband, 4

esquí acuático *(m.)* waterski, 8

esquiar to ski, 7

esquina *(f.)* corner

esta *(adj.)* this, 3; **— noche** tonight, 1

estacionar to park, 10
estación *(f.)* season, 2
estadio *(m.)* stadium
estado *(m.)* state; **en—** pregnant, 14
estadounidense *(m., f.)* U.S. *(used to denote citizenship)*, 1
estampilla *(f.)* stamp, 10
estar to be, 4; **está bien** all right, okay, 6; **— a dieta** to be on a diet; **— de moda** to be in style, 9; **— de vacaciones** to be on vacation, 5; **— en regla** to be in order; **— muerto(a) de hambre** to be starving, 6 **— seguro(a)** to be sure
estatura *(f.)* height, 4; **de — mediana** of medium height, 4
este, estos, esta(s) *(adj.)* this, these, 3
éste, éstos, ésta(s) *(pron.)* this (one), these, 3
estéreo *(m.)* stereo
estimarse to have self-esteem
esto *(neut. pron.)* this, 3
estómago *(m.)* stomach, 13
estrecho(a) narrow
estrella *(f.)* star, 8
estudiante *(m., f.)* student, 1
estudiar to study, 2
examinar to examine, to check, 14
exceso *(m.)* excess, 11; **— de equipaje** *(m.)* excess luggage *(charge)*, 11
excursión *(f.)* tour, excursion, 11
excusa *(f.)* excuse, 3
éxito *(m.)* success, 4; **todo un —** quite a success, 4
expresión *(f.)* expression
exterior *(m.)* exterior, 12
extranjero(a) foreigner
extraño(a) *(m., f.)* stranger

F

fácil easy, 8
fácilmente easily, 8
facultad *(f.)* college, 9
falda *(f.)* skirt, 9
falso(a) false
familia *(f.)* family, 3
famoso(a) famous, 6
farmacéutico(a) *(m., f.)* pharmacist
farmacia *(f.)* pharmacy, 14
favorito(a) favorite, 3
febrero February, 2
fechar to date *(a document)*, 10
feliz happy, 4
feo(a) ugly, 1
fiebre *(f.)* fever, 14
fiesta *(f.)* party, 4; **— de bienvenida** welcome party
fijarse en to check, to notice, 12
fin *(m.)* end; **— de semana** *(m.)* weekend, 7
firmar to sign, 10
física *(f.)* physics, 2
flan *(m.)* caramel custard, 5
flor *(f.)* flower
florero *(m.)* vase, 7
fogata *(f.)* bonfire, 8
folleto *(m.)* brochure, 12
fortaleza *(f.)* fortress
fractura *(f.)* fracture, 13
fracturar(se) to fracture
francés *(m.)* French *(language)*
franco(a) open
frecuentemente often, 8
fregar (e > ie) to wash *(dishes)*
freír (e > i) to fry
fresa *(f.)* strawberry, 6
frío(a) cold, 9
frito(a) fried, 8
fruta *(f.)* fruit, 5
fuente de ingresos *(f.)* source of income
fumar to smoke
funcionar to work, to function; **no funciona** it doesn't work, 12
fundado(a) founded

G

gamba *(f.)* shrimp, 5
ganado *(m.)* cattle
garaje *(m.)* garage, 3
garganta *(f.)* throat, 14
gastar to spend *(money)*, 9
general general, 8
generalmente generally, 8
género *(m.)* gender
gente *(f.)* people, 10
geografía *(f.)* geography, 2
geología *(f.)* geology, 2
gerente *(m., f.)* manager
ginecólogo(a) *(m., f.)* gynecologist, 14
giro postal *(m.)* money order, 10
gobierno *(m.)* government
golpear(se) to hit (oneself), 13
gordo(a) fat, 1
gota *(f.)* drop; **—s para la nariz** *(f. pl.)* nose drops
gracias thanks, 1; **muchas —** thank you very much, 1
grado *(m.)* degree *(temperature)*, 9; **hay . . . grados** it's . . . degrees, 9
grande big, 5; **gran** big, great
gratis free (of charge), 10
grave serious, 14
gripe *(f.)* flu, 14
gris gray, 1
gritar to shout, 4
grupo *(m.)* group
guante *(m.)* glove, 9
guapo(a) handsome, 1
guardar to keep
guatemalteco(a) Guatemalan, 4
guerra *(f.)* war
gustar to like, to appeal, 7
gusto *(m.)* pleasure, 1; **el — es mío** the pleasure is mine, 1; **mucho —** it's a pleasure to meet you; how do you do?, 1

H

Habana *(f.)* Havana
haber *(auxiliary verb)* to have, 10; **va a —** there is going to be, 12
había una vez once upon a time
habitación *(f.)* room, 12
hablar to speak, 2; **habla... (nombre)** this is . . . (name) speaking; **hablado** spoken, 10
hacer to do, to make, 3; **hace... . . . ago**, 9; **— buen (mal) tiempo** to be good (bad) weather, 9; **— calor** to be hot, 9; **— cola** to stand in line, 10; **— diligencias** to run errands, 10; **— ejercicio** to exercise; **— escala** to make a stop over, 11; **— frío** to be cold, 9; **— sol** to be sunny, 9; **— surfing** to surf, 8; **— una caminata** to go hiking, 8; **— una radiografía** to take an X-ray, 13; **— viento** to be windy, 9
hambre *(f.)* hunger, 3; **tener —** to be hungry, 3
hamburguesa *(f.)* hamburger, 5
hasta until, 7; even; **— la vista** (I'll) see you around, 1; **— luego** (I'll) see you later, 1; **— mañana** (I'll) see you tomorrow, 1; **— que** *(conj.)* until, 13
hay there is, there are, 1
hecho(a) made, done, 10

heladera *(f.)* refrigerator, 3
helado *(m.)* ice cream, 5
helado(a) frozen
herida *(f.)* wound, 13
herido(a) wounded
hermana *(f.)* sister, 3
hermanastra *(f.)* stepsister
hermanastro *(m.)* stepbrother
hermano *(m.)* brother, 3
hermoso(a) beautiful
hielo *(m.)* ice, 2
hija *(f.)* daughter, 4
hijastra *(f.)* stepdaughter
hijastro *(m.)* stepson
hijo *(m.)* son, 4
hijos *(m. pl.)* children, 3
hinchado(a) swollen, 13
historia *(f.)* history, 2
hola hello, hi, 1
hombre *(m.)* man, 1
hombro *(m.)* shoulder, 13
hora *(f.)* hour, time, 2; **¿qué — es?** what time is it?, 2; **¿a qué —?** at what time?, 2
horario de clases *(m.)* class schedule, 2
horno *(m.)* oven, 3; **al —** baked; **— de microondas** *(m.)* microwave oven, 3
hospedarse to stay, to lodge *(i.e., at a hotel)*, 8
hospital *(m.)* hospital, 13
hotel *(m.)* hotel, 8
hoy today, 2; **— mismo** this very day, 14
hubo there was, there were
huevo *(m.)* egg, 5
húmedo(a) humid, 9
huracán *(m.)* hurricane

I

ida *(f.)*: **de —** one-way, 11; **de — y vuelta** round-trip, 11
idea *(f.)* idea, 2
identificación *(f.)* identification
idioma *(m.)* language
iglesia *(f.)* church
impermeable *(m.)* raincoat
importarle (a uno) to matter, 6
impresora *(f.)* printer, 10
incluir to include, 11
infección *(f.)* infection
información *(f.)* information
informática *(f.)* computer science, 2
ingeniería *(f.)* engineering
inglés *(m.)* English *(language)*, 2
inglés(esa) *(m., f.)* English *(person)*
ingreso *(m.)* income
inodoro *(m.)* toilet, 12
insistir en to insist on, 12
inteligente intelligent, 1
interés *(m.)* interest
interesante interesting, 1
interior interior, 12
internacional international, 1
interrogativo(a) interrogative
invierno *(m.)* winter, 2
invitación *(f.)* invitation, 4
invitado(a) *(m., f.)* guest, 4
invitar to invite, 4
inyección *(f.)* shot, injection, 13; **— antitetánica** tetanus shot, 13
ir to go, 4; **— a** + *inf.* to be going to, 4; **— a acampar** to go camping, 8; **— de compras** to go shopping; **— de pesca** to go fishing; **— (se) de vacaciones** to go on vacation; **— se** to go away
istmo *(m.)* isthmus
italiano *(m.)* Italian *(language)*
izquierdo(a) left; **a la izquierda** to the left

J

jabón *(m.)* soap
jamás never, 6
jamón *(m.)* ham, 5
jarabe *(m.)* syrup, 14
jardín *(m.)* garden, 12
jefe(a) *(m., f.)* boss
joven young, 1
joya *(f.)* jewel; *(pl.)* jewelry
juego *(m.)* game, 7
jueves *(m.)* Thursday, 2
jugador(a) *(m., f.)* player
jugar (u > ue) to play *(i.e., a game)* 8; **— al golf** to play golf, 8; **— al tenis** to play tennis, 8
jugo *(m.)* juice, 2; **— de manzana** *(m.)* apple juice, 2; **— de naranja** *(m.)* orange juice, 2; **— de tomate** *(m.)* tomato juice, 2; **— de toronja** *(m.)* grapefruit juice, 2; **— de uvas** *(m.)* grape juice, 2
julio July, 2
junio June, 2
juntarse to get together, 8
junto(a) next (to)
juntos(as) together, 2
justo(a) fair, 7

L

la *(f. sing.)* the, 1; *(pron.)* her, you, it, 6
laboratorio de lenguas *(m.)* language lab
ladera *(f.)* hillside
lago *(m.)* lake, 8
langosta *(f.)* lobster, 5
lápiz *(m.)* pencil, 1
largo(a) long, 9
las *(f. pl.)* the, 1; *(pron.)* them, you, 6
lastimar(se) to hurt (oneself), 13
Latinoamérica *(f.)* Latin America
lavabo *(m.)* washbasin, 12
lavadora *(f.)* washing machine, 3
lavaplatos *(m. sing.)* dishwasher, 3
lavar to wash, 3; **—se** to wash (oneself), 7; **—se la cabeza** to wash one's hair
le (to) him, (to) her, (to) you *(form.)*, 7
lección *(f.)* lesson
leche *(f.)* milk, 2
lechuga *(f.)* lettuce, 6
lector(a) *(m., f.)* reader
leer to read, 3
lejía *(f.)* bleach, 6
lejos far (away)
lengua *(f.)* tongue, 13; language
lentamente slowly, 8
lento(a) slow, 8
les (to) them, (to) you *(pl. form.)*, 7
letrero *(m.)* sign
levantar to raise, 4; **levantarse** to get up, 7
libertad *(f.)* liberty
libre off, 6; vacant, available, 12; free
libreta de ahorros *(f.)* passbook, 10
libro *(m.)* book, 1
licencia para manejar (conducir) *(f.)* driver's license
licuadora *(f.)* blender, 3
ligero(a) light
limonada *(f.)* lemonade, 3
limpiar to clean, 3; **— el polvo** to dust, 3
limpio(a) clean, 12
lindo(a) pretty, 1
liquidación *(f.)* sale
lista *(f.)* list, 5; **— de espera** *(f.)* waiting list, 11
listo(a) ready
literatura *(f.)* literature, 2
llamada *(f.)* call, 11

llamar to call; **— a la puerta** to knock at the door
llamarse to be named, 1; **¿cómo se llama?** what is your *(form.)* name?, 1, **¿cómo te llamas?** what is your *(fam.)* name?, 1; **me llamo...** my name is . . . , 1
llave *(f.)* key
llegar to arrive, 3; **— tarde (temprano)** to be late (early)
llenar to fill, to fill out, 10
lleno(a) full, 12
llevar to take *(someone or something someplace)*, 4; to wear
llorar to cry, 13
llover (o > ue) to rain, 9
lluvia *(f.)* rain, 9
lo him, you, it, 6; **— importante** the important thing; **— mismo** the same thing, 11; **— que** what, that, which, 9; **— siento** I'm sorry, 1
los *(m. pl.)* the, 1; *(pron.)* them, you *(form.)*, 6; **— (las) dos** both, 2
lucirse to shine
luego later
lugar *(m.)* place, 12; **— de interés** *(m.)* place of interest, 12; **en — de** in place of
lujo *(m.)* luxury, 12
luna de miel *(f.)* honeymoon
lunes *(m.)* Monday, 2
luz *(f.)* light, 1

M

madera *(f.)* wood
madrastra *(f.)* stepmother
madre *(f.)* mom, mother, 4
madrina *(f.)* godmother, 4
madrugada *(f.)* early morning (pre-dawn)
maestro(a) *(m., f.)* teacher
magnífico(a) great
mal badly, 5; poorly
maleta *(f.)* suitcase, 11
maletín *(m.)* hand luggage, small suitcase, 11
malo(a) bad, 5
mamá *(f.)* mom, mother, 3
mami *(f.)* mommy
mandar to send, 4; to order; **¿mande?** *(Mex.)* pardon?, 1
mandón(ona) bossy, 3
manejar to drive
manga *(f.)* sleeve, 9
mano *(f.)* hand
mantel *(m.)* tablecloth, 5
mantequilla *(f.)* butter, 5
manzana *(f.)* apple, 2; block, 10
mañana tomorrow; morning, 2
mapa *(m.)* map, 1
mar *(m.)* ocean, 8
marca *(f.)* brand
marisco *(m.)* shellfish, 6
marrón brown, 1
martes *(m.)* Tuesday, 2
marzo March, 2
más more, 5; **— de** more than, 5; **— despacio** slower, 1; **— o menos** more or less, 1; **— ... que** more . . . than, 5; **— tarde** later, 5
matar to kill; **— dos pájaros de un tiro** to kill two birds with one stone
matemáticas *(f. pl.)* mathematics, 2
materia *(f.)* course, subject, 2
matrimonio *(m.)* married couple, 8
mayo May, 2
mayor older, 5; elderly; **(el, la) —** oldest, 5
me *(obj. pron.)* me, 6; (to) me, 7; *(refl. pron.)* (to) myself, 7; **— gusta...** I like . . . , 7; **— llamo...** my name is . . . , 1; **— voy** I'm leaving, 2
media hermana *(f.)* half sister
mediano(a) medium, 9
medianoche *(f.)* midnight, 2
medicina *(f.)* medicine, 9
médico(a) *(m., f.)* doctor, M.D., 11
medida *(f.)* measure
medio(a) half; **media hora** half an hour, 3; **y media** half past, 2
medio hermano *(m.)* half brother
mediodía *(m.)* noon, 2; **al —** at noon, 2
mejor better, 5; **(el, la) —** best, 5
mejorarse to get better, 14
melocotón *(m.)* peach, 6
melón de agua *(m.)* watermelon, 6
memoria *(f.)* memory, 10
menor younger, 5; **(el, la) —** youngest, 5
menos to, till, 2; less, 5; **—... que** less . . . than, 5; **— mal** thank goodness
mensaje *(m.)* **electrónico** e-mail, 10
mensual monthly
mentir (e > ie) to lie, 11
menú *(m.)* menu, 5
mercado *(m.)* market, 6; **— al aire libre** *(m.)* outdoor market, 6
merendar to have an afternoon snack, 7
merienda *(f.)* afternoon snack
mermelada *(f.)* jam, marmalade, 5
mes *(m.)* month, 2
mesa *(f.)* table, 3
mesero(a) *(m., f.)* *(Mex.)* waiter, 5
mexicano(a) *(m., f.)* Mexican, 1
mezcla *(f.)* mixture
mezclar to mix
mi(s) my, 2
mí *(obj. of prep.)* me, 5
microcomputadora *(f.)* laptop, 10
mientras while
miércoles *(m.)* Wednesday, 2
mil one thousand, 3
minuto *(m.)* minute, 2
mío(a), míos(as) *(pron.)* mine, 9
mirar to watch, to look at, 3
mismo(a) same; **a sí —** him/herself
mochila *(f.)* backpack, 1
modo *(m.)* way; **de — que** so, 6
momento *(m.)* moment, 3
moneda *(f.)* coin
monitor *(m.)* monitor, 10
montar: — a caballo to go horseback riding, 7; **— en bicicleta** to ride a bike, 7
montón: un montón de a bunch of, many, 12
morado(a) purple, 1
moreno(a) dark, brunet(te), 4
morir (o > ue) to die
mostrar (o > ue) to show, 12
mozo *(m.)* waiter, 5
muchacha *(f.)* young girl, 1; maid
muchacho *(m.)* young man, 1
mucho(a) much; **— gusto** it's a pleasure to meet you; how do you do?, 1; **no mucho** not much, 1
muchos(as) many, 3; **muchas gracias** thank you very much, 1
mudarse to move (relocate)
muebles *(m. pl.)* furniture, 3
muerto(a) dead, 10; **estar — de hambre** to be starving, 6

mujer *(f.)* woman; 1
muletas *(f. pl.)* crutches, 13
muñeca *(f.)* wrist, 13
museo *(m.)* museum, 7
música *(f.)* music, 2
muy very, 1; **— bien** very well, 1

N

nacer to be born
nada nothing, 6; **de (por) —** you're welcome, 1; **— más** nothing else
nadar to swim, 7
nadie nobody, no one, 6
naranja *(f.)* orange, 2
nariz *(f.)* nose, 13
navegar la Red to surf the net, 10
Navidad *(f.)* Christmas
necesitar to need, 2
negar (e > ie) to deny, 13
negativo(a) negative
negro(a) black, 1
nevada *(f.)* snowfall
nevar (e > ie) to snow, 9
nevera *(f.)* refrigerator, 3
ni. . .ni neither . . . nor, 6
niebla *(f.)* fog, 9
nieta *(f.)* granddaughter, 4
nieto *(m.)* grandson, 4
ningún, ninguno(a) none, not any, 6; no, 6
niño(a) *(m., f.)* child, 5
no no, not, 1; **— importa** it doesn't matter
noche *(f.)* night, 1; **esta —** tonight, 3
nocturno *(m.)* night *(adj.)*
norteamericano(a) *(m., f.)* North American, 1
nos *(obj. pron.)* us, 6; (to) us, 7; (to) ourselves, 7; **nos vemos** I'll see you, 1
nosotros(as) we, 1; *(obj. of prep.)* us, 5
nota *(f.)* grade
notar to notice
novecientos(as) nine hundred, 3
noventa ninety, 2
novia *(f.)* girlfriend (steady), 4
noviembre November, 2
novio *(m.)* boyfriend (steady), 4
nublado(a) cloudy, 9
nuera *(f.)* daughter-in-law, 4
nuestro(s), nuestra(s) *(adj.)* our, 2; *(pron.)* ours, 9
nueve nine, 1
nuevo(a) new, 2
número *(m.)* number, 1; **— de teléfono** phone number, 1
nunca never, 6

O

o or; **o... o** either . . . or, 6
obra *(f.)* work *(e.g., of art)*
ochenta eighty, 2
ocho eight, 1
ochocientos(as) eight hundred, 3
octubre October, 2
oculista *(m., f.)* oculist, 14
ocupación *(f.)* occupation, 3
ocupado(a) busy, 3; occupied, 12
oficina *(f.)* office; **— de correos** post office, 10
oído *(m.)* (inner) ear
ojalá I hope, 11
ojos *(m. pl.)* eyes, 4; **de — castaños** with brown eyes, 4
olvidar(se) (de) to forget, 12
ómnibus *(m.)* bus
once eleven, 2
oprimido(a) oppressed
ordenador (personal) *(m.)* *(Spain)* (personal) computer, 1
oreja *(f.)* (external) ear, 13
orilla *(f.)* shore
oro *(m.)* gold, 9
orquesta *(f.)* band, orchestra
ortiga *(f.)* nettle
os *(fam. pl. obj. pron.)* you, 6; (to) you, 7; (to) yourselves, 7
oso *(m.)* bear
otoño *(m.)* autumn, 2
otro(a) other, another, 10; **otra vez** again, 14
oye listen, 1

P

paciente *(m., f.)* patient, 13
padrastro *(m.)* stepfather
padre *(m.)* dad, father, 4
padres *(m. pl.)* parents, 3
padrino *(m.)* godfather, 4
pagar to pay, 5
país *(m.)* country, nation, 11
pájaro *(m.)* bird
palabra *(f.)* word; **— cariñosa** *(f.)* term of endearment
palo de golf *(m.)* golf club, 8
pan *(m.)* bread, 5; **— tostado** toast, 5
panadería *(f.)* bakery, 6
panqueque *(m.)* pancake, 5
pantalla *(f.)* screen, 10
pantalón *(m. sing.)*, **pantalones** *(m. pl.)* pants, trousers, 9
pantimedias *(f. pl.)* pantyhose
papa *(f.)* potato, 5; **—s fritas** french fries, 9; **puré de papas** *(m. sing.)* mashed potatoes, 5
papá *(m.)* dad, father, 3
papanicolaus *(m.)* pap smear
papel *(m.)* paper, 1; **— higiénico** toilet paper, 6
papi *(m.)* daddy
paquete *(m.)* package, 11
par *(m.)* pair, 9; **un — de días** a couple of days
para in order to, for, 3; **— que** in order that, so that, 13
paraguas *(m. sing.)* umbrella
paramédico(a) *(m., f.)* paramedic, 13
parar to stop
parecer to seem, 12
pareja *(f.)* couple, 4
parentesco *(m.)* relationship
pariente(a) *(m., f.)* relative
parque *(m.)* park; **— de diversiones** amusement park, 7
parrilla *(f.)* grill; **a la —** grilled, 5
parte *(f.)* part; **en —** in part, 11
partido *(m.)* game, 7; **— de básquetbol** *(m.)* basketball game
pasado(a) last, 7
pasaje *(m.)* ticket, 11; **— de ida** one-way ticket, 11; **— de ida y vuelta** round-trip ticket, 11
pasajero(a) *(m., f.)* passenger, 11
pasaporte *(m.)* passport, 11
pasar to happen, 13; to spend time, 8; **— a formar parte de** to become part of; **— la aspiradora** to vacuum, 3; **pasarlo bien** to have a good time, 4; **pase** come in, 1
pastel *(m.)* pastry, cake, 4, pie, 5
pastilla *(f.)* pill, 11
patata *(f.)* *(Spain)* potato, 5
patinar to skate, 7; **ir a —** to go skating, 7
patio *(m.)* patio, 12
pecho *(m.)* chest, 13
pedazo *(m.)* piece
pediatra *(m., f.)* pediatrician, 14
pedido *(m.)* order
pedir (e > i) to ask for, to order, 5; to request, 6; **— turno** to make an appointment; **— un préstamo** to apply for a loan, 6

película *(f.)* movie, film, 7
pelirrojo(a) red-haired, 4
pelo *(m.)* hair
penicilina *(f.)* penicillin
pensar (e > ie) to think, 5; — + *inf.* to plan to *(do something)*, 5
pensión *(f.)* boarding house, 12; **— completa** *(f.)* room and board, 12
peor worse, 5; **(el, la) —** worst, 5
pepino *(m.)* cucumber, 6
pequeño(a) small, 5; little, 8
pera *(f.)* pear, 6
perder (e > ie) to lose; **— el conocimiento** to lose consciousness, to faint, 13
perdón sorry, 1, pardon me, 1
perdonar to forgive
perfecto(a) perfect, 1
periódico *(m.)* newspaper
permiso excuse me, 1
pero but, 2
perro(a) *(m., f.)* dog; **— caliente** *(m.)* hot dog, 5
persona *(f.)* person, 12
pertenecer to belong
peruano(a) Peruvian, 12
pesar to weigh, 14
pescadería *(f.)* fish market, 6
pescado *(m.)* fish, 5
pescar to fish, to catch a fish, 8
peso *(m.)* weight
petróleo *(m.)* oil
picnic *(m.)* picnic, 7
pie *(m.)* foot, 13
pierna *(f.)* leg, 13
pijama *(m. sing.)***, pijamas** *(m. pl.)* pajamas, 9
pilotes *(m. pl.)* stilts
pimienta *(f.)* pepper, 5
pimiento *(m.)* green pepper, 6
pintor(a) *(m., f.)* painter
pintura *(f.)* painting
piña *(f.)* pineapple, 6
piscina *(f.)* swimming pool, 12
piso *(m.)* floor, 12
pizarra *(f.)* chalkboard, 1
plan de ahorros *(m.)* savings plan, 10
plancha *(f.)* iron, 3
planchar to iron, 3
planear to plan, 4
planilla *(f.)* form, 10
plata *(f.)* silver; money, 2
plátano *(m.)* banana, 6
platillo *(m.)* saucer, 5
plato *(m.)* dish, plate, 3
playa *(f.)* beach, 1
pluma *(f.)* pen, 1
pobre poor, 7
pobreza *(f.)* poverty
poco(a) little; **un — (de)** a little, 6
pocos(as) few
poder (o > ue) to be able to, can, 6
poema *(m.)* poem
pollo *(m.)* chicken, 5
polvo *(m.)* powder
ponche *(m.)* punch *(beverage)*
poner to put, to place, 4; to turn on; **— la mesa** to set the table, 3; **—se** to put on, 7; **— una inyección** to give a shot, 10; **— una película** to show a movie, 7; **ponerse de acuerdo** to come to an agreement, 11
por for; per; through, along, by, via; because of, on account of, on behalf of; in exchange for; during, in, for, 9; **— ciento** percent; **— favor** please, 1; **— fin** finally, 10; **— la tarde** in the afternoon, 2; **— noche** per night; **— si acaso** just in case, 8; **— suerte** luckily, 14;**— supuesto** of course; **— vía aérea** air mail
porque because, 2
¿por qué? why?, 2
posesivo(a) possessive
posible possible, 12
postre *(m.)* dessert, 5; **de —** for dessert, 5
practicar to practice
precio *(m.)* price, 12
preferir (e > ie) to prefer, 5
pregunta *(f.)* question
preguntar to ask *(a question)*, 7
preocuparse to worry
preparar to prepare, 3; **—se** to get ready, 7
presión *(f.)* pressure, (blood) pressure, 14
préstamo *(m.)* loan, 10
prestar to lend, 8
primavera *(f.)* spring, 2
primero *(adv.)* first, 10; **lo —** the first thing, 12
primero(a) first; **primera clase** *(f.)* first-class, 11; **primera vez** first time
primo(a) *(m., f.)* cousin, 4
privado(a) private, 12
probador *(m.)* fitting room, 9
probar(se) (o > ue) to try (on), 7
problema *(m.)* problem
profesor(a) *(m., f.)* professor, 1
programa *(m.)* program, 2
prometer to promise, 8
pronto soon, 8
propietario(a) *(m., f.)* owner, 12
propina *(f.)* tip *(for service)*, 5
propio(a) own
próximo(a) next, 12
psicología *(f.)* psychology, 2
puerta *(f.)* door, 1; **— de salida** *(f.)* boarding gate, 11
puertorriqueño(a) Puerto Rican, 2
pues then, 2; well, okay, 8; therefore
puesto(a) put, placed, 10
puesto de revistas *(m.)* magazine stand, 12
pulgada *(f.)* inch
pulmonía *(f.)* pneumonia, 14
punto *(m.)* stitch, 13
puré de papas *(m. sing.)* mashed potatoes, 5

Q

que who, 2; that, 2; than, 5; **— viene** next, 14; **— yo sepa** that I know of, 14
¿qué? what?, 2; **¿en — puedo servirle?** how may I help you?, 9; **¿— día es hoy?** what day is today?, 2; **¿— fecha es hoy?** what is today's date?, 2; **¿— hay de nuevo?** what's new?, 1; **¿— hora es?** what time is it?, 2; **¡— lástima!** too bad!, what a pity!?; **¿— quiere decir... ?** what does . . . mean?, 1; **¿— tal?** how is it going?, 1; **¿— temperatura hace?** what's the temperature?, 9; **¿— tiempo hace hoy?** what's the weather like today?, 9; **¿— más?** what else?, 6
quebrado(a) broken, 10
quedar to fit, to suit; **—le bien** to fit; **—le grande/chico(a) (a uno o una)** to be too big/small (on someone), 9
quedarse to stay, to remain
quejarse to complain, 7
quemar(se) to burn (oneself), 13

querer (e > ie) to want, to wish, 5; **— decir** to mean, 1; **¿quieres?** will you?, 12
querido(a) dear, 11
queso *(m.)* cheese
¿quién(es)? who?, 3; **¿a —?** whom?, 4; **¿con —?** with whom?, 2
química *(f.)* chemistry, 2
quince fifteen, 2; **— días** two weeks
quinientos(as) five hundred, 3
quitarse to take off, 7
quizás maybe, perhaps, 9

R

radiografía *(f.)* X-ray, 13
raíz *(f.)* root
rápidamente rapidly, 8
rápido(a) fast, 8
raqueta *(f.)* racket, 8
rascacielos *(m.)* skyscraper
rasurarse to shave, 7
rato *(m.)* while; **al —** a while later; **un —** a while, 3
ratón *(m.)* mouse, 10
rebuzno *(m.)* braying
recámara *(f.) (Mex.)* bedroom, 3
receta *(f.)* prescription, 14
recetar to prescribe, 14
recibir to receive, 3; **recibido(a)** received, 10
recién casados *(m. pl.)* newlyweds, 6
reciente recent, 8
recientemente recently, 8
recomendar (e > ie) to recommend, 11
recordar (o > ue) to remember, 6
refresco *(m.)* soft drink, soda
refrigerador *(m.)* refrigerator, 3
regadera *(f.) (Mex.)* shower, 12
regalo *(m.)* gift, 9
regatear to bargain
registro *(m.)* register
regresar to return
reina *(f.)* queen
reírse to laugh, 7
reloj *(m.)* clock, watch, 1
remar to row, 8
rentar to rent, 8
repaso *(m.)* review
represa *(f.)* dam
reproductor de discos compactos *(m.)* CD player
requisito *(m.)* requirement, 2
reservación *(f.)* reservation, 12
reservar to reserve, 12
resfriado *(m.)* cold
resfrío *(m.)* cold
residencia universitaria *(f.)* dormitory
respirar to breathe, 14; **— hondo** to take a deep breath, 14
respuesta *(f.)* answer, reply
restaurante *(m.)* restaurant, 5
revisar to check, 13
revista *(f.)* magazine
rico(a) rich, 1; tasty, 5
río *(m.)* river
riquísimo(a) very tasty; delicious
rodeado(a) surrounded
rodilla *(f.)* knee, 13
rojo(a) red, 1
romper to break, 7; **romperse** to break (a bone), 13
ropa *(f.)* clothes, 3; **— interior** *(f.)* underwear
rosado(a) pink, 1; rosé *(wine)*, 2
rostro *(m.)* face
roto(a) broken, 10
rubio(a) blond, 4
ruiseñor *(m.)* nightingale
ruso *(m.)* Russian *(language)*

S

sábado *(m.)* Saturday, 2
saber to know *(a fact, how to do something)*, 4
sacar to take out, 3
sacudir to dust, 3
sal *(f.)* salt, 5
sala *(f.)* living room, 3; **— de emergencia** *(f.)* emergency room, 13; **— de estar** *(f.)* family room, den; **— de rayos X (equis)** *(f.)* X-ray room, 13
saldo *(m.)* balance, 10
salida *(f.)* exit, 11; **— de emergencia** emergency exit, 11
salir to go out, 4
salsa *(f.)* sauce, 6; salsa *(dance)*, 5
salud *(f.)* health, 10; **¡—!** cheers, 4
saludar to greet
saludo *(m.)* greeting; **saludos a...** say hi to . . . , 1
salvavidas *(m., f.)* lifeguard, 8
sandalia *(f.)* sandal, 9
sandía *(f.)* watermelon, 6
sándwich *(m.)* sandwich
sartén *(f.)* frying pan, 3
se (to) herself, himself, itself, themselves, yourself, yourselves, 7; **— dice...** you say . . . , 1
secadora *(f.)* dryer, clothes dryer, 3
sección *(f.)* section; **— de (no) fumar** *(f.)* (non)smoking section
seco(a) dry, 9
sedante *(m.)* sedative, 14
sedativo *(m.)* sedative, 14
seguir (e > i) to continue, 6; to follow, 6
según according to, 9
segundo(a) second, 12
seguro(a) sure, 13
seguro *(m.)* insurance, 14; **— médico** *(m.)* medical insurance, 14; **— social** *(m.)* social security
seis six, 1
seiscientos(as) six hundred, 3
sello *(m.)* stamp, 10
selva *(f.)* rain forest
semana *(f.)* week, 7
semestre *(m.)* semester, 2
sentado(a) seated
sentar(se) (e > ie) to sit down, 7
sentir (e > ie) to regret, 11; **lo siento** I'm sorry, 1
señor (Sr.) *(m.)* Mr., sir, gentleman, 1; **los señores** Mr. and Mrs., 13
señora (Sra.) *(f.)* Mrs., lady, madam, 1
señorita (Srta.) *(f.)* miss, young lady, 1
septiembre September, 2
ser to be, 1; **— de** to be from, 1; **— la(s)...** to be . . . , 2
serio(a) serious, 14
servicio de habitación (cuarto) *(m.)* room service, 12
servilleta *(f.)* napkin, 5
servir (e > i) to serve, 6; **¿en qué puedo —le?** how may I help you?, 9
sesenta sixty, 2
setecientos(as) seven hundred, 3
setenta seventy, 2
si if, 12
sí yes, 1; **— mismo(a)** himself (herself)
siempre always, 3
siete seven, 1
siglo *(m.)* century
siguiente following, 5
silla *(f.)* chair, 1
simpático(a) charming, nice, fun to be with, 1
sin que without, 13
sino but

sistema *(m.)* system
situación *(f.)* situation
sobre about 12; **— todo** especially
sobrina *(f.)* niece, 4
sobrino *(m.)* nephew, 4
sociología *(f.)* sociology, 2
sofá *(m.)* sofa
sofá-cama *(m.)* sleeper sofa, 12
solamente only, 2
solicitar un préstamo to apply for a loan, 10
sólo only, 2
solo(a) alone
soltero(a) single, 4
solución *(f.)* solution
sombrero *(m.)* hat, 9
sombrilla *(f.)* parasol
sopa *(f.)* soup, 5
sorpresa *(f.)* surprise, 4; **¡qué —!** what a surprise, 4
su(s) his, her, its, their, your *(form.)*, 2
subir to go up; to board *(a vehicle)*, 11
suceder to happen, 13
sucursal *(f.)* branch *(of a bank)*, 10
suegra *(f.)* mother-in-law, 4
suegro *(m.)* father-in-law, 4
suerte *(f.)* luck; destiny; **fue una —** it was a stroke of luck
suéter *(m.)* sweater, 9
suficiente sufficient
sugerir (e > ie) to suggest, 11
sujetar(se) to hold
superlativo *(m.)* superlative
supermercado *(m.)* supermarket, 6
suyo(s), suya(s) *(pron.)* his, hers, theirs, yours *(form.)*, 9

T

tabla de mar *(f.)* surfboard, 8
tablilla de anuncios *(f.)* bulletin board, 1
tacón *(m.)* heel, 9
tal vez maybe, perhaps, 9
talla *(f.)* size *(of clothing)*, 9
talonario de cheques *(m.)* checkbook, 10
tamaño *(m.)* size, 9
también also, too, 2
tampoco neither, 6
tan as; so, **— ... como** as . . . as, 5; **— pronto como** as soon as, 13
tanto(a) so much; **tantos(as)** so many, 6
tarde late, 5; **ya es —** it's already late, 2
tarde *(f.)* afternoon, 2; **esta —** this afternoon, 4; **más —** later, 5
tarea *(f.)* homework
tarjeta *(f.)* card, 10; **— de crédito** *(f.)* credit card, 12; **— de embarque** *(f.)* boarding pass, 11; **— postal** *(f.)* postcard, 10
tarta *(f.)* cake, 4
taxi *(m.)* taxi, 12
taza *(f.)* cup, 2
tazón *(m.)* bowl, 3
te *(pron. fam.)* you, 6; (to) you, 7; (to) yourself, 7; **— gusta** you *(fam.)* like, 7
té *(m.)* tea, 2; **— helado, frío** iced tea, 2
teatro *(m.)* theater, 7
teclado *(m.)* keyboard, 10
tecnología *(f.)* technology
teléfono *(m.)* telephone; **llamar por —** to phone
telegrama *(m.)* telegram
telenovela *(f.)* soap opera, 3
televisión *(f.)* television, 2
televisor *(m.)* TV set, 12
tema *(m.)* theme
temer to be afraid, to fear, 11
temperatura *(f.)* temperature, 9; **¿Qué — hace?** what is the temperature?, 9
templado(a) warm, 9
temprano early, 7
tenedor *(m.)* fork, 5
tener to have, 3; **— acceso a la Red** to have access to the Internet, 10; **— ...años (de edad)** to be . . . years old, 3; **— calor** to be warm, 3; **— frío** to be cold, 3; **— ganas de...** to feel like . . . **— (mucha) hambre** to be (very) hungry, 3; **— lugar** to take place; **— miedo** to be afraid, scared, 3; **— muchas cosas que hacer** to have many things to do; **no — nada que ponerse** not to have anything to wear, 9; **— prisa** to be in a hurry, 3; **— que** to have to, 3; **— que ver** to have to do; **— razón** to be right, 3; **no — razón** to be wrong, 3; **— (mucha) sed** to be (very) thirsty, 3; **— (mucho) sueño** to be (very) sleepy, 3
terminar to end, to finish, to get through, 2
termómetro *(m.)* thermometer, 14
ternera *(f.)* veal, 6
terremoto *(m.)* earthquake
ti *(obj. of prep.)* you, 5
tía *(f.)* aunt, 4
tiempo *(m.)* time, 3; weather, 9
tienda *(f.)* store, 9; shop; **— de campaña** *(f.)* tent, 8; **— de regalos** *(f.)* souvenir shop, 12
tierra *(f.)* earth, land
tijeras *(f., pl.)* scissors, 14
timbre *(m.) (Mex.)* stamp, 10
tímido(a) shy, 5
tinto red *(wine)*, 2
tintorería *(f.)* dry cleaner's
tío *(m.)* uncle, 4
tipo *(m.)* type
tiro *(m.)* shot
título *(m.)* title
tiza *(f.)* chalk, 1
tobillo *(m.)* ankle, 13
tocar to play *(music, an instrument)*; **— a la puerta** to knock at the door, 3
tocino *(m.)* bacon
todavía yet, 3
todo everything, 12; **todo(a)** all, 3; **— un éxito** quite a success, 4
todos(as) all, 2
tomar to take *(a class)*, 2; to drink, 2; **— algo** to have something to drink; **— el sol** to sunbathe, 8; **tome asiento** have a seat, 1; **— una decisión** to make a decision, 11
tomate *(m.)* tomato, 2
tonto(a) dumb, 1
torcedura *(f.)* sprain, 13
tormenta *(f.)* storm
tornado *(m.)* tornado
toronja *(f.)* grapefruit, 2
torpeza *(f.)* stupidity
torta *(f.)* cake, 4; pancake, 5
tortilla *(f.)* omelette
tos *(f.)* cough, 14
toser to cough, 14
tostada *(f.)* toast
tostadora *(f.)* toaster, 3
trabajar to work, 2
trabajo *(m.)* work, 3; **los trabajos de la casa** housework, 3
traducir to translate, 4

traer to bring, 4
tráfico *(m.)* traffic
traje *(m.)* suit, 9; **— de baño** *(m.)* bathing suit, 8
trasbordar to change planes, ships, etc.
tratar (de) to try, 8
travieso(a) mischievous, 5
trece thirteen, 1
treinta thirty, 1
tres three, 1
trescientos(as) three hundred, 3
trigueño(a) dark, brunet(te), 4
trozo *(m.)* piece
tu(s) your *(fam. sing.)*, 1
tú you *(fam. sing.)*, 1
turista *(m., f.)* tourist, 12; **clase —** tourist class, 11
turno *(m.)* appointment, 14
tuyo(s), tuya(s) *(pron.)* yours, *(fam. sing.)*, 9

U

últimamente lately, 10
último(a) last *(in a series)*, 7
un(a) a, an, 1
unir to join
universidad *(f.)* university, 1
universitario(a) (related to) college, 1
uno one, 1
unos(as) some, 1
usar to use, to wear, 9
usted (Ud.) *(form. sing.)* you, 2; *(obj. of prep.)* you, 5
ustedes (Uds.) *(form. pl.)* you, 2; *(obj. of prep.)* you, 5
útil useful
uva *(f.)* grape, 2

V

vacaciones *(f. pl.)* vacation; **estar de —** to be on vacation, 5; **ir(se) de —** to go on vacation
vainilla *(f.)* vanilla, 5
valija *(f.)* suitcase, 11
valor *(m.)* value
vamos let's go, 4; **no —** we are not going, 2; **— a comer** let's eat, 8
varios(as) several, 13
vasallo(a) *(m., f.)* subject *(vassal, subordinate, feudal tenant)*
vaso *(m.)* glass, 2
vecino(a) *(m., f.)* neighbor
vegetal *(m.)* vegetable, 5
veinte twenty, 1
velero *(m.)* sailboat, 8
venda *(f.)* bandage, 14
vendedor(a) *(m., f.)* merchant
vender to sell, 8
venir (de) to come (from), 3
venta *(f.)* sale
ventana *(f.)* window, 1
ventanilla *(f.)* window *(bank, ticket, etc.)*
ver to see, 4
veranear to spend the summer (vacationing)
verano *(m.)* summer, 2
verdad *(f.)* truth; **es —** it's true; **¿—?** right?, true?, 2
verdadero(a) true
verde green, 1
verdulería *(f.)* vegetable market
verdura *(f.)* vegetable, 5
vermut *(m.)* vermouth, 5
vestíbulo *(m.)* lobby, 12
vestido *(m.)* dress, 9
vestir(se) (e > i) to dress (oneself), to get dressed, 7
vez *(f.)* time, 7; **a veces** sometimes, 6; **la última —** the last time, 10; **otra —** again, 14
vía aérea airmail
viajar to travel, 11
viaje *(m.)* journey; trip, 11; **¡buen —!** have a nice trip!, 11; **de —** on a trip
viajero(a) *(m., f.)* traveler
vida *(f.)* life, 2; darling
viejo(a) old, 1
viernes *(m.)* Friday, 2
vinagre *(m.)* vinegar
vino *(m.)* wine, 2; **— blanco,** 2; **— rosado** rosé wine, 2; **— tinto** red wine, 2
visa *(f.)* visa
visita *(f.)* visit, 7
visitar to visit, 7
vista *(f.)* view, 12; **— al mar** ocean view, 12
visto(a) seen, 10
vitamina *(f.)* vitamin, 14
vivir to live, 3
vocabulario *(m.)* vocabulary
volver (o > ue) to return, to go (come) back, 6
vosotros(as) you *(fam. pl.)*, 1; you *(obj. of prep.)*, 5
vuelo *(m.)* flight, 11
vuelto(a) returned, 10
vuestro(s), vuestra(s) *(adj.)* your *(fam. pl.)*, 2; yours, 9

Y

y and, 1; past, after, 2; **— media** half past, 2; **¿y tú?** and you?, 1
ya already, 4; **¡— es tarde!** it's (already) late!, 2; **¡— voy!** I'm going!
yerno *(m.)* son-in-law, 4
yo I, 1

Z

zacate *(m.) (Mex.)* lawn, 3
zanahoria *(f.)* carrot, 6
zapatería *(f.)* shoe store, 9
zapatilla *(f.)* slipper, 9
zapato *(m.)* shoe, 9
zoológico *(m.)* zoo, 7
zumo *(m.) (Spain)* juice, 2

English-Spanish

A

a, an un(a), 1; **— day** al día, 6
about de, 2; sobre, 12
access to the Internet acceso a la Red, 10
accident accidente *(m.)*
accompanied acompañado(a)
according to según, 9
account cuenta *(f.)*, 10; **on — of** por, 9
accounting contabilidad *(f.)*, 2
ache *(v.)* doler (o > ue), 13
activity actividad *(f.)*, 8; **outdoor —** actividad al aire libre, 8
add añadir
address dirección *(f.)*, 1; domicilio *(m.)*, 1
adhesive bandage curita *(f.)*, 14
admit admitir, 14
advise *(v.)* aconsejar, 11
adviser consejero(a) *(m., f.)*
aerobic dance danza aeróbica *(f.)*, 2
after después de, 9
afternoon tarde *(f.)*; **this —** esta tarde, 1
again otra vez, 14
agency agencia *(f.)*, 11
agent agente *(m., f.)*, 11
ago hace... , 9
agree on convenir en, 12
air aire *(m.)*; **— conditioning** aire acondicionado, 12
airline aerolínea *(f.)*, 11
airmail por vía aérea
airport aeropuerto *(m.)*, 11
all todos(as), 2
allergic alérgico(a), 13
almost casi, 13
alone solo(a)
along por, 9
alphabet alfabeto *(m.)*
already ya, 4
also también, 2
although aunque, 4
always siempre, 3
ambulance ambulancia *(f.)*, 13
amount cantidad *(f.)*
amusement park parque de diversiones *(m.)*, 7
and y, 1
ankle tobillo *(m.)*, 13
anniversary aniversario *(m.)*, 5
another otro(a), 10
antacid antiácido *(m.)*, 14
anthropology antropología *(f.)*, 2
antibiotic antibiótico *(m.)*, 14
any algún, alguno(a), algunos(as), 6; cualquier(a); **at — time** en cualquier momento
anyone alguien, 6
anything algo, 5; **— else?** ¿algo más?, 10
anywhere en alguna parte
apartment apartamento *(m.)*, 6
appetizer entremés *(m.)*, 4
apple manzana *(f.)*, 2
apply for a loan solicitar (pedir) un préstamo, 10
appointment turno *(m.)*, 14; **make an —** pedir turno, 14
April abril, 2
Argentinian argentino(a)
arm brazo *(m.)*, 13
arrive llegar, 3; **— late (early)** llegar tarde (temprano)
art arte *(m.)*, 2
as como, 9; **— if** como si, 14; **— much . . .** tanto(a)...; **— soon as** en cuanto, tan pronto como, 9
ask (for) pedir (e > i), 5; **— (a question)** preguntar, 7
aspirin aspirina *(f.)*
assistance ayuda *(f.)*
at en, 1; a, 2; **— any time** en cualquier momento; **— home** en casa; **— present** actualmente; **— what time . . . ?** ¿A qué hora... ?, 2
attend asistir
August agosto, 2
aunt tía *(f.)*, 4
automatic teller machine cajero automático *(m.)*, 10
automobile coche *(m.)*, automóvil *(m.)*, auto *(m.)*, carro *(m.)*, 10
autumn otoño *(m.)*, 2
available libre, disponible, 12
avocado aguacate *(m.)*, 6

B

back espalda *(f.)*, 13
backpack mochila *(f.)*, 1
bacon tocino *(m.)*
bad malo(a), 5; **too —!** ¡qué lástima!
badly mal, 5
baked al horno
bakery panadería *(f.)*, 6
balance saldo *(m.)*, 10
banana plátano *(m.)*, 6
band orquesta *(f.)*
bandage venda *(f.)*, 14
bank banco *(m.)*, 10
barefoot descalzo(a), 9; **to go —** andar descalzo(a), 9
bargain *(v.)* regatear
baseball béisbol *(m.)*, 7
basket cesta *(f.)*, 8
bathe bañarse, 7
bathing suit traje de baño *(m.)*, 8
bathroom baño *(m.)*, 3; cuarto de baño *(m.)*, 3
bathtub bañadera *(f.)*, 12
battlefield campo de batalla *(m.)*
be ser, 1, estar, 4; **— able to** poder (o > ue), 6; **— acquainted with** conocer, 4; **— afraid, scared** tener miedo, 3, temer, 11; **— bored** aburrirse, 7; **— born** nacer; **— cold** tener frío, 3, hacer frío, 9; **— from** ser de, 1; **— going to** ir a + *inf.*, 4; **— good (bad) weather** hacer buen (mal) tiempo, 9; **— hot** tener calor, 3, hacer calor, 9; **— (very) hungry** tener (mucha) hambre, 3; **— in a hurry** tener prisa, 3; **— late (early)** llegar tarde (temprano); **— okay** estar bien; **— pleasing** gustar, 7; **— right** tener razón, 3; **— (very) sleepy** tener (mucho) sueño, 3; **— sorry** sentir (e > ie), 1; **— sunny** hacer sol, 9; **— sure** estar seguro(a); **— (very) thirsty** tener (mucha) sed, 3; **— tight** apretar (e > ie), 7; **— too big/small (on someone)** quedarle grande/chico(a) (a uno o una), 9; **— windy** hacer viento, 9; **— wrong** no tener razón, 3; **— . . . years old** tener... años de edad, 3
beach playa *(f.)*, 1; **— resort** balneario *(m.)*
bear oso *(m.)*
beautiful hermoso(a)
because porque, 2; **— of** por, 9

bed cama *(f.)*, 12; **double —** cama doble *(f.)*, 12; **twin —** cama chica (pequeña) *(f.)*, 12
bedroom dormitorio *(m.)*, recámara (*Mex.*) *(f.)*, 3
beer cerveza *(f.)*, 2
before antes *(adv.)*, antes de *(prep.)*, 6, antes de que *(conj.)*, 13
begin comenzar (e > ie), empezar (e > ie), 5
behalf: on — of por, 9
believe creer, 13
bellhop botones *(m. sing.)*, 12
belong pertenecer
belt cinto *(m.)*, cinturón *(m.)*, 9
besides además *(adv.)*, 2; además de *(prep.)*
best (el, la) mejor, 5
better mejor, 5
between entre; **— meals** entre comidas
big grande, 5; gran
bigger más grande, 5
biggest (el, la) más grande, 5
bill cuenta *(f.)*, 10
biology biología *(f.)*, 2
bird ave *(f.)*, pájaro *(m.)*
birthday cumpleaños *(m. sing.)*, 4
black negro(a), 1
blackboard pizarra *(f.)*, 1
bleach lejía *(f.)*, 6
blender licuadora *(f.)*, 3
block cuadra *(f.)*, manzana *(f.)*, 10
blond rubio(a), 4
blouse blusa *(f.)*, 9
blue azul, 1
board *(v.)* abordar, 11; subir (a), 13
boarding gate puerta de salida *(f.)*, 11
boarding house pensión *(f.)*, 12
boarding pass tarjeta de embarque *(f.)*, 11
body cuerpo *(m.)*, 13
bonfire fogata *(f.)*, 8
book libro *(m.)*, 1
boot bota *(f.)*, 9
boring aburrido(a), 2
boss jefe(a) *(m., f.)*
bossy mandón(ona), 3
bottle botella *(f.)*, 2
bowl tazón *(m.)*, 3
boy chico *(m.)*, muchacho *(m.)*, 1
boyfriend novio *(m.)*, 4
branch *(of a bank)* sucursal *(f.)*, 10
brand marca *(f.)*
braying rebuzno *(m.)*
bread pan *(m.)*, 5
break romper, 7; **— (a bone)** romperse, 13
breakfast desayuno *(m.)*, 5
breathe respirar, 14
bring traer, 4
broccoli brócoli *(m.)*, 6
brochure folleto *(m.)*, 12
broken quebrado(a), roto(a), 10
brook arroyo *(m.)*
broom escoba *(f.)*
broth caldo *(m.)*, sopa *(f.)* *(Mex.)*, 5
brother hermano *(m.)*, 3
brother-in-law cuñado *(m.)*, 4
brown marrón, café, 1; *(hair or eyes)* castaño, 4
brunet(te) moreno(a), 4
bulletin board tablilla de anuncios *(f.)*, 1
buried enterrado(a)
burn (oneself) quemarse, 13
bus autobús *(m.)*, ómnibus *(m.)*
business administration administración de empresas *(f.)*, 2
busy ocupado(a), 3
but pero, 2; sino
butter mantequilla *(f.)*, 5
buy comprar, 6
by por, 9
bye chau, 1

C

cafeteria cafetería *(f.)*, 2
cake torta *(f.)*, pastel *(m.)*, tarta *(f.)*, 4
call llamar, 4; llamada *(f.)*, 11
camp *(v.)* acampar, 8
can *(v.)* poder (o > ue), 6
cancel cancelar, 11
canoe canoa *(f.)*, 8
capital capital *(f.)*, 11
car coche *(m.)*, carro *(m.)*, auto *(m.)*, automóvil *(m.)*, 10
caramel custard flan *(m.)*, 5
card tarjeta *(f.)*, 10; **credit —** tarjeta de crédito *(f.)*, 12; **I. D. —** cédula de identidad *(f.)*, 12
cardiologist cardiólogo(a) *(m., f.)*, 14
carrot zanahoria *(f.)*, 6
carry-on bag bolso de mano *(m.)*, 11
case caso *(m.)*; **in that —** entonces, en ese caso
cash efectivo *(m.)*; **— (a check)** cobrar (un cheque), 10
cattle ganado *(m.)*
celebrate celebrar, 4
celery apio *(m.)*, 6
central céntrico(a), 12
century siglo *(m.)*
cereal cereal *(m.)*
chain cadena *(f.)*, 9
chair silla *(f.)*, 1
chalk tiza *(f.)*, 1
chalkboard pizarra *(f.)*, 1
champagne champán *(m.)*, 4
change *(v.)* cambiar, 7; **— planes** trasbordar, cambiar de avión
charge cobrar, 10
charming simpático(a), 1, encantador(a), 4
check *(n.)* cheque *(m.)*, 10; cuenta *(f.)*, 5; **—up** chequeo *(m.)*, 14; *(v.)* examinar, revisar, 13; 14; **— out (of a hotel room)** desocupar, 12
checkbook talonario de cheques *(m.)*, 10
checking account cuenta corriente *(f.)*, 10
cheers! ¡salud!, 4
cheese queso *(m.)*
chemistry química *(f.)*, 2
cherry cereza *(f.)*, 6
chest pecho *(m.)*, 13
chicken pollo *(m.)*, 5
child niño(a) *(m., f.)*, 5
children hijos *(m. pl.)*, 3
chivalry caballería *(f.)*
chocolate chocolate *(m.)*, 2
choose elegir (e > i), 6; escoger, 6
chop: pork — chuleta de cerdo *(f.)*, 6; **veal —** chuleta de ternera *(f.)*, 6
Christmas Navidad *(f.)*
church iglesia *(f.)*
city ciudad *(f.)*, 3
claim check comprobante *(m.)*
class clase *(f.)*, 1; **— schedule** horario de clases *(m.)*, 2; **first —** primera clase, 11; **tourist —** clase turista, 11
classmate compañero(a) de clase *(m., f.)*, 1
classroom aula *(f.)*, 2
clean *(v.)* limpiar, 3; *(adj.)* limpio(a), 12
clear claro(a), despejado(a), 9
clerk empleado(a) *(m., f.)*, 9; dependiente(a) *(m., f.)*
climate clima *(m.)*, 9
climb mountains escalar montañas, 7

clock reloj *(m.)*, 1
close cerrar (e > ie), 5; **closed** cerrado(a), 10
clothes ropa *(f.)*, 3
cloudy nublado(a), 9
club club *(m.)*, 4; **golf —** palo de golf *(m.)*, 8
coat abrigo *(m.)*, 9
coffee café *(m.)*, 2; **— and milk** café con leche
coffee pot cafetera *(f.)*, 3
coin moneda *(f.)*
cold frío(a), 9; catarro *(m.)*, resfriado *(m.)*, resfrío *(m.)*
collar cuello *(m.)*, 13
college facultad *(f.)*, 9; universidad *(f.)*, 1
collide (with) chocar (con), 13
color color *(m.)*
come venir, 3; **— in** pase, 1
comfortable cómodo(a), 9
compact disc (CD) disco compacto *(m.)*, 4
complain quejarse, 7
computer computadora *(f.)*, ordenador *(m.) (Spain)*, 1; **— science** informática *(f.)*, 2
concert concierto *(m.)*, 7
conduct *(v.)* conducir, 4
confirm confirmar, 11
consciousness conocimiento *(m.)*, 13; **lose —** perder el conocimiento, 13
continue seguir (e > i), 6; continuar, 13
converse conversar, 2
cook *(v.)* cocinar, 6
cook *(n.)* cocinero(a), 6
corner esquina *(f.)*
cost costar (o > ue), 6; **— an arm and a leg** costar un ojo de la cara, 9
cotton algodón *(m.)*, 14
cough tos *(f.)*, 14; *(v.)* toser, 14
country *(as opposed to city)* campo *(m.)*; país *(m.)*
couple pareja *(f.)*, 4; **a — of days** un par de días
course asignatura *(f.)*; materia *(f.)*, 2
cousin primo(a) *(m., f.)*, 4
crab cangrejo *(m.)*, 6
cream crema *(f.)*, 5
crow cuervo *(m.)*
cruise crucero *(m.)*, 11
crutches muletas *(f. pl.)*, 13
cry *(v.)* llorar, 13
Cuban cubano(a) *(m., f.)*, 1; **— American** cubanoamericano(a), 2
cucumber pepino *(m.)*, 6
cup taza *(f.)*, 2
custom costumbre *(f.)*
cut cortar, 3; **— (oneself)** cortarse, 13
cyclone ciclón *(m.)*

D

dad padre *(m.)*, papá *(m.)*, 3
daddy papi *(m.)*
dam represa *(f.)*
dance *(v.)* bailar, 4; **shall we — ?** ¿Bailamos?, 4
dark moreno(a), trigueño(a), 4
darling mi vida, 8
date *(a document)* fechar, 10; *(appointment)* cita *(f.)*, 14
daughter hija *(f.)*, 4
daughter-in-law nuera *(f.)*, 4
day día *(m.)*, 1; **— before yesterday** anteayer; **per —** al día, 6; **(on) the following (next) —** al día siguiente, 5
dead muerto(a), 10
dear querido(a), 11
December diciembre, 2
decide decidir, 4
deer ciervo *(m.)*
degree *(temperature)* grado *(m.)*, 9
delicious riquísimo(a)
demonstrative demostrativo(a)
deny negar (e > ie), 13
department apartamento *(m.)*, 6
deposit *(v.)* depositar, 10
dermatologist dermatólogo(a) *(m., f.)*, 14
desk escritorio *(m.)*, 1
design programs diseñar programas
dessert postre *(m.)*, 5; **for —** de postre, 5
detergent detergente *(m.)*, 6
die morir (o > ue)
diet dieta *(f.)*
difficult difícil, 1
dining room comedor *(m.)*
dinner cena *(f.)*; **have —** cenar, 3
disaster desastre *(m.)*, 3
discount descuento *(m.)*
discovered descubierto(a)
disease enfermedad *(f.)*, 14
dish plato *(m.)*, 3
dishwasher lavaplatos *(m.)*, 3
disinfect desinfectar, 13
disinfectant desinfectante *(adj.)*, 14
disk disco *(m.)*
do hacer, 3
doctor doctor(a) *(m., f.)*, 1; médico(a) *(m., f.)*, 11
doctor's office consultorio *(m.)*, 14
document documento *(m.)*
dog perro(a); **hot —** perro caliente *(m.)*, 5
done hecho(a), 10
donkey borrico *(m.)*
door puerta *(f.)*, 1
dormitory residencia universitaria *(f.)*
double bed cama doble *(f.)*, 12
doubt *(v.)* dudar, 13
dozen docena *(f.)*, 6
dress vestido *(m.)*, 9; **— (oneself)** vestir(se) (e > i), 7
drink *(v.)* tomar, 2; beber, 3; bebida *(f.)*, 4
drive *(v.)* conducir, manejar, 4; *(n.)* **hard —** disco duro *(m.)*, 10
driver's license licencia para conducir (manejar) *(f.)*
drop gota *(f.)*
drugstore farmacia *(f.)*, 14
dry seco(a), 9; **— cleaner's** tintorería *(f.)*
dryer *(clothes)* secadora *(f.)*, 3
during por, 9; durante; **— the week** entre semana
dumb tonto(a), 1
dust *(v.)* sacudir, limpiar el polvo, 3

E

eagle águila *(f.)*
ear *(external)* oreja *(f.)*, 13; *(internal)* oído *(m.)*
early temprano, 7; **— morning** madrugada *(f.)*
earrings aretes *(m. pl.)*, 9; pendientes *(m. pl.)*, 9
earth tierra *(f.)*
earthquake terremoto *(m.)*
easily fácilmente, 8
easy fácil, 8
eat comer, 3
eaten comido(a), 10
egg huevo *(m.)*, 5; blanquillo *(m.) (Mex.)*, 5
eight ocho, 1
eight hundred ochocientos(as), 3
eighteen dieciocho, 2

eighty ochenta, 2
either . . . or o... o, 6
elbow codo *(m.)*, 13
elderly mayor
elegant elegante
elevator ascensor *(m.)*, 12
eleven once, 2
e-mail mensaje electrónico *(m.)*, 10
emergency emergencia *(f.)*, 11; **— exit** salida de emergencia *(f.)*, 11; **— room** sala de emergencia *(f.)*, 13
end *(v.)* terminar, 2
engineering ingeniería *(f.)*
English *(language)* inglés *(m.)*, 2; *(person)* inglés(esa) *(m., f.)*
enter entrar (en), 7
enthused animado(a), 4
eraser borrador *(m.)*, 1
errand diligencia *(f.)*; **to run —s** hacer diligencias
escalator escalera mecánica *(f.)*, 13
especially sobre todo
essay ensayo *(m.)*
esteem oneself estimarse
even hasta; **— if** aunque, 13
ever alguna vez, 6
everything todo, 12; **— is in order** todo está en regla
examine examinar, 14
excess exceso *(m.)*, 11; **— luggage (charge)** exceso de equipaje *(m.)*, 11
excursion excursión *(f.)*, 11
excuse excusa *(f.)*, 3; **— me** permiso; perdón 1
exercise hacer ejercicio; ejercicio *(m.)*
exit salida *(f.)*, 11
expand ampliar
expensive caro(a), 6
expression expresión *(f.)*
exterior exterior *(m.)*, 12
eyes ojos *(m. pl.)*, 4; **brown —** ojos castaños, 4

F

face cara *(f.)*, 13; rostro *(m.)*
faint perder el conocimiento, desmayarse, 13; desfallecer
fair justo(a), 7
fall otoño *(m.)*, 2; **— asleep** dormirse (o > ue); **— down** caerse, 13; **— in love (with)** enamorarse (de), 12
false falso(a)
family familia *(f.)*, 3; **— room** sala de estar *(f.)*
far (away) lejos
farewell despedida *(f.)*
fast rápido(a), 8
fasten the seat belt abrocharse el cinturón de seguridad, 11
fat gordo(a), 1
father padre *(m.)*, papá *(m.)*, 4
father-in-law suegro *(m.)*, 4
fear temer, 11
February febrero, 2
feel *(v.)* sentir(se) (e > ie), 10; **— like** tener ganas de
fever fiebre *(f.)*, 14
few pocos(as)
field campo *(m.)*
fifteen quince, 2
fifty cincuenta, 2
fill (out) llenar, 10
finally por fin, 10
find *(v.)* encontrar (o > ue), 6; **— out** averiguar, 11
fine bien, 1
finger dedo *(m.)*, 13
finish *(v.)* terminar, 2
finished acabado(a)
first primero *(adv.)*, 10; **— class** (de) primera clase, 11; **— time** primera vez
fish pescado *(m.)*, 5; **— market** pescadería *(f.)*, 6; *(v.)* pescar, 8
fishing rod caña de pescar *(f.)*, 8
fit *(v.)* caber, 4; quedar; quedarle bien
fitting room probador *(m.)*, 9
five cinco, 1
five hundred quinientos(as), 3
flight vuelo *(m.)*, 11; **— attendant** auxiliar de vuelo *(m., f.)*, 11, azafata *(f.)*, 11
floor piso *(m.)*, 12
flower flor *(f.)*
flu gripe *(f.)*, 14
fog niebla *(f.)*, 9
follow seguir (e > i), 6
food comida *(f.)*, 3
foot pie *(m.)*, 13
for para, 3; por, 9
foreign extranjero(a)
forest bosque *(m.)*
forget olvidarse (de), 12
forgive perdonar
fork tenedor *(m.)*, 5
form planilla *(f.)*, 10
fortress fortaleza *(f.)*
forty cuarenta, 2
founded fundado(a)
four cuatro, 1
four hundred cuatrocientos(as), 3
fourteen catorce, 2
fracture *(n.)* fractura *(f.)*, 13; *(v.)* fracturar(se), romper(se)
free gratis, 10; libre
French *(language)* francés *(m.)*; **— fries** papas fritas *(f. pl.)*, 9
Friday viernes *(m.)*, 2
fried frito(a), 8
friend amigo(a) *(m., f.)*, 2
friendship amistad *(f.)*
from de; desde
frozen helado(a)
fruit fruta *(f.)*, 5
fry freír (e > i)
frying pan sartén *(f.)*, 3
full lleno(a), 12
furniture muebles *(m. pl.)*, 3

G

game juego *(m.)*, partido *(m.)*, 7
garage garaje *(m.)*, 3
garbage basura *(f.)*, 3
gee! ¡caramba!, 1
gender género *(m.)*
general general, 8
generally generalmente, 8
gentleman señor *(m.)* (*abbr.* Sr.), 1; caballero *(m.)*
geography geografía *(f.)*, 2
geology geología *(f.)*, 2
German *(language)* alemán *(m.)*
get conseguir (e > i), 6; **— a haircut** cortarse el pelo; **— acquainted** conocer, 4; **— better** mejorarse, 14; **— dressed** vestirse (e > i); **— engaged (to)** comprometerse (con), 12; **— hurt** lastimarse, 13; **— married to** casarse (con), 12; **— ready** prepararse, 7; **— through** terminar, 2; **— up** levantarse, 7; **— worse** empeorar, 14
gift regalo *(m.)*, 9
girlfriend novia *(f.)*, 4
give dar, 4; **— a shot** poner una inyección, 13
glad: to be glad (about) alegrarse (de), 12
glass vaso *(m.)*, 2
glove guante *(m.)*, 9
go ir, 4; **— away** irse; **— back** volver (o > ue), 6;

— down bajar; **— fishing** ir de pesca; **— hiking** hacer una caminata, 8; **— in** entrar (en), 7; **— on vacation** ir(se) de vacaciones; **— out** salir, 4; **— shopping** ir de compras; **— to bed** acostarse (o > ue), 7; **— up** subir, 13
godfather padrino *(m.)*, 4
godmother madrina *(f.)*, 4
gold oro *(m.)*, 9
good bueno(a), 2; **— afternoon** buenas tardes, 1; **— evening** buenas noches, 1; **— morning** buenos días, 1; **— night** buenas noches, 1
good-bye adiós, 1
government gobierno *(m.)*, 1
grade nota *(f.)*
granddaughter nieta *(f.)*, 4
grandfather abuelo *(m.)*, 4
grandmother abuela *(f.)*, 4
grandparents abuelos *(m.)*
grandson nieto *(m.)*, 4
grape uva *(f.)*, 2
grapefruit toronja *(f.)*, 2
gray gris, 1
great magnífico(a)
great-granddaughter bisnieta *(f.)*
great-grandfather bisabuelo *(m.)*
great-grandmother bisabuela *(f.)*
great-grandson bisnieto *(m.)*
green verde, 1
greet saludar
greeting saludo *(m.)*
grilled a la parrilla, 5
groceries *(food items)* comestibles *(m. pl.)*
group grupo *(m.)*
grow crecer
guest invitado(a); **— room** cuarto de huéspedes *(m.)*, 14
gurney camilla *(f.)*
gynecologist ginecólogo(a) *(m., f.)*, 14

H

hair pelo *(m.)*
half medio(a); **— past** y media, 2; **— an hour** media hora, 3
half brother medio hermano *(m.)*
half sister media hermana *(f.)*
ham jamón *(m.)*, 5
hamburger hamburguesa *(f.)*, 5
hand mano *(f.)*
handbag bolso *(m.)*; cartera *(f.)*; bolsa *(f.)*
hand luggage maletín *(m.)*, 11
handsome guapo(a), 1
happen pasar, suceder, 13
happy feliz, contento(a), 4
hat sombrero *(m.)*, 9
have tener, 3, haber, 10; **— a seat** tomar asiento, 1; **— breakfast** desayunar, 5; **— dinner (supper)** cenar, 3; **— fun** divertirse (e > ie), 7; **— just (done something)** acabar de + *inf.*, 8; **— lunch** almorzar (o > ue), 6; **— many things to do** tener muchas cosas que hacer; **— to** deber, 3, tener que, 3; **— to do with** tener que ver con
he él, 1
head cabeza *(f.)*, 13
headache dolor de cabeza *(m.)*
health salud *(f.)*, 10
heart corazón *(m.)*, 13
heating calefacción *(f.)*, 12
heaven cielo *(m.)*
heel tacón *(m.)*, 9
height estatura *(f.)*, 4; **of medium —** de estatura mediana, 4
hello hola, 1
help *(v.)* ayudar, 12
her su(s) *(adj.)*, 2; ella *(obj. of prep.)*, 5; la *(dir. obj.)* 6; **(to) —** le *(ind. obj.)*, 7
here aquí, 5; **— it is** aquí está, 2
hers suyo(a), suyos(as), 9
herself se, 7; sí misma
hi hola, 1
high school escuela secundaria *(f.)*
hillside ladera *(f.)*
him él *(obj. of prep.)*, 5; lo *(dir. obj.)*, 6; **(to) —** le *(ind. obj.)*, 7
himself se, 7; sí mismo
his su(s) *(adj.)*, 2; suyo(a), suyos(as), 9
history historia *(f.)*, 2
hit (oneself) golpear(se), 13
hold *(v.)* sujetar(se)
holiday día feriado *(m.)*, 10
home hogar *(m.)*; **at —** en casa; **— appliances** aparatos electrodomésticos *(m. pl.)*; **— office** casa central, 10
homework tarea *(f.)*
honeymoon luna de miel *(f.)*
hope *(v.)* esperar, 11; **I —** ojalá; **I — so** espero que sí, 8
horseback riding montar a caballo, 7
hospital hospital *(m.)*, 13
host anfitrión *(m.)*
hostess anfitriona *(f.)*
hot cálido(a), 9; caliente, 12; **— chocolate** chocolate caliente *(m.)*, 2; **— dog** perro caliente *(m.)*, 5
hotel hotel *(m.)*, 8
hour hora *(f.)*, 2
house casa *(f.)*, 3; **—work** trabajos de la casa, 3
how cómo, 1; **— are you?** ¿cómo está usted?, ¿cómo estás?, 1; **— do you do?** Mucho gusto, 1; **— do you say . . . ?** ¿cómo se dice... ?, 1; **— is it going?** ¿qué tal?, 1; **— long?** ¿por cuánto tiempo?; **— many?** ¿cuántos(as)?, 2; **— may I help you?** ¿en qué puedo servirle?, 6; **— much?** ¿cuánto(a)?
humid húmedo(a), 9
hunger hambre *(f.)*, 3
hungry: to be hungry tener hambre, 3
hunt *(v.)* cazar, 8
hurricane huracán *(m.)*
hurry apurarse; darse prisa
hurt doler (o > ue), 13; **— (oneself)** lastimar(se), 13
husband esposo *(m.)*, 4
hydrogen peroxide agua oxigenada, 14

I

I yo, 1; **—'m going!** ¡Ya voy!
ice hielo *(m.)*; **— cream** helado *(m.)*, 5; **— water** agua con hielo *(f.)*, 2
iced tea té helado, té frío *(m.)*, 2
idea idea *(f.)*, 2
identification identificación *(f.)*
if si, 12
illiterate analfabeto(a) *(m., f.)*
important importante; **the — thing** lo importante
improve mejorar, 14
in en, 1; de, 11; por, 9; a, 11; **— exchange for** por, 9; **— order that** para que, 13; **— order to** para
inch pulgada *(f.)*
include incluir, 11
income ingreso *(m.)*
inexpensive barato(a), 9

infection infección *(f.)*
information información *(f.)*
injection inyección *(f.)*, 13
inside en, 11
insist on insistir en, 12
instead of en vez de, 7
insurance seguro *(m.)*, aseguranza *(f.)*, 14; **medical —** seguro médico, 14
insured asegurado(a)
intelligent inteligente, 1
interest interés *(m.)*
interesting interesante, 1
interior interior, 12
international internacional, 1
invitation invitación *(f.)*, 4
invite invitar, 4
invited invitado(a), 4
iron *(appliance)* plancha *(f.)*, 3; *(v.)* planchar, 3
isthmus istmo *(m.)*
it *(dir. obj. pron.)* la, 6; lo, 6
Italian *(language)* italiano *(m.)*
its su(s), 2
itself se, 7

J

jacket chaqueta *(f.)*, 9
jam mermelada *(f.)*, 5
January enero, 2
jewel joya *(f.)*
jewelry joyas *(f. pl.)*
join unir
joint account cuenta conjunta *(f.)*, 10
joke *(v.)* bromear, 7
journey viaje *(m.)*
juice jugo *(m.)*, zumo *(m.)* *(Spain)*, 2
July julio, 2
June junio, 2

K

keep guardar
keyboard teclado *(m.)*, 10
key llave *(f.)*
kid *(v.)* bromear, 7
kill matar; **— two birds with one stone** matar dos pájaros de un tiro
kitchen cocina *(f.)*, 3; **— utensils** batería de cocina *(f. sing.)*
knee rodilla *(f.)*, 13
knife cuchillo *(m.)*, 5
knight caballero *(m.)*
knock (at the door) tocar (llamar) a la puerta, 3
know conocer, 4; saber 4
known conocido(a)

L

lady señora *(f.)* (*abbr.* Sra.), 1
lake lago *(m.)*, 8
lamb cordero *(m.)*, 5
land tierra *(f.)*
language idioma *(m.)*, lengua *(f.)*
laptop microcomputadora *(f.)*, 10
last *(v.)* durar; *(adj.)(in a series)* último(a); pasado(a), 7; **— name** apellido *(m.)*; **— night** anoche, 7; **— time** la última vez *(f.)*, 10; **— year** el año pasado *(m.)*
late tarde, 5; **it's (already) —!** ¡ya es tarde!, 2
lately últimamente, 10
later después, más tarde, 5; luego; **see you —** hasta luego, 1
Latin America Latinoamérica *(f.)*
laugh *(v.)* reírse, 7
lawn césped *(m.)*, zacate *(m.)* *(Mex.)*, 3
lawyer abogado(a) *(m., f.)*
learn aprender (a), 11
leave dejar, 5; **I'm leaving** me voy, 2
lecture conferencia *(f.)*, 14
left izquierdo(a); **to the —** a la izquierda
leg pierna *(f.)*, 13
lemonade limonada *(f.)*, 3
lend prestar, 8
less menos, 5; **— . . . than** menos... que, 5
lesson lección *(f.)*
let dejar, 11
let's: —eat vamos a comer, 8; **— go** vamos, 4; **— see** a ver, 6
letter carta *(f.)*, 10
lettuce lechuga *(f.)*, 6
liberty libertad *(f.)*
library biblioteca *(f.)*, 1
license licencia *(f.)*
lie *(v.)* mentir (e > ie), 11
life vida *(f.)*
lifeguard salvavidas *(m., f.)*, 8
light luz *(f.)*, 1; ligero(a); claro(a)
like gustar, 7; como *(adv.)*, 9; **I — it** me gusta; **you — it** te gusta, 7
listen! ¡oye!, 1
literature literatura *(f.)*, 2
little *(adj.)* chico(a), 8, pequeño(a), 8; **a —** un poco, 6
live vivir, 3
living room sala *(f.)*, 3
loaded cargado(a)
loan préstamo *(m.)*, 10
lobby vestíbulo *(m.)*, 12
lobster langosta *(f.)*, 5
lock *(in a canal)* esclusa *(f.)*
lodge *(v.)* hospedarse, 8
long largo(a), 9
look at mirar, 3
look for (up) buscar, 9
lose perder (e > ie); **— consciousness** perder el conocimiento, 13
love *(n.)* amor *(m.)*; *(v.)* encantar, 8; **in —** enamorado(a), 4
luck suerte *(f.)*; **it was a stroke of — (v.)** fue una suerte; **luckily** afortunadamente, 14
luggage equipaje *(m.)*, 11; **— compartment** compartimiento de equipaje (*m.*), 11
lunch almuerzo *(m.)*, 5; **have —** *(v.)* almorzar (o > ue), 6
luxury lujo *(m.)*, 12

M

madam señora *(f.)* (*abbr.* Sra.), 1
made hecho(a), 10
magazine revista *(f.)*; **— stand** puesto de revistas *(m.)*, 12
maid criada *(f.)*, 6, muchacha *(f.)*
maiden name nombre de soltera *(m.)*
make hacer; 3; **— a decision** tomar una decisión, 11; **— an appointment** pedir turno
man hombre *(m.)*, 1
manager gerente *(m., f.)*, 13
many muchos(as), 3; un montón de, 12
map mapa *(m.)*, 1
March marzo, 2
market mercado *(m.)*, 6
marmalade mermelada *(f.)*, 5
married casado(a), 4; **— couple** matrimonio, 8
marry casarse (con), 12
mashed potatoes puré de papas *(m. sing.)*, 5
mathematics matemáticas *(f. pl.)*, 2
matter *(v.)* importar, 6; **it doesn't —** no importa
May mayo, 2
maybe quizás, tal vez, 9
M.D. médico(a) *(m., f.)*, doctor(a) *(m., f.)*, 11

me mí *(obj. of prep.)*, 5, me *(dir. obj.)*, 6; me *(indir. obj.)*, 7; me *(refl. pron.)*, 7
meal comida *(f.)*, 3
mean *(v.)* querer (e > ie) decir, 1
measure medida *(f.)*
meat carne *(f.)*, 6; **— market** carnicería *(f.)*
meatball albóndiga *(f.)*, 6
medicine medicina *(f.)*, 9
medium mediano(a), 9
memory memoria *(f.)*, 10
men's department departamento de caballeros *(m.)*
menu menú *(m.)*, 5
merchant vendedor(a) *(m., f.)*
Mexican mexicano(a) *(m., f.)*, 1
microwave oven horno de microondas *(m.)*, 3
midnight medianoche *(f.)*, 2
milk leche *(f.)*, 2
mine mío(a), míos(as), 9
minute minuto *(m.)*, 2
mischievous travieso(a), 5
Miss señorita *(f.)* (*abbr.* Srta.), 1
mix *(v.)* mezclar
mixture mezcla *(f.)*
mom madre *(f.)*, mamá *(f.)*, 3
moment momento *(m.)*, 3
mommy mami *(f.)*
Monday lunes *(m.)*, 2
money dinero *(m.)*, 2; **— order** giro postal *(m.)*, 10
monitor monitor *(m.)*, 10
month mes *(m.)*, 2
monthly mensual
more más, 5; **— . . . than** más... que, 5; **— than (number)** más de, 5
morning mañana *(f.)*, 2; **early —** madrugada *(f.)*
mother madre *(f.)*, mamá *(f.)*, 4
mother-in-law suegra *(f.)*, 4
mouse ratón *(m.)*, 10
mouth boca *(f.)*, 13
move *(v.) (relocate)* mudarse
movie película *(f.)*, 7; **— theater** cine *(m.)*, 7
mow (the lawn) cortar el césped, 3
Mr. señor *(m.)* (*abbr.* Sr.), 1; **Mr. and Mrs. . . .** los señores ...
Mrs. señora *(f.)* (*abbr.* Sra.), 1
much mucho(a)
museum museo *(m.)*, 7
music música *(f.)*, 2
must deber, 3
my mi(s), 2; **— name is** me llamo, 1
myself me, 7

N

name nombre *(m.)*; **my — is . . .** me llamo..., 1; **what is your —?** *(form.)* ¿cómo se llama usted?, *(fam.)* ¿cómo te llamas?, 1
napkin servilleta *(f.)*, 5
narrow estrecho(a)
near cerca (de), 6; **— here** cerca de aquí
neck cuello *(m.)*, 13
need *(v.)* necesitar, 2
negative negativo(a)
neighbor vecino(a) *(m., f.)*, 14
neighborhood barrio *(m.)*
neither ni, 6; tampoco, 6
nephew sobrino *(m.)*, 4
nettle ortiga *(f.)*
never jamás, nunca, 6
new nuevo(a), 2
newlyweds recién casados *(m. pl.)*, 6
newspaper diario *(m.)*, periódico *(m.)*
next próximo(a), 12; que viene, 14; **— to** junto a
nice simpático(a), 1
niece sobrina *(f.)*, 4
night noche *(f.)*, 1
nightclub club nocturno *(m.)*, 7
nightgown camisón *(m.)*, 9
nightingale ruiseñor *(m.)*
nine nueve, 1
nine hundred novecientos(as), 3
nineteen diecinueve, 2
ninety noventa, 2
no no, 1; ningún, ninguno(a), 6; **— one** nadie, ninguno(a), 6
nobody nadie, 6; ninguno(a), 6
none ninguno(a), 6
noon mediodía *(m.)*, 12; **at —** al mediodía, 2
no one nadie, ninguno(a), 6
North American norteamericano(a) *(m., f.)*, 1
nose nariz *(f.)*, 13; **— drops** gotas para la nariz *(f. pl.)*
not no, 1; **— any** ningún, ninguno(a), 6; **— now** ahora no; **— very well** no muy bien
notebook cuaderno *(m.)*, 1
nothing nada, 6; **— else** nada más, 6
notice *(v.)* notar; fijarse, 12
noun nombre *(m.)*
November noviembre, 2
now ahora, 4
number número *(m.)*, 1; **phone —** número de teléfono, 1
nurse enfermero(a) *(m., f.)*, 13

O

obtain conseguir (e > i), 6
occupied ocupado(a), 12
ocean mar *(m.)*, 8
October octubre, 2
oculist oculista *(m., f.)*, 14
of de, 2; **— course** cómo no, por supuesto
often a menudo, frecuentemente, 8
oil aceite *(m.)*; petróleo *(m.)*
okay bueno, 1; pues, 8
old viejo(a), 1; antiguo(a)
older mayor, 5
oldest (el, la) mayor, 5
omelette tortilla *(f.)*
on en, 1
once upon a time había una vez
one uno, 1; un(a), 1
one hundred cien (ciento), 2
one-way de ida, 11
onion cebolla *(f.)*, 5
only sólo, 2, solamente, 2
open *(v.)* abrir, 3; abierto(a), 10; franco(a)
oppressed oprimido(a)
or o
orange anaranjado(a), 1; naranja *(f.)*, 2
order pedir (e > i), 5; mandar *(v.)*, 11; pedido *(m.)*; **— drinks** pedir bebidas; **in — that** para que, 13
other otro(a), 10
our nuestro(s), nuestra(s), 2
ours nuestro(s), nuestra(s) *(pron.)*, 9
ourselves nos, 7
outdoor: — café café al aire libre; **— market** mercado al aire libre *(m.)*, 6
oven horno *(m.)*, 3
over en
overlooking con vista a, 12
own propio(a)
owner dueño(a) *(m., f.)*, propietario(a) *(m., f.)*, 12

P

package paquete *(m.)*, 11
pain dolor *(m.)*, 13

painkiller calmante *(m.)*, 14
painter pintor(a) *(m., f.)*
painting pintura *(f.)*
pair par *(m.)*, 9
pajamas pijama *(m.)*, pijamas *(m. pl.)*, 9
pancake panqueque *(m.)*, 5
pants pantalón *(m.)*, pantalones *(m. pl.)*, 9
pantyhose pantimedias *(f. pl.)*
pap smear papanicolaus *(m.)*
paper papel *(m.)*, 1
paramedic paramédico(a) *(m., f.)*, 13
parasol sombrilla *(f.)*
pardon? ¿cómo?, ¿mande? *(Mex.)*, 1
parents padres *(m. pl.)*, 3
park *(n.)* parque *(m.)*; *(v.)* estacionar, 10
part parte *(f.)*
party fiesta *(f.)*, 4
passbook libreta de ahorros *(f.)*, 10
passenger pasajero(a) *(m., f.)*, 11
passport pasaporte *(m.)*, 11
pastry pastel *(m.)*, 4
pay *(v.)* pagar, 5
peach durazno *(m.)*, melocotón *(m.)*, 6
pear pera *(f.)*, 6
pediatrician pediatra *(m., f.)*, 14
pen bolígrafo *(m.)*, pluma *(f.)*, 1
pencil lápiz *(m.)*, 1
penicillin penicilina *(f.)*
people gente *(f. sing.)*, 10
pepper *(green)* pimiento *(m.)*, ají *(m.)*, 6; *(black)* pimienta *(f.)*, 5
per por, 9; **— day** al día, 6; **— night** por noche
percent por ciento
perfect perfecto(a), 1
person persona *(f.)*, 12
personal computer computadora personal *(f.)*, ordenador personal *(m.) (Spain)*, 1
pharmacist farmacéutico(a) *(m., f.)*
pharmacy farmacia *(f.)*, 14
phone *(v.)* llamar por teléfono
physics física *(f.)*, 2
pick up *(v.)* buscar
picnic picnic *(m.)*, 7
pie pastel *(m.)*, 5
piece pedazo *(m.)*, trozo *(m.)*
pill pastilla *(f.)*, 11
pineapple piña *(f.)*, 6
pink rosado(a), 1
place *(v.)* poner, 4; lugar *(m.)*; **— of interest** lugar de interés, 12; **in — of** en lugar de
placed puesto(a), 10
plan *(v.)* planear, 4; **to — to (do something)** pensar (e > ie) + *infinitive*, 5
plane avión *(m.)*, 11
plate plato *(m.)*, 3
play *(a game) (v.)* jugar (u > ue), 8; *(music, an instrument)* tocar; **— golf** jugar al golf, 8; **— tennis** jugar al tenis, 8
player jugador(a) *(m., f.)*
please *(v.)* complacer
pleasure gusto *(m.)*, 1; **it's a — to meet you** mucho gusto, 1; **the — is mine** el gusto es mío, 1
pneumonia pulmonía *(f.)*, 14
poem poema *(m.)*
polite de cortesía
political science ciencias políticas *(f. pl.)*, 2
poor pobre, 7
poorly mal
pork chop chuleta de cerdo *(m.)*, 6
porridge avena *(f.)*
possessive posesivo(a)
possible posible, 12
postcard tarjeta postal *(f.)*, 10
post office correo *(m.)*, oficina de correos *(f.)*, 10
potato patata *(f.) (Spain)*, papa *(f.)*, 5; **mashed potatoes** puré de papas *(m.)*, 5
pour out echar
poverty pobreza *(f.)*
powder polvo *(m.)*
practice *(v.)* practicar
praise *(v.)* elogiar
prefer preferir (e > ie), 5
pregnant embarazada, 14
prepare preparar, 3
prescribe recetar, 14
prescription receta *(f.)*, 14
pressure presión *(f.)*, 14
pretty bonito(a), lindo(a), 1
price precio *(m.)*, 12
printer impresora *(f.)*, 10
private privado(a), 12
privateer corsario *(m.)*
problem problema *(m.)*
professor profesor(a) *(m., f.)*, 1
program programa *(m.)*, 2
promise prometer, 8
proprietor dueño(a) *(m., f.)*, 12
provided that con tal (de) que, 13
psychology psicología *(f.)*, 2
punch ponche *(m.)*
purple morado(a), 1
purse bolso *(m.)*, 7; cartera *(f.)*; bolsa *(f.)*
put poner, 4; puesto(a), 10; **— on** ponerse, 7; **— a cast on** enyesar; **— together** armar, 8

Q

quality calidad *(f.)*
quarter cuarto *(m.)*; **— past (or after) . . .** ...y cuarto, 2; **— to . . .** ...menos cuarto, 2
queen reina *(f.)*

R

racket raqueta *(f.)*, 8
rain *(v.)* llover (o > ue), 9; *(n.)* lluvia *(f.)*, 9
raincoat impermeable *(m.)*
rain forest selva *(f.)*
raise levantar, 4
rapid rápido, 8
rapidly rápidamente, 8
rate of exchange cambio de moneda *(m.)*
read leer, 3
reader lector(a) *(m., f.)*
ready listo(a), 9
realize darse cuenta (de), 12
receive recibir, 3
recent reciente, 8
recently recientemente, 8
recommend recomendar (e > ie), 11
record disco *(m.)*; **— player** estéreo, tocadiscos *(m.)*
red rojo(a), 1; carmín; **— wine** vino tinto, 2
red-haired pelirrojo(a), 4
refrigerator refrigerador *(m.)*, heladera *(f.)*, 3
register registro *(m.)*, 13
registered certificado(a), 10
relationship parentesco *(m.)*
relative pariente *(m., f.)*
remain quedarse
remember recordar (o > ue), 6; acordarse (o > ue) (de), 12
rent *(v.)* alquilar, 8
request *(v.)* pedir (e > i), 6
reservation reservación *(f.)*, 12
reserve *(v.)* reservar, 12
rest *(v.)* descansar, 3

restaurant restaurante *(m.)*, 5

return volver (o > ue), 6; regresar

returned vuelto(a), 10

review repaso *(m.)*

rice arroz *(m.)*, 5; **— pudding** arroz con leche, 5

rich rico(a), 1

ride a bike montar en bicicleta, 7

right derecho(a); **to the —** a la derecha; **— away** en seguida, 10; **— now** ahora mismo

river río *(m.)*

robe bata *(f.)*, 9

room cuarto *(m.)*; habitación *(f.)*, 12; **— and board** pensión completa *(f.)*, 12; **— service** servicio de habitación, 12

roommate compañero(a) de cuarto *(m., f.)*, 1

root raíz *(f.)*

rosé *(wine)* rosado, 2

round-trip de ida y vuelta, 11

row *(v.)* remar, 8

run correr, 3; **— errands** hacer diligencias, 10; **— into** chocar (con), 13

Russian *(language)* ruso *(m.)*

S

safe deposit box caja de seguridad *(f.)*, 10

said dicho(a), 10

sailboat velero *(m.)*, 8

salad ensalada *(f.)*, 3

sale liquidación *(f.)*; venta *(f.)*

salsa *(dance)* salsa *(f.)*, 5; sauce, 6

salt sal *(f.)*, 5

same mismo(a); **the — thing** lo mismo

sand arena *(f.)*, 8

sandal sandalia *(f.)*, 9

sandwich sándwich *(m.)*

Saturday sábado *(m.)*, 2

saucepan cacerola *(f.)*, 3

saucer platillo *(m.)*, 5

sausage chorizo *(m.)*

save *(money)* ahorrar, 10

savings: — account cuenta de ahorros *(f.)*, 10; **— plan** plan de ahorros *(m.)*, 10

say decir (e > i), 5; **how do you — . . . ?** ¿cómo se dice... ?, 1; **you — . . .** se dice... , 1

scarf bufanda *(f.)*, 9

schedule horario (de clases) *(m.)*, 2

school escuela *(f.)*, 9; **— year** año escolar *(m.)*

scissors tijeras *(f. pl.)*, 14

screech chillido *(m.)*

screen pantalla *(f.)*, 10

scuba dive bucear, 8

season *(food) (v.)* condimentar

season *(n.)* estación *(f.)*, 2

seat asiento *(m.)*, 11; **aisle —** asiento de pasillo, 11; **window —** asiento de ventanilla, 11

seated sentado(a)

second segundo *(m.)*, 12

section sección *(f.)*

sedative sedativo *(m.)*, sedante *(m.)*, 14

see ver, 4; **— (a patient) atender (e > ie)**, 13; **— you around** hasta la vista; **— you later** hasta luego, 1; **— you tomorrow** hasta mañana, 1

seem parecer, 12

seen visto(a), 10

sell vender, 8

semester semestre *(m.)*, 2

send mandar, enviar, 4

September septiembre, 2

servant criado(a), 6

serious grave, serio(a), 14

serve servir (e > i), 6

set the table poner la mesa, 3

seven siete, 1

seven hundred setecientos(as), 3

seventeen diecisiete, 2

seventy setenta, 2

several varios(as), 13

share *(v.)* compartir, 11

shave afeitarse, rasurarse, 7

she ella, 1

shellfish marisco *(m.)*, 6

shelter amparo *(m.)*

shine *(v.)* lucir(se)

shirt camisa *(f.)*, 9

shoe zapato *(m.)*, 9; **— store** zapatería *(f.)*, 9

shop tienda *(f.)*

shore orilla *(f.)*

short bajo(a), 5; corto(a), 9

shot *(injection)* inyección *(f.)*, 13; *(gun)* tiro *(m.)*; **tetanus —** inyección antitetánica *(f.)*, 13

shotgun escopeta *(f.)*, 8

shoulder hombro *(m.)*, 13

shout gritar, 4

show *(v.)* enseñar, mostrar (o > ue), 12

shower ducha *(f.)*, regadera *(Mex.) (f.)*, 12

shrimp camarón *(m.)*, gamba (Spain) *(f.)*, 5

shy tímido(a), 5

sick enfermo(a)

sign *(v.)* firmar, 10; *(n.)* letrero *(m.)*

silver plata *(f.)*

single soltero(a), 4

sir señor *(m.)* *(abbr.* Sr.), 1

sister hermana *(f.)*, 3

sister-in-law cuñada *(f.)*, 4

sit down sentarse (e > ie), 7

situation situación *(f.)*

six seis, 1

six hundred seiscientos(as), 3

sixteen dieciséis, 2

sixty sesenta, 2

size *(of clothing)* talla *(f.)*, tamaño *(m.)*, 9

skate *(v.)* patinar, 7

ski *(v.)* esquiar, 7

sky cielo *(m.)*, 9

skirt falda *(f.)*, 9

skyscraper rascacielo *(m.)*

slander calumnia *(f.)*

sleep dormir (o > ue), 6

sleeper sofa sofá-cama *(m.)*, 12

sleeping bag bolsa de dormir *(f.)*, 8

sleeve manga *(f.)*, 9

slender delgado(a), 1

slip combinación *(f.)*

slipper zapatilla *(f.)*, 7

slow despacio, 1; lento(a), 8; **—er, please** más despacio, por favor, 1

slowly lentamente, 8

small pequeño(a), 5; chico(a), 8

smaller más pequeño(a), 5

smallest (el, la) más pequeño(a), 5

smoke *(v.)* fumar; **(non) smoking section** sección de (no) fumar *(f.)*

snack (afternoon) merienda *(f.)*; **to have an afternoon —** merendar (e > ie), 7

snow *(v.)* nevar (e > ie), 9

snowfall nevada *(f.)*

so así que; tan; **— much** tanto(a); **— that** para que, 13

soap jabón *(m.)*; **— opera** telenovela *(f.)*, 3

soccer fútbol *(m.)*

Social Security Seguro Social

sociology sociología *(f.)*, 2

sock calcetín *(m.)*

soda refresco *(m.)*

sofa sofá *(m.)*; **sleeper —** sofá-cama *(m.)*, 12
soft drink refresco *(m.)*
solution solución *(f.)*
some unos(as), 1; algún, alguno(a), algunos(as), 6
someone alguien, 6
something algo, 6; **— to eat (drink)** algo para comer (tomar)
sometimes a veces; algunas veces, 6
somewhere en alguna parte
son hijo *(m.)*, 4
son-in-law yerno *(m.)*, 4
soon pronto, 8; **as — as** en cuanto, 9
sorry perdón, 1; **I'm —** lo siento, 1
soul alma *(f.)*
soup sopa *(f.)*, 5
source of income fuente *(f.)* de ingresos
souvenir shop tienda de regalos *(f.)*, 12
spaghetti espaguetis *(m. pl.)*, 6
Spanish *(language)* español *(m.)*, 1; *(person)* español(a)
speak hablar, 2; **this is . . . (name) speaking** habla... (nombre), 5
specialty especialidad *(f.)*, 5
spell deletrear
spelling deletreo *(m.)*
spend *(money)* gastar, 9; *(time)* pasar, 8; **— the summer vacationing** veranear
spoilsport aguafiestas *(m.)*, 2
spoken hablado, 10
spoon cuchara *(f.)*, 5
sport deporte *(m.)*
sprain torcedura *(f.)*, 13
spring *(season)* primavera *(f.)*, 2
stadium estadio *(m.)*
stairs escalera *(f.)*, 13
stamp estampilla *(f.)*, 10; sello *(m.)*, 10, timbre *(m.) (Mex.)*, 10
stand in line hacer cola, 10
star estrella *(f.)*
start comenzar (e > ie), empezar (e > ie), 5
starving muerto(a) de hambre, 6
state estado *(m.)*
stay quedarse; *(at a hotel)* hospedarse, 8
steak bistec *(m.)*, biftec *(m.)*, 5
stepbrother hermanastro *(m.)*
stepdaughter hijastra *(f.)*
stepfather padrastro *(m.)*
stepmother madrastra *(f.)*
stepsister hermanastra *(f.)*
stepson hijastro *(m.)*
stereo estéreo *(m.)*
stilts pilotes *(m. pl.)*
stitch punto *(m.)*, 13
stomach estómago *(m.)*, 13
stop *(v.)* parar; dejar de; **to — over** hacer escala, 11
stopover escala *(f.)*, 11
store tienda *(f.)*, 9; **to — information** archivar la información, 10
stork cigüeña *(f.)*
storm tormenta *(f.)*
strain *(v.)* colar (o > ue)
strainer colador *(m.)*, 3
stranger extraño(a) *(m., f.)*
strawberry fresa *(f.)*, 6
street calle *(f.)*, 1
stretcher camilla *(f.)*
student estudiante *(m., f.)*, 1; alumno(a) *(m., f.)*, 1
study *(v.)* estudiar, 2
stupidity torpeza *(f.)*
subject *(academic)* asignatura *(f.)*, materia *(f.)*, 2; *(person)* vasallo(a) *(m., f.)*
success éxito *(m.)*, 4; **quite a —** todo un éxito, 4
sufficient suficiente
sugar azúcar *(m.)*, 6; **— cane** caña de azúcar *(f.)*
suggest sugerir (e > ie), 11
suit traje *(m.)*, 9; *(fit)* quedar
suitcase maleta *(f.)*, valija *(f.)*, 11; **small —** maletín, 11
summer verano *(m.)*, 2
sunbathe tomar el sol, 8
Sunday domingo *(m.)*, 2
superlative superlativo *(m.)*
supermarket supermercado *(m.)*, 6
supper cena *(f.)*
sure seguro(a), cómo no, 13
surf *(v.)* hacer surfing, 8; **— the net** navegar la Red, 10
surfboard tabla de mar *(f.)*, 8
surgeon cirujano(a) *(m., f.)*, 14
surrounded rodeado(a)
survey encuesta *(f.)*
sweater suéter *(m.)*, 9
sweep barrer, 3
swim *(v.)* nadar, 7
swimming pool piscina *(f.)*, 12
swollen hinchado(a), 13
syrup jarabe *(m.)*, 14
system sistema *(m.)*

T

table mesa *(f.)*, 3
tablecloth mantel *(m.)*, 5
take *(v.)* tomar, 2; **— (someone or something someplace)** llevar, 4; **— care (of oneself)** cuidar(se), 14; **— charge** encargarse; **— out** sacar, 3 **— off** *(clothes)* quitarse, 7; **— place** tener lugar
talk *(v.)* conversar, 2
tall alto(a), 1
tape cinta *(f.)*, casete *(m.)*; **adhesive —** esparadrapo *(m.)*, 14
tasty rico(a), 5; **very —** riquísimo(a)
taxi taxi *(m.)*, 12
tea té *(m.)*, 2
teacher maestro(a) *(m., f.)*
tear out arrancar
teaspoon cucharita *(f.)*, 5
technology tecnología *(f.)*
telegram telegrama *(m.)*
telephone teléfono *(m.)*
television televisión *(f.)*, 2; *(set)* televisor *(m.)*, 12
teller cajero(a) *(m., f.)*, 10
temperature temperatura *(f.)*, 9; **what is the —** ¿qué temperatura hace?, 9
ten diez, 1
tent tienda de campaña *(f.)*, 8
tenth décimo(a)
term of endearment palabra cariñosa *(f.)*
test *(n.)* análisis *(m.)*, 13; examen *(m.)*
than que, 5
thanks gracias, 1
thank you gracias, 1; **— very much** muchas gracias, 1
thank goodness menos mal
that que *(rel. pron.)*, 3; ese, esa, eso, *(distant)* aquel, aquella, *(adj.)*, 3; eso, aquello, *(neut. pron.)*, 3; ése, ésa, aquél, aquélla, *(pron.)*, 3
the el *(m. sing.)*, la *(f. sing.)*, los *(m. pl.)*, las *(f. pl.)*, 1
theater teatro *(m.)*, 7
their su(s), 2
theirs *(pron.)* suyo(a), suyos(as), 9
them ellas *(f.)*, ellos *(m.)* *(obj. of prep.)*, 5; las *(f.)*, los *(m.)*, 6; **(to) —** les, 7
theme tema *(m.)*

themselves se, 7
then entonces, 2; después
there allí, 12; allá; **— is (are)** hay 1; **— was (were)** hubo
therefore pues
these estos(as) *(adj.)*, 3; éstos(as) *(pron.)*, 3
they ellos(as) *(m., f.)*, 1
thin delgado(a), 1
thing cosa *(f.)*, 3; **things to do** cosas que hacer, 3
think pensar (e > ie), 5; creer, **— so (not)** creer que sí (no), 13
thirteen trece, 1
thirty treinta, 1
this este, esta *(adj.)*, 3; esto *(neut. pron.)*, 3; **— one** *(pron.)* éste, ésta, 3
thistle cardo *(m.)*
those esos(as), aquellos(as) *(adj.)*, 3; ésos(as), aquéllos(as) *(pron.)*, 3
thousand mil, 3
three tres, 1
three hundred trescientos(as), 3
throat garganta *(f.)*, 14; **sore —** dolor de garganta, 14
through por, 9
Thursday jueves *(m.)*, 2
ticket billete *(m.)*, 11; pasaje *(m.)*, 11; **one-way —** billete de ida, 11; **round-trip —** billete de ida y vuelta, 11
tie corbata *(f.)*, 9
time tiempo *(m.)*, 3; hora *(f.)*, 2; vez *(f.)*, 7; **what — is it?** ¿qué hora es?, 2; **at what — . . . ?** ¿a qué hora... ?, 2
tip *(for service)* propina *(f.)*, 5
tired cansado(a), 4; **to get —** cansarse, 11
title título *(m.)*
to a, 2
toast *(n.)* pan tostado *(m.)*, 5; tostada *(f.)*; brindis *(m.) (at a celebration)*, 4
toast *(v.)* brindar, 4
toaster tostadora *(f.)*, 3
today hoy, 2
toe dedo del pie *(m.)*, 13
together juntos(as), 2
toilet inodoro *(m.)*, 12
tomato tomate *(m.)*, 2
tomorrow mañana
tongue lengua *(f.)*, 13
tonight esta noche, 1
too también, 2; **— bad** qué lástima; **— much** demasiado(a)
tooth diente *(m.)*, 13
tornado tornado *(m.)*
tour excursión *(f.)*, 11
tourist turista *(m., f.)*, 12
traffic tráfico *(m.)*
tranquilizer calmante *(m.)*, 14
translate traducir, 4
travel viajar, 11
travel agency agencia de viajes *(f.)*, 11
traveler viajero(a) *(m., f.)*
traveler's check cheque de viajero *(m.)*, 11
tree árbol *(m.)*, 13
trip viaje *(m.)*, 11; **have a nice —** buen viaje, 11; **on a —** de viaje
trousers pantalón *(m.)*, 9; pantalones *(m. pl.)*, 9
true cierto(a); verdadero; **it's —** es verdad, es cierto
trust *(v.)* confiar en, 12
truth verdad *(f.)*
try tratar de, 8; **— (on)** probar(se) (o > ue), 9
T-shirt camiseta *(f.)*, 9
Tuesday martes *(m.)*, 2
turn into convertirse (e > ie) en, 14
turn on poner
TV set televisor *(m.)*, 12
twelve doce, 2
twenty veinte, 2
two dos, 1; **there are — of us** somos dos
two hundred doscientos(as), 3
type tipo *(m.)*

U

ugly feo(a), 1
umbrella paraguas *(m. sing.)*
uncle tío *(m.)*, 4
under debajo de
undershorts calzoncillos *(m. pl.)*, 9
understand entender (e > ie), 5
underwear ropa interior *(f.)*
unfortunately desgraciadamente
university universidad *(f.)*, 1
unless a menos que, 13
unpleasant antipático(a), 1
until hasta, 5; hasta que, 13
us nosotros(as) *(obj. of prep.)*, 5; nos *(dir. obj.)*, 6; nos *(indir. obj.)*, 7
U.S. estadounidense *(m., f.) (used to denote citizenship)*, 1
use usar, 9
used to acostumbrado(a) a, 8
useful útil

V

vacant libre, disponible, 12
vacate desocupar, 12
vacation vacaciones *(f. pl.)*; **to be on —** estar de vacaciones, 5
vacuum *(v.)* pasar la aspiradora, 3
vacuum cleaner aspiradora *(f.)*
value valor *(m.)*
vanilla vainilla *(f.)*, 5
vase florero *(m.)*, 7
veal chop chuleta de ternera *(f.)*, 6
vegetable verdura, vegetal *(m.)*, 5; **— market** verdulería *(f.)*
very muy, 1; **— well** muy bien, 1
vest chaleco *(m.)*, 9
via por, 9
vinegar vinagre *(m.)*
visa visa *(f.)*
visit *(v.)* visitar, 7
vitamin vitamina *(f.)*, 14
vocabulary vocabulario *(m.)*

W

wait (for) esperar, 5
waiter camarero(a) *(m.)*; mozo *(m.)*, mesero(a) *(m.) (Mex.)*, 5
waiting list lista de espera *(f.)*, 11
waitress camarera *(f.)*, mesera *(f.) (Mex.)*, 5
wake up despertarse (e > ie), 7
walk *(v.)* caminar
wallet billetera *(f.)*, 9
want desear, 2; querer (e > ie), 5
war guerra *(f.)*
warm templado(a), 9
warning advertencia *(f.)*
wash *(v.)* lavar, 3; **— oneself** lavarse, 7; **— one's hair** lavarse la cabeza, 7
washbasin lavabo *(m.)*, 12
washing machine lavadora *(f.)*, 3
wastebasket cesto de papeles *(m.)*, 1
watch *(v.)* mirar, 3; reloj *(m.)*, 1
water agua (el) *(f.)*, 2; **—- ski** esquí acuático *(m.)*, 8; **ice —** agua con hielo, 2; **mineral —** agua mineral, 2
watermelon sandía *(f.)*, 6
way modo *(m.)*; **one — ticket** billete de ida, 11
we nosotros(as), 1

weak débil
wear usar, llevar, 7; **— a certain shoe size** calzar, 9
weather tiempo *(m.)*, 3; **to be good (bad) —** hacer buen (mal) tiempo, 9
wedding boda *(f.)*, 5; **— anniversary** aniversario de bodas *(m.)*
Wednesday miércoles *(m.)*, 2
week semana *(f.)*, 7
weekend fin de semana *(m.)*, 7
weigh pesar, 14
weight peso *(m.)*
welcome bienvenido(a), 1; **you're —** de nada, 1; **— party** fiesta de bienvenida *(f.)*
well pues, 8; bueno, 10; **very —** muy bien, 1; **not very —** no muy bien, 1
what? ¿qué?, 2; ¿cuál?, 13; **— a pity!** ¡qué lástima!; **— day is today?** ¿qué día es hoy?, 2; **— does . . . mean?** ¿Qué quiere decir... ?, 1; **— is . . . like?** ¿cómo es...?, 5; **— is today's date?** ¿qué fecha es hoy?, 2; **—'s new?** ¿qué hay de nuevo?, 1; **—'s your phone number?** ¿Cuál es tu número de teléfono?; **— is the rate of (monetary) exchange?** ¿a cómo está el cambio de moneda?, 11; **— is your name?** *(form.)* ¿cómo se llama usted?, *(fam.)* ¿cómo te llamas?, 1; **— time is it?** ¿Qué hora es?, 2
when cuándo, 2; cuando, 13
where ¿dónde?, 1; **— are you from?** ¿de dónde eres *(fam.)*?, 1; **— (to)?** ¿adónde?, 4
which ¿cuál(es)?, 1
while mientras; rato *(m.)*; **a —** un rato, 3; **a — later** al rato
white blanco(a), 1
who ¿quién(es)?, 3; que, 2
why? ¿por qué?, 2
wide ancho(a), 7
wife esposa *(f.)*, 4
window ventana *(f.)*, 1; *(bank, ticket, etc.)* ventanilla *(f.)*
wine vino *(m.)*, 2; **—glass** copa *(f.)*, 2
winter invierno *(m.)*, 2
wish *(v.)* desear, 2; querer (e > ie), 5
with con, 1; de, 11; **— brown eyes** de ojos castaños, 4; **— me** conmigo, 3; **— you** contigo, 3; **— whom?** ¿con quién?
within dentro de, 14
without sin que, 13
woman mujer *(f.)*, 1
wonder: no — con razón
wood madera *(f.)*
word palabra *(f.)*
work trabajo *(m.)*, 3; *(of art)* obra *(f.)*; *(v.)* trabajar, 2; **it doesn't —** no funciona, 12
worry preocuparse
worse peor, 5
worst (el, la) peor, 5
wound herida *(f.)*, 13
wounded herido(a)
wrist muñeca *(f.)*, 13
write escribir, 3; **— down** anotar; **— programs** diseñar programas
written escrito(a), 10

X

X-ray radiografía *(f.)*, 13
X-ray room sala de rayos X (equis) *(f.)*, 13

Y

year año *(m.)*, 2
yellow amarillo(a), 1
yes sí, 1
yesterday ayer, 7
yet todavía, 3
you tú, vosotros(as), usted(es) *(pron.)*, 1; ti, usted(es), vosotros(as) *(obj. of prep.)*, 5; la(s), lo(s), os, te *(dir. obj.)*, 6; le(s), os, se, te *(indir. obj.)*, 7; **—'re welcome** de nada, 1
young joven, 1; **— girl** chica *(f.)*, muchacha *(f.)*, 1
young lady señorita *(f.)*, 1
young man chico *(m.)*, muchacho *(m.)*, 1
younger menor, 5
youngest (el, la) menor, 5
your tu(s), 1; su(s); vuestro(s), vuestras(s), 2
yours suyo(a), suyos(as), tuyo(a), tuyos(as), vuestro(a), vuestros(as), 9
yourself se, te, 7
yourselves os, se, 7

Z

zoo zoológico *(m.)*, 7

Index

Photo and Art Credits

p. 2, Simon Wilkinson/Iconica/Getty Images; *p. 3 (TL),* © Richard Cummins/CORBIS; *p. 3 (BL),* Tony Anderson/Taxi/Getty Images; *p. 3 (BR),* © Richard Cummins/CORBIS; *p. 27,* © Royalty-Free, College Education/Getty/Images; *p. 44 (T),* Digital Vision/Getty Images; *p. 45,* Manch/Photodisc Red/Getty Images; *p. 46 (T),* © Lisa O'Connor/ZUMA/Corbis; *p. 46 (B),* © Reuters/CORBIS; *p. 47,* © Christopher Farina/Corbis; *p. 52,* Danita Delimont/Alamy; *p. 53 (T),* Oscar Ruiz; *p. 53 (BL),* © ML Sinibaldi/CORBIS; *p. 53 (BR),* © Margie Politzer/Lonely Planet Images; *p. 58,* © Royalty-Free/Corbis; *p. 59,* © Royalty-Free/Corbis; *p. 78,* © Royalty-Free, College Education/Getty Images; *p. 86,* © Royalty-Free, College Education/Getty Images; *p. 87,* © Royalty-Free, University Life/Getty Images; *p. 89,* © Morgan David de Lossy/Corbis; *p. 90 (T),* Beryl Goldberg; *p. 91 (TL),* © Jon Feingersh; *p. 91 (TR),* Robert Frerck/Odyssey Productions; *p. 91 (BL),* H. Huntley Hersch/DDB Stock Photography; *p. 91 (BR),* © Melanie Carr/Viesti & Associates; *p. 92 (T),* © Peter M. Wilson/CORBIS; *p. 92 (B),* © Robert Frerck/Odyssey/Chicago; *p. 93 (T),* © SIPA Press; *p. 93 (B),* Neil Julian/Alamy; *p. 98,* Plowes ProteaPix; *p. 99 (T),* © Blaine Harrington III/Corbis; *p. 99 (BL),* © Danny Lehman/CORBIS; *p. 99 (BC),* © Tony Arruza/CORBIS; *p. 99 (BR),* INSADCO Photography/Alamy; *p. 104,* © Royalty-Free, European People, Business and Lifestyle/Getty Images; *p. 119,* Robert Frerck/Odyssey Productions; *p. 125,* © Royalty-Free, College Education/Getty Images; *p. 137,* © Royalty-Free/Corbis; *p. 139,* Richard I'Anson/Lonely Planet Images/Getty Images; *p. 141,* © Royalty-Free/Corbis; *p. 142 (T),* Jan Csernoch/Alamy; *p. 142 (B),* Humberto Olarte Cupas/Alamy; *p. 143 (T),* Robert Francis/Robert Harding World Imagery/Getty Images; *p. 143 (B),* Brian Atkinson/Alamy; *p. 148,* Pablo Corral V/Corbis; *p. 148,* © Pablo Corral V/CORBIS; *p. 149 (TL),* © Patrick Robert/Sygma/CORBIS; *p. 149 (CL),* M. Timothy O'Keefe/Alamy; *p. 149 (BL),* © Bruce Adams; Eye Ubiquitous/CORBIS; *p. 149 (BR),* AP/Wide World Photos; *p. 155,* © Royalty-Free, Personnel File/Getty Images; *p. 169,* © Royalty-Free, College Education/Getty Images; *p. 171,* Image Source/Alamy; *p. 177,* © Royalty-Free, College Education/Getty Images; *p. 194 (T),* © 2006 Ulrike Welsch; *p. 194 (B),* © Omar Bechara Baruque; Eye Ubiquitous/CORBIS; *p. 195 (T),* © ANA MARTINEZ/Reuters/Corbis; *p. 195* (C), D. Donne Bryant/DDB Stock Photo; *p. 195 (B),* Kimberly White/Reuters/Corbis; *p. 200,* Patrick Pihl/Pixonnet.com/Alamy; *p. 201 (T),* © Amy Johnson; *p. 201 (BC),* © Amy Johnson; *p. 201 (BR),* Mike Goldwater/Alamy; *p. 227,* © Royalty-Free, College Education/Getty Images; *p. 240 (T),* © Stuart Westmorland/Corbis; *p. 240 (B),* © Amy Johnson; *p. 241 (T),* Eitan Simanor/Alamy; *p. 241 (B),* imagebroker/ Alamy; *p. 246,* Photri MicroStock™/De La Puente Imagen; *p. 247 (T),* Peter Adams Photography/Alamy; *p. 247 (BL),* © Theo Allofs/zefa/Corbis; *p. 247 (BR),* © Dave G. Houser/Post-Houserstock/Corbis; *p. 253,* © Royalty-Free/Corbis; *p. 265,* © Royalty-Free, College Education/Getty Images; *p. 273,* © Royalty-Free, University Life/Getty Images; *p. 281,* © Royalty-Free, College Education/Getty Images; *p. 286 (T),* The Granger Collection; *p. 286 (B),* © Amy Johnson; *p. 287 (T),* © Dave G. Houser/Post-Houserstock/Corbis; *p. 287 (B),* © Kit Houghton/CORBIS; *p. 292,* Blend Images/Alamy; *p. 293 (T),* Robert Frerck/Odyssey Productions; *p. 293 (BL),* © Patrick Ward/CORBIS; *p. 293 (BR),* Ken Welsh/Alamy; *p. 317,* © Royalty-Free/Corbis; *p. 334 (T),* Mark Antman/The Image Works; p. *334 (B),* © Patrick Ward/CORBIS; *p. 335 (T),* John Bigelow Taylor/Art Resource, NY; *p. 335* ©, Chris McLennan/Alamy; *p. 335 (B),* © Francesc Muntada/CORBIS

Maps courtesy of Patricia Isaacs, Parrot Graphics; simulated realia courtesty of Steve McEntee, McEntee Designs; lesson-opener dialogue illustrations courtesy of Ben Shannon/Magnet Reps; interior illustrations courtesy of Sean Flanagan, Diane Gray/Boomerang Studios Inc.

América del Sur
Mar Caribe
OCÉANO ATLÁNTICO
OCÉANO PACÍFICO
TRINIDAD Y TOBAGO
Puerto España
Barranquilla
Cartagena
Maracaibo
Caracas
La Guaira
San Carlos
Ciudad Bolívar
VENEZUELA
Río Orinoco
Georgetown
Paramaribo
Cayena
GUYANA
SURINAM
GUAYANA FRANCESA
Salto Ángel
Medellín
Río Magdalena
Zipaquirá
Bogotá
Cali
COLOMBIA
Popayán
San Agustín
Otavalo
Santo Domingo de los Colorados
Pichincha
Quito
ECUADOR
Chimborazo
Guayaquil
Ecuador
Río Negro
Manaos
Río Amazonas
Belén
Iquitos
CORDILLERA DE LOS ANDES
Río Madeira
Sipán
Trujillo
BRASIL
Recife
PERÚ
Callao
Lima
Machu Picchu
Cuzco
Lago Titicaca
Puno
La Paz
Arequipa
Tiahuanaco
Cochabamba
BOLIVIA
Río Paraguay
Brasilia
Salvador
Arica
Sucre
Potosí
Iquique
Bello Horizonte
Filadelfia
PARAGUAY
Asunción
Río Paraná
San Pablo
Santos
Río de Janeiro
Trópico de Capricornio
Antofagasta
Salta
San Miguel de Tucumán
Puerto Iguazú
Resistencia
CHILE
Río Uruguay
Puerto Alegre
Córdoba
Aconcagua
Mendoza
Viña del Mar
Valparaíso
Santiago
Rosario
URUGUAY
Montevideo
Buenos Aires
La Plata
Punta del Este
ARGENTINA
Río de la Plata
Concepción
Río Colorado
Mar del Plata
Bahía Blanca
ISLAS GALÁPAGOS
San Salvador
Santa Cruz
San Cristóbal
Isabela
Bariloche
Puerto Montt
PATAGONIA
Estrecho de Magallanes
Islas Malvinas
Punta Arenas
TIERRA DEL FUEGO
Cabo de Hornos
0 250 500 Km.
0 250 500 Mi.